The Disciples according to Mark

The Disciples according to Mark

Markan Redaction in Current Debate

SECOND EDITION

C. Clifton Black

WILLIAM B. EERDMANS PUBLISHING COMPANY

GRAND RAPIDS, MICHIGAN / CAMBRIDGE, U.K.

First edition © 1989 Sheffield Academic Press, Sheffield, England,
Journal for the Study of the New Testament Supplement Series 27

Second edition © 2012 C. Clifton Black

Published 2012 by
Wm. B. Eerdmans Publishing Co.
2140 Oak Industrial Drive N.E., Grand Rapids, Michigan 49505 /
P.O. Box 163, Cambridge CB3 9PU U.K.
www.eerdmans.com

Printed in the United States of America

17 16 15 14 13 12   7 6 5 4 3 2 1

Library of Congress Cataloging-in-Publication Data

Black, C. Clifton (Carl Clifton), 1955-
    The disciples according to Mark: Markan redaction in current debate /
    C. Clifton Black. — 2nd ed.
        p.   cm.   — (Journal for the study of the New
        Testament. Supplement series; 27)
    Includes bibliographical references and index.
    ISBN 978-0-8028-2798-2 (pbk.: alk. paper)
    1. Bible. N.T. Mark — Criticism, Redaction.
    2. Apostles.   I. Title.
    BS2585.52.B53   2012
    226.3′066 — dc23

                                        2012028325

The author and publisher gratefully acknowledge Oxford University Press for kind permission to
reprint excerpts from Ernest Best's review of *The Disciples according to Mark: Markan Redaction in
Current Debate* in *The Journal of Theological Studies* 41.2 (October 1990), pp. 602-07. © Oxford
University Press. All rights reserved.

To Harriet

Contents

List of Tables and Figures

List of Tables

List of Figures

Preface to the Second Edition

I am deeply grateful to the William B. Eerdmans Publishing Company for giving this volume a new lease on life. Because its original edition was very much a child of its time, early on it was decided that any attempt to revise the bulk of its contents would prove frustrating for both author and readers. In a new Afterword I have attempted to bring this book's issues and scholarship up to date.

In addition to those mentioned in the original Preface, I have incurred new debts to other colleagues and friends. Professor David J. Downs, now of Fuller Theological Seminary, provided me with technological assistance at a crucial time. Professors M. Eugene Boring, Texas Christian University, and Cilliers Breytenbach, Humboldt-Universität zu Berlin, kindly discussed with me aspects of the Afterword's shape and contents. A graduate colloquium at Princeton Theological Seminary offered me helpful responses to a draft of the Afterword. I am especially grateful to that group's convener, Professor J. Ross Wagner, for helping me clarify claims that were murky and in need of greater precision. Doubtless none of these scholars would agree with many of my conclusions, though all have shown me great courtesy in improving their articulation. The expertise of Ms. Kate Skrebutenas, Reference Librarian of the Princeton Seminary Library, never fails to astonish me. Ms. Maria denBoer compiled the indexes conscientiously and with good cheer. Ms. Linda Bieze, managing editor at Eerdmans, has been unfailingly gracious, supportive, and patient. My debt to Harriet, who has now lived with Mark's Gospel for almost as long as she has lived with me, remains beyond repayment.

C. C. B.
March 2012

Preface to the First Edition

The substance of the present study originally appeared in a doctoral dissertation that was presented to the faculty of Graduate Studies in Religion at Duke University in April, 1986. That work has been revised, and to some degree updated, for publication in this form.

My indebtedness to the full complement of New Testament researchers and interpreters of Mark is manifest in the pages that follow. A number of scholars, however, have made the personal contribution of wisdom and energy that merits special recognition and thanks. At the head of the list stands Professor D. Moody Smith, who guided the writing of my dissertation as well as most of my study at Duke. To him I owe an incalculable debt of gratitude for his characteristic erudition, sagacity, and unfailing kindness. The development of this project was further enriched by the comments and criticisms of Duke Professors James L. Price, Franklin W. Young, and David C. Steinmetz, and of Professor George A. Kennedy, of the University of North Carolina at Chapel Hill. During the transitional period from dissertation to monograph, Professor William Scott Green, of the University of Rochester, and Professor Beverly Roberts Gaventa, now of Columbia Theological Seminary, provided me with both critical insight and collegial support. For their encouraging reception of my work, and for the care with which they have seen it into print, my sincere thanks are due to the officers of Sheffield Academic Press, particularly to Dr. David E. Orton, Senior Editor, and to Dr. David Hill, Executive Editor of the series supplement to the *Journal for the Study of the New Testament*. Would that every apprentice to the guild of biblical scholarship had such mentors and friends as these! To each and all I am profoundly grateful; naturally, not they but I am responsible for whatever errors of fact and judgment remain in this book.

Still others have made invaluable contributions that are hereby grate-fully acknowledged. Mrs. Wanda Camp, Staff Assistant to the Department of Religion at Duke, typed the burdensome manuscript on which my revi-sions were based. In preparing the text and indices, I have profitted from the indispensable service of two friends and doctoral candidates at Duke, Messrs. Rollin G. Grams and Keith J. Newell. I am also indebted to the Board of Higher Education and Ministry of The United Methodist Church, whose generous assistance relieved me of financial worry during the years in which the preponderance of the research and writing of this study was undertaken. Finally, the dedication of this book recognizes the debt of affection and gratitude that I owe to my wife, Harriet, who for too many years has supported a preoccupied husband with patience, encour-agement, endurance, and grace.

C. CLIFTON BLACK II
September 1987

Abbreviations

AASF	Annales academiae scientiarum fennicae
AB	Anchor Bible
AnBib	Analecta biblica
AsSeign	*Assemblées du Seigneur*
ATANT	Abhandlungen zur Theologie des Alten und Neuen Testaments
ATR	*Anglican Theological Review*
AusCathR	*Australian Catholic Record*
b.	Babylonian Talmud (preceding the title of a tractate)
BAGD	W. Bauer, W. F. Arndt, F. W. Gingrich, and F. W. Danker, *Greek-English Lexicon of the New Testament*
B. Bat.	*Baba Batra*
BBB	Bonner biblische Beiträge
BBM	Baker Biblical Monograph
Bell.	Josephus, *Bellum Judaicum*
BET	Beiträge zur evangelischen Theologie
BETL	Bibliotheca ephemeridum theologicarum lovaniensium
BHT	Beiträge zur historischen Theologie
BJRL	*Bulletin of the John Rylands University Library of Manchester*
BNTC	Black's New Testament Commentaries
BR	*Biblical Research*
BT	*The Bible Translator*
BTB	*Biblical Theology Bulletin*
BU	Biblische Untersuchung
BZ	*Biblische Zeitschrift*
BZNW	Beihefte zur *Zeitschrift für die neutestamentliche Wissenschaft*
CalCom	D. W. Torrance and T. F. Torrance (eds.), Calvin's Commentaries
Cath	*Catholica*
CBQ	*Catholic Biblical Quarterly*
CBQMS	Catholic Biblical Quarterly — Monograph Series

CGTC	Cambridge Greek Testament Commentary
ConBNT	Coniectanea biblica, New Testament
CTM	*Concordia Theological Monthly*
DTT	*Dansk teologisk tidsskrift*
EHPR	Études d'histoire et de philosophie religieuses
EKKNT	Evangelisch-katholischer Kommentar zum Neuen Testament
ET	English translation
ETL	*Ephemerides theologicae lovanienses*
EvT	*Evangelische Theologie*
ExpTim	*Expository Times*
FB	Forschung zur Bibel
FBBS	Facet Books, Biblical Series
FRLANT	Forschungen zur Religion und Literatur des Alten und Neuen Testaments
Fur	*Furrow*
GBSNTS	Guides to Biblical Scholarship, New Testament Series
GBSOTS	Guides to Biblical Scholarship, Old Testament Series
GNS	Good News Series
GPS	Glazier Passion Series
H.E.	Eusebius, *Historia Ecclesiastica*
HNT	Handbuch zum Neuen Testament
HTKNT	Herders theologischer Kommentar zum Neuen Testament
HTR	*Harvard Theological Review*
HTS	Harvard Theological Studies
IBCTP	Interpretation, A Bible Commentary for Teaching and Preaching
IBS	*Irish Biblical Studies*
IDBSup	K. Crim (ed.), Supplementary volume to *The Interpreter's Dictionary of the Bible*
Int	*Interpretation*
IRT	Issues in Religion and Theology
JAAR	*Journal of the American Academy of Religion*
JBL	*Journal of Biblical Literature*
JBLMS	Journal of Biblical Literature — Monograph Series
JBR	*Journal of Bible and Religion*
Jee	*Jeevadhara*
JR	*Journal of Religion*
JSNT	*Journal for the Study of the New Testament*
JSNTSup	Journal for the Study of the New Testament, Supplement Series
JSOT	*Journal for the Study of the Old Testament*
JTS	*Journal of Theological Studies*
JTSA	*Journal of Theology for Southern Africa*
KBANT	Kommentare und Beiträge zum Alten und Neuen Testament
LB	*Linguistica Biblica*
LD	Lectio divina

List	*Listening*
LJS	Lives of Jesus Series
LQ	*Lutheran Quarterly*
LS	*Louvain Studies*
LumVie	*Lumière et vie*
m.	Mishnah (preceding the title of a tractate)
MeyerK	H. A. W. Meyer, Kritisch-exegetischer Kommentar über das Neue Testament
MNTC	Moffatt New Testament Commentary
MP	*Monatsschrift für Pastoraltheologie*
NCB	New Century Bible
NF	Neue Folge
NICNT	New International Commentary on the New Testament
NovT	*Novum Testamentum*
NovTSup	Novum Testamentum, Supplements
n.s.	new series
NTFF	New Testament Foundations and Facets
NTL	New Testament Library
NTS	*New Testament Studies*
NUSPEP	Northwestern University Studies in Phenomenology and Existential Philosophy
OBO	Orbis biblicus et orientalis
ÖBS	Österreichische Biblische Studien
o.s.	old series
ÖTKNT	Ökumenischer Taschenbuch Kommentar zum Neuen Testament
OTU	Old Testament Library
PC	Proclamation Commentaries
Pers	*Perspective*
Pesiq. R.	*Pesiqta Rabbati*
PGC	Pelican Gospel Commentaries
PRelS	*Perspectives in Religious Studies*
PSTJ	*Perkins School of Theology Journal*
PTMS	Pittsburgh Theological Monograph Series
RB	*Revue biblique*
RelS	*Religious Studies*
RelSRev	*Religious Studies Review*
RevExp	*Review and Expositor*
Sal	*Salesianum*
Sanh.	*Sanhedrin*
SANT	Studien zum Alten und Neuen Testament
SB	Stuttgarter Bibelstudien
SBL	Society of Biblical Literature
SBLDS	Society of Biblical Literature Dissertation Series
SBLSBS	Society of Biblical Literature Sources for Biblical Study

SBLSemSup	Society of Biblical Literature Semeia Supplements
SBM	Stuttgarter biblische Monographien
SBT	Studies in Biblical Theology
SE	Studia Evangelica
Sem	Semeia
SemSup	Semeia Supplements
SFEG	Schriften der Finnischen Exegetischen Gesellschaft
SJT	Scottish Journal of Theology
SNTSMS	Society for New Testament Studies Monograph Series
SNTW	Studies of the New Testament and Its World
SPB	Studia postbiblica
Spec	Speculum
SPIB	Scripta Pontificii Instituti Biblici
SRev	Sewanee Review
ST	Studia theologica
Sukk.	Sukka
SUNT	Studien zur Umwelt des Neuen Testaments
SWJT	Southwestern Journal of Theology
TBT	The Bible Today
TC	Thornapple Commentaries
TD	Theology Digest
TDNT	G. Kittel and G. Friedrich (eds.), Theological Dictionary of the New Testament
TGl	Theologie und Glaube
Theol	Theology
TJ	Theologische Jahrbücher
TLZ	Theologische Literaturzeitung
TS	Theological Studies
TST	Toronto Studies in Theology
TToday	Theology Today
TTS	Trier Theologische Studien
TTZ	Trier theologische Zeitschrift
UBSGNT	United Bible Societies Greek New Testament
USQR	Union Seminary Quarterly Review
VTSup	Vetus Testamentum, Supplements
WC	Westminster Commentaries
WF	Wege der Forschung
WMANT	Wissenschaftliche Monographien zum Alten und Neuen Testament
WUNT	Wissenschaftliche Untersuchungen zum Neuen Testament
ZKT	Zeitschrift für katholische Theologie
ZNW	Zeitschrift für die neutestamentliche Wissenschaft
ZTK	Zeitschrift für Theologie und Kirche

Introduction: Problem and Procedure

In his important monograph of 1956, *Der Evangelist Markus*,[1] Willi Marxsen constructed the methodological frame on which three decades of Markan study would be spun. He called this method *Redaktionsgeschichte* (literally, 'redaction history', but usually translated as 'redaction criticism') and proposed, contrary to the objectives of precursory source and form criticism, that the analysis of the Second Gospel should attend to the following:

> First, 'an individual, an author personality who pursues a definite goal with his work' and 'the particular interest or point of view of the evangelist concerned';[2]

> Second, 'the "framework", . . . the itinerary and scenic links' within the narrative, as well as 'textual transformations, to the extent we can recognize them';[3]

> Finally, 'the "third situation-in-life" [*Sitz im Leben*], . . . the situation of the community in which the gospels arose', as opposed to 'the "first situation-in-life" located in the unique situation of Jesus' activity' and

---

1. W. Marxsen, *Der Evangelist Markus: Studien zur Redaktionsgeschichte des Evangeliums* (FRLANT NF 49; Göttingen: Vandenhoeck & Ruprecht, 1956); ET *Mark the Evangelist: Studies on the Redaction History of the Gospel* (Nashville and New York: Abingdon, 1969).

2. Marxsen, *Mark the Evangelist*, pp. 18, 24.

3. Ibid., p. 23. Cf. pp. 23-24: 'With this approach, the question as to what really happened is excluded from the outset. We inquire rather how the evangelists describe what happened.'

1

'the "second situation-in-life" mediated by the situation of the primitive church'.[4]

Marxsen's perspective on the interpretation of Mark[5] caught the scholarly tide at its turning, and up to the present day redaction criticism continues to be the most influential methodological approach to the exegesis of the Second Gospel. In some respects this state of affairs is most curious. On the one hand, in order to apply redaction criticism to Mark with conviction, the discipline requires that the Gospel be perceived in the light of its traditions or written sources or both (without which the character and degree of the Evangelist's redaction cannot be determined). Since Mark usually has been considered to be the earliest of the canonical Gospels, such direct antecedents are unavailable, and there exists no clearly defined critical consensus on those antecedents that may be inferred.[6] On the other hand, despite some measure of agreement among Markan exegetes, their practice of *Redaktionsgeschichte* with the Second Gospel has produced a bewildering variety of interpretive results, many of which are mutually exclusive.[7] Both of these dimensions of the problem of Markan redaction criticism have been crystallized in Jack Dean Kingsbury's assessment: 'The

---

4. Marxsen, *Mark the Evangelist*, pp. 23, 24. Marxsen associated the ascertainment of the 'second situation-in-life' with *Formgeschichte*.

5. Only a brief, introductory chapter of Marxsen's book was devoted to issues of perspective and method. The rest of his study was given to the *redaktionsgeschichtlich* analysis of different aspects of Markan theology: the role of John the Baptist (pp. 30-53), the geographical outline of the Gospel (pp. 54-116), the meaning of εὐαγγέλιον (pp. 117-50), and the function of Mark 13 in the total narrative (pp. 151-206).

6. Marxsen was aware of this consideration yet never considered it especially problematic: 'And it is not absolutely necessary to [reconstruct the sources of Mark and the other Synoptics], since no one can dispute *that* Mark had sources. How accurately they can be singled out, however, is not too important for the *final* redaction which concerns us' (*Mark the Evangelist*, pp. 27-28). For two reasons this comment is puzzling: (1) If one intends to evaluate how an Evangelist has manipulated his sources, would it not be *vital* to establish what those sources were? (2) Marxsen implicitly answers this question in the affirmative, and thus seems to contradict himself, when, in describing his method, he states, 'First we shall go back behind Mark and separate tradition from redaction, then by way of construction, illumine and explain his composition' (*Mark the Evangelist*, p. 28).

7. Among recent *Forschungsberichte*, none demonstrates the breadth and depth of this exegetical jumble with greater clarity and concision than W. R. Telford's 'Introduction: The Gospel of Mark', in *The Interpretation of Mark* (ed. W. R. Telford; IRT 7; Philadelphia and London: Fortress/SPCK, 1985), pp. 1-41. See also S. P. Kealy, *Mark's Gospel: A History of Its Interpretation from the Beginning until 1979* (New York and Ramsey: Paulist, 1982), pp. 159-237.

debate over the alleged creativity of Mark as a redactor is largely the result of the inability of scholars to reach a consensus on the vexing problem of separating tradition from redaction'.[8]

This book aims to engage in that debate and to grapple with that problem. Our primary, though not exclusive, concern will be to venture, on the basis of a limited yet systematic analysis, an evaluation of the validity of the redaction-critical method in the interpretation of Mark's Gospel. By 'the validity of the method', I mean the degree to which the discipline's feasibility or practical usefulness is supported and corroborated by the objective evidence that arises from the method's application to Mark by generally accepted authorities.

From this statement of purpose, it should be clear that, in this study, *Forschungsbericht* functions as far more than a prolegomenon; it is the primary ingredient, since the validity of redaction criticism can be assessed only by careful observation of the manner in which Markan scholars have used that method. It is equally clear, however, that we must be selective in our coverage of the secondary literature, which embraces an enormous number of studies in the Second Gospel that employ *Redaktionsgeschichte*. Therefore, as a test-case on which we might focus our attention, I propose to consider an exegetical issue that has been the center of no little debate in recent Markan research: the Evangelist's presentation of the disciples. The heart of this study thus attempts to measure the effectiveness of Markan redaction criticism by observing and evaluating its application to a critical, interpretive issue: the role of the disciples in the Second Gospel. This analysis, in turn, serves as a springboard for pondering precise questions about the prospect for the refinement of Markan *Redaktionsgeschichte,* as well as larger issues pertaining to current methodological options in the study of Mark's Gospel.

In the light of these concerns, we shall proceed according to the following plan. Chapter 1 offers a general overview of the development of the discipline of redaction criticism and its employment with the Second Gospel; particular attention is paid to the antecedents of the *redaktionsgeschichtlich* approach in the modern history of New Testament exegesis as well as to recent efforts to devise a comprehensive method for Markan redaction criticism. Following a review of the primary evidence for the complex portrayal of the disciples in Mark, in Chapter 2 a *Forschungsbericht* of narrower scope is presented, which surveys the past three decades of schol-

---

8. J. D. Kingsbury, 'The Gospel of Mark in Current Research', *RelSRev* 5 (1979), p. 104.

arly research, conducted on redaction-critical premises, into the question of Markan discipleship. From this review of the secondary literature, three categories or 'types' of *redaktionsgeschichtlich* investigation emerge, varying in their general assumptions (usually about the Evangelist's relationship to history and tradition) and in their exegetical results (regarding the Evangelist's perspective on the disciples as principally positive, predominantly negative, or both positive and negative). With the emergence of this typology, the problem of Markan interpretation based on redaction criticism comes into sharp focus: why is there among scholars so little unanimity, and such remarkable divergence, on the subject of Mark's presentation of the disciples when all of their investigations have been carried out, ostensibly, with the use of a common method (redaction criticism) in the interpretation of a primary text that is common to all (the Second Gospel)?

The next four chapters of the monograph address this question. From among the scholars associated with the various categories of redaction-critical studies of Markan discipleship, defined in Chapter 2, three investigators are chosen as representative of the three different types. In Chapters 3, 4, and 5, the work of each representative is critically explored for its specific *redaktionsgeschichtlich* assumptions, for the particular aspects or components of its *redaktionsgeschichtlich* procedure, and for the distinctive exegetical results that arise from its use of the *redaktionsgeschichtlich* method. A comparative analysis of these three probes ensues in Chapter 6, which attempts to ascertain the extent to which the diverse interpretations of Markan discipleship, proposed by the three representative investigators, are actually dependent on their use of the redaction-critical method. Although I do not wish to anticipate the specific results that emerge from that comparative analysis, at this point it suffices to say that considerable doubt is raised about the capability of Markan redaction criticism either to control interpretive assumptions or to verify interpretive results.

Since it is possible that this negative conclusion might apply only to the investigators whose work is scrutinized in this study, it becomes necessary, in Chapter 7, to consider the research of other scholars who have embarked on the formidable project of making Markan redaction criticism more dependable. A critical analysis of that research suggests that the reliability of that method in the interpretation of the Second Gospel remains highly suspect. In Chapter 8, we return to the recent history of scholarship in the Gospels in an attempt to discern why so problematic a method as *Redaktionsgeschichte* has held sway over Markan exegesis. Once its *raison d'être* in the context of contemporary research has been clarified, it becomes possible (I suggest) to differentiate a cluster of redaction-critical *methods*, which, when applied to Mark, are fraught with procedural difficulties, from a redaction-critical *perspective*, which comprises both benefits and limitations. Finally, attempting to appropriate the insights of both the *redaktionsgeschichtlich* viewpoint and of other exegetical approaches to the Second Gospel, this study concludes by proposing a synthetic, methodological model for Markan interpretation.

In this synopsis I have not proposed a thesis, as such, to be tested. This is intentional. I entered the present study with a general notion of the problem of Markan redaction criticism and with the germ of an idea about how that problem might be explored; I did not begin with any deliberate, or at least conscious, prejudgment concerning the precise dimensions of the problem, the reasons for its existence, or its potential for resolution. In an investigation such as this, there is always the danger of discovering only that which one expects to find; one's preconceptions father the facts. Therefore, the preceding précis is intended to provide a general map of the terrain in the chapters that follow. Although a thesis will emerge as the investigation progresses, we need not feel enslaved to its defense from the start. Indeed, the adoption of a more inductive, rather than deductive, procedure offers us the opportunity of greater freedom in evaluating the evidence.

Having summarized the character, scope, and purpose of this study, perhaps I should indicate, as clearly as possible, what it does *not* intend to do. First, although the nature of the present investigation requires at numerous points a critical response to the work of various Markan interpreters, that which will come under sharpest criticism here is Markan *Redaktionsgeschichte* itself. The principal questions to be raised of the method will be not so much philosophical as practical. I am less interested in deliberating the hermeneutical appropriateness of the discipline (especially when viewed from the standpoint of other interpretive approaches, such as narratology or structuralism);[9] I am more concerned to ask a comparatively simple yet no less important question: When taken on its own terms, does Markan redaction criticism *work*? That is, does the method enable its practitioners to draw exegetical conclusions that are trustworthy and confirmable?

Second, the present work intends to wrestle with fundamental ques-

---

9. For a helpful comparison of structuralist analysis with conventional historical-critical methods, consult E. V. McKnight, *Meaning in Texts: The Historical Shaping of a Narrative Hermeneutics* (Philadelphia: Fortress, 1978), pp. 242-48.

tions, both of Markan interpretation and of method in the study of the Second Gospel; yet it is neither directly exegetical nor purely theoretical in orientation. The point of this study is neither to offer an original interpretation of the disciples in Mark nor to resolve 'the vexing problem of separating tradition from redaction'[10] in the Gospel. Mine is the more modest goal of using the exegetical issue as a point of reference for evaluating the methodological query: to offer, in short, an original survey and assessment of recent studies dealing with discipleship in Mark with an eye for their suggestiveness for redaction criticism and other interpretive methods of the Gospel as a whole.

This study does not present information that has hitherto been unknown; however, I hope to frame some old and perennially challenging questions in a fresh and different way and to arrive at some tentative answers and proposals that might contribute to our knowledge about the Second Gospel. Ultimately, whatever significance may be claimed for this investigation resides in its attempt to bring together a major exegetical issue and a methodological approach to Mark that has been virtually presuppositional for over a quarter of a century, in the hope that the one will shed some light on the other. There is a sense in which the time is ripe for an inquiry like this. On the one hand, despite the customary caveats acknowledged by thoughtful exegetes since the method's inception, redaction-critical investigations of the Second Gospel continue to be generated at a prolific rate. On the other hand, increasing skepticism over the feasibility or desirability of the *redaktionsgeschichtlich* study of Mark is motivating a growing number of scholars to adopt a plethora of other methods in the attempted interpretation of the text. And the role of the disciples in Mark's Gospel remains enigmatic or, at least, resistant to a solution that commands the assent of the majority of Markan interpreters.

Markan studies are in a state of transition and perhaps some confusion. If this monograph lends some clarity to this state and advances the study of method in Markan interpretation, it will have served a valid purpose. One thing is reasonably clear: both the contributions and the deficiencies of redaction criticism will need to be given serious consideration in the advancement of Markan interpretation and of method in Gospel research. As we turn now to the position of *Redaktionsgeschichte* in the history of New Testament exegesis, it is just such consideration that this study intends to give.

10. Kingsbury, 'Mark in Current Research', p. 104.

1. Redaction Criticism of the Gospel of Mark: A Selective Review of Its Disciplinary Bases, Precursors, and Methodological Explication

> Redaction criticism continues to enjoy a considerable vogue in New Testament studies, and some remarkable claims have been made on its behalf. . . . In view of the confidence and the wide scope of these claims, it is a little surprising that the presuppositions and method of redaction criticism itself have not received closer scrutiny than has hitherto been brought to bear on them.
>
> C. J. A. Hickling[1]

Redaktionsgeschichte[2] has been variously defined by biblical exegetes; however, for its brevity, comprehensiveness, and accuracy with respect to the history of the discipline's application, Norman Perrin's definition is probably unsurpassed: '[*Redaktionsgeschichte*] is concerned with studying the theological motivation of an author as this is revealed in the collection, arrangement, editing, and modification of traditional material, and in the composition of new material or the creation of new forms within the traditions of early Christianity'.[3] Implicit in this definition, and in twentieth-century redaction-critical analysis of the Synoptics, are two assumptions:

---

1. C. J. A. Hickling, 'A Problem of Method in Gospel Research', *RelS* 10 (1974), p. 339.

2. According to J. Rohde, *Rediscovering the Teaching of the Evangelists* (Philadelphia: Westminster, 1968), p. 10, the term *Redaktionsgeschichte* was first coined by Marxsen in a discussion of Conzelmann's *Die Mitte der Zeit* (Tübingen: J. C. B. Mohr [Paul Siebeck], 1953; ET *The Theology of St. Luke* [New York: Harper & Row, 1961] in *MP* 6 (1954), p. 254.

3. N. Perrin, *What Is Redaction Criticism?* (GBSNTS; Philadelphia: Fortress, 1969), p. 1. Cf. the similar definitions of R. T. Fortna, 'Redaction Criticism, NT', *IDBSup*, p. 733, and J. A. Wharton, 'Redaction Criticism, OT', *IDBSup*, p. 729.

first, that many biblical texts are, despite their appearance, collections of material that enjoyed a previous history of usage in the early church; second, that this prehistory can be detected and reconstructed with a certain measure of reliability. If these presuppositions could be claimed for the Gospel of Mark,[4] and if Mark was the earliest of all the canonical Gospels to be written (as was the prevailing scholarly opinion of the early twentieth century),[5] then redaction criticism of the Second Gospel had to be predicated upon one of two exegetical disciplines.

A. The Disciplinary Underpinnings of Markan Redaction Criticism

One course, pursued by some scholars, was to base the analysis of Mark's editiorial activity on the hypothesis of some written source or sources on which the Evangelist was dependent. Perhaps the parade example of this approach was Wilhelm Bussmann's three-part *Synoptische Studien*,[6]

4. Here and throughout this study, I use 'Mark' (as well as 'Matthew', 'Luke', and 'John') to designate both the Gospel and the Evangelist concerned. Such usage is purely for the sake of convenience and in no way implies any judgment about the traditional authorship of the Gospels.

5. For the original formulation and early development of the theory of Markan priority, consult C. G. Wilke, *Der Urevangelist: oder, Exegetische kritische Untersuchung über das Verwandtschaftverhältnis der drei ersten Evangelien* (Dresden and Leipzig: Fleischer, 1838); C. H. Weisse, *Die Evangelienfrage in ihrem gegenwärtigen Stadium* (Leipzig: Breitkopf & Härtel, 1856); and H. J. Holtzmann, *Die synoptischen Evangelien: Ihr Ursprung und geschichtlicher Charakter* (Leipzig: Engelmann, 1863). Owing largely to the vigor with which W. R. Farmer has argued for the recovery of the Griesbach hypothesis (in *The Synoptic Problem: A Critical Analysis* [New York: Macmillan, 1964]), the Synoptic problem has come to appear more problematic in recent years than it had during the century preceding: N.B. the cautious and critically equivocal study of E. P. Sanders, *The Tendencies of the Synoptic Tradition* (SNTSMS 9; Cambridge: Cambridge University Press, 1969); also H.-H. Stoldt, *History and Criticism of the Markan Hypothesis* (ed. D. L. Niewyk; Macon, GA: Mercer University Press, 1980). Nevertheless, at present it seems that the majority of New Testament interpreters would concur with D. M. Smith: 'For the task of exegesis, the hypothesis or paradigm that Mark was used by Matthew and Luke still seems the most satisfying, especially in comparison with the view that Mark conflated Matthew and Luke' (*Johannine Christianity: Essays on Its Setting, Sources, and Theology* [Columbia, SC: University of South Carolina Press, 1984], p. 126). Thus see W. G. Kümmel, *Introduction to the New Testament* (17th edn; Nashville: Abingdon, 1975), pp. 38-80; F. Neirynck, 'Synoptic Problem', *IDBSup*, pp. 845-48; and G. M. Styler, 'The Priority of Mark', in C. F. D. Moule, *The Birth of the New Testament* (3rd edn, rev., and rewritten; San Francisco: Harper & Row, 1982), pp. 285-316.

6. W. Bussmann, *Synoptische Studien* (Halle [Salle]: Buchhandlung des Waisenhauses,

which argued for a compilation of Mark in three stages: G *(die Grund-gestalt)*, B *(der erste galiläische Bearbeiter)*, and E (= Mark, *der zweite römische Bearbeiter)*. Source criticism of the Second Gospel was by no means relegated to Continental scholarship: the 1920s and 1930s saw significant contributions to the field made, in America, by Benjamin Wisner Bacon (1860-1932),[7] and, in Great Britain, by Arthur Temple Cadoux (1874-1948)[8] and John MacLeod Campbell Crum (1872-1958).[9] Source criticism of the Second Gospel remains something of a 'hardy perennial' of Markan scholarship, and new, ever more highly refined *Quellen*-hypotheses have been proposed in successive decades of the twentieth century.[10] Nevertheless, this particular discipline has failed to capture the imagination of Markan interpreters of more recent years. In part this has been owing both to the high degree of speculation inherent in the enter-

---

1925, 1929, 1931). This work is also notable for its once influential presentation of the now all-but-forgotten *Urmarkus* hypothesis, the vicissitudes of which are neatly sketched in V. Taylor, *The Gospel According to St. Mark: The Greek Text with Introduction, Notes, and Indexes* (2nd edn; TC; Grand Rapids, MI: Baker Book House, 1981), pp. 67-77.

7. B. W. Bacon, *The Beginnings of the Gospel Story: A Historico-Critical Inquiry into the Sources and Structure of the Gospel According to Mark, with Expository Notes upon the Text for English Readers* (New Haven: Yale University Press, 1920). Bacon argued that Mark had at his disposal both a primitive narrative and Q (ibid., pp. xx-xxii). In a variation of part of Bacon's thesis, R. Bultmann argued that Mark used an anti-Petrine source ('Die Frage nach dem messianischen Bewusstsein Jesu und das Petrusbekenntnis', *ZNW* 19 [1919/1920], pp. 165-74; repr. idem, *Exegetica: Aufsätze zu Erforschung des Neuen Testaments* [ed. E. Dinkler; Tübingen: J. C. B. Mohr (Paul Siebeck), 1967], pp. 1-9). B. H. Branscomb's *The Gospel of Mark* (MNTC; New York and London: Harper and Brothers, n.d.) is an interesting and learned example of an American commentary on the Second Gospel that is written from a predominantly source-critical point of view.

8. A. T. Cadoux, *The Sources of the Second Gospel* (New York: Macmillan, 1935). Cadoux argued that Mark was a compilation of three earlier Gospels: one, Palestinian Aramaic (A); one, Gentile (C); and the other, Alexandrian.

9. J. M. C. Crum, *St. Mark's Gospel: Two Stages of Its Making* (Cambridge: Cambridge University Press, 1936). The two stages were 'Mark I', written (ca. 36-60 CE) by an associate of Peter, and 'Mark II', reflecting a later Christology (ca. 65 CE) and affinities with Q and with the Septuagint.

10. Thus the postulation of a biographical 'Twelve-source' (W. L. Knox, *The Sources of the Synoptic Gospels: St. Mark* [1; Cambridge: Cambridge University Press, 1953]), a Palestinian Gospel core (Mark 1–13) to which was appended a later, Roman liturgical document (Mark 14–16; E. Trocmé, *The Formation of the Gospel According to Mark* [Philadelphia: Westminster, 1975]), and a βλέπετε-source, which cautions against the Jewish teaching class and apocalyptic pseudo-prophecy (P. Vassiliadis, 'Behind Mark: Towards a Written Source', *NTS* 20 [1974], pp. 155-60).

prise as well as to the relative lack of definable literary aporiae, within the Second Gospel, necessary in order to make such source-critical differentiations.[11] In even larger measure, however, Markan source criticism has been displaced by another, far more influential approach to pre-Markan traditions: *Formgeschichte*.

Although the inception of form criticism of the Gospels is usually associated with the pioneering works of Schmidt, Dibelius, and Bultmann, Norman Perrin has perceptively suggested that the main tracks, along which the form critics of the 1920s traveled, already had been laid nearly fifteen years earlier by Julius Wellhausen (1844-1918).[12] Indeed, one need only read Wellhausen's words, penned in 1905, to realize how truly prophetic were his insights:

> The ultimate source of the Gospels is oral tradition, but this contains only scattered material. The units, more or less extensive, circulate in it separately. Their combination into a whole is always the work of an author and, as a rule, the work of a writer with literary ambitions. . . . The separate units are often presented in lively fashion, without irrelevant or merely rhetorical means, but they usually stand side by side like anecdotes, *rari nantes in gurgite vasto* ['solitary swimmers in a vast whirlpool']. They are inadequate as material for a life of Jesus. . . . Mark does not write *de vita et moribus Jesu* ['about the life and conduct of Jesus']. He has no intention of making Jesus' person manifest, or even intelligible. For him it has been absorbed in Jesus' divine vocation. He wants to demonstrate that Jesus is the Christ.[13]

11. If one contrasts Markan and Johannine research at this point, the difference is telling: the attempt to limn a *sēmeia*-source behind the Fourth Gospel has been considered feasible, precisely because of the seemingly clearer presence of literary aporiae within the text of John. See, for instance, R. T. Fortna, *The Gospel of Signs: A Reconstruction of the Narrative Source Underlying the Fourth Gospel* (SNTSMS 11; Cambridge: Cambridge University Press, 1970), esp. pp. 19-22, and the balanced summary assessment of R. Kysar, *The Fourth Evangelist and His Gospel: An Examination of Contemporary Scholarship* (Minneapolis: Augsburg, 1975), pp. 13-37, 67-81.

12. Perrin, *What Is Redaction Criticism?*, pp. 13-14.

13. J. Wellhausen, *Einleitung in die drei ersten Evangelien* (Berlin: Reimer, 1905), pp. 3, 51-52; reproduced and translated by S. M. Gilmour and H. C. Kee in W. G. Kümmel, *The New Testament: The History of the Investigation of Its Problems* (London: SCM, 1972), pp. 282-83. Wellhausen's perspective is also evident in his commentary on the Second Gospel, *Das Evangelium Marci* (2nd edn; Berlin: Reimer, 1909).

Here, *in nuce*, we find the basic conceptual elements of what would become Gospel *Formgeschichte:* the original sources of the Gospels as having circulated orally and in discrete units, only later to be redacted by the Evangelists in light of the beliefs and circumstances of the primitive church.[14] The elaboration and refinement of these principles were accomplished by the renowned, aforementioned troika: Karl Ludwig Schmidt (1891-1956), who argued that the chronological and topographical framework of the Gospels was largely the construction of the Evangelists, who had taken pericopes of tradition and strung them together, like so many pearls on a string, in accordance with *urchristlich* cultic concerns;[15] Martin Dibelius (1883-1947), who first forged the tools for the form-critical distinction of traditional *Gattungen* — paradigms, tales, legends, myths, and sayings;[16] and Rudolf Bultmann (1884-1976), who executed an exhaustive and arguably definitive analysis of every individual unit of the Synoptics in their entirety, precisely identifying both the *Gattung* as well as the *religionsgeschichtlich Sitz* of each pericope.[17] In recent years Gospel *Formgeschichte* undeniably has undergone considerable rethinking and, in some cases, radical revision; as shall be witnessed more than once in the remainder of this study, such revision carries important implications for the practice and reliability of Markan redaction criti-

14. K. Koch, *The Growth of the Biblical Tradition: The Form-Critical Method* (New York: Charles Scribner's Sons, 1969), is the standard, general introduction to the discipline. Among overviews of New Testament form criticism, see R. Bultmann and K. Kundsin, *Form Criticism: Two Essays on New Testament Research* (New York: Harper & Brothers, 1962); and E. V. McKnight, *What Is Form Criticism?* (GBSNTS; Philadelphia: Fortress, 1969). Though over forty years old, W. G. Doty's 'The Discipline and Literature of New Testament Form Criticism' (*ATR* 51 [1969], pp. 257-321) remains an invaluable bibliographical essay, which includes a listing of 238 *formgeschichtlich* studies.

15. K. L. Schmidt, *Der Rahmen der Geschichte Jesu: Literarkritische Untersuchung zur ältesten Jesusüberlieferung* (Berlin: Trowitzsch & Sohn, 1919). Interestingly, Schmidt's denial of a strictly historical sequence of events in the Gospels, and the affirmation of their control by ecclesial theology, was anticipated by Cornelius à Lapide (ca. 1654; see idem, *The Great Commentary of Cornelius à Lapide: S. Matthew's Gospel — XXII to XXVIII; S. Mark's Gospel — Complete* [3rd edn; London: John Hodges, 1891], p. 364), John Calvin (ca. 1555; *A Harmony of the Gospels: Matthew, Mark, and Luke* [CalCom 1; Edinburgh: Saint Andrews, 1972], pp. xii-xiii), and even Jerome (ca. 390: 'Mark . . . related according to the truth of the things which were done, rather than the order in which they were done' [cited by à Lapide, ibid.]).

16. M. Dibelius, *From Tradition to Gospel* (New York: Charles Scribner's Sons, n.d.). The original German edition was published in 1919.

17. R. Bultmann, *The History of the Synoptic Tradition* (rev. edn; New York: Harper & Row, 1963 [original German edition, 1921]).

cism. Yet it is equally undeniable that form criticism has provided the conceptual framework for a number of influential Markan commentaries of the past half-century,[18] as well as the starting-point for practically every major study of the Markan passion narrative.[19] To the extent that 'redaction criticism proper is dependent upon the ability to write a history of the tradition',[20] *Redaktionsgeschichte* indeed presupposes the insights and methods of *Formgeschichte*.

B. The Movement toward *Redaktionsgeschichte*

For all of its dependence on *Formgeschichte*, redaction criticism was born in reaction to what was perceived as form-critical excesses. Although the contribution of the Evangelists in the final stage of the Gospel tradition was ignored by none of the pioneers of *Formgeschichte*, they did tend to undervalue or at least to underestimate that contribution. Thus the Gospels were construed as nonliterary cultic legends, produced through the collective creativity of the *urchristliche Gemeinde*;[21] the Evangelists, being 'vehicles of tradition' and 'only to the smallest extent authors',[22] were inadequate to the task of mastering the traditions that they collected and edited.[23] In time, such an understanding came to be challenged on three

18. Thus Taylor's *St. Mark*; E. Klostermann, *Das Markusevangelium* (4th edn; HNT 3; Tübingen: J. C. B. Mohr [Paul Siebeck], 1950); D. E. Nineham, *The Gospel of St. Mark* (PGC; Baltimore: Penguin Books, 1963).

19. Among others, note E. Linnemann, *Studien zur Passionsgeschichte* (FRLANT 102; Göttingen: Vandenhoeck & Ruprecht, 1970); D. Dormeyer, *Die Passion Jesu als Verhaltensmodell: Literarische und theologische Analyse der Traditions- und Redaktionsgeschichte der Markuspassion* (Münster: Aschendorff, 1974); W. Schenk, *Der Passionsbericht nach Markus: Untersuchungen zur Überlieferungsgeschichte der Passionstraditionen* (Gütersloh: Gerd Mohn, 1974); and L. Schenke, *Der gekreuzigte Christus: Versuch einer literarkritischen und traditionsgeschichtlichen Bestimmung der vormarkinischen Passionsgeschichte* (SB 69; Stuttgart: KBW, 1974).

20. Perrin, *What Is Redaction Criticism?*, p. 13.

21. K. L. Schmidt, 'Die Stellung der Evangelien in der allgemeinen Literaturgeschichte', in *Eucharisterion: Hermann Gunkel zum 60. Geburtstag* (ed. H. Schmidt; Göttingen: Vandenhoeck & Ruprecht, 1923), pp. 50-134; see esp. pp. 76, 124.

22. Dibelius, *Tradition*, p. 3.

23. Bultmann, *Synoptic Tradition*, p. 350. In fairness, Bultmann explicitly argued that Mark was not sufficiently master of his material (ibid.); Matthew's Gospel was a revision and enrichment of Mark's (ibid., p. 353), and the Gospel of Luke was in many ways 'the climax of the history of the Synoptic Tradition' (ibid., p. 367). Still, Bultmann (like Dibelius)

fronts. First, it was argued, to minimize the Evangelists' contribution to the Gospel tradition was to curtail precipitately the very history of the tradition that the form critics sought to reconstruct: 'Form history which bypasses the authors of the Gospels is somehow left hanging in the air'.[24] Second, to regard the Evangelists as little more than *Sammler* or 'scissors-and-paste men' in their assemblage of the various pericopes was to overlook the possibility that

> the 'scissors' were manipulated by a theological hand, and the 'paste' was impregnated with a particular theology. In contrast to the anti-individualistic view of the form critics, today the evangelists are recognized as individual theologians. . . . We are here dealing with individual authors not with the 'community'.[25]

Third, to focus one's attention almost exclusively on the various forms of the tradition, their history and their communal *Sitz*, was to run the risk of ignoring the Gospels as homogenous wholes: 'We grasp Mark's share of the work and thus his actual achievement (as well as that of the other evangelists) not in the material primarily but in the "framework"'.[26] To offset certain imbalances in the form-critical approach, therefore, a new strategy in the reading of the Gospels was called for, one accenting their unitary character as the creation of an Evangelist functioning as a genuine author and theologian.

As was the case with form criticism, the new approach that came to be called *Redaktionsgeschichte* was in fact the elaboration of certain insights that had been applied to the Gospels years before. The overall understanding of redaction criticism (that the Evangelists were not dominated by purely biographical or historical concerns but were guided by a theologically creative attitude toward the Gospel tradition) had been anticipated

---

regarded the redaction history of the Gospels as '[involving] nothing in principle new, but only [completing] what was begun in the oral tradition' (ibid., p. 321).

24. Marxsen, *Mark the Evangelist*, p. 21.

25. R. H. Stein, 'What Is *Redaktionsgeschichte?*', *JBL* 88 (1969), pp. 46, 49. No more satisfying, for the redaction critic, is the likening of the Evangelists' use of traditional material to some haphazard arrangement of pearls on a string: 'Any woman would have spotted at once the flaw in the analogy: pearls need to be carefully selected and graded. And gradually it has dawned on New Testament scholars that this is precisely what the evangelists have done with their material' (M. D. Hooker, *The Message of Mark* [London: Epworth, 1983], p. 3).

26. Marxsen, *Mark the Evangelist*, p. 23.

nearly two centuries earlier by the staunch German Deist and rationalist, Hermann Samuel Reimarus (1694-1768).[27] Over a century later, a similar intuition characterized the work of Martin Kähler (1835-1912), who lambasted the historicism of his day for treating the Gospels as though they were windows onto the inner life of Jesus; on the contrary, retorted Kähler, the Gospels were imbued with early Christian theology and were intended to awaken faith in Christ as Savior: 'To state the matter somewhat provocatively, one could call the Gospels passion narratives with extended introductions [*Passionsgeschichte mit ausführlicher Einleitung*]'.[28] However, there is little question that the most powerful, and ultimately most influential, precursor of the redaction-critical perspective was presented by William Wrede (1859-1906) in his seminal book, *Das Messiasgeheimnis in den Evangelien* (1901).[29] A landmark in Gospel research, Wrede's monograph contended that the secrecy motif in the Gospels, especially dominant in Mark, was quite without historical foundation: 'the messianic secret' was a theological idea, one of a number of dogmatic conceptions that stemmed from primitive Christian traditions antedating the Gospels[30] and controlling their creation.[31]

That Wrede opened the floodgates to a tide of christological research

27. 'However, I find great cause to separate completely what the apostles say in their own writings from that which Jesus himself actually said and taught, for the apostles were themselves teachers and consequently present their own views. . . .' (H. S. Reimarus, *Reimarus: Fragments* [ed. C. H. Talbert; LJS; Philadelphia: Fortress, 1970], p. 64).

28. M. Kähler, *The So-Called Historical Jesus and the Historic Biblical Christ* (Philadelphia: Fortress, 1964), p. 80 n. 11. In the context of this famous dictum, it is evident that Kähler had Mark's Gospel particularly in mind.

29. ET *The Messianic Secret* (Greenwood, SC: Attic, 1971).

30. Though the point has been clarified by others, it bears repeating that Wrede attributed the creation of 'the messianic secret' to the pre-Markan tradition epitomized by Acts 2.36, Rom. 1.4, and Phil. 2.6ff. (*Messianic Secret*, pp. 209-17). He explicitly and emphatically denied the conclusion that is carelessly attributed to him: that the messianic secret was an invention of the Second Evangelist ('The notion seems quite impossible', ibid., p. 145). Wrede was generally inclined to regard the creative theology of the Gospels as contributed by the community in which the Evangelists participated, rather than by the Evangelists themselves (ibid., esp. pp. 84, 145); in this respect he was in greater alignment with what came to be the form-critical, rather than the redaction-critical, perspective. The debate with Wrede on this point has most recently been renewed by R. Weber, 'Christologie und "Messiasgeheimnis": ihr Zusammenhang und Stellenwert in der Darstellungsintention des Markus' *EvT* 43 (1983), pp. 108-25.

31. 'In this sense the Gospel of Mark belongs to the history of dogma' (Wrede, *Messianic Secret*, p. 131).

that has yet to be stanched is well-known;[32] that many of these investigations have been occupied with challenging the vulnerable points in Wrede's presentation is also generally acknowledged.[33] For our purposes, the point of enduring interest is the *perspective* on the Gospels crystallized by Wrede and the force with which he communicated that perspective: that the Gospels were preeminently theological and not historical works, their creators being more interested in the cultivation of religious belief than in the presentation of historical facts. Though the accents of their respective presentations varied from Wrede's, all of the Continental form critics we have considered, as well as such Anglo-Saxon scholars as Benjamin Wisner Bacon[34] and James Hardy Ropes (1866-1933),[35] were significantly influenced by Wrede's position.

Wrede had suggested that a unified, traditional secrecy motif could be differentiated from the Second Gospel's own inchoate presentations of that motif;[36] however, he never satisfactorily clarified how such a differentiation could be achieved. In short, if Wrede anticipated a redaction-critical *perspective,* it was left for others to anticipate a redaction-critical *method.* Preeminent among those in quest of the latter was the Oxford don, Robert Henry Lightfoot (1883-1953). Lightfoot's Bampton Lectures, which today read with a remarkable freshness that belies their age (1934), are unmistakably indebted to Wrede in their case for the Gospels' thor-

32. A reliable and relatively thorough chronicle of research and debate on the subject is provided by J. L. Blevins, *The Messianic Secret in Markan Research, 1901-1976* (Washington, DC: University Press of America, 1981).

33. Among others, see H. J. Ebeling, *Das Messiasgeheimnis und die Botschaft des Marcus-Evangelisten* (BZNW 19; Berlin: Töpelmann, 1939); E. Sjöberg, *Der verborgene Menschensohn in den Evangelien* (Lund: C. W. K. Gleerup, 1955); G. Minette de Tillesse, *Le Secret Messianique dans l'Évangile de Marc* (LD 47; Paris: Cerf, 1968); H. Räisänen, *Das 'Messiasgeheimnis' im Markusevangelium* (SFEG 28; Helsinki: Länsi-Suomi, 1976); and the important collection of essays in *The Messianic Secret* (ed. C. Tuckett; IRT 1; Philadelphia and London: Fortress/SPCK, 1983).

34. Wrede's impact on Bacon seems most pronounced in the latter's understanding of a doctrinal development from Pauline to Markan theology, with direct and indirect Pauline influences being evidenced in Mark (B. W. Bacon, *The Gospel of Mark: Its Composition and Date* [New Haven: Yale University Press, 1925], pp. 221-71; idem, *Is Mark a Roman Gospel?* [HTS 7; Cambridge, MA and London: Harvard University Press, 1919], pp. 66-75).

35. J. H. Ropes, *The Synoptic Gospels* (Cambridge, MA: Harvard University Press, 1934), pp. 6, 9-10: 'To suppose that [Mark] was prompted by a primary historical purpose is to do it and its author a grave injustice. . . . [The] author's motive was only in a minor degree biographical[;] . . . its purpose . . . is theological'.

36. Wrede, *Messianic Secret,* pp. 145-49, 209-17.

ough commingling of history and theology;[37] yet Lightfoot moved beyond Wrede, as well as beyond most of Lightfoot's fellow form critics, by arguing that distinctive theological interests of Mark and of the other Evangelists could be identified in a good deal of the arrangement given by them to their traditional material. Developing in greater detail certain suggestions of the accomplished German form critic, Ernst Lohmeyer (1890-1946),[38] Lightfoot specifically called attention to a geographical scheme in the Second Gospel that (in his estimation) conveyed subtle but real theological significance: Mark had structured his narrative in such a way that Galilee represented the sphere of divine operation and redemption, and Judea symbolized the realm of misunderstanding, hostility, rejection, and ultimate disaster.[39] Quite different from Lightfoot's analysis were Austin Marsden Farrer's (1904-1968) attempts to discern in the Second Gospel esoteric, and extraordinarily complicated, numerological cycles and patterns;[40] and quite different again from the theories of both Lightfoot and Farrer was Philip Carrington's (1892-1975) argument that Mark's Gospel was structured in accordance with the Jewish seasonal and festal calendar and its accompanying synagogue lectionary, supposedly appropriated by the primitive church.[41] The effect of reviewing these multifarious attempts to educe some key pattern that purportedly mir-

37. R. H. Lightfoot, *History and Interpretation in the Gospels* (London: Hodder and Stoughton, 1935). N.B. ibid., p. 98: 'We have found reason to believe that, rightly regarded, [Mark's Gospel] may be called the book of the (secret) messiahship of Jesus'. Lightfoot's later volume of collected essays, *The Gospel Message of St. Mark* (Oxford: Clarendon, 1950), continued to tackle the question of history and theology in the Second and Fourth Gospels.

38. E. Lohmeyer, *Galiläa und Jerusalem* (Göttingen: Vandenhoeck & Ruprecht, 1936). Lohmeyer later contributed an important, form-critically oriented commentary on Mark: *Das Evangelium des Markus* (MeyerK 1/2; Göttingen: Vandenhoeck & Ruprecht, 1954).

39. R. H. Lightfoot, *Locality and Doctrine in the Gospels* (London: Hodder and Stoughton, 1938).

40. A. M. Farrer, *A Study in St Mark* (Westminster: Dacre, 1951); idem, *St Matthew and St Mark* (Westminster: Dacre, 1954). As Kealy (*Mark's Gospel*, p. 150) notes, Farrer later repudiated many of his own theories, not only because of their almost universal rejection as being too far-fetched, but also out of his concern that their pursuit would ultimately lead to a perception of the Gospels as works of pure fiction.

41. P. Carrington, *The Primitive Christian Calendar: A Study in the Making of the Markan Gospel* (Cambridge: Cambridge University Press, 1952); idem, 'The Calendrical Hypothesis of the Origin of Mark', *ExpTim* 67 (1956), pp. 100-103. More recent variations on Carrington's hypothesis have been worked out in considerable detail by J. Bowman, *The Gospel of Mark: The New Christian Jewish Passover Haggadah* (SPB 8; Leiden: Brill, 1965), and M. D. Goulder, *Midrash and Lection in Matthew* (London: SPCK, 1974).

rors the Evangelist's set purpose is somewhat mind-boggling. Apart from the internal plausibility of any one of them,[42] the existence of each tends to render the others suspect: surely Lightfoot, Farrer, and Carrington cannot all be right, though they may all be wrong. Still, at this juncture it is less important for us to adjudicate their results and more important to observe what they hold in common: the assumption that Mark was a creative arranger of his traditions, and the search for a method that would illuminate that arrangement.

Mark's authorial creativity and the methods appropriate for its assessment were sought along avenues other than traditional arrangement. Harking at least as far back to the work of Eduard Zeller (1814-1908),[43] numerous scholars on both sides of the Atlantic attempted to compile ever more exacting lists of the Synoptics' word-usage, with the aim of delineating the linguistic peculiarities of Mark and of the other Evangelists.[44] Nor was Markan literary style overlooked: beyond the pioneering study by Christian Gottlob Wilke (1756-1854) in 1843,[45] the period spanning the initiation of form criticism and the inception of redaction criticism was the era of the great synthetic studies of the Second Evangelist's grammar and syntax: Cuthbert Hamilton Turner's (1860-1930) influential series of articles on Markan usage,[46] Maximilian Zerwick's (1901-1975) *Untersuchung*

---

42. Of the critical reception to Farrer's essays I have already spoken in note 40 above. On the Lohmeyer-Lightfoot geographical hypothesis, see G. Stemberger, 'Galilee — Land of Salvation?', in W. D. Davies, *The Gospel and the Land: Early Christian and Jewish Territorial Doctrine* (Berkeley: University of California Press, 1974), pp. 409-38. On Carrington's calendrical hypothesis, consult W. D. Davies, 'Reflections on Archbishop Carrington's "The Primitive Christian Calendar"', in *The Background of the New Testament and Its Eschatology: Studies in Honour of C. H. Dodd* (ed. W. D. Davies and D. Daube; Cambridge: Cambridge University Press, 1956), pp. 124-52.

43. E. Zeller, 'Studien zur neutestamentlichen Theologie: 4. vergleichende Übersicht über den Wörtervorrath der neutestamentlichen Schriftsteller', *TJ* 2 (1843), pp. 443-543.

44. J. C. Hawkins, *Horae Synopticae* (Oxford: Clarendon, 1909); K. Grobel, 'Idiosyncrasies of the Synoptics in their Pericope-Introductions', *JBL* 59 (1940), pp. 405-10; R. Morgenthaler, *Statistik des Neutestamentlichen Wortschatzes* (Zürich: Gotthelf, 1958). L. Gaston's *Horae Synopticae Electronicae: Word Statistics of the Synoptic Gospels* (SBLSBS 3; Missoula, MT: SBL, 1973), which unlike its predecessors is avowedly concerned to identify redactional vocabulary items, will be treated at greater length in Chapter 7.

45. C. G. Wilke, *Die neutestamentliche Rhetorik* (Dresden and Leipzig: Arnoldische Buchhandlung, 1843).

46. C. H. Turner, 'Markan Usage: Notes, Critical and Exegetical, on the Second Gospel', *JTS* o.s. 25 (1923), pp. 377-86; 26 (1924), pp. 12-20, 145-56, 225-40, 337-46; 27 (1925), pp. 58-62; 28 (1926), pp. 9-30, 349-62; 29 (1927), pp. 257-89, 346-61.

zum Markus-Stil,[47] and John Charles Doudna's (1907-2009) *The Greek of the Gospel of Mark*.[48] Beyond the Evangelist's language, style, and creative patterning of traditions, almost all of the other assumed indicators of Markan authorial activity were covered in 1953 by Pierson Parker (1905-): insertions, additions, summaries, condensations, and transitions.[49]

To sum up: by the time redaction criticism, as a distinctive exegetical discipline, made its first bow in the mid-1950s, its way had been prepared, both conceptually and procedurally, by a host of researchers in the Synoptics. Although the redaction critics would highlight, as never before, the artistry of the Second Gospel and the creativity of its author, these insights had already been trumpeted by Morton Scott Enslin (1897-1980) some seven years before the redaction-critical discipline was known by that name:

> It is time to stop our talk about the artless and unpremeditated and unimaginative style of [Mark's] gospel. . . . The longer I study this gospel, the more I am impressed by the daring genius of its author. Far from being artless work, it bears on every page the evidence, will we but lose our presuppositions, of the author's creative design.[50]

C. The Pursuit of a Method for Markan Redaction Criticism

In the preceding discussion we have observed a distinction between the *perspective* and *procedure* of Markan redaction criticism in its embryonic form. This is a serviceable differentiantion insofar as it better enables us to

47. M. Zerwick, *Untersuchung zum Markus-Stil* (SPIB; Rome: Pontifical Biblical Institute, 1937).

48. J. C. Doudna, *The Greek of the Gospel of Mark* (JBLMS 12; Philadelphia: Society of Biblical Literature, 1961).

49. P. Parker, *The Gospel Before Mark* (Chicago: University of Chicago Press, 1953), pp. 52-59.

50. M. S. Enslin, 'The Artistry of Mark', *JBL* 66 (1947), pp. 385-99; citation, pp. 387-88. Although a number of contemporary critics would share Enslin's sentiments (e.g. see D. Rhoads and D. Michie, *Mark as Story: An Introduction to the Narrative of a Gospel* [Philadelphia: Fortress, 1982]), there has been no dearth of aspersions cast on Mark's literary ability: contrast the rather less generous appraisals of A. E. J. Rawlinson, *The Gospel According to St. Mark* (WC; London: Methuen, 1942), p. xxxii); M. Smith, 'Comments on Taylor's Commentary on Mark', *HTR* 48 (1955), p. 38; and J. C. Meagher, *Clumsy Construction in Mark's Gospel: A Critique of Form- and Redaktionsgeschichte* (TST 3; New York and Toronto: Edwin Mellen, 1979); cf. idem, '*Die Form- und Redaktionsungeschickliche Methoden:* The Principle of Clumsiness and the Gospel of Mark', *JAAR* 43 (1975), pp. 459-72.

understand what is going on in the secondary literature on the subject; this distinction I shall maintain in the comments that follow. Later in this study (Chapter 8) we shall have occasion to reflect at length on the *redaktionsgeschichtlich* point of view, the reasons for its popularity among exegetes of the mid-twentieth century, and its contributions and liabilities. For now, however, I wish to concentrate on the actual procedure or method of the discipline as that has been hammered out by its practitioners in the course of interpreting Mark. On the basis of our discussion to this point, we may assume as a working definition that redaction criticism is an exegetical discipline with an explicit interest in the Gospels as literary wholes, in the Evangelists as genuine authors who have imposed upon their traditions a distinctive theological stamp, and in the communities of which those Evangelists were members. With this operational definition in mind, it should be emphasized that my objective in the following paragraphs is *not* to present a comprehensive review of all redaction-critical research in Mark's Gospel of the past three decades; such an enterprise is neither pertinent to my present goals nor needful in light of the plethora of *Forschungsberichte* on the subject that already exists and is readily accessible.[51] Here I wish only to present and to document the principal criteria that have been customarily invoked by New Testament scholars in their attempts to separate tradition from redaction in the Second Gospel.

51. Although every redaction-critical study of Mark neither is nor can be included in a single *Forschungsbericht,* the following studies cover both the breadth of the research and its most important specimens: H.-D. Knigge, 'The Meaning of Mark: The Exegesis of the Second Gospel', *Int* 22 (1968), pp. 53-70; F. J. Matera, 'Interpreting Mark — Some Recent Theories of Redaction Criticism', *LS* 2 (1968), pp. 113-31; Rohde, *Rediscovering,* pp. 113-52; H. C. Kee, 'Mark's Gospel in Recent Research', *Int* 32 (1978), pp. 353-68; R. P. Martin, *Mark: Evangelist and Theologian* (Grand Rapids, MI: Zondervan, 1972); Kingsbury, 'Mark in Current Research'; Kealy, *Mark's Gospel,* pp. 159-237; Telford, 'Introduction: The Gospel of Mark'; W. O. Seal, Jr, 'Norman Perrin and His 'School': Retracing a Pilgrimage', *JSNT* 20 (1984), pp. 87-107. One should also consult the bibliographies of the standard redaction-critical commentaries on Mark: E. Schweizer, *The Good News According to Mark* (Richmond, VA: John Knox, 1970); W. L. Lane, *The Gospel According to Mark: The English Text with Introduction, Exposition, and Notes* (NICNT; Grand Rapids, MI: Eerdmans, 1974); H. Anderson, *The Gospel of Mark* (NCB; Grand Rapids, MI and London: Eerdmans/Marshall, Morgan & Scott, 1976); R. Pesch, *Das Markusevangelium* (2 vols.; 2nd rev. edn; HTKNT 2; Freiburg: Herder, 1976, 1977); J. Gnilka, *Des Evangelium nach Markus* (2 vols.; EKKNT II. 1-2; Zürich, Einsiedeln, and Cologne: Benzinger/Neukirchener Verlag, 1978, 1979); W. Schmithals, *Des Evangelium nach Markus* (2 vols.; OTKNT 2; Wörzburg/Gütersloh: Gerd Mohn/Gütersloher & Echter Verlag, 1979); C. S. Mann, *Mark: A New Translation with Introduction and Commentary* (AB 27; Garden City, NY: Doubleday, 1986).

Not many years ago the task of systematizing Markan redaction-critical method would have been formidable indeed. Relatively soon after Harald Riesenfeld (1913-1981)[52] and Willi Marxsen (1919-1993) ignited scholarly interest in the discipline's application to the Second Gospel, redaction critics began to adopt a *redaktionsgeschichtlich* perspective on Mark without articulating their *redaktionsgeschichtlich* method.[53] There were exceptions: early on Eduard Schweizer (1913-2006) had settled on typical vocabulary, themes, and narrative structure as significant in determining Markan redaction;[54] and in 1961 Johannes Schreiber (1927-) enunciated four 'methodische Grundsätze', which he hoped would facilitate a proper understanding of Mark.[55] However, *Grundsätze* such as Schreiber's were as much redaction-critical points of orientation as they were specific criteria;[56] and while particular criteria were proposed by Schweizer and others, virtually no efforts were made to synthesize and to systematize the methodological options. Thus, some fourteen years after the pioneering work of Riesenfeld and Marxsen, Georg Strecker (1929-1994) could complain that 'the method-

52. H. Riesenfeld, 'Tradition und Redaktion im Markusevangelium', *Neutestamentliche Studien für Rudolf Bultmann zu seinem siebzigsten Geburtstag* (ed. W. Eltester; Berlin: Töpelmann, 1954), pp. 157-64; repr. in *Das Markus-Evangelium* (ed. R. Pesch; WF 411; Darmstadt: Wissenschaftliche Buchgesellschaft, 1979), pp. 103-12.

53. Characteristic of many in this regard was J. M. Robinson, who later confessed this to be a methodological deficiency of his monograph, *The Problem of History in Mark* (SBT 21; London: SCM, 1957). See his 'The Problem of History in Mark, Reconsidered', *USQR* 10 (1965), pp. 131-47, esp. pp. 132-35.

54. E. Schweizer, 'Anmerkungen zur Theologie des Markus', *Neotestamentica et Patristica: Freundesgabe O. Cullmann* (Leiden: E. J. Brill, 1962), pp. 35-46; idem, 'Die theologische Leistung des Markus', *EvT* 24 (1964), pp. 337-55; *Good News*, passim.

55. J. Schreiber, 'Die Christologie des Markusevangeliums: Beobachtungen zur Theologie und Komposition des zweiten Evangeliums', *ZTK* 58 (1961), pp. 154-55: '1. Alle Verse des Markusevangeliums, die mit Hilfe analytischer Untersuchungsmethoden der Redaktion des Markus zuzuschreiben sind, ergeben den Ausgangspunkt für die Erhebung seiner Theologie. . . . 2. Wo Matthäus oder Lukas oder gar beide Evangelisten den Markustext in einem bestimmten Punkt, womöglich über das ganze Evangelium hin, ändern, liegt sehr wahrscheinlich eine theologische Aussage des Markus vor, die sie ablehnen. . . . 3. Die Auswahl und Anordnung der Tradition im Markusevangelium erlaubt ebenfalls Rückschlüsse auf die Redaktion des Evangelisten. 4. Die . . . Theologie des Markus muß . . . auch in einer bestimmten religionsgeschichtlichen Situation sinnvoll sein'.

56. The same could be said for J. Delorme, 'Aspects Doctrinaux du Second Evangile', *ETL* 43 (1967), pp. 77-79, and Q. Quesnell, *The Mind of Mark: Interpretation and Method through the Exegesis of Mark 6, 52* (AnBib 38; Rome: Pontifical Biblical Institute, 1969), pp. 46-57 (despite Quesnell's express concern for 'scientific rigor in method' [p. 45]).

ological problem of redaction criticism [of Mark] has not yet been worked out in a clear presentation and remains a matter of urgent importance'.[57]

The gauntlet thrown down by Strecker in 1967 was taken up the following year by Robert Harry Stein (1935-) in a Th.D. thesis submitted to the faculty of Princeton Theological Seminary.[58] Stein's procedure was straightforward and clear: after conducting a descriptive review of the explicit or implicit criteria employed by three precursors of *Redaktionsgeschichte*[59] and by three more recent practitioners of the discipline,[60] Stein prescribed thirteen criteria, based on the collective wisdom of his predecessors, that corresponded with the various ways in which Mark had edited his traditional materials and thus could be used reliably in ascertaining a Markan redaction history. (One of these, 'the direct address of Mark to his reader', was later dropped, leaving an even dozen criteria in Stein's revised presentation.)[61] 'Unless we first isolate the Markan redaction from the tradition', warned Stein, 'we shall become confused between the theology of the Markan tradition and the particular theology of the Evangelist'.[62] The capability of his criteria to make this preliminary isolation and to avoid such confusion validated (in Stein's own opinion) the fittingness of his methodology for ascertaining a Markan *Redaktionsgeschichte*.

Whether or not Stein's twelve canons, taken singly or collectively, actually fulfill his promise of a 'proper methodology' is of little concern to me at the moment: the chapters which follow will constitute the proof of the

57. G. Strecker, 'The Passion and Resurrection Predictions in Mark's Gospel', *Int* 22 (1968), p. 423 n. 5. (The German original of this article, 'Die Leidens- und Auferstehungsvoraussagen im Markusevangelium (Mk 8, 31; 9, 31; 10, 32-34)', appeared in *ZTK* 64 [1967], pp. 16-39).

58. R. H. Stein, 'The Proper Methodology for Ascertaining a Marcan *Redaktionsgeschichte*' (Th.D. Diss., Princeton Theological Seminary, 1968), the heart of which was revised for publication as 'The Proper Methodology for Ascertaining a Markan Redaction History', *NovT* 13 (1971), pp. 181-98. Hereafter, 'Proper Methodology' will refer to Stein's thesis; 'Markan Redaction History' will designate Stein's article in *NovT*.

59. W. Wrede (*The Messianic Secret*), E. Lohmeyer (*Galiläa und Jerusalem*), and R. H. Lightfoot (principally, *Locality and Doctrine*).

60. J. M. Robinson (*The Problem of History in Mark*), W. Marxsen (*Mark the Evangelist*), and E. Best (*The Temptation and the Passion: The Markan Soteriology* [SNTSMS 2; Cambridge: Cambridge University Press, 1965]).

61. The revised presentation was, of course, 'Markan Redaction History' (see above, note 58). Presumably, Stein discarded 'Mark's direct address' as a criterion owing to its limited usefulness: in his dissertation he could document only one instance of its occurrence in the Second Gospel (Mark 13.14; cf. 'Proper Methodology', pp. 186-88).

62. Stein, 'Proper Methodology', p. 249.

pudding. For now, I would claim only that Stein's presentation is probably unsurpassed as a precise, synthetic, and comprehensive description of how exegetes have, in fact, applied redaction criticism to the Gospel of Mark.[63] This should become clear as we review Stein's criteria and witness their appropriation by Markan investigators whose work has antedated as well as postdated Stein's own research.

1. On the customary form-critical assumption that the Second Evangelist received his traditional material in the form of disconnected units, a generally recognized means by which scholars have attempted to ascertain the distinctive editorial activity and the unique theological interests of Mark is the investigation of *Markan seams*.[64] Marxsen tacitly appealed to

---

63. Relatively few redaction critics have attempted the sort of project that Stein has carried out, and none, to my knowledge, has executed it as well. Quesnell (*Mind of Mark*, pp. 46-57) has presented a number of significant hermeneutical principles to be exercised in reading Mark (e.g., that one should stick closely to the existing text, that intelligible unity can be used as an interpretive norm, and so forth), but these are rather general and in any case need not be confined to a *redaction-critical* reading of the Second Gospel. Subject to neither of these criticisms are Perrin's methodological suggestions (the focus upon Markan vocabulary and style, thematic concerns, compositional techniques, and usage of traditional units), but these lack precision and do not cover the full range of customary *redaktionsgeschichtlich* methods ('The Christology of Mark: A Study in Methodology', *JR* 51 [1971], pp. 174-75). The same could be said of W. G. Doty's helpful but cursory treatment (*Contemporary New Testament Interpretation* [Englewood Cliffs, NJ: Prentice-Hall, 1972], pp. 70-75). In the introduction to his magisterial commentary on the Second Gospel, Pesch offers a careful discussion and critique of redaction-critical technique; however, his own interpretive predilections lead him to emphasize only one of the customary redaction-critical options (the analysis of overarching thematic constructs, *Spannungsbögen*) and to reject or to ignore other options that are exercised, notwithstanding Pesch's objections, by other Markan redaction critics (e.g. editorial insertions or outright creations; Pesch, *Des Markusevangelium*, pp. 15-32). Equal in thoroughness to Stein's presentation is the genuinely helpful discussion by H. Zimmermann in *Neutestamentliche Methodenlehre: Darstellung der Historisch-Kritischen Methode* (2nd rev. edn; Stuttgart: Kath. Bibelwerk, 1968), pp. 214-57, esp. pp. 221-30; however, Zimmermann is more generally concerned with Synoptic *Redaktionsgeschichte* in its breadth and, unlike Stein, does not consistently zero in on the problems peculiar to the discipline's application to the Second Gospel on the assumption of Markan priority. To repeat: I know of no study other than Stein's that accurately describes the full range of techniques associated with Markan redaction criticism.

64. The most detailed methodological study of this aspect of Markan redaction has been undertaken by Stein himself: 'The "Redaktionsgeschichtlich" Investigation of a Markan Seam (Mc 1.21f)', *ZNW* 61 (1970), pp. 70-94, a revision of Stein's discussion of the same subject in his Princeton dissertation (pp. 108-45).

Here and throughout, my documentation of Markan scholars' use of these redactional criteria should be taken as illustrative, not exhaustive.

this canon when he argued, 'We grasp Mark's share of the work and thus his actual achievement . . . not in the material primarily but in the "framework"'.[65] More explicit was Ernest Best's (1917-2004) observation that 'the most obvious place to look for Mark's hand is in the words, phrases, and sentences which join together the various incidents of the Gospel'.[66] As with the other criteria to be discussed, Markan seams were not probed in order to satisfy purely literary or form-critical curiosity: 'the investigation of the way the Evangelists cemented together the various isolated materials available to them must reveal something of their unique theological interests'.[67]

2. Long attracting the attention of *redaktionsgeschichtlich*-oriented researchers have been the *Markan insertions (Zwischenbemerkungen)*, those (putative) foreign statements placed by the Evangelist within pericopes in order to explain or to comment upon the inherited tradition, thereby aligning it with his main theological purposes.[68] Somewhat surprisingly, bold exegetical interpretations have been made to turn upon the purported presence of a Markan insertion: long before Norman Perrin and his students seized upon the verses, Mark 14.28 and 16.7 were interpreted by Ernst Lohmeyer to be Markan *Zwischenbemerkungen* in reference to the *parousia*, not the resurrection;[69] those same verses were pivotal in Marxsen's theory that Mark was a Galilean Gospel exhorting Christians to flee to Pella to await the *parousia*.[70]

3. Aside from seams, the earliest established and best-known structural features of the framework of the Second Gospel are those recurring statements that summarize the mission, message, or fame of Jesus and his followers (Mark 1.14-15, 21-22, 32-34, 39; 2.13; 3.7-12; 5.21; 6.6b, 12-13, 30-33, 53-56; 10.1).[71] Markan scholars are not in complete accord on the function

65. Marxsen, *Mark the Evangelist*, p. 23, cf. pp. 54-55, 63. Thus also Schweizer, *Good News*, pp. 13-14.

66. Best, *Temptation*, p. 63, cf. pp. 63-102.

67. Stein, 'Markan Redaction History', p. 184. Cf. Lohmeyer (*Galiläa und Jerusalem*, p. 26) and Lightfoot (*Locality and Doctrine*, p. 112), both of whom argue for the theological significance of Galilee on the basis of the region's repeated reference in the Markan seams (e.g., 1.28, 39; etc.).

68. Best, *Temptation*, p. ix; Stein, 'Proper Methodology', p. 145; cf. Schweizer, *Good News*, p. 14.

69. Lohmeyer, *Galiläa und Jerusalem*, pp. 26, 36. Cf. W. O. Seal, Jr, 'The Parousia in Mark: A Debate with Norman Perrin and His "School"' (Ph.D. diss., Union Theological Seminary [New York], 1982).

70. Marxsen, *Mark the Evangelist*, pp. 75-95.

71. Schmidt, *Der Rahmen*, pp. 160-61 et passim; W. Marxsen, 'Redaktionsgeschichtliche

served by these *summaries,* or *Sammelberichte;*[72] that Mark was responsible for their composition, and fashioned them according to his theological purposes, is still generally assumed by redaction critics of the Gospel.[73]

4. If it be granted that such elements of the Second Gospel as seams, insertions, and summaries are attributable to the Evangelist's creative activity, then it could be the case that Mark was further responsible for *the creation of pericopes.* Although some Markan interpreters flatly reject this possibility,[74] and others (including Stein) acknowledge the difficulty in substantiating such a claim,[75] Stein is correct to include this in a descriptive listing of redactional criteria: it is indeed the case that a number of scholars accord to Mark a high degree of compositional freedom and creativity.[76]

5. In addition to the possibility of Mark's creation of new material, and his creation of a new framework for old traditions, many redaction critics think that the Evangelist may have engaged in *modification (Abwandlung) of his material:* that is, actual changes made by Mark to his inherited sayings

---

Erklärung der sogenannten Parabeltheorie des Markus', *ZTK* 52 (1955), pp. 255-71, esp. p. 258. The verses to be included in any listing of summaries will vary from scholar to scholar; those indicated above are representative.

72. For example, they have been regarded as essentially transitional devices in Mark's Gospel (N. Perrin, 'Towards an Interpretation of the Gospel of Mark', *Christology and a Modern Pilgrimage: A Discussion with Norman Perrin* [ed. H. D. Betz; Philadelphia: Fortress, 1971], pp. 3-5), as both summarizing and transitional passages (H. C. Kee, *Community of the New Age: Studies in Mark's Gospel* [Philadelphia: Westminster, 1977], pp. 56-62), and as fundamentally narrative devices, intended to broaden and to intensify the effects of Jesus' ministry (C. W. Hedrick, 'The Role of "Summary Statements" in the Composition of the Gospel of Mark: A Dialog with Karl Schmidt and Norman Perrin', *NovT* 26 [1984], pp. 289-311).

73. Among others, see Strecker, 'Passion and Resurrection Predictions', p. 423; Schweizer, *Good News,* p. 14; Anderson, *Gospel of Mark,* p. 39; P. J. Achtemeier, *Mark* (2nd edn; PC; Philadelphia: Fortress, 1986), pp. 28-29.

74. Thus Pesch, *Des Markusevangelium* (I, p. 22): 'der Redaktor Markus ist kein Inventor, sondern Bearbeiter von Tradition . . .'

75. Stein, 'Markan Redaction History', pp. 185-86.

76. For instance, both J. Lambrecht (*Die Redaktion der Markus-Apokalypse: Literarische Analyse und Strukturuntersuchung* [AnBib 28; Rome: Pontifical Biblical Institute, 1967]) and J. R. Donahue (*Are You the Christ? The Trial Narrative in the Gospel of Mark* [SBLDS 10; Missoula, MT: SBL, 1973]) argue that Mark has played a major role, not only in modifying traditions, but also in composing new material. The Evangelist's creative freedom is also evident in two collections of essays on the passion narrative: Linnemann's *Studien zur Passionsgeschichte* (above, note 19) and *The Passion in Mark: Studies on Mark 14–16* (ed. W. H. Kelber; Philadelphia: Fortress, 1976).

and stories in order to bring them into conformity with his own point of view.[77] On the assumption of Markan priority, the implementation of this criterion is fraught with enormous difficulties, since it requires that the investigator must first ascertain the character of the pre-Markan tradition in order to evaluate the nature and degree of its redactional modification. 'The situation is not entirely hopeless, however', avers Stein, 'because several additional means of detecting the Markan modification of the tradition are available'.[78] These subcriteria, as flagged by Stein in the secondary literature, are three: (a) the comparison of Mark with Matthew and Luke; (b) the investigation of 'misformed' pericopes; and (c) the investigation of the inconsistency between Mark's account and what actually happened.

A few observations on each of these canons for ascertaining Markan modification are in order. Moving in reverse order, the noting of inconsistencies between the Gospel account and historical fact (insofar as the latter is patient of demonstration) is, of course, a keynote in the work of one of the earliest precursors of *Redaktionsgeschichte,* William Wrede. The inquiry into 'misformed' pericopes operates on two large bases of presupposition: first, that certain 'rules' or 'laws' have governed the transmission and formation of the pre-Markan tradition, just as the form critics have suggested, such that departures in Gospel material from 'pure forms' can be recognized; second, that the Second Evangelist could be sufficiently incautious or even sloppy at certain points so as to 'misform' such material.[79] Finally, the best-known proponent of the view that a specifically Markan concept or prejudice can be inferred from its alteration by Matthew or Luke is Johannes Schreiber;[80] though the logic of Schreiber's position has been contested,[81] Stein maintains that this subcanon of Synoptic

---

77. Among others, note K. Tagawa, *Miracles et Évangile: La Pensée personnelle de l'Évangeliste Marc* (EHPR 62; Paris: Universitaires de France, 1966), passim; and Rohde, *Rediscovering,* pp. 14-15.

78. Stein, 'Markan Redaction History', p. 187. In addition to those that follow, in his Th.D. thesis (pp. 196-98) Stein also included, as a subcriterion of Markan modification, 'the way in which Mark uses Q'; however, Stein concluded that the many problems surrounding this approach impugned its validity. Cf. B. H. Throckmorton, 'Did Mark Know Q?', *JBL* 67 (1948), pp. 319-29.

79. The example offered by Stein of a pericope so modified by redactional 'misformation' is Mark 11.27-33: 'the anacoluthon of verse 32 would have been impossible to transmit orally. It is therefore probably due to the hand of Mark' ('Markan Redaction History', p. 189).

80. Schreiber, 'Christologie', pp. 154-55, quoted in note 55 above.

81. Among others, Stein himself has questioned it: 'When the particular theological viewpoints of Matthew and Luke clash with Mark, their change of Mark reveals not so much

comparison is still admissible if employed cautiously and in conjunction with other redactional criteria.[82]

6. While agreeing with Ernest Best that every pericope included in the Second Gospel need not betoken a special theological interest or point of view of the Evangelist,[83] Stein holds that 'Nevertheless in general the *selection [Auswahl] of material* made by Mark must of necessity reveal something of his own particular theological interests'.[84] This is akin to James McConkey Robinson's (1924-) dictum that arguments for Mark's distinctive theology and narrative shape should be 'built upon what Mark clearly and repeatedly has to say . . .'.[85]

7. If some of Mark's theological emphases are revealed by what material he chose to include in his Gospel, then the converse should also hold true: that his interests are betrayed by his intentional *omission (Auslassung) of material.* However, if Markan priority be assumed, then we are at the considerable disadvantage of having no certain knowledge of what materials Mark may have chosen to omit.[86] For Stein, this is clearly a criterion that cannot be expected to shoulder great weight; still, he wishes to retain it since 'this method gives some hints as to areas of the tradition which Mark chose not to stress'.[87]

---

a Markan redaction history as a Matthean or Lukan one' ('Markan Redaction History', p. 187 n. 2).

82. Stein, 'Markan Redaction History', p. 188. In the interest of clarity, a distinction should be drawn between, on the one hand, comparing the Second Gospel with the other Synoptics in order to illuminate by contrast Mark's special interests and concerns, and, on the other hand, comparing Mark with Matthew and Luke in order to form *traditionsgeschichtlich* judgments about Mark's distinctive theology. The latter, which is Schreiber's position, has not been widely accepted among scholars; the former, however, is frequently essayed, with fruitful results (see e.g. Wrede, *Messianic Secret*, pp. 151-207; Marxsen, *Mark the Evangelist,* pp. 44-53, 95-111, 117-50, 189-206; Tagawa, *Miracles et Évangile,* pp. 3-5; and P. J. Achtemeier, '"He Taught Them Many Things": Reflections on Marcan Christology', *CBQ* 42 [1980], pp. 472-76).

83. Best, *Temptation,* pp. 103-11.

84. Stein, 'Markan Redaction History', p. 190, emphasis mine. Cf. Hooker, *Message,* pp. 21-22.

85. Robinson, *Problem,* p. 12. Cf. Schreiber, 'Christologie', p. 155.

86. N.B. Best, *Temptation,* p. 103.

87. Stein, 'Markan Redaction History', p. 191. As an example of what is meant by this comment, Stein observes that James Robinson might be faulted for laying too much stress on the element of Jesus' continuous struggle with the demonic powers (*Problem,* pp. 33-42) in light of the relative paucity of stories of exorcism in Mark's Gospel. Thus also Best: 'In actual fact the demonic slowly fades out of Mark, highly concentrated at the beginning, it

8. We are equally in the dark about the extent to which certain traditions existed in cycles or in clusters prior to their arrangement by Mark. Scholarly opinion reflects the breadth of this uncertainty: on the one hand, it has been contended that the Evangelist's compositional freedom was limited by the existence of a kerygmatically standardized, pre-Markan order of Gospel events;[88] on the other hand, it has been theorized that Mark's composition was free, consciously artistic, and even esoterically architectonic.[89] Between these extremes, various complexes of pre-Markan traditions have been proposed, especially with reference to the passion narrative,[90] certain miracle stories,[91] and the seed parables in Mark 4.1-32.[92] Nevertheless, many exegetes continue to hold that *the arrangement (Anordnung, Gliederung) of the material* in the Second Gospel is attributed in some measure to Mark and that that arrangement betokens, at least to some extent, the Evangelist's distinctive theological concerns.[93] As with the criterion of modification, Stein suggests three subcriteria that Markan redaction critics have frequently employed in their evaluation of the Gospel's arrangement:

---

gradually disappears [i.e., in Stein's terms, 'is omitted'] so that in the Passion story it escapes mention altogether' (*Temptation*, p. 22). Robinson has raised another possibility: 'But even if one cannot determine that the omission [of a given tradition from a Gospel] was deliberate, since the traditions in question may not have been available [to the Evangelist] for consideration, still such a lacuna in the tradition itself has implications' ('The Literary Composition of Mark', *L'Évangile selon Marc: Tradition et rédaction* [ed. M. Sabbe; BETL 34; Duculot and Gembloux: Leuven University Press, 1974], p. 13).

88. C. H. Dodd, 'The Framework of the Gospel Narrative', *ExpTim* 43 (1932), pp. 396-400.

89. Farrer, *A Study in St Mark*, passim.

90. Dibelius, *Tradition*, pp. 178-217.

91. P. J. Achtemeier, 'Toward the Isolation of Pre-Markan Miracle Catenae', *JBL* 89 (1970), pp. 265-91; idem, 'The Origin and Function of the Pre-Marcan Miracle Catenae', *JBL* 91(1972), pp. 198-221.

92. H.-W. Kuhn, *Ältere Sammlungen im Markusevangelium* (SUNT 8; Göttingen: Vandenhoeck & Ruprecht, 1971), pp. 99-146. Kuhn postulates three other pre-Markan collections: the four controversy stories on discipleship in Mark 2; three apophthegmata conjoined with instruction on discipleship in Mark 10; and six epiphanic *Novellen* in Mark 4–6.

93. Schreiber, 'Christologie', p. 155; Best, *Temptation*, pp. 112-33; Rohde, *Rediscovering*, pp. 14-15; Achtemeier, *Mark*, pp. 22-30; Hooker, *Message*, pp. 22-33. L. E. Keck's estimate is typical: 'it is clear that much more attention must be paid to the relation between the structure of Mark's thought and the structure of his text. Though it is much easier to select a theological theme to analyse in Mark, it is much more fruitful and doubtless more accurate — though more intricate and the results more tenuous — to investigate Mark's theology through the ordering of all the material' ('The Introduction to Mark's Gospel', *NTS* 12 [1966], p. 369).

(a) the arrangement of individual pericopes;[94] (b) the placing of one pericope inside another (referred to, variously, as 'intercalations', 'interpolations', 'interlaminations', 'sandwiches', *Schwalbenschwanztechnique*', '*Einschachtelung*');[95] and (c) the geographical scheme of Mark.[96]

9. Stein observes that, if the introductions to Matthew, Luke, and John are telling with regard to their authors' theological orientations, the same must be true of Mark as well.[97] Although there is little agreement among scholars on the Second Evangelist's precise intentions in *the introduction* (or, for that matter, on the actual extent of the introduction),[98]

94. Surely the portion of Mark that has been most extensively probed on the basis of this criterion has been the Gospel's central section, 8.22-10.52. Its subtle interconnections between Christology, discipleship, and suffering have been scrutinized by a host of investigators, including Wrede, *The Messianic Secret*, pp. 82-100; Best, *Temptation*, pp. 121-25; Strecker, 'The Passion and Resurrection Predictions'; Schweizer, *Good News*, pp. 165-225; and Perrin, 'Towards an Interpretation', pp. 6-21. As another example, Norman Perrin's celebrated characterization of Mark as 'an apocalyptic drama in three acts' is based upon his assessment of Mark's careful arrangement of traditional stories and sayings depicting the recurrent 'preaching' and 'delivering up' of the Baptist, Jesus, and Jesus' followers (Mark 1.7, 14; 9.31; 13.10, 9-13; N. Perrin and D. Duling, *The New Testament: An Introduction* [2nd edn; New York: Harcourt Brace Jovanovich, 1982], pp. 237-39).

95. The following exemplify this oft-cited technique: Mark 2.1-5a + 2.10b-12/2.5b-10a (the healing of the paralytic + Jesus' authority to forgive); 3.1-3 + 3.5b-6/3.4-5a (the man with a withered hand + healing on the sabbath); 3.20-21 + 3.31-35/3.22-30 (Jesus' family in opposition + Beelzebul and forgiveness); 5.21-24a + 5.35-43/5.24b-34 (Jairus' daughter + the hemorrhaging woman); 6.6b-13 + 6.30/6.14-29 (the mission of the twelve + the death of the Baptist); 11.12-14 + 11.20-25/11.15-19 (the cursing of the fig tree + the cleansing of the temple); 14.53-54 + 14.66-72/14.55-65 (Peter's denial + the Sanhedrin trial); 15.6-15 + 15.21-32/15.16-20 (Jesus' sentencing and execution + the soldiers' mockery). For discussion, see, among others, Klostermann, *Des Markusevangelium*, pp. 36, 50; Taylor, *St. Mark*, pp. 191-92; Donahue, *Are You the Christ?*, pp. 41-45, 58-63; Achtemeier, *Mark*, pp. 31-32; Kee, *Community*, pp. 54-56.

96. With respect to this canon, the lion's share of attention has been devoted to the theological function of 'Galilee' and 'Jerusalem' in Mark: Lohmeyer, *Galiläa und Jerusalem*; Lightfoot, *Locality and Doctrine*; Marxsen, *Mark the Evangelist*, pp. 54-116; Best, *Temptation*, pp. 174-75; Lambrecht, *Markus-Apokalypse*, pp. 256-60; Perrin, 'Towards an Interpretation', pp. 26-31; J. M. van Cangh, 'La Galile dans l'évangile de Marc: un lieu théologique?', *RB* 79 (1972), pp. 59-75; and W. H. Kelber, *The Kingdom in Mark: A New Place and a New Time* (Philadelphia: Fortress, 1974). For a sharp critique of scholars' attempts to read historical or geopolitical significance out of a fundamentally narrative opposition between 'Galilee' and 'Jerusalem', see E. S. Malbon, 'Galilee and Jerusalem: History and Literature in Marcan Interpretation', *CBQ* 44 (1982), pp. 242-55.

97. Stein, 'Markan Redaction History', p. 195.

98. A convenient summary and assessment of the variety of positions (pre-1966) are provided by Keck, 'Introduction', pp. 353-58.

most Markan redaction critics would concur with Leander Keck that, 'when the extent and the intent of the prologue are clarified, the thrust and purpose of Mark as a whole fall into clearer perspective and must no longer be treated in isolation from the key-signature which Mark placed at the beginning'.[99]

10. If the introduction to Mark be accorded significance in discerning the Evangelist's purpose, so too, one might think, should be *the Markan conclusion*. In principle, Stein agrees with this; however, he wavers on the reliability of Mark's conclusion as an indicator of redactional orientation, owing to the well-known objections that have been raised against the Gospel's ending at 16.8.[100] To be sure, if Mark 16.8 is not the original conclusion of the Gospel, then its value is diminished for redaction-critical purposes. On the other hand, at present scholarly opinion may be moving more closely to consensus on this issue than it was when Stein first suggested this criterion. In spite of occasional reclamations of the argument that Mark must have intended his Gospel to continue past 16.8,[101] and the provocative but unpersuasive attempt of William R. Farmer to dispel the shadow of doubt cast over the authenticity of Mark 16.9-20,[102] a majority of critics, many of whom approach the issue from different methodological perspectives,[103] appear to favor 16.8 as the end of Mark's Gospel.[104] Although the issue defies complete resolution, Stein's appraisal is surely de-

99. Ibid., p. 369; cf. also Hooker, *Message,* p. 24.

100. Stein, 'Markan Redaction History', pp. 196-97. For a summary of the debate, with full documentation, see Kümmel, *Introduction,* pp. 98-101.

101.Thus B. M. Metzger, *The Text of the New Testament: Its Transmission, Corruption, and Restoration* (2nd edn; New York and Oxford: Oxford University Press, 1968), pp. 226-29; idem, *A Textual Commentary on the Greek New Testament* (n.p.: United Bible Societies, 1971), pp. 122-26; Schweizer, *Good News,* pp. 365-71.

102. W. R. Farmer, *The Last Twelve Verses of Mark* (SNTSMS 25; Cambridge: Cambridge University Press, 1974). A penetrating review of this monograph is provided by J. N. Birdsall in *JTS* n.s. 26 (1985), pp. 151-60.

103. Cf. the conclusions of N. R. Petersen's literary-critical study, 'When Is the End Not the End? Literary Reflections on the Ending of Mark's Narrative', *Int* 34 (1980), pp. 151-66, with the 'socio-rhetorical' assessment of V. K. Robbins, *Jesus the Teacher: A Socio-Rhetorical Interpretation of Mark* (Philadelphia: Fortress, 1984), pp. 191-93.

104. See the balanced assessment of Anderson, *Gospel of Mark,* pp. 351-54. For all of the exegetical problems that it raises, most interpreters would regard 16.1-8 as the ending with which they must wrangle, if for no other reason than that once voiced (in another connection) by T. A. Burkill: 'The primary duty of the exegete is to elucidate the gospel as it stands, not as he thinks it ought to be . . .' (*Mysterious Revelation: An Examination of the Philosophy of St. Mark's Gospel* [Ithaca, NY: Cornell University Press, 1963], p. 5).

fensible: in theory at least, the conclusion of the Second Gospel (16.1-8) is a potentially significant locus of redaction-critical investigation.

11. From its inception, the redaction criticism of Mark has been guided by the pursuit of a distinctive *Markan vocabulary*, on the assumption that the language most regularly employed by the Evangelist would communicate important clues to his theological emphases: thus Marxsen devoted an entire chapter of his programmatic study to the meaning of εὐαγγέλιον in the Second Gospel;[105] Robinson's analysis of the baptism, temptation, and exorcism narratives took as its point of orientation the Evangelist's 'cosmic language of a struggle between the Spirit and Satan' which '[transcends] historical immanence and yet [participates] in the history Mark records';[106] and Schweizer suggested that Mark's use of certain terms (among others, κηρύσσειν, διδάσχειν, παραβολή) be considered a primary *Ausgangsbasis* for distinguishing redaction from tradition within the Gospel.[107] The investigation of vocabulary was also fueled by scholars' discovery of what they considered to be characteristic Markan terminology in those parts of the Gospel having already been established as redactional on other grounds: seams, insertions, and summaries. In time, redaction critics were conversing with one another, easily and frequently, about 'Markan words' and 'characteristic Markan vocabulary'. If the language of the secondary literature — to say nothing of Mark's own language — is to be trusted, then 'vocabulary' has been one of the most dominant criteria in the *redaktionsgeschichtlich* interpretation of Mark.

12. Ernest Best once observed that Matthew and Luke appear to have exercised considerable freedom to retain or to alter the titles of Jesus that they found in Mark. The inferences drawn from this by Best were (a) that Mark probably exercised comparable freedom in using or reworking the Christological titles in his own source material, and (b) 'that [Mark's] choice of titles for Jesus may reveal something of his theology'.[108] Although there seems to have been almost as many different interpretations of Mark's Christology as the number of exegetes proposing them,[109] Stein's

105. Marxsen, *Mark the Evangelist*, pp. 117-50.

106. Robinson, *Problem*, p. 33.

107. Schweizer, 'Die theologische Leistung', pp. 339-42; idem, 'Anmerkungen', pp. 35-46.

108. Best, *Temptation*, pp. 160-77; quotation, p. 160.

109. Among the raft of alternatives: the Markan understanding of 'Son of God' as patterned after an ancient Egyptian ritual in which the king is 'adopted', presented, and enthroned (P. Vielhauer, 'Erwägungen zur Christologie des Markusevangeliums', *Zeit und Geschichte: Dankesgabe an Rudolf Bultmann zum 80. Geburtstag* [ed. E. Dinkler; Tübingen:

inclusion of *the Markan Christological titles* appears justified in a descriptive catalogue of criteria most frequently used by Markan redaction critics.

It should be noted that Stein was not inclined to regard all of these twelve criteria as being equally valuable. The Markan creation of pericopes, omission of material, and conclusion were accorded by him little if any weight; the first two because of the seeming impossibility of their demonstration, the third owing to the reigning confusion over the Gospel's ending.[110] Conversely, Stein was prepared to consider some canons as being especially valuable as well as representative of most Markan redaction criticism: the investigation of seams, insertions, and summaries; the modification, selection, and arrangement of material; and Mark's introduction, vocabulary, and Christological titles.[111] Nevertheless, Stein finally concluded that all twelve of these canons were both theoretically valid and of demonstrated usefulness among scholars in pursuit of a Markan redaction history.

Robert Stein's catalogue of *redaktionsgeschichtlich* criteria remains an accurate and nearly exhaustive assessment of the specific ways in which the discipline has been applied to the Gospel of Mark. It is, however, not quite complete: there are, I think, two other criteria, to which Markan redaction critics have often resorted, which should be appended to Stein's catalogue, or included as extensions of two canons mentioned by him.

J. C. B. Mohr (Paul Siebeck), 1964], pp. 155-69); Mark's use of 'Son of God' as establishing rapport with his readers and 'Son of man' as correcting a false Christology among them (N. Perrin, 'The Creative Use of the Son of Man Traditions by Mark', *USQR* 23 [1967/1968], pp. 357-65; idem, 'Christology of Mark'); the Markan 'Son of God' as reflecting either the *alttestamentlich* emphasis on obedient sonship (L. S. Hay, 'The Son-of-God Christology in Mark', *JBR* 32 [1964], pp. 106-14) or the royal Messianism of the Old Testament and Qumran literature (J. R. Donahue, 'Temple, Trial, and Royal Christology (Mark 14.53-65)', *Passion in Mark*, pp. 61-79); Mark's prevailing emphasis on 'the suffering Son of man' (E. Schweizer, 'Towards a Christology of Mark?', *God's Christ and His People: Studies in Honour of Nils Alstrup Dahl* [ed. J. Jervell and W. A. Meeks; Oslo: Universitetsforlaget, 1977], p. 39); and Mark's establishment of Jesus as the teacher whose power is made manifest in his mighty works (Achtemeier, '"He Taught Them Many Things"'). For a critical survey of these and other possibilities, consult Schweizer, 'Towards a Christology of Mark?', pp. 29-42.

110. Stein, 'Markan Redaction History', p. 198.

111. Ibid. Stein further observed that, in some cases, these most important means of obtaining a Markan redaction history overlap: thus an analysis of Mark's introduction would entail the investigation of any seams, insertions, summaries, modifications, arrangements, and characteristic words or titles found in the introduction ('Markan Redaction History', p. 198 n. 2).

First, it seems to me that the third of Stein's subcriteria for the canon of Markan arrangement is somewhat inaccurately defined. 'The geographical scheme of Mark' is really a species of a much larger genus of investigation, quite common in Markan *Redaktionsgeschichte* but otherwise unaccounted for in Stein's presentation: Mark's arrangement of material in the service of *overarching theological themes*. The geographical polarity of 'Galilee' and 'Jerusalem' is, to be sure, one thematic arrangement that has played an important role in the history of Markan research, but there are many others: the secrecy motif and its attendant commands to silence;[112] the interplay between the secret fact of Jesus' messianic status in the first half of the Gospel and the mysterious meaning of that fact revealed in the second;[113] the astonishment and fear evoked by Jesus' miracles and mighty works;[114] the supposed eucharistic symbolism of the feeding stories;[115] true discipleship as defined by the example of Jesus as the suffering Son of man.[116] However each of these themes is ultimately to be evaluated in the exegesis of Mark, it is evident that they and others have been perceived by scholars as governing the manner in which the Second Evangelist arranged his traditions.[117]

Second, I suggest that Stein's eleventh criterion be broadened beyond Markan vocabulary to embrace, in addition, *Markan literary style* (that is, such features as Mark's use of the historic present, pleonasms, and καί-parataxis, to name but a few).[118] As we have already witnessed, Markan syntax defines a time-honored field of investigation that, while omitted

---

112. Wrede, *The Messianic Secret,* pp. 24-149. Revisionist interpretations of the locus of 'the secret' in Mark have been tendered, among others, by U. Luz, 'Das Geheimnismotiv und die Markinische Christologie', *ZNW* 56 (1965), pp. 9-30, and Räisänen, *Das 'Messiasgeheimnis',* pp. 159-68.

113. Burkill, *Mysterious Revelation,* pp. 1-6, 319-24, et passim.

114. Tagawa, *Miracles et Évangile,* p. 116, et passim.

115. Quesnell, *Mind of Mark,* p. 276, et passim.

116. Schweizer, 'Die theologische Leistung', pp. 337-55; idem, 'The Portrayal of the Life of Faith in the Gospel of Mark', *Int* 32 (1978), pp. 387-99.

117. Cf. Pesch (*Das Markusevangelium,* I, p. 59): 'Die so gesehene 'theologische Leistung' des Markus ist nun besonders in der übergreifenden Komposition greifbar, mit welcher der Evangelist über die einzelnen Traditionen hinaus Spannungsbögen schafft, die das ganze Evangelium umfassen'. The three *Spannungsbögen* upon which Pesch settles are 'der Weg Jesu' (ibid., pp. 59-60), 'die aretalogische Wirkung Jesu' (pp. 60-61), and 'die fortschreitende himmlische Offenbarung der Würde Jesu' (pp. 61-62).

118. For a convenient listing of the syntactical features most commonly cited, see Taylor, *St. Mark,* pp. 44-66.

from Stein's discussion, continues to be harvested by Markan redaction critics.[119]

In the interest of clarity, let me recall a caveat previously entered: it is *not* my intention, at least at this point, to argue that either Stein's criteria or my suggested additions to them can enable interpreters to separate tradition from redaction in the Second Gospel, or even to argue that they are uniquely *redaktionsgeschichtlich* in character. Although Stein made such claims, in the light of which he prescribed the use of his method,[120] for the moment I am prepared to do neither. What I *am* suggesting is that Stein's twelve canons for ascertaining a Markan redaction history provide us with a comprehensive and useful paradigm for understanding the variety of ways in which Markan redaction critics of recent decades have actually gone about their business — even when they have neglected to be as clear about their procedure as Stein has been. In understanding the history of Markan *Redaktionsgeschichte,* Stein's presentation has undeniable *descriptive* value, quite apart from whatever objections may be lodged against its cogency or *prescriptive* force.

In sum, were we to undertake an analysis of the precise manner in which Markan *Redaktionsgeschichte* has been practiced by its advocates, with the goal of assessing the validity of that method, we could do worse than to measure their work by the procedural yardstick that Stein has provided. However, so popular has *Redaktionsgeschichte* been among Markan scholars that it is manifestly impossible for any study to consider every redaction-critical analysis of the Second Gospel: if attempted, the results would be either analytically superficial or hopelessly unwieldy. To circumvent both of these outcomes, at least two things are needful: (1) concentration on a single exegetical issue that has proved to be significant in Markan discussion of the past three decades, and (2) the determination of some means by which the dimensions of that issue might be appropriately whittled down to a manageable size. These are the qualifications that, in the next chapter, I shall consider and attempt to satisfy.

---

119. Two recent examples must suffice: Donahue's extensive appropriation of such data in his influential study of Mark 14 (*Are You the Christ?,* esp. pp. 53-102) and F. J. Matera's appeal to similar evidence in his complementary investigation of Mark 15 (*The Kingship of Jesus: Composition and Theology in Mark 15* [SBLDS 66; Missoula, MT: Scholars, 1981], pp. 38-39 et passim).

120. Stein, 'Proper Methodology', pp. 242-49.

2. Mark's Presentation of the Disciples and Discipleship: A Selective Review of Redaction-Critical Research

While a work which begins with the statement 'the good news of Jesus, Messiah, Son of God', (Mk 1.1) has an obvious Christological thrust, with the sayings and deeds of Jesus in the forefront, the story of the disciples occupies a strong second position. . . . The gospel of Mark tells us not only who Jesus is, but what it is to be involved with him.

John R. Donahue[1]

From time to time, New Testament interpreters have been disposed to describe particular books of the canon as 'storm centers' in contemporary scholarship.[2] At the risk of overworking that metaphor, it could reasonably be argued that the role of the disciples has defined a true storm center in recent *redaktionsgeschichtlich* investigation of Mark. This is not to suggest that all research in the Second Gospel has been focused on the question of discipleship: perhaps the *locus classicus* of Markan redaction-critical study has been the Evangelist's understanding of the role of Jesus, or Christology,[3] and a goodly portion of scholars' attention has also been

1. J. R. Donahue, *The Theology and Setting of Discipleship in the Gospel of Mark* (The 1983 Pere Marquette Theology Lecture; Milwaukee: Marquette University Press, 1983), p. 2.

2. So W. C. van Unnik, 'Luke-Acts, A Storm Center in Contemporary Scholarship', *Studies in Luke-Acts* (ed. L. E. Keck and J. L. Martyn; Philadelphia: Fortress, 1980), pp. 15-32; and (more recently) G. Stanton, 'Introduction: Matthew's Gospel: A New Storm Centre', *The Interpretation of Matthew* (ed. G. Stanton; IRT 3; Philadelphia and London: Fortress/ SPCK, 1983), pp. 1-18.

3. Among the most recent, major contributions are H. Baarlink, *Anfängliches Evangelium: Ein Beitrag zur näheren Bestimmung der theologischen Motive im Markusevangelium*

attracted to the character of Markan eschatology.[4] Nevertheless, Mark's presentation of the disciples and of discipleship has scarcely been ignored, and few topics in Markan interpretation have generated alternative exegeses as sharply defined, even polarized, as the function of the disciples in that Gospel.[5]

(Kampen: J. H. Kok, 1977); C. R. Kazmierski, *Jesus, the Son of God: A Study of the Markan Tradition and Its Redaction by the Evangelist* (FB 33; Würzburg: Echter Verlag, 1979); and H.-J. Steichele, *Der Leidende Sohn Gottes: Eine Untersuchung einiger alttestamentlicher Motive der Christologie des Markusevangeliums* (BU 14; Regensburg: Friedrich Pustet, 1980).

4. Again, only a few monographs may be cited as representative: L. Hartman, *Prophecy Interpreted: The Formation of Some Jewish Apocalyptic Texts and the Eschatological Discourse Mark 13 Par.* (ConBNT 1; Lund: Gleerup, 1966); Lambrecht, *Markus-Apokalypse;* A. M. Ambrozic, *The Hidden Kingdom: A Redaction-Critical Study of the References to the Kingdom of God in Mark's Gospel* (CBQMS 2; Washington, DC: Catholic Biblical Association of America, 1972); and R. Pesch, *Naherwartungen: Tradition und Redaktion in Mk 13* (KBANT; Düsseldorf: Patmos, 1968).

5. One of the many debated questions in Markan interpretation is whether 'the twelve' (eleven occurrences in Mark) are distinct (e.g. K. Stock, *Boten aus dem Mit-Ihm-Sein: Des Verhältnis zwischen Jesus und den Zwölf nach Markus* [AnBib 70; Rome: Pontifical Biblical Institute, 1975], esp. pp. 200-201) or indistinguishable (e.g. E. Best, 'Mark's Use of the Twelve', *ZNW* 69 [1978, pp. 11-35) from other 'disciples' (forty-six occurrences). Without intending to imply a premature resolution of the problem, I find the latter argument more persuasive, given the facts that Mark (a) sometimes appears to merge the twelve with a larger group (4.11; 10.32), (b) often does not rigorously differentiate, at least at a terminological level, 'the twelve' from 'the disciples' (6.35-44; 7.17; 9.28; 10.10), and (c) frequently attributes behavior associated with 'the twelve' or with 'disciples' to those not expressly singled out as such (1.45; 2.15; 5.20; 7.37; 9.38-40; 10.52; 14.1-9; 15.42-47; 16.1-8). Hereafter, therefore, I shall follow what I take to be Mark's lead and use the terms 'the twelve' and 'the disciples' interchangeably. Similarly, the Fourth Evangelist does not clearly differentiate 'the twelve' (four occurrences) from 'the disciples' of Jesus (seventy-eight occurrences). Nor, it would appear, does Matthew: notice that the crowds are among the auditors (along with 'the disciples' [seventy-three occurrences]) of the Sermon on the Mount (Matt 5.1; 7.28-29), which anticipates the calling of the twelve (eight occurrences) in Matthew by at least two chapters (10.1-4). Among the Evangelists, Luke seems to be more explicit in differentiating the twelve (seven occurrences in the Gospel, one in Acts) as 'apostles' (six occurrences in Luke, twenty-eight in Acts) from the rest of the 'disciples' (thirty-seven occurrences in Luke, twenty-eight in Acts): in this regard, note especially Luke 6.13; 19.37; Acts 6.2; 11.26 (although Barnabas and Paul are atypically designated as ἀπόστολοι in Acts 14.4, 14). For detailed discussion, see G. Klein, *Die Zwölf Apostel: Ursprung und Gehalt einer Idee* (Göttingen: Vandenhoeck & Ruprecht, 1961); A. Schulz, *Nachfolgen und Nachahmen: Studien über das Verhältnis der neutestamentlichen Jüngerschaft zur urchristlichen Vorbildethik* (SANT 6; Munich: Kösel, 1962); and H. D. Betz, *Nachfolge und Nachahmung Jesu Christi in Neuen Testament* (BHT 37; Tübingen: J. C. B. Mohr [Paul Siebeck], 1967).

A. The Disciples in the Four Gospels:
A Review of the Textual Evidence

Such divergent interpretations of the disciples characterize Markan research in a manner not evidenced in the study of the other canonical Gospels.[6] In large measure this fact is accountable to the relatively greater clarity, or at least more obvious internal consistency, with which the other Evangelists have rendered their portraits of Jesus' followers.

In *Matthew* the disciples seemingly exemplify the fundamental qualities of Christian existence. Though susceptible to incomprehension and failure (Matt 15.16; 16.5-11, 21-23; 26.6-13, 40-46), the disciples do understand Jesus and penetrate the mystery of his teaching and identity (13.23, 51; 14.33; 16.12, 16-19). Though it be of little degree, they do display faith (ὀλιγόπιστος: 8.26; 14.31; 16.8; 17.20) and are encouraged in unflagging vigilance for their master's unexpected *parousia* (24.15-51; 25.1-13). Though capable of doubt and defection (14.28-33; 26.14-16, 20-25, 33-34, 47, 56b, 69-75; 28.17), ultimately the disciples in Matthew display obedience to Christ and are united with him (4.18-22; 8.18-22; 9.9; 10.1-4, 37-39, 40-42; 18.18-20; 19.28; 21.6; 26.17-19; 28.7, 10, 16-20).[7]

Although its nuances are somewhat different, the character of discipleship in *Luke-Acts* is just as sharply defined. Exemplary of all true disciples, the twelve are those who follow in 'the Way' of Jesus (Luke 5.11, 27-28; cf. Acts 9.2; 19.9, 23; 22.4; 24.14, 22) and who bear witness to the risen Christ (Luke 24.48; cf. 1.2; Acts 1.8; 2.32; 3.15b; 5.32; 10.39-41; 13.31; cf. Acts 22.15; 26.16). They are admonished to be, or in fact are, perpetually engaged in prayer (Luke 10.2; 11.1; 18.1-8; 22.46; Acts 1.14; 2.42; 4.24-31; 6.4, 6;

---

6. Cf. Donald Senior: 'A number of scholars have offered detailed studies of discipleship in Matthew, and there seems to be considerable consensus about the broad features of this part of the Gospel' (*What Are They Saying About Matthew?* [New York and Ramsey: Paulist, 1983], p. 70). Earle Ellis observes a similar consensus among Lukan scholars on the identity and role of the twelve and the apostles in Luke-Acts, while demurring on some aspects of that consensus (*The Gospel of Luke* [NCB; Grand Rapids, MI, and London: Eerdmans/Marshall, Morgan & Scott, 1981], pp. 132-35). The role of the disciples in John is virtually absent from Kysar's comprehensive review, surfacing only in his cursory discussion of 'The Church' (*Fourth Evangelist*, pp. 241-48).

7. On the role of the disciples in Matthew, see G. Bornkamm, G. Barth, and H.-J. Held, *Tradition and Interpretation in Matthew* (NTL; Philadelphia: Westminster, 1963), pp. 105-24, 181-92, 200-206; U. Luz, 'Die Jünger im Matthäusevangelium', *ZNW* 62 (1971), pp. 141-71; and J. Zumstein, *La Condition du Croyant dans L'Évangile selon Matthieu* (OBO 16: Göttingen: Vandenhoeck & Ruprecht, 1977).

10.9, 30; 11.5; 12.5, 12; 14.23; cf. Acts 9.11; 20.36; 21.5; 22.17; 24.14; 27.23), in the proper stewardship of material possessions (e.g. Luke 6.35; 8.3; 11.41; 12.33; 14.33; 16.13; cf. 3.11; Acts 2.44-45; 4.35, 37; 9.36; 10.2, 4, 31; 20.35; cf. 5.2-11; 6.1-7; 8.18-20), and in the proclamation of a *kerygma* that demands faith (Acts 10.43; 16.31), repentance, conversion and forgiveness (e.g. Luke 24.47; Acts 3.19; 5.31; 26.20), and baptism (e.g. Acts 2.38; 8.12, 37; 9.18; 10.48; 22.16b).[8]

So, too, does *the Fourth Gospel* present a relatively clear and coherent portrait of the disciples. Albeit (understandably) imperfect in their comprehension of the Johannine Jesus (John 2.21-22; 4.27, 33; 6.60; 9.2; 10.6; 11.8, 11-15; 12.16; 13.36; 14.5, 8, 22; 16.17-18), the disciples, particularly the twelve (6.67, 70; 13.18; 15.16, 19; cf. 6.64, 66), are characteristically those who, from the beginning, recognize and rightly acclaim Jesus for who he truly is (1.41, 45, 49; 6.69; 13.13; 20.28-31; 21.7, 12b; cf. 20.31). They believe in his claims (2.11, 22b; 6.68), and convey faith in Jesus to others (1.41-42, 45-48; 12.20-22; cf. 4.2). Moreover, the Johannine disciples receive Jesus' service (13.1-11), practice brotherly love (13.14-15, 34-35; 15.12-17; 19.26-27), abide with Jesus and do not forsake him (11.54; 12.16, 20-26; 14.20; 15.1-11; 17.10-12, 23-24; 19.25-27, 38-42; 20.1-10; cf. 6.67; 8.31; 18.8-11), and are ultimately inspired and appointed by the risen Christ to positions of pastoral leadership and trustworthy witness (15.27; 17.18; 20.19-23; 21.15-19, 24).[9]

At the risk of oversimplification, we might conclude that there is a basic clarity and coherence in the overall presentation of the disciples in Matthew, Luke-Acts, and John. That the same may be said of Mark is debatable. On the one hand, the disciples in the Second Gospel are cast in a favorable light. The first four of them (Simon and Andrew, James and John) are called to discipleship at the initiative of Jesus,[10] prior to the performance of any of his mighty works (and thus without the incentive

---

8. On discipleship in Luke-Acts, consult E. Repo, *Der 'Weg' als Selbstbezeichnung des Urchristentums: Eine traditionsgeschichtliche und semesiologische Untersuchung* (AASF B132/2; Helsinki: Suomalainen Tiedeakatemia, 1964), pp. 55-138, 150-58, 167-80; M. Sheridan, 'Disciples and Discipleship in Matthew and Luke', *TBT* 3 (1973), pp. 235-55; and J. A. Fitzmyer, *The Gospel According to Luke (I–IX)* (AB 28; Garden City, NY: Doubleday, 1981), pp. 235-51.

9. The Johannine perspective on the disciples has not received the attention it deserves, but note Schulz, *Nachfolgen und Nachahmen*, pp. 137-44, 161-76, and the discussion of church and ministry in the Fourth Gospel by Smith, *Johannine Christianity*, esp. pp. 209-22.

10. Contrast the rabbinic tradition of the pupil (תלמיד) as seeking out a teacher (רב) under whom he might apprentice for a long period (e.g. *m. 'Abot* 1.6). See K. H. Rengstorf, 'μανθάνω, κ.τ.λ', *TDNT* IV (1967), pp. 431-41; Robbins, *Jesus the Teacher*, pp. 87-108.

that such might have provided: Mark 1.16-20; cf. Luke 4.31–5.11; John 1.35-42).[11] Purely at the word of Jesus, they leave their occupation and family (1.18, 20b; a fact of which Peter pointedly reminds Jesus, later in the Gospel: 10.28)[12] and follow the one who has called them, to assume for themselves Jesus' own mission (1.17, 20a; N.B. καὶ ποιήσω ὑμᾶς γενέσθαι ἁλιεῖς ἀνθρώπων).[13] Following a whirlwind campaign of exorcisms (1.21-28, 34, 39), healings (1.29-31, 34, 40-45; 2.11-12), preaching (1.38-39; 2.1-5), teaching (2.13; cf. 1.27), and debate with certain scribes (2.6-10), Jesus issues a similar call to Levi, the son of Alphaeus, to leave the revenue office and follow him, and Levi complies (2.14).[14] Subsequent to the summons of Levi, Mark recounts in rapid succession a series of controversies between Jesus and various Jewish factions (criticism for eating with sinners and tax collectors, 2.15-17; the dispute over fasting, 2.18-22; the controversy over abrogation of sabbath laws, 2.23-27); in each of these cases, Jesus explicitly defends his disciples against some criticism leveled at them (2.16-17, 18-19, 24-26; cf. 7.5-13), even as he rescues the disciples from the wind and waves when their boat is in danger of being swamped (4.35-41). In the shadow of various forces that already threaten his well-being (3.6, 9; cf. 2.20; 3.19a), Jesus constitutes the twelve[15] in a manner that echoes the initial summons of the four in 1.16-20: once more he initiates the call (προσκαλεῖται), and the disciples respond positively (3.13); once more they are summoned 'to be with him', leaving behind their old familial or political associations (3.14; cf. the references to Zebedee, Alphaeus, and

11. Compare Philostratus's *Life of Apollonius of Tyana* (1.19), wherein Damis (on whose diary Philostratus's work seems to have been based) is persuaded, at least in part, to become a disciple of Apollonius on the strength of the latter's claim to understand all languages, though never having studied any.

12. For discussion, see G. Theissen, '"Wir haben alles verlassen" (Mk x. 28): Nachfolge und soziale Entwurzelung in der jüdisch-palästinischen Gesellschaft des I. Jahrhunderts n.Ch.', *NovT* 19 (1977), pp. 161-96.

13. The most thorough treatment of the sociological background of Mark 1.16-20 and its parallels is provided by W. Wuellner, *The Meaning of 'Fishers of Men'* (NTL; Philadelphia: Westminster, 1967).

14. The exemplary power of this pericope is explored by P. Lamarche, 'The Call to Conversion and Faith: The Vocation of Levi (Mk 2,13-17)', *LumVie* 25 (1970), pp. 301-12.

15. Both the twenty-sixth edition of the Nestle-Aland text and the third edition of the *UBSGNT* preserve, in Mark 3.14, the clause οὕς καὶ ἀποστόλους ὠνόμασεν in brackets, reflecting the balance of superb manuscript attestation (e.g. א B cop^sa,bo) and the suspicion of scribal interpolation from Luke 6.13. In any case, most scholars concur that the selection of twelve disciples mirrors the twelve tribes of Israel: see K. H. Rengstorf, 'δώδεκα', *TDNT* II (1964), pp. 321-28.

'the Cananaean' in 3.17-18);[16] once more their ministry and authority reflect that of Jesus ('authority to cast out demons', 3.15). The same motifs recur in Jesus' commissioning of the twelve for their missionary task (6.6b-13):[17] again the disciples are called by Jesus (προσκαλεῖται, 6.7; cf. also 8.1; 12.43); again they are charged by him to adopt the life-style of a particular social group (that of itinerant preachers: 6.7-11);[18] again their authority and mission are commensurate with Jesus' own (preaching, healing, and casting out of demons: 6.7, 12-13).[19] In contrast with 1.16-20 and 3.13-19a, here Mark states that the twelve carry out their mission (6.12-13, 30), and this is in line with other positive affirmations made of the disciples throughout the Gospel. Notice, for instance, that they receive private and comprehensive explanation from Jesus of his parabolic teaching (4.10-12, 34), as well as detailed instruction on discipleship (8.34-9.1; 9.35-50; 10.42-45), ethics, faith, and prayer (10.10-12; 11.22-26), stewardship (12.43-44; cf. 10.23-31), and the end of the age (13.1-37; cf. 8.31; 9.9-13, 30-31; 10.32b-34). Further, they are uniquely privy to certain miraculous occurrences (5.37, 40; 6.37a, 41; 6.45-52; 8.6; 9.2-8; 11.14, 20-21) and special fellowship with Jesus (6.31-32; 14.17-25; cf. 14.32-33). Almost to the very end, they continue to follow Jesus (4.36; 5.1; 6.1, 53; 8.22; 9.30, 33; 10.32, 46; 11.1) and to act in obedience to him (6.45-46; 8.6-7; 9.20; 11.2-7; 14.12-16)[20] in the face of steadily mounting, hostile forces (3.6, 22,

16. Although the 'Cananaeans' (τὸν Κανανοῖον = קַנְאָן; cf. *m. Sanh.* 9.6) have usually been identified with the 'Zealots' of 66-70 CE (e.g. BAGD, p. 403), recent research suggests that it is prochronistic to equate the former Jewish resistance movement with the latter. See M. J. Borg, 'The Currency of the Term "Zealot"', *JTS* n.s. 22 (1971), pp. 504-12; M. Smith, 'Zealots and Sicarii: Their Origins and Relation', *HTR* 64 (1971), pp. 1-19.

17. Questions concerning the historicity of the sending of the twelve and its significance for Jesus make Mark 6.6b-13 one of the most controversial of all the discipleship pericopes in the Gospel. For full discussion, see C. E. B. Cranfield, *The Gospel According to St. Mark* (CGTG; Cambridge: Cambridge University Press, 1959), pp. 197-203; Schulz, *Nachfolge*, pp. 97-116; Pesch, *Das Markusevangelium*, 11.1, pp. 325-32.

18. The going in pairs (6.7) reflects Jewish custom (cf. Mark 11.1; 14.13; Luke 7.18; John 1.35; Acts 11.30; 15.40 et al.). The πήραν in Mark 6.8 could refer, not just to a knapsack, but to the 'beggar's bag' that was part of the Cynic preacher's equipment (BAGD, p. 656b). The spartan accoutrements are somewhat reminiscent of Josephus' description of the Essenes when journeying (*Bell.* 2.125).

19. For the parallelism among the calling and commissioning narratives in Mark, I am particularly indebted to Donahue, *Discipleship*, pp. 13-21. See also J. Donaldson, '"Called to Follow": A Twofold Experience of Discipleship in Mark', *BTB* 5 (1975), pp. 67-77.

20. Ironically, even when Peter forsakes his master in Mark 14.50, 66-72, he does so in compliance with Jesus' prediction of the same in 14.27, 30. It should also be observed that the

31; 5.17; 6.2-6a, 14-29; 7.1-5; 8.11, 31; 9.14, 31; 10.2-9, 33-34; 11.18, 27-33; 12.1-27; 13.8-23; 14.1-2, 10-11, 43-49, 53-72). Prior to their abandoning of him, the potential for the disciples' reconciliation with Jesus is forecast at the supper (14.28); after their desertion, it is reasserted at the empty tomb (16.7).

Representative of this favorable picture of the disciples is Simon Peter, who by any estimate figures prominently in Mark's Gospel.[21] The first of the disciples (along with his brother, Andrew) to be called (1.16-18) and the first of the disciples to be renamed (3.16-17), Peter stands at the head of the list of the twelve (3.16-19a) and is always the first to be mentioned among an inner group of disciples (1.29; 5.37; 9.2; 13.3; 14.33). Typically, he functions, for good or ill, as the spokesman for the twelve (1.36; 8.29; 9.5-6; 10.28; 11.21; 14.29-31). In a variety of ways he is singled out for special attention in the Second Gospel: as the son-in-law of one of the first persons healed by Jesus (1.29-31); as the only follower whose desertion is explicitly foretold (14.30) and narrated in detail (14.66-72); as the disciple who, among all others, follows Jesus longest (14.54), openly repents of his desertion (14.72), and is explicitly named by the young man at the empty tomb as an intended recipient of the news of Jesus' resurrection (16.7). A positive role in Mark's Gospel is played, therefore, by the disciples in general and by Simon Peter in particular.

For all that, however, one is inclined to agree with Paul Achtemeier that, 'If there is any progression in the picture Mark paints of the disciples, it appears to be from bad to worse'.[22] This seems to be especially the case with their understanding of Jesus, his intentions, and his teaching — an understanding that diminishes as the Gospel narrative progresses. The earliest glimmering of this appears in 1.35-39: Jesus' withdrawal from the crowds for solitude and prayer is interrupted by Simon and the other disciples, who announce that everyone is searching for (ζητοῦσιν) Jesus (1.37).[23]

---

terse statement of the disciples' defection in 14.50 immediately follows Jesus' injunction that the scriptures should be fulfilled (14.49b; cf. 9.12; 14.21).

21. A detailed consideration of the Petrine passages in Mark is provided in *Peter in the New Testament: A Collaborative Assessment by Protestant and Roman Catholic Scholars* (ed. R. E. Brown, K. P. Donfried, and J. Reumann; Minneapolis and New York: Augsburg/Paulist, 1973), pp. 57-73.

22. Achtemeier, *Mark*, p. 105.

23. As Anderson (*Mark*, p. 95) notes, ζητέω occurs nine times in Mark (1.37; 3.32; 8.11, 12; 11.18; 12.12; 14.1, 11, 55) in the sense of 'seeking someone or something out from wrong or hostile motives'.

Preceding his explanation of the parable of the sower, there is a trace of surprise or impatience in Jesus' questions of the twelve, οὐχ οἴδατε τὴν παραβολὴν ταύτην, καὶ πῶς πάσας τὰς παραβολὰς γνώσεσθε; (4.13);[24] perhaps this is owing to the disparity (at least as perceived by Mark) between the disciples' comprehension and the assurance that to them has been given τὸ μυστήριον τῆς βασιλείας τοῦ θεοῦ (4.11). Even more bluntly, Jesus questions the disciples on the cause of their fear and lack of faith following the stilling of the storm (4.40), and, for their part, the awe-stricken disciples can only wonder with whom they are dealing (4.41). They are no more perspicacious at 5.31, when they chide Jesus for asking who touched his garments (the reproof being omitted in Matt 9.20-22 and toned down in Luke 8.45), or at 6.37, when they (sarcastically?) suggest to Jesus that they would require two hundred denarii (= two hundred days' wages for a laborer) to purchase enough bread to feed the multitude of five thousand (cf. also 8.4).[25] Mark underlines their thickheadedness after Jesus' walking on the water: καὶ λίαν [ἐκ περισσοῦ] ἐν ἑαυτοῖς ἐξίσταντο, οὐ γὰρ συνῆκαν ἐπὶ τοῖς ἄρτοις, ἀλλ᾽ ἦν αὐτῶν ἡ καρδία πεπωρωμένη (6.51b-52).[26] Nor do they understand, as one might have expected of them, Jesus' teaching on the things that defile (7.17-18), the 'leaven' of the Pharisees and of Herod (8.14-21), or the passion and vindication of the Son of man (9.31-32).[27] Three times Jesus predicts his death and resurrection (8.31; 9.31; 10.33-34) and the implications of his passion for discipleship (8.34–9.1; 9.35-37; 10.42-45); three times the disciples miss the point, usually by bickering amongst themselves about their desire for exalted status (8.32-33; 9.33-34; 10.35-41). No greater discernment is demonstrated in the disciples' behavior: their faith is insufficient to heal the epileptic child (9.18c-19; cf. 9.28-29); they unwarrantably reprove an exorcist who operates in the name of Jesus without joining the ranks of those who follow him (9.38-41); they

24. Thus also Nineham, *St. Mark,* p. 139. Notice that the suggestion of reproach is removed in the Matthean (13.18) and Lukan (8.11) parallels.

25. Matthew and Luke eliminate the tone of disrespect in the disciples' questions at both Mark 6.37 (cf. Matt 14.17; Luke 9.13) and Mark 4.38 (cf. Matt 8.25; Luke 8.24).

26. The most extensive treatment of this obscure statement in the Second Gospel has been executed by Quesnell, *Mind of Mark.* To conclude, as does Quesnell, that 'The full meaning of the Eucharist is the full meaning of Christianity', and that it is this *sensus plenior* to which Mark 6.31-44 and 8.1-10 point (ibid., p. 276), is ultimately as unpersuasive as it is imprecise; still, Quesnell explores in meticulous detail the undeniable eucharistic overtones in those pericopes, and his monograph is filled with fascinating insights.

27. It is worth noting the irony that permeates the wording of Peter's first denial in the high priest's courtyard: Οὔτε οἶδα οὔτε ἐπίσταμαι σὺ τί λέγεις (14.68a).

41

scold and hinder children who would touch Jesus, thus incurring his indignation (10.13-16); they persist in amazement and fear (10.32) and sleep during their master's 'dark night of the soul' (14.32-42). One of the twelve betrays him (14.10-11, 43-46), another denies him not once but thrice (14.66-72), and all of them forsake him and flee at his arrest (14.50-52).[28] Given the remarkable fact that the last words of a disciple recorded in Mark are Peter's devastating denial, οὐχ οἶδα τὸν ἄνθρωπον τοῦτον ὅν λέγετε (14.71), many scholars might ultimately ask of the twelve, in the exasperated words of Jesus, 'Do you not yet perceive or understand? Are your hearts hardened? Having eyes do you not see, and having ears do you not hear? And do you not remember?' (8.17b-18).[29]

Individually, Simon Peter fares no better than the disciples as a whole. As spokesman for the twelve, he intrudes upon Jesus' prayerful solitude (1.35-37), rebukes his master for the teaching about the suffering Son of man (8.32), reacts incongruously to the transfiguration (9.5-6), and avows a steadfastness with Jesus that proves to be as shallow as it is vehement (14.29-31). Mark singles out Peter, chief among the disciples, in ways most uncomplimentary: alone among the twelve, Peter is associated with satanic opposition to Jesus (8.33);[30] he is directly remonstrated in Gethsemane for his inability to stay awake and alert (14.37); and only Peter's rejection of Jesus is narrated in such uncomfortable detail (14.66-72). In short, if Peter

28. I take this to be the point of the mysterious anecdote about the young man who fled naked from the garden (cf. P. J. Achtemeier: 'His panicked flight simply emphasizes the total abandonment of Jesus to his enemies' [*Invitation to Mark: A Commentary on the Gospel of Mark with Complete Text from the Jerusalem Bible* (Image Books; Garden City, NY: Doubleday, 1978), p. 207]; see also H. T. Fleddermann, 'The Flight of the Naked Young Man (Mark 14.51-52)', *CBQ* 41 [1979], pp. 412-18). The range of speculation, from Ambrose to Frank Kermode, about the identity of the lad and the meaning of the passage is helpfully summarized by L. Williamson, Jr, *Mark* (IBCTP; Atlanta: John Knox, 1983), p. 262.

29. These words of rebuke by Jesus to the twelve, following the warning about the leaven of the Pharisees (8.15) and the disciples' baffled discussion about bread (8.16), are in themselves remarkable: as almost all of the commentators note, Jesus' accusation in 8.17b-18 (considerably mitigated in Matt 16.9 and conspicuously absent from Luke 12.1) precisely aligns the disciples with 'those on the outside' (ἐκείνοις τοῖς ἔξω), who, unlike the twelve, have not been given the secret of the kingdom of God (Mark 4.11-12).

30. B. A. E. Osborne has proposed the intriguing hypothesis that the rebuke of Peter in Mark 8.33 reflects a subtle, rabbinic interconnection of three ideas: (a) the stone of stumbling possibly suggested by πέτρος (= כיפא; cf. *Pesiq. R.* 165a), (b) the evil יצר associated with that stumbling-block (cf. *b. Sukk.* 52a), and (c) the identification of the evil impulse with 'Satan' (cf. *b. B.Bat.* 16a). See Osborne's 'Peter: Stumbling-Block and Satan', *NovT* 15 (1973), pp. 187-90.

typifies the positive characteristics of the disciples in Mark, he also embodies their incomprehension and failure.

To be sure, as Mark recounts the story of Jesus, the disciples are not alone in their failure to understand the teacher from Nazareth. The crowds who witness his mighty works and hear his authoritative teaching are the same multitudes who impose on Jesus' leisure and meal times (3.20; 6.31b) and even endanger his life (3.9);[31] later, after their 'shepherd' has been stricken, those who had previously been milling about like lost sheep not only scatter but also are swayed to demand the release of Barabbas and the execution of Jesus (14.27; 15.8-15; cf. 6.34).[32] Of course, the most pervasive incomprehension of who Jesus is and what he is about is demonstrated by those who also mount against him the deadliest attack: the Jewish religious authorities. Threatened by Jesus' authority (2.6-10; 3.22-30; 6.14; 8.11-13; 11.15-19, 27-33; 12.35-37), by his liberal stance toward social mores and prescriptions of the law (2.15-28; 3.2-5; 7.1-23; 10.29; 12.13-27), and by his outright attacks on their own character and position (7.6; 12.1-12, 38-40), the Jewish leaders (referred to, variously, as Pharisees, Sadducees, Herodians, chief priests, and the high priest)[33] are engaged in perpetual, usually hostile, opposition to Jesus throughout the narrative (2.7, 16, 18, 24; 3.2, 22; 7.5; 8.11; 10.2; 11.27-28; 12.12, 13-15a, 18-23; 14.43-46, 53, 55-65; 15.1, 10, 11). As early as 3.6 the Jewish leaders are explicitly engaged in a plot on Jesus' life, the hatching of which pervades the rest of the narrative (8.31; 9.31; 10.33-34; 11.18; 12.7-8; 14.1-2, 64bc; 15.31-32).

However, like Simon Peter and the rest of the twelve, these other figures cut like a double-edged blade: they also present another, more positive, response to Jesus. This is obviously the case with the crowds,[34] who enthusi-

31. Among the crowd are Jesus' family and hometown acquaintances, all of whom, like the disciples, prove that proximity to Jesus guarantees no special insight into his identity or ministry (3.19b-21, 31-35; 6.1-6a), For discussion, see in particular J. D. Crossan, 'Mark and the Relatives of Jesus', *NovT* 15 (1973), pp. 81-113; and J. Lambrecht, 'The Relatives of Jesus in Mark', *NovT* 16 (1974), pp. 241-58.

32. For this insightful linkage of the crowds ('the little people') with Mark 14.27, I am indebted to Rhoads and Michie, *Mark as Story*, pp. 134-35.

33. On Mark's less than rigorously historical differentiations among the various Jewish groups, see M. J. Cook, *Mark's Treatment of the Jewish Leaders* (NovTSup 51; Leiden: Brill, 1978).

34. P. S. Minear has suggested that, while the μάθηται in Mark's Gospel have been given special authority for performing special tasks, the ὄχλος represents followers of Jesus who are obedient to God's will and are able to hear and to comprehend (to varying degrees) the word taught by Jesus ('Audience Criticism and Markan Ecclesiology', *Neuen Testament und*

astically receive Jesus both in Galilee (1.27-28, 45; 2.1-2, 13; 3.7-8, 10, 33-35; 4.1; 5.21, 24b; 6.33-34, 44, 54-56; 7.36-37; 8.1-3, 9; 9.14-15; 10.1, 13, 16, 36) and in Jerusalem (11.8-10; 12.12, 37b).[35] More to the point, the special status of the disciples is indirectly compromised by the presence of a larger, motley cast of characters who in many ways exhibit the sort of exemplary behavior that one might justifiably expect of the twelve: the grateful service of Peter's mother-in-law (1.31); the faith of the leper (1.40), of the paralytic and his escort (2.3-5), of Jairus the ἀρχισυνάγωγος (5.22-23; cf. 5.36) and the woman with the hemorrhage (5.25-28), of the epileptic child's father (9.24; cf. 9.19), and of blind Bartimaeus (10.46-52); the yearning for discipleship of the erstwhile demoniac (5.18, cf. 17); the solicitous dedication of the Baptist's disciples (6.29); the self-renunciation of the Syro-Phoenician woman (7.25-28);[36] the perceptiveness of men healed of blindness (8.22-26; 10.46-52); the receptiveness of children (9.36-37; 10.13-16); the generosity of the widow (12.41-44); the loving extravagance of the woman who anointed Jesus (14.3-9); the courage of Joseph of Arimathea (15.42-46); and the loyalty of Mary Magdalene and the other women in Jesus' entourage (15.40-41, 47; 16.1-8).[37]

Geschichte: Historisches Geschehen und Deutung im Neuen Testament. Oscar Cullmann zum 70. Geburtstag [ed. H. Baltensweiler and B. Reicke; Zürich and Tübingen: Theologischer Verlag/J. C. B. Mohr (Paul Siebeck), 1972], pp. 79-89). Cf. also A. W. Mosley, 'Jesus' Audiences in the Gospels of St. Mark and St. Luke', *NTS* 10 (1963), pp. 139-49.

35. This amounts to one of several pieces of evidence against the Lohmeyer/Lightfoot hypothesis of a thoroughgoing pattern in Mark of Jesus' 'Galilean springtime' of acceptance and his total rejection in Jerusalem (see e.g. Lightfoot, *Locality and Doctrine*, pp. 124-25).

36. A thorough examination of the context, literary congruence, and *Sitz im Leben* of this finely etched *Streitsgespräch-cum-Wundernovelle* is offered by T. A. Burkill, *New Light on the Earliest Gospel: Seven Markan Studies* (Ithaca, NY, and London: Cornell University Press, 1972), pp. 48-120.

37. The role of the women *vis-à-vis* the disciples has been a source of debate in recent Markan scholarship. The interpretive options range from the suggestion of a strong female constituency and power base in both the ministry of Jesus and the Markan church (W. Munro, 'Women Disciples in Mark?', *CBQ* 44 [1982], pp. 225-41), to the argument that the women in Mark's narrative function chiefly as models of fidelity in contrast to the fickleness of the twelve (M. J. Schierling, 'Women as Leaders in the Marcan Communities', *List* 15 [1980], pp. 250-56; M. J. Selvidge, '"And Those Who followed Feared" (Mark 10.32)', *CBQ* 45 [1983], pp. 396-400), to the position that both male and female followers of Jesus in Mark conduct themselves in ways good and bad (J. J. Schmitt, 'Women in Mark's Gospel', *TBT* 19 [1981], pp. 228-33; E. S. Malbon, 'Fallible Followers: Women and Men in the Gospel of Mark', *Sem* 28 [1983], pp. 29-48). Although the various exegetical issues cannot be pursued and resolved at this time, the total evidence of the Second Gospel suggests that the third of these options is the better balanced and most persuasive.

In many respects these 'little people' in Mark's narrative serve as foils for the disciples, fulfilling a number of the functions expected of Jesus' followers; if they do not supplant the twelve, they do at least incarnate Jesus' repeated maxim that those who are servants and least of all become, within the context of the narrative, truly great (cf. 9.35; 10.42-45). Even a scribe, a member of the Jewish officialdom that is otherwise antagonistic to Jesus, proves capable of acknowledging without reservation the authority of Jesus and the demands of God's law — for which he is amply commended by Jesus (12.28-34). In summary, then, misunderstanding, antagonism, and failure are not unique to the disciples in Mark, but neither are faith, insight, and allegiance to Jesus. To the extent that these latter attributes, not only their negative counterparts, are displayed by figures other than the twelve — that is, to the degree that 'discipleship' is evinced by those not directly called or trained to be disciples — the status of Peter and his cohorts appears correspondingly equivocal.

B. The Disciples in the Second Gospel:
A Review of Recent Redaction-Critical Alternatives

From the preceding it should be evident that, if the role of the disciples in Mark is problematic, New Testament scholars have not invented the problem. The image of the twelve in the Second Gospel is complex and ambiguous; in trying to limn that image it is scarcely surprising that Markan exegetes have produced a body of interpretation that is multifarious and to some extent self-contradictory. What *is* striking, however, is the sometimes radical disparity in exegesis that emerges from the application to Mark of a single method of interpretation — namely, redaction criticism. In other words, if the majority of Markan scholars had customarily adopted different exegetical strategies, which entailed their assessment and weighting of different types of textual evidence, we could understand why they might end up drawing very different exegetical conclusions; however, it is much more difficult to understand and to explain how such radically divergent exegetical conclusions could have arisen from the adoption of a *single* exegetical strategy — *Redaktionsgeschichte* — which, by even the most conservative reckoning of the evidence presented in Chapter 1, has surely been the most widespread and influential method of reading the Gospel of Mark during the past thirty years. To put the matter pointedly: if redaction criticism is truly as serviceable as its practitioners have implicitly or explicitly claimed, why has its usage consistently produced exegetical outcomes that scatter in different directions rather than cohere and coalesce?

It is not difficult to substantiate the claim that redaction critics have wrought radically divergent interpretations of the disciples in Mark. The review of research in the field speaks for itself. Although the lineaments of the scholarly debate would be detectable in a chronological review of the leading studies of Markan discipleship, those contours become even more sharply defined with the presentation of a thematic *Forschungsbericht*, which groups those investigations into larger categories. Although allowance must always be made for the specific nuances of particular scholars' interpretation, I would suggest that for heuristic purposes most of the redaction-critical explorations of 'the disciples' or 'discipleship' in the Second Gospel may be grouped according to the following categories or types.

Type I: The 'Conservative'[38] *Position.* Much of the research in Markan discipleship falls into a category whose perspective might be defined as follows: Consonant with church tradition and historical fact, Mark's theology incorporates a generally favorable estimation of the disciples. Notice that this perspective consists of two components: a *traditio-historical* judgment (that Mark's representation is congruent with historical fact or early Christian tradition, or both) and a *theological* judgment (emphasizing the positive status of the disciples in the Second Gospel). This first category may be conceived therefore, in terms of *a generally positive understanding of Mark's attitude toward history, tradition, and the role of Jesus' disciples.*

Even among scholars who accept the fundamentally theological orientation of the redaction-critical method, there has been no dearth of assertions that Mark's narrative preserves concrete, historical data about the disciples generally, and about Peter in particular. Thus, on the basis of geographical feasibility (cf. Mark 8.27a), the internal coherence of Mark 8.27b-29ab with the foregoing Markan narrative (N.B. 3.6; 6.14-16), and the historical plausibility of an apolitical but prophetic-messianic accla-

---

38. To clarify the argument developed in this study, it seems necessary to describe each of the forthcoming 'types' in some abbreviated manner. I am not entirely comfortable with the adjectives on which I have settled ('conservative', 'mediate', 'liberal'); however, I am unable to come up with more satisfactory alternatives. At any rate, in characterizing Type I as 'conservative', I refer only to these scholars' *de facto* proximity to more traditional claims for the positive historicity of Mark's portrayal of Jesus and the twelve. Neither this nor any of the adjectives used to describe forthcoming 'types' implies any value judgment whatever as to a category's inherent 'rightness'; nor does the use of the term here necessarily betoken a 'conservative' theological perspective on the part of scholars grouped in this category.

mation of Jesus by Peter (8.29b), Rudolf Pesch has argued at length both for a pre-Markan passion narrative undergirding Mark 8.27-30 as well as for the essential historicity of Peter's confession behind that pre-Markan *Vorlage*.[39] While departing from Pesch's claim for the historicity of Peter's confession at 8.29, Josef Ernst is otherwise one with Pesch in claiming that the Second Evangelist allows us to perceive some of the contours of the historical Peter, especially his preeminence among the twelve, his characteristic vacillation, his witness to the resurrected Lord, and his function as missionary and transmitter of the Jesus-tradition.[40] And one of the outcomes of a national dialogue conducted in 1971 between Lutheran and Roman Catholic theologians in the United States was that, through the emphasis on Peter in 3.16 and 16.7, 'Mark may be giving implicit testimony to the tradition that, by the will of Jesus, Peter had real importance for the church'.[41] In short, as these examples testify, the adoption of a redaction-critical perspective in interpreting Mark does not necessarily preclude the assumption of the Gospel's linkage with early Christian tradition or historical fact.

Nor does the adoption of a redaction-critical perspective, along with the assumption of Mark's historical or traditional reliability, preclude a positive assessment of the disciples' role in the Second Gospel. Among those who arrive at this general interpretation, greater or lesser weight is given to different positive attributes of the twelve: thus John Coutts lays special emphasis on the authority to exorcise demons, enjoyed by Jesus and conferred by him upon the twelve,[42] whereas (in exploring a passage like Mark 1.16-20) Pesch stresses Mark's preoccupation with the disciples'

---

39. R. Pesch, 'Das Messiasbekenntnis des Petrus (Mk 8,27-30): Neuverhandlung einer alten Frage', *BZ* 17 (1973), pp. 178-95 + *BZ* 18 (1974), pp. 20-31. In *Das Markusevangelium* (2/2, pp. 1-27), Pesch contends that the entire second half of the Gospel (Mark 8.27–16.8) faithfully reproduces a pre-Markan passion narrative that is characterized by both thematic coherence and historical accuracy.

40. J. Ernst, 'Simon-Kephas-Petrus: Historische und typologische Perspektiven im Markusevangelium', *TGl* 71 (1981), pp. 438-56; cf. idem, 'Die Petrustradition im Markusevangelium — Ein altes Problem neu angegangen', *Begegnung mit dem Wort: Festschrift für Heinrich Zimmermann* (ed. J. Zmÿewski and E. Nellessen; BBB 53; Bonn: Hanstein, 1980), pp. 35-65.

41. Brown, Donfried, and Reumann, eds., *Peter in the New Testament*, p. 72. Cf. O. Cullmann, *Peter, Disciple-Apostle-Martyr: A Historical and Theological Study* (Philadelphia: Westminster, 1953), esp. pp. 17-32.

42. J. Coutts, 'The Authority of Jesus and of the Twelve in St. Mark's Gospel', *JTS* n.s. 8 (1957), pp. 111-18.

witness to Jesus' activity and their own missionary endeavor.[43] A number of investigations emphasize the unashamed association and intimate fellowship enjoyed in Mark between Jesus and the disciples.[44] In their important monographs on Markan discipleship, Günther Schmahl and Klemens Stock arrive at essentially the same exegetical conclusion: Mark depicts the twelve as carrying out and extending within the post-Easter community Jesus' ministry of word and deed.[45] Stock and other scholars (in particular, Wim Burgers[46] and Karl Kertelge[47]) draw an even more positive conclusion from the role of the twelve as eyewitnesses, associates, and representatives of Jesus: the twelve become, for Mark, the foundation for and the authentication of the truth of the gospel, as well as the basis for apostolic authority in the post-Easter church.[48] That the disciples occupy a place of such importance in the Second Gospel is not to suggest that they usurp Jesus as the leading figure: all of the researchers listed here would concur

43. R. Pesch, 'Berufung und Sendung, Nachfolge und Mission: Eine Studie zu Mk 1,16-20', *ZKT* 91 (1969), pp. 1-31; cf. idem, *Das Markusevangelium,* 2/1, pp. 108-16. Interestingly, Pesch goes so far as to conclude that the Second Gospel may best be described as a *Missionsbuch (Das Markusevangelium,* 11.1, p. 61).

44. For example, see W. Au, 'Discipleship in Mark', *TBT* 67 (1973), pp. 1249-51; H. F. Peacock, 'Discipleship in the Gospel of Mark', *RevExp* 74 (1978), pp. 555-64.

45. Thus G. Schmahl, *Die Zwölf im Markusevangelium: Eine redaktionsgeschichtliche Untersuchung* (TTS 30; Trier: Paulinus, 1974), p. 143: 'Durch diese Zusammenschau [in Mark 1.14-15; 3.7-12, 14-15; 6.7-12] der geschichtlich-eschatologischen Sendung Jesu und der Funktion der Zwölf stellt Markus den Zwölferkreis als jene Größe vor, die für die Durchführung des Werkes Jesu in der nachösterlichen Kirche verantwortlich ist'. N.B. also idem, 'Die Berufung der Zwölf im Markusevangelium', *TTZ* 81 (1972), pp. 203-13 (on Mark 3.13-19). Cf. K. Stock, *Boten,* p. 191: 'Aus dieser Verteilung und aus dem Zusammenhang der Texte [pertaining to the twelve] ergibt sich als Grundstruktur der 12-Existenz: von Jesus zu den Menschen mit der ganzen Botschaft Jesu, und: für die Menschen bei Jesus. Sie sind von Jesus berufen, sie sind Weggenossen Jesu, sie sollen Diener sein wie Jesus, ihre personale Beziehung zu Jesus wird sichtbar vor allem in der Krise der Passion. Sie sind Abgesandte zu den Menschen und sie sollen die Diener allen sein'.

46. W. Burgers, 'De Instelling van de Twaalf in het Evangelie van Marcus', *ETL* 36 (1960), pp. 625-54.

47. K. Kertelge, 'Die Funktion der 'Zwölf' im Markusevangelium: Eine redaktionsgeschichtliche Auslegung, zugleich ein Beitrag zur Frage nach dem neutestamentlichen Amtsverständnis', *TTZ* 78 (1969), pp. 193-206.

48. Stock (*Boten,* p. 70) is among the most explicit in making this point. Kertelge ('Die Funktion') is careful to argue that, in Mark's Gospel, the twelve do not so much exercise an 'official [ecclesial] authority' *(Amtsautorität)* as they guarantee the historical and theological continuity between Jesus and the church in the midst of historical change. Cf. also Minear, 'Audience Criticism', pp. 88-89.

with Schmahl that the significance of the twelve in Mark remains relative to the normative person and work of Jesus;[49] and (according to a number of interpreters) it is precisely by way of Mark's Christology in general, and the messianic secret in particular, that blemishes on the disciples' character and conduct should be accounted for.[50] Notwithstanding these understandable smirches, the disciples (as regarded by Type I exegetes) are the object of the Second Evangelist's favor and play, throughout his Gospel, a consistently positive role.

Few Markan exegetes exemplify both aspects of this position (Mark's historical and traditional reliability, and the Gospel's commendation of Jesus' disciples) as well as Robert Paul Meye (1929-). Much of Meye's research in the Second Gospel has defended the thesis that a didactic motif is preeminent in Mark, especially in the Gospel's editorial sectors;[51] a corollary to this thesis, for Meye, is the favorable status assumed by the disciples in Mark.[52] According to Meye's exegesis, the twelve are the beneficiaries of Jesus' special appointment and his private and persistent instruction;[53] they respond by remaining with Jesus to the end, unquestioningly obedient to his word,[54] as well as by bearing witness to their master through advancing his authoritative ministry of preaching and healing.[55] In sum, the

---

49. Thus Schmahl, 'Die Berufung', p. 213.

50. Thus Minette de Tillesse, *Le Secret Messianique*, pp. 227-78; J. Roloff, 'Das Markusevangelium als Geschichtsdarstellung', *EvT* 29 (1969), pp. 73-93; idem, *Apostolat-Verkündigung-Kirche: Ursprung, Inhalt, und Funktion des kirchlichen Apostelamtes nach Paulus, Lukes, und der Pastoralbriefen* (Göttingen: Vandenhoeck & Ruprecht, 1970), pp. 138-68; K. Kertelge, 'Die Epiphanie Jesu im Evangelium (Markus)', in *Gestalt und Anspruch des Neuen Testaments* (ed. J. Schreiner; Würzburg: Echter Verlag, 1969), pp. 153-72; J. Ernst, 'Noch einmal: Die Verleugnung Jesu durch Petrus (Mk 14,54.66-72)', *Cath* 30 (1976), pp. 207-26; idem, 'Petrusbekenntnis-Leidensankündigung-Satanwort (Mk 8,27-33): Tradition und Redaktion', *Cath* 32 (1978), pp. 46-73; M. Fitzpatrick, 'Marcan Theology and the Messianic Secret', *AusCathR* 59 (1982), pp. 404-16. N.B. the neat encapsulation of this perspective by Pesch (*Das Markusevangelium*, 11.1, p. 276): '. . . für den Weg Jesu ans Kreuz, der zugleich zur Norm des Weges des Jüngers werden soll (8,34). Unter diesem Aspekt werdien Messiasgeheimnis und Jüngerunverständnis verknüpft'.

51. R. P. Meye, *Jesus and the Twelve: Discipleship and Revelation in Mark's Gospel* (Grand Rapids, MI: Eerdmans, 1968), pp. 13, 30-87, 92; idem, 'Messianic Secret and Messianic Didache in Mark's Gospel', *Oikonomia: Heilsgeschichte als Thema der Theologie* (O. Cullmann Festschrift; ed. F. Christ; Hamburg-Bergstedt: Reich, 1967), pp. 57-68, esp. p. 60.

52. Meye 'Messianic Didache', pp. 60, 65, 67; idem, *Jesus*, pp. 20, 194, 197, 210, 211.

53. Meye, *Jesus*, pp. 71-73, 78, 105, 123-62, 219-22.

54. Ibid., pp. 48, 102-103; cf. idem, 'Messianic Didache', pp. 62-65.

55. Meye, *Jesus*, pp. 55-56, 109, 115, 179-81.

disciples function for the Markan church as the all-important guarantors of the gospel and authoritative mediators of a messianic διδαχή.[56] Although Mark thereby intends to validate existing Christian tradition by showing that it arose from a band of witnesses specially selected and equipped by Jesus,[57] Meye does not conclude that the Evangelist has simply fabricated such a glowing portrayal of the disciples; on the contrary, this positive presentation is a historically acceptable portrait of those about Jesus and one that is entirely compatible with the early ecclesial tradition, associated with Papias, that the Second Gospel was produced by the ἑρμηνευτής of Peter.[58] Overall, Meye's redaction-critical research is a model of what I denote as the Type I position: a scholarly slant on Mark's Gospel that emphasizes its traditio-historical veracity and its thoroughgoing, positive depiction of Jesus' disciples.

Type II: The 'Mediate'[59] *Position.* The point of view just described is not shared by all students of the Second Gospel or is adopted only with qualifications. For other interpreters, the Evangelist is not in every case so firmly bound to tradition or to history, and his depiction of the disciples is inherently equivocal, giving equal weight both to their defects of character and of conduct and to their more attractive attributes. Thus might this interpretive position be defined: Indebted but not enslaved to church tradition and historical fact, Mark's theology incorporates both a positive and a negative, an alternating favorable and unfavorable, estimation of the disciples. Once again, we are dealing with a position that embraces both an exegetical assessment (the ambiguous role of the disciples in Mark) as well as a traditio-historical assumption (the Evangelist's flexibility toward history and tradition). In this second category of Markan research we are dealing with scholars who propound *a positive but significantly qualified attitude of the Evangelist toward history, tradition, and the role of Jesus' disciples.*

Scholars tending to subscribe to Type II would agree with Meye, Pesch, and the researchers surveyed in our first category that both the historical facts of Jesus' ministry and the early Christian interpretation of those facts have exercised a genuine influence on the Second Evangelist; as

---

56. Ibid., pp. 102-103, 135-36, 182-83, 190-91; idem, 'Messianic Didache', pp. 66, 68.

57. Meye, *Jesus,* p. 216.

58. Ibid., pp. 33, 92, 209, 225-27; cf. Eusebius, *H.E.* 3.39.15.

59. 'Mediate' in this context refers only to the fact that the perspectives and interpretations of the scholars in this category fall somewhere in the middle of my typological spectrum, between the extremes demarcated by Types I and III. See also my comments in note 38, above.

Hugh Anderson has put it, 'there are Gospel "moments" when the Church is not so much completely master of the tradition as mastered and controlled by the primary data of tradition emanating from Jesus himself'.[60] However, for representatives of this 'mediate' position, such 'Gospel "moments"' are counterbalanced by other instances in the Gospel in which Mark is just as clearly master of his materials, shaping them in accordance, not so much with historical or even traditional veracity, but with his own perception of theological truth. Thus Joachim Gnilka: 'Markus kann als theologischer Geschichtserzähler, nicht als literarischer Geschichtsschreiber vorgestellt werden. . . . [So] kann sein Werk mit 'Bericht als Verkündigung oder im Dienst der Verkündigung' umschrieben werden'.[61] In alignment with this point of view, and with special reference to the disciples, Walter Schmithals has hypothesized that the call and commissioning of the twelve (Mark 3.13-19; 6.7-13), along with the narrative of the transfiguration (9.2-8) and a portion of the longer ending of the Gospel (16.15-20), may in fact have constituted the conclusion of Mark's source; however, the call, commissioning, and transfiguration narratives were transplanted to their present, pre-Easter locations by the Evangelist for the sake of his larger *Geheimnistheorie*.[62] Also focusing on Mark 6.7-13, Jean Delorme has stressed Mark's typological rendering of the mission of the twelve, a presentation sensitive to the responsibilities and hardships of Christian missionaries of the Evangelist's own time.[63] Similarly, Eta Linnemann has argued that the theologically powerful story of Peter's de-

---

60. Anderson, *Gospel of Mark*, p. 20; cf. pp. 8-24.

61. Gnilka, *Das Evangelium*, 1.1, p. 24; cf. pp. 17-24 and p. 25, where Gnilka summarizes his view of Mark as 'ein gemäßigter Redaktor'. Cf. also Schweizer, *Good News*, pp. 11-27.

62. W. Schmithals, 'Der Markusschluss, die Verklärungsgeschichte und die Aussendung der Zwölf', *ZTK* 69 (1972), pp. 379-411. That Schmithals's theory is extraordinarily speculative need not detain us at present; as with the other interpreters here, I am more concerned, for the moment, with representative points of view, not exegetical cogency. Schmithals's understanding of Mark's redaction of his sources is also exemplary of the overall perspective displayed by Type II scholars (though departing from them on specific matters of hypothetical detail): with the aid of his *Messiasgeheimnistheorie*, Mark has creatively fused an already existing *Grundschrift* (a confessional account of an implicitly messianic 'life of Jesus') with a sayings-tradition (*Logienüberlieferung* Q^I) that presented a non-messianic portrayal of Jesus' ministry and death as a martyred prophet of God. With its assumption of the reciprocal restraints exercised by Mark and his traditions, Schmithals's perspective becomes the framework on which his recent, two-volume Markan commentary hangs. For Schmithals's redaction-critical theory, N.B. *Das Evangelium*, II.1, pp. 52-61.

63. J. Delorme, 'La mission des Douze en Galilée: Mk 6,7-13', *AsSeign* 46 (1974), pp. 43-50.

nials of Jesus (Mark 14.54, 66-72) was creatively woven by the Evangelist, using threads found by him in the traditional narrative of Jesus' prediction of the disciples' desertion (Mark 14.27-31).[64] Other examples of this perspective on Mark as both servant and master of history and tradition could be multiplied; these should suffice to typify a redaction-critical understanding that has been given apt expression by Sherman Johnson:

> Sometimes the evangelist imposed . . . ideas on his source material, but he nevertheless derived them from certain elements in the gospel tradition. . . . Therefore the earliest gospel is not a mere compilation of earlier accounts, nor on the other hand an artificially constructed scheme. Although the order of events is sometimes determined by dogmatic ideas and teaching devices, the evangelist has gathered from his anonymous informants a broad outline of the life of Jesus and a sense of the dramatic movement of his ministry. This may explain the combination of art and apparent artlessness, of simple verisimilitude and theological reflection, which tends to make the gospel difficult to analyse.[65]

Given such a nuanced perspective on Mark's relation to history and tradition, a similarly nuanced, if not complicated, reading of Markan discipleship should not surprise us. This is, indeed, what we encounter among the interpreters representative of the Type II, or 'mediate', position. Congenial with the exegesis of the scholars considered in our first category are those interpretations that stress the positive role of the disciples in Mark: their distinctive calling and commissioning by Jesus, intimately sharing in their master's ministry and destiny;[66] their unique insight into the divine plan for history (corresponding to מַשְׂכִּילִים of some apocalyptic writ-

---

64. E. Linnemann, 'Die Verleugnung des Petrus', *ZTK* 63 (1966), pp. 1-32.

65. S. E. Johnson, *A Commentary on the Gospel According to St. Mark* (BNTC; London: Black, 1960), p. 19. Likewise, Rolf Busemann: 'Sicherlich kommt der literarischen Produktivität des Evangelisten ein Stellenwert zu, der sich etwa in der Mitte einpendelt: Markus ist weder ein 'literarisch unproduktiver' und 'konservativer' Redaktor, für den R. Pesch ihn hält, noch ist seine literarische Leistung überzogen hoch zu veranschlagen' (*Die Jüngergemeinde nach Markus 10: Eine redaktionsgeschichtliche Untersuchung des 10. Kapitels im Markusevangelium* [BBB 57; Bonn: Hanstein, 1983], p. 228).

66. See especially S. Freyne, *The Twelve: Disciples and Apostles — A Study in the Theology of the First Three Gospels* (London and Sydney: Sheed and Ward, 1968), pp. 106-50; F. J. Moloney, 'The Vocation of the Disciples in the Gospel of Mark', *Sal* 43 (1981), pp. 487-516; E. L. Taylor, Jr, 'The Disciples of Jesus in the Gospel of Mark', Ph.D. diss., Southern Baptist Theological Seminary, 1979, pp. 193-94.

ings);[67] their authority nonpareil in the post-Easter, missionary *Sitz* because of their contact with the risen Lord, implied in Mark 16.7, 8b.[68] In these and other ways,[69] according to this line of interpretation, the twelve function as a model for believers in the Evangelist's own time: 'Mark's community', observes Edward Lynn Taylor, 'therefore knows a positive example of what it means to represent Jesus in their own day'.[70] This, however, is not the full story: as is frequently pointed out, the disciples also exemplify the world's misunderstanding of, and blindness toward, Jesus, leading to their descent into unbelief and defection.[71] As explained by scholars in this camp, the resolution of these positive and negative characteristics of the disciples is ultimately to be attributed to demonstrable tensions in Mark's theology.[72] For instance, Camille Focant cautions interpreters against speaking too hastily or too glibly about the Markan theme of the disciples' lack of understanding: although certainly capable of carrying a negative valence (cf. Mark 4.13; 6.50-52; 7.18; 8.16-21), their incomprehension can also connote a positive response to the magnitude of a miracle (4.40-41; 5.31; 6.37; 8.4), to the severity of Jesus' teaching (8.32-33; 9.32; 10.24, 34), or to an epiphany involving Jesus (9.5-6). Thus, for Focant, the disciples show themselves to be tending toward perfection,

---

67. S. Freyne, 'The Disciples in Mark and the *maskilim* in Daniel: A Comparison', *JSNT* 16 (1982), pp. 7-23.

68. D. Catchpole, 'The Fearful Silence of the Women at the Tomb: A Study in Markan Theology', *JTSA* 18 (1977), pp. 3-10.

69. Even so harsh and embarrassing a thing as Peter's denial of Jesus has been construed in fundamentally positive terms, due to the message of subsequent reconciliation for which it prepares the reader (cf. Mark 14.28; 16.7). In a fascinating study ('St. Peter's Denial', *BJRL* 55 [1973], pp. 346-68), G. W. H. Lampe has suggested the existence of a certain tension between Peter's forgiveness and the warning about blaspheming against the Holy Spirit (Mark 3.28-29); Lampe further explores the impact of these two poles of thought upon patristic arguments for leniency during periods of persecution as well as for the rigorism of the Novationists and Donatists.

70. Taylor, 'Disciples', p. 194.

71. Among others, see Schweizer, 'Die theologische Leistung'; P. J. Achtemeier, ' "And he followed him": Miracles and Discipleship in Mark 10.46-52', *Sem* 11 (1978), pp. 115-45.

72. With other exegetes in our 'mediate' category, Freyne does not rule out the possibility that the equivocal status of the disciples in the Second Gospel reflects historical fact: For all their endowment with the powers requisite for propagation of the gospel, 'This aspect of the Twelve [viz., their weakness and lack of comprehension] best corresponds with the gospel portrayal of the life of Jesus which Mark gives, and perhaps it is the most historical picture of the Twelve that we get in the New Testament' (*Twelve*, p. 149). 'Yet', concludes Freyne (with other Type-II scholars), 'Mark's preoccupation is mainly theological' (ibid.).

though not yet having attained it completely.[73] Similarly, David J. Hawkin suggests that a distinction is drawn by Mark between the disciples and the οἱ ἔξω of 4.11: the disciples are privileged recipients of revelation and are thereby given the means to pierce the secret of Jesus' identity (8.27-30); what they fail to grasp is the mystery of Jesus' destiny, into which they are called to enter.[74] Edward Taylor concedes that the disciples in the Second Gospel fail miserably to come to grips with Jesus and his ministry; 'One can even speak of total discipleship failure'. Yet, according to Taylor, this cannot be the last word, for Jesus' predictions of the disciples' own ministry in the last days (Mark 13.9-13, 30-31) evidently betoken a future for them.[75] Beyond these encouraging forecasts in the 'Little Apocalypse', Welton Seal reminds us of Mark 14.27-28, which depicts the scandalization of the twelve as scriptural and divinely necessitated as well as predicts its ultimate reversal, and Mark 16.7, which presages the reversal of the disciples' fecklessness.[76] However it is defined, the scholars of Type II would underscore the tension in Mark's presentation of discipleship, and they would undoubtedly concur with Donald Senior's judgment that Mark is 'a story of representative Christian existence, an existence embracing both failure and reconciliation'.[77]

Like their Type I colleagues, these 'mediate' scholars hypothesize the circumstances in the Markan *Sitz* from which this understanding of discipleship may have arisen. Thus Francis Moloney argues that the disciples' failure in the Second Gospel undercuts any temptation to highlight their supposed virtuousness: Christian discipleship is summoned and sustained

---

73. C. Focant, 'L'incompréhension des disciples dans le deuxième Évangile: Tradition et rédaction', *RB* 82 (1975), pp. 161-85 (a condensed English translation of which appears as 'The Disciples' Blindness in Mark's Gospel' in *TD* 24 [1976], pp. 260-64). As the subtitle of the original article suggests, Focant attempts to identify those expressions of the motif or incomprehension that occurred in the pre-Markan tradition (Mark 4.40-41; 5.31; 6.37; 8.4; 9.19; maybe 4.13 and 7.18) and to suggest a reason for Mark's redactional development of that motif (to underscore for his readers the difficulty of understanding the mystery of Jesus and his cross).

74. D. J. Hawkin, 'The Incomprehension of the Disciples in the Marcan Redaction', *JBL* 91 (1972), pp. 491-500.

75. Taylor, 'Disciples', p. 321.

76. Seal, 'Parousia', pp. 181-82; cf. also Hooker, *Message*, pp. 115-21.

77. D. P. Senior, 'The Struggle to Be Universal: Mission as Vantage Point for New Testament Investigation', *CBQ* 46 (1984), p. 78. Cf. H. T. Fleddermann, 'The Central Question of Mark's Gospel: A Study of Mark 8.29', Ph.D. diss., Graduate Theological Union, 1978, pp. 209-10.

by the power and love of God, exhibited in Jesus.[78] Similarly, Eta Linnemann interprets Mark 14.54, 66-72 as a kind of fable of grace: 'Im Glauben machen die Jünger die Erfahrung, daß sie sich nicht in der Hand haben, daß sie über die eigentliche Entscheidung nicht verfügen, sondern mit ihrer ganzen Existenz ausgesetzt sind. . . . Auch da, wo wir uns selbst nicht in der Hand haben, sind wir in Gottes Hand'.[79] For other interpreters, the paradoxical position of the disciples in the Second Gospel corresponds with Mark's understanding of the paradoxical character of discipleship itself: a following of Jesus that entails lowliness, service, and a peaceful equanimity,[80] as well as suffering and a clear-eyed awareness of the possibility of martyrdom.[81] Whatever theological freight Mark uses the disciples to convey, there seems to be little question among these investigators that the Evangelist writes, not from purely literary or even abstractly theological motivations, but out of pastoral,[82] didactic,[83] or apologetic[84] concerns for his own Christian community in the latter half of the first century.

Even as the work of Robert Meye epitomizes the research in Markan discipleship surveyed under our 'conservative' (Type I) heading, the studies

78. Moloney, 'Vocation', pp. 515-16; cf. S. Freyne, 'At Cross Purposes: Jesus and the Disciples in Mark', *Fur* 33 (1982), pp. 331-39.

79. Linnemann, 'Die Verleugnung', p. 32.

80. H. T. Fleddermann, 'The Discipleship Discourse (Mark 9.33-50)', *CBQ* 43 (1981), pp. 57-75.

81. Among many others, see E. Haenchen, 'Die Komposition von Mk vii 27–ix 1 und Par.', *NovT* 6 (1963), pp. 81-109; H. Simonsen, 'Mark 8,27–10,52: Markusevangeliets kompositions', *DTT* 27 (1964), pp. 83-89; Achtemeier, *Mark*, pp. 97-100; Gnilka, *Das Evangelium*, II.2, pp. 9-112; R. Kühschelm, *Jüngerverfolgung und Geschick Jesu: Eine exegetisch-bibeltheologische Untersuchung der synoptischen Verfolgungsankündigungen Mk 13, 9-13 par und Mt 23, 29-36 par* (ÖBS 5; Klosterneuburg: Österreichisches Katholisches Bibelwerk, 1983).

82. Thus Busemann, *Die Jüngergemeinde*, p. 228: in the face of persecution, 'Markus ist der Seelsorger der Jüngergemeinde. . . .'

83. Freyne, *Twelve*, pp. 129, 149 (speaking of Mark's 'catechetical reasons' for portraying the twelve in particular ways); H. Simonsen, 'Zur Frage der grundlegenden Problematik in form- und redaktionsgeschichtlicher Evangelienforschung', *ST* 26 (1972), pp. 1-23; W. Bracht, 'Jüngerschaft und Nachfolge: Zur Gemeindesituation im Markusevangelium', *Kirche im Werden: Studien zum Thema Amt und Gemeinde im Neuen Testament* (ed. J. Hainz; Munich: Schöningh, 1976), pp. 143-65.

84. Freyne, *Twelve*, p. 149; cf. the similar but not altogether redaction-critical judgment of C. F. D. Moule, 'The Intention of the Evangelists', *New Testament Essays: Studies in Memory of T. W. Manson* (ed. A. J. B. Higgins; Manchester: University of Manchester Press, 1959), pp. 165-79.

of Ernest Best (1917-2004) nicely exemplify this second, or 'mediate', category. In accord with most Type II investigators, Best believes that the Second Gospel emerged from a dialectical process, in which Evangelist and traditions about the historical Jesus exerted equal and (to some degree) opposite forces, one upon the other: '[Mark] remained a real author, not just a recorder of tradition',[85] and 'He used the historical material with a theological purpose in mind';[86] yet 'He is not wholly master of his material; as well as controlling it in the way he arranges and modifies it he is also controlled by it'.[87] From such a compositional process arose Mark's Gospel and the slant on discipleship presented therein: discipleship as 'following Jesus', not in the sense of 'imitating' Christ, but as undertaking a journey in which believers pursue a path, not only of suffering and persecution, but also of mission to the world.[88] '[The] role of the disciples in the gospel is then to be examples to [Mark's] community'[89] of such discipleship. While it is indisputable that the disciples appear in a bad light, 'it is because Mark wishes to use them as a foil: their failure to understand is sometimes introduced in order to allow Jesus to give further and fuller instruction; their fearfulness is brought out in order that Jesus may show them the sources of calm and courage; their desire for positions of importance is stressed in order that Jesus may teach them about the meaning of service'.[90] Mainly because the pre-Markan tradition depicted him as such, Peter is representative of the disciples' failure and shortcomings; yet even this is not allowed to stand in the Gospel without qualification, since Mark typically lifts much of the stain off Peter by associating other disciples with him.[91] Finally, in Best's judgment, the disciples are not presented in the Gospel for their own sake, by reason of their merit or lack thereof. 'Mark's purpose was pastoral. He wrote primarily to build up his readers in faith.'[92] As such, 'Any apparent attack on [the twelve] normally ends not in the negative side of their failure,

---

85. Best, *Temptation*, p. xi.

86. E. Best, *Following Jesus: Discipleship in the Gospel of Mark* (JSNTSup 4; Sheffield: JSOT, 1981), p. 10.

87. Ibid., p. 203.

88. E. Best, 'Discipleship in Mark: Mark 8.22–10.52', *SJT* 23 (1970), pp. 323-37; idem, *Temptation*, p. 121; *Following Jesus*, pp. 246-50; *Mark: The Gospel as Story* (SNTW; Edinburgh: Clark, 1983), pp. 83-92.

89. E. Best, 'The Role of the Disciples in Mark', *NTS* 23 (1977), p. 401.

90. Best, 'Role', p. 399; cf. idem, *Mark*, pp. 44-50.

91. Idem, 'Peter in the Gospel According to Mark', *CBQ* 40 (1978), pp. 547-58, esp. 557-58.

92. Idem, *Mark*, p. 51; cf. *Following Jesus*, pp. 13-14.

but in positive teaching on the part of Jesus which will assist Mark's community . . . [and] be a source of great comfort to his readers'.[93] In sum, few scholars have articulated more clearly or consistently than Ernest Best the tensive relationship between Mark and his historical traditions or the Evangelist's own tensive portrayal of the disciples.

Type III: The 'Liberal'[94] *Position.* The degree of tension characterizing Mark's presentation of the twelve and his own position relative to history and tradition — that tension often absent from the interpretation of Meye and other Type I researchers, yet pervasive in the work of Best and his confreres in Type II — tends once again to be diminished in a third general category of Markan scholarship. The Second Evangelist is increasingly perceived by this group as an independent author in his own right, unfettered from the bonds of his traditions or historical fact; as *Schriftsteller,* he is free to devise a theologically creative and consistent picture of the disciples in his Gospel. Incorporating *a consistently positive or negative interpretation of the disciples with the perception of a loose relationship between the Evangelist and his source material,* this third category might be defined as follows: More or less indifferent to church tradition or history or both, Mark's theology reveals a thoroughgoing estimation, either positive or negative, of the disciples.

As in our previous categories, implicit in the first half of this definition lies a traditio-historical assumption: that Mark as redactor operates more or less independently of his source materials and historical details about the life and ministry of Jesus. Rather than being largely (cf. Meye) or even partially (cf. Best) restrained by his traditions, Mark is regarded by Type III scholars as a near autonomous author, 'as master of the material whose purpose is found in the composition of material and creation of new forms'.[95] Postulated here is a very loose fit between the traditions inherited

---

93. Idem, 'Role', p. 339; cf. 'Discipleship', p. 337.

94. The adjective harbors no value judgment about the essential goodness or correctness of this position (see above, note 38); here, 'liberal' refers only to the freedom, or 'liberality', with which (in these scholars' perception) Mark employed or disregarded his traditions in his (equally free) rendition of the twelve. To refer to scholars in this camp as 'liberal' entails no assumptions about their general theological perspectives, if any; neither does the term 'liberal', as used here, have anything directly to do with those intellectual currents in nineteenth-century Protestantism associated with such theologians as Schleiermacher, Ritschl, and Harnack.

95. J. R. Donahue, 'Introduction: From Passion Traditions to Passion Narrative', in *Passion* (ed. Kelber), p. 16.

by the Evangelist and the Gospel that he produces and, by inference, a correspondingly loose fit between Mark's story of Jesus and historical facts about Jesus. Thus the Second Gospel comes to be understood atemporally, if not ahistorically: 'The Jesus who addresses the disciples in Galilee is addressing the members of the church for which Mark writes. . . . In the gospel of Mark, past, present, and future all flow together'.[96] Though closely associated with Norman Perrin and his students,[97] this perspective is not unique to them: it tacitly underlies Friedrich Gustav Lang's view of Mark's Gospel as an ancient drama in five acts,[98] as well as Karl-Georg Reploh's assessment that 'die Jünger sind für [Markus] gar nicht mehr vornehmlich die irdischen Begleiter Jesu, sondern in ihnen sieht er die in der "heutigen" Nachfolge Jesu stehenden Jünger, die Glaubenden seiner Gemeinde'.[99] Still, it is one of Perrin's students, Werner H. Kelber, who expresses most clearly the historical and traditional assumptions here in force:

In principle, it could well be assumed that in this process of adjustment and transformation an evangelist's loyalties were strongly on the side of the historical Jesus [cf., e.g., Meye], or divided at best, belonging as much to the Jesus of the past as to concerns for imaginative interpretation [cf., e.g., Best]. Could not one suppose particular adjustments to authentic Jesus materials while preserving the overall framework of the life of Jesus? *Yet this is precisely what redaction criticism has attempted to disprove.* . . . In [the] process of selecting, arranging, and producing [literary material] each evangelist was motivated by a logic which was neither that of the historical life of Jesus, nor that of any single unit or of the sum total of the units of tradition. The masterplan according to which he operated, the new logic into which he integrated the diversity of viewpoints, was the evangelist's very own. . . . His loyalties belong neither to the historical Jesus *per se,* nor to fragmentary reflections on him, but *entirely* to his own constructive conceptualization of the Jesus of the past.[100]

96. Perrin and Duling, *New Testament,* pp. 237, 238.

97. See the essays collected in *Passion* (ed. Kelber).

98. F. G. Lang, 'Kompositionsanalyse des Markusevangeliums', *ZTK* 74 (1977), pp. 1-24.

99. K.-G. Reploh, *Markus — Lehrer der Gemeinde: Eine redaktionsgeschichtliche Studie zu den Jüngerperikopen des Markus-Evangeliums* (SBM 9; Stuttgart: Katholisches Bibelwerk, 1969), p. 196.

100. W. H. Kelber, 'Redaction Criticism: On the Nature and Exposition of the Gospels', *PRelS* 6 (1979), p. 12 (emphasis mine).

Certainly the evidence marshalled in our discussion of Types I and II contradicts Kelber's blanket assertion that redaction criticism *as such* has attempted to disprove any relationship between history or tradition and the Evangelist's editorial activity. That this is how Kelber himself understands the matter, there can be little doubt. And in this belief he is not alone.

Once severed from its moorings in tradition and history, Mark's depiction of the disciples angles in one of two directions, according to Type III exegetes. Though they may interpret it differently, some perceive a generally high regard of the disciples in the Second Gospel: thus Thomas L. Budesheim suggests that, in editing his traditions, the Evangelist has elevated both Jesus and the twelve to the honor of *theioi andres* in order that they might stand out from the teachers of official Judaism;[101] thus Karl-Georg Reploh proposes that the disciples, transparent to the weal and woe of Mark's church, constitute the channel through which the Evangelist communicates to first-century Christians Jesus' teaching on suffering, prayer, and fruitful discipleship.[102] Like the 'conservative' positions surveyed in Type I, these 'liberal' interpretations stress a more or less positive role of the disciples in Mark; unlike our Type I exegetes, little or no interest is evinced by Budesheim and Reploh in demonstrating continuity between Mark's redactional activity and the historical Jesus and the twelve.

A similar discontinuity is presupposed in the other exegetical tack that is taken by Type III scholars: the interpretation of Mark as being, in some measure, a polemic against the disciples and the sort of Christian witness that they represent. To be sure, derogatory aspects of the disciples' character or conduct in Mark are recognized by Best, Focant, and the other Type II exegetes; in their reading of the Second Gospel, however, such negative traits are balanced against other, more positive qualities exhibited by the twelve. For Type III investigators, this balance is lost: rejecting a Markan portrait of the disciples with 'warts and all', many of these interpreters focus exclusively on 'the warts' — and assume that Mark's focus is just as exclusive. Put differently, if the exegetical tendency of Type I scholars be toward a rather sunny portrayal of the disciples in Mark, the following investigators tend to conclude that the Evangelist has unremittingly cast the disciples in the shadows.

The earliest redaction-critical movements in this direction were un-

---

101. T. L. Budesheim, 'Jesus and the Disciples in Conflict with Judaism', *ZNW* 62 (1971), pp. 190-209.

102. Reploh, *Markus.*

dertaken by researchers who couched their work in historical terms; that is, they understood Mark to be aware of, and underlining, a signal difference between his own point of view and that of the historical disciples or the traditions about them. In such terms Alfred Kuby contended in 1958 that the Second Gospel comprises two main divisions: 1.16–8.21, dealing with the disciples' incomprehension *(Nichtbegreifen)* of Jesus' identity, and 8.22–14.72, treating their misunderstanding *(Misverständnis)* and unwillingness to grasp the fact that the Messiah must suffer.[103] Three years later, Joseph B. Tyson advanced a similar argument: Mark thought that the historical disciples had completely misunderstood Jesus' messiahship, not in terms of suffering, but as a nationalistic, royal messiahship that would yield benefits for themselves; thus the Evangelist was engaged in pricking this 'inflated understanding of their own position', and 'one of Mark's chief purposes was to call attention to the ways in which the disciples fell short in their understanding and proclamation of the Christian gospel'.[104] In the same year that Tyson's article appeared, Günter Klein published a traditio-historical analysis of the Gospel narratives of Peter's denials, in which he argued that the story of the denials originally stemmed from a larger, anti-Petrine segment of the pre-Markan tradition; despite its contradiction of the universal flight of the twelve in 14.27, 50, the story was then coopted by Mark (14.54, 66-72) in order to score certain edifying theological points.[105] A consistent feature of these various scholarly interpretations is the notion that Mark's portrayal of the disciples emerged from some interaction of tradition with history — even if that interaction were one of *Auseinandersetzung.*

In time, however, in the judgment of some exegetes, even this slender historical or traditional connection with the Gospel grew increasingly more attenuated, to the point that it virtually snapped altogether. By the 1970s it had become commonplace in certain quarters to speak of the decidedly negative role played by the disciples in Mark and to explain that role, not by reason of any historical or traditional axes that the Evangelist supposedly wished to grind, but in terms of certain antagonistic narrative functions or undesirable theological positions that the twelve were assumed to represent. A consensus was never reached on the exact content of

103. A. Kuby, 'Zur Konzeption des Markus-Evangeliums', ZNW 49 (1959), pp. 52-64.

104. J. B. Tyson, 'The Blindness of the Disciples in Mark', *JBL* 80 (1961), pp. 261-68 (quotations, p. 268).

105. G. Klein, 'Die Verleugnung des Petrus: Eine traditionsgeschichtliche Untersuchung', *ZTK* 58 (1961), pp. 285-328.

the 'heresy'[106] that, owing to Mark's inventive portrayal, was espoused by the disciples: most frequently mentioned was a false Christology, most probably of the (so-called) *theios-anēr* type;[107] occasionally suggested was a false (that is, overly realized) eschatology.[108] In either case, it was assumed that Mark had made the disciples into advocates of a triumphalist *theologia gloriae*, the refutation of which had been provided by the Evangelist through sayings set upon the lips of Jesus.[109] Whatever controversy underlay his redaction, Mark (so it was argued) made the most of every opportunity to spotlight the disciples' flaws and failures. Thus Werner Kelber underscored these aspects: the Evangelist's deadly serious charge that the disciples' hearts were hardened (6.52, '[putting] the disciples into the role of opposition . . . [intimating] disobedience, loss of redemption, and even death');[110] Mark's further accusation of their blindness and deafness (8.18, signifying 'that they are about to forfeit their privileged position as insiders');[111] the disturbing midsection of the Gospel (8.22–10.52, wherein 'Mark spares no effort to illustrate the persistent and incorrigible failure of the disciples, the Twelve, and the triumvirate [of Peter, James, and

---

106. Despite its anachronistic quality, I use the term 'heresy', not only because it vividly captures the idea of 'false teaching when viewed from an authoritative point of view', but also because it is sometimes employed by the Markan interpreters considered here.

107. Among many others, see L. Schenke, *Studien zur Passionsgeschichte des Markus: Tradition und Redaktion in Markus 14, 1-42* (FB 4; Würzburg: Echter Verlag, 1971), esp. p. 564; and V. K. Robbins, 'Last Meal: Preparation, Betrayal, and Absence (Mark 14.12-25)', in *Passion* (ed. Kelber), pp. 21-40. Johannes Schreiber ('Die Christologie') appears to have first proposed the now widely circulated notion that there were two competing Christologies in Mark, a *theios-anēr* type and Mark's own Christology of suffering. After having been cross-pollinated with Dieter Georgi's *Die Gegner des Paulus im 2. Korintherbrief* (WMANT 11; Neukirchen-Vluyn: Neukirchener Verlag, 1964), Schreiber's theory was taken up and developed by Markan scholars too numerous to mention. In at least one striking instance the theory was made to stand on its head: Budesheim's 'Conflict with Judaism' argues that Mark redacted his sources so as *to highlight and to honor* Jesus and the disciples' status as *theioi andres*!

108. Kelber, *The Kingdom in Mark: A New Place and a New Time*, N.B. pp. 83-84, 13-37. The 'new place' of the subtitle is Galilee (not Jerusalem) and the 'new time' is the *parousia* (contrary to the supposed claim of certain heretical groups that the *parousia* had already occurred with the destruction of the Holy City).

109. R. A. Edwards, 'A New Approach to the Gospel of Mark', *LQ* 22 (1970), pp. 330-35. Cf. T. J. Weeden, Sr, who suggests that 'Mk [*sic*] is combatting a divine man Christology conjoined with a realized eschatology which depicts Jesus as the destroyer of the old temple and builder of the New' ('The Cross as Power in Weakness (Mark 15.20b-41)', in *Passion* [ed. Kelber], p. 128; therein the entire quotation is italicized).

110. W. H. Kelber, *Mark's Story of Jesus* (Philadelphia: Fortress, 1979), p. 37.

111. Ibid., p. 41.

John]');[112] and the callous sleep of that triumvirate in Gethsemane (14.32-42, demonstrative of the disciples' 'recurrent and incorrigible blind-ness').[113] In an essay on Peter's denials (Mark 14.53-54, 66-72), Kim E. Dewey suggests that, in denying Jesus, Peter denies his own identity and becomes subject to Jesus' curse in Mark 8.38, with the effect that 'Jesus and Peter have cursed each other'; by expanding the number of denials to three, 'A weak Peter is transformed [by Mark] into a hostile Peter, an opponent' whose antagonism to Jesus is even more pronounced than Judas'.[114] Nor, according to this line of interpretation, does the resurrection offer any relief from Mark's dark vision of the disciples; for Norman Perrin, Mark 14.28 and 16.7 imply no restitution of the twelve following their abysmal failure of Jesus, for the appearances of the Lord described therein refer, not to the resurrection, but to the judgment of an imminent *parousia*.[115] Moreover, as conceived by John Dominic Crossan, the story of the empty tomb (Mark 16.1-8) is 'a totally new tradition . . . created most deliberately' by Mark in order to oppose the credal assertion that the risen Lord had appeared to Peter and the apostles (cf. 1 Cor. 15.5-7); the unvarnished consequence of the women's fearful silence in 16.8 is to impugn the position of the Jerusalem community led by Peter and the disciples, since the latter never received, and therefore never accepted, the call of the exalted Lord to meet him in Galilee.[116]

112. Ibid., p. 52. As a result of his 'confrontation' with Jesus at Caesarea Philippi, Peter 'qualifies himself as his master's leading opponent' (Kelber, 'The Hour of the Son of Man and the Temptation of the Disciples (Mark 14.32-42)', in *Passion* [ed. Kelber], p. 50).

113. Kelber, 'Hour', p. 50; cf. idem, 'Mark 14.32-42: Gethsemane — Passion Christology and Discipleship Failure', *ZNW* 63 (1972), pp. 166-87. Kelber contends that Gethsemane marks a parting of the ways: Jesus chooses death and, through death, enters into life; 'The disciples . . . abandon Jesus at the occasion of his arrest and thus forfeit their last chance for entering upon the way to the Kingdom' (*Mark's Story*, p. 77). For Kelber's most recent formulation of the conflict in Mark between 'orality' and 'textuality', see *The Oral and the Written Gospel: The Hermeneutics of Speaking and Writing in the Synoptic Tradition, Mark, Paul, and Q* (Philadelphia: Fortress, 1983), esp. pp. 90-139.

114. K. E. Dewey, 'Peter's Curse and Cursed Peter (Mark 14.53-54, 66-72)', in *Passion* (ed. Kelber), pp. 96-114 (quotations, pp. 101, 108, 110).

115. N. Perrin, *The Resurrection According to Matthew, Mark, and Luke* (Philadelphia: Fortress, 1977), pp. 30-31.

116. J. D. Crossan, 'Empty Tomb and Absent Lord (Mark 16.1-8)', in *Passion* (ed. Kelber), pp. 135-52 (quotation, p. 146). For the notion that, with the empty tomb, Mark invented an 'anti-resurrection story' emphasizing Jesus' absence, Crossan is most directly indebted to N. Q. Hamilton, 'Resurrection Tradition and the Composition of Mark', *JBL* 84 (1965), pp. 415-21.

Probably no scholar has presented more forcefully, and with greater impact on Markan interpretation, the traditio-historical and exegetical dimensions of this third category than Theodore John Weeden, Sr (1933-). Weeden begins his research with a number of assumptions, all of which are more 'liberal' than those that would normally be claimed by the exponents of our Types I and II: first, 'that the Evangelist is no longer concerned with the facts of 30 A.D. but rather with the specific problems of his own community of the late 60's';[117] second, that the theological interests of Mark's sources and of the Evangelist himself are not necessarily congruent, with the result that Mark may have drawn upon his traditions in the interest of discrediting them;[118] third, that far from being a mere editor or preserver of tradition, 'Mark exercised an author's freedom and creativity in composing the Gospel', even to the point of intentionally '[staging] the christological debate of his community in a "historical" drama in which Jesus serves as a surrogate for Mark and the disciples serve as surrogates for Mark's opponents'.[119] The latter presupposition sets the tone for Weeden's interpretation of the disciples in the Second Gospel: representative of a *theologia gloriae*, a divine-man Christology and realized eschatology that is advocated by Mark's opponents in a debate of his own day, the disciples are repeatedly attacked and thoroughly disgraced by the Evangelist.[120] The Second Gospel is orchestrated to accent their precipitous deterioration from imperceptiveness of Jesus' messiahship, through its misconception, to its utter rejection.[121] The obtuseness, obduracy, and recalcitrance displayed by the disciples is epitomized in the figure of Peter: his persistence in viewing Jesus' messiahship from a *theios-anēr* perspective is rebuked as satanic (cf. Mark 8.27-33); the denial of his master (14.54, 66-72) 'underscores the complete and utter rejection of Jesus and his messiahship by the disciples'.[122] Because the women at the empty tomb never overcame their frightened silence, Peter and the disciples never received word of Jesus' *parousia* in Galilee (cf. 16.7); thus they were robbed of

---

117. T. J. Weeden, Sr, 'The Heresy that Necessitated Mark's Gospel', *ZNW* 59 (1968), p. 149 n. 7.

118. T. J. Weeden, 'The Conflict between Mark and His Opponents over Kingdom Theology', *SBL 1973 Seminar Papers* (ed. G. MacRae; Cambridge, MA: SBL, 1973), p. 206.

119. T. J. Weeden, Sr, *Mark — Traditions in Conflict* (Philadelphia: Fortress, 1971), pp. 1, 163.

120. Ibid., pp. 50-51, 163-64.

121. Ibid., pp. 26-51; idem, 'Heresy', pp. 146-47.

122. Weeden, 'Heresy', pp. 155-56; idem, *Mark*, pp. 64-69; quotation, p. 38.

their apostolic credentials and were never rehabilitated from their apostasy.[123] For the status of the disciples in the Second Gospel, Weeden's final judgment, like many of the Type III investigators, is nothing short of devastating:

> The disciples are reprobates. They obstinately hold on to a christology that Jesus has branded as heretical. In rejecting Jesus they themselves are rejected (8.38). They are no more than heretics. In Mark's scheme the disciples remain heretics even unto his own day.[124]

C. A Proposed Procedure for Evaluating Alternative Redaction-Critical Interpretations of the Disciples in Mark

At least one thing should be clear from the foregoing *Forschungsbericht:* if we seek an exegetical issue that has proved to be both significant and heavily controverted in the *redaktionsgeschichtlich* interpretation of Mark, we need search no further than the role of the disciples in that Gospel. Indeed, in a most striking and fascinating way, this particular topic poses the conundrum, broached in Chapter 1, of Markan redaction-critical method: for, when comparing the exegetical results of the scholars represented in the three categories considered above, one is driven to ask why there seems to be so little unanimity on Mark's presentation of the disciples — especially since the various investigations ostensibly stem from the implementation of a common critical method. Is it owing to the investigators' different understandings of that method or of its application, irrespective of their agreement on the fruitfulness of redaction criticism? To frame the question differently: in their practice of *Redaktionsgeschichte,* precisely what sort of *redaktionsgeschichtlich* criteria are these various exegetes invoking, and what kind of judgments are they making? Do they invoke the same criteria and make the same judgments? On the basis of what presuppositions about the Gospel of Mark and its underlying traditions are different criteria being selected and different judgments being made? When viewing each of the three interpretive categories outlined in this chapter, is there a discernible correlation between the exegetical results of its proponents' investigations and the specific manner in which each 'type' of

123. Weeden, *Mark,* p. 44.
124. Ibid., p. 164.

scholar has applied the redaction-critical method? To return to the fundamental question: on the issue of Markan discipleship, how *can* we account
for the wide array of divergent, even mutually exclusive, interpretations
that, if their advocates' claims are to be accepted, arise from the application
of one and the same exegetical method?

At stake with such questions as these is nothing less than the practical
validity[125] of redaction criticism as applied to Mark's Gospel. But this
presents for us a dilemma: although the validity of the method can be assessed only by carefully observing how it has been employed by Markan
scholars, it is manifestly impossible to scrutinize, within the bounds of a
single monograph, all of the *redaktionsgeschichtlich* investigations into
Markan discipleship that have been mentioned. The way out of this pre-
dicament seems clear: we cannot examine the redaction-critical procedure
of all the scholarly studies under review, but we can inspect the method of
three studies representing each of the broad types of interpretation that we
have discovered. Already I have indicated three scholars whose research in
Markan discipleship is in many ways typical of others in their respective
categories; therefore, I propose that we consider, at length and in detail, the
redaction-critical work of Robert Meye (as representative of Type I, the
'conservative' position), Ernest Best (characteristic of Type II, the 'mediate'
position), and Theodore Weeden (representing Type III, the 'liberal' position). Although other investigators have made distinguished contributions
to the redaction-critical study of the disciples in the Second Gospel, the
work of Meye, Best, and Weeden seems peculiarly well-suited for our purposes. Each of the three scholars brings to the interpretive task a differently
(and explicitly) nuanced set of assumptions about redaction criticism and
the Gospel of Mark, and each emerges with a sharply defined exegesis of
Markan discipleship that is distinct from the others. Each of the three has
contributed, from his distinctive point of view, both a major redaction-
critical monograph as well as several shorter studies on the role of the disciples in Mark (thus giving us sufficient data to analyze). Each is reflective
of, or has been heavily influenced by, relatively distinct streams within the

---

125. Of course, any number of objections could be, indeed have been, advanced against
Markan *Redaktionsgeschichte*: that such a traditio-historical method is inappropriate in the
interpretation of narrative literature; that the kind of data yielded by the method is, in the
end, trivial; and so forth. Although such criticisms will be addressed in Chapter 8, they will
not command our attention in the bulk of this study. My interest here is in the *utility* or *feasibility* of the method: its capability for producing reliable and confirmable exegeses of the
Second Gospel.

general flow of international scholarship (thus lending even greater ideological breadth to our discussion). Finally, each has produced scholarship of obvious merit, as gauged by its capacity for generating international conversation among Markan researchers.

What specific questions, germane to the purpose of this study, should be addressed to our three representative redaction critics? The following three areas of inquiry seem, to me, essential: *First,* how may each exegete's general *redaktionsgeschichtlich* perspective on Mark's Gospel be defined? *Second,* what are the specific aspects or components of each investigator's redaction-critical method? *Third,* what exegetical results, significant for understanding Mark's presentation of the disciples, emerge from each interpreter's application of his method? The typology presented in this chapter reflects the distinct redaction-critical assumptions and exegetical results adopted by the major camps within Markan scholarship; thus it should help us in answering the first and third of these questions. To give order to our treatment of the second question — consideration of the particular redaction-critical criteria of Meye, Best, and Weeden — we shall appeal to Robert Stein's systematic and comprehensive statement of 'the proper methodology for ascertaining a Markan redaction history', the elements of which were reviewed in Chapter 1. Thus much of our attention will be concentrated on how Meye, Best, and Weeden employ (or disregard) the following twelve *redaktionsgeschichtlich* criteria:

1. Markan seams
2. Markan insertions
3. Markan summaries
4. Markan creation of pericopes
5. Markan modifications of traditional material, embracing
   a. The comparison of Mark with Matthew and Luke
   b. The investigation of 'misformed' pericopes
   c. The investigation of the inconsistency between Mark's account and what actually happened
6. Markan selection of material
7. Markan omission of material
8. Markan arrangement of material, including
   a. The arrangement of individual pericopes
   b. The placing of one pericope inside another
   c. The geographical scheme, and other thematic devices, in Mark
9. The Markan introduction

10. The Markan conclusion
11. Markan vocabulary and style
12. Markan Christological titles

With the use of Stein's categories, and on the basis of a careful reading of the research of Meye, Best, and Weeden, the answers to our questions of perspective, method, and results — and the manner in which those answers are observed to interrelate — should shed greater light on the practical value of that method which all three presentations hold in common: Markan redaction criticism.

This study's observations and conclusions on redaction criticism will be limited almost exclusively to the method's use with the Gospel of Mark, which, on the assumption of Markan priority, presents a set of circumstances and difficulties not characteristic of the other Synoptics; our results, therefore, should not be hastily and unreflectively generalized as applicable to Matthew and Luke.[126] Nor should we be premature in generalizing our conclusions regarding the studies of Meye, Best, and Weeden, as though all scholars of their various types could be commended for the same virtues displayed by their representatives (or tarred with the same brush for their shortcomings). The merits and faults of the work of Meye, Best, and Weeden are not in themselves demonstrative of those same qualities in the research of scholars with whom they share certain understandings; however, the gains and limitations of the redaction-critical exegeses of these three may well be suggestive of the gains and limitations of the types of Markan scholarship that they represent.

---

126. The results of this study might have some transfer value for redaction criticism of Matthew's Gospel that is predicated on the Griesbach hypothesis: there, as in the case of Markan *Redaktionsgeschichte* that assumes Markan priority, the interpreter is confronted with the problem of identifying an Evangelist's editorial activity when his sources are considered indeterminate. As for the Fourth Gospel, Lloyd R. Kittlaus has noted analogous difficulties between Markan and Johannine *Redaktionsgeschichte* ('John and Mark: A Methodological Evaluation of Norman Perrin's Suggestion', *SBL Seminar Papers* [II; Missoula, MT: Scholars, 1978], pp. 269-79).

3. Type I: The 'Conservative' Position of Robert P. Meye

Die Beziehung der 12 zu Jesus läßt sich zusammenfassend wohl formulieren als eine totale Bindung an ihn, als eine totale Übergabe in seinen Einflußbereich und in seine Verfügungsgewalt. Sie werden dieser Beziehung nicht gerecht, als Jesus sein Leiden und seinen Tod antritt; sie versagen. Doch ist mit ihrem Versagen nicht alles ausgelöscht, und der Auferweckte stellt von sich aus diese Bindung in einer neuen Form wieder her.

Klemens Stock[1]

Written under the direction of Bo Reicke and Oscar Cullmann, and accepted by the University of Basel in 1962, Robert P. Meye's doctoral dissertation on the role of the disciples in Mark bore much fruit: it served as the basis, not only for two articles on the subject,[2] but also for a monograph, published in 1968 as *Jesus and the Twelve: Disciples and Revelation in Mark's Gospel*. At the time of its appearance, Meye's book was hailed as 'a significant contribution to the study of Markan theology',[3] and as 'an important contribution to Marcan studies and to NT [*sic*] theology' that 'no serious interpreter of Mk [*sic*] can ignore'.[4] As John Donahue has noted,[5] it was not until 1981, with Ernest Best's *Following Jesus: Discipleship in the Gospel*

---

1. Stock, *Boten,* p. 197.
2. R. P. Meye, 'Mark 4,10: "Those About Him with the Twelve"', *SE* 2 (1964), pp. 211-18; idem, 'Messianic Didache'.
3. H. C. Kee, review in *Int* 24 (1970), p. 117.
4. R. Kugelman, review in *CBQ* 31 (1969), p. 590.
5. J. R. Donahue, reviewing E. Best's *Following Jesus* in *JBL* 103 (1984), p. 114.

of Mark, that Meye's monograph enjoyed a major scholarly successor in English. Such positive appraisals of the book, coupled with its assumption of the redaction-critical method and a distinctive approach to the interpretation of the Second Gospel, make an examination of Robert Meye's contribution to Markan research appropriate to our task.

A. General Perspective

Meye approaches the exegesis of Mark with a clearly formulated set of historical presuppositions about the Gospel as well as about the Evangelist's own estimate of history. Emanating from the Pauline sphere of influence,[6] Mark's Gospel was in all likelihood the first to arise within the early Christian community; this makes its portrait of Jesus and the twelve 'historically extremely significant, and [deserving] of the historian's most careful attention'.[7] For Meye, there are at least two primary historical facts with which scholars must conjure. First, Jesus was, among other things, a teacher; both the fact and the content of his teaching have been deliberately preserved in the Gospel record.[8] Second (and correlatively), 'the Twelve were an extremely important group in the early church'; in particular, 'Mark's readers had a special interest in those who had confessed allegiance to the historical Jesus', either because of some later, existential identification with those first followers, or because the disciples were regarded by Mark's church as exemplary representatives of the way that must be followed.[9] In Meye's judgment, then, neither the historical Jesus nor the historical disciples belong to the realm of 'historical adiaphora'; the very creation by Mark of a new literary form, the Gospel, was intended 'to give *historical expression* to his faith in a *historically* meaningful ministry of Jesus'.[10]

---

6. 'Messianic Didache', p. 59, following M. Werner, *Der Einfluß paulinischer Theologie im Markusevangelium: Eine Studie zur neutestamentlichen Theologie* (BZNW 1; Gießen: Töpelmann, 1923). For a critique of this theory, see F. C. Grant, *The Earliest Gospel: Studies of the Evangelic Tradition at Its Point of Crystallization in Writing* (New York/Nashville: Abingdon, 1943), pp. 188-206.

7. 'Messianic Didache', p. 60; see also ibid., pp. 59, 63; *Jesus,* pp. 16-19, 89, 192-209.

8. *Jesus,* pp. 17, 97.

9. 'Messianic Didache', pp. 60, 62; cf. ibid., pp. 66, 68; *Jesus,* pp. 91, 197.

10. *Jesus,* p. 33 (Meye's italics). 'By setting the words and deeds of Jesus in an account that has connections to historical places, persons, and events, Mark shows himself to be a theologian of history' (ibid.).

From such a perspective, it is scarcely surprising that Meye would be sensitive to the division among New Testament scholars regarding the authenticity of the Gospel's portrait of the historical Jesus: 'it seems clear enough that these differences will be reduced whenever scholarship as a whole divests itself of all sorts of presuppositions and increasingly devotes its attention to the concrete figure of Jesus in the New Testament'.[11] Similarly, Meye mounts an extensive rebuttal against the reluctance (associated with Bultmann) to view the twelve as a historical community of disciples: the evidence of 1 Cor. 15.5, which hardly suggests a later, anachronistic imposition upon the earliest tradition; the evidence of Mark itself, the earliest narrative of Jesus' ministry, which already accords to the twelve a prominent place even as it preserves material unflattering to the disciples; the judgment that a serious blow would be delivered to the worth of the Gospel tradition in general if the existence of the twelve were assigned a nonhistorical value.[12] Equally disputable is the ideological basis of such an assessment: 'the critical attack [associated with Bultmann and others] is largely governed by the *presupposition* that Jesus did not have a company of twelve disciples'.[13] The alternative, for Meye, is far superior: there actually were twelve disciples whose principal activity was to be with the historical Jesus and to receive his teaching; and, with respect to the Gospel witness, 'one must suppose a decisive continuity, barring clear evidence to the contrary, between Mark's description of Jesus' pre-Easter preparation of the Twelve and his understanding of their actual post-Easter activity'.[14]

On the other hand, Meye does not suggest that every detail in Mark is historically accurate. Because the Second Gospel is akin to a sermon that proclaims both the historical and the cosmic at one and the same time, described therein are events (such as the baptism, the temptation, and the transfiguration) that simply resist characterization as 'historical' and certain representations (such as the disciples' unrelenting obtuseness) that betoken a more theological, and less historical, importance for Mark.[15] Thus one can and should speak of a Markan redaction — the Evangelist's 'concept', 'intention', or 'use' — that is distinguishable from historical factors.[16] Insofar as the purpose of Meye's work on discipleship is 'to call at-

11. *Jesus*, p. 17; cf. pp. 92, 129-31; 'Messianic Didache', p. 57.

12. *Jesus*, pp. 192-209.

13. Ibid., p. 205; see also pp. 139, 209.

14. *Jesus*, pp. 184-85; 'Messianic Didache', p. 66.

15. *Jesus*, pp. 33-34, 75.

16. 'Those About Him', p. 212 n. 4; *Jesus*, pp. 143, 177-78; cf. 'Messianic Didache', p. 60.

tention to the role of the didactic motif in Mark's Gospel narrative of Jesus' ministry', 'how the Second Gospel is significantly shaped by a didactic understanding of Jesus' ministry', then '[the] decisive goal must be to uncover adequately the Marcan conception'.[17] For Meye, this does not automatically exclude the possibility that historically reliable data are reflected in the redactional passages of the Gospels; he steadfastly 'does *not* assume that what is theologically meaningful is relatively worthless as history'.[18] Indeed, the historical control on redactional (that is, theologically oriented) material resides in 'the historical continuity between the first disciples and the community which *knew* and formed the tradition, and which continued to function as the transmitting Church'.[19]

Such an assessment leads directly to the question of the Evangelist's freedom of composition relative to the constraints of his inherited tradition. On the one side, Meye suggests, 'Mark is already determined by the tradition that he has received'.[20] There are two reasons for this judgment: first, the assumed richness, variety, and complexity of pre-Markan tradition, which would militate against the Evangelist's control of his narrative outline such that everything moved clearly and directly to a single (Markan) end; second, the scholarly *opinio communis*, which, despite its diversity of interpretive approach, 'persistently [points] to the fact that the evangelists were indeed controlled by purposes and conceptions which can still be uncovered by diligent study'.[21] On the other side, Meye contends that Mark obviously chose to use traditions which emphasized Jesus as one who went about teaching; thus the Evangelist can be regarded, at least to some degree, as 'the master and arranger of the materials of his narrative', with the implicit freedom to alter or to ignore some details of his tradition.[22]

Granted, therefore, that Mark exercised some editorial influence over his traditions, and that *Redaktionsgeschichte* is a useful tool in identifying

17. *Jesus*, pp. 13, 30, 172. Meye calls to task scholars such as J. Weiss, K. L. Schmidt, and E. Lohmeyer for not clearly separating Mark's viewpoint from that of the pre-Markan tradition (ibid., pp. 145-46).

18. *Jesus*, p. 92 (Meye's emphasis).

19. Ibid. Cf. H. Simonsen, 'Zur Frage der grundlegenden Problematik in form- und redaktionsgeschichtlicher Evangelienforschung', *ST* 26 (1972), pp. 1-23.

20. *Jesus*, p. 72. In Meye's view, 'the whole problem of tradition' is one of the chief matters with which biblical scholars should be concerned (ibid., pp. 18-20).

21. Ibid., pp. 63, 72. N.B. p. 63 n. 2, where Meye paraphrases, with implicit approval, the opinion of W. Wrede, R. H. Lightfoot, and T. A. Burkill that 'Mark had only a slight ability to control his materials', not having 'achieved mastery of his material'.

22. *Jesus*, pp. 28, 38; cf. 'Those About Him', p. 215.

the Evangelist's distinctive outlook, what specific methodological presuppositions does Meye bring to the exegetical task? To begin with, he suggests that the circularity of the interpretive process is hard if not impossible to escape: 'it is difficult to determine what aspect . . . Mark intended to stress'.[23] Second, Meye frankly admits the real bugbear of redaction-critical investigation of Mark's Gospel: 'attempts to differentiate between that which is Marcan and that which is traditional are at best precarious'.[24] It is apparently for this reason that, at certain points, Meye simply forsakes the attempt: 'The methodology employed in [Meye's article, 'Messianic Secret and Messianic Didache'] simply elevates the *total content* of that gospel to the status of Marcan theology'.[25] Nevertheless, 'the data called upon [in Meye's analysis] is firmly located within the redactional sectors of Mark's gospel', which may be identified by references to the disciples and emphasis on Jesus' διδαχή.[26] In dealing with either evidently redactional or putatively traditional material in Mark, one canon of interpretation explicitly assumes a position of special importance for Meye: 'one must simply concentrate upon what Mark clearly and repeatedly says and not upon what are at best questionable exceptions to the clear thrust of the narrative'.[27]

Before scrutinizing Meye's redaction-critical method, we should reflect on certain aspects of his perspective and presuppositions. As we have seen, Meye is inclined to accord historical reliability to Mark's account by virtue of its relative proximity to the life of Jesus:

> The first assumption is that Mark's gospel is the first gospel to arise within the early Christian community. It is at least the earliest gospel of which we have knowledge. This means that the picture presented by the second gospel is, after the writings of Paul, our earliest document from the primitive church. The Marcan portrait is historically extremely significant, and deserves the historian's most careful attention.[28]

23. Ibid., pp. 58-59; cf. p. 25.

24. Ibid., p. 38.

25. 'Messianic Didache', p. 60 (italics mine).

26. Ibid., p. 60; cf. *Jesus*, p. 92.

27. 'Messianic Didache', p. 65; cf. 'Those About Him', p. 215; *Jesus*, pp. 39, 41, following Robinson, *Problem*, p. 12. Note also Meye, 'Those About Him', p. 217: 'Alternative interpretations must be chosen not only on the basis of their possibility, but also with regard to their ability to avoid problems found in other interpretations as well as *supporting what is clearly indicated elsewhere in the context*' (my emphasis).

28. 'Messianic Didache', pp. 59-60.

Aside from the questions that have been raised by W. R. Farmer and the revisionist Griesbach theoreticians, and in spite of its surface plausibility, the logic of this assessment is problematic. Meye seems to assume, fallaciously, that what is earliest is *for that reason* historically trustworthy. Although Mark indeed merits 'the historian's most careful attention', there is much in that Gospel that transcends historical considerations, a fact of which Meye is well aware.[29] Whether the Second Evangelist shares with modern interpreters the same understanding of 'history' remains debatable;[30] in any case, the historical trustworthiness of Mark's Gospel is not a necessary consequence of its temporal proximity to historical events.

As we have witnessed, Meye counters the charge of historical unreliability in the Gospels' redactional passages by arguing for the maintenance of historical continuity by 'the transmitting Church, [which] had knowledge of the unifying background . . . [and] *knew* and formed the tradition. . . .'[31] At least two assumptions underlie this rebuttal: first, that the pre-Markan church was guided in its transmission of tradition by concerns that were *fundamentally* historical; second, that *Mark,* the Evangelist and redactor, was implicitly guided by such concerns.[32] The latter assumption may be valid; yet it is curious that Meye's defense of historicity in the Markan redaction is based, at this point, on a *traditionsgeschichtlich* argument that does not directly address *the Evangelist's* redactional intentions. As for the former presupposition (that historical concerns governed the transmission of tradition), there is substantial form-critical evidence which suggests that some emergent genres of the earliest church tradition were influenced by concerns more theological or imaginative than historical (for example, miracle stories and legends).[33] Meye's rejoinder to skepticism concerning the historicity of pre-Markan tradition — that it amounts to 'a serious blow . . . struck at the worth of the tradition in

---

29. Even so, Meye occasionally blurs historical and theological considerations: thus he concludes a lengthy redaction-critical study of Mark 15.40-41, 43 by asserting, not only that Mark did not elevate the women at the tomb to the status of disciples, but also that there were no female disciples of the historical Jesus (*Jesus,* p. 171).

30. J. M. Robinson, *A New Quest of the Historical Jesus* (SBT 25; London: SCM, 1971), pp. 26-32, 66-72.

31. *Jesus,* p. 92.

32. Ibid., pp. 16-17, 192-209 et passim; 'Messianic Didache', p. 68. That Jesus and the twelve are not to be classified as 'historical adiaphora' (*Jesus,* pp. 33, 194) appears to be, not only a reconstruction of the Markan perspective, but a statement of Meye's own position.

33. Dibelius, *Tradition,* pp. 70-132.

general'[34] — seems to be little more than special pleading, similar to his call for scholarship to divest itself of presuppositions that would challenge the historical authenticity of the Gospels' portrait of Jesus. Although Meye is driven to acknowledge that perhaps such presuppositions are inevitable, there is a tendency in his presentation to brand as 'ideological' attacks on the historicity of the Markan account,[35] as though Meye's own conservative defense of historicity were not equally ideological in its premises and argumentation.

With respect to Meye's procedural assumptions, his work clearly intends to be a study in redaction criticism.[36] Yet Meye retains some doubt about the possibility of separating tradition and redaction in Mark's Gospel: such attempts are 'at best precarious'. It is apparently for this reason that Meye prefers to base his reconstruction of Markan discipleship on 'what Mark clearly and repeatedly has to say', that is, 'the *total* content and form by which [Mark] expresses the "gospel of Jesus Christ". . . . [Thus] it is a justifiable procedure to seek the Marcan theology in the entirety of his Gospel'.[37] Though such a position is commonsensical, the method described here is only loosely, if at all, redaction-critical: *Redaktionsgeschichte* presupposes that tradition and redaction *can* and *should* be distinguished when analyzing the theology of the Gospels.[38] In terms of methodological assumptions, then, Meye's research purports to be redaction-critical even though it leans towards a broader, more literary-critical procedure. Meye stresses that his close reading of the whole Gospel finds exegetical support in particular, redactional sectors of Mark, but his criterion for defining these 'sectors' (namely, locating portions in which the disciples or the Messianic *didache* are emphasized) only assumes what he is attempting to prove exegetically: that 'the Second Gospel is significantly shaped by a didactic understanding of Jesus' ministry'.[39]

Finally, we might note the tension, if not self-contradiction, that exists in Meye's presuppositions concerning Mark's freedom of composition rel-

---

34. *Jesus,* p. 194, refuting the claim that 'the twelve' was a creation of the early church. Cf. ibid., pp. 16-17, 139.

35. Ibid., pp. 205, 209; cf. p. 139.

36. Thus ibid., pp. 21-29.

37. Ibid., p. 25; cf. p. 38; 'Messianic Didache', p. 60.

38. Interestingly, J. M. Robinson, the source for Meye's exegetical canon of 'the clear and the repeated' in Mark, ultimately rejected this principle as insufficiently sensitive to redaction-critical concerns ('History in Mark, Reconsidered', pp. 133-35).

39. *Jesus,* p. 20; cf. p. 13; 'Messianic Didache', p. 60.

ative to the dictates of pre-Markan tradition. On some occasions Meye speaks of Mark's compositional freedom of choice; the Evangelist is, to some degree, 'the master and arranger of the materials of his narrative'. At other times, the Evangelist is considered to be determined or controlled by his traditions and 'has not achieved a mastery of his material'.[40] Precisely how this conflict in Meye's perspective is resolved, if in fact it finds resolution, should become clearer in the next part of this chapter; for now, let us note that this tension in Meye's understanding of Markan 'freedom' and 'determination' is commensurate with the exegetical tension, recurring throughout *Jesus and the Twelve*, between *redactional* inquiry and *historical* investigation.

B. Method

'In one sense, methodology is everything in the study of any given literary document', says Meye in a section on method that introduces his monograph.[41] After observing 'the circular relationship existing between history and the interpretation of history',[42] Meye presents his understanding of redaction criticism: first, that it represents a positive extension of the form-critical method, directly concerned with the theological and sociological *Sitz* of the Evangelist; second, that it justifiably encompasses the total content and form by which the Evangelist has expressed 'the gospel of Jesus Christ'; third, that the Evangelist's particular historical situation is reflected primarily in his selection of traditional materials, the terminology used, the structure of the narrative, and its specific emphases.[43] The principal criteria suggested by Meye for assessing these elements, and thus for interpreting Mark's Gospel, are 'the clear statements of purpose found in the mouth of Jesus', through which is derived the meaning of Markan discipleship, repetition of certain narrated events and terminology, and the structure of the Gospel narrative (which incorporates many of the preceding elements).[44]

We might observe that, of the seven exegetical criteria that Meye proposes, four have rough parallels in Stein's 'proper methodology for ascer-

40. *Jesus*, p. 28; contrast ibid., p. 63 n. 2.
41. *Jesus*, pp. 21-29; quotation, p. 21.
42. Ibid., pp. 22-23.
43. Ibid., pp. 24-26.
44. Ibid., pp. 26-29.

taining a Markan redaction history': Mark's selection of traditional materials (criterion 6 considered below, pp. 80-81), terminology or vocabulary (criterion 11, pp. 91-96 below), narrative structure (= 'arrangement of material', criterion 8, pp. 81-89 below), and orientation to purposes expressed by Jesus (approximating 'Markan Christological titles', criterion 12, pp. 96-97 below). Meye's canon of thematic emphasis may be considered an extension of Stein's eighth category, Markan arrangement, and Meye's criterion of repetition of action and terminology conflates Stein's categories of Markan summaries[45] (criterion 3, p. 77 below) and vocabulary (again, criterion 11, pp. 91-96 below). The remaining criterion suggested by Meye, for which Stein presents no counterpart, is 'the clear statements of purpose found in the mouth of Jesus'. Precisely how such statements can be identified as issuing from tradition or redaction Meye does not explain. At worst, this is not an inherently redaction-critical criterion at all, but a more literary-critical appraisal of how narrative point of view is communicated through character; at best, this 'interpretive clue' could be subsumed under Markan selection or inclusion of material (Stein's category 6, pp. 80-81 below). Overall, though, most of Meye's explicit redactional criteria correspond to Stein's breakdown of the method. Now let us consider each of these in turn, as well as others that are implicit in Meye's study.

1. Five verses and one complex of verses appear to be implicitly regarded by Meye as *Markan seams*: 4.2; 4.10-12; 10.32; 11.18; 12.38.[46] Even though Meye designates each of these as distinctively 'Markan', he never refers to them as 'seams'; however, the apparent function of each in linking traditional pericopes renders this ascription appropriate. Of these five putative seams, Meye gives no specific reason for believing that 10.32 originated with Mark and not with pre-Markan tradition; for the remainder, the determination is based on vocabulary (κατὰ μόνας, παραβολάς, δώδεκα in Mark 4.10) or, more frequently, on the theme or terminology of 'teaching' found therein (4.2; 11.18; 12.38). In two of these instances (4.2, 10ff.), redactional status is confirmed for Meye by the received opinion of scholarship.

Clearly Markan seams do not loom large in Meye's redaction-critical enterprise; those few cited are not even designated as such. Yet at least two

45. Cf. ibid., p. 26: 'Repetition may also be expressed by the Markan summary statements. The summaries of Jesus' actions, just because they are repeated, are an especially good index to Mark's understanding of Jesus'.

46. Meye's references to these verses occur, respectively, in *Jesus,* p. 44; 'Those About Him', p. 211; *Jesus,* pp. 160, 44, 45.

things should be observed: (1) Where Meye supplies a rationale for the redactional character of these verses, none of the reasons — whether of terminology, theme, or scholarly corroboration — actually grapples with the possibility that the verses could as easily have stemmed from the pre-Markan tradition. (2) In his claim that these seams are Markan because of their emphasis on Jesus' διδαχή, Meye exhibits a tendency to assume as valid what he is attempting to prove: namely, that Mark's narrative evinces a peculiarly didactic emphasis.

2. When Meye suggests that the clause οἱ δὲ ἀκολουθοῦντες ἐφοβοῦντο in Mark 10.32 is 'a Marcan after-thought (cf. 2.15) or explanation (cf. 7.3, 19b)' that provides 'added commentary' on the action within the narrative,[47] tacitly he may be invoking Stein's criterion of *Markan insertions*. However, these are the only allusions to insertions that I discovered in a review of Meye's research; moreover, in none of these cases does Meye defend his assignment of such an identification. That they are 'Markan', with the implication of being '*distinctively* Markan redaction', is simply assumed, not substantiated.

3. Because they are repeated, *Markan summaries* of Jesus' action are considered by Meye to be an especially good index to the Evangelist's understanding of Jesus.[48] In light of this assessment, two facts are striking: first, Meye appeals to putative *Sammelberichte* almost as rarely as he refers to Markan seams and insertions; second, in one of the few instances where he explicitly identifies a passage in Mark (1.14-15) as a 'summary statement' (or at least concedes the possibility of such an identification by scholars), he considers that designation redaction-critically problematic: '. . . *there is not a single instance in the remaining chapters of Mark where Jesus' work is described with kerygmatic terminology*', which suggests that Mark declines to elaborate on κηρύσσων in 1.14.[49] This datum is used by Meye in support of his basic assumption concerning the content of *Sammelberichte*: 'the term *didaskein* regularly appears in the Marcan summaries [e.g. 2.13b; 6.6b, 34; 10.1]':[50] thus the theme of 'teaching', not 'proclamation', is the distinctive redactional characteristic of Markan summaries. Like his use of Markan seams, Meye's references to *Sammelberichte* are infrequent, imprecise in distinguishing redaction from tradition, and suggestive of exegetically circular reasoning.

---

47. *Jesus*, p. 164.
48. Ibid., p. 26.
49. Ibid., p. 52 (Meye's italics).
50. Ibid., p. 38 (Meye's transliteration); cf. p. 26; 'Messianic Didache', p. 61.

4. In my review of his work, I discovered no instances whatever of Meye's argument for Mark's *creation of pericopes*. This may indicate either Meye's disinclination to accord such freedom of composition to the Evangelist, or his regard of this criterion as nearly valueless in reconstructing a redaction history, or both.

5. With respect to the *Markan modification* of traditional material, the evidence in Meye's various studies is mixed. As far as I can determine, he makes no reference to pericopes in the Second Gospel that are (by form-critical conventions) so 'misformed' that they must be attributed, not to oral transmission, but to the hand of the Evangelist. (Whatever the absence of this criterion may suggest, surely it does not reflect a high valuation of Mark's literary or narrative style, about which Meye says virtually nothing.)

Early in his monograph, Meye offers an interpretive judgment that appears to esteem Stein's other two subdivisions of Markan modification: 'For it is only by comparing Mark with the other Gospels, and with the historical course of the mission of Jesus, that the unique proclamation of Mark can be determined'.[51] The comparison (or, in Stein's terminology, 'inconsistency') of Mark's account with what actually happened is in fact employed not at all by Meye in educing 'the unique proclamation of Mark'. There seem to be two reasons for this. First, Meye recognizes the inherent circularity of this criterion, which hampers its usefulness: 'our understanding of Jesus' ministry is based to a considerable degree upon Mark's Gospel'.[52] Second, implicit in Meye's entire treatment of Mark is the general historical trustworthiness of that Evangelist's portrait of Jesus and the twelve; thus we would expect Meye's aversion to detailing inconsistencies between the Markan account and historical fact.

Of all the methodological criteria considered thus far, 'the comparison of Mark with the other Synoptic Gospels' turns out to be the one most frequently used by Meye. And in every case where this *redaktionsgeschichtlich* principle is invoked, it is to promote the understanding of what is for Meye a consistent Markan *Tendenz*: 'Matthew and Luke were not as obviously and consciously concerned to depict Jesus *as a teacher* as was Mark'.[53] For

---

51. *Jesus*, p. 25.

52. Ibid., p. 25.

53. Ibid., p. 39 (Meye's italics). Meye's defense of this interpretation, in the face of such non-Markan material as the Sermon on the Mount (Matt 5–7) and the Sermon on the Plain (Luke 6.20-49) is that '*Fullness of teaching* is not at all the same as *emphasis upon the activity of teaching*' (ibid., p. 42). For a different assessment, consult J. P. Meier, *The Vision of Mat-*

Meye this is made plain by a wealth of data: the divergence from, or the outright omission of, Mark's distinctive use of 'didactic terminology' by the other Synoptics (that is, διδαχή, διδάσκαλος, διδάσχειν, λέγειν); Matthew and Luke's omission of the Markan thematic emphasis on discipleship and Jesus' esoteric instruction, as well as their relative stress on themes left unemphasized by Mark (such as Jesus' healing activities); the other Synoptics' restructuring or rewording of Markan passages that highlight Jesus' didacticism (for example, Mark 4.35-41; 6.45-52; 8.14-21; 10.46-52).[54] While conceding the inherent ambiguity of the term μαθητεύειν, Meye frequently attempts to clarify the Markan conception of discipleship by noting its similarity to Matthew's understanding and by delineating its dissimilarity to Luke and John's interpretation (both of whom, for Meye, display a much broader understanding of discipleship than does Mark).[55] On occasion Meye admits that the Synoptic parallels offer no direct benefit in interpreting Mark;[56] however, the implication of this acknowledgment is that elsewhere, as a rule, the comparison with Matthew and Luke does afford such help.

Regardless of how persuasive one finds Meye's interpretation of the theme of 'teaching' in Mark, some definite assessments may be made of his use of Matthew and Luke in isolating that Markan theme. First, if indeed the redaction history of a Gospel is attested by modifications among the Synoptics, then Matthean and Lukan alterations of the Markan account would bear witness in the first instance to *their* redaction history rather than to Mark's.[57] Second, Meye's somewhat overstated suggestion, 'it is only by comparing Mark with the other Gospels . . . that the unique proclamation of Mark can be determined', is not so much a *redaction-critical* judgment — nor does it function as such in Meye's research — as it is a commonsense *heuristic* principle for the interpretation of any piece of literature that deals in a distinctive way with material common to other literary works.[58]

---

thew: *Christ, Church, and Morality in the First Gospel* (New York: Paulist, 1979), pp. 45-51 et passim.

54. 'Messianic Didache', p. 61; *Jesus,* pp. 36-47, 65-67, 78, 133, 167-69.

55. *Jesus,* pp. 138, 228-30; cf. 'Messianic Didache', p. 65 n. 40; *Jesus,* pp. 148-49, 185-89.

56. *Jesus,* pp. 149, 160.

57. As noted by Stein, 'Markan Redaction History', pp. 187-88.

58. *Jesus,* p. 25. In like manner, and with no intention of making any redaction-critical case, a critic of English literature might claim, 'It is only by comparing Chaucer's *Troilus and Criseyde* with Chapman's version of the *Iliad* and Shakespeare's *Troilus and Cressida* that the unique statement of Chaucer can be determined'.

6. As I have already noted, Meye considers especially important *Mark's selection, or inclusion, of material:* among others, this criterion '[reflects] the particular historical situation of the Evangelist'.[59] On the basis of redactional selection, exactly what are the contours of the Markan *Sitz im Leben?* For Meye, the answer is obvious: it is a setting in which the twelve are the object of great interest and curiosity. Thus Mark includes considerable material in his narrative that identifies the membership of the disciples, emphasizes their private instruction by Jesus, and describes their companionship with their master even during his last days.[60] Meye is well aware that such inclusion of material, while perhaps distinctive of Mark, need not betoken uniquely Markan interests; the pre-Markan tradition could have harbored the same concerns. And that is why Meye finds this criterion especially useful: 'As in many other instances, it can be argued that Mark is simply following the tradition [at 6.30]. Regardless of *this* fact, it is this tradition that he follows — and one must reckon with the Marcan intention in using it'.[61]

Yet it is precisely with the Markan intention that the criterion of inclusion seems unable to reckon: for how can the canon of selection determine the Evangelist's distinctive concerns if implicit in that criterion is the *convergence,* if not identity, of traditional and redactional interests? Meye's response seems to be this: one must scout for repetition of consistent themes in the Gospel in order to distinguish *Markan* concerns. Thus, with respect to Mark 1.14, he urges that 'it is necessary to compare this text with the remainder of Mark's Gospel. The question is: What is in fact the consistent Marcan depiction of Jesus?'[62] However, might we not respond: does a consistent depiction of Jesus (or of anything else) in the Second Gospel necessarily betray a uniquely or even distinctively *Markan* concern? Could not much of the information, recounted by Mark about Jesus, have been included simply because it was well-known? Could not other such information have been connected in the pre-Markan tradition, such that its inclusion would signify no intention on Mark's part of emphasizing it? In the end, one strongly suspects that Meye approves of this criterion, not because

---

59. *Jesus,* p. 28.

60. Ibid., pp. 134, 139, 142, 183; cf. 'Those About Him', p. 214.

61. *Jesus,* p. 55. Cf. Wrede: 'At least partially, the [theological] motifs themselves will not be the property of the evangelist, but the way he concretely uses them is at all events his own work. . . . The way traditional material and Mark's own are apportioned in individual circumstances will also not be uniformly capable of being settled by a special investigation. It has to be left as it is — an admixture' (*Messianic Secret,* p. 146).

62. *Jesus,* p. 53.

of its extraordinary helpfulness in establishing a Markan redaction history, but rather because it *sidesteps* the redaction-critical contretemps presented by the Second Gospel: 'Attempts to differentiate between that which is Marcan and that which is traditional are at best precarious. More recently significant is the obvious fact that Mark chose to utilize traditions in which Jesus generally appeared as one who went about teaching'.[63] From a literary or narrative point of view, this makes good interpretive sense; in effect, however, it amounts to the near abandonment of redaction criticism.

7. 'It is a more appropriate procedure to read Luke's understanding of the purpose of the Twelve from his description of their work, than it is to assign a meaning to the Lucan narrative contrasting to that of Mark on the basis of Luke's *non*inclusion of a statement of purpose in the account of their appointment'.[64] Insofar as he would render the same judgment in elucidating the Markan purpose, the criterion of *Mark's omission of material* would seem to be rejected by Meye as an invalid *argumentum e silentio;* indeed, that *redaktionsgeschichtlich* canon plays no evident role in Meye's analysis of the Second Gospel. Moreover, according to Meye, Mark's seeming omission of traditional material can actually lead one to draw an improper deduction about Mark's didactic interest: 'the *relative* lack of didactic material in Mark has often led to a depreciation of oral content in Mark's understanding of the Gospel'.[65]

On the other hand, occasionally Meye is inclined, and possibly constrained, to draw meaning from Markan silence. Thus 'It is significant that notes describing the future course of the Gospel are not a part of Jesus' public teaching';[66] 'Mark never specifically states that Jesus had many disciples (as in Lk. 6,17; 19,37; Jn 6,66) . . . [and] Mark does not clearly posit the existence of other disciples'.[67] Neither of these observations is exegetically questionable; what they make clear, however, is Meye's willingness, when it suits his purpose, to argue on the basis of what Mark omits to say, even as he would maintain, in principle, the problems associated with such an exegesis.

8. Perhaps no redactional criterion assumes greater pride of place in Meye's work than *the Markan arrangement of material.* While urging that 'great caution must be employed in developing arguments based upon structure', Meye maintains that the 'didactic shape of the Second Gospel'

63. Ibid., p. 38; cf. pp. 24, 41.
64. Ibid., p. 188.
65. Ibid., p. 51 (Meye's emphasis).
66. Ibid., p. 183.
67. 'Those About Him', pp. 214-15.

may be perceived with unusual clarity in Mark's terminology and in the structure of the Gospel, even though 'only the Gospel itself can guide us in our appeal to structure as a bearer of meaning'.[68] Meye suggests specific techniques of Markan arrangement or structure, most of which have counterparts in Stein's analysis of this category.

a. *The arrangement of individual pericopes* is the subset of Markan *Anordnung* most frequently invoked by Meye; arguably, it is the most frequently exercised of all his redactional canons. Critical for Meye in discerning Markan meaning is 'the manner in which certain actions are clearly bound together in the ongoing narrative'.[69] The examples, proposed by Meye, of such narrative binding are numerous:

i. Mark 1.16-20. *'Mark first placed this pericope at the head of all the stories of the public ministry'*, and, in so doing, 'lays great stress upon the fact of a chosen circle of disciples' who are obedient to Jesus' call.[70]

ii. With its summons to be 'fishers of men', Mark 1.17 initiates a narrative cycle in the Second Gospel, composed by the Evangelist, which finds its 'midpoint' in Jesus' appointment of the twelve (3.13-19) and its completion in the mission of the twelve (6.7-13, 30).[71]

iii. Mark 3.35 and 10.28-30 complement each other in communicating Mark's understanding that discipleship entails a new familial relationship.[72]

iv. The three narratives of a sea-crossing (Mark 4.35-41; 6.45-53; 8.13-21) share a common and interrelated function, conceived by Mark, which comes into focus in 'the didactic motif'.[73]

v. At 6.30 Mark is manifestly concerned to link the mission of the twelve (6.6b-13) with the feeding of the five thousand (6.30-44).[74]

vi. The first feeding of the multitude and the second crossing of the sea (6.45-52) are interwined by their references to 'the loaves' as well as by the common theme of not understanding the identity of Jesus (in v. 49) or the meaning of the loaves (in v. 52, referring to 6.30ff.).[75]

vii. Similarly, 'bread' and 'understanding' dominate the events de-

---

68. *Jesus*, pp. 26-27; cf. p. 20.
69. Ibid., p. 27.
70. 'Messianic Didache', p. 62 (Meye's emphasis).
71. *Jesus*, pp. 178, 189; cf. pp. 107-109.
72. Ibid., p. 151.
73. Ibid., pp. 63-67; cf. p. 27: 'The manner in which certain actions are repeated . . . or characteristic of Jesus' ministry [should be noted]'.
74. Ibid., pp. 110-12.
75. Ibid., pp. 67-68.

scribed in 8.1-10 and 8.14-21; thus 'the context is provided by the evangelist's own arrangement'.[76]

viii. The thematic progression from those with eyes to see, yet who are blind, to one who is blind, yet is made to see clearly, is established by Mark's juxtaposition of 8.14-21 and 8.22-26; by Markan design, a parallel juxtaposition recurs in 10.35-45 and 10.46-52.[77]

ix. With its emphasis on the heart of the Christian gospel, the cross and the resurrection, as well as its repetitive pattern of Jesus' revelation of private or secret teaching to benighted disciples, 'Mark 8.27–10.52 has a programmatic flavor'.[78]

x. In chs. 9 and 10 the disciples' concern for special position and their implicit knowledge of themselves as privileged hark back to their special appointment and their endowment by Jesus with special authority, depicted earlier in the Second Gospel.[79]

xi. '[There] is a strong link between [the] repeated elements of the passion narrative and the initial chapters of Mark's narrative where Jesus assembles a community of disciples about him as a teacher, but one with authority. . . .'[80]

For all of the structural sophistication that he discovers in Mark's arrangement of individual pericopes, it should be noted that Meye is conscious of the danger of imposing patterns where none exists: 'Even when patterns or programs are seen, it is wise to refrain from attempts to force everything under a given heading'.[81] Moreover,

> [It] is important that one neither expects too much refinement in Mark's development of his narrative nor ignores patterns or emphases actually there. Many treatments of Mark's Gospel have suffered from attributing to the Gospel highly developed plans similar to what one might expect in a modern novel. . . . Such expectations have no place in Gospel interpretation.[82]

76. Ibid., pp. 68-69.
77. Ibid., pp. 70-71, 77.
78. Ibid., p. 73; cf. pp. 51, 71-72, 74, 103, 112-13, 160-62.
79. Ibid., pp. 180-81.
80. Ibid., p. 62.
81. Ibid., p. 72.
82. Ibid., pp. 62-63. Thus Meye can conclude (ibid., p. 86) that Mark 11–13 appears not to contain as clear a didactic pattern as that which may be discerned in the Gospel's earlier chapters.

Nevertheless, in his attempt to pinpoint Mark's theological intentions, Meye treats the arrangement of pericopes in the Second Gospel with utmost seriousness.

Before proceeding further, we might pause to reflect on some of the implications of Meye's method up to this point. First, it could be argued that he is not utterly consistent in his appraisal of the control exercised by the Second Evangelist over the arrangement of individual pericopes. Thus, while it is evident from the preceding list that he attributes to Mark considerable structural control over the Gospel narratives, Meye broaches, but does not directly refute, Philipp Vielhauer's judgment that a 'loose' narrative style characterizes the Second Gospel.[83]

Second, a seeming inconsistency within the putative Markan arrangement, recognized by Meye, tends to work against the cogency of this redaction-critical canon. Thus Meye expends great effort in uncovering the careful 'didactic' pattern in the first ten chapters of Mark, only to observe — without suggesting any explanation for the phenomenon — that the arrangement of chs. 11–13 does not appear to maintain this pattern.[84]

Third, the tension already witnessed in Meye's assumptions concerning Markan editorial freedom relative to the constraints of tradition arises again with the issue of the Gospel's structure: Meye wishes to argue *both* for 'the programmatic framework' of the feeding/sea-crossing complex *and* for the varied and complex character of the tradition, which would diminish Mark's complete control over the narrative outline.[85] Similarly, Meye contends that Mark 8.27–10.52 has a 'programmatic flavor', even as he cautions interpreters against forcing all Markan material under a given heading.[86] In both of these cases, the problem is not that Meye wishes to hold in tension redactional freedom and traditional limitation; the prob-

---

83. Meye (ibid., pp. 197-98) challenges the implication drawn from this by Vielhauer (namely, that this 'loose' literary structure suggests historical inauthenticity); he does not respond to Vielhauer's exegetical assessment of Markan arrangement, which seems to contravene Meye's own position.

84. *Jesus*, p. 86. At least two factors might account for the phenomenon witnessed by Meye: (1) Chapters 11–13 may reflect the pre-Markan passion tradition and for this reason may have been more resistant to the redactor's adaptation than material in earlier chapters; (2) the didactic emphasis is not entirely lacking in chs. 11–13, since both the beginning and conclusions of this section are marked by Jesus' dialogue with, or discourse to, the disciples.

85. *Jesus*, p. 72. Presumably, it is this lack of editorial control that prompts Meye's warning that one should not read Mark with an eye for the narrative patterns expected of a modern novel.

86. *Jesus*, pp. 72-73.

lem is that he does not define the nature of their conjunction as precisely as one would like. Indeed, on those rare occasions when Meye does defend his *redaktionsgeschichtlich* assessment of Mark's arrangement of pericopes, the defense lacks rigor: his appraisal of 'the programmatic structure' of the feeding/sea-crossing complex is substantiated by his discernment of 'the didactic motif' — that is, by the very exegetical thesis that his monograph aims to prove; and the principal defense for 'the programmatic flavor' of Mark 8.27–10.52 is the 'decisive agreement among scholars today'.[87]

Fourth and finally, I would argue that, while Meye has presented a plausible case for an intentional structuring of the Gospel narrative, he has not demonstrated that *the Evangelist* is responsible for that structure. In theory, why could not 'the didactic motif' have been a pre-Markan, *traditional* theme, already integrating various pericopes, which Mark simply let stand or shifted only slightly in his representation of the tradition?[88] I am not suggesting that such a tradition-critical explanation is necessarily more persuasive, or for that matter amenable of demonstration, than Meye's redaction-critical argument. My point is that Meye usually does not consider this alternative and rarely defends his consignment of certain structural patterns to the Evangelist's redaction.

b. *The placing of one pericope inside another,* or '[the] device of *inclusio*[,] seems to be a Marcan favorite also', according to Meye.[89] Thus '[the] fact that Mark brackets the exorcism (1.23-26) with notes on Jesus' teaching' suggests that 'The power of the word of teaching is manifest in Jesus' power over the unclean spirits'; 'there seems to be a nexus between the friends of 3.21 and the family of 3.31'; the sandwiching of Mark 6.14-29 between the two references to the mission of the twelve (6.6b-13; 6.30) 'is Mark's way of indicating that Jesus' fame was broadcast even through the

---

87. Ibid., p. 73. However, Meye does refer to the pattern of the thrice-repeated predictions by Jesus of the passion and resurrection of the Son of man (Mark 8.31; 9.31; 10.33-34).

88. Even among interpreters sympathetic to *Redaktionsgeschichte*, this possibility is not far-fetched. For example, P. J. Achtemeier has proposed that certain thematic considerations were responsible for the *pre-Markan* grouping of the pericopes in Mark 4.35–6.44 and 6.45–8.10 ('Toward the Isolation of Pre-Markan Miracle Catenae'; 'The Origin and Function of the Pre-Marcan Miracle Catenae'). Similarly, according to H.-W. Kuhn (*Ältere Sammlungen*), Mark may have received, from among his available traditions, whole collections of material that already had been organized thematically: controversy stories (reproduced in Mark 2), seed-parables (Mark 4), epiphanic *Novellen* (Mark 4–6), and instruction about discipleship (Mark 10).

89. *Jesus,* p. 27.

work of the disciples'.[90] Aside from a certain obscurity in his rationale for the third instance of intercalation,[91] these are credible interpretations of the effect created by some of the Gospel's interpolations of pericopes.

Ultimately, though, we are confronted by the same problem that was encountered in Meye's treatment of the Markan arrangement of pericopes: how does he know that *the Evangelist-redactor* is responsible for these 'sandwiches' of tradition? Meye's only defense rests on an interpretive precedent set forth by R. H. Lightfoot with respect to such passages as Mark 3.20-22, 4.10ff., 5.25-34, 8.34–9.1, and 11.15-19. All of these, for Meye (appealing to Lightfoot), are examples of the redactor's handiwork, 'without touching the question of the original state of the tradition'.[92] But if one is to make the redaction-critical judgment that Mark is demonstrably responsible for these intercalations, is not this *precisely* the question that Meye's investigation should touch?

c. Meye expresses skepticism regarding the attempt to disclose *the geographical scheme of Mark,* or, for that matter, any all-encompassing scheme. Comparison of the many possible plans that have been attributed to a given Gospel suggests that warning flags need to be raised: one should not be sanguine about any attempt to uncover a 'plan' or 'pattern' in the narrative of a Gospel.[93] Elsewhere in his discussion, however, Meye suggests that 'Galilee' is no mere datum of the gospel tradition but conveys, for Mark, extraordinary theological significance: 'in those texts where Jesus promises his disciples that he will go before them to Galilee (14.28; 16.7) . . . there is a visible parallel to and extension of the narrative pattern culminating in the Messianic affirmation at Caesarea Philippi (cf. 4.35-41; 6.45-52; 8.14-21) and continuing in the way of the cross after Caesarea Philippi (8.31; 9.31f.; 10.32-34)'.[94] More specifically, according to Meye, Gal-

90. The quotations are excerpted from *Jesus,* respectively pp. 46, 150, 179.

91. Meye's principal argument for the interpolation of Mark 6.14-29 between 6.6b-13 and 6.30 — namely, that by it Mark wished to highlight Jesus' exorcisms and ever-increasing fame — accounts for 6.14 but for little else in the pericope introduced by that verse. Moreover, if that were the main point that Mark intended to score by means of 6.14-29, it could just as easily, and perhaps more effectively, have been made by conjoining that pericope with Mark 1.28, 39, 45, or 5.20. A more plausible explanation of the 'sandwich' in ch. 6 is suggested by the theme of 6.14-29, the death of the Baptist: the world's hostility to mission, crystallized in John's execution, implicitly colors the twelve's own mission and presages Jesus' fate (8.31; 9.31; 10.33-34).

92. *Jesus,* p. 179 n. 9, citing Lightfoot, *Gospel Message,* p. 61.

93. *Jesus,* p. 29.

94. Ibid., p. 81.

ilee becomes the place of the disciples' reformation, reconstitution, and restoration to Jesus; it is the locus of the Gospel's beginning and ending (cf. 1.1 [*sic*]; 16.7), where *'the cycle of encounter with the divine Teacher is completed'* and after which the disciples 'really understand'.[95]

Three features should be noted in Meye's use of this subdivision of the criterion of redactional arrangement. (1) It is curious that Meye practically disavows the attempt to detect in the Second Gospel a particular plan or pattern — only to introduce just such a plan, centered on Galilee, into his discussion. (2) Once again, Meye has neither substantiated nor even attempted to substantiate his argument that the concept of 'Galilee' conveys for the redactor any theological significance greater than that conveyed in the tradition — if, indeed, it bears *theological* significance at all.[96] (3) Certain aspects of Meye's interpretation of 'the Galilean plan' in Mark are at best inferential and at worst specious: Mark 14.28 and 16.7 state only that, after his resurrection, Jesus will go before the disciples into Galilee, where they will see him; neither these passages nor any text in Mark expressly recounts the scattered twelve's 'reformation, reconstitution, and restoration to Jesus' following the resurrection.[97] This may be a valid exegetical *inference;* but when Meye argues that after Easter the disciples 'became transformed from those taught into proclaimers of the gospel of Jesus Christ, the Son of God (Mark 1.1)',[98] he does so without manifest textual support.

Meye's emphasis on the significance of 'Galilee' in the Second Gospel abumbrates a larger redaction-critical canon that is not explicitly proposed by Stein: the presence of distinctive, recurrent themes that characterize the theology and structure of Mark. Those that figure most prominently in Meye's analysis are presented in the following list.

Christology: Jesus as
    The one who is alone with the twelve,[99]
    The one with authority,[100]

---

95. Ibid., p. 85 (Meye's italics); cf. p. 84.

96. Mark 1.9 and 16.7 may simply reproduce traditional geographical data, without intending to suggest a 'cycle of encounter with the divine teacher'.

97. Excluding 16.9-20, which is almost certainly a later addition to the original ending of the Gospel at 16.8 (contra Farmer, *Last Twelve Verses*).

98. *Jesus,* p. 85.

99. Ibid, p. 152.

100. Ibid., pp. 178-79.

The divine teacher,[101]

Enunciating 'clear statements of [Markan] purpose' that 'are of decisive importance';[102]

Discipleship: The disciples as

Obedient to Jesus' call,[103]

Being with Jesus,[104]

Those whose understanding of Jesus' teaching is expected to evolve, as symbolized by the three sea-crossings,[105]

Led onward by Jesus in a didactic program that focuses on the way of the cross;[106]

Miscellaneous:

The Markan emphasis on 'teaching', conveyed (among other ways) in the repeated crossings of the sea;[107]

The dynamic process involved in Jesus' ministry to the disciples,[108] captured by the terminology of Jesus' initiatory 'going ahead' and the disciples' 'following' (i.e., engaged in a work similar to that of Jesus);[109]

The conceptual linkage of 'seeing' or 'being given eyes to see' with 'understanding' or 'knowing';[110]

'Discipleship' as distinguished from 'faith', 'following', and 'ministry';[111]

'The messianic secret' and the concept of 'the twelve' as correlative;[112]

'Fear' or 'astonishment' as reflecting a provisional lack of understanding or as a response to the numinous;[113]

---

101. Ibid., p. 72 et passim.
102. Ibid., p. 26; cf. pp. 49-50.
103. 'Messianic Didache', p. 62; cf. *Jesus,* pp. 158-59, 183.
104. *Jesus,* p. 167.
105. Ibid., pp. 67, 72.
106. Ibid., pp. 73-74, 112, 115.
107. Ibid., pp. 45, 66-67.
108. Ibid., pp. 87, 219.
109. Ibid., pp. 82, 108-9, 163, 178, 180-81.
110. Ibid., pp. 78-80, 220.
111. Ibid, pp. 79, 151, 157, 171.
112. Ibid., pp. 130-34, 215.
113. Ibid., pp. 75-77, 162, 218.

> The Holy Spirit as discloser of the divine word and originator of Christian testimony;[114]
>
> A repeated concern for 'the many' who are beneficiaries of Jesus' feedings and covenantal sacrifice.[115]

Taken collectively, the items in this list seemingly represent a fair and accurate measure of Mark's Gospel. On the other hand, it is an incomplete appraisal: in particular, the negative traits of the disciples' response (for example, their ignorance or failure) are conspicuous by their absence. There is an even more serious difficulty: once again, Meye does not clearly demonstrate the *redactional*, or distinguishably Markan, character of these themes. For instance, when he appeals to Jesus' injunction and Bartimaeus' response in Mark 10.52 in order to support his claim that 'faith', 'following', and 'discipleship' are not equivalent terms in Mark, Meye's contention is based, not on the differentiation of tradition and redaction, but rather on a 'close reading' of the text. Without question, the latter is a commendable method, worthy of use by Meye's successors; at issue here is whether this is in fact a *redaction-critical* method, as Meye seems to think: 'the specific emphases [of Mark's Gospel] reflect *the particular historical situation of the Evangelist*.[116] At best, this makes Meye's delineation of themes a subset of the larger criterion of Markan inclusion, the problems of which we have already considered; at worst, Meye has not demonstrated at all the *redactional* significance of these Markan themes.

9. Conceived as either 1.1-13 or 1.1-15, *the Markan introduction* offers comparatively little to Meye in understanding Markan discipleship beyond a reasonable inference drawn from 1.1: 'The very first line of Mark's Gospel bids the reader to view every aspect of the Gospel from a Christological perspective. And from this perspective, "discipleship" for Mark is discipleship to Jesus *the Christ*.[117] Mark 1.16-20 sheds greater light on Markan discipleship: the four fishermen's summons to be ἁλιεῖς ἀνθρώπων (1.17) sets the stage, both for Jesus' and the disciples' ministry to 'the many' and for Jesus' leadership of the twelve 'from one level of understanding to another until their final encounter with him as the risen Lord in Galilee'.[118] That the disciples attain that ultimate level of understanding after Easter is, of

---

114. Ibid., p. 221.
115. Ibid., p. 82.
116. Ibid., p. 25 (emphasis mine).
117. Ibid., p. 30 (Meye's italics).
118. Ibid., p. 213; cf. pp. 83-84, 100, 107, 211-12.

course, never explicitly stated in Mark 16.1-8; elsewhere Meye backs off from such an exegesis by suggesting that the 'program for discipleship' in Mark 1.17 is an agenda for the future, left unfulfilled in the Gospel.[119]

10. Meye's treatment of *the Markan conclusion* accords with his general understanding of Markan discipleship. Negatively, a careful reading of Mark 16.7 suggests that the women at the tomb are not considered by the Evangelist to be 'disciples'.[120] Positively, by the conclusion of the Gospel, the disciples have been fully prepared for the resurrection, the culminating event of Jesus' ministry. Their encounter with the risen Lord, a reunion to which only the twelve are privy, will be based on their obedience in following Jesus (as evidenced throughout the Gospel and anticipated as early as Mark 1.17). Their seeing the risen Jesus at Galilee is climactic, leading to final understanding on their part. 'Thus rather than being an ending with unaccepted negative overtones, Mark 16.7, 8 constitutes a positive and glorious affirmation not only of the resurrection of Christ but of his continued presence in the Christian community in the power of his word.'[121]

When one remembers that Meye accepts Mark 16.8 as the Gospel's end,[122] his interpretation of the Markan conclusion seems remarkably sweeping. In dealing with this section, Meye speaks, not of the potential for reconciliation between the risen Jesus and the twelve in Galilee, but of its actual accomplishment — almost as though Matt 28.16-20 could be used to fill the vast silence that follows Mark 16.8.[123] Likewise Meye states, 'In Mark's account only the Twelve are witnesses to the risen Lord':[124] the possibility presented by Mark 16.7 becomes, in Meye's exegesis, an indicative *fact*. In short, we witness in Meye's treatment of the Markan conclusion the abandonment, not only of any attempt at redaction criticism, but also of a close and careful reading of the text.

11. Among the redactional landmarks that, for Meye, point to the par-

---

119. 'Messianic Didache', p. 66; cf. *Jesus*, pp. 99-100.

120. *Jesus*, p. 171.

121. Ibid., pp. 218-19; cf. pp. 83, 100, 107, 182, 218, 220.

122. R. P. Meye, 'Mark 16.1-8 — The Ending of Mark's Gospel', *BR* 14 (1969), pp. 33-42.

123. Cf. *Jesus*, p. 220, and note the tenses of Meye's verbs: '[The disciples'] seeing [of the risen Lord] was climactic. It created the final understanding, which led to the confession of Jesus as the Christ and their proclamation of this gospel in all the world'. Contrast the subtler exegesis of T. E. Boomershine, who posits that, while Mark 16.7-8 amounts to an apostolic commission to proclaim the gospel, the ending of Mark concretizes the conflict between proclamation and silence, between responsibility and fearful flight ('Mark 16.8 and the Apostolic Commission', *JBL* 100 [1981], pp. 225-39).

124. *Jesus*, p. 182.

ticular historical situation of the Evangelist, 'the terminology used', or *Markan vocabulary*, is often emphasized. In the following list I have tabulated those words or phrases that are specifically mentioned by Meye as indicative of distinctive or typical Markan concerns.

TABLE 1   Meye's Identification of Markan Redactional Vocabulary

Verbal Unit	Frequency in Gospels[125]	Page Reference in Meye[126]
ἀκούειν		49-50
διδάσκαλος	12-12-17[-8]	35, 45; cf. 78, 87; 'Messianic Didache', 61-62
διδάσκειν	14-17-17[-9]	41, 45, 59-60
διδαχή	3-5-1[-3]	44, 45
δώδεκα		180-81, 213; 'Those About Him', 211
ἐκθαμβεῖσθαι/θαμβεῖσθαι	0-7-0-0	161
θέλειν		186
κατὰ μόνας		152, 'Those About Him', 211
κατ' ἰδίαν		133, 152, 155; 'Those About Him', 212
κηρύσσειν	9-12-9[-0][127]	52-53
λαλεῖν		49
λέγειν		48
λόγος		49
μαθηταί	73-46-37-78	62-63, 98
ὄχλος	48-37-39[-20][128]	'Those About Him', 214

125. Only on those occasions that Meye indicates a term's frequency of occurrence in the Gospels have I reproduced such information here. Bracketed numbers indicate frequency of occurrence in the Fourth Gospel, which Meye customarily does not give.

126. Unless otherwise identified, all citations are from *Jesus*.

127. Morgenthaler *(Statistik, s.v.)* counts 14 occurrences of κηρύσσειν in Mark, rather than 12 (contra Meye).

128. Morgenthaler *(Statistik, s.v.)* lists the Synoptic occurrences as 49-38-41.

Verbal Unit	Frequency in Gospels	Page Reference in Meye
παραβολή		'Those About Him', 211
πᾶς ὁ		'Those About Him', 214
ποιεῖν [δώδεκα/ὑμᾶς]		107, 113
πολύς		'Those About Him', 214
ῥαββι/ῥαββουνί		78; 'Messianic Didache', 61
φοβεῖσθαι	[18-]12[-23-5][129]	161

Meye also suggests certain items of vocabulary *not* characteristic of Mark or denotative of redaction: reference to the twelve as ἀπόστολοι (occurring only at Mark 6.30),[130] ἀκολουθεῖν as a *terminus technicus* for discipleship,[131] the many references to a 'boat',[132] and indications that there were 'many' disciples (*à la* Luke and John).[133]

Less frequently Meye proposes some features of Markan style that he considers to be redactionally significant:

TABLE 2 Meye's Identification of Mark's Redactional Style

Element of Style	Page Reference in Meye
Repetition, embracing such features as parataxis, pleonasm, tautology, the infinitive-absolute construction, the redundant participle	144, cf. 163
Frequent use of ἄρχομαι in the narrative	74
Parallelism in vocabulary and style	83, 144; 'Those About Him', 218
Narrative doublets	64 n. 3
Preference for καί over δέ as a conjunctive particle	162

129. In *Jesus*, p. 161, Meye gives the number of occurrences of this word in Mark but not in the other Gospels.

130. *Jesus*, p. 175.

131. Ibid., pp. 120-25; 'Those About Him', p. 214.

132. *Jesus*, p. 102.

133. Ibid., p. 120.

Element of Style	Page Reference in Meye
An easy alternation between μαθηταί and δώδεκα	198; 'Those About Him', 213; 'Messianic Didache', 63
περί used locatively, σύν as indicative of 'attachment'	152-56; 'Those About Him', 216-17

When tabulated in this manner, Meye's suggested redactional vocabulary of Mark seems impressive. Let us assess the items in these lists and the rationale behind their tabulation.

(1) Usually implicit, and often explicit, in Meye's verbal statistics is the assumption that a given word's frequency of occurrence in Mark, relative to its occurrence in the other Gospels, is suggestive of a distinctively Markan-redactional concern. For instance, Meye claims: 'the Second Gospel is significantly shaped by a didactic understanding of Jesus' ministry. This may be seen with particular clarity in the Marcan terminology . . .', a basically didactic terminology, in the employment of which '[Mark] exceeds the other Synoptists relatively if not absolutely'.[134] To judge from the statistical data, however, it is a real question whether this statement is defensible in any meaningful sense: διδαχή occurs but five times in Mark's Gospel, only twice more than in Matthew or John; the number of occurrences of διδάσκειν (17) is the same in Mark and in Luke, only thrice more than in Matthew; Mark and Matthew are tied in their frequency of usage of διδάσκαλος (12), and Luke surpasses both of them in his use of this word (17 occurrences). Clearly, except in the case of διδαχή, Mark's use of 'didactic terminology' does not absolutely exceed that of the other Synoptists; while the frequency of occurrence of such terminology is, arguably, greater in Mark than in Matthew and Luke, relative to their respective length and total number of words, in fact there exist only 34 occurrences of 'didactic terminology' (διδάσκαλος, διδάσκειν, or διδαχή) in the whole of the Second Gospel. Similarly, one wonders about the redactional significance of ἀκούειν (63-44-65-58), θέλειν (42-24-28-23), λαλεῖν (26-21-31-60), λέγειν (289-202-217-266), λόγος (33-24-33-40), μαθηταί (73-46-37-78), ὄχλος (48-37-39-20), παραβολή (17-13-18-0), and φοβεῖσθαι (18-12-23-5): all, or all but one, of the Evangelists use each of these words more frequently than does Mark. On a numerical basis, one must further wonder

134. Quotations from, respectively, *Jesus,* p. 20, and 'Messianic Didache', p. 61.

93

why Meye is inclined to categorize 'boat' (πλοῖον) as traditional rather than redactional when it is used in Mark as frequently, both absolutely and relatively to the other Gospels, as διδάσκειν, which for Meye is redactional (πλοῖον: 13-17-7-7; διδάσκειν: 14-17-17-9).

(2) The foregoing observation raises another, larger question about Meye's assessment of Markan terminology: how can he be reasonably sure that the vocabulary, tabulated above, reflects the Evangelist's particular concerns[135] rather than the concerns of the tradition to which Mark is indebted? Often Meye confesses that he cannot be sure: thus the Second Gospel may bear witness both to a pre-Markan 'boat' tradition as well as to the Evangelist's redactional interest in Jesus' teaching of the disciples in a boat; whereas ἀκούειν, for Mark, relates positively to Jesus' teaching ministry, the term can have a broader (that is, not redactionally significant) connotation; although 'Mark continually envisions a large, pressing crowd' as the audience of Jesus' teaching, 'there is no reason to suppose that this picture has not come down to him within the tradition of the Church'.[136] If the line between tradition and redaction in these cases be fuzzy, or even incapable of being drawn, how, then, can Meye be so confident that *Mark* is responsible for the repetitive depictions of Jesus' being alone or teaching in private, that doublets (such as 4.35-41/6.45-52) suggest 'a specific purpose on the part *of the evangelist*', that 'to speak the word' is 'a typically *Marcan* expression', that '*Mark* shows a preference for such terms as ὄχλος, πολύς, and πᾶς ὁ'?[137] On other occasions Meye's differentiation of tradition and redaction is both confusing and confused: thus Mark makes use of kerygmatic terminology, as evidenced by the twelve occurrences of κηρύσσειν in the Second Gospel (cf. nine instances in both Matthew and Luke); nevertheless, 'Mark shows a fivefold preference for διδάσκειν over κηρύσσειν in his description of Jesus' activity'.[138] The implication of this curious argument is that, somehow, Meye feels equipped to determine that some things in Mark, while redactional, are less redactionally significant than others. Elsewhere, Meye asserts that any attempt to differentiate the usage of θαμβεῖσθαι and φοβεῖσθαι is futile: 'the two terms overlap in their usage by Mark [at 9.32 and 10.32] . . . and both passages may be regarded as

135. Recall *Jesus*, p. 25: '[Among other criteria,] the terminology used [reflects] *the particular historical situation of the Evangelist*' (emphasis mine).

136. Ibid., pp. 50, 102, 120 (quotation, p. 120).

137. 'Those About Him', pp. 212, 214 (emphasis mine); *Jesus*, pp. 49, 64 n. 3 (emphasis added).

138. *Jesus*, p. 53; cf. pp. 59-60.

Marcan redaction'.[139] At best, Meye has omitted a step in this argument and has drawn a redaction-critical conclusion without substantiation. At worst, this reasoning is fallacious: the similarity in meaning of two different terms constitutes no irrefutable demonstration of a redactional tendency, since one could just as easily argue that the words' likeness in usage was characteristic of the pre-Markan (traditional) level, or that one term was traditional and the Evangelist introduced only the other, similar term into his narrative.

(3) As we have seen, Meye frequently bases his argument for the redactional character of some words on their frequency of occurrence in the Second Gospel: thus Meye is careful to note that μαθηταί 'appears frequently', a frequency that swells with the inclusion of all pronominal references to the disciples; thus as many as eleven references to the twelve can be counted; 'Mark makes frequent use of *archō* = begin in his narrative'; 'terms such as κατὰ μόνας, παραβολή, and δώδεκα . . . are otherwise frequent in the Marcan redaction'.[140] Although the frequency of occurrence of various words in a Gospel may indirectly suggest something about an Evangelist's predilections (since he has seen fit to include those words in his account), such frequency in itself cannot *prove* that certain concepts or concerns (such as 'the didactic emphasis') are uniquely or even distinctively Markan, since it is impossible to determine how frequently or infrequently those concerns characterized the Second Evangelist's tradition.[141]

(4) While one may doubt that 'frequency of occurrence' is a reliable indicator of Markan redactional vocabulary, it is at least a verifiable datum. An even larger problem with many of Meye's identifications of 'Markan vocabulary' is that he offers for such designations no reason or substantiation at all. Hence it is not uncommon for Meye to make assertions like the following with little, if any, justification: 'Most of the Marcan references [to οἱ δώδεκα] appear within sections probably belonging to the

---

139. Ibid., p. 161.

140. 'Messianic Didache', pp. 62-63; *Jesus*, p. 74 (Meye's transliteration); 'Those About Him', p. 211.

141. Already we have observed (p. 93) that Meye minimizes the argument of 'frequency of occurrence' when it impedes a redaction-critical point that he wishes to make. Notice also the rationale for Meye's contention ('Those About Him', pp. 216-17) that σὺν τοῖς δώδεκα (Mark 4.10) denotes 'attachment', supporting a 'locative' nuance of οἱ περὶ αὐτόν in the same verse: ultimately 4.10 must be regarded as 'a special case' in Mark for so construing σύν since elsewhere the preposition never conveys that precise sense and, in any case, is *infrequent* in Mark (6 occurrences).

Marcan redaction'; 'both [δώδεκα and μαθηταί] fall within the redactional 'sectors' of Mark's Gospel'; 'twice [θέλειν] appears in typical *Marcan* sections'.[142] In these and other instances Meye merely declares some material to be 'Marcan' without defense or explanation, without attempting to distinguish redaction from tradition.

(5) Finally, a good test of the reliability of the criterion of vocabulary is its verification in research of other Markan redaction critics. While the preceding questions cast a dark shadow of doubt over Meye's attempt to establish a Markan redactional vocabulary, final judgment should be suspended until we can observe the degree to which Meye's results are reproduced in the work of Ernest Best and Theodore Weeden.

12. In Meye's study of Markan discipleship, *the Markan Christological titles* assume a position of importance greater than might be expected. While concurring with other scholars that 'Son of God' and the self-sacrificing 'Son of man' are fundamental to Mark's understanding of Jesus,[143] Meye holds that the motif of Jesus as *teacher* has been underestimated in the Second Gospel, inasmuch as '"Messianic Didache" is . . . Mark's description . . . of Jesus' office and Jesus' most prominent action. . . . [On the basis of Mark 3.6, 6.1ff., 11.18, 14.49], Mark makes it abundantly clear that the rejected Messiah is rejected as one who itinerated among Israel as a teacher'.[144] For Meye, the implication of this Christological understanding is clear: since in Mark the disciple receives his meaning from Jesus, and because the Second Evangelist's concept of Jesus' ministry demanded that he emphasize Jesus' didactic work, the key to the meaning of Markan discipleship is, therefore, the devotion of the twelve to Jesus as their Lord and Teacher.[145] 'Discipleship' is correlative to the concept of Jesus as the revealer of a Messianic secret and Messianic διδαχή, and this, in Meye's judgment, is true for Mark's historical context as well as for the Evangelist's own faith.[146]

Of the Second Evangelist, Paul Achtemeier has said, 'It would be difficult to put more emphasis on Jesus as teacher than Mark does'.[147] Insofar as most Markan scholars would agree with this assessment, part of the

---

142. These quotations are taken from, respectively, 'Those About Him', p. 213; *Jesus*, p. 99 and p. 186 (Meye's italics).

143. *Jesus*, pp. 30-32, 112.

144. 'Messianic Didache' p. 58 n. 5, 62; cf. *Jesus*, pp. 26, 31, 38, 61, 87, 105, 210, 213-14.

145. *Jesus*, p. 26; cf. pp. 32, 57, 103.

146. Ibid., pp. 32, 130-31.

147. Achtemeier, *Mark*, p. 74.

credit must go to Meye for casting the spotlight so unrelentingly upon this aspect of Markan Christology. The idea that such an understanding of Jesus shapes the manner in which Mark intends for the disciples to be perceived is, if not self-evident, at least commonsensical. However, to what degree has *redaction criticism* as such driven Meye to this conclusion? His deductions seem to be the result of a close, insightful reading of the text, rather than of the differentiation and assessment of traditional and redactional elements in the Second Gospel.

Summary: We have subjected Meye's redaction-critical procedure to detailed, perhaps even tedious, scrutiny. Before proceeding to the final part of this chapter, a review of Meye's exegetical conclusions and their dependence on the practice of *Redaktionsgeschichte,* let us sum up the recurring critical problems that appear to be associated with Meye's *redaktionsgeschichtlich* method.

First, there is the persistent problem of *unsubstantiated claims:* in defending the existence of Markan insertions, arrangement of pericopes, intercalations, or vocabulary, Meye's arguments often are based solely on the *opinio communis* of New Testament scholarship. On other occasions Meye's defense is grounded on no evidence whatever.

Second, though Meye himself is sensitive to its danger, a large measure of *circular reasoning* characterizes his claims. For instance, the seams, summaries, and arrangement of the narrative in the Second Gospel are identified as redactional because they are characterized by distinctively Markan themes or vocabulary, or both. Then, when one asks how such themes and vocabulary may be identified as distinctively Markan, the invariable response is that they are located in Markan 'sectors' or 'sections' — that is, the Gospel's seams, summaries, and arrangement. The degree to which this poses a problem in Meye's treatment of Mark is, of course, commensurate with the extent to which those particular criteria are employed; unfortunately, arrangement, themes, and vocabulary constitute those aspects of redaction criticism to which Meye habitually resorts.

Third, and in line with the preceding two criticisms, frequently *no clear distinction between pre-Markan and Markan editorial work* is invoked or even attempted. Seams, *Sammelberichte,* words, and elements of style are commonly decreed as 'Markan' without any cogent explanation of how this decision was reached.

Fourth, there are broad elements of *internal inconsistency* in Meye's argumentation. One might recall the following examples: a concern both to distinguish tradition from redaction and to blur all such distinctions and to focus ultimately upon the complete, undifferentiated content of the Gospel and what the Evangelist has opted to include; a distrust of building exegetical arguments on what Mark omits to say, even while judging some omissions or silences as pregnant with meaning; the simultaneous acceptance and rejection of 'loose structure' in the Markan narrative; the assumption that a sophisticated redactional arrangement in the Second Gospel can be discerned against an equally complex pre-Markan tradition; a wariness in identifying programmatic plans in the Gospel while at the same time holding to a clear 'Galilean' plan, on which the narrative is purportedly structured; exegetical caution in suggesting that the disciples' vocation is not fulfilled in the course of the Gospel narrative, coupled with the argument that the disciples *do* come to full understanding after Easter (cf. 16.1-8); and finally, a lack of consistency in dealing with the implications of certain words' frequency of occurrence in the Second Gospel, relative to their frequency in the other Synoptics or relative to words of equal frequency within Mark itself.

Fifth, and related to the problem just described, there is an appreciable tension in Meye's exegesis between *a meticulous and insightful reading* of Mark on some points (see his treatment of διδάσκαλος as a significant Christological title) and *a lax and dubious interpretation* of the Gospel on other points (for example, Galilee as 'the place of enlightenment'; a categorically positive interpretation of the narrative's equivocal conclusion, with all of Mark's mystery dispelled).

Sixth and finally, much that is methodologically sound and most persuasive in Meye's work is, despite its casting as such by the author, not actually redaction-critical: often Meye has elected to interpret the text along broader, literary-critical lines.[148] So it is with Meye's penetrating, thematic insights, his aforementioned treatment of the Markan Christological titles, his illumination of the Second Gospel through heuristic comparisons with Matthew and Luke. Correlative to this lack of thoroughgoing adherence to

---

148. Reviewing *Jesus* in *JBL* 88 (1969), pp. 361-62, R. A. Edwards criticized Meye as making no attempt to distinguish between tradition and redaction, with the results that (a) Mark is made to appear internally consistent at every point and (b) Meye's research advances no further than the pre-form-critical study of Mark's theology. Regardless of whether Meye, writing in 1968, was methodologically arrested at a *vorformgeschichtlich* stage (as Edwards believed), or whether he was anticipating the literary-critical approach of the 1980s, it should be noted that, at the time of its appearance, Meye's research was recognized as being at some points only nominally redaction-critical.

Redaktionsgeschichte is Meye's repeated stress on the criterion of inclusion — 'what Mark clearly and repeatedly says' — which tends to ignore or to obliterate redaction-critical distinctions. We might also recall, in this connection, the presuppositional tension in Meye's understanding of Mark as both 'free in composition' and 'restrained by the dictates of historical tradition'. At some points in his work, therefore, it is as though Meye's explicit and specific distrust of redaction-critical attempts at limning a 'pattern' or 'plan' in the Gospel narrative has been generalized to embrace a wider wariness of the redaction-critical method overall.

C. Exegetical Results

Presuppositional for Meye's exegesis is the idea that Mark and the Markan community were profoundly interested in the teaching of the historical Jesus, who was now worshipped as the Christ: they were committed, in short, to the Messianic διδαχή. This, for Meye, explains the Second Gospel's emphasis on Jesus' teaching: a διδαχή that is new, authoritative, and essentially esoteric, shrouded in secrecy.[149] Congenial with such parabolic teaching is Jesus' parabolic activity and presentation of messiahship, which is conceived by Meye as 'the Way of the Cross' that engenders antagonism among the multitudes and even among the disciples.[150]

Indeed, so thoroughly parabolic is Jesus' discourse that, time and again in the Second Gospel, the twelve fail to understand with an 'almost impossible blindness and hardness', notwithstanding the fact that Jesus' explanations are invariably addressed to them.[151] As Meye is well aware, such ineptitude on the disciples' part has been attributed to a hypothetical Markan or Hellenistic-Christian polemic against the twelve.[152] For Meye, the theory that Mark intends to depict the disciples as villains is incredible. Basically this is for two reasons. First, the total content of the Gospel, which presents the disciples in a favorable as well as unfavorable light,

---

149. *Jesus,* pp. 47, 50-51, 60, 71, 74, 80, 126, 178, 210; 'Messianic Didache', p. 58.

150. 'Messianic Didache', p. 62; cf. *Jesus,* pp. 47, 71, 74, 122-24, 214. N.B. ibid., p. 48: 'In summary, one could say that Jesus' way as a teacher is for Mark a direct cause of the way of the cross'.

151. *Jesus,* pp. 43, 99; cf. pp. 12, 60, 70, 114.

152. See 'Messianic Didache', p. 65, where Meye associates this position with R. Bultmann and J. Schreiber; N.B. also *Jesus,* pp. 222-24, where Meye so characterizes S. Sandmel's position.

works against the plausibility of such a theory: 'one must suppose that had Mark set out to establish for the first time the authoritative place of the Twelve for the later Church, or to undermine a position they already held, a less ambiguous picture would have resulted'.[153] Second, the hypothesis of a Markan vendetta against the disciples flouts the precise intention of the Gospel, as Meye construes it: 'If one views Mark as an anti-Twelve polemic he robs the struggling (and sinning) Marcan community of the very hope that a *gospel* is calculated to bring'.[154] Therefore, 'in view of the Messianic appointment of the Twelve and in view of the central place occupied by the Twelve in every phase of the Messianic ministry, it is simply impossible to believe that the Marcan Church did or could have loved the Messiah and hated the Twelve'.[155]

Such a position is, in Meye's view, patently absurd in any case: the presentation of the disciples in the Second Gospel is too consistently positive to allow the notion of an 'anti-twelve polemic' a leg on which to stand.[156] After all, the disciples receive nothing less than a special appointment from Jesus: '*the primary activity of those called* (1.16-20; 2.14) is to be with Jesus. . . . And it must be remembered that it is the Twelve who are with Jesus as disciples to the end'.[157] Despite their hardness of heart and denial of Jesus, Mark is careful 'to speak of Jesus' *persistent* (and private) unfolding of his teaching *to them*'; in the course of their evolving appreciation of messiahship, up to and beyond Caesarea Philippi (8.27–9.1), it is Jesus' didactic leadership that at every step of the way brings them to understanding.[158] Ultimately, the disciples are made to understand everything (cf. 4.11, 34).[159] Through their unique encounter with the very Son of God —

153. *Jesus*, pp. 181-82. Also note, ibid., p. 223: 'Does the negative picture [of the disciples] of Mark's Gospel really negate this decisive [i.e., Christologically determined] place of the Twelve?'

154. 'Messianic Didache', p. 65; cf. p. 67.

155. *Jesus*, p. 224. If the Evangelist fingers any group as 'the bad guys', it is the Pharisees, whose evil disposition leads them to seek from Jesus a sign when great signs (such as repeated feedings of the multitudes) have already been given (*Jesus*, p. 69).

156. *Jesus*, p. 209; cf. 'Messianic Didache', p. 65.

157. *Jesus*, pp. 102-3 (Meye's emphasis); cf. pp. 105, 107, 123, 182-83, 210. Cf. M. F. Kirby, 'Mark's Prerequisite for Being an Apostle', *TBT* 18 (1980), pp. 77-81, who argues (perhaps to the point of overstatement) that 'companionship' is Mark's primary contribution to the theology of discipleship.

158. *Jesus*, pp. 71-73, 78, 123, 162; quotation from 'Messianic Didache', p. 65 (Meye's emphasis).

159. *Jesus*, pp. 44, 210.

by seeing, hearing, and being with Christ — the disciples become the unique recipients of that revelation which, for Mark, distinguishes Jesus' ministry.[160]

How does the Second Evangelist depict the disciples' response to their special selection by, and association with, Jesus? One response has already been mentioned: they remain with Jesus to the end. Implicit here is another, broader pattern of behavior: that of unquestioning obedience, a 'whole-souled identification with Jesus' word (Mark 8.34-38)'.[161] This entails the disciples' embarking on a ministry similar to Jesus' own, one in which preaching is the dominant activity (at least according to Mark's portrayal [3.13-19; 6.7-13, 30]) and Jesus' authority to cast out demons is exercised (3.15; 6.7, 13, 30). In brief the twelve, like Jesus, 'are ministers to the needs of men' (cf. 1.17).[162] Nevertheless, 'If the main activity of the historical disciples was to be with and to receive his teaching, this would then suggest that their primary function for the Marcan Church would be that of witness to the person and word and deed of Jesus'.[163] From this understanding of the disciples as witnesses to Jesus, Meye draws a crucial inference: if the words of Jesus are accorded a place in the Markan community alongside the Christ himself (8.38), and if an encounter with the gospel is an encounter with Jesus' own words, then the disciples function for Mark and his church *as authoritative mediators and guarantors* of the words of Jesus:

> The specific office of the Twelve is to receive the word and witness the deeds of the historical Jesus who functioned as their teacher. . . . As such they are the guarantors of the total 'gospel of Jesus Christ, the Son of God' (1.1). . . . [The] Messianic Secret is [the Markan community's] precisely because it was [affirmed to have been] disclosed to the Twelve[!] in the form of a Messianic Didache.[164]

For Meye, the implication of this is indubitable: it is the twelve who constitute the nexus between the historical Jesus and the Markan church. '[It]

160. Ibid., pp. 219-22; 'Messianic Didache', pp. 65-66.

161. *Jesus*, p. 48; cf. 'Messianic Didache', pp. 62, 65.

162. *Jesus*, p. 104; cf. pp. 55-56, 109, 115, 179-81; 'Messianic Didache', pp. 62, 65.

163. 'Messianic Didache', p. 66. N.B. in this quotation how easily Meye can shift from a redactional to a historical assessment. On the Markan disciples as 'witnesses' to Jesus, see also *Jesus*, pp. 102-3, 182.

164. 'Messianic Didache', p. 68; see also *Jesus*, pp. 60, 135-36, 173, 183, 190-91, 210, 214.

was to his chosen disciples that Jesus revealed himself and . . . it is through them that he now reveals himself to the Marcan Church.'[165] From this assessment Meye educes two further inferences, one pertaining to the purpose of the Second Gospel and the other touching on the perception of the disciples by the Markan community. Regarding its purpose, 'Mark's narrative is an account of the apostolic foundation or beginning (1.1) of the gospel proclaimed by the church'.[166] The Second Gospel was written to validate the existing tradition by showing that it stemmed from a community of witnesses handpicked and prepared by the church's Lord himself. Because they were witnesses specially selected and equipped, the disciples are exalted by the company of believers who have received the tradition: the twelve are accorded an 'all-important' status or 'the highest possible position within the ministry of the historical Jesus', a place of 'central significance' that is 'the very foundation upon which the Church is built'.[167]

If this be true, why, then, are the disciples often presented by Mark in such unflattering terms? Meye suggests that there may have been three reasons. First, their ineptitude functions as a Christological foil: 'The blindness and the fear of the disciples consistently underscores the glory of the Messianic revelation'.[168] Therefore, when the disciples misapprehend who Jesus is in a pericope like 6.45-52, that misinterpretation sets the stage for the Christological issue in which Mark is primarily interested (namely, that the disciples need have no fear, once they recognize the figure on the sea as Jesus).[169] According to Meye, Christology is not being used to highlight the disciples' misapprehension, since the Evangelist is careful to show that, in the end, only the disciples were made by Jesus to understand everything and were enabled to guard the mysterious διδαχή with which they had been entrusted.[170] Second, the blemishes on the disciples' behavior are intended by Mark to make plain their full humanity, to extend (as it were)

165. *Jesus*, p. 134; cf. pp. 182-83.

166. Ibid., p. 87.

167. *Jesus*, pp. 20, 194, 210-11, 216; 'Messianic Didache', pp. 65, 67. Along the same line, S. Légasse has suggested that Mark 10.35-40 is intended to illustrate the glory of Christ and of his disciples in general, although that glory is to be realized, apocalyptically, only in the future ('Approche de l'Épisode préévangélique des Fils de Zébédée (Marc x. 35-40 par.)', *NTS* 20 [1974], pp. 161-77).

168. *Jesus*, p. 224. Here Meye indicates his indebtedness to Ebeling, *Das Messiasgeheimnis*.

169. *Jesus*, p. 64; see especially n. 4 on that page.

170. Ibid., pp. 44, 127, 134-35, 210, 214-15. Note also p. 71: '[The disciples'] understanding is dependent upon . . . the one who explains everything to [them]'.

the Evangelist's understanding of the incarnation.[171] Third, and following upon the second reason, the humanness of the twelve makes a tacitly poignant statement about steadfastness in the face of persecution: 'in their blindness, hardness, and faithlessness [the Markan community, like the disciples,] can hope to persevere and to encounter the Son of man unashamed (cf. Mark 8.35, 38)'.[172]

Ultimately, there can be no gainsaying Mark's positive portrayal of the twelve, and 'there is no escaping the fact that the Marcan presentation as it stands, theological though it is, is a historically acceptable portrait of those about Jesus'.[173] By emphasizing the disciples' customary position as that of a small, improbable but favored group,[174] the Second Evangelist effectively limits discipleship to the twelve, making of them an apostolic, quasi-institutional, 'official teaching collegium', upon which the Markan church might rest assured 'that it had and would continue to have the Messianic word in its midst'.[175] For Meye, at least two implications of this analysis are significant. First, the Papias tradition about Mark's Gospel (Eusebius, *H.E.* 3.39.15) is (at most) historically valid or (at least) a justified, interpretive inference.[176] Second, modern scholarship must reverse its view that there was a dogmatically determined narrowing in the early church's understanding of discipleship to Jesus; on the contrary, the restriction of discipleship to the twelve originated with the historical Jesus, and the historical and theological conception of the early church (at least in its Markan and Matthean expressions) remained consistent with Jesus' original understanding.[177]

By way of critical assessment, we might respond to Meye's exegetical results by posing three broad questions. First, *is his exegesis of Mark cogent?* Much in his analysis is satisfying: the 'parabolic' character of Jesus' life and ministry, as portrayed in the Second Gospel; the ambiguity in the presen-

---

171. Ibid., pp. 223-24.

172. Ibid., p. 224. Cf. 'Messianic Didache', p. 66: 'Thus, the Twelve, even when depicted in negative fashion, become bearers of hope to the Marcan community'.

173. *Jesus*, pp. 23, 209.

174. Ibid., pp. 136, 154-55, 185. Meye further suggests (pp. 116-17) that Simon Peter's primacy in the Gospel mirrors Mark's stress on the primacy of the disciples as a group.

175. *Jesus*, pp. 190, 217. On the apostolic and incipiently institutional character of the twelve, see ibid., pp. 189, 203; on the equation of 'twelveship' and discipleship, see 'Those About Him', pp. 214, 217; 'Messianic Didache', pp. 63-66; *Jesus*, pp. 115-16, 172, 186, 188, 210; cf. ibid., pp. 145, 147, 153.

176. *Jesus*, pp. 225-27.

177. Ibid., pp. 228-30.

tation of the disciples, which argues against any single-minded (and historically improbable) vendetta perpetrated against the twelve by the Markan community; the 'didactic' use to which Mark apparently puts the disciples' weakness (as a foil for the Evangelist's Christology; as a means of inspiring hope in a beleaguered church). Perhaps none of these would qualify as 'assured results in Markan interpretation', precluding the need for further research, refinement, or restatement; still, such exegetical conclusions seem to square with the whole of Mark's Gospel.[178] Nevertheless, there are demonstrable weaknesses in Meye's interpretation. (a) In spite of the recurrent descriptions of Jesus as teaching (1.21; 2.13; 4.1-2; 6.2; 10.1; et al.) and the frequent references to Jesus as a teacher (e.g., 9.38; 12.14, 19, 32), there is surprisingly little content of Jesus' teaching in the Second Gospel. Unless we assume that Mark had access to teaching material no more comprehensive than that now reproduced in his Gospel, Meye's presentation of Mark as displaying a *thoroughgoing* emphasis upon Jesus' teaching should be chastened. (b) It also could be argued that Meye has blunted the keen edge of Mark's own treatment of the disciples. To state (as does Meye) that the disciples remained with Jesus to the end,[179] that they were ultimately made to understand everything,[180] and that their function in Mark's narrative is to bear witness to the person and deed of Jesus[181] is to move beyond the evidence of the Gospel[182] and to defuse a considerable degree of

178. Many of Meye's insights have been validated by successive interpreters: cf. J. R. Donahue, 'Jesus as the Parable of God in the Gospel of Mark', *Int* 32 (1979), pp. 369-88; and R. C. Tannehill, 'The Disciples in Mark: The Function of a Narrative Role', *JR* 57 (1977), pp. 386-405.

179. *Jesus*, p. 123; contrast Mark 14.50, 66-72.

180. *Jesus*, p. 44; contrast Mark 4.11, 34. Mark 4.11 says that the secret of the kingdom of God has been given to the disciples; it does not say that the disciples accepted that gift, nor does the remainder of Mark's Gospel suggest that the twelve boast greater perspicacity into the mystery that Jesus presents. Similarly, Mark 4.34 says only that Jesus privately explained everything to his disciples; there is no indication that the disciples *understood* or *accepted* such explanations (indeed, contrast 6.52; 8.14-21, 32-33; 9.32). Elsewhere (*Jesus*, p. 134) Meye states that the disciples decisively differed from the crowds in the former's consistent guarding of the messianic secret; however, it is a fine question whether one may guard something that he has never fully received to start with.

181. 'Messianic Didache', p. 66; contrast Mark 8.32b-33; 9.18, 34, 38; 10.13, 35-37; 14.66-72.

182. Meye has made a reasonable case for Mark's limitation of discipleship to the twelve ('Those About Him', pp. 211-18; *Jesus*, pp. 88-136 et passim). However, at least two points might be raised in rebuttal. (1) A number of passages seem to challenge this exegesis (among them, Mark 2.18-22; 4.10-11; 9.38; 10.32) and, while Meye responsibly deals with each (*Jesus*, pp. 137-72), he himself admits that his arguments may not satisfy at every point (ibid., pp.

the ambiguity inherent in the Markan presentation of the twelve.[183] Wherever possible, critical exegesis should strive to clarify; however, no service is rendered by the exegetical attempt to dispel ambiguity or obscurity when either is an ingredient of the text.

A second question that may be raised concerns *the extent to which Meye's exegesis is genuinely dependent on the redaction-critical method.* In viewing his work from the standpoint of method, we observed that much of Meye's approach resembles a kind of broader, literary criticism. The same result emerges when we survey his exegetical results and ask how they were arrived at: thus Meye repeatedly attributes to Mark a variety of concepts or themes — Jesus' persistent and private teaching of the twelve, the disciples as possessing unique authority, 'being with Jesus' and preaching as the dominant activities of the twelve, Peter's primacy as reflective of the primary position of the disciples at large — without ever justifying their ascription to *Mark,* rather than to the tradition upon which the Evangelist was presumably dependent. Likewise, to my knowledge, Meye never deduces one of his more critical conclusions — that discipleship in the Second Gospel is limited to the twelve — by separating Mark's point of view from that of the Evangelist's materials; on the contrary, Meye's rationale for this exegesis is patent: 'If one uses "what Mark clearly and repeatedly has to say" as a canon of interpretation, then the balance is in favor of limiting Markan discipleship to the Twelve'.[184] Without question, this is a sound canon of interpretation; it is *not* distinctively redaction-critical, as the method is typically understood.

Third and finally, one must enquire *to what extent Meye's presuppositions about, and general perspective on, the Gospel of Mark have slanted or controlled his exegetical results.* 'To a great extent indeed' would seem to be the answer. As we have observed, Meye begins with the assumption that Jesus' teaching and his identification as a teacher were important for the primitive church; he ends with the exegetical judgment that Mark empha-

---

171-72). (2) Can discipleship really be so restricted to the twelve in a Gospel wherein Jesus makes the extraordinarily open-ended claim, 'For he that is not against us is for us; for whoever gives you a cup of water to drink because you bear the name of Christ will by no means lose his reward' (Mark 9.40-41, a text never discussed by Meye)? In the end it seems that (at best) Meye may have attempted to clarify a conception that Mark cares little to make clear; (at worst) he may have imposed a rigid consistency upon Mark's understanding of discipleship that the Evangelist is uninterested in maintaining.

183. An ambiguity whose existence is conceded by Meye (*Jesus,* pp. 181-82).

184. 'Those About Him', p. 215.

sizes the function of Jesus as the Teacher.[185] Meye starts with the presupposition that Jesus' disciples assumed a position of exceptional significance in the early church; he finishes by suggesting that the Markan community regarded the twelve as the dignified source, mediator, and guarantor of the proclamation of its Lord.[186] Meye commences with the view that Mark's Gospel was intended to generate hope within his community; Meye thereby concludes that the Gospel could not have functioned as a polemic against the twelve.[187] At no point have we witnessed an application by Meye of the redaction-critical method in a manner that controls, much less corrects, his interpretive presuppositions. In fact, another of Meye's assumptions seems to militate against the very practice of redaction criticism: by subscribing to a belief in the pervasive, historical continuity between Jesus and his disciples, the disciples and the earliest Christian tradition, and the tradition and Mark's community and Gospel, Meye is virtually forced to ignore many aspects of the redaction-critical method, which is predicated upon the possibility of discerning *dis*continuity and *dis*similarity. Ultimately, I believe that it is this unresolved tension between Meye's implicit assumptions and his ostensible method that gives rise to his predominantly holistic, literary-critical approach, to his intermittent confusion of theological and historical results, and — in spite of his assertions to the contrary — to his seeming dissatisfaction with the redaction-critical method in interpreting the Gospel of Mark.

In sum, there are genuine tensions and problems in Robert Meye's redaction-critical study of discipleship in Mark's Gospel. Are these tensions idiosyncratic to Meye's research, or are they indicative of a more fundamental problem, inherent in Markan *Redaktionsgeschichte*? In order to answer these questions, we now turn from Meye, and the 'conservative' type of exegetical perspective that he represents, to another interpreter: one who also explores Markan discipleship redaction-critically, yet does so on the basis of slightly different assumptions and with somewhat different exegetical results.

---

185. *Jesus*, pp. 17, 97; 'Messianic Didache', p. 58; cf. *Jesus*, p. 210.
186. *Jesus*, pp. 91, 197; 'Messianic Didache', pp. 60, 62, 66, 68; cf. *Jesus*, p. 211.
187. 'Messianic Didache', p. 65.

4. Type II: The 'Mediate' Position of Ernest Best

[The way of the cross] is the way that Jesus went, and it is the way that his disciples must go also. True, in the Gospel [of Mark], they cut a sorry figure. Yet, in the end, they will follow him. You will drink my cup, says Jesus. You will be handed over for my sake. You will *not* be ashamed of me.

Morna D. Hooker[1]

In considering both the role of the disciples in Mark and the role of *Redaktionsgeschichte* in Markan interpretation, few scholars have been as influential as Ernest Best, and none has been more prolific. Published over forty years ago, Best's first monograph on the Second Gospel was a groundbreaking exercise in Markan redaction criticism.[2] Although discipleship was considered only cursorily in that work, the topic was explored by Best in greater detail in a series of important redaction-critical articles that appeared in the 1970s.[3] The synthesis and culmination of that research was achieved in 1981, with the publication of Best's monograph, *Following Jesus: Discipleship in the Gospel of Mark*.[4] A remarkable consistency of inter-

---

1. Hooker, *Message*, pp. 117-18 (Hooker's emphasis).

2. *The Temptation and the Passion: The Markan Soteriology* (1965).

3. 'Discipleship in Mark: Mark 8.22–10.52' (1970); 'The Role of the Disciples in Mark' (1977); 'Peter in the Gospel According to Mark' (1978); 'Mark's Use of the Twelve' (1978). A considerable portion of Best's 'Mark: Some Problems' (*IBS* 1 [1979], pp. 77-98) is devoted to a redaction-critical consideration of the nature of Mark's authorship.

4. Even this sizeable monograph has not proved to be Best's last word on the subject: both redaction criticism and the disciples in Mark consume much of Best's attention in his

pretive perspective, method, and results has emerged from the scholarly contributions of Ernest Best. Those contributions merit our scrutiny in this chapter.

A. General Perspective

As we observed in Chapter 2, certain traditio-historical assumptions are held by Markan scholars who occupy the Type II, or 'mediate', position. Specifically, these interpreters tend to understand the relationship between the Evangelist and his traditions as characterized by tension: Mark was indebted to his traditional materials and thus was their servant; yet he exercised freedom and theological creativity in molding these materials and thus was their master. Both of these assumptions are given clear expression by Best in the following redaction-critical principle (which, though enunciated in 1965, he has never forsaken): 'In many ways Mark was thus bound by the tradition which came to him, but yet he remained a real author, not just a recorder of tradition'.[5]

To understand Best's approach, both elements in this double-pronged assertion must be taken seriously. On the one hand, 'Mark was bound by the tradition' (which came to the Evangelist in the form of discrete pericopes or larger complexes of related pericopes);[6] hence Best speaks of the Evangelist as being 'tied by the tradition', 'forced . . . by the tradition' to use uncharacteristic terminology, presented by the tradition with 'only a very limited number of possibilities' in arranging given traditional material.[7] This does not imply (for Best) that the Evangelist stands in an adversarial relationship with his tradition; 'on the contrary he had a real respect for the tradition',[8] a deference that may be detected when Mark leaves unaltered

---

Mark: The Gospel as Story (1983). *Disciples and Discipleship: Studies in the Gospel According to Mark* (Edinburgh: T. & T. Clark, 1986) is a collection of Best's essays, including most of those listed in the previous note.

5. *Temptation,* p. xi.

6. *Following Jesus,* p. 10; *Gospel as Story,* pp. 16-20.

7. Quotations excerpted from, respectively, *Following Jesus,* p. 19; 'Mark's Use', p. 29; *Following Jesus,* p. 194. Cf. also 'Mark's Use', p. 26.

8. *Following Jesus,* p. 140. Interestingly, the idea that Mark regarded the disciples as heretics (or as representative of heretics in his community) is rebuffed by Best on the grounds that 'Mark depends in the final issue on the reliability of the disciples in handing on the material he has used. . . . If he attacks those who transmitted [that material] he attacks the value of what he himself writes' (*Gospel as Story,* p. 48).

certain details that conflict with his own theological purposes.[9] Overall, then, '[Mark] is not wholly master of his material; as well as controlling it in the way he arranges and modifies it he is also controlled by it'.[10]

Though he may have been restrained by his traditions, Mark is, on the other hand, 'a real author'. Because the early church was not interested sheerly in the life and times of the historical Jesus, Mark 'used the historical material with a theological purpose in mind'.[11] This is not to suggest that Mark fabricated incidents or created whole pericopes; Mark's contribution, rather, was the reshaping and internal modification of those pericopes in order to fit them into his account and to draw certain points that he wished to make.[12] Indeed, according to Best, 'Before Mark went to work most of the [oral] material lacked within itself a principle by which it could be ordered'. Since only an individual can provide and work out such an organizational principle, 'Mark's great achievement was to take the material and to give it an order'.[13]

In Best's judgment, the modifications to which the Second Evangelist has subjected his traditions have been minimal: they may be relegated largely to Markan seams and summaries, in the writing of which 'he has been quite obviously creative'.[14] As will become evident in the next section of this chapter, Best also thinks that Markan editing of the tradition is discernible, and that the discernment of such editorial contributions can help the interpreter to identify 'a clear pattern' of Markan theology.[15] It is for

9. Such details include the demon's confession of Jesus as 'the holy one of God' (1.24), which Mark allows to stand in place of his preferred designation for Jesus, 'the Son of God'; the predictions of the resurrection 'after three days' (8.31; 9.31; 10.33-34) rather than 'on the third day', the normal liturgical phrase during Mark's period; and Jesus' promise to Peter, a fisherman, concerning those who have left family and *lands* (10.28-29). For discussion and additional examples, see Best, 'Some Problems', pp. 79-80; *Gospel as Story*, pp. 12-13.

10. *Following Jesus*, p. 208.

11. 'Some Problems', p. 84; *Following Jesus*, p. 10. Doubtless owing to this assumption, Best prefaces one of his earlier investigations of Markan discipleship with the following disclaimer: 'Indeed no attempt will be made to answer any of the questions about the historical relationship of Jesus to the actual disciples he had on earth; our concern lies with what Mark thinks a disciple ought to be' ('Discipleship', p. 323).

12. *Following Jesus*, pp. 10, 25; 'Some Problems', p. 80; *Gospel as Story*, p. 12.

13. Quotations, 'Some Problems', pp. 81, 82; cf. *Gospel as Story*, p. 6.

14. 'Mark's Preservation of the Tradition', *L'Évangile selon Marc* (ed. Sabbe), p. 33.

15. *Temptation*, p. 63; 'Role', p. 384. Mark's editorial embellishments are not as easily discerned, however, as the Matthean or Lukan redaction of Mark. In light of this, recently Best has suggested that, 'If we speak of what [Matthew and Luke] did as "redaction" then we ought, perhaps, to speak of Mark's work as "composition" and the way we deal with it as

this reason that Best's praise tends to be lavished on scholars who undertake the difficult task of ascertaining Markan redactional style, and his criticism is directed either to those who separate without precision Markan redaction from tradition or to those who attempt such separation not at all.[16] At stake with the redaction-critical method is nothing less than the proper exegesis of the Second Gospel: 'Without the control which [Markan style and vocabulary] supply it is possible to make Mark mean almost anything'.[17]

To sum up: For Best, Mark's editorial contribution is both ascertainable and exegetically indispensable in isolating the Evangelist's theology. The redactor stands in constructive tension with his inherited traditions: like an artist putting together a collage, Mark creates a new literary unity out of existing material; yet his creativity is not unbridled.[18]

> A better illustration [than that of the artist and his collage] may be that of a composer who brings together folk songs or sea shanties to make a new unity. Just as each of the original tunes is clearly recognisable but each has also been subtly changed to accommodate to it what precedes and follows so Mark created a new and exciting whole out of the material available to him in the tradition. He has conserved material, but it would be wrong to say that this was what he primarily set out to do. He has used the tradition, but used it creatively.[19]

So well balanced, carefully nuanced, and reasonable is Best's *redaktionsgeschichtlich* perspective that an extended critique seems out of order. At this stage in our discussion, we might question only the internal consistency of Best's point of view: in giving full consideration to the tensions that supposedly characterized the relationship between redactor and traditions, does there always emerge a coherent understanding of Mark's task as

---

"composition criticism" rather than "redaction criticism"' (*Gospel as Story*, p. 14; cf. Haenchen, *Der Weg Jesu*, p. 24).

16. See, for instance, his commendation (in *JSNT* 4 [1979], pp. 69-76) of E. J. Pryke's *Redactional Style in the Marcan Gospel: A Study of Syntax and Vocabulary as Guides to Redaction in Mark* (SNTSMS 33; Cambridge: Cambridge University Press, 1978). Contrast, in *Following Jesus*, his reproof of R. P. Meye (p. 92 n. 16), T. J. Weeden (pp. 59 n. 17, 237, 241), and 'some scholars' in general (p. 222 n. 16).

17. *Following Jesus*, p. 241.

18. 'Mark's Preservation', p. 33.

19. *Gospel as Story*, pp. 121-22.

Evangelist and of our task as redaction critics? For instance, it is conceivable that Mark could have been *both* theologically forthright in shaping his traditions in accordance with a Son-of-God Christology *and* so theologically inhibited by that tradition that he permitted the demon's confession of 'the holy one of God' to stand in 1.24 (cf. 3.11);[20] however, does Best's redaction-critical perspective enable us to understand *why* such a tension would have been, for the Evangelist, incapable of resolution? Is there not also an inconsistency in Best's suggestion (on the one hand) that Mark's editorial handiwork can and should be differentiated from the traditions at his disposal and (on the other hand) that such differentiation is sufficiently fraught with difficulty that our dealings with the Second Gospel perhaps should be less *redaktionsgeschichtlich* and more *kompositionskritisch*?[21] In other words, the more cautious Best is to reckon with the ambiguities pertaining to Mark and to Markan redaction criticism, the more equivocal his viewpoint sometimes appears.

B. Method

Although he had been producing important *redaktionsgeschichtlich* studies on the Gospel of Mark for over twenty years, Best's most detailed treatment of the redaction-critical method *per se* was not published until 1983, in *Mark: The Gospel as Story*.[22] Best prefaces his discussion with two observations, both of which are common to many such methodological studies: first, redaction criticism depends on the form critics' reconstruction of the form of the Gospel material in the pre-Markan stage; second, 'The [redaction-critical] method of study is inevitably circular but as the work has proceeded certain important procedures have appeared'.[23] Best groups these procedures into three categories: the identification of Markan seams and summaries, used by the Evangelist to connect discrete pericopes to each other and characterized by favorite Markan words, idioms, and

20. Ibid., p. 12.

21. Ibid., p. 14; see above, note 15.

22. Ibid., pp. 9-15. To say that this treatment represents Best's most comprehensive methodological statement to date is not to suggest that heretofore he has ignored all methodological discussion. In 'Mark's Preservation', Best proposes several possible indicators of the content of pre-Markan tradition; in *Temptation*, he devotes entire chapters to the seams, selection, and order of material in the Markan passion narrative.

23. *Gospel as Story*, p. 10.

themes; the isolation of Mark's brief, explanatory insertions; and a sensitivity to the order in which Mark has grouped his material.[24] Owing to our uncertainty about the fund of traditions at his disposal, speculations about the reasons for Mark's inclusion and (putative) omission of material are of little help to the interpreter, and 'There is no indication that [Mark] ever invented individual incidents'.[25]

It is interesting to notice how closely Best's criteria correspond to Stein's 'proper methodology for ascertaining a Markan redaction history': seams (criterion 1, considered immediately below), summaries (criterion 3, p. 114 below), vocabulary and style (criterion 11, pp. 124-31 below), themes (my extension of Stein's criterion of arrangement, pp. 117-23 below), insertions (criterion 2, pp. 113-14 below), and arrangement of material (criterion 8, pp. 117-23 below). Three more of Stein's criteria are mentioned by Best, albeit with reservations about their usefulness: Mark's inclusion of material (criterion 6, pp. 116-17 below), omission of material (criterion 7, p. 117 below), and invention of material (criterion 4, p. 114 below).

Best's specification of redaction-critical criteria is important, not only for its correlation with Stein's analysis, but also for what it says about Best's assumptions in the process of his own interpretation. As a rule, he does not systematically lay out his *redaktionsgeschichtlich* method; even in his recent monograph on Markan discipleship, which is a model of exegesis based on a redaction-critical rationale, the precise aspects of Best's method usually must be deduced by the reader. With the aid of Stein's twelve canons of redaction criticism, this is precisely the task that must now be performed.

1. At least in theory, *Markan seams* play a substantial role for Best in obtaining a redaction history of that Gospel: 'The most obvious place to look for Mark's hand is in the words, phrases, sentences which join together the various incidents of the Gospel'.[26] Nevertheless, the investigation of such seams does not figure significantly in Best's study of discipleship in Mark, even though their demonstrable existence is sometimes presupposed in his discussion.[27] A good example of how seams are handled by Best occurs in his discussion of Mark 10.1-12: verse 1 is assumed to be a Markan seam on the basis of its distinctive vocabulary, its verbal iden-

24. Ibid., pp. 10-11, 14.
25. Ibid., pp. 12, 14.
26. *Temptation,* p. 63. Cf. *Gospel as Story,* p. 10: 'the first place to look [for Mark's handiwork] is at the connecting seams by which Mark joins one pericope to another'.
27. See e.g. *Following Jesus,* pp. 28, 49 n. 54, 102 nn. 7, 10, 190, 212 n. 4, 230, 231-32.

tity with another putative seam (7.24a), and its characteristically Markan style and theme.[28] Save for the second, each of these criteria will be examined later in this chapter; for now we need note only that Best presupposes the existence of redactional seams in Mark's Gospel but does not require that they bear the brunt of his exegetical conclusions.[29] Moreover, the consideration of seams is usually introduced to support Best's establishment of a Markan vocabulary and grammar; the analysis almost never moves in the opposite direction.

2. As with seams, so with *Markan insertions:* Best explicitly accords *Zwischenbemerkungen* exegetical significance in theory, though in practice they play a role of subordinate importance (at least in his studies of Markan discipleship).[30] However, where they do appear in his discussion, 'insertions' raise important questions for Best's procedure and exegetical results. For instance, in an article published in 1977, Best (without explanation) classified Mark 6.7-13 as pre-Markan tradition;[31] a year later 6.7 was reasssigned (on the basis of vocabulary and style) to Markan redaction that is 'almost certainly' dependent upon pre-Markan tradition in 3.13-15.[32] While no one would forbid Best the right to change his mind, a sliding scale of criteria for the evaluation of conjectural entities seems to be in use. The potential significance of this methodological laxity becomes apparent in Best's exegesis of a verse like Mark 16.7, which he construes as an insertion stressing the high esteem in which Peter is held by the Evangelist. Despite his awareness that other scholars regard the verse as an original part of the tradition reflected at 16.1-8[33] or consider only the reference to Peter

28. Ibid., p. 100. Notice that these criteria for identifying seams comport with those suggested by Stein, '"Redaktionsgeschichtlich" Investigation'. Elsewhere, Best's definition of seams is not as easy to follow: see, for example, 'Mark's Use', pp. 25-26, on Mark 11.11.

29. Sometimes Best expresses confidence in recognizing, not only Markan editing, but also the pre-Markan material being edited: 'Mark . . . often incorporates existing [pre-Markan] introductions to pericopae' (*Following Jesus*, p. 125; cf. pp. 139, 141, 180).

30. *Temptation*, p. ix: '[To single out the Markan contribution,] we also examine the explanatory additions Mark may have made within incidents in order to align them with his main purpose'; cf. also *Gospel as Story*, p. 11. Nevertheless, in *Following Jesus* I counted only four allusions to insertions (at pp. 150, 175, 183, 210), though it is possible that I missed others. Elsewhere ('Some Problems', p. 92) Best states that the final clause in Mark 14.72 'is almost certainly due to Mark'.

31. 'Role of the Disciples', p. 385 (Table 1).

32. 'Mark's Use', p. 15.

33. Thus R. Pesch, 'Der Schluss der vormarkinischen Passionsgeschichte und des Markusevangeliums: Mk 15.42–16.8', in *L' Évangile selon Marc* (ed. Sabbe), pp. 365-409.

in v. 7 as Markan,[34] the only reason offered by Best for his consignment of 16.7 to the redactor is the received opinion of scholars.[35] In fine, Markan insertions do not loom large in Best's redaction-critical work on the disciples, but at times they are asked to display a redactional pattern more consistent than would be expected of an entity so chameleon-like.

3. 'Of course [Mark] created the *summaries*', Best declares; thus *Sammelberichte* (such as Mark 3.7-12) or passages akin to those summaries (like Mark 2.13) are more or less assumed by Best to have originated with the redactor.[36] Such assessments in fact play a minimal role in Best's investigations of Markan discipleship. However, the identification of redactional summaries is indirectly important for Best, since (as he thinks) the *Sammelberichte* display various features of Markan vocabulary and style, which may then be discerned in Markan passages germane to the disciples.[37] Beyond this circularity of reasoning, which will become especially evident in our consideration of Markan vocabulary, a shadow of doubt is cast over this 'contribution' of *Sammelberichte* since, as Best himself observes, Mark may use terminology *uncharacteristic* of his redactional vocabulary in such summary statements.[38] The inconsistency is patent: Markan summaries are considered valuable to the redaction critic because they provide clues to the Evangelist's distinctive vocabulary; yet, it is granted, they harbor atypical words that Mark has accepted from his tradition.

4. Already we have noted that, in Best's view, Mark is a conservative redactor: 'there is no real evidence in the Gospel that Mark either composed extensive sections, other than summaries, or created actual incidents'.[39] Consistently adhering to this dictum, Best therefore rejects the redactional criterion of *the Markan creation of pericopes*.

5. Although inclined to give 'great value' to *the Markan modification of the material* as a redactional canon, Stein recognized its fundamental weakness: it depends upon prior determination of that pre-Markan material in order to establish the redaction.[40] Of the three subdivisions of Stein's criterion, Best invests no confidence in 'inconsistencies between Mark's account and what actually happened': like Stein, Best understands

---

34. So Dormeyer, *Die Passion Jesu als Verhaltensmodell*, pp. 224-26.

35. 'Peter', pp. 555-56; see esp. p. 555 n. 49; cf. *Gospel as Story*, p. 44.

36. *Following Jesus*, p. 14 n. 6 (italics mine); cf. pp. 175, 230.

37. Ibid.; cf. *Gospel as Story*, pp. 10-11.

38. Thus *Following Jesus*, p. 197 n. 19 (on δαίμων).

39. Ibid., p. 78; see also pp. 66, 146, and *Gospel as Story*, p. 12.

40. Stein, 'Markan Redaction History', pp. 186, 198.

that the demonstration of historical inconsistency does not amount to proof of the Evangelist's modification of the tradition.[41] In Stein's second subdivision, 'the investigation of "misformed" pericopes', Best seems to express some methodological interest by his occasional reference to grammatical 'clumsiness' as an indicator of Markan redaction;[42] on the other hand, the value of this canon seems impugned by the equal number of instances in which Best either attributes such clumsiness to Markan tradition or calls into question the very standard of 'clumsiness' when applied without proper discrimination to non-classical (Hellenistic) Greek.[43] Somewhat more extensively employed by Best is Stein's first canon of modification, 'the comparison of Mark with Matthew and Luke'. In comparing the Second Gospel with the other Synoptics, Best is more persuasive when he argues that an agreement between Matthew and Luke against Mark in the form of a logion (for example, Mark 8.34b) probably points to a different form of the tradition than that attested in Mark, or when he states that the changes of the Markan account by the other Synoptists bear witness to a Matthean and Lukan redaction history.[44] Best is least convincing when he suggests that the absence in Matthew and Luke of certain words or verses present in Mark betokens a Markan emphasis:[45] this is nothing more than an *argumentum e silentio* that begs the question. However, for all its weakness, this is precisely the sort of argument needed to make the case for a *Markan* redaction history: which is to say that, if one assumes the Markan hypothesis (as Best does), the comparison of Mark with the other Synoptics yields the most persuasive results for a redaction history of Matthew and Luke, *but not of Mark.*

Some of Best's observations on the Markan modification of traditional material do not correspond to any of Stein's major subdivisions of that criterion; as described by Best, they are modifications by way of insertion. For example, Best argues that Mark has consistently rendered Peter's traditional weaknesses less glaring (a) by widening the scope of the disciple's fear at the transfiguration through introducing into the account James and John

41. *Following Jesus*, p. 172 n. 1; cf. Stein, 'Markan Redaction History', p. 189.

42. *Following Jesus*, pp. 63, 114, 155, 178 n. 2. In 'Mark's Use', p. 24, Best refers to the Evangelist's 'neat balancing' of parallel participles in 10.32. This raises an interesting question: can the same author be so 'neat' as well as so 'clumsy'?

43. *Following Jesus*, pp. 62, 81, 141, 152.

44. Ibid., pp. 34-35, 45-46 n. 4, 76, 115 n. 2.

45. Ibid., pp. 40, 56, 114; cf. pp. 144 n. 7, 188 n. 22. Note Best's own awareness of the indeterminacy of such results: ibid., p. 221 n. 5.

(Mark 9.6) and (b) by (possibly) creating the reference to Peter's weeping after his denials of Christ (14.72c).[46] Substantiation for the latter is so tenuous[47] that Best ultimately backs down from it, suggesting instead that Mark 14.72c was present in the tradition but stressed by the Evangelist as the final item of importance.[48] Support for Best's claim for a Markan insertion at 9.6 rests on nothing firmer than the unsubstantiated possibility that James and John did not originally appear with Peter in 9.2.[49]

To summarize: Best's weakest arguments for Mark's modification of traditional material arise when he possesses no standard for the shape of that tradition other than what he preconceives it to be. His strongest arguments emerge when he has clearly defined any publicly accessible material against which Mark can be compared, such as Matthew and Luke. Unfortunately, those strongest arguments do not address the redaction history of the very Synoptist whose theology Best is at pains to discern.

6. To judge from some of his comments, one might have anticipated that *the Markan selection, or inclusion, of material* would assume an important role in Best's reconstruction of the Gospel's redaction history: 'Most of the statements however came to Mark in the [traditional] material and his inclusion of them is at least secondary evidence for his own point of view; if they had definitely cut across it he would either not have included them or would have modified them. . . . [Thus] we may still ask why he has included the material that he has'.[50] In fact, this *redaktionsgeschichtlich* criterion is of minor importance in Best's investigation and is employed chiefly, if not exclusively, in his rebuttal of the exegetical positions of others: thus (*contra* T. J. Weeden) Mark can scarcely be attacking a false Christology that is preoccupied with mighty works if the miracles occupy more than a quarter of his gospel;[51] thus Peter can hardly be the object of Mark's special disap-

46. 'Peter', pp. 550, 554; 'Some Problems', p. 92.

47. 'As we have seen [Mark] regularly adds a brief but important independent clause at the end of pericopes' ('Peter', p. 554; cf. p. 553 n. 39). See also *Following Jesus*, pp. 44, 221-22 n. 12.

48. Best's interpretation is plausible, but his argument is invalid: it presupposes an exegetical conclusion in order to support a redactional analysis which leads to that conclusion.

49. 'Peter', p. 550, on which basis he then renders an analogous judgment concerning the presence of James and John in Gethsemane (Mark 14.33, 38; 'Peter', pp. 550-51). Equally fragile is Best's claim that Peter was introduced at 10.29-30 by the Evangelist, because the reference is 'inappropriate . . . to Peter who left his nets and not his fields' ('Peter', p. 554; cf. 'Some Problems', p. 80; *Gospel as Story*, p. 12).

50. *Temptation*, pp. 134, 103.

51. *Following Jesus*, p. 241.

proval if his name already appeared in the traditional story of the denial.[52] Best himself offers one reason why so little heed is paid to the criterion of inclusion: since we cannot know the total extent of the tradition available to the Evangelist, to appeal to Mark's selection is to attempt the measurement of the unknown by the uncertain.[53] There may be at least two other reasons for the virtual absence of this canon in Best's research: first, a principle of 'selection', with its implied power of choice, does not comport well with presumption of a tradition that exerts certain 'forces' on the Evangelist; second, Best's customary procedure is oriented to distinguishing that which is characteristically Markan for the tradition he has used — and that is precisely what this criterion cannot afford the investigator.[54]

7. For similar reasons, *the Markan omission of material* is all but discarded as a guide to the Evangelist's redaction:

> If we knew that Mark had a great amount of material about the teaching of Jesus, say a 'copy' of Q and only three exorcism accounts, and chose to omit most of the teaching and put in all three exorcisms, this would obviously lead us to conclude that for him exorcisms were most important. Equally had he at his disposal only the teaching of Jesus which he has inserted and a hundred exorcism stories from which he selected the present three then we would come to quite a different conclusion about the importance of the exorcisms for Mark. Unfortunately we are not in a position to draw either conclusion.[55]

Consequently, Best employs the criterion of omission rarely, carefully, and usually to address issues of less than momentous import.[56]

8. On the other hand, Best considers *the Markan arrangement of the material* a useful indicator of the Evangelist's theological emphases.

52. 'Peter', p. 552. However, this sort of argument cuts both ways: if the tradition behind Mark 16.7 had already singled out Peter for restoration (an assumption rejected by Best), could one then say that Peter was the object of Mark's special approval (thus Best, ibid., p. 556)?

53. *Following Jesus*, pp. 141-42, 197 n. 29; *Gospel as Story*, p. 14.

54. Stein ('Markan Redaction History', p. 190) issues a further caution: 'It must be admitted from the start that Mark need not have chosen every pericope in his gospel because it contained his particular theology or point of view. He may have included some simply because they were well known'.

55. *Temptation*, p. 103. Cf. *Gospel as Story*, p. 14.

56. See *Following Jesus*, p. 188 n. 27 (on '[the] twelve' in Mark 3.13-19); 'Peter', p. 552 (on the possible omission of 'Christ' in 14.71).

a. *The arrangement of individual pericopes* is noteworthy.[57] Thus the seemingly premature call of the disciples (Mark 1.16-20) has been carefully placed by the Evangelist into his narrative in order to emphasize Jesus' compelling nature and the disciples' total commitment; the complex consisting of 3.7-12, 3.13-19, and 3.20-35 was also constructed by Mark (for reasons unspecified by Best); and instruction on the proper understanding of discipleship controls the cyclical sequence of Christological disclosure (via the passion predictions or the transfiguration) alternating with the incomprehension of the disciples (8.27–10.46).[58]

b. Attention is also paid to Markan 'sandwiches', *the placing of one pericope inside another* in order that they might interpret each other. Some of Best's examples of this phenomenon are persuasive: the linkage of 3.20-21 and 3.31-35, suggesting Jesus' alienation from his family (cf. the explicit hostility in 3.22-30); the framing of 8.31–9.1 by 8.27-30 and 9.2-8, as a signifier of suffering at the heart of Markan Christology; the two healings of the blind (8.22-26; 10.46-52) as a commentary on the stages of the disciples' own blindness (8.27–10.45); the intertwining theme of judgment in 11.12-14/20-21 and 11.15-19; and the intercalated trials and testimonies of Jesus and Peter at the high priest's house (14.53-72).[59] Other proposed interpolations seem more tendentious: the insertion of the Baptist's death (6.14-29) between the dispatch and return of the twelve (6.7-13, 30) in order that Jesus might not be depicted as acting apart from the disciples during their absence;[60] the bracketing of 14.3-9 with 14.1-2 and 14.10-11.[61]

c. Following the lead of Lohmeyer and Lightfoot, Best is convinced that *the geographical scheme of Mark* has been arranged in accordance with

57. 'Mark's great achievement was to take the material and to give it an order' (Best, 'Some Problems', p. 82).

58. *Following Jesus*, pp. 169, 189 n. 35; cf. pp. 68, 77, 123; *Temptation*, pp. 92, 121-25; 'Discipleship', passim. Likewise, Best interprets the widow's generosity in the face of the temple's impending destruction (Mark 12.41-44; cf. 13.22) as appropriate behavior in an apocalyptic situation, an interpretation suggested (he argues) by Mark's arrangement of pericopes (*Following Jesus*, pp. 155-56).

59. E. Best, 'Mark III.20, 21, 31-35', *NTS* 22 (1975/1976), pp. 309-19; *Following Jesus*, pp. 64, 134-35, 216; 'Mark's Use', pp. 25-26; 'Peter', p. 552.

60. *Following Jesus*, p. 192. If Best's explanation is correct, why would Mark have thought such an insertion necessary? Why did he not resort to the expedient of making a narrative jump in time from the dispatch to the return of the twelve?

61. 'Mark's Use', p. 27. Except perhaps for the allusions to Jesus' death, what reciprocal interpretation could Mark have had in mind here?

the Evangelist's theology. Hence Best speaks of the Second Evangelist as creating 'the artificial geography of the journey to Jerusalem', with (for example) the reference to Capernaum in 9.33 as introduced by the Evangelist for no reason other than 'to increase the verisimilitude of a journey'.[62] Likewise, Best assumes that 'the use of Galilee is largely redactional in Mark's Gospel' and that 'Galilee has theological significance for Mark'[63]:

> Galilee is not just a place. . . . In the gospel there is a sharp division between Galilee and Jerusalem; the former is the place of mission; the latter is the place of death. Once [the disciples] are through death they are sent back on the mission with Jesus at the head.[64]

For Best, it is logical that 'Galilee' should be associated with the post-Easter Gentile mission: 'Galilee, where the commission is given, is Galilee of the Gentiles', which squares with 'the emphasis Mark lays on the gospel as a gospel for Gentiles'.[65]

Best's heavy redaction-critical reliance on Mark's arrangement of the tradition raises for us a number of issues, necessitating a somewhat longer critique. First, with respect to the subcriterion of 'the arrangement of individual pericopes', one might challenge Best's assumption that it is in fact *the Evangelist* who has executed the arrangement: aside from conventional form-critical suppositions, is it not possible that much of the tradition circulated in prearranged form and was reproduced by Mark undisturbed? Best himself concedes such a possibility: thus the patterning of Jesus' repeated return to the sleeping disciples in Gethsemane (Mark 14.32-42) may be attributed to the penchant for 'threefold schemas' exhibited either by the Evangelist or in the folk-literature that he inherited.[66] Moreover, if the lengthy complex of material in 9.33-50 came to Mark as a traditional unit — as Best believes — can we be certain that other such complexes in the Gospel did not come to Mark prearranged?[67]

---

62. *Following Jesus*, p. 76; cf. pp. 73-76, 100, 120, 135; 'Mark's Use', p. 19.

63. *Following Jesus*, pp. 200, 167; cf. *Temptation*, pp. 174-77.

64. 'Discipleship', p. 336; cf. *Gospel as Story*, p. 92.

65. *Following Jesus*, pp. 171, 218.

66. Ibid., pp. 148, 150, 158 n. 26; cf. p. 85.

67. Ibid., p. 75. Of course, my criticism might be inverted: how cogent are Best's criteria for identifying pre-Markan tradition? For instance, could not one argue that certain 'catchwords', attributed by Best to pre-Markan tradition (ibid., pp. 81, 90-91 n. 2, 130 n. 6), originated in the Markan redaction (thus Kuhn, *Ältere Sammlungen*, p. 34)? Except perhaps for

Second, save for some of his less plausible suggestions, noted above, Best has presented a strong case for 'interlaminations' of pericopes as being the handiwork of the Evangelist and indicative of his theological concerns — *if* the original character of the tradition precluded such intercalation at a pre-Markan stage, and *if* in every case the common themes permeating the 'sandwiched' traditions are uniquely reflective of Mark's theology. The latter qualification I shall address momentarily. Regarding the former, we should bear in mind that the originally disconnected character of the Gospel tradition, its transmission in discrete pericopes, is a *hypothesis* of form and redaction criticism, not a demonstrated fact. While Mark may have been responsible for intermingling pericopes, conceivably these intercalations could have been formed before the Evangelist received the tradition. If this seems to run roughshod over conventional form-critical sensibilities, one might recall Paul Achtemeier's thesis involving double pre-Markan catenae identical in their arrangement of a sea miracle, three healing miracles, and a feeding miracle.[68] If pre-Markan tradition could have attained this level of complexity and sophistication, then why could it not have been intercalated as well? Whether or not we accept Achtemeier's theory is beside the point; in any case, Best accepts it. Why, then, would he doubt the existence of possible pre-Markan intercalations — a far less complicated form-critical hypothesis?

Third, 'the geographical scheme of Mark' as an indicator of the Evangelist's theological concerns is perhaps the least convincing of the sub-canons of Markan arrangement. Given our ignorance of the details and arrangement of traditions available to the redactor, Best's claim for the Markan creation of an 'artificial geography of the journey to Jerusalem' is unverifiable and implausible: we need not accept C. H. Dodd's thesis of a predetermined framework for the Gospel narrative to suppose that certain geographical references were furnished by the tradition rather than created by Mark in the interest of 'verisimilitude'.[69] Furthermore, the association

---

vv. 42 and 45, is the presence of 'Semitic interference' in Mark 9.33-50 incontestable (see E. C. Maloney, *Semitic Interference in Marcan Syntax* [SBLDS 51; Missoula, MT: Scholars, 1981], pp. 246-52)?

68. Achtemeier, 'Toward the Isolation'; 'Origin and Function'. Cf. Best, 'Mark's Use', p. 31; *Following Jesus*, p. 233 n. 4. Aspects of Achtemeier's proposal are challenged by R. M. Fowler, *Loaves and Fishes: The Function of the Feeding Stories in the Gospel of Mark* [SBLDS 54; Chico, CA: Scholars, 1981]).

69. Best himself grants this point with respect to Jericho and Gethsemane (*Following Jesus*, pp. 139, 147). For Dodd's proposal, see idem, 'Framework'; for its most extensive rebut-

of 'Galilee' and 'Jerusalem' with, respectively, 'mission' and 'death' is somewhat pat and insufficiently nuanced: as T. A. Burkill observed years ago, Galilee in the Second Gospel is in some measure the scene of hostility (Mark 2.1–3.6; 3.20-35; 6.1-6; 7.1-23), and Jerusalem is to some extent the arena of Jesus' favorable reception (cf. Mark 11.18; 12.12, 37; 14.2).[70]

With 'Galilee', however, another dimension of Best's procedure comes into focus: the use of *themes* to adduce redactional tendencies. Indeed, as we may observe from the following selective list, the delineation of distinctively Markan motifs is one of Best's favorite methods for obtaining a redaction history of the Second Gospel.

Christology: Jesus as
> The teacher (despite a paucity of actual teaching),[71]
> The one who can save,[72]
> Wishing to escape attention,[73]
> Enjoining silence,[74]
> The Risen One, present in the community,[75]
> Qualitatively different from the disciples (no *imitatio Christi*);[76]

Discipleship: The disciples as
> Isolated from the crowd, often for special instruction,[77]
> Amazed,[78]

---

tal, see D. E. Nineham, 'The Order of Events in St. Mark's Gospel — An Examination of Dr. Dodd's Hypothesis', in *Studies in the Gospels: Essays in Memory of R. H. Lightfoot* (ed. D. E. Nineham; London: Basil Blackwell, 1955), pp. 223-39.

70. Burkill, *Mysterious Revelation*, pp. 252-57. It is curious that Best should cite with approval Günter Stemberger's research on the theological significance of Galilee, since the thrust of Stemberger's essay contravenes Best's orientation ('Galilee — Land of Salvation?', in Davies, *The Gospel and the Land*, pp. 409-38; N.B. p. 434: 'There is no proof of a thoroughgoing Galilean redaction in Mark'). In fairness, it should be said that Best disavows certainty about 'the precise geographical meaning and extent of Galilee for Mark' (*Following Jesus*, p. 203 n. 11).

71. *Following Jesus*, pp. 100, 175, 211, 217.

72. Ibid., p. 145 n. 31; cf. *Gospel as Story*, pp. 55-65.

73. *Following Jesus*, pp. 73, 74 n. 4.

74. Ibid., pp. 62, 140; 'Discipleship', p. 328.

75. *Following Jesus*, pp. 232, 237-42.

76. Ibid., pp. 58, 80, 108; 'Discipleship', pp. 334-35.

77. *Following Jesus*, pp. 56, 68, 70 n. 14, 73, 75, 100, 101, 232, 235.

78. Ibid., pp. 120, 217 (cf. p. 71 n. 27 [referring to the crowd]).

Fearful,[79]

Silent (often followed by discussions among themselves),[80]

Ignorant,[81]

Failing to understand, if not to act,[82]

Epitomized by Peter, in whom a special interest is shown,[83]

Epitomized by 'the three' (with James and John included to remove the exclusive stigma from upon Peter);[84]

Miscellaneous:

Retiring to 'a house' (the locus for special instruction);[85]

'A ship' (the locus for separation of Jesus and the disciples from the crowd);[86]

'The sea';[87]

'The mountain';[88]

The importance of 'hearing';[89]

'The demons' or (more frequently) 'unclean spirits';[90]

Judgment on old Israel.[91]

Best has rendered genuine service in alerting us to these and other themes in Mark. However, while these motifs are clearly characteristic of Markan theology, *they are not necessarily indicative of Markan redaction,* inasmuch as any or all of them could be congruent with the theology of the traditions used by Mark. Indeed, Best acknowledges that some of the above — the command to silence, the disciples' ignorance, 'the mountain', 'the house', and 'the ship' — appeared in the pre-Markan material.[92] It is likely, *a fortiori,* that others did as well. How, then, may we determine whether a

---

79. Ibid., pp. 56, 73, 120, 219; 'Peter', p. 550.

80. *Following Jesus,* p. 76.

81. Ibid., pp. 56, 73, 134, 148.

82. Ibid., pp. 57, 62, 66, 67, 73, 150-51, 232.

83. Ibid., pp. 112, 113, 148; 'Peter', passim.

84. *Following Jesus,* pp. 147, 150, 152; 'Peter', passim.

85. *Following Jesus,* pp. 66, 75, 100, 175, 226-27.

86. Ibid., p. 230.

87. Ibid., p. 175.

88. Ibid., p. 100.

89. Ibid., p. 56.

90. Ibid., pp. 182, 191, 186 n. 13.

91. Ibid., p. 219.

92. Respectively, pp. 140, 131 n. 11, 180, 126, and 230 of *Following Jesus.*

given theme is traditional or redactional? For Best, there seem to be two major (if not always explicit) criteria: its frequency of appearance and its conjunction with other Markan redactional features. More will be said of the former in our consideration of Markan vocabulary; suffice it to say that 'frequency of appearance' is a plausible criterion but not without problems. With regard to the latter criterion, the 'conjoined redactional feature' that is sometimes pressed in defending a theme as redactional is 'distinctively Markan arrangement'.[93] But in so arguing, Best completes a perfect circuit around the hermeneutical circle: the redactor's arrangement is fixed by identifying the controlling themes, which themselves have been determined redactional through analysis of the arrangement.

Before we leave this topic, let me be clear: I am not rejecting the existence of either particular themes or certain patterns of material arrangement in Mark. The issue here is whether in every case these themes or patterns signify *Markan redaction,* as Best seems to think. If Stein has cautioned us that a theological purpose need not lie at the root of every Markan arrangement, I would add the caveat that every theological tendency in the Gospel need not have originated with the redactor.[94]

9. In Best's work on the disciples, *the Markan introduction* plays only a minimal role. This disregard is a function of the particular topic being considered: discipleship as such does not clearly enter the picture until Mark 1.16-20, about which Best naturally has more to say.[95] In the main, the introduction of Mark serves to orient him to the Evangelist's general understanding of a 'gospel' (a historical narrative, rather than a sermon or series of kerygmatic statements), and to alert him to certain Markan devices that will become plainer, by comparison or contrast, elsewhere in the narrative.[96]

10. Notwithstanding scholarly dispute over the ending of the Second Gospel at 16.8, *the Markan conclusion* takes on redaction-critical importance in Best's research. This is owing, in large measure, to his exegesis of 16.7: a new responsibility — the Galilean (= Gentile) mission — has been given by the risen Lord to his disciples, who represent the entire church.

---

93. For example, see ibid., p. 68.

94. Cf. Stein, 'Markan Redaction History', p. 191. Of course, Best is aware of this: 'A differentiation must therefore be made between the theology of the Gospel of Mark and Mark's theology (i.e., the theology of the gospel may be uneven, reflecting tensions between theologies of tradition and redactor)' ('Mark's Preservation', p. 34).

95. *Following Jesus,* esp. pp. 166-74. See also pp. 112, 175-76, 177-78, 184, 204, 246.

96. Ibid., pp. 11, 16, 57; *Gospel as Story,* pp. 37-43.

'Jesus goes at the head of his community in a mission to Galilee of the Gentiles'.[97] This interpretation follows from Best's analysis of the Gospel as a whole, as does his exegesis of 16.1-8 as consummating the Markan themes of continued 'movement' in mission and suffering and the sustained fellowship of Christians with Christ.[98] Best is impressed by the absence in Mark of any formal commission to the disciples after the resurrection, *à la* Matt 28.16-20; he speculates that Mark 16.7 may function in this way or that there may have been an actual commission in a supposed lost ending of the Gospel.[99]

This is no place for a detailed response to Best's interpretation of Mark 16.1-8, but a couple of observations are in order. First, we might notice the degree to which Best's redaction-critical judgments about the conclusion of the Second Gospel depend on the identification of putative Markan themes ('the mission to Galilee of the Gentiles', 'suffering', 'the disciples' continued fellowship with Christ'). Here, as I have suggested, Best's reasoning is flawed: the identification of such themes in Mark is not tantamount to a demonstration that they are *redactional* (as Best seems to propose). Second, the specific details of Best's interpretation of the conclusion are contingent, not so much on *redaktionsgeschichtlich* analysis, as on his overall understanding of Markan discipleship. It may be debated whether or not Mark associates 'Galilee' with a mission to the Gentiles; it may even be debated whether or not the thrust of the Gospel is toward the unimpeded communion of the disciples with Jesus after the resurrection. It is beyond debate, however, that such themes are not *unequivocally* stated in Mark 16.1-8.[100]

11. For Best, no redaction-critical canon is more important than the discernment of special *Markan vocabulary*. Over and again in his studies of

97. *Following Jesus*, p. 218; see also pp. 201-2, 205-6; 'Discipleship', pp. 336-37.

98. *Following Jesus*, pp. 121, 204, 239; cf. 'Discipleship', pp. 326-27, 336-37; 'Some Problems', p. 87; *Gospel as Story*, p. 47. N.B. *Following Jesus*, p. 11: 'The resurrection, no appearances are [*sic*] narrated, is so presented that it is also the beginning; from it new life opens out; when the book is read and its message lived the risen Christ is present'.

99. *Following Jesus*, pp. 171-72.

100. Contrast R. H. Smith's exegesis: while agreeing with Best that Mark 16.1-8 is intended to provoke discipleship, Smith thinks that the Gospel is intentionally open-ended, in order to maintain a tension between the resurrection and the incomplete consummation of the kingdom ('New and Old in Mark 16.1-8', *CTM* 43 [1972], pp. 518-27). Cf. also D. O. Via's observation that 'for Mark the paradox of concealed revelation is never resolved [in 16.1-8]. . . . We get as much in the ending as the narrative gives us reason to expect' (*The Ethics of Mark's Gospel — In the Middle of Time* [Philadelphia: Fortress, 1985], pp. 55, 57).

discipleship, Best is careful to argue that a particular word or phrase is 'Markan', with the implication that it is 'distinctively' or even 'uniquely' Markan. Because many (though not all) of these words are derived from the (putative) seams and summaries, Best in effect assembles a Markan redactional vocabulary. The significance of this criterion for Best may be witnessed by tabulating those verbal units that he denotes as Markan.

TABLE 3   Best's Identification of Markan Relational Vocabulary

Verbal Unit	Frequency in Gospels[101]	Page Reference in Best[102]
ἀκολουθεῖν	[25-18-17-19]	112, 139, 175, 178 n. 2; 'Discipleship', 327; 'Mark's Use', 22
βλέπειν	[20-15-15-17]	11, 116 n. 18
γρηγορεῖν	[6-6-1-0]	152
διαλογίζεσθαι	3-7-6-0	'Mark's Use', 19 n. 49
διαστέλλεσθαι	1-4-0-0	62, 64 n. 3
διδάσκειν	[14-17-17-9]	23, 74 n. 2, 190, 193
δύνασθαι (preferred over ἰσχύειν)	27-33-26-36	67, 147, 157 n. 14
δυνατός	3-5-4-0	157 n. 14
εἶδον	[58-42-67-36]	168, 175
ἐκεῖθεν	[12-5-3-2]	100
ἐκθαμβεῖσθαι	0-4-0-0	116 n. 20, 156 n. 7; 'Role', 387; 'Mark's Use', 22 n. 70
ἐκπλήσσεσθαι	4-5-3-0	'Role', 387
ἐκπορεύεσθαι	6-11-3-2	110

101. Where Best does not indicate a word's frequency, the figures are bracketed. My additions to Best's listing are based largely on Morgenthaler, *Statistik,* which Best also employs (*Following Jesus,* p. 49 n. 51, et passim).

102. Unless otherwise specified, all citations are from *Following Jesus.*

Verbal Unit	Frequency in Gospels	Page Reference in Best
ἐξουσία	[10-10-16-8]	152, 191, 187 n. 15; 'Mark's Use', 15
ἐπερωτᾶν	8-25-17-2	66, 70 n. 11, 74 n. 2, 100, 104 n. 23, 175, 228 n. 13; 'Mark's Use', 17 n. 32, 19 n. 47
ἐπιτιμᾶν + (ἵνα)	6-9-12-0	106, 108 n. 5, 138 n. 7
ἔρημος τόπος	[2-5-2-0][103]	233 n. 6
εὐαγγέλιον (used absolutely)	[0-3-0-0]	40, 114, 164
εὐθύς (used adverbially)	7-42-1-3	68, 139, 143 n. 4, 172 n. 14
θαμβεῖσθαι	0-3-0-0	116 n. 20; 'Role', 387; 'Mark's Use', 22 n. 70
θαυμάζειν	[7-4-12-6]	'Role', 387
κρατεῖ	12-15-2-1	219, 225 n. 55
λόγος (used absolutely)	[1-7-0-0][104]	62
μετά (preferred over σύν)	[70-55-63-55]	182; 'Peter', 548
ὅσος	15-14-10-9	193, 197 n. 32
ὄχλος (preferred over λαός)	20-37-25-22	28-29, 38, 46 nn. 10,13, 212, 222 n. 14, 231
ὀψέ	1-3-0-0	'Mark's Use', 25 n. 94
ὀψία	7-5-0-2	'Mark's Use', 25 n. 94
πάλιν	17-28-3-43	100, 102 n. 11, 104 n. 22, 157 n. 22, 178 n. 5; 'Mark's Use', 22 n. 75; Gospel as Story, 105

103. Without τόπος, ἔρημος has a frequency in the Gospels of 6-4-8-5.

104. Reckoning of the occurrences of absolute λόγος may vary. Reflected in my frequency count are the parallels in Matt/Luke/John to Mark 2.1; 4.14ff., 33; 8.32; 9.10; 10.22; 14.39 (cf. Following Jesus, p. 64 n. 7).

Verbal Unit	Frequency in Gospels	Page Reference in Best
παραβολαί (in the plural when referring to only one parable)	[2-3-0-0]	218
παραπορεύεσθαι	1-4-0-0	74 n. 2
περιβλέψεσθαι	0-6-1-0	'Mark's Use', 25 n. 94
(ἐκ/ὑπερ)περισσῶς	0-4-0-0	111, 116 n. 13
πνεύματα ἀκάθαρτα (preferred over δαιμόνια, 10-12-10-4[105])	2-10-6-0	196 n. 12; 'Mark's Use', 15 n. 26
πολλά (used adverbially)	[6-9-3-0]	155, 214
πολλοί (as substantive substitute for ὄχλοι)	[9-6-2-10]	46 n. 13, 144 n. 18
προάγων	6-5-1-0	'Mark's Use', 22 n. 71
πρὸς ἑαυτούς	0-7-2-2[106]	62, 64 n. 4 (cf. 116 n. 14)
προσκαλεῖσθαι (preferred over φωνεῖν)	6-9-40	28, 45 n. 3, 76, 123, 130 n. 8, 155, 180, 191, 236 n. 1
συζητεῖν	0-6-2-0	62, 64 n. 5, 217
συνάγειν	24-5-6-7	49 n. 51, 193
φέρειν	[6-15-4-17]	138 n. 4
φοβεῖσθαι	[18-12-23-5]	'Mark's Use', 22
Verbs of motion generally (ἄγειν, βαίνειν, [προσ]- ἔρχεσθαι, [ἐκ]- πορεύεσθαι)	425 out of 18,278, 307/11,229, 363/19,404, 360/15,420	49 n. 51; cf. 19, 35-36, 73, 100, 110, 120, 135, 139, 147, 149, 166-68, 171, 181, 190; 'Discipleship', 326

Of equal importance to Best in ascertaining a Markan redaction history is the isolation of a distinctive Markan literary style. The following table lists those features of Markan grammar that, for Best, betray the redactor's hand.

105. Here Best's frequency count disagrees with Morgenthaler's (11-13-23-6).
106. Best incorrectly records the frequency of this unit as 0-5-2-0 in *Following Jesus*, p. 116 n. 14.

TABLE 4   Best's Identification of Markan Redactional Style

Element of Style	Page Reference in Best
Repetition of γάρ (in clauses)	30, 51 n. 86, 91 n. 7, 107, 110, 131 n. 22, 148, 159 n. 48, 166, 175, 178 n. 2, 222 n. 12; 'Peter', 551.
καί-parataxis	19, 100, 106, 110, 123, 135, 139, 147-49, 167, 181, 190, 212; 'Some Problems', 81
Asyndeton	117 n. 28
Singular verb with a plural subject	20
Plural verb followed by a singular participle	139
Compound verb followed by the preposition of the compound	66, 70 n. 10, 167; 'Mark's Use', 25 n. 94, 28 n. 166; *Gospel as Story*, 105
Frequent use of the imperfect tense, often periphrastically	74 n. 2, 110, 120, 175, 187 n. 20, 190; 'Mark's Use', 22, 26 n. 96; 'Peter', 553
Historic present tense	100, 102 n. 9, 148, 156 n. 11; 'Mark's Use', 29
Mixing of historic present and past tenses	32-33, 39, 149-50
Pleonastic or redundant participles (usually in aorist, introducing pericopes)	100, 110, 130 n. 8, 155, 166, 175, 178 n. 10, 201, 212; 'Peter', 551
Repeated use of ἄρχεσθαι plus the infinitive	23, 25-26, 112, 123, 147, 191, 211, 218; 'Mark's Use', 22, 24, 28 n. 106; 'Peter', 551, 554
Impersonal plural constructions	103 n. 15, 108 n. 4, 138 n. 4; cf. also 143 n. 2
Repetition of καὶ ἔλεγεν αὐτοῖς	31, 74 n. 2, 175, 190, 217; 'Mark's Use', 17
Introduction of OT reference with γέγραπται	63, 65 n. 12, 217

Element of Style	Page Reference in Best
Customary use of παρακαλεῖν + a verb of saying	'Mark's Use', 24-25
Introduction of a translation with ὅ ἐστιν [μεθερμηνευόμενον]	141, 144 n. 23
ὅτι *recitativum*	74 n. 2
Use of εἰς for ἐν	104 n. 20
Repetition of ἐν τῇ ὁδῷ	100, 120, 142; 'Mark's Use', 19, 21
Frequent use of κατ' ἰδίαν [μόνους]	56, 66, 159 n. 53, 223 n. 6; 'Mark's Use', 17, 18 n. 40
Use of direct speech	147
'Duality' in expression	40, 50 n. 71, 56, 89, 143 n. 2, 167, 201, 217; 'Mark's Use', 23-24
Parenthetical clauses	168
'Vivid concrete detail'	78

Insofar as these listings provide a genuine redactional vocabulary and grammar of Mark, we owe Best our thanks for a significant exegetical service. Nevertheless, some questions arise from Best's achievement.

(1) A number of the words appearing in Table 3 (ἀκολουθεῖν, βλέπειν, διαλογίζεσθαι, δύνασθαι, μετά, ὄχλος, ὀψία, πάλιν, προσέρχεσθαι, προσκαλεῖσθαι) appear, by Best's own concession, in pre-Markan material as well as in the redaction.[107] Similarly, in Table 4, many of the stylistic traits presumed to be characteristic of Mark are acknowledged by Best to have occurred in the tradition: paratactic καί, γάρ-connectives, use of the historic present tense, introductory participles, auxiliary ἄρχεσθαι, the formula καὶ ἔλεγεν αὐτοῖς, references to ὁδός, vivid detail, and 'double' expressions.[108] Arguably, other words and stylistic features might fall into the

---

107. See (respectively), *Following Jesus*, pp. 172-73 n. 15, 135; 'Mark's Use', p. 19 n. 49; *Following Jesus*, pp. 67-68, 182, 211; 'Mark's Use', p. 25 n. 95; *Following Jesus*, pp. 148, 157 n. 13, 130 n. 8, 180, 191; and 'Mark's Use', p. 15 n. 22.

108. See (respectively) *Following Jesus*, pp. 81, 111, 51 n. 81, 180, 111, 130 n. 8, 147, 17 n. 8, 111, 267, 191. 'Duality' as a redactional indicator has been called into question by F. Neirynck, *Duality in Mark: Contributions to the Study of Markan Redaction* (BETL 31: Leuven: Leuven University Press, 1972).

same category: not uniquely Markan but characteristic of both traditional and redactional stages. Are the tools of redaction criticism keen enough to permit us such refinement as Best attempts?[109]

(2) There seem to be some instances of internal inconsistency in Best's procedure. For example, does ὀψέ display a more statistically significant frequency rating (1-3-0-0) than ἀδημονεῖν (1-1-0-0), such that Best can deem the former to be Markan but the latter, non-Markan?[110] Why is παραπορεύεσθαι (with four occurrences in Mark) considered exemplary of that Gospel's vocabulary, whereas ἐμβλέπειν (with the same number of occurrences) 'can hardly be described as one of [Mark's] favourite words'?[111] Why does Mark twice use δαίμων redactionally in putative Markan summaries (1.34, 39) when, according to Best's analysis, one would expect to find πνεύματα ἀκάθαρτα instead?[112] If the *plural* παραβολαί in reference to only one parable especially signifies Markan redaction, why, in a similar state of affairs (at 7.17), is the singular παραβολή to be regarded as a redactional tip-off?[113] Stylistically, how can καὶ ἔλεγεν αὐτοῖς be a 'sign of Markan redactional activity', yet 'not normally Markan'?[114]

(3) As suggested in Table 3, a fundamental criterion for Best of 'characteristic' or 'favorite' Markan vocabulary is the frequency of a given word's occurrence. While at first blush this might seem a reasonable guide, it does create problems. For example, there are a number of cases in which a word appears 'frequently' in Mark but occurs with equal or greater frequency in other Gospels, thus throwing into question its distinctively Markan character: γρηγορεῖν (6-6-1-0), ἐξουσία (10-10-16-8), ἔρημος τόπος (2-5-2-0), θαυμάζειν (7-4-12-6), κρατεῖν (12-15-2-1), προάγων (6-5-1-0). In some instances a so-called 'Markan' word actually appears *less* frequently in that Gospel than in some of the others: εἶδον (58-42-67-36) and συνάγειν (24-5-6-7)! At first sight baffling, Best's reasoning here evidently conforms to the manner in which he deals with other words, such as βλέπειν, ἐκεῖθεν, ἐπιτιμᾶν, ὅσος, and συζητεῖν: they are judged redactional, not only for their frequency of occurrence, but also owing to their appearance in putatively 'redactional passages' (often

---

109. Note, for example, how confidently Best can assign Mark 10.32 as one-third tradition and two-thirds redaction ('Mark's Use', pp. 21-22)!

110. Cf. 'Mark's Use', p. 25 n. 94 with *Following Jesus,* p. 156 n. 10.

111. Contrast *Following Jesus,* p. 74 n. 2 and pp. 135, 138 n. 9.

112. See ibid., p. 197 n. 19.

113. Contrast ibid., p. 218 with 228 n. 13.

114. Contrast ibid., p. 196 with p. 104 n. 24 (cf. 'Mark's Use', p. 20).

Markan seams).[115] The problem with such a defense is that it 'proves' only what has already been assumed: certain words are stamped as Markan because they appear in seams, which have been identified as such (more often than not) on the basis of their distinctively Markan vocabulary.

(4) Finally, suspicions should be raised about the entire procedure of postulating a Markan redactional vocabulary on the grounds of 'frequency of occurrence'. Exactly what do Best's (or Morgenthaler's) word-statistics prove? They prove that a given word appears in Mark, or in the other Gospels, a certain number of times — nothing less, nothing more. They cannot prove which words are distinctive of, or unique to, Mark, since we cannot know how frequently (or infrequently) they occurred in his traditions. When Best asserts (on the basis of frequency) that certain words are 'Markan favorites',[116] he creates the impression that they (and the themes they suggest) were favored by Mark over others. This *may* be the case, but we cannot know that it *is* the case — and all the *Statistiken des Markuswortschatzes* cannot make it otherwise.

To summarize: Best's meticulous attention to the vocabulary and grammar of Mark's Gospel is worthy of praise. However, one must ask whether the evidence elicited by this criterion is cumulatively as strong as at first it might appear. In any event, here as elsewhere, we should beware of the self-deception that we *do* know more than we can know about the vocabulary and style of either tradition or redaction in the Second Gospel.

12. As our focus is on his research in discipleship, it comes as no surprise that *the Markan Christological titles* play a comparatively minor role in Best's redaction-critical endeavor. In line with the common *redaktionsgeschichtlich* interpretation of Mark 8.29, Best opines that Peter's confession of Jesus as Christ (a datum available to Mark in his tradition) betokens an accurate but incomplete understanding (cf. 8.22-26); only later in the Gospel will a true confession be linked to a true understanding of discipleship.[117]

Summary: The foregoing discussion should indicate, if nothing else, the careful, systematic, and impressive manner in which Best has attempted to ply redaction criticism in his quest of Mark's understanding of discipleship. Best's work commands respect; for that reason, in my analysis and re-

---

115. *Following Jesus*, pp. 62, 100, 106, 108 n. 5, 111, 116 n. 18, 168, 175, 193, 197 n. 32, 217.
116. Ibid., pp. 108 n. 5, 138 n. 4, 193.
117. Ibid., pp. 21, 25; see also *Temptation*, pp. 160-77.

flections I have striven to be equally attentive to matters of detail. Rather than rehearse all of the questions raised previously, I close this section with three general observations.

First, I find it striking, if not surprising, just how much editorial activity Best invites us to witness in the Gospel of Mark. It is remarkable on Best's own terms: his general perspective on the Evangelist-redactor is that of an author 'bound by the tradition', modifying it minimally. Yet the image of Mark that emerges from Best's own *redaktionsgeschichtlich* analysis is of an author who displays unusual thoroughness and finesse in interweaving disparate materials with his own theological *Tendenzen*. As a result (in Best's judgment), the traditions about Jesus preserved in the Second Gospel are demonstrably riddled with distinctively Markan themes, style, and vocabulary. Hence my query: Does Best's redaction-critical *analysis* — emphasizing Mark's freedom in tailoring traditions to his own point of view — outrun his redaction-critical *perspective* on Mark as 'a conservative redactor', limited by his traditions? Does the tension in Best's 'mediate' type of *Redaktionsgeschichte* dissolve into paradox?

Second, three of the criteria we have explored seem to be especially important for Best: the thematic, the linguistic, and the stylistic. Insofar as the first is usually inferred from the second, we are left with vocabulary and grammar as Best's paramount *redaktionsgeschichtlich* canons. Given the problems associated with these criteria — the debatable significance of frequent occurrence, the persistent doubts about the shape of a pre-Markan tradition no longer directly recoverable, and instances of Best's own inconsistency in analysis — one wonders if they are strong enough to bear the burden of Best's redaction-critical enterprise. It could be argued[118] that Best's case is bolstered by the collocation, in a given passage, of several Markan characteristics: thus the evidence of style and wording is said to be supported by the appearance of those traits in definable Markan constructions (such as seams, insertions, and summaries), which also evince distinctive Markan themes. While in some restricted cases this might be true, in general the cogency of such a 'criterion of coherence' is diminished by the inherent circularity of Markan redaction criticism: we can adduce the Evangelist's grammar and vocabulary because we know what his themes and arrangements of material look like; we can deduce the themes and arrangements because we know what his grammar and vocabulary look like. When dealing with a Synoptic whose priority is assumed

118. Best himself has argued thus (*Following Jesus*, p. 130 n. 8).

(or with a Gospel, like John, whose creation, in all likelihood, was literarily independent of the others), I see no way of escaping this hermeneutical circle.

All of this leads to a final question about Best's method: if there is no way off this merry-go-round of distinguishing tradition and redaction in the Second Gospel, why climb aboard to begin with? Best has an immediate riposte: despite the difficulty of assessing Markan style and vocabulary, 'without the control which these supply it is possible to make Mark mean almost anything'.[119] This raises a serious exegetical issue, to which later we must return. For now, we might respond (with John Donahue),[120] that such a control might be as effectively provided by a 'close reading' and narrative analysis of the Gospel. If our concern is for the final shape of the text rather than for its tradition-history, what need is there for so fine a redactional separation as Best undertakes? Indeed, on occasion, Best himself admits that such analysis is too difficult to be performed with reasonable certainty and is ultimately profitless.[121] What stands in the Gospel of Mark, Mark has let stand; whether it stems from tradition or from his own hand may be of less exegetical consequence than has often been supposed.

C. Exegetical Results

Underlying Best's exegesis are his assumptions about the Markan *Sitz im Leben*: the Gospel was written in Rome just before or just after 70 CE, for a church that had already undergone persecution and saw more on the horizon. Although the community was characterized by apocalyptic expectation, its chief problem was not that of living too much in light of the end, but that of living too little in light of the cross.[122] Therefore, Mark's primary purpose was neither informational (that is, conveying facts about Jesus) nor polemical (attacking certain heretics or recognized heretical positions). Mark's principal objective was pastoral; 'to build up his readers as Christians and show them what true discipleship is', namely,

---

119. Ibid., p. 241.

120. Donahue, review of *Following Jesus* in *JBL* 103 (1984), p. 116.

121. Thus *Following Jesus*, p. 213: 'If Mark received [14.58 and 15.29] in the tradition he had ample opportunity to drop one occurrence; he must therefore have thought it important. If he received it once and inserted it a second time he obviously thought the same'.

122. 'Role', pp. 378-79; *Following Jesus*, pp. 9-14, 50 n. 66. Alternative reconstructions of the Markan *Sitz* are presented and refuted by Best in *Gospel as Story*, pp. 21-36.

'[as] apparent only in the light of the cross, and not in the light of Jesus' mighty acts'.[123]

For Best, discipleship in Mark's Gospel is fundamentally to be understood as 'following Jesus', a dynamic pilgrimage 'towards suffering, persecution and a Cross'.[124] This is not to be confused with an *imitatio Christi*, which is precluded by the centrality given to Jesus' unique mission, executed through his passion and death.[125] The means of 'getting in and staying in' the community of Jesus' followers is faith. Discipleship is not thereby removed from the good and evil of the world; it remains in tension with it, sustained in that tension by the baptism of the Holy Spirit, the presence of Jesus, the grace of God, and fellowship with other disciples.[126] The mission of the community is 'to deal with the sin of men' through healing the sick and preaching repentance; itself a body ransomed, forgiven, and saved, the community is called 'to bring others into the position in which they themselves are'.[127] That status is not only one of suffering and self-denial; it is also a position 'in which they are forgiven and may be finally victorious'.[128]

Given this framework for understanding discipleship, what role do 'the twelve', 'the disciples', and 'Peter' play in the Gospel of Mark? Because there is no easily identifiable center of the disciples' views in the Second Gospel, they are not 'such acknowledged villains or enemies of the church'.[129] In-

123. 'Some Problems', p. 88; *Following Jesus*, pp. 11-14; *Gospel as Story*, pp. 93-99.

124. 'Discipleship', pp. 326-27; *Temptation*, p. 121; *Following Jesus*, pp. 246-48; *Gospel as Story*, pp. 86-99. For a lengthy assessment of the Markan motif of 'following in the way of Jesus', see E. Manicardi, *Il cammino di Gèsu nel Vangèlo di Marco: Schema narrativo e tema cristologico* (AnBib 96; Rome: Biblical Institute, 1981). On suffering as the key to Markan discipleship, see P. S. Pudussery, 'The Meaning of Discipleship in the Gospel of Mark', *Jee* 10 (1980), pp. 93-110; and D. P. Senior, *The Passion of Jesus in the Gospel of Mark* (GPS 2; Wilmington, DE: Glazier, 1984), pp. 148-50.

125. *Temptation*, p. 182; *Following Jesus*, pp. 18, 39, 127, 248; *Gospel as Story*, pp. 85-86. Cf. 'Discipleship', p. 335: 'The example of Jesus is the pattern for the disciple and yet the disciple cannot really be like Jesus; there is a dimension into which he is unable to enter. The disciple of the rabbi in due time becomes a rabbi; the apprentice philosopher becomes a philosopher, but the disciple of Christ never becomes a Christ'. For further discussion of the difference between discipleship and *imitatio Christi*, consult Schulz, *Nachfolge und Nachahmen*.

126. *Temptation*, pp. 180-87; *Gospel as Story*, p. 99; cf. S. Légasse, 'Tout quitter pour suivre le Christ: Mc 10,17-30', *AsSeign* 59 (1974), pp. 43-44.

127. *Temptation*, pp. 179, 188. Cf. *Following Jesus*, pp. 170, 243; and H. T. Fleddermann, 'The Discipleship Discourse (Mark 9.33-50)', *CBQ* 43 (1981), pp. 57-75.

128. 'Some Problems', p. 88; cf. 'Discipleship', pp. 329-30; *Gospel as Story*, pp. 86-87.

129. 'Role', p. 395. Cf. ibid., pp. 383, 393-96; *Gospel as Story*, pp. 44-48.

deed, when compared to the dark shadows cast by the scribes, rulers, and Pharisees, the disciples appear relatively luminous. Far from being the blackguards in the narrative, the disciples are used by Mark as a foil for Jesus' positive example and teaching; their failures were not created by the Evangelist but were emphasized by him for the purpose of assisting his own community and reassuring it of God's continued love and strength in the midst of its own failure. '[The] role of the disciples in the gospel is then to be examples to the community.'[130] Similarly, Mark does not attack the historical Peter. The high point of any such assault must have happened at the pre-Markan stage, for the Evangelist maintains a consistently favorable or neutral outlook toward Peter, who exemplifies the disciples even as they collectively exemplify the church.[131] As for 'the twelve', they are virtually interchangeable with 'the disciples' in role and function, except for the twelve's peculiar (that is, full-time) missionary activity. Normally in Mark's Gospel the twelve do not constitute a special subgroup of disciples, restricting discipleship or representing church officials; 'in Mark's eyes the Twelve are typical believers'.[132]

If one grants his presuppositions about the Markan *Sitz* and the Evangelist's pastoral purpose, then Best's exegesis squares with most of the evidence of the Second Gospel and is, for that reason, convincing. Of course, there are minor points in Best's interpretation with which we might quibble. (1) Is there any solid evidence to support Best's allegation that Peter was so unfavorably regarded in the tradition that Mark would have thought it necessary to 'rehabilitate' him in his Gospel? (2) Is there a contradiction between Best's assertion (on the one hand) that the disciples' activity, as described in the Second Gospel, carries implications for the missionary task of the Markan church and his observation (on the other hand) that 'the twelve' are distinguished as missionaries in a way that 'the disciples' are not? (3) In a Gospel where discipleship is epitomized as self-

---

130. 'Role', p. 401; cf. ibid., pp. 394-99; 'Some Problems', p. 94; *Gospel as Story*, p. 47. Note also 'Discipleship', p. 337: 'Mark writes to explain to the church the position of those who seem willfully blind, but even more to explain the position of those who claim to be Christians and yet whose discipleship is impoverished and inadequate, who follow and yet may be scared off when persecution comes, or may be tempted off by the desire for wealth or popularity or success'.

131. 'Peter', pp. 556-58; *Following Jesus*, p. 2.

132. *Temptation*, p. 178; cf. 'Role', p. 398; *Following Jesus*, pp. 184-85, 194-95, 204-5; *Gospel as Story*, pp. 49-50. N.B. 'Mark's Use', p. 32: 'Mark distinguishes to some extent between the twelve and the disciples, the latter being the wider group'.

denial and taking up one's own cross (Mark 8.34), is the boundary between 'following Jesus' and *imitatio Christi* as hard and fast as Best suggests?[133] Nevertheless, the main contours of Best's interpretation are persuasive: had Mark wished to indulge in sheer history or polemic, one would have expected a very different literary work than what we have received from him. That the Evangelist produced his narrative with pastoral concerns in mind, to encourage a struggling church to pursue proper paths of discipleship, is indeed a plausible hypothesis. And if one accepts that hypothesis, then the disciples appear to function in the Second Gospel precisely as Best indicates: as foils for Jesus and his instruction about discipleship as the way of the cross.

To what degree does Best's exegesis of Markan discipleship depend on his thoroughgoing separation of tradition and redaction? This is a difficult question to answer. Perhaps we might tackle it by examining a segment of Best's research for the correlation between method and interpretive results.

In his article, 'The Role of the Disciples in Mark' (1977),[134] Best argues, on the basis of redaction-critical analysis, that three general points of view can be sorted out in the Second Gospel: that of the pre-Markan tradition which the Evangelist retains but does not extend, that of the tradition which is given emphasis by the redactor, and that of the redactor which is entirely redactional, not deriving from the tradition. Under the first heading, tradition retained but not amplified by Mark, Best lists Jesus' defense of the disciples in response to outsiders' attacks (Mark 2.18, 23-24; 7.2, 5), the disciples' mediation between Jesus and others (3.14; 6.7-13, 41; 8.6), and the disciples' actions for or on behalf of Jesus (11.1; 14.13, 14, 16). In the second category, distinctive Markan emphases as gauged by the redactional development of traditional motifs, Best includes the following: the disciples as foils for Jesus' teaching and action (redaction: 2.16; 7.17; 8.17; 9.11, 33;

133. Best is absolutely right when he says that Mark never conceives of a disciple as actually becoming a Christ ('Discipleship', pp. 334-35). However, Best seems to assume that just such *identity with* Christ is necessarily implied in the *imitation of* Christ. I think this unlikely. In speaking, respectively, of an *imitatio Pauli* and an *imitatio Dei*, would the writers of 1 Thess 1.6 and Eph 5.1 have intended to suggest that their addressees actually should (or could) become Paul or God? For detailed discussion, see W. Michaelis, 'μιμέομαι, κ.τ.λ.', *TDNT* IV (1967), pp. 659-74.

134. The following précis summarizes Best's conclusions in 'Role', pp. 384-89, and the charts presented therein. In those cases where Best expresses doubt over the assignment of certain verses to either tradition or redaction, I have tried to group the material according to the general tenor of his argument.

10.10, 28; 11.12, 21; 12.43; 13.1, 3; tradition: 6.35; 8.27b, 29; 9.39; 10.35-39, 41; 14.12); the disciples as recipients of private instruction (redaction: 4.34, 36-41; 7.17; 8.15-21; 9.9, 29, 31; 10.11f., 23ff.; 12.43; 13.3; 14.17, 33; tradition: 4.10; 9.35; 10.32-34; 10.41-45); the disciples as journeying with Jesus (redaction: 3.7, 9; 6.1, 45; 8.10, 27; 9.30, 33; 10.46; 11.1; tradition: 10.32; 11.11; 14.17); the disciples as fearful, failing to understand, and subject to Jesus' rebuke (redaction: 4.41; 6.45, 50, 52; 7.17; 8.15-21, 32; 9.6, 32; 10.32; 14.33, 54, 72; 16.8; tradition: 5.31; 6.37, 49; 8.4, 33; 9.18, 35-37, 39; 10.13, 37, 40, 41; 14.27, 29, 31, 66, 67, 70); the disciples as failing in action (redaction: 14.37, 50; tradition: 9.18); and the disciples as called by Jesus (the redactor's distinctive placement of the tradition behind 1.16-20 and 2.14). Best's third category, uniquely redactional additions to the tradition, comprises the amazement of the disciples (10.24, 26, 32), their being told not to disclose information (8.30; 9.9), the conferral on them of a position in the post-resurrection period (9.9; 16.7), and Mark's mention of them without their presence being regarded as exceptional in any way (1.29-31; 2.15; 3.7, 9; 6.1; 14.10, 20, 43 [though the last three references, plus 8.27ab, may be traditional]).

Which of the criteria considered in this chapter have been most important for Best in separating tradition from redaction, so as to arrive at these exegetical conclusions? For seven of the images of the disciples discussed by him in this article — their role as Jesus' foil, their receipt of private instruction, their post-resurrection position, their failure in action, their unexceptional presence, their mediatory role, and their actions for or on behalf of Jesus — Best offers no supporting redaction-critical evidence.[135] *Markan vocabulary and style* seem to underlie Best's consignment, to the Evangelist's redaction, of the disciples' amazement and their journey with Jesus (characterized by vivid detail).[136] *Mark's arrangement of pericopes* emphasizes the disciples' fear, misunderstanding, and rebuke (cf. 8.27–10.46), and the early call of the four fishermen and the tax-collector (the resemblance of the call narratives also suggesting Mark's dualistic style).[137] 'The disciples as exhorted not to disclose information to outsiders' is a typical *Markan theme;* possibly the Evangelist was unable to extend the theme of Jesus' defense of the disciples against outsiders because 'he

---

135. That is, in reference to these themes, Best states only that they are traditional or redactional in origin, and that they are or are not emphasized or extended by the redactor, without providing any clear indication of how he has arrived at that judgment (see 'Role', pp. 384, 385, 388-89).

136. 'Role', p. 387.

137. Ibid., pp. 387-88, 389.

had no material in which to develop this aspect' (an implicit argument against the Markan creation of pericopes).[138]

Best has undertaken an ambitious project: he has isolated fifteen themes, manifested in the Second Gospel and germane to the role of the disciples, and, on the basis of commonly accepted redaction-critical criteria, has attempted to classify those themes as either 'traditional' or 'redactional'. Moreover, in this exercise Best proves to be consistent in using those criteria that are theoretically most important for him (arrangement, themes, vocabulary and style). On reflection, however, one wonders if Best's achievement is really as convincing as it appears. At least five questions might be raised.

First, two themes ('the disciples' amazement' and 'the disciples' journeying with Jesus') are identified by Best as redactional on the basis of vocabulary and style, which assumes that the words or details associated with those themes would have been unlikely to appear in the tradition. Best may be correct that the detail of Jesus' movements with the disciples, from Caesarea Philippi to Jerusalem, would not have been preserved at the oral stage of transmission;[139] yet, if we can conceive (with Best) of a pre-Markan passion narrative, is it impossible to conceive that other connected complexes of the Jesus-story might already have coalesced during the oral stage, complexes requiring (or inviting) statements of Jesus' journeying with the disciples? As for the other theme, Best's statement that 'the amazement of the disciples . . . , though entirely redactional, is not heavily emphasized'[140] seems, at first blush, almost ludicrous: unless one assumes that the Gospel narrative was a complete invention of the Evangelist (a suggestion Best would never countenance), one wonders how any element that was *not* heavily emphasized could ever be recognized as being *entirely* redactional. Evidently, Best's confidence stems from the appearance, in verses describing the disciples' astonishment, of vocabulary that he takes to be redactional (θαυμάζειν; θαμβεῖσθαι; ἐκπλήσσεσθαι). I shall not rehearse my earlier comments about Best's *redaktionsgeschichtlich* arguments based on vocabulary; here it suffices to say that there is no reason why any or all of these words, whether in reference to the disciples or to others, could not have appeared in the pre-Markan tradition.

Second, 'Jesus' defense of the disciples against outsiders' attacks' and

138. Ibid., pp. 388-89.
139. Ibid., p. 387.
140. Ibid.

'Jesus' mandate to the disciples not to disclose information' appear to have been classified by Best as, respectively, pre-Markan and Markan on the grounds of thematic arrangement: that is, on no basis other than the expectation that a particular theme comports with the point of view assumed of the tradition or of the redactor. Such an argument is tautologous.

Third, almost one-third of the themes discussed by Best ('the disciples as called', 'afraid', 'rebuked', and 'failing to understand') are classified as traditional themes that have been given redactional emphasis through Mark's arrangement of pericopes. This datum is not as significant as it may appear once we realize that, when viewed from the perspective of Best's presuppositions, these themes could hardly have been categorized in any other way. The classification of 'traditional, not emphasized or extended by Mark' is precluded, since (a) a thematic arrangement of pericopes implies a certain emphasis or extension of an idea (without which the arrangement would never be perceived as such) and (b) Best tends to assume that most of the Evangelist's source-material circulated in discrete pericopes (that is, without arrangement).[141] The classification of 'entirely redactional additions to the tradition' is precluded, since Best assumes that the materials arranged by the Evangelist are not of his own creation.

Fourth, as nearly as I can determine, seven of the fifteen themes that are proposed by Best (about 47%) are identified as redactional on no *redaktionsgeschichtlich* grounds whatever. Among these are themes that are crucial in Best's understanding of the disciples in Mark: their function as foils to Jesus and as privy to his confidential instruction, their failure in action, as well as their assumption of an important role after the resurrection.

Finally, we might note that over one-half of the themes pertaining to the disciples, pinpointed by Best in the Second Gospel, (a) fall in the category of material preserved in the tradition yet given redactional amplification and (b) incorporate both favorable and unfavorable traits of the disci-

---

141. Here a tension within Best's position must be admitted. On the one hand, he speculates that already in the oral stage of the tradition some of the separate incidents had come together, such as the parables in Mark 4 and the miracles in Mark 4.35–5.43 (*Gospel as Story*, p. 16). On the other hand, because he doubts that pericopes or complexes 'would necessarily have joined themselves up to one another by some natural process of evolution' (ibid.), Best tends to attribute significant and discernible arrangements of material in the Gospel to the Evangelist. 'It is this conscious step [from the complexes to the first Gospel] which we attribute to Mark and it is this which makes him more than a collector of material. . . . [He] carefully unifies the material in such a way as to produce a total effect' (ibid.).

ples. Given Best's assumptions, about both Markan discipleship and Markan redaction criticism, can this result be purely coincidental?

For all of the care exercised by Ernest Best in his redaction-critical study of the disciples in the Second Gospel, it is clear that his work is no less fraught with problems than is the research of Robert Meye. Indeed, their investigations appear to share many of the same tensions, even though their presuppositions and exegetical results do not agree at every point. Let us now consider how Markan *Redaktionsgeschichte* and Markan discipleship fare in the research of a third noted scholar, whose assumptions and interpretation are at sometimes dramatic variance with those of our 'conservative' and 'mediate' exegetes.

5. Type III: The 'Liberal' Position of Theodore J. Weeden, Sr

The misunderstanding, misconception, and failure of the disciples is perhaps the most surprising motif we have discovered in the past twenty years of Markan studies. Those of us who had a hand in this exploration have been subjected to sharp and bitter criticism. In part, this is understandable, since Christian investment in and sympathy with Peter and the Twelve is deep and heavy. The evangelist seems well acquainted with the traditional high estimation of the disciples, but he chooses to object to it. In his view, those who should have known best knew least of all. If, therefore, one looks up to the Twelve for guidance, one is likely to court disaster and invite one's own destruction. The author skillfully derails his readers from the traditional track of discipleship and reorients them onto the way of Jesus.

Werner H. Kelber[1]

The preceding quotation aptly summarizes the primary aspects of a third major type of *redaktionsgeschichtlich* analysis of Markan discipleship: that exegetical position which (a) assumes a hiatus between the Evangelist's tradition and redaction and (b) frequently arrives at a negative reconstruction of the disciples' role in the Second Gospel. Perhaps no interpreter has presented these assumptions and conclusions more provocatively and with greater force than Theodore J. Weeden, Sr. Appearing in 1968, Weeden's first notable essay in this area of research[2] was a condensation of his Clare-

---

1. Kelber, 'Redaction Criticism', pp. 5-6.
2. Weeden, 'The Heresy That Necessitated Mark's Gospel' (1968).

mont doctoral dissertation, written four years earlier under the direction of James M. Robinson. From this foundational work arose Weeden's other redaction-critical articles on Markan theology and the Markan *Sitz im Leben*.[3] However, his most comprehensive, and most influential, statement about Markan discipleship and the Evangelist's *redaktionsgeschichtlich* technique appeared in 1971 as *Mark — Traditions in Conflict*, a book that was lauded by one reviewer as 'an extremely creative approach to the interpretation of the Gospel of Mark'.[4] Whatever else may be said of Weeden's contribution to the study of the Second Gospel, it has certainly been creative, stimulating, and exemplary of what I have classified as the Type III, or 'liberal', approach.

A. General Perspective

At least in 1971, Weeden's praise of Markan redaction criticism was lavish, if not excessive: 'Redaction criticism has placed in our hand the key for unlocking the mysteries behind the Gospel of Mark and its creation'.[5] However, in applying this tool to the Second Gospel, Weeden recognizes difficulties both of perspective and of method.

First, redaction criticism is troublesome (maintains Weeden) because it has altered our perspective on Mark the Evangelist.

> . . . [As] long as one limits the role of the evangelist to that of an editor, one can assume that he has for the most part reproduced his material untouched, exhibiting his own particular biases only at those points where his editorial hand was required to link the received material together in some meaningful composition. . . . [But] in postulating a much freer hand for Mark in the composing process, redaction makes the lines which are drawn by form criticism between Markan created material and Markan received material look less sharply defined, the distinctions less assured.[6]

---

3. Germane to the present study are Weeden, 'The Conflict Between Mark and His Opponents over Kingdom Theology' (1973), and idem, 'The Cross as Power in Weakness (Mark 15.20b-41)' (1976).

4. V. K. Robbins, in a review published in *JBL* 91 (1972), pp. 417-20 (quotation, p. 417).

5. *Mark*, p. 1.

6. Ibid., pp. 2-3.

Notice that, for Weeden, it is Mark's *redactional* activity that has blurred the lines between the character of the Evangelist's traditions and his own handiwork. Why is this so? Weeden's answer lies in his postulation of 'a much freer hand for Mark in the composing process'. That 'Mark exercised an author's freedom and creativity in composing the Gospel' is, for Weeden, not only 'a sound postulate with which to begin a Markan study', but also to be identified as the fundamental premise of redaction criticism.[7] Hence, throughout his research, Weeden stresses the Evangelist's freedom of thought and liberty in composition: Mark is 'a much more deliberate theologian than had earlier been assumed', possessing 'the freedom to shape his material as he felt necessary'.[8] While conceding that, in chapter 13 (for example), Mark built his composition upon an apocalyptic source, Weeden denies that Mark felt bound to that source in any subservient way; on the contrary, Mark in effect 'created' chapter 13.[9]

If the Evangelist exerts such mastery over his material, why should the interpreter even care to attempt the distinguishing of source and redaction? The answer, for Weeden, evokes another of his assumptions about Mark: the Evangelist did not regard with favor all of the theological emphases in all of his sources. Therefore, 'It is necessary that we who are involved in redaction criticism sharpen our analytical probings and be more conscious of the distinction which must be made among (1) the theological biases of the sources which Mark draws upon, (2) Mark's own peculiar theological intent and (3) the effect that the theological position of the sources may have of an unintentional nature upon Mark's position once these sources are put to work by the evangelist for his own purpose'.[10] In short, the distinction between tradition and redaction is necessary, in Weeden's view, because a negative or antagonistic relationship between Mark and his traditions could and did exist.

In assessing the difficulty of *Redaktionsgeschichte* that arises from his perspective on the redactional freedom of Mark, Weeden recognizes another problem: 'Without help from the evangelist and without clear-cut knowledge of his sources, deriving a *methodology* that will take us to the heart of the Markan purpose is an extremely difficult task'.[11] Citing with

7. Ibid., p. 1.

8. Ibid., pp. 3, 73 n. 4.

9. Ibid., pp. 73, 101, following Lambrecht, *Markus-Apokalypse*, and Pesch, *Naherwartungen*.

10. 'Conflict', p. 206.

11. *Mark*, pp. 4-5.

approval Johannes Schreiber's four principles for ascertaining Markan redaction, Weeden notes the limitations of three of them: the Matthean and Lukan alteration of the Second Gospel may not indicate those Evangelists' correction of *Markan* theological prejudices; the Markan selection and arrangement of tradition presupposes, without possibility of verification, the existence of material that the Evangelist chose to ignore; and the presence of a unified, theological conception is not immediately verifiable from the data of the Second Gospel.[12] Curiously, Weeden does not evaluate Schreiber's fourth principle: that Markan redactional theology be shown to possess not only inner consistency but meaningful coherence 'in terms of a given situation in the history of religion'.[13]

Given these handicaps, 'What is needed is a methodological approach that will guide one in the accurate interpretation of the data amassed from exegetical study of the Gospel, and that will help safeguard one from the hermeneutical snare of reading into the Gospel preconceived ideas that do violence to the author's intent'.[14] For Weeden, the only such approach is 'to read [the Evangelist's] work with the analytical eyes of a first century reader', allowing the peculiarities of Mark to speak for themselves apart from prejudicial knowledge of the other Gospels and without supplying the consensus of New Testament tradition.[15] Because the Gospel approximates the style of contemporaneous Greek drama and popular biographies, both of which used the literary device of characterization to communicate the writer's thoughts and moral judgments, 'The twentieth century reader must start with the Markan characters', who 'hold the key to the mystery surrounding the creation of the Gospel'. In this way, Weeden believes, the twentieth-century reader can share with his or her first-century counterpart 'the same hermeneutical approach . . . , a common compass setting'.[16]

Significant repercussions for Weeden's view of history in Mark issue from this approach. If the Gospel is to be understood in terms of a first-century Hellenistic drama, then (infers Weeden) the Evangelist may be responsible for 'intentionally staging' a variety of events.[17] Specifically (and

12. Ibid., pp. 6-8, responding to Schreiber, 'Die Christologie'.

13. *Mark,* p. 5; cf. pp. 5-8.

14. Ibid., pp. 10-11. N.B. p. 8: 'The hermeneutical point of departure one chooses is of critical importance'.

15. Ibid., pp. 11 (quotation), 114; cf. 'Heresy', p. 148.

16. Quotations, ibid., pp. 18, 19; cf. pp. 12-19 for Weeden's full discussion.

17. 'Heresy', pp. 150, 155; *Mark,* pp. 97, 155 n. 23.

here we must anticipate one of Weeden's exegetical results),[18] in his Gospel Mark 'dramatizes' a dispute over Christology and discipleship occurring in his own time and place, with Jesus representing one point of view (that of Mark) and the disciples, the other side in the debate (that of Mark's opponents).[19] As there is no historical basis for a dispute of this nature having taken place between Jesus and his disciples, the possibility exists 'that the Evangelist is no longer concerned with the facts of 30 A.D. but rather with the specific problems of his own community in the late 60's.'[20] This inference propels Weeden to the further conclusion that any number of events in Mark's Gospel — for instance, Peter's confession at Caesarea Philippi (8.27-30) and the apocalyptic discourse in chapter 13 — 'can be understood only in view of the evangelist's own situation.'[21] For Weeden, this is in no wise surprising, since 'The Gospel is not a chronicle of the past but preaching for the present'.[22] Thus, while the Second Gospel may be the product of a 'historical redactor-theologian', the accent in Weeden's understanding falls heavily on the second half of that designation.[23]

Weeden's overall perspective on *Redaktionsgeschichte* and the redaction history of Mark invites our critical reflection. At least five observations might be made. First, in view of the development of the redaction-critical perspective, and in light of its evolution from form criticism in particular, can Weeden's contention for Mark's maximal role in fabricating the Gospel be allowed to pass without any defense whatever? This is not to fault Weeden because he shares a point of view that we have associated with Type III exegetes; it is, however, to ask why he has elected to present his understanding of Mark's redactional activity in relative isolation from those general perspectives of Type I or Type II interpreters, which allow for

18. Even as Weeden himself tends to do in his prolegomena: see 'Heresy', p. 145.

19. 'Heresy', p. 147; *Mark,* pp. 100, 162-63.

20. 'Heresy', p. 149 n. 7; ibid., p. 150; *Mark,* p. 69. Here cf. Reploh, *Markus — Lehrer der Gemeinde:* unlike Weeden, Reploh presupposes no polemic in the Markan *Sitz;* like Weeden, Reploh thinks that the Second Gospel is transparent to the concerns of the Evangelist's community and thus is virtually unhistorical.

21. 'Heresy', p. 149 n. 7; *Mark,* pp. 70-72; cf. p. 155.

22. 'Conflict', p. 205; cf. Marxsen: '. . . for Mark the gospel is the (or a) form in which Jesus is made present' (*Mark the Evangelist,* p. 129).

23. Cf. *Mark,* p. viii. Acknowledging the influence of D. O. Via, Jr, by 1976 Weeden was beginning to relocate his methodological starting-point away from redaction criticism proper to 'a literary critical investigation of motifs and thematic configurations' ('Cross', p. 115; cf. ibid., p. 130). However, Weeden continued to invoke *Redaktionsgeschichte* to support insights derived from the practice of literary criticism.

the possibility that certain forces were exerted on the Evangelist by his traditional material.[24] Stated differently, it seems problematic that Weeden should overtly align himself with Rudolf Pesch's research on Mark 13 without an equally overt discussion of the real dissimilarities in their respective understandings of Mark's role as redactor.[25]

Second, we might return to a question that has been adumbrated: why does Weeden not proffer any criticism of Schreiber's fourth redaction-critical principle — namely, that the Markan message must make sense in a *religionsgeschichtlich* context? Such a principle is valuable to the degree that it prevents redaction-critical results from being made to dangle in midair, without any grounding in a plausible historical or religious setting. On the other hand, not all proposed *Sitze* are equally plausible. Precisely how does one's redaction-critical analysis arbitrate the credibility of the different religious settings that have been suggested? To frame the question negatively, how does one guard against cutting the message of Mark to fit this year's scholarly fashion in *Religionsgeschichte*? It may be that Weeden himself has not exercised sufficient caution in this regard: the idea of a 'debate' in the Markan church over Christology and discipleship may owe less to evidence in the Second Gospel, unearthed by means of redaction criticism, than to the unquestioned assumption that, because Paul sometimes hammered out his theological position in debate with certain opponents, Mark and his putative interlocutors must have done the same.[26]

Third, we might recall Weeden's exhortation 'to read Mark without

24. Curiously, Ernest Best's different point of view on the character of Markan redaction — to say nothing of Best's dissimilar interpretation of the disciples in Mark — is (as far as I can determine) never mentioned, much less discussed, by Weeden. At the time of his monograph's publication, some reviewers took exception to what they perceived to be Weeden's selective coverage of the secondary literature (see, for example, J. P. Martin's review of *Mark* in *Int* 26 [1972], pp. 361-62).

25. Contrast Pesch, *Das Markusevangelium*, 11.1, pp. 15-32.

26. W. L. Lane's observation seems as pertinent now as it was almost forty years ago ('*Theios Anēr* Christology and the Gospel of Mark', in *New Dimensions in New Testament Study* [ed. R. N. Longenecker and M. C. Tenney; Grand Rapids, MI: Zondervan, 1973], p. 159): 'It is necessary to recognize that NT [*sic*] studies tend to pass periodically through phases of concern with particular issues. The climate for research today is controlled by a wholesale concern with the polemical character of the documents and the identification of the opponents encountered by Paul and others. . . . In the absence of such references [to deviant points of view, like those found in Paul's letters], however, it would be unwise to assume that the presence of opponents within the community accounts for the character of the statement in a given document'.

bringing to it . . . an awareness of the other Gospels and the rest of the New Testament which, by virtue of our knowledge of this material, must color, if not in some cases distort, any reading or interpretation of Mark'.[27] While we grant the potential for such distortion, as well as the need to remain sensitive to Mark's distinctive theology, the soundness of this hermeneutical principle should be challenged on at least two fronts. On the one hand, there is the matter of practical exegesis: by reading Mark in complete isolation from the other Gospels, one risks exaggerating or distorting the significance of certain Markan themes.[28] On the other hand, at a theoretical level, such an isolation of the Second Gospel from the rest of the New Testament seems to vitiate Weeden's own *religionsgeschichtlich* perspective: for how can Mark be located within the developing religious thought of the time if the Gospel is sealed off from other early Christian literature?

Fourth, the interpretive key that, for Weeden, finally unlocks the Gospel of Mark is the dramatic role played by its characters in communicating different theological points of view. This is crucial to Weeden's understanding of Mark and merits careful reflection. (a) It should be said that reading the Second Gospel as a Greek drama, or as history written in accordance with Greek dramatic conventions, is a plausible and even suggestive manner of interpretation; however, it is certainly not the only way to read Mark, in either the first or the twenty-first century. Weeden implies that there was no other hermeneutical principle available to first-century Christians, but that is not so: surely they would have known the stories of the Old Testament and especially the prophetic narratives, which bear a marked resemblance to the Gospel narratives yet operate independently of hermeneutical principles presupposed in Hellenistic drama and history.[29]

27. 'Heresy', p. 148.

28. Thus Lane suggests that 'Weeden's attempt to sharpen the impression that the presentation of the unperceptiveness of the disciples is "peculiarly Markan" . . . by pointing to the more positive impression of the Twelve in Matthew and Luke is overdrawn' ('*Theios Anēr* Christology', p. 151).

29. One might recall such passages as Mark 1.2-3; 2.25-26; 6.15, 30-44; 7.6-7, 10; 8.1-10, 17-18, 28; 9.4-5, 11-13; 10.3-4, 6-7; 11.9-10, 17; 12.10-11, 26, 29-33, 36; 13.14; 14.1, 62; 15.24, 34-35, all of which presuppose no little knowledge of the Old Testament (cf. A. Suhl, *Die Funktion des alttestamentlichen Zitate und Anspielungen in Markusevangelium* [Gütersloh: Gütersloher Verlagshaus, 1965]). A number of scholars have considered the particular parallels between the Markan narrative and the stories of Elijah and Elisha in 1 and 2 Kings: among others, see R. Pesch, 'Berufung und Sendung'; R. E. Brown, 'Jesus and Elisha', *Pers* 12 (1971), pp. 85-104; and E. Schweizer, 'Neuere Markus-Forschung in USA', *EvT* 33 (1983), pp. 533-37. Robbins, *Je-*

(b) If Mark was trying to convey his point of view by means of a drama-tized dispute between Jesus (speaking for the Evangelist) and the disciples (representing Mark's antagonists), then he botched the job rather badly: as we shall see below, Jesus' own activity is ultimately responsible for throw-ing the disciples off the right track.[30] (c) Finally, the analysis of character in discerning a narrator's sympathies is a time-honored aspect of literary criticism,[31] and one that other biblical critics have fruitfully exploited;[32] indeed, it may be potentially helpful in the interpretation of the Second Gospel.[33] However, it should be clear that such an exercise is not necessar-ily integral to redaction criticism, as that method has been customarily un-derstood and practiced.[34]

Fifth, we might conclude these reflections on Weeden's general per-spective by considering the measure of history tolerable in his understand-ing of redaction criticism. Though we shall have opportunity to pursue this later in the chapter, for now let us note that Weeden seems to draw his position of historical skepticism from the presupposition of *Redaktions-geschichte* itself:

> But with the possibility that the evangelist is no longer concerned with the facts of 30 A.D. but rather with the specific problems of his own community in the late 60's . . . , the content of the confession [of Peter at Caesarea Philippi] can be understood only in view of the evange-list's own situation, not in terms of whatever content may have been

---

sus the Teacher, calls attention to the commingling of Hebrew and Greek narrative patterns in the Second Gospel.

30. As pointed out by D. O. Via, Jr, *Kerygma and Comedy in the New Testament: A Structuralist Approach to Hermeneutic* (Philadelphia: Fortress, 1975), p. 75. Alternatively, Via suggests that the disciples may reflect 'the existential problem of the difficulty of man's grasping the revelation of God in a suffering messiah, the difficulty of appropriating exi-stentially what one has been instructed about intellectually' (ibid., pp. 75-76).

31. See, for instance, R. Scholes and R. Kellogg, *The Nature of Narrative* (London: Ox-ford University Press, 1966), pp. 160-206.

32. Analogous to Weeden's perspectives on the Second Gospel as 'drama' and on char-acterization as a window through which historical conflict may be viewed is J. L. Martyn's approach to John, most notably articulated in *History and Theology in the Fourth Gospel* (rev. and enlarged; Nashville: Abingdon, 1979).

33. See Rhoads and Michie, *Mark as Story,* esp. pp. 101-36.

34. Weeden is not as clear on this point as one might wish: notice how he speaks of *both* redaction criticism *and* the Markan characters as 'the key' for unlocking the mystery of the Gospel's creation (*Mark,* pp. 1 and 18).

behind a confession made originally in 30 A.D. — if such a confession was made.[35]

This statement presents two problems. First, Weeden's reasoning is somewhat reckless: it is fallacious to argue from 'the possibility' of Mark's lack of historical concern to the certainty of an exclusively theological intention of the Evangelist. Second, by suggesting that Mark was interested *only* in theology, and *not at all* in history, has not Weeden posed the alternatives more sharply than is necessary for the practice of redaction criticism?[36]

B. Method

Although Weeden regards *Redaktionsgeschichte* as nothing less than 'the key for unlocking the mysteries behind the Gospel of Mark and its creation', as a rule he does not explicate the specific methods or strategies that are to be used in reading that Gospel redaction-critically. As I have noted, he cites with qualified approval Schreiber's criteria of Matthean and Lukan alterations of Mark (cf. Stein's fifth criterion; below, pp. 153-57), Markan selection of tradition (cf. Stein's sixth criterion; below, pp. 157-58), and Markan arrangement of tradition in accordance with 'a unified theological conception' (cf. Stein's eighth criterion; below, pp. 158-63). Nevertheless, the precise aspects of Weeden's *redaktionsgeschichtlich* procedure usually must be inferred from his work. It is to the task of drawing and systematizing such inferences that we now turn.

1. In reviewing Weeden's research, the only reference to a *Markan seam* that I have noted occurs in his discussion of the empty-tomb narrative (Mark 16.1-8). Weeden contends that the story could not have been originally connected to the burial account (15.42-47), since the latter in no way indicates the incompleteness of preparations for interment implied by 16.1 (namely, the bringing of spices by the women for the anointment of the corpse). If 16.1 were a redactional seam linking the two accounts, Weeden further argues, this would explain 'the awkward, redundant time references' created by the juxtaposition of 16.1 and 16.2 ('when the Sabbath was

35. 'Heresy', p. 149 n. 7.

36. As R. P. Martin comments, 'It is not impossible that [Mark] should be *both* sensitive to the historical traditions he has received *and* concerned so to interpret and angle these traditions as to bring home to the Christians of his day the meaning of Christ' (*Mark: Evangelist and Theologian*, p. 153 [Martin's emphasis]).

over'/ 'very early on the first day of the week . . . when the sun had risen'). So it is that 'Mark made the decision to link the empty-tomb story to the burial story'.[37]

Since Weeden's analysis at this point bears little fruit in his exegesis of 16.1-8 (see below), we need not belabor the matter. Two points may be mentioned in response. (a) Leaving aside for the moment the issue of awkward connectives, I see no reason why the burial and empty-tomb narratives could not have been joined at the pre-Markan stage. Although the narrative(s) of Jesus' resurrection appearances well might have antedated the empty-grave story,[38] once the latter was introduced into the tradition we might reasonably suppose that it would have been made to follow the burial account even as the narrative of the crucifixion had been made to precede it. In theory I can see neither justification nor advantage in arguing that Mark, not his source, was responsible for the connection of the empty-tomb and burial accounts.[39] (b) On the other hand, if one wishes to follow Weeden in attributing 16.1 to the Evangelist and 16.2 to his source, then those verses' 'awkward, redundant time references' present a curious argument for such a division: since 'awkward [temporal] redundancies' are often regarded as stylistic indicators of Markan redaction (compare, for example, 1.32), why could not one argue that verses 1 *and* 2 of chapter 16 constituted a 'Markan seam'? Exegetically, I have no particular interest in defending such an argument; I mention it only to indicate how analytically fickle our criteria for Markan redaction can sometimes be.

2. *Markan insertions* play a larger role in Weeden's work. There are four sections of the Gospel in which he finds significant redactional *Zwischenbemerkungen*. (i) In the parable complex of Mark 4, vv. 11-12 constitute a Markan insertion (note the formula καὶ ἔλεγεν αὐτοῖς) of traditional material that originally was used by Mark's opponents (proclaiming the disciples' receipt of esoteric knowledge from Jesus), whereas 4.13 is wholly Markan, lambasting as it does the disciples' dearth of discernment.[40] Also

37. *Mark*, pp. 103-105; quotations on pp. 104, 105.

38. Thus Bultmann, *Synoptic Tradition*, pp. 289-91. Bultmann (ibid., pp. 284-85) anticipates Weeden's argument that 16.1 precludes the possibility of the original coupling of the burial and empty-tomb stories; however, it does not follow from this form-critical deduction that their subsequent linkage had to have been made by *Mark*.

39. Indeed, if Mark composed his Gospel 'with [the] consummate skill' attributed to him by Weeden (*Mark*, p. 163), it would make more sense to credit the tradition with the 'clumsy' conjoining of 15.46-47 and 16.1.

40. *Mark*, pp. 148-49 (N.B. 149 n. 7), 150 n. 17; 'Conflict', pp. 212, 213, 221.

in ch. 4, vv. 21-24 constitute a clear reflection of Mark's belief (as construed by Weeden) that Jesus' teaching was characterized by openness and lucidity.[41] (ii) Following the transfiguration, Mark 9.9 'is a remark inserted by the evangelist in the service of a polemic against the disciples and their representatives in the Markan community. The point of 9.9 is to explain why an experience of Peter, James, and John during the public ministry, held by tradition to be a resurrection appearance, was mistakenly interpreted to be a resurrection experience'.[42] (iii) Into a Jewish-Christian apocalyptic core consisting of 13.7-8, 14-20, and 24-27, the Second Evangelist has inserted 13.5-6, 9-13, 21-23, and 28-37; that this material is insertional is suggested by the Markan key word βλέπειν, by characteristic redactional themes (the blunting of the apocalyptic edge and the caution against messianic pretenders who would lead the community astray), and by the general consensus of Markan exegetes.[43] (iv) Into the traditional empty-tomb story (16.1-8) Mark has inserted v. 7, which both fulfills the prophecy inserted by the Evangelist at 14.28 as well as shifts the emphasis of the pericope away from the resurrection of Jesus and onto the message to the disciples of his reappearance in Galilee. Mark 16.8b is also to be understood as an editorial insertion, inasmuch as φοβεῖσθαι in that concluding snippet of verse suggests a negative, cowardly fear (as opposed to the positive *mysterium tremendum* implicit in 16.8a; compare 6.51/6.52).[44]

The evidence supplied by Weeden for distinguishing all of the above as Markan *Zwischenbemerkungen* varies in kind and cogency. With respect to 4.11-12, 21-25; 13.5-6, 9-13, 21-23, 28-37, and 16.8b, Weeden's contention rests in part on ostensibly Markan vocabulary, which will be assessed below (pp. 166-68). In addition, thematic considerations have been invoked regarding 4.21-25, the verses from Mark 13, and 16.7; like vocabulary, this criterion demands more extensive evaluation (below, pp. 158-63). Therefore, while certain criticisms can be made at this juncture, it should be stressed that Weeden's most important indicators for Markan insertions are so-called Markan vocabulary and themes; if one considers these criteria to be sound, one may be inclined to accept as equally valid Weeden's claim for redactional insertions.

However, other factors must be taken into account. First, some of

---

41. *Mark*, p. 144; 'Conflict', pp. 212, 221.
42. *Mark*, pp. 122-23.
43. 'Heresy', pp. 150-58; *Mark*, pp. 71-100.
44. *Mark*, pp. 47-50.

Weeden's arguments for Markan insertions lack methodological rigor. For instance, he defends 16.7 as an insertion on the ground that 14.28 (which, admittedly, exhibits similarity in content) is also an insertion; however, (a) no evidence is presented to support his allegation that 14.28 *is* an insertion, except that such a position is 'espoused by a number of exegetes',[45] which in turn suggests that (b) Weeden's argument is invalid since he is 'substantiating' one conjecture only by the presupposition of another, similar conjecture. Likewise, the suggestion that Mark 13.5-6, 9-13, 21-23, and 28-37 are 'generally agreed' among scholars to be redactional scarcely amounts to proof; indeed, it contradicts Weeden's own admission that the interpretive problems in Mark 13 have been amenable to a diversity of solutions.[46] Second, at certain points Weeden's strongest defense for editorial insertions is, in fact, his cluster of *traditionsgeschichtlich* presuppositions about the passage. For example, his contention that Mark 9.9 serves only 'as an explanatory remark to the reader, explicating why the resurrection story of the evangelist's opponents could not have been a bona fide resurrection experience'[47] depends on a chain of unproven and arguably shaky assumptions: (a) that the transfiguration originally circulated as a resurrection-appearance narrative, (b) which was appropriated as such by some opponents of the Evangelist, who in turn (c) moved the account into the narrative of the earthly Jesus' life (d) with the aim of disproving, in the minds of his readers, those opponents' claims for its character as a resurrection appearance. Similarly ingenious are Weeden's claims for Mark 4.11-12: while Mark is responsible for the insertion of these verses into a chapter of predominantly traditional (and anti-Markan) material, they actually derive from his *opponents'* tradition, which Mark has appropriated and placed here on Jesus' lips for ironic effect![48] Aside from the question of exegetical plausibility, plainly Weeden is bolstering certain redaction-critical claims with some of his exegetical results (or preconceptions). Whatever one makes of the conclusions drawn by Weeden from such a procedure, the method being employed is suspect.

45. Ibid., p. 105. Weeden does not name these exegetes.

46. Contrast 'Heresy', p. 150, with *Mark*, p. 72.

47. *Mark*, p. 139.

48. Ibid., pp. 141-49; 'Conflict', p. 222. According to Weeden's interpretation, Jesus is to be regarded as the mouthpiece for Markan orthodoxy; thus it is strange that here the Evangelist would have Jesus spouting heresy (as Weeden construes it). In arguing for 'Markan irony' at 4.11-12, it appears that Weeden has made a virtue (Mark's literary sophistication) of necessity (squaring *Jesus'* pronouncement of 4.11-12 with Weeden's decoding of the Gospel).

3. As far as I can determine, Weeden's sole reference to the redactional significance of *Markan summaries* is his description of Mark 1.32ff., 3.7ff., and 6.53ff. as the Evangelist's interspersed 'summaries on [Jesus'] θεῖος ἀνήρ activity'.[49] Concerning this ascription, three things should be noted: (a) these passages are virtually assumed to be redactional, an assumption supported only by appeal to another scholar's research;[50] (b) once again Weeden focuses on a particular theme that, in his estimation, denotes Markan redaction; and (c) that theme is 'θεῖος ἀνήρ activity', which Weeden equates with Jesus' performance of miracles (an equation that will be discussed presently).

4. In the literature surveyed I have discovered no reference by Weeden to *Mark's creation of pericopes*. This is surprising in light of Weeden's aforementioned perspective on the Evangelist as exerting 'an author's freedom and creativity in composing the Gospel'. Nonetheless, in his redaction-critical analysis Weeden appears reticent to attribute to Mark the fabrication of pericopes out of whole cloth; instead he prefers to consider how thoroughly the redactor has reworked malleable traditions for his own ends.

5. Weeden has considerably more to say about *the Markan modification of material*, in all of Stein's suggested aspects. Most frequently, Weeden attempts to isolate Markan redaction by comparing material in the Second Gospel with its later modifications in the other Synoptics. According to Weeden, both Matthew and Luke delete or alter Markan passages (for example, 4.13; 5.29-31; 6.52; 7.17; 8.4, 14-21) 'in favor of a better picture of the disciples' acumen', thereby substantiating 'that this obtuse character of the disciples is a distinctively Markan motif'.[51] It is not a uniquely Markan motif, inasmuch as the Fourth Evangelist also depicts a sometimes dissonant relationship between Jesus and the disciples; nevertheless, we can attribute to Markan bias 'the thoroughgoing programmatic denigration of the disciples'.[52] Other distinctively Markan emphases become detectable through comparison of the Second with the First and Third Gospels: the stress on the false Christs' performance of 'signs and wonders' (13.21-22, deleted in the Lukan parallel owing to the Third Evangelist's own proclivity for *theios-anēr* theology),[53] the primitive conception of Jesus' ascent to

49. 'Heresy', p. 148. The indefinite primary citations ('ff.') are Weeden's own.
50. L. E. Keck, 'Mark 3.7-12 and Mark's Christology', *JBL* 84 (1965), pp. 341-48.
51. 'Heresy', p. 146 n. 4; see also *Mark*, pp. 28-32, 35-38, 39-40.
52. *Mark*, pp. 40-41.
53. 'Heresy', p. 152 n. 25.

enthronement at the *parousia* in Mark 13.24-27 (rather than the Matthean and Lukan image of Christ's glorious descent to earth),[54] and Mark's attestation of Jesus' resurrection by means of the story of the empty grave (as over against the appearance narratives in the other Gospels).[55]

In response to this component of his procedure, it might be said, first, that Weeden's most persuasive arguments involve a judgment, not about Mark's intentions, but on what Matthew and Luke may be doing redactionally. Thus it is more tenable that Luke omitted Mark 13.21-22 from his version of the apocalyptic discourse (Luke 21.8-36), owing to his theological predilection for 'signs and wonders' performed by Jesus' successors (compare Acts 3.1-10; 4.29-31; 5.12-16; 6.8; *et passim*), than that Mark 13.21-22 points to the Second Evangelist's struggle with *theioi andres* in his community (concerning which Mark explicitly says nothing). Second, the other Synoptists' modifications of Mark do not always move in directions that are congenial with Weeden's understanding of their intentions. For instance, it seems odd to attribute to Luke unhappiness 'about the Markan insinuation that Jesus played an inactive role in this [post-resurrection] period, thereby leaving it to the Spirit to guide the faithful',[56] since this is precisely the state of affairs that obtains in the book of Acts (Acts 1.8-9; 2.4; 9.31; 10.19; 20.22-23; 21.4; compare 16.7). Moreover, it is difficult to accept Weeden's claim that Matthew and Luke always tone down Mark's maligning of the disciples: Peter's denial looks every bit as bleak, if not bleaker, in Matthew (26.69-75) and in Luke (22.54-62, notwithstanding 22.31-34); Judas' macabre end, unmentioned by Mark, is vividly (albeit divergently) recounted by the other Synoptists (Matt 27.3-10; Acts 1.15-20); the disciples remain every bit as arrogant in the Third Gospel (9.46-55) as in the Second;[57] and, despite their rosy portrayal by Luke, in Acts Jesus' followers remain slow to act (Acts 1.11), slow to understand (Acts 10.9-17), and even persecutory of Jesus in a manner never described by Mark (Acts 8.1; 9.4-5).[58] Third, whatever may be gained from the redaction-critical strategy of observing the other Evangelists' modification of Mark, it is rather surprising that Weeden should countenance, much less adhere to, such a procedure: after all, he advocates an in-

---

54. *Mark,* pp. 124-37.

55. Ibid., pp. 102-3.

56. Ibid., p. 87.

57. This point is acknowledged by Weeden (ibid., p. 37).

58. It is true that Mark 6.52, 7.17, and 8.4, 14, 16-21 do not appear in Luke; however, since these verses are part of Luke's 'Great Omission' of Mark 6.45–8.26, it is difficult to know what, if anything, this implies about Luke's treatment of discipleship material in Mark.

terpretation of the Second Gospel that does not '[bring] to it consciously or unconsciously an awareness of the other Gospels and the rest of the New Testament literature which . . . must color, if not in some cases distort, any reading or interpretation of Mark'.[59]

Inasmuch as the Evangelist's composition is appraised by Weeden as being 'crystal clear', exhibiting 'consummate skill',[60] it is fitting that the 'misformation' of pericopes would be all but absent from his discussion of Markan modification. The clearest instance of such 'misformation' seems to occur in Weeden's consideration of the empty-grave story: following Ludger Schenke, Weeden argues that Mark 16.3-4 is redactional for two reasons. (a) Abruptly appearing only in response to 15.46, the problem of the stone's removal is left unresolved by Mark. (b) The close syntactical parallelism of 15.46 and 16.3 suggests that Mark created the latter, tailoring it to the syntax of the former.[61] This analysis may be correct. Nevertheless, three things should be borne in mind: (i) Weeden's argument assumes but does not demonstrate that *Mark* was responsible for the connection of the burial and resurrection narratives.[62] (ii) If the Evangelist inserted 16.3-4 only because he thought the issue of the tomb's seal needed to be addressed, then he did not do a thorough job of dealing with that problem.[63] (iii) The creation of 16.3 on the basis of 15.46 is credible, though it flouts the more customary redaction-critical argument that Mark is responsible for both halves of the stylistic duality recurrent in his Gospel.

Although not explicitly treated as such, in one sense the investigation of the inconsistency between Mark's account and what actually happened (Stein's third subcriterion of Markan modification) undergirds Weeden's entire project: 'Since there is no historical basis for a dispute [over *theios-anēr* Christology] having taken place between Jesus and the disciples, the only conclusion possible is that the *Sitz im Leben* for this dispute is Mark's own community and that Mark has intentionally staged the dispute in his Gospel using the disciples to play the role of his opponents and presenting

---

59. 'Heresy', p. 148. Notice also the appeals to 2 Corinthians for support of Weeden's theory of the *theioi andres* (*Mark,* pp. 41-44, 144-45).

60. *Mark,* pp. 163, 164.

61. Ibid., pp. 104-5; cf. L. Schenke, *Auferstehungsverkündigung und leeres Grab* (SB 33; Stuttgart: Katholisches Bibelwerk, 1969), pp. 30-55.

62. Concern over removal of the stone could have been part of the pre-Markan tradition behind 16.1-8.

63. As Weeden admits, 'No mention is made of how [the stone] was rolled away or by whom' (*Mark,* p. 105).

Jesus as the advocate of the evangelist's own position'.[64] To this assertion two responses might be made. First, if there be such incongruity between history and the Gospel, then the notion that Mark is wholly responsible for it is by no means 'the only conclusion possible': it is equally possible that this historical inconsistency could have arisen within any of the intermediate stages (embraced by Marxsen's second *Sitz im Leben*) between the historical event and Mark's Gospel. Stated differently, both the passion narrative (14.1–16.8) and the Gospel's central section on Christology and discipleship (8.27–10.45) could have been prefabricated and theologically charged, at least to some degree, before Mark ever received them (in the same way that — according to Weeden — the miracle narratives were subjected to pre-Markan retooling by the *theioi andres*).[65] Second, the nature of, and reasons for, the breach between history and theology in Mark do not appear to have been clearly or coherently worked out by Weeden. On the one hand, he argues that the heretics combatted by Mark claimed that their position went back to the disciples themselves (a hypothesis for which Weeden offers no evidence whatever); on the other hand, *Mark* is considered to be the scenarist who has placed the heretical lines on the disciples' lips, making of the twelve surrogates for the Evangelist's opponents.[66] On the one hand, there is no historical basis for the occurrence of a Christological dispute between Jesus and the disciples; on the other hand, Weeden maintains that Mark appealed for support of his position to the *historical* Jesus.[67] On the one hand, Jesus speaks as a proxy for Mark and the disciples represent Mark's antagonists; on the other hand, the Evangelist has Jesus proclaim the parabolic teaching in 4.3-32, all but six verses of which (vv. 13, 21-25) espouse the *opponents'* theology and chief hermeneutical principle (4.11-12).[68]

To summarize this subsection: Weeden's redaction-critical arguments involving the Markan modification of material are rarely based on the 'misformation' of pericopes and are least convincing when they detail putative inconsistencies between historical events and the Evangelist's replication of those events. His strongest arguments stem from the comparison of Mark with Matthew and Luke, even though (i) these arguments directly

---

64. 'Heresy', p. 150; cf. *Mark*, p. 69.

65. As aptly noted by Hickling, 'Problem of Method', pp. 342-43.

66. 'Heresy', p. 155; *Mark*, p. 148; contrast *Mark*, pp. 162-63.

67. *Mark*, p. 162. For this point I am indebted to Martin, *Int* 26 (1972), p. 362.

68. *Mark*, pp. 139-51. If the preponderance of Mark 4 represents the heretics' perspective, why did Mark, as dramatist, not give those lines *to the disciples* (as one would expect on the basis of Weeden's theory)?

inform, not Markan, but Matthean or Lukan theology, and (ii) they seem inconsistent with Weeden's injunction that the Second Gospel be investigated in isolation from the rest of the New Testament.

6. On two occasions Weeden alludes to *Mark's selection of material:* first, with reference to the saturation of the first half of the Gospel with wonder-working activities of Jesus; and second, with regard to the futurist eschatology in Mark 13.24-27.[69] As deduced by Weeden, the *redaktions-geschichtlich* significance of these two passages is very interesting: (a) Mark imbues the first half of his Gospel with miracles in order to lead the disciples (narratively speaking) and his readers (didactically speaking) to the conclusion that Jesus is a *theios-anēr* Christ (only to reverse that position from 8.30 on).[70] (b) The inclusion of 13.24-27 signals Mark's preoccupation with the future Son of man, not with the risen Christ in the present experience of the church.[71] I concur with Weeden that Mark's inclusion of the miracles and eschatological material may flag some of the Evangelist's theological concerns; however, I disagree with him on what the nature of those concerns might be. With regard to 13.24-27, Mark manifestly exhibits a futurist eschatological orientation; its being held in tension with a realized eschatological perspective is not, however, thereby precluded (see 1.14-15; 16.6).[72] With respect to the spate of miracles in Mark 1–8, a number of difficulties color the conclusion drawn by Weeden. First, the bifurcation of the Gospel into distinct halves, wonder-working (1.1–8.29) and suffering (8.30–16.8) will not withstand scrutiny: there are as many indications of hostility toward Jesus in the first half (for instance, 3.6, 19b-35; 5.17; 6.1-6a) as there are references to miracles in the second (for example, 9.2-8, 14-29; 10.46-52; 11.12-14; 16.6). Second, *if* in the first half of his Gospel Mark has concentrated attention on Jesus' role as a *theios anēr,* and *if* the disciples themselves represent *theioi andres* (as Weeden contends), it is simply inconceivable — on Weeden's own terms — that Peter and company would not 'get the point' until Caesarea Philippi. Third, if we assume Weeden's

---

69. 'Heresy', p. 148; *Mark,* pp. 91-92.

70. 'Heresy', pp. 148-49. Cf. *Mark,* p. 5: 'There is absolutely no hint in the first half of the Gospel that authentic messiahship should contain any other Christological dimension [than that of the *theios anēr*]'.

71. *Mark,* pp. 90-96.

72. In *Mark* (pp. 106-11), Weeden expends great energy and ingenuity in making a case for 16.1-8 as a translation or 'anti-appearance' narrative. However, there is no escaping the fact that 16.6 says, not only that Jesus is not there, but also that 'he has risen' — and resurrection from the dead is, indubitably, an eschatological event.

point of view, then, through Mark's selection of the miracle material and his favorable presentation of it in the first half of the Gospel, the Evangelist has made Jesus himself responsible for his misidentification by the disciples as a *theios anēr*.[73]

7. As a redaction-critical criterion, *the Markan omission of material* plays a minimal role for Weeden. Indeed, it plays a rather veiled role: hence, when he considers cases in which Matthew and Luke used their non-Markan sources to add complimentary touches to their portrayal of the disciples (e.g. Matt 10.40-42; Luke 5.1-11; 10.23-24), Weeden seems to imply that Mark could have done the same but refrained from so doing.[74] Of course, this presupposes that Mark indeed had other sources, similar to Q and L, the use of which he omitted when the disciples were cast in a positive light. Unfortunately, we know nothing so definite about the material available to Mark that would support such an allegation.[75]

8. If one considers the delineation of themes as a factor in the broader assessment of *Mark's arrangement of material*, then no criterion looms larger than this in Weeden's attempt to recover a Markan redaction history. For him, one of the surest signs of Mark's theological interests is the Evangelist's geographical scheme. This geographical arrangement is centered on Galilee, which is

> a region of immense theological import for Mark. It is the locus where Jesus proclaimed the authentic christology and eschatology (1.14-15; 8.27-31; 9.30ff.) and where he was opposed by those advocating a *theios anēr* christology (8.27-33). It is the locus of the parousia event (16.7).[76]

Explicit in this defense of Galilee's significance for Mark are other themes that, in Weeden's judgment, characterize the Evangelist's theology and arrangement of material. We may systematize these motifs as follows:

---

73. Thus Via, *Kerygma and Comedy*, p. 75.

74. *Mark*, pp. 30, 36, 38.

75. If Mark's Gospel bespeaks the sort of tensions postulated by Weeden, it is a wonder that the Evangelist did not omit any number of things that run against the grain of his theology: the authority conferred on the disciples to exorcise demons (3.15; 6.7) and their success in doing so (6.30), the esoteric teaching of 4.11-12, and the transfiguration (9.2-8), to name but a few. Weeden's wonted rebuttal is that such theological infelicities had to be conceded by Mark in order for him to score points off his opponents (see e.g. *Mark*, p. 168 n. 9), but to me this seems tenuous at best and at worst special pleading.

76. *Mark*, pp. 109-10; cf. pp. 95, 110 n. 11, 112.

Christology:
>   Jesus as the one whose identity is the object of continuous
>   speculation ('the identity motif');[77]
>   The correction of a *theios-anēr* Christology by a Christology
>   that emphasizes suffering;[78]
>   The delay of Jesus' exaltation until the *parousia;*[79]

Discipleship: The disciples as
>   Assuming a position of privilege, yet held specially responsible
>   and often unable to perform responsibly,[80]
>   A foil for Jesus' teaching concerning true (that is, suffering) dis-
>   cipleship,[81]
>   Stupid and abandoning Jesus, as epitomized by Peter,[82]
>   Those whose position deteriorates as the Gospel narrative pro-
>   gresses,[83]
>   Generally the object of Mark's 'blackwashing';[84]

Miscellaneous:
>   Retiring to 'a house';[85]
>   'The mountain';[86]
>   A 'desert place';[87]
>   'Salvation'.[88]

If asked how these themes may be adjudged characteristically Markan,
Weeden explains that they are highlighted by the Evangelist's arrangement
of individual pericopes: thus Mark manipulated whole blocks of material
in order to depict the disciples' progressive deterioration *vis-à-vis* Jesus
(1.16–8.26; 8.27–14.9; 14.10–16.8), to adjoin contrasting theologies of glory

77. Ibid., p. 57.
78. Ibid., pp. 56, 58-59, 68-69, 73, 160 n. 1.
79. Ibid., pp. 112-24; cf. pp. 88, 93-97.
80. 'Conflict', pp. 217-18, 220-21; *Mark*, p. 150 n. 17.
81. *Mark*, pp. 59, 64 n. 18, 84.
82. Ibid., p. 38. Cf. p. 123: at the transfiguration Mark 'portrays Peter as a dunce'.
83. 'Heresy', pp. 145-47; *Mark*, pp. 26-51.
84. 'Heresy', p. 145.
85. *Mark*, pp. 157-58.
86. Ibid., p. 158.
87. Ibid., p. 156.
88. Ibid., pp. 84, 99.

and suffering (1.1–8.29 and 9.2-8 versus 8.30–9.1), and to apply the brakes on an overwrought apocalyptic fervor (by dividing his material into two consecutive yet different spheres of action, 13.5-23, 28-37 and 13.24-27).[89] Similarly (according to Weeden), Mark has carefully planted specific verses so as to undercut otherwise heretical points of view: the juxtaposition of 4.13 against 4.11-12 vividly dramatizes 'the strident dissonance between the disciples' so-called favored position [vv. 11-12] and the actual nature of the disciples' performance [v. 13]'; the exhortation at 4.24 has been put there by the Evangelist to emphasize the disciples' responsibility, shifting the focus away from their special privilege (in 4.25).[90] The same point is driven home by Mark's sandwiching of the parables in ch. 4 (with their stress on the disciples' privileged information) into the context of pericopes that emphasize the special responsibility of followers of Jesus (3.31-35/8.35-38; 9.33-41; 10.13-16, 35-45; 14.32-42, 66-72).[91]

Obviously, 'the Markan arrangement of material' is, for Weeden, an extraordinarily important *redaktionsgeschichtlich* criterion. For this reason, a more detailed criticism of this aspect of his procedure is demanded.

(a) Regarding first the thematic significance of Galilee (and the larger geographical arrangement that it suggests), Weeden has not made a convincing case that 'Galilee' bears distinctively *redactional* import, that is, any significance other than that connoted in the pre-Markan tradition. On three aforementioned grounds, Weeden would disagree with my assessment; of these I find none especially persuasive, even on his own terms. First, if (as Weeden suggests) Galilee is 'the locus for authentic Christology', it is equally the locus for what amounts to inauthentic Christology in his reconstruction: Galilee is, after all, the principal venue for Jesus' miraculous, (so-called) *theios-anēr* behavior. Second, if Galilee is the site 'where [Jesus] was opposed by those advocating a *theios-anēr* Christology', then so too is Judea (that is, Jerusalem). Third, if Mark 14.28 and 16.7 refer, not to the *parousia*, but to the resurrection,[92] then Galilee would allude (in

---

89. See, respectively, 'Heresy', pp. 146-47 ('a carefully formulated polemical device'); ibid., p. 155; *Mark,* pp. 58-59, 84, 112-21; *Mark,* p. 88; cf. pp. 93-94, 97.

90. Quotation from *Mark,* p. 150 n. 7; 'Conflict', pp. 217-18.

91. 'Conflict', p. 221.

92. *Pace* Weeden and others, there are good reasons for thinking that these verses have Jesus' resurrection as their referent: (a) The verb, ὁράω, is used in the active voice, and not just in the passive, for experiences of the risen Lord (cf. John 20.18, 25, 29; 1 Cor. 9.1). (b) In Mark 9.9-13 the limit set for the disciples' silence about Jesus' glory is, not the *parousia*, but the resurrection. (c) In using Mark 16.7, Matthew construed the promise of the young man

Weeden's terms) to 'triumphalism' — precisely the reverse of his argument. In brief, the questions surrounding the true theological significance (if any) of 'Galilee', both in the tradition and in its redaction, dilute Weeden's claim that that region conveys 'immense theological import for Mark'.

(b) The difficulties entailed in separating tradition from redaction and in adjudicating theological significance bedevil Weeden's proposal of other 'Markan themes'. For example, he admits that the 'house' and 'mountain' motifs in the Second Gospel testify to a confused pattern of (i) Markan derivation, (ii) traditional derivations, and (iii) traditional derivations subsequently co-opted by Mark for his own theological purposes.[93] In all probability, other themes from the list compiled above originate from an equally complex tradition history that would defy Weeden's (or anyone's) efforts to sort out.

(c) In his treatment of the Evangelist's arrangement of individual pericopes, Weeden does not always provide the clearest analysis either of what Mark is doing redactionally or of the theological motives to be inferred from that redaction. For instance, even on a surface reading of the text, Mark 13.5-23, 28-37 and 13.24-27 do not suggest, *pace* Weeden, the redactor's arrangement of material into 'two consecutive spheres of action' (namely, world history and cosmic occurrences). On the contrary: if it be a separable unit at all, 13.24-27 constitutes not a consecution but an intercalation, material laminated between vv. 23 and 28. If we are to make anything theologically of this, it is scarcely that Mark envisions dichotomous epochs of worldly and cosmic happenings; more likely, the intercalated verses reflect an 'intercalated eschatology' that holds in tension events *both* present *and* future. To take another example of Markan arrangement suggested by Weeden: the threefold devolution of the disciples, from imperceptiveness (1.16–8.26) to misconception (8.27–14.9) to rejection (14.10-72), is just not as tightly structured and demarcated as Weeden would like. Were his analysis correct, we would hardly expect to find (i) sufficient perceptiveness among the disciples for them to ask about, and to receive instruction concerning, the parables (4.10, 11); (ii) Jesus' implicit confidence in the twelve, attested by their selection and missionary dispatch (3.13; 6.7, 12); (iii) an unknown exorcist (that is, one displaying so-called *theios-anēr*

---

at the tomb as referring to an appearance of the resurrected Lord (Matt 28.7-20). For a careful sifting of the evidence, consult Seal, 'Parousia'.

93. *Mark*, pp. 157-58.

behavior) being ranged 'on our side' by Jesus (9.38-41); or (iv) a continuing association of the disciples with Jesus (14.12-16, 28, 32, 47, 54; 16.7).[94]

(d) The persuasiveness of Weeden's suggestion that Mark 4.13 and 24 have been strategically placed by the Evangelist in order to reverse the flow of some opposing argument (esoteric instruction as the foundation of special privilege) will be directly proportional to the credence given to Weeden's hypothesized Markan setting and *modus operandi*. It is easier for me to accept Weeden's suggestion that ch. 4 is a compilation of heterogenous materials than to credit his explanation of that phenomenon.[95] In any case, Weeden does not consistently follow through with this sort of redaction-critical reasoning: 4.34, which caps the entire Markan parable chapter, is attributed, not to Mark (as one might expect on the basis of Weeden's previous contention), but to pre-Markan tradition which the Evangelist has let stand. Apparently, Weeden is forced to shift his argument at this point, not because v. 34 creates no conflict with what has preceded, but because it produces dissonance with his peculiar interpretation of ch. 4: 4.34 speaks of Jesus' exclusively parabolic instruction and of his confidential, complete explanations to the disciples, and Weeden's theory of the Evangelist's intentions will tolerate neither of these ideas. The best that Weeden seems able to do is to chalk up 4.34 as 'a minor case of an editorial oversight'.[96]

(e) I have indicated one of the few allusions made by Weeden to Markan intercalations; the claim that ch. 4, with its supposed theology of 'special privilege', was purposefully inserted by Mark into the midst of surrounding pericopes that highlight instead special responsibility (3.31-35; 8.35-38; 9.33-41; 10.13-16, 35-45; 14.32-42, 66-72). Weeden's argument runs thus: (i) the Evangelist favors special responsibility and rejects special privilege (prerogatives claimed by *theioi andres*); (ii) Mark 3.31-35 emphasizes responsibility ('doing the will of God'), whereas (iii) corresponding passages, from 8.35ff. on, portray the disciples' loss of their special relationship to Jesus because they reject such responsibility; therefore, (iv) the message of special privilege in Mark 4 has been interpolated into these passages in order to set in context and thereby discredit a theology based on special privilege.[97] To this pro-

---

94. For some of these observations I am indebted to Martin, *Mark: Evangelist and Theologian*, p. 152.

95. If Mark enjoyed as much freedom over his material as Weeden suggests (*Mark*, pp. 1-3), why did the Evangelist settle for small insertions that create such subtle, even vague, dissonances?

96. *Mark*, pp. 143-44.

97. 'Conflict', p. 221.

posal I would respond as follows: Thesis (i) cannot be plainly demonstrated from the verses involved and would have to be tested throughout the Gospel before being accepted as valid; thesis (ii) is a legitimate, if incomplete, interpretation of 3.31-35; neither element of thesis (iii) is credible (in 8.35–9.1 and elsewhere the disciples neither abdicate all responsibility nor lose their special relation to Jesus); Weeden's conclusion (iv) is specious inasmuch as (first) 8.35–9.1 and passages beyond are too far distant from ch. 4 to be reckoned as constituent of a Markan intercalation, as the term is customarily understood,[98] and (second) Markan interpolations typically serve to interweave themes common to different pericopes, not to discredit one theme by the juxtaposition of another.[99]

(f) By way of concluding this subsection, it should be said that, in Weeden's analyses, a circular interplay appears to exist between the isolation of distinctively Markan themes and the distinguishing of distinctively Markan arrangements. Weeden is able to discern Markan themes because he is familiar with characteristically Markan arrangements; he can identify Markan arrangements as editorial constructions because he has learned to recognize typical Markan themes. Given the exigencies of Markan redaction criticism, so circular a procedure may be unavoidable; however, such circularity becomes vicious when the criterion of Markan arrangement merely sanctions the critic's assumptions, whatever they might be, about matters of thematic interest to Mark.

9. As far as I am aware, *the Markan introduction* does not figure in Weeden's redaction-critical work on the disciples. For our purposes, this criterion may be safely ignored.

10. *The Markan conclusion* is considered at greater length by Weeden. His proposal incorporates the following steps: (a) A greater likelihood that 16.8 is the actual ending of the Gospel is argued on the basis of (b) linguistic possibility, (c) thematic coherence with the rest of the Gospel (N.B. the continued denigration of the disciples; a *parousia* prediction at 16.7), and (d) the evidence of possible Markan insertions at 16.7, 8b.[100] To anticipate

---

98. Cf. the proximity of 3.1-3/3.5b-6 (the healing of the man with the withered arm) to 3.4-5a (healing on the Sabbath), 6.6b-13/6.30 (the sending and return of the twelve) to 6.14-29 (the death of John), and 14.53-54/14.66-72 (Peter's denial) to 14.55-65 (the Sanhedrin hearing).

99. Cf. 2.1-5a/2.10b-12 (authority to heal the paralytic) and 2.5b-10a (authority to forgive sins); 3.20-21/3.31-35 (the opposition of Jesus' family) and 3.22-30 (the opposition of the scribes from Jerusalem); 11.12-14/11.20-25(?) (the cursing of the fig tree) and 11.15-19 (judgment upon the temple).

100. *Mark,* pp. 45-51, 101-17.

certain exegetical results, for Weeden all of this adds up to the following conclusion: the ending of Mark's Gospel is best understood as a translation or 'removal' story, 'an anti-appearance-tradition narrative' that emphasizes Christ's absence. The announcement of the angel in 16.7 refers, not to the resurrection, but to Christ's *parousia,* which will occur in Galilee ('Mark's favorite geographical spot'). The cowardly silence of the women (16.8b), designedly inserted by Mark, 'robs the disciples of their apostolic credentials': since they never received the message of 16.7, the conclusion of the Gospel constitutes 'the evangelist's final thrust in his vendetta against the disciples and his commitment to discredit them completely'.[101]

Our evaluation of Weeden's procedure and results at this point may be abbreviated, since the various aspects of his method already have been considered (under insertions and putative themes) or will be discussed presently (see below, on vocabulary). For now we should observe that these three methodological components do not function independently of each other: there is an inherent circularity in their operation, in that the insertions are ascertained chiefly on the basis of their distinctive vocabulary, which in turn is deemed distinctive because of the themes suggested by that vocabulary (for example, 'Galilee', 'cowardly fear'). Given the sweep of his exegetical results, it is worth mentioning that Weeden invests considerably more confidence in the Gospel's actual ending at 16.8 than does Robert Stein, who, while accepting the Markan conclusion as a *redaktionsgeschichtlich* criterion, ultimately regards it as 'an enigma [which] offers little assistance in the investigation of a Markan redaction history'.[102]

11. *Markan vocabulary and style* constitute another dimension of Weeden's method. Table 5 lists those linguistic units that, for Weeden, are key Markan words. Table 6 presents a shorter list of words that are denoted by Weeden as 'pre-Markan' or even 'non-Markan' (in the sense of being theologically antagonistic to Mark).[103] By my reckoning, Weeden's only reference to an element of distinctively Markan literary style occurs in his

---

101. Ibid., pp. 11-17, 106-11, 117; cf. pp. 50-51, 95.

102. Stein, 'Markan Redaction History', p. 197. In his review of Weeden's monograph (*TS* 33 [1972], pp. 754-56), Schuyler Brown has noted an interesting historical paradox raised by Weeden's exegesis of the Markan conclusion: 'if the message of [16.7] was never delivered, how is the Evangelist in on it, so that he can use it both to authenticate the Resurrection and to assure his community that they will see the Son of Man at the parousia?' (ibid., p. 755).

103. Although I may have overlooked some aspect of Markan vocabulary cited by Weeden, in both tables I have striven for completeness. Weeden does not indicate each word's frequency of occurrence in the Gospels; consequently, I have not done so.

TABLE 5   Weeden's Identification of Key Markan Words

Verbal Unit	Page Reference in Weeden[104]
βλέπειν (especially in the imperative mood)	22, 72-73; 'Heresy', 151
γινώσκειν (with the connotation of 'perception or penetrating insight')	140
διδάσκειν	150 n. 18
διδαχή	150 n. 18
ἔνεκεν (ἐμοῦ)	84
ἐπιτιμᾶν	66 n. 22
εὐαγγέλιον (especially as identified with Jesus)	82; 'Heresy', 157; 'Conflict', 205
καὶ ἔλεγεν αὐτοῖς	149 n. 17; 'Conflict', 208, 211, 221, 240 n. 61
κηρύσσειν	150 n. 18
οὐδείς (followed by the negative of a verb in the indicative)	49
ὄχλος	22 n. 7
πλῆθος	22 n. 7
πνεῦμα ἅγιον	'Heresy', 157-58
πολλοί (as a substantive substitute for ὄχλοι)	22 n. 7
σημεῖα καὶ τέρατα	74-74; 'Heresy', 152
φοβεῖσθαι (especially in the third person plural, imperfect tense, passive voice)	49 n. 6

discussion of Mark 8.29-33, wherein an intentional, antithetical parallelism is detected (arguably a form of Markan duality).[105]

What comments or criticisms are elicited by Weeden's employment of the redaction-critical criterion of vocabulary and style?

(a) First, we might note a certain tension in Weeden's research: al-

104. Unless otherwise indicated, all citations are from *Mark*.
105. *Mark*, pp. 65-66.

TABLE 6 Weeden's Identification of Pre-Markan or Non-Markan Words

Verbal Unit	Page Reference in Weeden
ἔκστασις	48
λαλεῖν	150 n. 18
λόγος (used absolutely)	150-51, 165; 'Conflict', 218, 239 n. 46
παραβολή	150 n. 18
τρόμος	48

though he expresses confidence in the evidence afforded by 'Markan key words', in fact the criterion of vocabulary and style does not play as important a role in Weeden's *redaktionsgeschichtlich* practice as in the work of other Markan redaction critics.[106] For now I only take note of this fact; the critical assessment to be made of it is relative to the confidence one has in the use of linguistic or stylistic statistics for obtaining a Markan redaction history.

(b) Apart from how it compares with the redaction-critical work of others, Weeden's investigation is not without its inherent difficulties. For example, he admits that certain words identified by him as redactional probably appeared in the pre-Markan tradition as well (ὄχλος, πλῆθος, πολλοί; cf. λαλεῖν).[107] Weeden's trust in his own ability to sort these words into piles of 'tradition' and 'redaction' raises another problem to be considered presently. In any case, our ignorance of the precise shape and features of pre-Markan tradition opens the possibility that other items on Weeden's list of 'Markan vocabulary' also might have appeared in the tradition.

(c) On occasion Weeden proposes that a given word's frequent occurrence is a reliable indicator of its redactional character (for example, φοβεῖσθαι).[108] Here we encounter two problems. First, as I have already

106. Contrast 'Heresy', p. 151. Best has pointedly chastised Weeden for this: '. . . it is important to point out the all but total absence from [Weeden's] work of redactional evidence; he moves almost entirely in the world of ideas without discussing the, admittedly, more difficult facts of Markan style and vocabulary' (*Following Jesus*, p. 241).

107. *Mark*, pp. 22 n. 7, 151. Following J. Jeremias (*The Parables of Jesus* [2nd rev. edn; New York: Charles Scribner's Sons, 1973], p. 14), Weeden claims that καὶ ἔλεγεν is a traditional formula, but καὶ ἔλεγεν αὐτοῖς is redactional. Since so much of what we know about the pre-Markan tradition is conjectural, are we really able to make such fine distinctions?

108. *Mark*, p. 49 n. 6.

stressed, frequency of occurrence indicates only how often a word appears; in itself it cannot distinguish the origin of those occurrences as either pre-Markan or Markan. Second, Weeden is sometimes inconsistent in his use of the argument of verbal frequency: ἔκστασις and τρόμος are rejected as part of Mark's vocabulary because they appear only once or twice in the Gospel; yet ἕνεκεν ἐμοῦ and σημεῖα καὶ τέρατα are reckoned redactional even though they occur in Mark, respectively, only thrice and once.[109]

(d) Other criteria used by Weeden for tagging certain words as redactional are at times equally tenuous. For instance, he argues that βλέπειν in the imperative mood is 'apparently a Markan key word as consultation with a concordance shows and the tendency of Matthew and Luke to omit or substitute προσέχω . . . underscores'.[110] The reference to 'consultation with a concordance' suggests, once again, the problematic argument of frequency of occurrence. That Matthew or Luke modifies a word appearing in Mark may be suggestive of the other Synoptists' linguistic biases; it tells us nothing definite about *Markan* predilections. Elsewhere, Weeden asserts that διδάσκειν, διδαχή, and κηρύσσειν 'are often found in redactional passages' without telling his reader why *those* passages are to be considered redactional.[111] If, from his citations of Mark 3.7-9 and 4.1 (for instance), one infers that Weeden is alluding to Markan summaries and seams, then that hardly constitutes proof of redaction: after all, the reason usually given for those passages' 'redactional character' is their 'Markan' vocabulary.

(e) On other occasions Weeden employs what might be termed a *thematic* criterion for ascertaining a Markan redactional vocabulary: hence ἐπιτιμᾶν carries for the Evangelist 'the intense connotation of rebuke . . . against a demonic adversary'. Although occurring only three times in the Gospel (8.35; 10.29; 13.9), ἕνεκεν ἐμοῦ is probably Markan since in all of its occurrences 'Thematically the question of salvation is of vital concern'; though appearing only at 13.22, σημεῖα καὶ τέρατα 'signifies a reference to θεῖος ἀνήρ activity', against which the Second Gospel is presumably directed.[112] Obviously, such thematic considerations carry such conviction for Weeden that they override the argument of frequency of occurrence; moreover, insight into the nuances of these themes enables Weeden to dis-

---

109. Contrast ibid., p. 48, against pp. 74-75 and 84.

110. 'Heresy', p. 151 n. 15.

111. *Mark,* p. 22 (N.B. n. 7).

112. Quotations from, respectively, *Mark,* p. 6 n. 22; ibid., p. 84; 'Heresy', p. 152.

tinguish pre-Markan and Markan usages of the *same* word: because the pre-Markan connotation of λόγος is that of a 'secret gospel' of the *theioi andres,* in redactional passages λόγος has been emptied of such esoteric meaning and replenished with the motif of suffering Christology.[113]

To this thematic criterion for establishing Mark's vocabulary two responses seem appropriate, and with these we shall conclude this subsection of our analysis of Weeden's method. First, though a final judgment should be delayed, pending our review of his exegetical results, one senses that the quest of a Markan redactional vocabulary has been made to serve Weeden's sometimes unconventional themes, when in the interest of methodological integrity it should be the other way around. Second, in his application of this important criterion, Weeden's research manifests marked inconsistencies between his method and results. For example, if παραβολή in the singular (with its connotation of 'riddle' or 'mystery') opposes Mark's theology of an open, unconcealed gospel, why has Mark allowed it to stand, with reference to Jesus' teaching, in the conclusion of the parable chapter?[114] If pneumaticism characterizes *theios-anēr* activity, then why is πνεῦμα ἅγιον a *Markan* key word?[115] If Mark is unrelenting in his portrayal of the disciples as blockheads, why is γινώσκειν (suggestive of 'penetrating insight') used at least twice by the Evangelist in recounting an address of Jesus *to the disciples* (13.28, 29)?[116]

12. With reference to discipleship, Weeden's investigation takes into account *the Markan Christological titles* at three points at least. (a) From the presentation of Jesus at the beginning of the Gospel up to 8.29, no other conclusion can be drawn than that Peter proclaims Jesus to be a *theios anēr* when, at Caesarea Philippi, he confesses him to be 'the Christ'.[117] (b) Throughout the Gospel, it is precisely this designation that Jesus muzzles; by contrast, 'The Son-of-man position is the one christological title that is not suppressed in the Gospel', and 'The only points at which Mark will allow a *theios-anēr* title to stand unsilenced is when the title has been properly reinterpreted in terms of Son-of-man christology'.[118] (c) The term ἐγώ εἰμί is a recognized title of Jesus that, to judge from Mark 13.6,

---

113. *Mark,* pp. 150-53.
114. Ibid., p. 150 n. 18.
115. Contrast ibid., p. 60, with 'Heresy', pp. 157-58.
116. *Mark,* p. 140 n. 5.
117. 'Heresy', pp. 148-49; cf. *Mark,* p. 99.
118. *Mark,* pp. 67, 155; cf. pp. 154, 165.

has been misappropriated by messianic pretenders in Mark's community who are disposed to a *theios-anēr* Christology.[119]

On reflection, I would say that the first half of proposition (c) is probably true, although its second half is not evincible from Mark 13 (and even less demonstrable is the further claim that *theioi andres* were in some way associated with the disciples). Proposition (b) outruns the evidence of the Gospel: the introductory assertion in Mark 1.1 that Jesus is 'the Christ' and 'the Son of God'[120] and the *bath-qôl* in 1.11 are by no means silenced, nor is the announcement of Jesus' miraculous feats suppressed in 5.20 or 7.37.[121] Weeden seems to weight Markan Christology *exclusively* in favor of the suffering Son of man in a way that the Evangelist does not. Finally, Weeden's proposition (a) is passing odd: if Mark wanted to dramatize Peter's confession as the mistaken acclamation of Jesus as a Hellenistic divine-man, why did he resort to the title 'Christ' when either 'Lord' or 'Son of God' would have accomplished his purpose more effectively? Indeed, as Jack Dean Kingsbury has suggested, the problem with this argument is that, by assuming Mark's intention that Peter come off poorly, Weeden has set up the issue in 8.29-31 as one of mutually exclusive or alternative Christologies; Mark, on the other hand, apparently intends that both titles — 'messiah' *and* 'Son of man' — be accepted as complementary descriptions of who Jesus is and what he is about.[122]

Summary: To judge from the foregoing analysis, one thing seems reasonably clear: by and large Weeden wishes to apply many of the *redaktionsgeschichtlich* tools systematized by Stein. Yet one is left wondering how essential most of these tools are to Weeden's procedure. Certainly one exegetical canon stands out in his work: the criterion of 'distinctive Markan themes'. Weeden obliquely indicates this to his reader when he makes the following comments:

---

119. Ibid., pp. 77-78; see also Weeden's comments on 'in the name' (Mark 13.6), ibid., pp. 79-81.

120. Of course, there is the thorny text-critical problem of deciding whether or not υἱοῦ θεοῦ appeared in the original text: its absence from א* Θ 28ᶜ et al. may be owing to scribal oversight; its presence in B D W et al. may be the result of scribal inclination to expand the *nomina sacra*.

121. The last word in both of these pericopes is one of disclosure, not of concealment (cf. *Mark*, p. 155 n. 23).

122. See Kingsbury's excellent discussion in *The Christology of Mark's Gospel* (Philadelphia: Fortress, 1983), pp. 91-102.

> Where one began looking in the Gospel for help in interpreting chapter 13 would be *the key methodological issue*. *The soundest methodological procedure* would be to seek help in understanding the *concerns* of chapter 13 in that section of the Gospel where *the same concerns* are most likely clearly addressed. This would inevitably lead one to 8.34–9.1. It is here more than any other passage in Mark that one finds *the closest thematic correspondence* to chapter 13. . . . [123]

In this statement I suspect that Weeden is disclosing more than a process for interpreting Mark 13; he is enunciating his method for the exegesis of the Gospel in its entirety. How does one interpret Mark? One identifies, correlates, and construes its *themes:* the ultimacy of suffering Christology and suffering discipleship, the denigration of a triumphalist Christology and discipleship, and so forth. It is for this reason that the reader may have sensed an almost constant prolepsis of Weeden's exegetical results in this section on method: as a rule Weeden himself tends to anticipate those results, expressed in the form of theological themes, in his determination of Markan insertions, modification of material, arrangement, vocabulary, and Christological titles. In effect if not by design, Weeden has made all of these and Stein's other redaction-critical criteria subservient to the methodological quest for Markan 'thematic correspondence'.

This, however, is not all. Weeden is convinced, and throughout operates on the assumption, that some of the themes to be identified and correlated are *contradictory,* in fact mutually exclusive. Mark is a *polemical* document, an attack waged against the Evangelist's opponents, whose views must be inferred from the document itself. Aside from the confusion which this injects into the interpretation of the Second Gospel, the legitimacy of this assumption should be challenged. Conceivably, some New Testament documents are amenable to the approach that Weeden proposes; 2 Corinthians, for example, manifests obvious bones of contention (see, for instance, 2 Cor. 11.4-5, 7; 12.1, 11-13), implicit accusations (2 Cor. 10.1, 10), explicit, even passionate, rebuttals (2 Cor. 11.2, 13, 21b-33; 12.2-10), and in general enough objective data with which we can begin to reconstruct the character of what we know to have been a real controversy. But the Second Gospel is not 2 Corinthians; since, on any surface reading, it does not give the impression of being polemical, Mark calls for a different approach.[124]

---

123. *Mark,* p. 99 (emphasis mine).
124. N. B. Best's observation: 'There is [in Mark] little of the personal abuse of oppo-

C. J. A. Hickling has put his finger on the problem: 'Weeden has applied techniques which have been perhaps somewhat over-used in the interpretation of the Pauline letters to a document which is in itself far less susceptible to treatment of this kind'.[125]

Since 'thematic correspondence' is, at best, only one aspect of the redaction-critical method, and 'the reconstruction of polemic' is no constituent of the method at all, why does Weeden seem to be so absorbed in both? The answer is given to us by the scholar himself:

> It is my opinion that . . . a christological dispute [was] raging in Mark's community, a dispute which had reached such a critical point that Mark felt he could settle it only by dramatizing the two sides through his presentation of the interaction between Jesus and his disciples. Thus, Jesus represents one point of view and the disciples the other. If the points of view can be identified, the dispute is revealed, and the need for the polemic explained.[126]

The reason for Weeden's methodological preoccupation with 'themes' and 'intra-Gospel polemics' lies in his presupposition that Mark was composed, and therefore should be read, as a 'Greek drama'. That Weeden has chosen this model for the Gospel as his starting-point is, I believe, significant: for a Greek drama not only conveys certain moral judgments through characterization; a drama necessarily entails some measure of *conflict*. I suspect that Weeden's reasoning runs something like this: If Mark is a drama, and if drama implies conflict, *then there must be a conflict*, 'a dispute', within that Gospel (thereby justifying the 'pursuit of polemic' in Mark). And if there is such a debate being dramatized in Mark, then the Evangelist must be setting up *conflicting points of view* that can be discerned (thereby justifying the 'pursuit of themes' in the Gospel). Once he identifies the dispute and defines the points of view, all that is left for Weeden to do is to postulate 'a given situation in the history of religion' in

---

nents found in the Pastorals, or even in Galatians. People have read the Gospel for centuries without this idea ever coming into their heads. It is probably a scholar's mirage created by the attitude they take up to other scholars' writings; they are so used to writing polemically against one another that they assume it is the only reason why people write!' (*Gospel as Story*, pp. 45-46).

125. Hickling, 'Problem of Method', p. 342; cf. also the similar criticisms of Lane, '*Theios Anēr* Christology', pp. 153-54.

126. 'Heresy', p. 147.

which that controversy can be plausibly located: a battle joined by Mark the Evangelist (proponent of a *theologia crucis*) and certain *theioi andres* (adherents of a *theologia gloriae*).

One might ask: What has all this *directly* to do with redaction criticism? The answer, obviously, is 'little or nothing'. And that is precisely the point: in his research on the disciples, Weeden's procedure is supported by redaction-critical arguments of varying degrees of cogency, but at the end of the day that procedure does not depend on the strict application of the redaction-critical method.

C. Exegetical Results

Weeden's reconstruction of Mark's message, and his understanding of the disciples' function in the Gospel narrative, are well known. Weeden envisions the Evangelist and his community in the throes of a persecution that shows no signs of abating. The delay of the *parousia* has added insult to injury. Into such a setting have entered proponents of a triumphalist, 'divine-man' *(theios-anēr)* Christology, a 'heretical' form of belief emphasizing the performance of miracles, a realized eschatology, and a 'secret gospel' as definitive of Christian existence. Such pernicious ideas have been rendered even more insidious by their proponents' misappropriation of orthodox traditions to buttress their own positions: the miracle stories, narratives of Jesus' post-resurrection appearance and spiritual presence in the midst of the community, and accounts of Jesus' private instruction of the disciples (whose 'specially privileged' successors the 'false Christs and false prophets' claim to be). The members of Mark's community have received these heretics with great enthusiasm, and orthodox faith has been stretched to the breaking point (cf. Mark 13.5-6, 9-13, 21-22).[127]

Faced with such a crisis, Mark hits upon an ingenious solution: he combats the heresy by appealing to a figure whose authority surpasses that of the disciples — Jesus. With Jesus articulating the Evangelist's own position, the Gospel of Mark becomes, in effect, a Christological polemic of 'devastating thoroughness' that redresses the imbalance created by this he-

---

127. *Mark*, pp. 76, 82, 89-90, 95, 98, 112, 139, 160-62; cf. 'Conflict', pp. 217, 225-26, and 'Cross', p. 128. In 'Conflict' (pp. 226-28) Weeden speculates that the opponents belonged to a branch of Christianity associated with Stephen.

retical *theologia gloriae*.[128] At many points the Evangelist outmaneuvers
the heretics by employing their own traditions against them: thus Jesus'
teaching is presented as thoroughly open and non-exclusionary. In addition, Mark neutralizes his opponents' heightened apocalyptic and realized
eschatology by historicizing the more apocalyptic features of the crucifixion account and by emphasizing the future exaltation and return of Jesus
as the Son of man. Against overwrought claims for Jesus' glorious presence
with the *theioi andres,* Mark stresses the absence of Christ from his church
in the present, retelling the empty-tomb story in a manner which underscores that absence while acknowledging Jesus' resurrection. The opponents' account of Jesus' glorious resurrection appearance is comman-
deered by the Evangelist and inserted into the story of the earthly Jesus as
an incident of transfiguration, framed in an appropriate context by the orthodox theological emphasis on the suffering Son of man.[129]

Far and away, Mark's polemical master-stroke was his character assassination of those whom his opponents claimed as mentors, the disciples.
Whereas Jesus is presented as exhorting an inclusive, suffering discipleship
commensurate with an open, suffering messiahship, the disciples are cast
as advocates of a *theios-anēr* Christology: they hold in contempt such humiliation as Jesus teaches, brandishing instead their own exclusive superiority over others. Throughout the Gospel Jesus and the twelve remain at
loggerheads over the proper understanding of messiahship and discipleship; 'It is a christological conflict that is never resolved'. This being the
case, 'Mark is assiduously involved in a vendetta against the disciples. He is
intent on totally discrediting them'. Thus in spite of the fact that the disciples are special agents for extending Jesus' ministry, and even though they
are peculiarly well-placed confidants of Jesus and recipients of special revelation, their position relative to Jesus progressively and precipitously de-
teriorates throughout the Gospel, from unbelivable imperceptiveness (1.1–
8.26), through ever-widening misconception (8.27–14.9), to complete rejection (14.10–16.8).[130] Surprisingly, Judas plays only a subordinate role in

---

128. 'Heresy', p. 145; *Mark,* pp. 98, 101, 157, 162-68; 'Conflict', pp. 223-25; 'Cross', pp. 116-
21. '[There] pulsates through the Mkan [*sic*] narrative a dialectic characterized by the clash
of two opposing ways to attain and sustain personal well-being' ('Cross', p. 132).

129. 'Heresy', pp. 151 n. 17, 155, 157; *Mark,* pp. 85, 89, 92-99, 102, 107-12, 114-31, 134, 144-47,
152, 161, 165; 'Conflict', pp. 208, 219-23; 'Cross', p. 131.

130. 'Heresy', pp. 146-47, 150, 158; *Mark,* pp. 23, 26-59, 63-68, 138-40, 144, 159, 163-64;
'Conflict', p. 231 n. 11. Quotations excerpted from *Mark,* pp. 34 and 50. Had the 'vendetta'
been as assiduous as Weeden describes, one wonders why Mark would have let slip into his

these proceedings; the real villain of the piece, the figure in whom are crystallized all of the disciples' obtuseness and hostility, is Simon Peter. The watershed passage of the Gospel, the point at which the disciples' true colors are unfurled, occurs at 8.27-33: at Caesarea Philippi, Peter, acting as spokesman for the twelve, confesses Jesus to be 'a messiah of the θεῖος ἀνήρ type', an ascription flatly denounced by Jesus (= Mark) as satanic. The other shoe finally drops with Peter's denial of Jesus at 14.66-72: 'It is the denial of Peter that underscores the complete and utter rejection of Jesus and his messiahship by the disciples'. After that denial 'there is no indication by Mark that the disciples were rehabilitated, that apostolicity *was* conferred upon them after their apostasy'. On the contrary, the Gospel's ending at 16.8, with the silence of the women, suggests that the disciples never received the message about Jesus' *parousia* in Galilee (16.7) and thus were robbed of their apostolic credentials.[131] 'Mark 16.8b is the evangelist's final thrust in his vendetta against the disciples and his commitment to discredit them completely.'[132]

For our present purposes we need not engage in lengthy debate with Weeden over his exegetical reconstruction; already I have called many aspects of it into question, and other dimensions of Weeden's interpretation have been copiously reviewed and criticized in the scholarly literature.[133] Our primary concern here is to ask if Weeden's exegetical results are dependent on his application of the redaction-critical method. If Weeden's

---

narrative such passages as 9.9, 13.10, 14.28, and 16.7, all of which imply (Weeden's interpretations notwithstanding) a return to Galilee and the possibility of the disciples' rehabilitation following the resurrection.

131. 'Heresy', pp. 146-47; *Mark*, pp. 33, 56, 64-69, 164; 'Conflict', pp. 222, 224-25; 'Cross', pp. 117, 119. Quotations from, respectively, 'Heresy', pp. 155-56; *Mark*, pp. 38, 44. If Weeden is correct, then primitive Christianity completely miscalculated the relationship between Peter and Mark the Evangelist. In particular, the testimony of Papias that Mark was Peter's interpreter (Eusebius, *H.E.* 3.39.14-15) must be rejected as both historically incredible and theologically misguided. On the other hand, if Peter's behavior is to be considered representative of all the disciples, then why is his weeping after the denial (14.72c) not symptomatic of all of the disciples' contrition?

132. *Mark*, p. 117; cf. p. 47. One may question whether the ending of Mark's Gospel is as conclusive as Weeden's (and others') interpretation would suggest; and, 'if the ending is open and inconclusive, then the disciples cannot be irrevocably rejected' (Via, *Ethics of Mark's Gospel*, p. 125 n. 12).

133. In addition to the reviews (cited previously) by Schuyler Brown, William Lane, James P. Martin, Ralph P. Martin, and Vernon K. Robbins, see also the reviews by Doug Ezell (in *SWJT* 15 [1973], p. 98), Howard Rhys (in *ATR* 54 [1972], pp. 368-69), and Roy A. Harrisville (in *Dialog* 12 [1973], pp. 233-34).

exegesis was anticipated in the last subsection, then so, too, was its critique and thus the answer to our question: No. In fact, Weeden's interpretation of Mark appears to have been arrived at by means largely independent of redaction criticism, even though certain characteristics of that method are invoked to lend credence to his results. This allegation can be supported by the consideration of one last example, concerning a matter of no little consequence for Weeden's reading of Mark.

The putative appearance of *theioi andres*, 'divine men', on the Markan horizon is really the linchpin of Weeden's reconstruction: without the postulation of the *theioi andres*, we would not recognize the contours of the implied heresy in Mark; and without that, we could appreciate neither the nature of the conflict, the reason for the Evangelist's polemic, nor the blackwashing of the disciples in the Second Gospel. On what, then, does Weeden base his belief for the existence of heretical 'divine men' behind the Second Gospel? Essentially his substantiation boils down to Mark 13.22: 'False Christs and false prophets will arise and show signs and wonders to lead astray, if possible, the elect'. Weeden argues that 13.21-23 comes from Mark's hand (as do 13.5-6, 9-13, 28-37, all of which are given hortatory punch with the Markan imperative, βλέπετε). Although appearing only twice in the Synoptics (Mark 13.22; Matt 24.24), elsewhere in the New Testament (in Acts, John, and 2 Corinthians) the phrase 'signs and wonders', σημεῖα καὶ τέρατα, functions as a *terminus technicus* in describing *theios-anēr* activity, as that has been defined by Dieter Georgi in his monograph on 2 Corinthians.[134]

> Thus the evidence strongly suggests that the use of the terms in combination in the New Testament, and as they appear in Mark, signifies a reference to θεῖος ἀνήρ activity. The descriptive clause ποιήσουσιν σημεῖα καὶ τέρατα pinpoints the 'false Christs' and 'false prophets' of 13.22 as θεῖοι ἄνδρες.[135]

From this Weeden draws the bold conclusion that all allusions elsewhere in Mark to 'signs and wonders', that is, to mighty works or extraordinary activity of any kind, are allusions to *theios-anēr* behavior; and it is because Peter had this sort of activity in mind at Caesarea Philippi that his confession of Jesus as 'Christ' signifies a *theios-anēr* perspective that must be squelched.[136]

134. Georgi, *Die Gegner,* pp. 145-67, 192-200.
135. 'Heresy', p. 152.
136. See, for example, ibid., pp. 155-56; *Mark,* pp. 59-100.

There are a host of difficulties with this argument. First, it asks one to accept a colossal hypothesis, built on the scanty foundation of a single verse (Mark 13.22). Second, for the connotation of 'signs and wonders' as expressive of the activity of primitive Christian 'divine men', the argument reaches beyond the confines of the Second Gospel in a manner that, elsewhere, Weeden refuses to countenance.[137] Third, several studies postdating Weeden's work have demonstrated that the *theios anēr* — the foundational concept for Weeden's classification of Mark's 'opponents' — is a modern (and misbegotten) scholarly construct; there was no paradigmatic figure of a divinized miracle-worker in Hellenistic Judaism.[138] Fourth, Weeden's proposition that all allusions to miraculous 'signs and wonders' in the Second Gospel, beyond 13.22, are intended by Mark to refer precisely to such heretical activity is a *non sequitur:* it does not follow from the Evangelist's acknowledgment that the elect could be misled *by means of* signs and wonders that *the very performance* of such miracles was deemed heretical by him (cf. Deut. 13.1-2, of which there is an echo in Mark 13.22).[139] The notion that such a heresy lies behind Peter's confession is supported, not expressly by the text, but only by Weeden's assumptions about a doctrinal *Auseinandersetzung* in the Markan *Sitz.* Indeed, a straightforward reading of the Second Gospel seems to contradict Weeden's hypothesis precisely at this point: for if Mark associated signs and wonders with heresy, then why did he include sixteen miracle stories

137. Recall *Mark,* p. 114, where Weeden exhorts interpreters '[to permit] the peculiarities of Mark to speak for themselves, . . . [to read] Mark alone, without supplying the consensus of New Testament tradition'.

138. See Lane, '*Theios Anēr* Christology', pp. 145-49, and the more detailed studies of D. L. Tiede, *The Charismatic Figure as Miracle Worker* (SBLDS 1; Missoula, MT: Scholars Press, 1972) and C. R. Holladay, Theios Anēr *in Hellenistic Judaism: A Critique of the Use of This Category in New Testament Christology* (SBLDS 40; Missoula, MT: Scholars Press, 1977). In the preface to the paperback edition of *Mark* (p. vii), Weeden acknowledges Holladay's work but maintains that, while the category, *theios anēr,* may be unsatisfactory in describing Mark, the phenomenon that it represents remains applicable to the Second Gospel.

139. As pointed out by Brown in *TS* 33 (1972), pp. 754-55. *Pace* Weeden, many exegetes argue for the positive implications in Mark of Jesus' mighty works: their eschatological edge (Schweizer, 'Neuere Markus-Forschung in USA', pp. 533-37), their congeniality with Jesus' power in teaching (P. J. Achtemeier, '"He Taught Them Many Things": Reflections on Marcan Christology', *CBQ* 42 [1980] pp. 465-81), their usefulness as a tensive counterpoint to the secrecy motif in the Gospel (U. Luz, 'Das Geheimnismotiv und die Markinische Christologie', *ZNW* 56 [1965], pp. 9-30), and their profound witness to Jesus as the compassionate healer, 'the one who cares' (Best, *Gospel as Story,* pp. 55-65).

in his Gospel?[140] In short, Weeden's case is hypothetically intriguing, but textually improbable in the extreme.

But how has Weeden's argument been honed by the use of *redaction criticism?* Very little, as far as I can tell: appeals are made only to Markan vocabulary (βλέπειν and perhaps σημεῖα καὶ τέρατα) and, in a supplementary way, to the Christological title in 8.29. And that is all. The presupposition of a pervasive heretical conflict, its linkage to 'signs and wonders', its definition as a *theios-anēr* Christology, and its association with the disciples: none of this, as far as I can determine, has been directly suggested to Weeden *by the practice of redaction criticism*. Weeden does use specific criteria associated with the method in the hope of discerning data in the Gospel of Mark; but the significance and proper understanding of those data seem to have been suggested to Weeden by means other than *Redaktionsgeschichte*.

Weeden's interpretation of the disciples in Mark is decidedly different from those of other exegetes we have considered in this study; yet have we not witnessed similar tensions and difficulties, associated with the practice of Markan redaction criticism, in the work of our 'conservative', 'mediate', and 'liberal' interpreters? It is to the fine-tuning of both the differences and the similarities evinced in the studies of Weeden, Best, and Meye that we turn, in the chapter that follows.

---

140. As Gerd Theissen observes, 'It seems a rather clumsy way of [warning against belief in miracles]' (*The Miracle Stories of the Early Christian Tradition* [Philadelphia: Fortress, 1983], p. 294); see also D. J. Hawkin, 'The Symbolism and Structure of the Marcan Redaction', *EvQ* 49 (1977), pp. 98-110. With particular reference to Mark 4.11-12, 6.52, 7.17-18, and 8.14-21, Best has noted another irony in Weeden's position: 'It is impossible on the one hand to stress the blindness of the disciples in respect of the cross and argue that they represent a christology which emphasizes the miracles and wisdom of Jesus when at the same time they do not understand the miracles or his teaching' ('Some Problems', p. 86).

6. The Three Types Collated: A Comparison and Contrast of the Perspective, Method, and Results of Meye, Best, and Weeden

> Perhaps the greatest danger before the redaction critic, however, is that of imposing his own philosophy upon the material, and seeing the gospel in the light of his own situation. . . . We try to put ourselves into the evangelist's shoes, and only succeed in forcing him into ours!
>
> Morna D. Hooker[1]

Let us summarize our inquiry to this point. We have seen how most of the redaction-critical explorations of 'the disciples' and 'discipleship' in Mark's Gospel can be grouped, for heuristic purposes, into one of three categories: the 'conservative' position, the 'mediate' position, or the 'liberal' position. This typology reflects the existence, not only of three widely varying exegeses of Mark, but also of three disparate clusters of presuppositions concerning the Second Evangelist's relationship to history and tradition. Thus the work of Robert P. Meye has been considered reflective of the Type I, or 'conservative', stance: the notion that Mark's theology incorporates a positive and favorable estimation of the disciples, consonant with ecclesial tradition and historical fact. With the research of Ernest Best I have associated the Type II, or 'mediate', position, which suggests that Mark's theology incorporates an alternately favorable and unfavorable estimation of the disciples that is indebted but not enslaved to history and tradition. Finally, the interpretation of Theodore J. Weeden, Sr has functioned for us as representative of the Type III, or 'lib-

---

1. M. D. Hooker, 'In His Own Image?', *What About the New Testament? Essays in Honour of Christopher Evans* (ed. M. Hooker and C. Hickling; London: SCM, 1975), pp. 35, 38.

eral', outlook: largely oblivious to ecclesial tradition and historical fact, Mark's theology incorporates a negative and unfavorable estimation of the disciples.[2]

The primary factor held in common by these different 'types' of scholarship has been an avowed acceptance of the redaction-critical method. Therefore, throughout this investigation, a pivotal question for us has been, To what degree has these scholars' practice of *Redaktionsgeschichte* informed, refined, or corrected their exegetical perspective and results? How might we characterize the interrelation of perspective, method, and results in the respective contributions of Meye, Best, and Weeden?

In the chapters preceding, some answers to these questions have been ventured. Now the time has come to draw these threads together. Some repetition of what we have witnessed will necessarily be entailed, not for redundancy's sake, but in the interest of accuracy and clarity. My goal in this chapter, then, is to compare and contrast the general perspective, method, and exegetical results of our three representative interpreters, in order to derive synthetic conclusions about the redaction-critical method and its application to the Second Gospel.

A. General Perspective

Allowing for the distortion that will inevitably plague any typology, I would suggest that the positions denoted by the somewhat infelicitous rubrics of 'conservative', 'mediate', and 'liberal' have proved serviceable in our exploration of the perspectives exemplified by Meye, Best, and Weeden. Whereas these three exegetes ostensibly agree on the value of *Redaktionsgeschichte,* they dramatically disagree in their presuppositions about that method, about the influence exerted by Markan theology on the Gospel, about the character of the pre-Markan tradition, and about the degree to which the Second Evangelist has been influenced by historical factors. Moving in inverse order, let us briefly consider each of these.

1. *The measure of history in the Gospel of Mark.* From among our representative interpreters, Meye is prepared to grant the greatest degree of historical veracity in the Second Gospel: 'The Marcan portrait is historically

---

2. It should be remembered that, based on similar, Type III assumptions, some scholars deduce more positive exegetical results. See above, Chapter 2, on T. L. Budesheim and K.-G. Reploh.

extremely significant, and deserves the historian's most careful attention'. For Meye this is true, not only because Mark's is the first Gospel to arise within the early Christian community, but also because Mark's very creation of the genre of 'Gospel' intends 'to give *historical expression* to his faith in a historically meaningful ministry of Jesus'. As for the disciples, the decisive continuity between the Evangelist's depiction of Jesus' pre-Easter preparation of the twelve and his understanding of their post-Easter activity is but a function of that larger historical continuity existing between the first disciples and the traditions about them, formed by the earliest Christians, as well as between those traditions and the beliefs of the Markan church, reflected in the Second Gospel.[3]

Weeden, on the other hand, begins his consideration of the disciples in Mark from precisely the opposite point of view and immediately moves in a direction 180 degrees away from Meye: because the Second Evangelist was (for Weeden) akin to an ancient Hellenistic dramatist, he 'intentionally staged' all sorts of episodes described in the Gospel — among others, the conflict between Jesus and Peter at Caesarea Philippi (Mark 8.27-30) and the apocalyptic discourse (13.5-37) — that bear little or no resemblance to historical reality.[4] By comparison, Best's presentation falls somewhere between those of Weeden and Meye (with greater inclination toward the latter): Best assumes, without discussion, that the traditions appropriated by Mark contained 'historical material' (*à la* Meye); yet Best evinces little interest in probing the historical implications of the Second Gospel, being far more engaged by the theological use to which the Evangelist put that material (*à la* Weeden).[5]

2. *The character of the pre-Markan tradition.* Already we have noted the tension within Meye's perspective on the traditions available to Mark: although he is prepared to grant that the Evangelist was, at least to some extent, 'the master and arranger of the materials of his narrative', Meye tends to conceive of Mark as 'already determined by the tradition that he has re-

---

3. Meye, 'Messianic Didache', pp. 59, 60 (first quotation); *Jesus,* pp. 16-19, 33 (second quotation), 92, 184-85, 192-209.

4. Weeden, 'Heresy', pp. 149 n. 7, 150, 155; *Mark,* pp. 70-72, 97, 155 n. 23. It should be recalled, however, that at a critical point — namely, his conclusion that the putative Markan heretics claimed to have traced their position back to the historical disciples — Weeden's presentation becomes internally inconsistent and thus more closely aligned with Meye's assumption of historical continuity (if not with Meye's understanding of the nature of that continuity; 'Heresy', p. 155; cf. 'Conflict', pp. 226-28).

5. Best, *Following Jesus,* p. 10; 'Discipleship', p. 323; *Gospel as Story,* p. 48.

ceived'.[6] The same internal tension characterizes Best's presuppositions: the Second Evangelist was bound by inherited tradition yet remained a true author, not merely a recorder of tradition. Whereas Meye stresses the degree to which Mark was mastered or bound by his sources — an assumption with which Best agrees — the latter is inclined to emphasize the Evangelist's creative authorship: working with materials for which he has 'a real respect', Mark's creativity is discernible, not in his fabrication of incidents or pericopes, but in his arrangement and minimal modification of tradition, especially in seams and summaries.[7] Weeden agrees with Best that the Evangelist demonstrates a genuinely creative capacity; however, Weeden goes beyond both Best and Meye in according to Mark 'a much freer hand . . . in the composing process'. For Weeden, the tradition functioned as no restraint whatever upon the Evangelist, who did not feel subservient to his source material. Indeed, in Weeden's judgment, Mark did not respect certain elements of his traditions, inasmuch as they harbored theological themes to which the Evangelist was hostile. Thus (*contra* both Best and Meye) Mark's role cannot be confined to the editorial linkage of traditions; for Weeden, 'Mark exercised an author's freedom and creativity in composing the Gospel'.[8]

3. *The influence of Markan theology upon the Gospel.* Once again, Best emerges as a bridge between the two extremes typified by Meye and Weeden. Far from being merely a recorder of tradition, Mark (in Best's view) is 'a real author' who 'used the historical material with a theological purpose in mind', a clear pattern of that purpose being detectable in Markan editorial activity.[9] From this mediating position, one can observe Meye and Weeden moving in diametrically opposite directions. Meye grants that, while Markan redaction does bespeak a theological intention of the Evangelist, such theology remains grounded upon and controlled by historical fact.[10] For Weeden, Mark is 'a much more deliberate theologian

6. Meye, *Jesus*, pp. 28, 72; cf. p. 63.

7. Best, *Temptation*, p. xi; *Gospel as Story*, pp. 121-22; *Following Jesus*, pp. 10, 19, 25, 140 (quotation), 208; 'Mark's Preservation', p. 33. N.B. 'Some Problems', pp. 81-82: 'Before Mark went to work most of the material lacked within itself a principle by which it could be ordered. . . . Mark's great achievement was to take the material and to give it an order'.

8. Weeden, *Mark*, pp. 1-2 (quotations), 3, 73 n. 4; 'Conflict', p. 206. On occasion Weeden seems to contradict his own point of view in this regard, such as when he speculates that ὁ λόγος (which, for him, is a 'non-Markan' word) may have been 'lodged' at Mark 1.45 and 2.2 beyond the Evangelist's capacity to edit out (*Mark*, p. 151 n. 19).

9. Best, *Following Jesus*, p. 10; 'Role', p. 384; *Gospel as Story*, p. 16; 'Some Problems', p. 82.

10. Meye, 'Those About Him', p. 212 n. 4; *Jesus*, pp. 92, 143, 174-78.

than had earlier been assumed', an Evangelist whose Gospel is preaching for the present and not a chronicle of the past. '[The] Evangelist is no longer concerned with the facts of 30 A.D. but rather the specific problems of his own community in the late 60's.'[11]

4. *Redaction criticism as a method appropriate for Markan investigation.* All three of these authors agree, in principle, on the theoretical validity and practical utility of *Redaktionsgeschichte:* for Meye, it is 'a positive extension of the detailed method of form criticism, . . . directly concerned with the theological situation and work of the evangelist and the living community of which he is a part'; according to Best, 'in any particular incident we have to separate Mark's view of the incident from its original place in the life of Jesus and also from the varying modifications which thereafter it may have received in the early Church'; 'Redaction criticism', Weeden proclaims, 'has placed in our hand the key for unlocking the mysteries behind the Gospel of Mark and its creation'.[12] However, after having paid homage to this interpretive tool, these exegetes go their separate ways in articulating general presuppositions about that method's application to the Second Gospel.

Of the three, Best is, in a sense, the most straightforward and sanguine regarding both the feasibility and value of redaction criticism; the former is simply assumed, and the latter is evident in his assertion that 'Without the control which [Markan style and vocabulary] supply it is possible to make Mark mean almost anything'.[13] While never avowedly forsaking the method, both Meye and Weeden are more circumspect in their assessments of its practicality. Both scholars recognize the difficulty of distinguishing tradition and redaction, but for different reasons: for Meye, the difficulty stems from the built-in circularity of the method;[14] for Weeden, the problem lies in the material to which the method is applied, since the lines between tradition and redaction have been blurred by the Evangelist's thoroughgoing compositional activity.[15] Because of this ambivalence in

---

11. Weeden, *Mark,* p. 3; 'Heresy', p. 147. Cf. idem, 'Conflict', p. 205.

12. Meye, *Jesus,* p. 23; Best, *Temptation,* p. ix; Weeden, *Mark,* p. 1.

13. Best, *Following Jesus,* p. 241; cf. ibid., pp. 9-10; *Temptation,* pp. 63-133.

14. Meye, *Jesus,* pp. 38, 58-59. On occasion Best confesses that clear and precise results are not forthcoming on the basis of redaction criticism (for example, *Following Jesus,* p. 213); however, such lack of confidence tends to be the exception rather than the rule.

15. *Mark,* pp. 2-3; in this respect Weeden might be considered a forerunner of the revisionist *traditionsgeschichtlich* thinking of E. Güttgemanns, *Candid Questions Concerning Gospel Form Criticism: A Methodological Sketch of the Fundamental Problematics of Form and Redaction Criticism* (PTMS 26; Pittsburgh: Pickwick, 1973), and Kelber, *Oral and Written*

their methodological presuppositions — approving of redaction criticism yet vaguely distrustful of its feasibility — Meye and Weeden tend to presume overarching yet different hermeneutical principles with which they believe *Redaktionsgeschichte* can be accommodated: for Meye it is the elevation of the Second Gospel's total content to the status of Markan theology, with particular attention to 'what Mark clearly and repeatedly says'; for Weeden, it is the ascription to Mark of the conventions of Hellenistic drama, with special sensitivity to the literary device of characterization in communicating the Evangelist's beliefs and judgments.[16] Both Meye and Weeden seem convinced that, by framing their *redaktionsgeschichtlich* studies in these different contexts, they can sidestep the pitfall against which Best cautions: the eisegesis of preconceived ideas into the text, doing violence to the Evangelist's intent.[17]

In summary: though there is a surface perspectival similarity in the works of Meye, Best, and Weeden — that is, in their common claim of indebtedness to redaction criticism in interpreting the Second Gospel — they differ among themselves, in their presuppositions, at four fundamental points: in their preconception of the method itself, and in their understanding of the relationship between the Gospel and history, between the Gospel and tradition, and between the Gospel and the Evangelist's own theology.[18]

B. Exegetical Results

Not only do Meye, Best, and Weeden disagree in their perspectives on Mark and its redactional underpinnings; they are also at wide variance in their exegetical conclusions regarding the figure of the disciples and the

---

Gospel. Although Best would agree with Weeden that precise differentiation between tradition and redaction is difficult, to my knowledge Best never claims that the redactional process itself has rendered *Redaktionsgeschichte* more difficult. In fact, such a view would run counter to Best's entire procedure, which is predicated on the belief that characteristically Markan touches, denoting distinctively Markan concerns, *can* be distinguished.

16. Meye, 'Messianic Didache', pp. 60, 65; 'Those About Him', 215, 217; Weeden, *Mark,* pp. 11-19.

17. Cf. Weeden, *Mark,* pp. 10-11, with Meye, 'Those About Him', p. 217, and *Jesus,* pp. 39, 41.

18. This is to say that their analyses and weighting of Marxsen's three *Sitze im Leben* (that of Jesus, the primitive church, and the Markan community) are divergent across the board (Marxsen, *Mark the Evangelist,* pp. 23-24).

role of discipleship in the Second Gospel. In preceding chapters this fact has been explored and documented; here we need only recapitulate each scholar's principal deductions, highlighting the differences of each through comparison and contrast with the others.

1. *Mark's portrayal of Christ.* On one issue, at least, all of our exegetes concur: as Mark presents it, Jesus' mission and teaching are ultimately defined in terms of humiliation, suffering, and death — in short, by the cross.[19] However, these investigators shade their exegeses of this common subject in different ways. In a manner congenial with his more 'conservative' outlook, Meye emphasizes Mark's concern to present the historical teaching of Jesus, a 'parabolic' life and ministry that engenders no little antagonism.[20] For Weeden, the Second Evangelist exhibits little or no interest in historical verisimilitude: in the context of the gospel narrative, Jesus is little more than a mouthpiece for Mark's point of view, giving voice to the Evangelist's own Christological polemic against an esoteric and heretical *theologia gloriae* by means of open and nonexclusionary teaching that emphasizes Jesus' exalted glory as a future reality.[21] Assuming a more moderate position, Best avers that Mark's purpose was neither 'primarily informational in the sense of conveying information either about Jesus or the true faith of the church' nor 'primarily polemical in that he wrote to attack certain heretics or recognized heretical positions'; Mark's objective was principally pastoral, intending to provide edification for Christians on the true meaning of discipleship in light of the cross.[22]

2. *Mark's portrayal of the disciples.* Here we have witnessed wide variance among the treatments of Meye, Best, and Weeden with respect to every dimension of discipleship in the Second Gospel:

a. *'The disciples' and 'the twelve':* Meye ventures the 'conservative' claim that the Second Evangelist relegates discipleship to the twelve and, in so doing, renders a portrait of those about Jesus that is historically acceptable: a depiction of the twelve as an apostolic, quasi-institutional body, appointed by the historical Jesus to function as an 'official teaching collegium'.[23] Best interprets the evidence otherwise: tailoring historical

---

19. Cf. Meye, 'Messianic Didache', p. 62; *Jesus*, pp. 48, 73-80; Best, *Following Jesus*, pp. 12-14; *Temptation*, p. 123; Weeden, *Mark*, pp. 52-54.

20. Meye, *Jesus*, pp. 52-80; 'Messianic Didache', p. 58.

21. Weeden, 'Heresy', p. 145; *Mark*, pp. 92-99, 118-31, 144-47, 162-68.

22. Best, *Following Jesus*, pp. 11-12; cf. *Gospel as Story*, pp. 93-99.

23. Meye, *Jesus*, pp. 115-16, 188-90, 203, 209, 228-30; 'Those About Him', pp. 214, 217; 'Messianic Didache', pp. 63-66.

material to a theological design, Mark presents 'the twelve' as virtually interchangeable with 'the disciples' in role and in function. Although in a narrower sense the twelve are distinguished by the Evangelist as specially consecrated for full-time missionary service, in a broader sense they collectively exemplify Christians in general as 'typical believers rather than [as] officials of the Church'.[24] As far as I can determine, Weeden does not probe the relationship between 'the disciples' and 'the twelve', and, as we have seen, he is as unconcerned with the historicity of the Markan portrayal of the disciples as he supposes the Evangelist to be.

b. *Mark's general perspective on the disciples:* As Meye sifts the data, the Markan presentation of the twelve is almost completely complimentary: the disciples are specially summoned by Jesus to be with him, and they remain with him until the very end; persistently and privately instructed by Jesus, they are the unique beneficiaries of a revelation that they consistently guard; their understanding of Jesus' identity develops progressively throughout the Gospel, to the point that ultimately they understand everything.[25] With this interpretation Weeden could not disagree more completely. Their special appointment and their extraordinarily advantageous position to receive special revelation to the contrary notwithstanding, the disciples in Mark are portrayed in a consistently pejorative manner: as contemptuous of Jesus' message of humiliation and suffering, as arrogating to themselves an insufferable superiority, and as steadily deteriorating in their relationship to Jesus from imperceptiveness, through misconception, to total rejection.[26] Between the extremes defined by Meye and Weeden, once again Best stands somewhere in the middle: both success and failure, features positive and negative, characterize the disciples in Mark; nevertheless, Peter, representative of the twelve, is introduced by the Evangelist in a favorable or at least neutral light, and 'The total structure of the second half of the gospel supports a positive evaluation of the role of the disciples'.[27]

c. *The reasons for the inauspicious figure of the disciples in Mark* are crystal-clear for Weeden: symbols of a *theios-anēr* Christology, the disciples are the villains of the piece, against whom 'Mark is assiduously involved in a vendetta . . . intent on totally discrediting them'.[28] To this both

24. Best, *Temptation*, p. 78; 'Role', pp. 398, 401; 'Mark's Use', p. 32; *Following Jesus*, pp. 10-11, 184-85, 194-95, 204-5.
25. Meye, *Jesus*, pp. 71-73, 102-5; 'Messianic Didache', p. 65.
26. Weeden, 'Heresy', pp. 150-55; *Mark*, pp. 26-69.
27. Best, 'Role', pp. 393-96 (quotation, p. 394); 'Peter', pp. 557-58.
28. Weeden, *Mark*, p. 50, et passim.

Meye and Best protest: 'it is simply impossible to believe that the Markan Church did or could have loved the Messiah and hated the Twelve' (Meye); 'The disciples were not such acknowledged villains or enemies of the church' (Best).[29] Meye and Best are in accord on two further points: (i) Mark casts the Pharisees in a role far darker than that in which he presents the disciples; (ii) by depicting the disciples' blindness and ineptitude, Mark aims both to emphasize by contrast Jesus' lustrous example and teaching as well as to reassure the Markan community of God's love and steadfastness in the midst of the community's own insecurity and failure.[30]

d. More moderate than those of his colleagues represented here are Best's conclusions on *the implications for discipleship to be drawn from Mark's portrayal of the twelve:* the mission of all followers of Jesus is to combat human sin by healing the sick, preaching repentance, and bringing others to a state of forgiveness. Mark's Gospel (as Best conceives it) is intended to build up its readers as Christians, who strive to follow Jesus in the way of the cross while living in tension with the good and evil of this world.[31] With this characterization of the Second Gospel Meye would not disagree;[32] however, he contributes a more 'conservative' nuance that is absent from Best's presentation: because the twelve resolutely remained with Jesus until the end, they were perceived as the exalted, all-important witnesses to Jesus and as the accredited mediators and guarantors of his teaching. Thus Mark's narrative is nothing less than an account of the apostolic foundation of the church's gospel.[33] To such a conclusion Weeden, of course, is diametrically opposed: the Christological conflict personified by Jesus and the disciples remains unresolved in the Second Gospel; and, since they never received word of Jesus' resurrection and impending return to Galilee (cf. Mark 16.7-8), the disciples remained apostate to the last, without apostolic accreditation or rehabilitation.[34]

In brief: At virtually every exegetical point in their presentations of Markan Christology and discipleship, Meye and Weeden draw interpretive conclusions so radically different that one can hardly believe that they are

29. Meye, *Jesus*, p. 224; Best, 'Role', p. 395.

30. Meye, *Jesus*, pp. 64, 69, 224; Best, 'Role', pp. 394, 399. Meye further suggests that the disciples' fully human failings are intended to extend Mark's incarnational theology (*Jesus*, pp. 223-24).

31. Best, *Temptation*, pp. 182-89.

32. Cf. Meye, *Jesus*, pp. 55-56, 104-9, 179-80; 'Messianic Didache', p. 65.

33. Idem, 'Messianic Didache', pp. 65-68; *Jesus*, pp. 87, 102-3, 134.

34. Weeden, *Mark*, pp. 34, 44, 117.

reading the same literary work. Although more generally in agreement with Meye than with Weeden, Best's interpretation of Markan discipleship is identical to neither. In his attempt to articulate a more finely nuanced and 'mediate' exegesis, an interpretation holding together various elements in tension, Best, too, goes his own way.

C. Method

For all their differences in general perspective and exegetical results, the common denominator in the work of Meye, Best, and Weeden would appear to be their use of the redaction-critical method. Their appropriation of *Redaktionsgeschichte*, their understanding and practice of it, must now be analyzed, compared, and contrasted. Three major areas of questioning merit investigation:

1. *The question of procedure:* Precisely how do these three scholars employ this method? Are they in agreement in this employment? Does one or more of the dozen redaction-critical criteria appear to be dominant, either overtly or covertly?
2. *The question of internal and external consistency:* Is there consistent evidence of internal contradictions in the redaction-critical method as exhibited by these interpreters? Are any such internal, methodological inconsistencies in the work of one scholar replicated in the practice of the method by the other(s)? Does the utilization of *Redaktionsgeschichte* by one exegete find corroboration or refutation in the work of the other(s)?
3. *The question of correlation:* Is there a discernible correlation between each scholar's general perspective and the manner in which he applies redaction criticism? Is there a discernible correlation between that manner of application and each scholar's exegetical results?

1. Let us begin with *the question of procedure.* Aside from their avowed acceptance of redaction criticism, are Meye, Best, and Weeden alike in their practice of that method? In order to address that question, Table 7 summarizes our findings from the preceding chapters' inquiries into method.

Even a cursory look at Table 7 suggests some comparative deductions regarding the redaction-critical procedure of Meye, Best, and Weeden.

TABLE 7   A Comparative Summary of the Manner of Application of Redaction Criticism in the Studies of Markan Discipleship by Meye, Best, and Weeden

	Seams	Insertions	Summaries
Meye	Used infrequently: 5 such determinations, made on the basis of vocabulary and themes (somewhat slanted toward Meye's presuppositions and the thesis he is defending). No clear differentiation between tradition and redaction attempted (pp. 76-77).	Used infrequently: 4 such determinations, implicitly designated (cf. Marken 'afterthoughts'). No demonstration or differentiation from pre-Markan tradition (p. 77).	Accorded theoretical significance but used infrquently: approximately 4 such determinations, made on the basis of 'distinctively Marken themes'. Demonstration includes no clear differentiation of Markan and pre-Markan material and tends to beg exegetical questions (p. 77).
Best	Accorded theoretical significance but playing relatively minor role in practice. 8 instances of material classified as seams without demonstration. Where proof is attempted, it is primarily on the basis of ostensibly distinctive vocabulary and characteristic themes (pp. 112-13).	Accorded theoretical significance but playing relatively insignificant role in practice. 4 instances of Markan material assumed to be insertional, with weak (i.e., only secondary) if not contradictory demonstration (pp. 113-14).	Simply assumed to be indicative of Mark's handiwork; yet assessment of summaries amounts to little in investigating Markan discipleship. Principal importance seems to be in ostensibly fixing certain words and elements as characteristic of Markan vocabulary and style; yet summaries manifest *both* tradition *and* redaction (p. 114).
Weeden	Used infrequently: 1 instance noted, with questionable justification (no differentiation of tradition from redaction; the evidence of 'awkward redundancy' as designating seams contradicts Weeden's redaction-critical assumption that Mark is a 'consummately skilled writer' whose style is characterized by duality: pp. 149-50).	Used frequently: 10 instances cited, based on Markan vocabulary and themes, which are in turn based on presumed existence and character of other insertions, the scholarly *opinio communis*, and unproven traditiohistorical assumptions about the pre-Markan and Markan *Sitze* (pp. 150-52).	Used infrequently: 3 instances cited, with questionable justification (unproven traditiohistorical assumptions and an *argumentum ad vericundiam*; p. 153).

TABLE 7 *(continued)*

	Creation of Pericopes	Modification of Material	Selection (Inclusion) of Material
Meye	No instances discovered (p. 78).	1. Numerous instances of comparison of Mark and Matthean/Lukan modifications of Mark (though seems to be more of a heuristic principle). Remains unclear how Markan *Tendenz* is thus discerned. 2. No instances of 'misformed' pericopes discovered. 3. Though conceded redactionally significant, inconsistency between history and Gospel not assumed (pp. 78-79).	Avowedly significant, betokening a concern for the twelve in the Markan *Sitz;* problematic in that it leads to unsupported inferences about the significance for Mark of material included by him. Criterion tends to homogenize tradition and redaction (pp. 80-81).
Best	No instances discovered; explicitly rejected as a criterion (p. 114).	1. Several instances of comparison of Mark with Matthean/Lukan modifications of Mark. Demonstration weak: arguments from silence. Unclear how Markan redaction is thus discerned. 2. 4 instances of grammatical 'clumsiness' discovered; argumentation weakened by uncertainty about shape of tradition. 3. No confidence invested in historical inconsistencies (pp. 114-16).	Accorded explicit importance yet rarely employed (typically in rebuttal of others' exegeses), owing to its unverifiability, its implication for tradition's 'mastery' over the Evangelist, and its tendency to homogenize tradition and redaction (pp. 116-17).
Weeden	No instances discovered, in spite of redaction-critical presumption of Markan creativity that would have rendered creation of pericopes possible (p. 153).	1. Approximately 9 instances of comparison of Mark with Matthean/Lukan modifications; arguments encumbered by Weeden's presuppositions and by lack of clarity about discernment of Markan *Tendenz.* 2. Only 1 instance of narrative awkwardness cited, without clear differentiation of tradition and redaction. 3. Historical inconsistencies presuppositional (pp. 153-57).	4 instances cited, but Weeden's inferences concerning significance of Markan inclusions are suspect (pp. 157-58).

TABLE 7 *(continued)*

	Omission of Material	Arrangement of Material	Introduction
Meye	Disavows criterion and inferences to be drawn from it; yet Meye occasionally susceptible to redactional *argumenta e silentio* (p. 81).	1. Arrangement of individual pericopes the most frequently exercised criterion (11 instances). Problems: question of Markan laxity and editorial freedom; the delineation of redaction from tradition. 2. Only 3 instances of intercalations, not all of equally cogent demonstration. 3. Geographical scheme: ambivalence about its existence. 4. Various themes (pp. 81-89).	Of little use, beyond reasonable concern for discipleship at Mark 1.16-20 (pp. 89-90).
Best	Explicitly distrusted as a criterion; used rarely and carefully concerning minor details (p. 117).	1. 4 instances of Markan arrangement of pericopes; redactional uncertainty admitted. 2. 6 instances of intercalations cited, with unequally cogent defense. 3. Heavy emphasis on geographical scheme, with respect to narrative and theological implications. Argumentation questionable. 4. Various themes (pp. 117-23).	Of little use to Best, beyond orientation to nature of a Gospel and certain thematic concerns (p. 123).
Weeden	Plays a minimal, even veiled, role in Weeden's analysis, with results sometimes exegetically embarrassing to Weeden's argument (p. 158).	1. Approximately 4 instances of arrangement of pericopes, usually discussed in context of educing Markan themes. Reasoning often circular, subject to dispute. 2. 1 (tendentious) instance of intercalation cited. 3. Decided emphasis on Galilean geographical scheme, without convincing defense. 4. Various themes (pp. 158-63).	Of no use to Weeden (p. 163).

	Conclusion	Vocabulary and Style	Christological Titles
Meye	Cited chiefly to support what are perceived to be characteristic Markan themes. No attempt made to separate tradition from redaction (p. 90).	Extensively used and exegetically emphasized. Defense questionably based on 'frequency of occurrence', internally inconsistent argumentation, lack of clear rationale for consigning such material to redactional level (pp. 90-96).	In addition to customary titles 'Jesus as teacher' is stressed. No clear demonstration on the basis of redaction-critical separation (pp. 96-97).
Best	Cited chiefly to support what are perceived to be characteristic Markan themes. Attempts made to separate tradition from redaction (pp. 123-24).	Most extensively used of all criteria and exegetically emphasized. Defense questionably based on 'frequency of occurrence', lack of clear rationale for consigning such material to redactional level (pp. 124-31).	Of minor importance to Best; only 1 instance cited germane to discipleship, supported thematically but not redaction-critically (p. 131).
Weeden	Cited chiefly to support what are perceived to be characteristic Markan themes. Attempts made to separate redaction from tradition on basis of insertions and vocabulary; process of separation moves circularly with respect to thematic concerns (pp. 163-64).	Markan style scarcely cited at all; vocabulary extensively cited but less frequently emphasized, exegetically, than in Meye and Best. Defense questionably based on 'frequency of occurrence', lack of clear rationale for consigning such material to redactional level, and Weeden's unconventional understanding of Markan themes (pp. 164-68).	Rarely cited, only 3 instances noted, supported thematically and (ostensibly) traditio-historically, but not redaction-critically (pp. 168-69).

TABLE 7 *(continued)*

First, a number of Stein's suggested redactional criteria are of minor importance for all three scholars, at least in their respective studies of the disciples in Mark: seams (criterion 1), summaries (3), creation of pericopes (4), omission of traditional material (7), the Markan introduction (9), and Christological titles (12). In one instance, Markan insertions (2), a criterion is relatively insignificant for two of the scholars (Meye and Best) and more frequently employed by the third (Weeden). *Second,* four of Stein's redactional canons are avowedly important for, or are frequently used by, the exegetes in question: Markan modification of traditional material (5) as discerned through comparison with Matthew and Luke, Mark's arrangement of traditional material (8; particularly the ordering of individual pericopes and arrangement in accordance with particular themes), the Markan conclusion (10), and Markan vocabulary and style (11). For Meye and Best the criterion of selection, or inclusion (6), is deemed significant, whereas Weeden lays less emphasis on it. *Third,* in general each scholar places stress on, or more customarily invokes, a different criterion from among those four most commonly employed: Weeden, the modification of material (5; especially comparisons of Mark with Matthew and Luke, and with historical fact); Meye, the arrangement of material (8; in virtually all of its forms); Best, vocabulary and style (11). Nevertheless, it appears to be the case that (a) a pattern in the employment of particular *redaktionsgeschichtlich* tools by these interpreters is discernible and that (b) these exegetes are in general, or at least superficial, agreement among themselves on the manner in which redaction criticism is used in the interpretation of Mark.

We can be even more precise. Evidently, there is one hermeneutical principle that, for all of our investigators, is methodologically dominant, one interpretive canon that tends to direct the manipulation of all the others: *the determination of Markan themes.* As we have seen, it is Meye's isolation of distinctive Markan motifs that enables him to detect the Second Gospel's seams, its modifications through comparison with the other Synoptics, its selection or inclusion of material, its arrangement, its introduction and conclusion, and the proper understanding of its Christological titles. So it is with Weeden: his identification of particular themes — both reflective of and antagonistic to the Evangelist's position — permits him to pinpoint Markan insertions, summaries, modifications, selections and arrangements of material, vocabulary, and the proper interpretation of the Gospel's conclusion and Christological titles. Similarly, Best's perception of (ostensibly) characteristic Markan themes informs his handling of that

Gospel's seams and summaries, introduction and conclusion, Christological titles, and even its vocabulary: for Best's inferences regarding
'Markan' verbal units ultimately rest on his presumption of certain redactional motifs signified by those words.

There is something odd about all of this. For the sake of convenience
and comprehensiveness, we have extrapolated Stein's subcriterion of geographical arrangement in order to take into account our investigators'
broader thematic considerations. In point of fact, however, *the determination of the Gospel's themes is not a uniquely redaction-critical criterion,* although it can be incorporated into a larger redaction-critical paradigm.
This focus on a fundamental interpretive canon that is not inherently
redaction-critical engenders two problems, both of which we have witnessed time and again:

a. Such a procedure tacitly short-circuits the necessity, in each investigator's research, of differentiating tradition from redaction: the need is no
longer apparent since it is assumed that the material in the Second Gospel
which conveys 'the characteristic theme(s)' is, *by definition,* redactional.
This may explain why Meye, Best, and Weeden plump for the practice of
redaction criticism yet often stop short of its execution: that is, why they
are sometimes lax in separating redaction from tradition, or negligent in
demonstrating the distinctively *Markan* character of putative seams, insertions, summaries, modifications, inclusions, arrangements, the Gospel's
introduction and conclusion, vocabulary, and Christological titles (recall
Table 7). By tacitly precluding further *redaktionsgeschichtlich* investigation
of the bases for delineating 'Markan themes', the investigators are thus relieved of the burden of executing a redaction-critical analysis of Mark in
the strict sense — which, as the evidence below suggests, is an arguably impossible task in any case.

b. This stress on ostensible themes, rather than on redaction-critical
analysis as such, seems to account moreover for those occasions when
Meye, Best, and Weeden resort to appeals to the 'received wisdom' of
Markan scholars for 'substantiating' their identifications of seams, insertions, summaries, arrangements, and the like. In place of proof, *argumenti
ad verecundiam* substitute a certain scholarly like-mindedness: thus, in
certain instances, Meye claims to be in exegetical alignment with R. H.
Lightfoot; Best, with Eta Linnemann; Weeden, with Ludger Schenke.[35]
This tactic seemingly obviates the need for redaction-critical substantia-

---

35. Meye, *Jesus,* p. 179 n. 9; Best, 'Peter', p. 555 n. 49; Weeden, *Mark,* pp. 104-5.

tion: it suffices to spotlight the proper theme and to remind one's readers that others have hit upon it as well.

In a moment we shall explore why Meye, Best, and Weeden have chosen the themes that they have, and the degree to which those themes agree. For now, let this much be clear: Meye, Best, and Weeden appear essentially to agree on those aspects of redaction criticism to which they will give comparatively short shrift; more important, they have evidently decided on a thematic hermeneutic — in itself not distinctively *redaktionsgeschichtlich* — in structuring their respective redaction-critical presentations.

2. *The question of internal and external consistency.* It seems reasonable to inquire about the internal coherence of the method exhibited by our case-studies. Do they logically and consistently carry out the redaction-critical exercise that they have set for themselves?

Let us start by reviewing the work of Best, which in many respects is a model attempt to implement redaction criticism. In spite of the methodological care that Best exercises, we have observed over a dozen instances in which his redaction-critical arguments are, at best, suspect and, at worst, flatly illogical.[36] In some cases his presentation is *internally inconsistent.* For example, seams and insertions are considered by Best to be the most obvious places to discern Mark's handiwork and purpose, yet these segments are employed relatively rarely in defining Markan discipleship. *Sammelberichte* constitute a treasure-trove for Markan vocabulary, yet harbor non-Markan words as well. On several occasions the Markan misformation of pericopes, or 'clumsiness', is conceded to exist, only to be impugned as a proper redaction-critical criterion owing to Mark's 'neatness' elsewhere, to the arguable 'clumsiness' of pre-Markan, traditional phraseology, and to the inappropriately value-laden character of this criterion. 'Inclusion' seems to be set forth as a significant *redaktionsgeschichtlich* criterion, at least in theory, yet is used only sporadically in the refutation of other exegetical positions. Certain examples of distinctively Markan vocabulary, adjudged by their frequency of occurrence, in fact appear in that Gospel no more frequently than other, putatively non-Markan words, or appear with equal frequency in some other Gospels. Finally, Best ends up perceiving far more redactional activity, overall, in the Second Gospel than one might expect on the basis of his 'mediate' presuppositions. Some other arguments ventured by Best are *non sequiturs:* the case

---

36. For documentation of each of the following, the reader is referred to my discussion of Best's method in Chapter 4.

that Matthean and Lukan redaction of Mark informs our understanding of the *latter's* redaction history; the position that the consecutive and intercalative arrangement of pericopes in the Second Gospel is necessarily an indicator of *redactional* activity; the seeming assumption that a given word's frequency of occurrence *demonstrates* its redactional character. Finally, one might recall instances of *circular reasoning,* or *petitio principii,* on Best's part: the determination of Markan seams by means of distinctive vocabulary — and the identification of distinctive vocabulary by means of attention to Markan seams; the delineation of redactional arrangements on the basis of characteristic themes — and the distinguishment of certain themes as characteristically Markan on the grounds of their recurrence in (so-called) redactional arrangements; and the confirmation of Gospel material that has been circularly defined as redactional by the supposed 'controls' of 'frequency of occurrence' and 'conjunction of redaction-critical criteria'.

From these comments it should not be inferred that Best is being specially targeted for criticism, or that his redaction-critical argumentation is more slipshod than others. In their use of the tools of Markan *Redaktionsgeschichte,* both Meye and Weeden fall prey to many of the same difficulties, as we have already observed.[37] In the work of both we have encountered, for example, *internally inconsistent arguments:* claims for the significance of certain redaction-critical criteria, coupled with a general disregard for those criteria; the disavowal of other *redaktionsgeschichtlich* canons, accompanied by the invocation of their usage later; attributions to the Second Gospel of both tightness and slackness of structure, of both awkwardness and smoothness; and self-contradictory contentions regarding the frequency of occurrence of particular elements of vocabulary, the relationship between actual history and Markan reportage, the correlation of Markan vocabulary and themes, and the implicit use of the criterion of inclusion as a way of bypassing the redaction-critical process altogether. As with a number of Best's claims, many of Meye's and Weeden's *arguments do not follow logically:* the notion that comparison of Mark with Matthew and Luke can inform us, even indirectly, of the Second Evangelist's redactional intentions; the idea that a theme's constancy throughout Mark or a term's frequency of occurrence actually proves anything about the Second Gospel's redaction history. And some of

---

37. The reader should consult the sections on 'Method' in Chapters 3 and 5 for evidence of the following problems.

Weeden's and Meye's *arguments tend to beg the question* as well: the definition of seams and summaries by means of themes, which themselves are deemed redactional on the basis of their appearance in seams and summaries; the identification of Markan insertions on the basis of the putative existence of other *Zwischenbemerkungen;* and the thoroughly circular interplay of Markan themes with such redaction-critical canons as arrangements and themes.

I do not wish to be misunderstood. By no means should these remarks be construed as a blanket indictment of the competence or quality of the studies of Meye, Best, and Weeden. The truth is just the opposite: allowing for the inconsistencies that will ordinarily occur in any comprehensive work, these investigators' contributions are well-researched, provocatively argued, serious scholarly contributions that merit the attention that has been given them. The internal inconsistency that plagues each of their studies is attributable, I believe, to an interpretive method that (at least in its application to Mark) is as graspable as quicksilver. Little wonder it is that all three of these exegetes have gravitated to a hermeneutical principle, the exposition of Markan themes, which (they assume) will counteract the slipperiness of redaction criticism when applied to Mark.

Unfortunately, in and of itself a thematic criterion cannot fulfill this promise. As we have witnessed, Best, Weeden, and Meye wildly disagree among themselves in their identifications and treatment of distinctive themes in the Second Gospel. If we cross-check our earlier compilations of Markan themes suggested in the work of Meye (whose list comprises 16 items), Best (with 21 items), and Weeden (with 12 items),[38] the following, rather telling, facts emerge:

a. Upon no single theme (from among Christology, discipleship, and miscellaneous motifs in those listings) do Meye, Best, and Weeden all agree.

b. Upon no single theme do both Meye and Weeden agree; in those listings, only upon 'Jesus as the teacher' and the motif of 'the [crossing of the] sea' do Meye and Best agree.

c. Upon a total of only four themes do Best and Weeden agree (the disciples as somehow 'specially removed' and 'ignorant' or 'stupid'; the miscellaneous motifs of 'the mountain' and 'retiring to a house').

---

38. Compare and contrast the lists presented above, pp. 87-89, 121-22, and 159.

Given the breadth of these scholars' research, and their tendency to stress thematic concerns, I submit that this scarcely constitutes a significant corroboration of results. However, in cross-checking the same three lists, all of which are supposedly derived from (or at least are supported by) redaction-critical analysis, the really surprising things to note are the patent *contradictions* among these scholars' findings:

TABLE 8	Contradictions in Dominant Themes		
	Meye	**Best**	**Weeden**
Christology	—	Jesus as risen and present in the community	The delay of Jesus' exaltation until the *parousia* and his absence from the community
	The disciples as being with Jesus	—	The disciples as abandoning Jesus
Discipleship	The disciples as progressively advancing in understanding	The disciples as failing to understand	The disciples as progressively deteriorating in understanding

This is not a matter of nit-picking: it is often upon just these discrepant thematic interpretations that our scholars' characteristic exegeses turn.

What measure of reciprocal corroboration is found in the assessments of Markan vocabulary and style by Meye, Best, and Weeden? If we compare and contrast our previous tabulations of Markan stylistic features, as suggested by Meye (whose list contains 11 items), Best (with 24 items), and Weeden (1 item),[39] we discover the following results:

a. Upon no single stylistic element do Meye, Best, and Weeden all agree.
b. Upon no single stylistic element do Meye and Weeden agree; only upon a certain 'duality of Markan expression' do Best and Weeden agree.
c. Out of a total of 36 items suggested between them, upon only three elements of Markan style do Meye and Best agree: parataxis, redundant participles, and some repetitive form of ἄρχεσθαι.

Once again, corroboration among the investigators is meager. Even more striking, in light of their unanimous emphasis on Markan vocabulary, is

39. See above, Tables 2 and 4, pp. 92-93, 128-29; cf. pp. 164-65.

the relative lack of agreement among Weeden, Best, and Meye on those terms that should be considered redactional:[40]

a. Upon only three verbal units do Meye, Best, and Weeden all agree: διδάσκειν, ὄχλος, and φοβεῖσθαι.
b. Upon only three additional verbal units[41] do Meye and Best agree: ἐκθαμβεῖσθαι, θαμβεῖσθαι and λόγος.
c. Upon only four additional verbal units do Best and Weeden agree: βλέπειν, ἐπιτιμᾶν [plus ἵνα], εὐαγγέλιον, and πολλοί (in place of ὄχλοι, in some instances).
d. Upon only two additional verbal units do Meye and Weeden agree: διδαχή and κηρύσσειν.

Even as we observed in considering Markan themes, this scanty redaction-critical corroboration is virtually undercut by the flat *contradictions* that persist among the three scholars' presentations of redactional and non-redactional vocabulary:

TABLE 9   Contradictions in Redactional and Nonredaction Vocabulary

Meye	Best	Weeden
ἀκολουθεῖν (non-Markan technical term for discipleship)	ἀκολουθεῖν (Markan technical term for discipleship)	—
λαλεῖν (Markan)	—	λαλεῖν (non-Markan)
λόγος (Markan)	λόγος (Markan)	λόγος (non-Markan)
παραβολή (Markan)	[παραβολαί: (Markan)]	παραβολή (non-Markan)

To the information presented in Table 9, one final, curious datum might be appended: Meye and Weeden (but not Best) explicitly identify a total of nine words that, in their opinion, are *not* redactional — and *none* of the items in their respective listings agree![42]

40. Meye's listing contains 21 items (see above, Table 1, pp. 91-92); Best's, 44 items (above, Table 3, pp. 125-27); Weeden's, 16 items (above, Table 5, pp. 164-65).
41. This total would be increased to five if one included the cognates παραβολή (Meye)/ παραβολαὶ (Best) and πολύς (Meye)/πολλά (used adverbially; Best).
42. Meye: ἀπόστολοι (referring to the twelve), ἀκολουθεῖν (as a *terminus technicus* for discipleship), πλοῖον and πολλαὶ [μαθηταί]; Weeden: ἔκστασις, λαλεῖν, ὁ λόγος, παραβολή, τρόμος.

To summarize the results of this subsection: the redaction-critical methods of Meye, Best, and Weeden are internally inconsistent and externally incoherent with each other. The various dimensions of each interpreter's redaction-critical procedure do not significantly corroborate other such dimensions; nor does the practice of redaction criticism in the work of one exegete find significant corroboration in the work of the others.

3. *The question of correlation.* Is there a discernible correlation between the general perspectives of Meye, Best, and Weeden and their respective implementations of the redaction-critical method? Put differently, if not pessimistically: have these scholars' general points of view slanted their particular practice of *Redaktionsgeschichte* in any detectable way?

This is a complex question. The complex answer elicited by it, I believe, is this: Although each of the interpreters has subtly put redaction criticism to use in a manner congenial with his presuppositions, by and large those assumptions do not appear to have determined the scholars' choice of *redaktionsgeschichtlich* criteria. Let me clarify what I mean. Meye is inclined to view historical fact, tradition, and Gospel in continuity; as a Type I critic, he tends to favor a redaction-critical approach that highlights the homogenization of these elements, elevating the total content of the Second Gospel — 'what Mark clearly and repeatedly says' — to the status of Markan theology. In light of this understanding, it is not altogether surprising that Meye emphasizes, more than do Best and Weeden, certain redaction-critical criteria that regard the Gospel more holistically: namely, the canons of inclusion and arrangement of material. On the other hand, Weeden, a Type III exegete, is disposed to finding radical disjunctions between history and tradition, between tradition and Gospel, and between history and Gospel; thus it is not out of character that he should devote somewhat more attention than his 'conservative' or 'mediate' colleagues to such *redaktionsgeschichtlich* criteria as insertions and modifications of material, as discerned through comparison with the other Synoptics (both of which criteria are predicated on a certain discontinuity or difference). The Type II position, which presumes a tensive conjunction of history, tradition, and theology in a Gospel, is perhaps reflected in the slight dominance given by Best, in principle, to the criterion of inclusion (which is compatible with the theory of continuity between history, tradition, and theology in Mark) and, in practice, to the criterion of vocabulary and style (which, by its allowance for the discrimination of characteristically Markan touches, reflects a measure of the Evangelist's discontinuity with history and tradition).

For all of these subtle distinctions, and despite the fact that Meye, Best, and Weeden begin their work with very different presuppositions about the measure of history in Mark, the character of the pre-Markan tradition, the influence of the Evangelist's theology, and the redaction-critical method itself, we have also observed a striking *agreement* in their actual practice of *Redaktionsgeschichte,* as measured by their customary implementation of many of the same redaction-critical criteria: Markan modification of traditional material as discerned through comparison with Matthew and Luke, Markan arrangement of traditional material (especially of individual pericopes), the Markan conclusion, and Markan vocabulary and style. In other words, insofar as these interpreters' essays exhibit particular hallmarks of the redaction-critical method, they tend to exhibit the *same* hallmarks. This is not to suggest that they ply each of these critical canons with equal care, or that the exegetical results achieved by one scholar in applying the method are supported by results achieved by the others. It is not even to suggest that these critics' interpretations of Markan discipleship are in every case directly dependent on their attempted employment of similar redaction-critical criteria. Two things *are* being suggested: stated negatively, neither Meye, Best, nor Weeden appears to be abusing the redaction-critical method or wrenching its practice to conform with either a 'conservative', 'mediate', or 'liberal' point of view. Stated positively, notwithstanding their differences in general perspective, Meye, Best, and Weeden gravitate toward the same criteria encompassed by the redaction-critical method. In general, all three exegetes are attempting to implement the same *redaktionsgeschichtlich* tools (modifications, arrangements, the conclusion, vocabulary, and style).

A second question must be considered: Is there a discernible correlation between the manner in which each of these interpreters has applied redaction criticism to Mark's Gospel and that interpreter's exegetical results? In all three cases, the answer appears to be No. We might begin with the obvious: If there were a detectable correlation between method and results, then we would logically expect Meye, Best, and Weeden to arrive at roughly similar interpretive conclusions, since they are apparently applying the same or quite similar exegetical tools to the same piece of literature, the Gospel of Mark.[43] In fact what we have discovered is that, in spite of

---

43. Of course, it would be unreasonable to expect *identity* of exegetical results to emerge from the application of the redaction-critical method by different scholars to a common Gospel. Always there will be many points that are debated, since different interpreters will

their general similarity in method (that is, their concurrence in the use of certain redaction-critical criteria), these investigations scatter far and wide in their exegeses of Markan discipleship: in their adjudication of historical (Meye), polemical (Weeden), and pastoral (Best) presentations of Jesus; in their perception of the disciples as figures positive (Meye), negative (Weeden), or both positive and negative, or neutral (Best); in their assessment of the ramifications of Markan discipleship in terms of apostolic foundation (Meye), theological polemic by means of character assassination (Weeden), and exemplary edification of the church (Best). Moreover, we might recall that the same problem of correlation between method and results has arisen within each of the preceding chapters on Meye, Best, and Weeden: while each scholar's exegetical results are not theoretically incompatible with the practice of redaction criticism, we have seen that none of their interpretations is ultimately dependent on their attempted utilization of the method.

Upon what, then, have these scholars' disparate exegeses been dependent? If anything has shaped or controlled the interpretive results of Meye, Best, and Weeden, surely it is the collection of distinctive *themes* or *motifs* that they have uncovered when reading the Gospel of Mark.[44] Has their application of redaction criticism driven them to these themes? For two reasons, I think not: first, as I have already suggested, on many occasions it appears that these scholars have fallen back on certain motifs as a way of making redaction-critical sense out of the Markan text (that is, as a means for determining Markan seams, insertions, vocabulary, and so forth); thus the themes have suggested their interpretation of the evidence, and the hermeneutical circle has begun spinning from that point. That this is almost certainly the case is suggested by a second fact: there is virtually no corroboration of one scholar's slate of distinctive Markan themes in the

---

formulate their studies differently and will perceive common issues from different angles of vision. Still, even under those circumstances, is it unreasonable to expect a greater degree of convergence than we have witnessed among scholars who explore Markan discipleship?

44. Though the connection is never made by Meye, Best, or Weeden, their hermeneutical approach is, at this point, strangely reminiscent of what Anders Nygren describes as 'structural analysis' or 'motif-research': 'an investigation which seeks to penetrate to the fundamental motif that governs a particular outlook', the discernment of 'the basic idea or the driving power of the religion concerned, or what it is that gives it its character as a whole and communicates to all its parts their special content and colour' (A. Nygren, *Meaning and Method: Prolegomena to a Scientific Philosophy of Religion and a Scientific Theology* [London: Epworth, 1972], pp. 351-78 [first quotation, p. 362]); idem, *Agape and Eros* [Parts I and II; Vol. I; Philadelphia: Westminster, 1938], pp. 34-40 [second quotation, p. 35]).

others' research. Yet it is precisely such corroboration that one would expect to find if the themes had been suggested by the practice of *Redaktionsgeschichte,* inasmuch as Meye, Best, and Weeden concur in their selection and attempted application of the same *redaktionsgeschichtlich* criteria.

What, then, has been the source of these various themes, which our 'conservative', 'mediate', and 'liberal' investigators have employed to guide their attempted redaction-critical studies of Markan discipleship? From all appearances, *the motifs have their origin in the general perspective and assumptions that each scholar has brought with him to the method and to the text.* Meye has assumed of the pre-Markan and Markan *Sitze* a historical concern for, and favorable estimation of, the disciples; he has discerned in the text of Mark such themes as the disciples' authority and proximity to Jesus; he has concluded, therefore, that the Markan community regarded the twelve as mediators and guarantors of the apostolic faith. Best has assumed of the pre-Markan and Markan *Sitze* an interplay between historical and theological concerns, with the tradition binding Mark even as the Evangelist, a creative theologian, shaped that tradition; he has discerned in the text of Mark such themes as the disciples' special status with respect to Jesus the teacher, as well as their fears and failings; he has concluded, therefore, that the Markan community regarded the twelve as typical believers rather than as historical authorities or as heretical opponents. Weeden has assumed of the pre-Markan and Markan *Sitze* a traditio-historical conflict between opposing theologies, the heretical version of which came to be associated with Jesus' disciples; he has discerned in the text of Mark such themes as the disciples' increasing incompetence, stupidity, and abandonment of Jesus; he has concluded, therefore, that Mark wished for his community to regard the disciples as rogues who were completely discreditable. In every case, the 'conservative', 'mediate', or 'liberal' presuppositions held by each scholar appear to have tacitly directed the investigation of each, to have informed their manipulation of redaction-critical tools, and, doubtless unconsciously, to have molded their exegetical outcomes. In no case of which I am aware (from among the studies considered) has the acceptance of the redaction-critical method or its application to the Second Gospel demonstrably challenged or corrected the presuppositions of either of these three investigators. In no case of which I am aware has the acceptance of the redaction-critical method or its application to the Second Gospel by one scholar demonstrably corroborated or corrected the work of the others.

The conclusion seems irresistible, albeit sobering: judged on the basis of careful examinations of Robert Meye, Ernest Best, and Theodore Weeden, redaction criticism of Mark's Gospel appears to be a method of interpretation that is radically if not fatally flawed. The evidence suggests that it is internally inconsistent, methodologically questionable, and virtually impossible to apply to the Second Gospel with rigor and with consistency. When that application is attempted, the method seems incapable of producing confirmable, exegetical results that can be replicated by researchers of divergent points of view, using the same criteria to analyze the same material. In the end, the *redaktionsgeschichtlich* analysis of Markan discipleship appears to function less as a critical control by which the exegete's assumptions may be disciplined and his exegesis may be informed; it appears to function more as a conduit, along which the investigator's assumptions can flow, without check or impediment, into particular exegetical conclusions to which he may be predisposed.

7. The Rehabilitation of the Redaction-Critical Method?

In view of the wide variety of opinions which the data of the Gospel seems to support — at least to the satisfaction of the proponents themselves — it has become increasingly clear that a methodology is required which will not only win the support of all those investigating Mk. [sic] but which will produce relatively agreed results. The last twenty years of Markan research has witnessed a number of alternative methods, has produced a conflicting range of deductions about the purpose of the final redactor, and . . . has resulted in a wide range of inferences about the particular *Sitz im Leben* of the Gospel. More recently, however, the trend has been to clarify the issue of the exact location of the redactional activity in the Gospel: the issue of *where* Markan redaction is to be found and *how* it is to be identified.

James C. Little[1]

The metaphor of a conduit was used in the preceding chapter to describe the practical effect of Markan redaction criticism. Another analogy might be that of a looking glass: in the interpretation of the Second Gospel, *Redaktionsgeschichte* appears to function less as a reliable, exegetical control, and more as a mirror by which the interpreter's assumptions and point of view are reflected in the exegesis. At what points does this conclusion appear vulnerable?

First, it might be argued that our judgments to this stage have been

---

1. J. C. Little, 'Redaction Criticism and the Gospel of Mark with Special Reference to Mark 4.1-34' (Ph.D. diss., Duke University, 1972), p. 31.

built on a foundation too narrow. In other words, it is possible to challenge the *redaktionsgechichtlich* studies of Robert Meye, Ernest Best, and Theodore Weeden without necessarily impugning the overall usefulness of Markan redaction criticism when employed by other interpreters. This is a reasonable objection: it would be unjust indeed to subject all practitioners of *Redaktionsgeschichte* to wholesale condemnation on the sole basis of questions surrounding its exercise by only three exegetes. Such a rebuttal would carry added weight if it could be shown that the use of the method by Meye, Best, and Weeden had been inhibited by factors, peculiar to their studies, for which adequate controls had not been instituted in my analysis.[2] Still, the force of this objection is diminished by the fact that we have surveyed, not just any three interpretations selected at random, but the work of three investigators whose research in Markan discipleship has made a significant contribution to New Testament scholarship. If the studies of Meye, Best, and Weeden do not exhaust the possibilities of Markan redaction criticism, at least they do represent, and have exerted influence on, both customary usage of that method and the variety of ways in which discipleship in Mark's Gospel has been understood.

To judge from our consideration of Meye, Best, and Weeden, it appears that their exegetical disagreements are *not* dependent on, or correlative to, their disagreement in the practice of *Redaktionsgeschichte*. In fact, these scholars are consistent in the criteria to which they appeal. Their radically divergent exegeses appear to arise, not from their inappropriate manipulation of redaction criticism, but from some flaw or flaws in the method itself. Though logical, this is not the only possible deduction. Hence the second objection to our study thus far: it might be argued that, while Meye, Best, and Weeden are procedurally consistent among themselves, their practice of redaction criticism is consistently lacking in methodological rigor. If this could be verified, then the better recommendation would be the refinement, rather than the renunciation, of Markan redaction criticism. In its application to the Second Gospel, can this method be made more reliable?

This question is important and merits further reflection. Though I am not inclined to propose a plan by which Markan *Redaktionsgeschichte* might be rendered more trustworthy, in this chapter it is necessary to review and to assess the work of those who have attempted such a project.

---

2. I am aware of no such mitigating factors; yet I am willing to concede the possibility of their existence.

A. The Pursuit of a Refined Method
for Markan Redaction Criticism

As we have witnessed throughout this study, the work of Robert Stein offers a lucid and accurate description of the manner in which Markan redaction critics have plied their craft from the late 1960s to the present. We would be wrong to conclude, however, that all methodological reflection on Markan *Redaktionsgeschichte* ceased with Stein. On the contrary, the ensuing years have seen various, intermittent endeavors to refine the method; curiously, the lion's share of this work has been undertaken within Anglo-Saxon scholarship. Let us now review six notable attempts to refine the redaction criticism of Mark.[3]

James Crichton Little

In a 1972 dissertation on the Markan parable chapter that deserves wider recognition than it has received,[4] James C. Little offered an early response to Stein's ground-breaking contributions to Markan redaction-critical method. Like Stein, Little understands the basic methodological issue to be '*where* Markan redaction is to be found in the Gospel and *how* it is to be identified'.[5] With Stein, Little agrees that certain *redaktionsgeschichtlich* criteria are comparatively less dependable (namely, Markan creation, omission, and selection of pericopes); primary attention should be devoted to Mark's arrangement of his material, since (as Stein observes in a statement quoted with emphatic approbation by Little) 'the theological emphasis . . . results from the arrangement of the material'.[6] An unusually significant specimen of Markan arrangement is, for Little, the interlaminations or intercalations; he also accords qualified significance to the Markan introduction and conclusion, the purpose of which may be informed by interests deduced from the Gospel's overall arrangement.[7]

---

3. Limitations of space forbid consideration of recent attempts by Kuhn, Güttgemanns, and others to rethink or to refine form-critical assumptions concerning the processes by which oral traditions may have been transmitted. Such investigations indirectly bear on the redaction-critical task; however, unlike the studies surveyed in this chapter, they do not directly set out to resolve the problems encumbering Markan *Redaktionsgeschichte*.

4. For bibliographical data, see note 1 above.

5. Little, 'Redaction Criticism', p. 31 (author's emphasis).

6. Stein, 'Markan Redaction History', p. 191; cf. Little, 'Redaction Criticism', p. 36.

7. Little, 'Redaction Criticism', pp. 36-39.

Of four redactional indicators on which Stein places high value — Markan transitions (that is, seams, insertions, summaries), modification of material, vocabulary, and Christological titles[8] — Little expresses greater reservations.

Little's misgivings about the validity of these last criteria may be summarized under three headings. First, on the grounds of *logic,* Little harbors reservations about Stein's tendency to regard the high frequency of supposed Markan vocabulary, style, and themes in *possible* redactional transitions as demonstrative of the *probability* that those transitions are redactional. Similarly, Little questions the wisdom of ascertaining Markan modifications of tradition by comparing Matthew and Luke's putative modification of Mark, and he rightly evaluates suggestions that the Second Evangelist has altered pre-Markan tradition as question-begging, since we have no inductive knowledge of such tradition apart from the Gospel itself.[9] Second, Little distrusts the *traditionsgeschichtlich* dependability of such criteria as supposed Markan seams, insertions, and summaries: each of these presupposes 'that the pre-Markan units of tradition were so fixed as to limit Mark's freedom and that a case of insertion [for example] is bound to leave tell-tale traces'.[10] Third, on *statistical* grounds, Little questions Stein's uncritical acceptance of Kendrick Grobel's attempted delineation of redactional vocabulary in Markan seams.[11] Beyond some minor errors in Grobel and Stein's procedure (concerning mistakes in verses and verse-divisions and subjectivity in the selection of putative seams),[12] Little exposes the inadequacy of Grobel and Stein's statistical method to demonstrate that the higher frequency of so-called Markan words, stylistic traits, and themes are owing to factors other than chance. Employing a 2 x 2 Chi-square test[13] of the ratio of characteristic words to total words in the

---

8. On Markan Christological titles, see Little's discussion in ibid., pp. 48, 88-89. Ultimately, Little concedes that 'The actual structure of Mk. is itself suggestive of an internal Christological interpretation' (ibid., p. 53).

9. Ibid., pp. 44-48.

10. Ibid., p. 41; cf. also pp. 45, 49.

11. Grobel, 'Idiosyncrasies of the Synoptists'.

12. Little, 'Redaction Criticism', pp. 170-73.

13. A Chi-square test is a statistical technique that can be used to determine whether there is a significant difference between some theoretical or expected frequency and a corresponding observed frequency in two or more categories of data that are independent of each other. (For example, based on the laws of probability, one would expect a 50-50 split in the number of heads and tails that occurs in 100 tosses of a coin; however, if the result of the tosses was a 45-55 split, one might ask whether this observed deviation from the expected

Markan and non-Markan universes (as defined by putative Markan seams), Little carefully and convincingly shows that only four of Mark's 'favorite terms', as tabulated by Grobel and Stein (διδάσκω, ἔρχομαι [most statistically significant], πάλιν, and συνάγω), and only two of Mark's 'stylistic characteristics' (the genitive absolute and the impersonal plural), appear in the Markan seams with a statistically significant, higher frequency.[14] Moreover, Little remains skeptical about the redaction-critical

---

frequency was significant: that is, owing to factors other than chance.) The calculation of a so-called one-way Chi-square classification is based on the following formula:

$$\chi^2 = \text{sum of } \frac{(\text{observed frequency - expected frequency})^2}{\text{expected frequency}}$$

Once the value for Chi-square is calculated, it must be interpreted for its significance. This interpretation is made on the basis of two other pieces of information: first, a value for the degrees of freedom (df) of the researcher's sample, which is equal to the number of categories being compared minus 1; second, a predetermined level of significance, which accounts for the possibility that test results are owing to sampling error (thus results that are significant at the 5% level probably occur by chance only 5% of the time or less). With the use of a standard Chi-square table, the researcher then compares his Chi-square value with the value listed in the table for his degrees of freedom and level of significance. If the value of Chi-square calculated by the researcher on the basis of his data is equal to or greater than the standard value of Chi-square in the table, then it may be concluded that the observed frequency is significantly different from the frequency that would be expected on the basis of chance alone.

A two-way Chi-square classification (of which Little's 2 × 2 test is a specific example) determines the significance of the difference between expected and observed frequencies of occurrence in two or more categories (c) with two or more groups (r). (For example, in a 2 × 2 test for the significance of difference in the educational level of male and female faculty members at a university, one might compare two categories [faculty members holding either a master's or a doctoral degree] with two groups [males and females among the faculty holding one of the two degrees].) The procedure for a two-way classification is the same as that for a one-way classification; before the calculation of the Chi-square value, an expected frequency is decided and a level of significance is selected; after the calculation of Chi-square, the value for the degrees of freedom is set (using the formula, df = [c-i] [r-1], in a two-way classification); and the final interpretation of the data for its significance is made with the use of a statistical table that presents standard values for Chi-square. As in the one-way classification, a significant Chi-square value in a two-way test is one that reflects a difference between expected and observed frequencies that must be explained on the basis of factors other than chance. For further information on the rationale and procedure of the Chi-square test, see A. E. Bartz, *Basic Statistical Concepts* (2nd edn; Minneapolis: Burgess, 1981), pp. 319-29; and D. Freedman, R. Pisani, and R. Purves, *Statistics* (New York and London: W. W. Norton, 1978), pp. 470-86.

14. Little, 'Redaction Criticism', pp. 173-80.

conclusions that can be deduced from this meager harvest of terms and stylistic characteristics: higher frequency levels, even those that are statistically significant, are not in themselves demonstrative of Markan compositional techniques; and other evidence suggesting a substantially consistent spread of Markan Greek style throughout the Gospel renders linguistic and stylistic factors alone undependable indicators of specifically Markan redaction.[15]

From this critique, Little draws the following conclusions regarding the proper method for obtaining a Markan redaction history:

> At the risk of making statistics prove anything, the present author would suggest that the foregoing analysis better supports the assumption that Mark has 'markanized' his sources rather than the assumption that he has been restricted by fixed traditions to introductions and seams [and the distinctively Markan vocabulary purportedly discerned therein] for his major input. . . . Markan redaction criticism should begin with what is most obvious in Mk: the arrangement and relationship of the stories and sayings which, acording to the conclusions of form criticism, had a probable independent existence in the period of oral transmission. Conclusions drawn from this analysis may then be confirmed and supplemented by analysis of the Markan Introduction and Conclusion. In the same way, certain motifs (for example, among the christological titles) may be shown to confirm and supplement already clearly identifiable Markan interests.[16]

On this basis, and primarily in consideration of the Markan complex at 8.22–10.52, Little concludes that 'Mark's arrangement of his material is constantly suggestive of emphasis on specific themes', namely, the paradigm of Jesus' suffering messiahship and its necessary consequences for the community's discipleship.[17]

That which is perhaps most salutary about Little's dissertation, if not extraordinary for the time at which it appeared, is its skepticism: while

---

15. Ibid., pp. 45, 180. In defense of Markan stylistic and verbal homogeneity, Little cites the research of Doudna, *The Greek of the Gospel of Mark*. Cf. the more recent, corroborative assessment of Neirynck, *Duality in Mark*, p. 37: 'There is a sort of homogeneity in Mark, from the wording of sentences to the composition of the gospel. After the study of these data one has a strong impression of the unity of the Gospel of Mark'.

16. Little, 'Redaction Criticism', pp. 49-50, 180.

17. Ibid., p. 66; cf. pp. 51, 53.

confident of the value of *Redaktionsgeschichte*, Little casts a critical eye on some of its methodological deficiencies and suggests means by which they might be eliminated or at least controlled. His judgments, especially his demonstration of the statistical insignificance of most of the perennial arguments for verbal frequency of occurrence, are cogent and clear. Still, one wonders if Little's criticisms go far enough:

1. As we have seen, Little doubts that pre-Markan tradition was as firm and fixed, and thus as resistant to the Evangelist's redaction (save for transitional devices), as many form critics have supposed. But the fundamental issue that he raises — namely, that our understanding of Markan redaction should not be shackled to indemonstrable *formgeschichtlich* presuppositions — boomerangs on Little when he bases his contention for the methodological primacy of redactional arrangement upon the equally indemonstrable, form-critical assumption that pre-Markan tradition existed only in independent units, stories, and sayings. Even at the time of Little's writing this premise was being challenged and substantially revised;[18] since then its tenability has been rendered even more suspect by those, like Erhardt Güttgemanns and Werner Kelber, who argue that the pre-Markan tradition could have diverged in manifold forms and directions, many of which were discontinuous with the redactor's written Gospel.[19] Insofar as Little would concur with Norman Perrin's judgment that 'redaction criticism proper is dependent upon the ability to write a history of the tradition',[20] and inasmuch as scholars are increasingly dubious about writing, to say nothing of achieving consensus on, such a *Traditionsgeschichte*, one must wonder if Markan redaction criticism as proposed by Little is any longer a viable prospect.

2. On the other hand, just how large a role such form-critical assumptions practically play in Little's own study is debatable: by according methodological pride of place to Markan arrangement, Little seems less inter-

---

18. Thus, for instance, Kuhn, *Ältere Sammlungen*.

19. Güttgemanns, *Candid Questions*, pp. 291-92, 323, 338-42; W. H. Kelber, 'Mark and Oral Tradition', *Sem* 16 (1979), pp. 7-55; cf. W. G. Doty, 'Fundamental Questions about Literary-Critical Methodology: A Review Article', *JAAR* 40 (1972), pp. 521-27. The positions represented by Kelber and Güttgemanns are not identical: the former posits a sharp discontinuity between the oral *kerygma* and the written Gospel; the latter understands 'Mark's taking up of the pen [as] therefore not a real act of composition but a variant of the oral, to be conceded in its form of appearance, uniqueness, and consequences' (*Candid Questions*, p. 138).

20. Perrin, *What Is Redaction Criticism?*, p. 13.

ested in the hypothetical separation of tradition and redaction and more concerned with what Ernst Haenchen has termed *Kompositionskritik*.[21] Striking, too, is the basis on which Little attempts to discern Markan composition: 'a *theological* principle of organization', concerning which 'reasonable deductions regarding Mark's special emphases' can be made.[22] For Little, no less than for Meye, Best, or Weeden, the identification of distinctive Markan *themes* is a fundamental if not paramount redactional canon: 'Mark's arrangement of his material is constantly suggestive of emphasis on specific themes'.[23] As has been suggested, however, the isolation of specific themes is not so much constitutive of *redaction* criticism as it is characteristic of many forms of narrative criticism.

3. Finally, if the main problem with many exercises in Markan *Redaktionsgeschichte* is the impossibility of verifying the contours of the pre-Markan tradition so as to identify contradistinctive redaction (as Little correctly points out), then the difficulty with Little's own understanding of the method is that its thoroughgoing application actually renders redaction criticism pointless. The paradox is this: the more successfully Little is able to show that the Second Evangelist has completely 'markanized' his sources, the less convincingly he is able to demonstrate this on the grounds of *redaction* criticism since, *ex hypothesi,* it is precisely the 'nonmarkanized' inconsistencies that enable him to determine that the redactor exists at all! 'Evidence that will show how sources have been edited to the point where all inconsistencies between them have been removed is also evidence that there never was a diversity of sources in the first place.'[24]

---

21. Haenchen, *Der Weg Jesu*, p. 24.

22. Little, 'Redaction Criticism', p. iii.

23. Ibid., p. 66.

24. J. Barton, *Reading the Old Testament: Method in Biblical Study* (Philadelphia: Westminster, 1984), pp. 57-58. Barton refers to this paradox as 'the disappearing redactor' (p. 57): 'The trick is simply this. The more impressive the critic makes the redactor's work appear, the more he succeeds in showing that the redactor has, by subtle and delicate artistry, produced a simple and coherent text out of the diverse material before him; the more also he reduces the evidence on which the existence of those sources was established in the first place.... Thus, if redaction criticism plays its hand too confidently, we end up with a piece of writing so coherent that no division into sources is warranted any longer; and the sources and the redactor vanish together in a puff of smoke, leaving a single, freely composed narrative with, no doubt, a single author'.

Lloyd Gaston

Although Lloyd Gaston's *Horae Synopticae Electronicae: Word Statistics of the Synoptic Gospels* does not intend to be exclusively oriented to the refinement of Markan redaction criticism, Gaston alludes to that method as an impetus for his compilation of Synoptic verbal statistics:

> With the current popularity of redaction criticism, the question often arises of a word or phrase being a 'favorite' expression of one of the Evangelists. . . . A student interested in a particular word cannot restrict himself to Hawkins' statistics, the listings in a concordance, or Morgenthaler's *Statistik*. One must distinguish between those cases where a redactor has simply taken over a word from a source and those in which he has written it of his own accord, as it is clear that the latter cases are the most significant for the preferences of the later writers.[25]

To measure the nature and degree of Matthean and Lukan redactional activity, Gaston presupposes the two-source theory in compiling his statistical data, 'since words that Matthew and Luke have added to (or subtracted from) Mark form the chief basis for determining their editorial preferences.'[26] But what of the redaction of the Second Gospel, on the assumption of Markan priority? In this case Gaston is compelled to start by combing through 'certain passages commonly agreed to be redactional', which, for him, consist of the following 'editorial sentences': Mark 1.1-2a, 14, 21-22, 28, 32-34, 39, 45; 2.1-2, 13; 3.6-16, 30; 4.1-2, 12-21a, 33-36; 5.21; 6.1, 6b-7, 8a, 12-13, 30-34, 45-46, 52-56; 7.3-4, 14a, 17, 20-24, 31; 8.1, 11-12a, 13-15a, 16-22a, 27a, 31a, 32-34a; 9.9a, 10-11, 14-15, 30-31a, 32-34; 10.1, 10, 23a, 24a, 26-27a, 28, 32, 41-42a, 46a; 11.11-12, 15a, 18-20, 27a; 12.1a, 9b-10a, 12-13, 34c, 37b-38a; 13.3-4; 14.9.[27] Drawing from this list material thought to be redactional, and taking into account every word, as printed in Aland's *Synopsis,* that occurs at least four

---

25. Gaston, *Horae Synopticae Electronicae,* p. 1.

26. Ibid., p. 4. On the same page Gaston suggests that those not assuming Markan priority can use his tables after making 'the necessary terminological adjustments, e.g. reading Mk sub[traction] for Mt add[ition]'. In my summary of Gaston, I shall not attend to his consideration of 'sources' other than Mark (that is, Q, QMt, QLk, M, L, Mt add, Lk add) or of 'forms' other than Mark Editorial (that is, Matthew Editorial, Luke Editorial, Legends, Apothegms, Miracle stories, Parables, Prophetic sayings, Rule or law sayings, Wisdom sayings, Christological sayings [*Ich-Wort*], Explicit Old Testament quotations, Hymns).

27. Gaston, *Horae Synopticae Electronicae,* pp. 6, 14; cf. p. 11. Gaston adopts a similar procedure in assessing Q, M, and L material (p. 14).

times (except for the definite article), Gaston compiles an inventory of 32 words characteristic of 'Mark Editorial'[28] as well as a supplementary list of 20 more 'editorial' words of questionable character.[29] Some of the items in these two catalogues appear in a longer table of 85 words that are considered by Gaston to be significantly characteristic of the possible source(s) of Mark;[30] Gaston's assignment of sentences (not pericopes) to this source is made on the basis of words appearing at least four times in Mark and in two, one, or no other Synoptic in a parallel sentence.[31] Out of a total of 32,996 words in all of the Synoptic sources surveyed, Gaston calculates that 9,582 words (29%) appear four or more times in the Second Gospel, and, of that number, 1,578 (approximately 16.4%) appear four or more times in the Markan editorial passages.[32] In addition to the sheer number of occurrences, Gaston's procedure also considers each word's relative percentage of occurrence and standard deviation from the norm that would be expected on a random distribution of words throughout the Second Gospel.[33]

It is easy to admire the thoroughness and care with which Gaston has

28. ἀκούω, ἄρχω, Γαλιλαία, γινώσκω, δαιμόνιον, διδάσκω, διδαχή, δώδεκα, εἰς, ἐμβαίνω, ἐξέρχομαι, θάλασσα, ἴδιος, Ἱεροσόλυμα, καί, κηρύσσω, λαλέω, λόγος, μαθητής, ὅριον, ὅτε, ὄχλος, πάλιν, παραβολή, πέραν, πλοῖον, πόλις, πολύς, πρός, προσκαλέω, σπείρω, συνάγω (Gaston, *Horae Synopticae Electronicae*, pp. 58-59).

29. ἀπέρχομαι, ἄρτος, αὐτός, ἐκεῖνος, ἐκπορεύομαι, ἐπερωτάω, ἔρχομαι, εὐθύς, ἔχω, κρατέω, ὅλος, ὅπου, ὅρος, ὅσος, παρά, πᾶς, περί, Φαρισαῖος, φοβέω, ὥστε (Gaston, *Horae Synopticae Electronicae*, pp. 59-60).

30. αἴρω, ἀκάθαρτος, ἀκολουθέω, ἀλλά, ἄλλος, Ἀνδρέας, ἄνεμος, ἀπαρνέομαι, ἄρτος, ἀρχιερεύς, ἀρχισυνάγωγος, ἄρχω, ἀσκός, αὐτός, ἀφίημι, βαπτίζω, Βηθανία, γραμματεύς, γρηγορέω, διαλογίζομαι, διαστέλλω, διδαχή, δύναμαι, δώδεκα, εἰς, εἰσπορεύομαι, ἐκθαμβέω, ἐκπορεύομαι, ἐξέρχομαι, ἐπερωτάω, ἐπιτιμάω, ἑπτά, ἔρχομαι, ἐσθίω, εὐαγγέλιον, εὐθύς, ἔχω, Ἠλίας, θάλασσα, Ἰάκωβος, ἴδε, ἱμάτιον, ἵνα, Ἰωάννης, καθεύδω, καί, κηρύσσω, κλάσμα, κοινόω, κοράσιον, κράβαττος, κρατέω, λέγω, μαθητής, μηδείς, μηκέτι, μνῆμα, Ναζαρηνός, ξηραίνω, οἶδα, ὅπου, οὐκέτι, οὔπω, πάλιν, παραδίδωμι, παράδοσις, παραλυτικός, παραπορεύομαι, πάσχα, πέραν, περιβλέπω, Πέτρος, πλοῖον, πολύς, προσκαλέω, πρωΐ, σινδών, σιωπάω, σπείρω, σταυρός, συζητέω, τοιοῦτος, φέρω, φωνεῖν, χείρ (Gaston, *Horae Synopticae, Electronicae*, pp. 18-21).

31. Ibid., pp. 3, 4.

32. Ibid., pp. 11, 18, 58.

33. To use the example given by Gaston (ibid., p. 13), καί appears 2,839 times in all of the Synoptic sources and 1,073 times in Mark alone: this amounts to 250 more occurrences than would be expected (29% × 2,839 = 823) and 10.2 times the standard deviation. (Standard deviation, or SD, is equal to the square root of the sample size multiplied by both the probability of a word's occurrence in a subgroup and the probability of its nonoccurrence; thus $\sqrt{2,839} \times .29 \times .71 = \pm24$.) For further discussion, see Gaston, *Horae Synopticae Electronicae*, pp. 12-14.

attempted to update and to refine Hawkins' *Horae,* within self-imposed limitations, as well as the refreshing humility with which he views his accomplishment: 'It should be emphasized that the work is in no sense the result of Synoptic research but only a tool for it'.[34] Moreover, Gaston is commendably candid and circumspect about the assumptions on which his statistical analysis rests: 'It is clear that any of the tables, read as an argument in itself in isolation from other factors, would be a circular argument. Even if used as a supplementary tool, the tables are of value only insofar as the initial assumptions are approximately correct on other grounds'.[35] One is loath to appear critical of a well-executed project that is so appropriately self-critical; nevertheless, Gaston's analysis raises some significant questions about the value of this kind of study for the refinement of Markan *Redaktionsgeschichte:*

1. To begin with a relatively minor point: there are some errors in Gaston's presentation. Some are seemingly typographical: for instance, comparing the tables detailing 'Markan source' and 'Mark editorial', the sums of the number of Markan words indicated therein are discrepant by a value of one (9,581 versus 9,582),[36] and the total number of occurrences of καί is discrepantly presented as 1,073 in one table and 1,078 in the other. Other errors appear to be of omission: accepting Gaston's standard of admitting into consideration words that appear in Mark four or more times, he should have included, in his tabulation of the Markan source, ἐκεῖθεν (6 occurrences, including κἀκεῖθεν), ἐκπλήσσομαι (5), θεραπεύω (5), κακῶς (4), κώμη (6), and παραλαμβάνω (6).[37]

2. Were we to lend the greatest benefit of doubt to Gaston's judgments concerning the significant frequency of certain words in putative 'Mark editorial', conceivably we might wish to allow verbal occurrences less than four to be considered significant (since the extent of 'Mark editorial' is, for Gaston, no more than one-sixth of the total Gospel — 1,578/9,582).[38]

34. Ibid., p. 3.
35. Ibid., p. 15.
36. Ibid., pp. 18-21 and pp. 58-60, respectively. Given his introductory discussion (ibid., p. 11), the latter appears to be accurate.
37. For these additions I am indebted to F. Neirynck, 'The Redactional Text of Mark', *ETL* 57 (1981), p. 145.
38. Thus, following Neirynck (ibid., p. 145), one might include Βηθανία (Mk4/Mk Ed2), διαλογίζεσθαι (7/3), διαστέλλομαι (5/2), εἰσπορεύομαι (8/3), ἐκεῖθεν (6/4), ἐκπλήσσομαι (5/3), ἐπιτιμάω (9/3), εὐαγγέλιον (7/3), θεραπεύω (5/3), κακῶς (4/3), κώμη (6/3), μηκέτι (4/2), οὔπω (5/2), παραλαμβάνω (6/3), παραπορεύομαι (4/2), περιβλέπω (6/2), συζητέω (6/3).

3. Still there is room for skepticism concerning the means by which Gaston is virtually forced to define and to isolate Markan redactional sectors: namely, the 'common agreement' among investigators that certain passages are redactional. In order that his analysis might proceed, it is reasonable that Gaston be allowed this as a working hypothesis; still, such a hypothesis is conditioned by the subjective, if not potentially arbitrary, preferences of scholars who determine the climate of opinion at any given time.

4. Moreover, there is reason to wonder whether, as Gaston implies, such a consensus of opinion or 'common agreement' on Markan redactional passages actually exists. In a review article as interesting as it is meticulously crafted, Frans Neirynck shows, on the basis of a comparative study of their commentaries (all roughly contemporaneous with Gaston's work), that Rudolf Pesch, Joachim Gnilka, and Walter Schmithals concur with Gaston's reckoning of Markan redactional verses — and with each other's reckonings — only 13% of the time (16 out of 127 verses or verse-fragments).[39] Indeed, given Pesch's principle of *in dubio, pro traditio*,[40] one could scarcely expect a much greater consensus.

5. To what extent is Markan redaction suggested, not merely by the statistical frequency of a word's occurrence, but also by the particular nuance of that word in certain instances? Gaston's statistical presentation does not, and cannot, clarify this. That is to say, Gaston tells us that 50% of the occurrences of Γαλιλαία (6 appearances) show up in purportedly 'Mark editorial', but this in itself cannot determine for us whether, or in what way, 'Galilee' holds for the Second Evangelist special theological significance, beyond its obvious function as a geographical indicator. To select another issue, with which we have conjured in previous chapters: Gaston's presentation of 46 occurrences in Mark of μαθητής, 16 of which appear to be editorial, is in itself of little or no help to us in adjudicating the merit of Meye's argument (that Markan discipleship is restricted to 'the twelve') over against Best's contention (that there is little distinction, and thus greater flexibility, in the manner that Mark uses 'the twelve' and 'the disciples').[41] In short, raw statistical data are insufficient to answer or

---

39. Neirynck, 'Redactional Text', p. 145. The verses, or portions of verses, that all four judge to be redactional are 1.1, 34c, 45b; 3.15; 4.21a, 34a; 6.13a, 30-31, 52; 8.13, 17b-21; 12.38a; 13.3c, 4b.

40. Pesch, *Das Markusevangelium*, I, pp. 15-32, 63-68 et passim.

41. Cf. Meye, 'Those About Him', p. 215, with Best, 'Mark's Use', p. 32.

even to address many of the redaction-critical issues that exercise Markan scholars.[42]

6. Similarly, it is worth pondering how tabulations of the sort compiled by Gaston enable us to interpret Mark in any significant way. It is one thing to be told that καί appears 1,073 times in Mark, arguably 210 of which occur in editorial passages, or that αὐτός occurs 746 times, 135 of which are possibly editorial. But it is difficult for me to envision specific cases in which these data, in themselves, can enable us better to understand Markan discipleship, Christology, or any of the other topics that have tantalized redaction critics.

7. As previously noted, Gaston is admirably sensitive to the circularity of much of his procedure (most notably, the assumption of Markan redaction, and of its amenability to discernment, in order to gauge the verbal character of that redaction). Still, he maintains that, 'If [such an initial assumption] is approximately correct on other grounds, then the resultant word lists can be used to test a specific sentence and thus arrive at a much more critical approach to the questions of redaction, possible sources, and possible forms. Therefore, even if the argument is circular, if it results in confirming the initial assumptions, it is legitimate.'[43] However, as H. F. D. Sparks has observed, a defense such as this only invites further questions:

> What if an initial assumption should turn out not to be 'correct on other grounds', even 'approximately'? Does the use of tables 'refine' an incorrect assumption as effectively as it 'refines' a correct one? And (what is much more important) can it ever help us to decide which is which?[44]

8. Finally, we might recall the principal *raisons d'être* for Gaston's revision of Hawkins' *Horae Synopticae:* the determination of expressions that are characteristic of a particular source,[45] and the differentiation of expressions appearing in a source and those occurring in editorial passages. It is dubious that Gaston's statistical analysis ultimately affords us the basis

---

42. Of this Gaston seems to be aware (*Horae Synopticae Electronicae*, p. 6). No scholar has done more to alert us to the importance of context in interpreting particular words than J. Barr, *The Semantics of Biblical Language* (London: SCM, 1983).

43. Gaston, *Horae Synopticae Electronicae*, pp. 15-16.

44. H. F. D. Sparks, review of Gaston in *JTS* n.s. 26 (1975), pp. 146-49 (citation, p. 148).

45. Gaston, *Horae Synopticae Electonicae*, p. 13: 'it is precisely this which would be the most helpful for both source and redaction criticism'.

for ascertaining either with assurance. Gaston argues that sentences in the Second Gospel that contain words appearing four or more times throughout Mark may be attributed to the Evangelist's sources; yet I fail to follow this reasoning: why could not those sentences have issued as easily from the redactor? And how does the fact that the repetitive words in those sentences appear in parallel sentences in two, one, or no other Synoptic(s) help one decide that the sentences originated from Mark's *source* and not from the Markan *redaction?* Nor, as we have seen, is Gaston's establishment of an editorial field of investigation any more compelling: in fact, Gaston himself admits the weakness of his treatment at this point:

> Assignment [of sentences] to form-critical categories [among which Gaston includes the Synoptists' editorial sentences] was even more difficult than that to sources, and indeed often had to be made rather arbitrarily. . . . The inclusion of this feature should be considered only as an experiment. . . . Even more than is the case with redaction critics, considerations of style and theology are much more important [in such form-critical distinctions] than statistics.[46]

With Gaston's evaluation I concur, except for his distinction (in the last sentence) between form and redaction criticism in assessing the reliability of his study: for, in the end, Gaston's determination and categorization of 'Mark editorial' are but extrapolations of those form-critical judgments, 'often . . . made rather arbitrarily'. In short, Gaston's statistical analysis can verify the existence and extent of certain quantitative data on the basis of certain initial assumptions; however, his analysis cannot verify those assumptions. And it is precisely such verification that is needful in the practice of Markan redaction criticism. Save for some discrepancies, Gaston has given us a statistical tool that is internally consistent, and this may be the most that can be hoped for; yet if a well-executed, self-confirming, circular argument *is* the most that one can expect, of Gaston or of any other scholar, then it is just there that the fundamental problem of Markan redaction criticism resides.

46. Ibid., p. 6.

Charles Joseph Reedy

In a doctoral dissertation presented in 1976 to the Faculty of Theology at St. Michael's College in Toronto, Charles J. Reedy investigated the motif of the messianic secret in Mark as a means for raising larger questions about the redaction-critical method and its potential for refinement.[47] '[The] need for a method [for discerning Markan redaction] remains', Reedy suggests, inasmuch as 'Redaction criticism . . . comes to recognize that the redaction in the Gospels represents a valid dimension which ought to be explored not as a kind of literary luxury or curiosity but as a matter of logical necessity'.[48] Acknowledging certain obstacles that have blocked the refinement of the method when applied to the Second Gospel — our ignorance of Mark's sources, the insufficiency of an analysis based solely on putative editorial arrangement, and deficiencies in previous studies to identify distinctively Markan vocabulary — Reedy wishes to devise that which, in his judgment, has heretofore eluded Markan researchers: a redaction-critical method that is truly sound.[49]

To that end, Reedy's proposal runs like this:

1. Drawing on what he takes to be a scholarly consensus at the time of his writing, Reedy isolates those passages in the Second Gospel that are most likely editorial: 'methodologically the Gospel seams constitute the basis for reconstructing Markan redaction', and the summaries 'likewise represent a major zone of Mark's redaction'.[50] The summaries (and, by implication, the seams) perform editorial functions: for example, they serve as transitions between 'the pre-Gospel material that . . . came to [Mark] in the form of isolated units'; therefore, it can be assumed that these editorial transitions 'did not exist before [Mark]. . . . In any case it is clear that Mark is the final redactor of these summaries'.[51]

---

47. C. J. Reedy, 'Redaction and the Messianic Secret in Mark: A Study of the Redaction Critical Method' (Ph.D. diss., University of St. Michael's College, 1976).

48. Ibid., pp. 86, 42.

49. Ibid, pp. 87, 253. Note also p. 255: 'It has become obvious that future redaction critics must become aware of the faulty methodological foundation of traditional studies of Markan editorial characteristics'.

50. Ibid., pp. 94, 96. Reedy's selection of supposed Markan seams is a compilation of suggestions offered by R. Bultmann, V. Taylor, A. Ambrozic, R. Pesch, and J. Lambrecht (ibid., pp. 123-27); a compendium of *Sammelberichte* suggested by Bultmann, M. Dibelius, C. H. Dodd, X. Léon-Dufour, B. H. Streeter, and Taylor constitutes Reedy's own field of investigation.

51. Reedy, 'Redaction', pp. 120 and 107. The piecemeal character of the tradition is regarded by Reedy as a fact 'established' by form criticism (p. 120).

2. Thus having defined his redactional field, Reedy catalogues every 'significant' word[52] that occurs in the seams and summaries and arrives at a percentage that represents the observed frequency of each word's occurrence relative to its occurrences elsewhere in Mark 1–13. Words that occur 100% of the time in the Markan seams and summaries are assumed to be statistically significant in frequency and, therefore, distinctively Markan by virtue of that fact.[53] Employing a one-way Chi-square classification,[54] Reedy then attempts to determine the statistical significance of words that fall within the seams and summaries either 40%-95% of the time, 30%-39% of the time, or 25%-29% of the time. On the basis of his statistical tests (the results of which are tabulated in the form of computer printouts), Reedy concludes that, in addition to the words that appear 100% of the time in purportedly redactional sectors of Mark, the vocabulary that falls within the ranges of both 40%-95% and 30%-39% (a total of 67 words) is statistically significant at the 1% level of significance.[55]

3. The procedure just outlined with respect to Markan vocabulary is repeated for Markan grammar, or stylistic traits. Reedy concludes that only those grammatical constructions that occur 35%-95% of the time in Markan seams and summaries, as over against their occurrence elsewhere in Mark 1–13, may be considered statistically significant at the 1% level of significance.[56]

4. Employing a z-test and a normal distribution curve,[57] Reedy then

52. Reedy's catalogue omits conjunctions, prepositions, particles, and pronouns, 'which were felt to be generally insignificant' (ibid., p. 131).

53. Ibid., p. 147: Βηθανία, Βηθσαϊδά, διαπεράω, ἐγγίζω, Ἡρῳδιανοί, Καφαρναούμ, οἰκοδόμας, πέραν, ποταπός, Σιδών, Τύρος.

54. On the Chi-square test, and the difference between one-way and two-way classifications, see above, note 13.

55. Reedy, 'Redaction', pp. 135-47. In this context, a 1% level of significance means that the appearance of a given word with a certain percentage of occurrence in the seams and summaries can be attributed to chance only 1% of the time.

56. Reedy, 'Redaction', pp. 148-53. In Reedy's judgment, these 'statistically significant' constructions are the genitive absolute, ἄρχειν as an auxiliary verb, ἄν plus the indicative, periphrasis, the impersonal plural, and δύναμαι as an auxiliary verb.

57. The z-test is a test of statistical significance, the purpose of which is to determine whether the difference between the observed and expected frequencies of data is real or owing to chance variation. In this respect, the z-test is similar in purpose to a Chi-square test. A primary difference between them is that, unlike the Chi-square classification, a z-test assumes that the distribution of the data being analyzed approximates the normal (or 'bell-shaped') curve. Data whose distribution approximates the normal curve can be compared to that mathematical model, the known properties of which can then be used to describe and

tries to establish either the statistical significance or the overall importance of twenty-six themes that recur in the Markan redactional areas (the seams and summaries).[58] Four themes emerge as statistically significant; six are deemed 'important'.[59] In addition, three other themes may be considered probably editorial inasmuch as each offers an 'interpretative overview of Jesus' Ministry . . . [that] goes far beyond its particular context [in a seam or summary]'.[60]

5. Thus having analyzed Markan vocabulary, grammar, and themes in the primary redactional zones, and having suggested that Markan redaction can be assumed where any two or more such editorial characteristics are present, Reedy concludes, in general, 'that we have sufficiently surmounted the traditional obstacles to attaining a sound redaction-critical analysis. Proceeding from a sound methodological basis, redaction critics should have less difficulty and more reliability in determining Markan redactional interests' — one of which is the motif of messianic secrecy that is found throughout the Second Gospel.[61]

To his credit, Reedy recognizes a significant problem with most of his predecessors' *redaktionsgeschichtlich* investigations: the inability, or seeming unwillingness, to make the method more rigorous, more 'objective', and thus more dependable in distinguishing redactional from traditional concerns. Moreover, Reedy refuses to work in a vacuum: he attempts to sharpen the tool of redaction criticism in conversation with other scholars.

Nevertheless, Reedy's work bristles with problems, both of conception and of execution:

First, if we take seriously one of the hindrances to Markan redaction criticism acknowledged by Reedy, namely, our ignorance of the Evangelist's sources, would not this cast from the start a considerable shadow of

---

to predict the outcome or significance of the researcher's data. For more information, see Freedman, Pisani, and Purves, *Statistics*, pp. 437-53.

58. Reedy, 'Redaction', pp. 154-59. 'Importance' is assessed by Reedy on the basis of these themes' more frequent occurrence than the average theme in the seams and summaries.

59. 'Significant' themes are the enthusiasm of the crowd, secret teaching, the presence of the disciples with Jesus, and the fame of Jesus. 'Important' themes are the conflict between Jewish officials and Jesus, statements about privacy, the presence of the twelve with Jesus, the presence of the crowd or multitude with Jesus, Jesus as teacher, and the temple motif (ibid., p. 159).

60. Ibid., p. 160: the failure of the disciples to understand, injunctions to silence, and the inside/outside motif.

61. Quotation, ibid., p. 162. The questions of why Mark depicted the disciples 'in such sinister shades' is raised but left unanswered by Reedy (ibid., pp. 255-56).

doubt on the refinement of a method that, by its very nature, demands some (if but hypothetical) knowledge of the shape and substance of pre-Markan material in order to establish 'a distinction between editorial contribution and the tradition of the primitive church'?[62] Nor is the restraint on investigatory subjectivity invoked by Reedy, the appeal to a *consensus omnium* regarding Markan seams and summaries, as secure as one might wish: it is debatable whether the scholarly concurrence cited by Reedy is as thoroughgoing as he intimates.[63]

Second, although many Gospel researchers continue to assume as a working hypothesis the fragmentary state of pre-literary tradition, there is, as we have noted, increasing skepticism concerning the idea that no larger collections of material (other than the passion narrative) might have been forged prior to Mark's editorial activity. If, indeed, the Second Evangelist received some pre-arranged compilations of stories and sayings, then he may have received *from the tradition* (and, *pace* Reedy, may not have created outright) some of the seams and summaries that linked them together. Were this the case, the assumption on which Reedy's statistical analysis is based, the 'primary redactional zones', would be rendered yet more dubious.[64]

Third, a host of questions surround the 'editorial characteristics' that Reedy claims to discover in the putative seams and summaries:

a. With respect to *Markan style*, Reedy neglects to indicate both the considerable disagreement among scholars regarding actual occurrences in Mark of a number of these stylistic features, as well as the high degree of selectivity in his own listing.[65]

---

62. Reedy, 'Redaction', p. 149.

63. Using Taylor's listing of *Sammelberichte* as a base (*St. Mark*, p. 85) and the indices of Bultmann's *Synoptic Tradition* and Dibelius' *Tradition* as cross-references, I spot-checked the degree of consensus on the identification of Markan summaries among these three scholars (to all of whom Reedy appeals). Out of 45 summaries designated by Taylor, Bultmann is in agreement with 32 of them; 11 out of Taylor's 45 are replicated by Dibelius. Dibelius proposes 3 *Sammelberichte* that Taylor omits; Bultmann suggests 8 not found in Taylor. On at least one occasion Dibelius denotes as traditional a verse which Taylor considers editorial; on at least three occasions Bultmann and Taylor disagree on a verse's traditional or redactional character. It is possible that similar discrepancies could be evidenced among the other scholars cited by Reedy as constitutive of as 'consensus'. Thus there is justification in asking if such precision in detecting 'primary redactional zones' is possible or can be agreed on by Markan scholars.

64. It profits Reedy nothing to argue that, even if some seams and summaries derived from the tradition, 'In any case . . . Mark is the final redactor of [them]' ('Redaction', p. 120). Of what part of the Gospel could such a judgment not be made?

65. Cf., for example, Taylor's consideration of the impersonal plural and pleonasms

b. Even more dubious is Reedy's analysis of *Markan themes*. First, Reedy assumes that any themes to be found in the seams and summaries are distinctively Markan. This is fallacious, since, in theory, Mark may be reproducing a theme or themes that originated in his traditions. Second, Reedy's use of the z-test is predicated on the assumption 'that a particular theme will follow a normal distribution pattern'.[66] The twenty-six themes listed by Reedy vary in their appearance within Markan seams and summaries from one to twelve occurrences; with so few occurrences, any given theme can hardly approximate the normal curve. Indeed, when plotted on a graph, the percentage of occurrence of Reedy's twenty-six themes corresponds to the pattern, not of a normal curve, but of an irregularly shaped curve that is positively skewed. Therefore, Reedy cannot use the z-test to determine what he refers to as 'the statistical significance of each theme'.[67] Third, for yet another reason the z-test cannot be employed in this case: the execution of a z-test depends, in part, on the determination of an expected frequency value, independent of the data being analyzed (in this case, the average occurrence of Markan themes in seams and summaries), against which the observed frequency value can be compared. Because Reedy neither identifies nor appeals to an expected frequency value for the average occurrence of Markan themes outside of the seams and summaries, his appeal to the z-test is invalid. Fourth, on consideration of his data, tabulated in a computer printout, one discovers that Reedy has in fact calculated the *standard deviation* of the number of occurrences of the twenty-six Markan themes in putative redactional sectors; despite his assertion, Reedy has not performed a z-test at all! Finally, even if he had selected an appropriate statistical test and had executed it properly, Reedy's attempt to be methodologically rigorous would be undercut: in the end he sweeps into his purview so-called 'important' themes that provide an 'interpretative overview', thus departing from the use of only those themes that occur with a frequency that is, even putatively, 'statistically significant'.[68]

c. Like his treatment of Markan themes, and for all of its seeming objectivity and verifiability, Reedy's statistical approach to *Markan vocabulary* is riddled with problems and errors. This is not the place to present a

(*St. Mark*, pp. 47-48, 50-52). Although he refers to the work of C. H. Turner and M. Zerwick, Reedy's own catalogue of Markan stylistic elements precisely corresponds to neither of them.

66. Reedy, 'Redaction', p. 157.

67. Ibid., pp. 154-56; cf. Bartz, *Basic Statistical Concepts*, p. 35.

68. Reedy, 'Redaction', pp. 159-60; for his table of themes, see pp. 157-58.

complete rebuttal of Reedy's statistical analysis of Markan words; however, the following preliminary observations should suffice to indicate the difficulties in accepting his conclusions:

(1) In cataloguing the frequency of occurrence of words in Mark's seams and summaries, Reedy omits words 'felt to be generally insignificant': conjunctions, prepositions, particles, and pronouns. On what basis has Reedy appraised such words as 'insignificant'? He never explains. Nor is this, potentially, any small matter, for a number of words often considered to be characteristic or distinctive of the Second Evangelist are linguistic units that Reedy thereby excludes: conjunctions (καί, used paratactically), prepositions (εἰς, ἐν, ἐκ, ἀπό), particles (various uses of ὅτι), and pronouns ([πρὸς] αὐτούς).[69]

(2) Reedy offers no rationale for his decision to compare the frequency of various words' occurrence in only the first thirteen chapters of Mark. Presumably, this reflects the older, *formgeschichtlich* judgment that the passion narrative (Mark 14–16) underwent only minimal editorial reworking by the Evangelist. However, writing in 1976, Reedy's assessment of this matter is already dated: he demonstrates no awareness of the possibility that Mark 14–16 might have been as exhaustively redacted as the rest of the Gospel.[70]

(3) The manner in which Reedy frames his hypothesis for statistical analysis and sets up his statistical tables is, at best, confusing.[71] For example, Reedy repeatedly presents computer printouts of his Chi-square test without any labeling of the various columns of figures within those tables; this militates against both a clear understanding of the type of mathemati-

69. Cf. Taylor, *St. Mark*, pp. 48-49; Turner, 'Markan Usage', *JTS* o.s. 26 (1924), pp. 14-20, 58-62; *JTS* o.s. 27 (1925), pp. 9-15; *JTS* o.s. 28 (1926), pp. 280-82.

70. Contrast Donahue, *Are You the Christ?*, and the various essays in Kelber, ed., *The Passion in Mark*. In the latter, note especially Kelber's comments ('Conclusion: From Passion Narrative to Gospel', pp. 157-58, author's emphasis): '*From the perspective of the history of tradition there exists no appreciable difference between Mk 14–16 and what is known about the literary genesis and composition of Mk 1–13. Mk is no more tradition-bound in Mk 14–16 than he is in Mk 1–13.* He edits and unifies individual traditions, composes new material, and creates the total narrative sequence in Mk 14–16 in the same manner in which he edits and unifies individual traditions, composes new material, and creates the total narrative sequence in Mk 1–13'.

71. Reedy, 'Redaction', p. 135: 'Of the total times that they occur in the Gospel, words occurring 40%-95% of the time in the Markan seams and summaries do not occur by chance more frequently in the seams and summaries than in the rest of the text of Mark 1–13'. For Reedy's statistical tables, see ibid., pp. 137-39, 141, 143, 151, 157-58.

cal data being presented, as well as the likelihood of an independent observer's capability of replicating the tests.

(4) In order to perform a Chi-square test, one must be able to compare an item's observed frequency with its expected frequency. As Reedy has structured his tests, the observed frequency is the number of occurrences of a word (or stylistic feature or theme) in Markan seams and summaries. How does he determine how frequently one should *expect* to find such an item in the Gospel? 'The expected [frequency] value . . . is 18% which is the percentage of seam and summary verses in relation to total verses in Mark 1–13. Thus the expected frequency of occurrence of a word in 18% of the total would be 18%'.[72] Aside from the fact that Reedy never actually demonstrates that 18% of the total verses in Mark 1–13 is made up of seams and summaries, the second sentence in the explanation just quoted does not logically follow from the first: it is fallacious to assume a one-to-one correspondence between verses and words and to deduce thereby an expected frequency of *words* on the basis of the expected frequency of *verses*. In other words, Reedy is comparing peaches to pears in a manner that can only distort the rest of his statistical results.

(5) A necessary assumption for use of the Chi-square technique is that the sum of the observed frequencies must equal the sum of the expected frequencies.[73] In fact, in Reedy's test of words in the 40%-95% range, these sums are not equal: the sum of his observed frequencies is 188, while the sum of his expected frequencies is 349. Somewhere, Reedy has made a basic computational error (perhaps in the expected frequency column since, as I have indicated, these values are questionable). Whatever the reason, any Chi-square test that proceeds from unequal total values of observed and expected frequencies cannot help but be invalid.[74]

(6) Finally, even if greater care had been exercised in gathering the

---

72. Ibid., p. 137.

73. Bartz, *Basic Statistical Concepts*, p. 329.

74. Another requirement for the use of the Chi-square test is an adequate sample size. Specifically (according to some statisticians), no more than 20% of the categories considered can have expected frequency values of less than 5 (thus Bartz, *Basic Statistical Concepts*, pp. 323, 328). This requirement presents a problem for Reedy's analysis: in his consideration of vocabulary in the 40%-95% range within seams and summaries, 11 out of his 44 words, or 25%, have expected frequencies of less than 5 (Reedy, 'Redaction', pp. 137-39). However, in fairness to Reedy, it should be said that statisticians are not of one mind in insisting on this requirement, and some consider it too stringent (see, for example, B. S. Everitt, *The Analysis of Contingency Tables* [New York: Wiley, 1977]).

data and implementing the Chi-square test, and even if Reedy's contention had been substantiated — that certain words appear in putative Markan passages with a statistically significant, greater frequency than other words — the thorny problem of interpreting the *significance* of that fact would remain. Reedy judges these words to be reliable indicators of Mark's own handiwork, but this is by no means incontrovertible. Four years prior to Reedy's study, James Little implemented a more sophisticated version of the Chi-square technique (a two-way classification, entailing double the number of categories and groups for comparison than that surveyed by Reedy): not only did Little's study corroborate the statistical significance of *no more than four* of Reedy's 'Markan' words (ἔρχομαι, συνάγω, διδάσκω, and πάλιν); Little also pointed out that the higher frequency in seams of words like ἔρχομαι and διδάσκω might simply be explained by the higher frequency of verbs of motion and communication in those passages.[75] Similarly, it is fallacious to assume that any word that appears exclusively (that is, 100% of the time) in seams and summaries must be indicative of 'redactional' vocabulary: almost one-half of all such words indicated by Reedy are place-names (Bethsaida, Bethany, Capernaum, Tyre, Sidon) that arguably derived from the tradition, none of which occurs more than four times in the Gospel and one of which appears only twice!

In short, Reedy's attempt to refine Markan *Redaktionsgeschichte* seems well-intentioned; however, when judged in terms of the statistical rigor that it advocates, his analysis is radically flawed. Whether or not redaction criticism of the Second Gospel is, as Reedy opines, 'a matter of logical necessity'[76] may be debated; that Reedy has not succeeded in establishing this exegetical tool on 'a sound methodological basis' is, sadly, beyond dispute.

William Oliver Walker, Jr

A few scholars have attempted to provide criteria for distinguishing between tradition and redaction in Mark, but, for the most part, these at-

75. Little, 'Redaction Criticism', pp. 174, 176, 180. Curiously, reference is never made by Reedy to Little's dissertation.

76. Reedy, 'Redaction', p. 42. Interestingly, when Reedy leaves his methodological chapter and moves to the exegesis of the Second Gospel, his study takes the form of a *thematic* analysis, bolstered with only secondary and tertiary references to putative Markan vocabulary and style (much as we have observed to be the case with Meye, Best, and Weeden); cf. ibid., pp. 163-255.

tempts are weakened by their presupposition of Marcan priority and, most significantly, by their failure to establish any 'control' as a starting point for a redactional study of the gospel. . . . The first task of redaction criticism, therefore, is the discernment of a method for identifying a 'hard core' of redactional passages in the gospel under study; once this is done, the identification of additional passages as redactional can proceed in an 'organic' matter.

With these words William O. Walker introduces his suggested 'Method for Identifying Redactional Passages in Matthew on Functional and Linguistic Grounds'.[77] Although his principal field of inquiry is the First Gospel rather than the Second, Walker's contribution merits discussion in this review, since (a) he does not assume Markan priority in dealing with Matthean redaction (and thus regards the *redaktionsgeschichtlich* problems with that Gospel as being formally the same as those with Mark), and (b) he anticipates 'that the method to be developed here will also apply *mutatis mutandis* to Mark and Luke (and probably also John)'.[78] In addition to his agnosticism regarding the precise nature and extent of the Synoptics' interrelationship, Walker begins with the following presuppositions: that the general insights of form criticism are valid (namely, that the Gospels were dependent for their basic source material on primitive, oral traditions, classifiable according to recognizable *Gattungen,* which circulated as discrete pericopes or in combination as earlier collections); that 'there is, at least in principle, a very real [and discernible] distinction between traditional and redactional materials in Matt [*sic*]'; and that the burden of proof rests with the investigator who would claim that a given passage is redactional, not traditional.[79]

Walker's proposed method for distinguishing tradition and redaction proceeds according to a series of stages. The first stage entails isolating, on the basis of 'common sense considerations', those passages (that is, paragraphs, sentences, or clauses) in the Gospel that can plausibly be regarded

77. Published in *CBQ* 39 (1977), pp. 76-93; quotation, pp. 80-81.
78. Ibid., p. 76; cf. p. 78. Walker's article actually comprises three separate but interrelated goals: the proposition of a method for distinguishing Matthean tradition and redaction; the suggestion of criteria for differentiating the work of earlier and final redactors of Matthew; and the implications of this research for resolution of the Synoptic problem. Inasmuch as refinement of the redaction-critical method is of immediate importance in this book, my discussion will be relegated to Walker's first goal.
79. Walker, 'Method', pp. 78-79 (quotation, p. 79).

as redactional, rather than traditional, on functional grounds. Thus one compiles a 'Maximal List' of passages, 'almost universally regarded as redactional by modern critical scholarship', whose function is either to interpret, to summarize, to anticipate, or to provide transitions between accompanying material, often including brief indications of time, place, or circumstances.[80]

Rigorously applying the criterion that the burden of proof must be assigned to the claim that a given passage is redactional, in the second stage the investigator trims the Maximal List to a 'Minimal List', which includes only those passages that, on functional grounds, can be considered *almost certainly* redactional, not traditional. In other words, the generous benefit of doubt invoked in the previous stage is revoked in this stage: all passages that even conceivably might be traditional (for example, those with temporal or locational 'situation indicators') are eliminated.[81]

Thus having obtained a hard core of almost certainly redactional passages, in the third stage the researcher assembles a list, arranged in order of decreasing frequency, 'of all significant linguistic phenomena [that is, individual words, phrases, and syntactical constructions] which occur twice or more in the passages on the Minimal List, noting the specific passages in which each phenomenon occurs'. Walker does not assume that all such linguistic phenomena are thereby decidedly redactional in origin; he claims only that such phenomena in almost certainly redactional passages may be considered 'more or less' characteristic of the redactor.[82]

In the fourth stage the investigator returns to the Maximal List, compiled in Stage One, and identifies those passages, provisionally omitted from the Minimal List (of Stage Two), which contain the significant linguistic phenomena ascertained in Stage Three. Because such linguistic considerations may be considered as corroborating evidence originally gathered on a functional basis, an 'Expanded List' now can be compiled that includes (a) passages on the Minimal List and (b) additional passages on the Maximal List that exhibit linguistic phenomena appearing twice or more in passages on the Minimal List.[83]

The fifth stage is the compilation of a list, in order of decreasing frequency, of all linguistic phenomena occurring twice or more in passages

---

80. Ibid., pp. 81-82 (citations, p. 81).
81. Ibid., pp. 82-83.
82. Ibid., pp. 83-84.
83. Ibid., pp. 84-85.

on the new Expanded List, noting the specific passages in which each phenomenon occurs. In other words, this stage repeats the procedure of Stage Three — only this time the field of investigation has been widened to include items on the new Expanded List, not originally incorporated in the Minimal List.[84]

In the sixth stage the remaining passages on the Maximal List are examined for the presence of those significant linguistic phenomena ascertained in Stage Five (that is, on the basis of the Expanded List). This leads to the compilation of a fourth or 'Further Expanded List', which consists of (a) passages on the Expanded List and (b) additional passages on the Maximal List that display linguistic phenomena appearing twice or more in passages on the Expanded List.[85]

The seventh stage continues the process outlined in Stages Three through Six as long as it produces results. 'The final list of passages thus produced (the 'Final Expanded List') will contain passages which, on functional grounds confirmed where necessary by linguistic grounds, are regarded as almost certainly redactional rather than traditional, and the final list of significant linguistic phenomena thus produced will contain phenomena which are regarded as almost certainly characteristic of a redactor'.[86]

A number of things are to be admired in Walker's methodological proposal. While sympathetic to the work of previous scholars through his employment, as a redaction-critical canon, of those passages 'almost universally regarded as redactional by modern critical scholarship',[87] Walker is attempting to hammer out an original, controlled method of Synoptic *Redaktionsgeschichte* that will identify a 'hard core' of redactional passages in the Gospel under investigation. More so than many of his colleagues in this area of research, Walker has also grasped the fact that essays in the identification of tradition and redaction are essentially exercises in logic: as a result, Walker is sensitive to the perils of circular reasoning in this enterprise;[88] he observes caution in drawing inferences and formulating deductions.[89] In all of these respects, Walker's work is to be applauded.

84. Ibid., p. 85.
85. Ibid., pp. 85-86.
86. Ibid., p. 86.
87. Ibid., p. 81.
88. N. B. ibid., p. 80: '. . . there is a serious danger of circular argumentation, in which certain passages are regarded as redactional because they exhibit redactional features, but the features are regarded as redactional because they occur in redactional passages'.
89. Thus, for example, ibid., p. 86 n. 28: 'The mere recurrence of significant linguistic

However, one must ask if these advances are equal to the potential drawbacks in Walker's proposal. 1. For him, the criterion of 'function' manifestly assumes a major, indeed preeminent, role in the demonstration of a Synoptist's editorial activity: 'It is important that functional categories (i.e., how a particular passage functions within the gospel as a whole or within a given section of the gospel) form the initial basis for identifying passages as redactional rather than traditional.'[90] Yet this statement sparks a number of questions. First, is such a definition of 'function' (how a passage operates in the Gospel, in part or *in toto*) sufficiently narrow, sufficiently precise, and sufficiently sturdy to bear the brunt of all the many stages that then unfold in Walker's suggested method? In other words, if we grant the soundness of his principle that an established 'control' is needed as a starting-point for redaction-critical study, is Walker's own functional starting-point sufficient to provide such a control? Second, is it really the case, as Walker suggests, that the function of a given passage can be decided on the grounds of 'common-sense considerations' that are almost universally 'clear' to modern critical scholars?[91] Is it not the case that the transitions between pericopes in Mark, and the functions performed by those transitions, are at many points confoundedly difficult to identify?[92] Third, even on the assumption that a consensus could be reached on the function of a given passage, I fail to see how that would directly identify *whose* purposes — the tradition's or the redactor's — underlay that function. Knowledge of a passage's function, its form and content, cannot be equated with knowledge of the *origin* of the material.

2. The aforementioned problem stimulates reflection on Walker's form-critical hypotheses. Beholden to Bultmann, Dibelius, and others, Walker begins with the classic assumptions: the Evangelists' dependence on

---

phenomena is no guarantee that the passages containing the phenomena are redactional, even if, on functional grounds, the passages are regarded as potentially redactional'. Note also ibid., p. 84.

90. Ibid., p. 77.

91. Ibid., pp. 77 n. 5, 81, 83 n. 18. For critical disagreements on the demarcation and function of certain Markan transitions, see (among others) Keck, 'The Introduction to Mark's Gospel', and Hedrick, 'The Role of "Summary Statements"'.

92. N. B. D. Juel's assessment (*An Introduction to New Testament Literature* [Nashville: Abingdon, 1978], p. 53): 'The outstanding feature of Mark's style, as noted earlier, is its lack of any real transition from one scene to another. He provides little background information; he does little to place scenes in context, and to explain how they are related to what has preceded and to what follows. In many instances he fails to provide even information that would seem essential to the story'.

traditions that circulated, orally, in discrete units, reflecting recognizable genres. Once again, it is precisely such insights as these that are being challenged in revisionist *traditionsgeschichtlich* scholarship, some of which suggests that the process of literary redaction may have obscured, if not obliterated, the very 'forms' upon whose perception Walker's type of redaction criticism is predicated. Another sort of problem is created by Walker's admission that the pericopes on which the Gospels draw for their source material may have circulated, not merely as independent units, but also in previously combined, pre-literary collections. Though a point well-taken, this constitutes a major concession: for if we admit the possibility of such *ältere Sammlungen,* then who is to say that some of the transitional sutures and summaries between pericopes in Mark — precisely those areas of 'functional' importance for Walker — were not already in existence in the pre-Markan tradition? Finally, with regard to his form-critical assumptions, Walker's method seems grounded to a lesser extent on actual *formgeschichtlich* laws, by means of which tradition and redaction can be convincingly distinguished, and to a greater degree on the scholarly *opinio communis* on such matters: thus 'certain passages . . . [are to be] almost universally regarded as redactional by modern critical scholarship'. A criticism that once was voiced, in another connection, by Morna Hooker is equally applicable in this case: 'The real criterion being used here is *not the principle of dissimilarity, but the scholar's own understanding of the situation*'.[93]

3. In his quest for a 'hard core' of generally agreed-upon redaction, has not Walker circumscribed the Synoptists' editorial acitivity more severely than most scholars would find acceptable? The functions with which he associates 'redactional passages' (interpretation, summarization, anticipation, transition, indications of time and place) effectively relegate his search for Synoptic redaction to those areas referred to by Stein and others as seams, insertions, and summaries.[94] For Walker, these are the areas where the Synoptists' input is most susceptible to discernment, and it is the existence of only these redactional sectors that Walker's method would theoretically allow us to confirm. (One could not readily extrapolate Walker's *redaktionsgeschichtlich* conclusions for the rest of a Synoptic, since his various lists of passages and linguistic phenomena could never be

---

93. M. D. Hooker, 'On Using the Wrong Tool', *Theol* 75 (1972), p. 577 (Hooker's italics).

94. As Walker himself indicates ('Method', p. 81 nn. 13, 15). In a narrow sense, 'the foreshadowings or anticipation of events' (with which Walker associates the passion predictions of Matt 16.21; 17.22-23; 20.17-19; 26.1-2) could be considered a form of the modification of material.

compiled on the basis of Gospel material outside the boundaries of the original Maximal List). Aside from the necessary but constrictive circularity of such a proposal — a circularity no less serious than that which Walker chides in other investigators' procedure — this method provokes major problems for many Markan redaction critics. First, it assumes that the Synoptists' creativity has been bound by their fidelity to fixed traditions (a notion unattractive, if not unacceptable, to Type II and III interpreters like Best and Weeden). Second, despite Walker's protestations to the contrary, it seems to reduce the Synoptists' role to that of 'scissors-and-paste' craftsmen, or, at least, to restrict our knowledge of their activity to the establishment of a 'scissors-and-paste' framework for their source materials. In other words, the more rigorously Walker controls redaction criticism, the more confined is our understanding of the editorial tacks being taken by the Evangelists.[95]

4. For all of the care displayed in Walker's presentation, some procedural ambiguities remain. For instance, precisely what is the means by which 'plausibly' redactional material (on the Maximal List of Stage One) is distinguished from 'almost certainly' redactional material (on the Minimal List of Stage Two)? Walker never explicates this. The assumption seems to be that a more skeptical stance is adopted in Stage Two than in Stage One; however, one should not expect all scholars to be equally skeptical at every point. The definition of the 'significance' of various linguistic phenomena constitutes another gray area. Walker is sensitive to the problem:

> 'Significant' obviously means something other than what is necessary, ordinary, or commonplace. In some cases, a phenomenon may not appear to be 'significant' until its recurrence in another passage is noted. Thus, the definition of 'significant' must remain subject to continual revision.[96]

Unfortunately, this obscures as much as it clarifies. What norm of necessity or ordinariness is presupposed here? Is it a valid norm? The second sentence in the excerpt above intimates that a certain word's frequency of occurrence is at times necessary in clinching its significance, although,

---

95. Nor would even this amount to 'assured' knowledge: as Walker rightly grants, '. . . at times, tradition and redaction are so interwoven as to be practically inseparable' ('Method', p. 79 n. 8).

96. Ibid., pp. 83-84 n. 21.

elsewhere, Walker correctly observes that such recurrence cannot guarantee a word's status as redactional.[97] Moreover, as Walker himself acknowledges, this criterion of 'significance' does not resolve the potentially knotty problems of 'whether linguistic phenomena must be identical or merely similar and, if merely similar, just how similar'.[98]

5. Finally, two unanswered but important questions loom large with respect to Walker's methodological proposal. First, his procedure assumes that functional considerations not only take precedence over, but also are independent of, linguistic considerations, and that the latter can provide confirmatory evidence of redactional passages that have been isolated on the basis of the former. Is it the case, however, that such linguistic and functional criteria *are* necessarily independent of each other? For example, if (following Walker) we identify verses such as Mark 1.35 and 1.40 as redactional because they create transitional shifts in time, place, and circumstance, does the recurrence in those verses of ἔρχομαι and its cognates independently corroborate the 'Markan character' of those verses? Does not the function of Mark 1.35, 40 *depend*, at least in some measure, on such linguistic features as verbs of motion, which (along with other words) signal those 'transitional shifts in time, place, and circumstance'? Second, were a number of Markan scholars to implement Walker's procedure, it would be interesting to observe whether their catalogued 'significant linguistic phenomena' appeared, not only in the so-called functional passages, but throughout the Gospel as well.[99] To the extent that such phenomena did occur throughout the Gospel, one might question whether Mark was actually as tied to his traditions as Walker's method assumes.

In summary, therefore, Walker's proposal for the refinement of redaction criticism incorporates a number of helpful insights and valuable cautions. Nonetheless, after all of his caveats have been entered, *Redaktionsgeschichte* remains essentially circular, methodologically questionable on various counts, and fundamentally similar to — though a far sight narrower than — the procedure outlined by Stein and others.

---

97. See above, note 89. To the extent that frequency of occurrence does figure in Walker's proposal, has that criterion been made adequately rigorous? On the basis of either Little's or Gaston's analysis, a word's occurrence twice or more would not be regarded as statistically significant.

98. Walker, 'Method', p. 84 n. 24.

99. Some evidence suggests that this might well be the result: recall Little, 'Redaction Criticism', p. 45.

Edgar John Pryke

This is a valuable and important piece of work; no one who attempts to examine Mark redactionally will in the future be able to ignore it. It is a task which needed to be done and once done will not require to be done again for some considerable time because it has been carried through so thoroughly.[100]

In its present form, in short, the book may be safely ignored by students of the Gospel of Mark. More's the pity, since the research underlying the book, had it been organized tightly, and argued cogently and coherently, might have been able to make a contribution to the quest for the theology of the second Evangelist.[101]

When two accomplished Markan scholars render such widely discrepant judgments of the same book, we may rest assured that, at the very least, the work under review is an interesting one. So it is with E. J. Pryke's *Redactional Style in the Marcan Gospel*, which is based on the author's doctoral thesis, produced under the supervision of C. F. Evans at King's College, London. Before casting our lot with either Best or Achtemeier and their respective evaluations, we need to review the procedure of Pryke's attempted refinement of Markan *Redaktionsgeschichte*.

Pryke introduces his project by laying out some major assumptions. First, he acknowledges indebtedness to the 'certain objectivity' of the studies of Markan linguistic usage undertaken earlier in the twentieth century by Hawkins, Turner, and others.[102] Rejecting Farrer's thesis of Mark's inspired creation of his own pericopes, Pryke presupposes the basic principles of form criticism (especially the belief that the Gospels' source material circulated in the form of discrete pericopes). 'Since redaction-history is concerned with the linking passages of a redactor-editor who pulls his sources into a logical and coherent form, purely linguistic features may also provide criteria by which the accuracy of the literary delineation may be tested or rejected'.[103] In essence, then, the purpose of Pryke's study is to 'integrate both linguistics and literary studies as independent ways of dis-

---

100. E. Best, review in *JSNT* 7 (1979), p. 70.
101. P. J. Achtemeier, review in *CBQ* 41 (1979), p. 657.
102. Pryke, *Redactional Style*, pp. 1-2.
103. Ibid., p. 6.

tinguishing editorial and source material in the Gospel so as to lead on to a detection of the theology of the evangelist as redactor'.[104]

Pryke's investigation adopts the following procedure:

1. He offers a list of over 400 verses that, in whole or in part, purportedly have been identified as redactional in the secondary literature by such scholars as Best, Bultmann, Marxsen, and Pesch. To this list he appends bibliographical citations as well as categorizations of these verses according to nine separate classifications (for example, 'Chronology', 'Editorial', 'Explanatory Comment', 'Saying Link', 'Topography').[105]

2. Following a cursory review of 'Marcan Linguistic Studies Since Hawkins and Turner', Pryke provides extensive notes on fourteen 'Syntactical Features [That Are] Considered as Possible Guidelines to the Author's Style': parenthetical clauses, the genitive absolute, the participle used as a main verb, accusative use of πολλά, the clause λέγω ὅτι, ἄρχομαι plus the infinitive, εὐθύς and καὶ εὐθύς, πάλιν, the redundant participle, periphrastic tenses, impersonals, ὥστε plus the infinitive, the use of two or more participles before or after the main verb, and γάρ used as an 'explanatory'.[106] In all fourteen cases Pryke begins by assigning, on 'literary or higher critical grounds',[107] the Markan verses containing that syntactical feature to either R (redaction) or S (source). After briefly discussing the occurrences of each redactional feature in these 'source' or 'redactional' passages, and basing his arguments on the syntax and vocabulary of those sections, Pryke suggests that almost 100 verses, typically regarded as source passages, should in fact be considered redactional. Moreover, he concludes that all fourteen of the syntactical features studied occur much more frequently in Markan redactional passages than in Markan source passages.[108]

3. Based on the assignment of passages to either 'source' or 'redaction', as confirmed by ostensible scholarly agreement (see above, §1) and as corrected by Pryke's additions to redactional material of passages usually consigned to Mark's sources (see above, §2), Pryke then provides a register of

---

104. Ibid., p. 25.

105. Ibid., pp. 10-24. For instance, Mark 1.26-28 is identified with citations of Best, Bultmann, Burkill, and eight other scholars (p. 10); 1.26 and 1.27-28 are later classified, respectively, as 'Editorial', and 'S.S.P.' ('Summary Statement of Progress', p. 24).

106. Ibid., pp. 32-134.

107. Ibid., p. 64.

108. For instance, 29 out of 29 Markan genitive absolutes are determined to be redactional, as well as 26 out of 26 instances of ἄρχομαι plus the infinitive, and 29 out of 30 occurrences of periphrastic tenses (see Pryke, *Redactional Style*, p. 135).

140 words, arranged alphabetically, that can be classified as 'Markan redactional vocabulary' on the grounds of their occurrence at least five times in the Second Gospel, with not less than 50% of those occurrences in redactional passages.[109]

4. Thus having ascertained, to his own satisfaction, characteristically Markan syntactical features (above, §2) and most frequently used vocabulary (§3), Pryke lists 263 complete verses and 148 partial verses that can be identified as Markan redaction. Thus Pryke notes that Mark 1.9a, 10-11a are not only redactional but also contain four instances of Markan vocabulary (ἀναβαίνειν, εὐθύς, καταβαίνειν, and φωνή) as well as two characteristically Markan stylistic traits (πολλά accusative; multiple participles preceding and following the main verb).[110]

5. Finally, drawing on the results of the preceding list, Pryke presents what he considers to be the redactional text of Mark: that is, all passages from the Greek text, set out and arranged in the sequence in which they occur in the Gospel, that (according to Pryke's analysis) may be attributed to the redactional activity of the Evangelist.[111]

Of all recent attempts to lend greater precision to Markan *Redaktionsgeschichte*, Pryke's is probably the best known. This is not without justification: *Redactional Style in the Marcan Gospel* is distinguished by prodigious labor, as well as by extensive conversation between the author and his most significant predecessors in the fields of form and redaction criticism.

Other strengths of this monograph are worth noting. First, there is methodological wisdom in Pryke's beginning with a minimal definition of Markan *Redaktionsgeschichte*: namely, the putative 'sutures' that stitch pericopes to one another.[112] If one concurs with Pryke in presupposing the atomistic character of the pre-Markan tradition, such seams would appear to possess a stronger claim to verifiable Markan redactional activity, thus functioning as a relatively 'known' quantity from which broader, less certain *redaktionsgeschichtlich* conclusions might be extrapolated.

Second, the overarching principle governing Pryke's discussion is laudable: the desire to conjoin different methods — form and redaction criticism, vocabulary and literary (stylistic) studies — so as to corroborate

---

109. Ibid., pp. 136-38.

110. Ibid., pp. 139-48; on Mark 1.9-11a, see p. 189.

111. Ibid., pp. 149-76.

112. Ibid., pp. 30-31: 'Naturally it is at the beginnings and endings of pericopae (the so-called "seams") where redaction is mainly to be found'. On p. 30 n. 7, Pryke indicates that he is following Best in this assumption.

or to disavow common, heretofore unvalidated, redaction-critical judgments pertaining to the Second Gospel. In other words, Pryke is cognizant of the complexity of the problem facing Markan redaction critics, and he is groping for a method that will allow him and others some control over that complexity. That he should attempt to determine whether or not so-called 'Markan vocabulary' actually occurs more frequently in purportedly 'Markan compositions' is by no means a nonsensical enterprise.

Third, the manner in which Pryke has envisioned the Markan redaction-critical task has, in the estimation of some scholars, proved beneficial in supplementing previous studies of Markan language.[113] Moreover, Pryke's method, based on the convergence of different critical approaches, has stimulated at least one interesting attempt to evaluate the authenticity of an excerpt from the so-called *Secret Gospel of Mark*, discovered by Morton Smith in a letter of Clement of Alexandria.[114]

Overall, then, Pryke's study raises some intriguing points and possibilities. Critics of his work have been duly forewarned, by William Farmer, against 'the kind of shooting from the hip that can so easily characterize the judgment of book reviewers who in the nature of the case are not expected to *work* with a book or get down in the well with its author and dig where he is digging before passing judgment upon it'.[115] Still, after contemplating the perspective and tools brought to the task by Pryke, as well as after some 'digging' of my own, I find that a considerable number of nagging questions persist.

1. To begin with, Pryke invests great confidence in the 'objectivity' of previous linguistic studies undertaken by such investigators as Hawkins, Turner, and Taylor. Is such trust well-founded? Already we have recognized the compilation of Lloyd Gaston's *Horae Synopticae Electronicae,* some five years prior to the publication of Pryke's study, in order to rectify some of the imprecision of Hawkins' work (most notably, the latter's failure to distinguish words and phrases in Markan redaction from those in Markan tra-

---

113. Thus W. R. Farmer, reviewing Pryke's work in *PSTJ* 32 (1978), p. 47: 'It will join but not replace Hawkins and the handful of commentaries and other useful Marcan studies that one must presently consult if he is to do redaction-critical work on Mark'. Similarly, Neirynck ('Redactional Text', p. 152) considers Pryke serviceable 'as a supplementary detector of characteristic words not yet found in the lists of Hawkins, Morgenthaler, and Gaston'.

114. Thus (in *JSNT* 7 [1979], pp. 71-76) Best, who concluded that this non-canonical Mark was not written by the canonical Evangelist. Cf. M. Smith, *Clement of Alexandria and a Secret Gospel of Mark* (Cambridge, MA: Harvard University Press, 1973).

115. Farmer, *PSTJ* 32 (1978), p. 48.

dition — a matter of prime importance for Pryke). In addition, Hawkins employed no valid statistical analysis to arrive at his results: his only criteria for distinguishing Markan linguistic phenomena were (a) the occurrence, at least three times in Mark, of a word or phrase that (b) was found not at all in Matthew or in Luke or (c) occurred more frequently in Mark than in the other Synoptics combined.[116] Turner's research also was at some distance removed from 'objectivity': much of his careful study is predicated on the fallacious assumption that linguistic phenomena not characteristic of Matthew or Luke are therefore 'Markan' (again, without differentiating between the Second Evangelist's tradition and redactional activity).[117]

2. Are Pryke's basic form-critical assumptions tenable? For instance, if some of the pericopes underpinning the Second Gospel were already sutured together at the pre-Markan stage, would not this challenge, even undercut, the locus of Pryke's initial investigation? Apart from his confidence in the work of Ernest Best, how does Pryke know that *Mark* was responsible for these seams, that it is the Evangelist's vocabulary and style that are being observed?[118]

3. Are Pryke's primary methodological assumptions unassailable? As we have seen, his procedure assumes that linguistic (vocabulary) and syntactical (literary) evidence are independent of each other, and that, when there is a coincidence of the two in a given passage, the redactional character of that passage is thereby substantiated. However, it is a fine question whether or not these two sorts of evidence, the 'linguistic' and the 'literary', are actually independent of one another, as Pryke suggests. As David Peabody has observed,

> In fact, the 'linguistic studies' that Pryke utilizes as a norm for his work, namely those of Hawkins and Turner, are the very studies that influ-

116. Hawkins, *Horae Synopticae*, p. 10.

117. Turner, 'Markan Usage', *JTS* o.s. 25 (1923), pp. 377-78 et passim. To the extent that Pryke is heavily indebted to Vincent Taylor's research in Markan vocabulary and syntax, and to the degree that Taylor acknowledges significant indebtedness to Turner (Taylor, *St. Mark*, pp. 44-52), Pryke's *Redactional Style* seems inordinately dependent, directly or indirectly, on the work of C. H. Turner.

118. For that matter, the question could be inverted: how can Pryke be sure that the passion narrative in Mark underwent a lesser degree of creative sculpting by the Evangelist than the rest of the Gospel? '[Pryke] operates unquestioningly on the assumption that there was a continuous pre-Markan passion narrative, an assumption acceptable when the research was being undertaken [the 1960s], but not when the volume was published' (Achtemeier, review in *CBQ* 41 [1979], p. 656).

enced at least some of the authors of 'literary studies' that Pryke cites as normative for establishing redactional passages in Mark.[119]

4. Although his ostensible field of examination is the Markan text, in fact much of Pryke's dialogue is conducted with a wide-ranging yet selective representation of pre-1978 secondary literature rather than with the primary source. Even more problematic, however, is the undisclosed principle underlying Pryke's choice of scholars in his first step, described above: as Robert Mowery has demonstrated, one cannot assume that all of Pryke's scholarly citations, in support of his establishment of certain verses as 'redactional', actually reflect those scholars' agreement on such a designation.[120] This *prima facie* case for discernible Markan redaction is, of course, the foundation for Pryke's analysis; once its instability is revealed, the structure on which it rests begins to totter.

5. A similar fuzziness bedevils Pryke's discussion at other crucial points. For instance, early on he states that the end toward which his investigation moves is a consideration of the Evangelist's theology: yet Pryke's study never grapples with Markan theology in any cohesive way. Another example: by the end of his lengthy consideration of syntactical features as 'Possible Guidelines to the Author's Style', Pryke's argument, buttressed with 'final statistics', virtually assumes those guidelines to be 'probable' if not 'certain'.[121] Another puzzlement arises from Pryke's initial sorting of passages that contain each of the fourteen syntactical features into separate piles of 'redactional material' and 'source material': on what basis does he make such assignments? Pryke never explains or defends his preliminary reckoning of 29 out of 29 verses containing the genitive absolute as redac-

---

119. D. B. Peabody, *Mark as Composer* (New Gospel Studies 1; Macon, GA: Mercer University Press, 1987), p. 7. In addition, it should be noted that Pryke's repeatedly suggested 'conversions' of S into R material have the effect of inflating his final list of Markan redactional vocabulary (words appearing five or more times in the Gospel).

120. R. L. Mowery, reviewing Pryke's study in *JBL* 99 (1980), p. 616: 'Astonishingly enough, Pryke never explained the significance of these citations [of secondary bibliography]. Although the reader might initially assume that these citations support the identification of 1.26-28 [for example] as redactional verses, such is not the case; only four of the eleven scholars cited argue that all of 1.28 is redactional, only six of the eleven argue that even a portion of 1.27 is redactional, and none of the eleven argues that any portion of 1.26 is redactional. Pryke's failure to explain the function and limitations of these and many other citations in Part A [described in Step 1, above] represents one of the glaring weaknesses of his book'.

121. See, for example, Pryke, *Redactional Style*, pp. 134-35.

tional.[122] It is confusing to be told, at various points in the discussion, that such verses as Mark 1.26; 9.3, 26; 14.65; 15.27 should be *reclassified* as redactional passages, instead of as source passages, when, early in Pryke's monograph, those verses were listed as redactional to start with.[123]

6. A number of reviewers have commented on the numerous errors and inaccuracies that crop up in Pryke's presentation.[124] For example, in his list of Markan passages containing the genitive absolute, he fails to include Mark 4.17; 5.18; 15.33; 16.1, 2. Furthermore, why does Pryke insist that a word must appear at least five times in the Gospel in order to be included in his final list of Markan redactional vocabulary, when (a) 9 words appear five or more times in Mark, yet do not show up on Pryke's list,[125] and (b) 36 out of the 140 words listed in fact occur less than five times in Mark?[126]

7. Ultimately, Pryke concludes that 98 passages should not be regarded as emanating from Mark's source but should be 'converted' to the 'redactional' category; however, not one passage normally assigned to 're-daction' is (to my knowledge) ever reclassified by Pryke as issuing from the 'source'. As William Farmer has observed, this is a curious result:

> But it is troublesome to think that there seem to be no passages usually classified as 'Redactional' which could be converted to 'Source', whereas there are numerous passages which seem to go the other way. Is this just the way the cookie crumbles? Or is this a consequence of the way the test was set up? Or why is it?[127]

---

122. So Mowery (*JBL* 99 [1980], p. 616): 'Amazingly enough, [Pryke] made no attempt to explain or justify his assignments of verses to one group or the other. . . . Did he assume that Part A [presented as Step 1 in my review] had provided an adequate defense of such claims? Such is not the case, for Part A failed to provide any discussion of the evidence. The inadequacies of Part A therefore undermine the credibility of Part B [the discussion of the fourteen syntactical features]'.

123. Contrast Pryke, *Redactional Style,* pp. 79, 104, 113, 117, 121 with ibid., pp. 10, 17, 22, 23.

124. See, for example, the reviews by Neirynck ('Redactional Text') and Achtemeier (*CBQ* 41 [1979], pp. 655-57). To their discussions I am indebted in what follows.

125. ἐκεῖθεν (6 occurrences), ἐπιτιμάω (9), θεραπεύω (5), ὅσος (14), ὅτε (12), οὔπω (5), παρά (16), πᾶς (66), περί (22).

126. ἀγρεύω, ἄλαλος, ἀμφιβάλλω, ἄμφοδον, ἀναπηδάω, ἀφρίζω, γναφεύς, δύσκολος, ἐκθαμβέομαι, ἐκθαυμάζω, ἐναγκαλίζομαι, ἐνειλέω, ἐξάπινα, ἐξουδενέω, θαμβέομαι, θυγάτριον, καταβαρύνομαι, κατακόπτω, κατευλογέω, κατοίκησις, κυλίομαι, μογιλάλος, παιδιόθεν, περιτρέχω, πρασιά, προσάββατον, προσκεφάλαιον, προσκυλίω, προσπορεύομαι, ῥάπισμα, στίλβω, συμπόσιον, συνθλίβω, συλλυπέομαι, τρυμαλιά, ὑπολήνιον.

127. Farmer, *PSTJ* 32 (1978), p. 48.

8. Ernest Best, perhaps the most laudatory of all of Pryke's reviewers, raises another significant point: Pryke does not examine what remains of the source material after he extracts the redactional matter.[128] This is more than a matter of fussiness: had Pryke scrutinized the residue in Mark's source after the redactional touches have been excised, he might have been hard pressed to explain, for example, how the pericope of Jesus' baptism (Mark 1.9-11) could have circulated with only the traditional words, ἦλθεν Ἰησοῦς ἀπὸ Ναζαρὲτ τῆς Γαλιλαίας καὶ ἐβαπτίσθη εἰς τὸν Ἰορδάνην ὑπὸ Ἰωάννου. . . . Σὺ εἶ ὁ υἱός μου ὁ ἀγαπητός, ἐν σοὶ εὐδόκησα.[129] In order for the last statement to make any sense, would not the tradition — Mark's *source* — have needed some if not all of the circumstantial indicators of the ascent of Jesus from the water, the descent of the spirit, and the designation of the voice from heaven?

9. If James Little's redaction-critical approach suffers from the paradox of 'the disappearing redactor' (to use John Barton's expression), then the same problem plagues Pryke, and to a far greater extent. By Pryke's reckoning, well over half of Mark's Gospel (411 whole or partial verses out of a total of 666 verses) is the direct product of the Evangelist-Redactor. But this conclusion creates, or should create, a significant dilemma for Pryke: if the Second Evangelist has as thoroughly 'markanized' his traditions as Pryke suggests, then how (on the one hand) can he believe that Mark is more an editor than an author,[130] and why (on the other hand) should it be needful or desirable, in the end, to practice *redaction* criticism at all?[131]

To conclude: Pryke's study of Markan redactional style ultimately raises more questions than it answers. This suggests that neither Best's nor Achtemeier's evaluations, quoted at the opening of this review, seems totally accurate: Pryke's monograph is not the near definitive statement of Markan redaction criticism, as Best proposes; nor, *pace* Achtemeier, does it deserve to be completely ignored. It should be read and pondered, if for no

128. Best, *JSNT* 4 (1979), p. 70.

129. Thus filling in the ellipses in Pryke's reconstruction of the Markan redactional text (*Redactional Style*, p. 151).

130. Pryke, *Redactional Style*, pp. 29-31.

131. Cf. G. B. Caird's assessment (reviewing Pryke's study in *ExpTim* 90 [1978], p. 56): 'But once we admit that any of the redactional material is simply Mark's version of the substance which he found in other words in his sources, on what grounds can we regard any verse in the gospel as merely editorial? Do we not find ourselves back with the old-fashioned and highly unpopular view that the whole of Mark is Markan?'

other reason than that it crystallizes so many of the problems of the method that it aims to refine.

David Barrett Peabody

In the pursuit of a more refined Markan *Redaktionsgeschichte,* one of the most recent proposals has been tendered by David B. Peabody. In a monograph based on his doctoral dissertation, presented in 1983 to the graduate faculty in religion at Southern Methodist University, Peabody states as his goals '(1) the collection and systematic display of potentially redactional features of the text of Mark as a whole and (2) the isolation of those redactional features within this larger body of potentially redactional material that have the highest probability of coming from the hand of the author/composer of the gospel'.[132] Like William Walker, Peabody wishes to achieve his objectives without assuming any particular resolution of the Synoptic problem; unlike Walker, Peabody wishes to proceed with only minimal presuppositions about 'passages that function redactionally' within the Gospel under scrutiny, because of the tendency to circular reasoning in evaluating literary and redactional features in passages.[133] The target at which Peabody aims is, not 'redactional passages', but 'redactional features', defined as 'favorite or habitual expressions' of the Second Evangelist. Peabody is specifically concerned with recurrent language or phraseology in Mark's Gospel, by which he means 'all of the combinations of two or more literary elements that recur within the gospel of Mark two or more times', rather than recurrent vocabulary, grammar, or syntactical features as such.[134]

132. Peabody, *Mark as Composer,* p. xv. Peabody's study was originally presented as 'The Redactional Features of the Author of Mark: A Method Focusing on Recurrent Phraseology and Its Application' (Ph.D. diss., Southern Methodist University Press, 1983).

133. Peabody, *Mark as Composer,* pp. xv, 3-10 (quotation, p. 8). As an example of circular reasoning, Peabody cites, and disagrees in large measure with, the work of E. J. Pryke. Interestingly, in the 1977 article discussed earlier in this chapter, W. O. Walker indicated that Peabody had 'begun the task of applying the method proposed in [Walker's] paper to the Gospel of Mark' ('Method', p. 76 n. 2). If the culmination of that task came to be Peabody's dissertation and monograph, then they ultimately diverged from Walker's approach in several respects.

134. Peabody, *Mark as Composer,* pp. 15, 19. Peabody acknowledges the similarity of his work with that of Frans Neirynck, which Peabody hopes to extend, refine, and complement (ibid., pp. 14-17).

Peabody's method essentially comprises two stages, each of which may be broken down into several, supporting criteria. The first stage entails the identification of redactional features within the Markan text, which can be achieved through the employment of three criteria: (a) observation of the frequency of a feature's occurrence; (b) observation of the number of elements in that frequently occurring, putative redactional feature (supported by the attendant assumption that the greater the number of elements, the more likely the feature's origination with the redactor); and (c) observation of the conjunction of the previous two criteria (their coincidence suggesting a more significant probability of Markan redaction).[135] After a detailed and extensive analysis of the Markan text, presenting 252 tables of linguistic phenomena that constitute the heart of his monograph,[136] Peabody concludes that the recurring phrase for which the highest certitude of redactional character can be claimed is πάλιν used retrospectively uniting two or more separate pericopes (occurring 52 times in Mark); in addition, a similar claim of relative certainty can be made for πάλιν used retrospectively uniting two verses within a single pericope (23 occurrences in Mark).[137] Peabody notes that these πάλιν-passages create in the Gospel narrative 'a geographical framework, a sense of development, and a coherent portrait of Jesus' ministry'.[138]

The second stage of Peabody's method is the differentiation of redactional features in Mark from the traditions most likely to have been employed by the Evangelist. Again, three criteria guide the execution of this stage. First to be implemented is the criterion of compositional function: the isolation of recurrent phrases, discerned in Stage One, in material whose function is to link independent units by providing some foreshadowing of, or retrospection on, those surrounding units. Peabody grants that Mark might have inherited source material in which such linkages already had been introduced; to establish a control for this, Peabody suggests observing (a) those compositional links that connect passages not found in immediate succession, but which may be separated by any number of pericopes; and (b) the manner in which such links provide 'some structure for the gospel narrative' in a way that 'a certain development is to be seen in the gospel from one pericope to the next . . . through a number of liter-

135. Peabody, *Mark as Composer*, pp. 20-21. Peabody points out that frequency of occurrence by itself cannot guarantee Markan redaction.
136. Ibid., pp. 31-113.
137. Ibid., pp. 56-57, 95.
138. Ibid., p. 125.

ary contexts'.[139] The second criterion used in distinguishing redactional features from Mark's tradition is that of distribution: the identification of recurrent phrases throughout the Gospel, both within passages functioning compositionally as well as within different types of material (as defined by form criticism).[140] Third, Peabody suggests as a clue to Mark's handiwork the criterion of interlacing: the extent to which separable redactional features of a single author appear together within the same immediate literary context.[141] Based on the results garnered in Stage One, the constant factor or starting-point from which such interlacing can be measured is 'the use of πάλιν retrospectively, uniting two or more separated pericopes'. Therefore, Peabody deduces, 'If the interlaced features are also frequent and extensive so as to qualify as potentially redactional features in Stage [One] of this research, and if they not only interlace with this usage of πάλιν but also are well distributed and/or interlace with one another and/or function compositionally and/or appear in passages that function compositionally then the fact that they come from the hand of the author of Mark will be substantially confirmed'.[142] In short, Peabody is arguing for the validity of results on the grounds of their coherent satisfaction of different criteria, as was the case with criterion (c) in Stage One, described above. The remainder of his book[143] is devoted to the execution of this second stage, on the basis of these criteria.

After completing this two-stage analysis, Peabody draws two major conclusions. First, he tabulates a list of (at least) 39 or (at most) 44 redactional features of the text of Mark that have the highest probability of coming from the hand of the Evangelist.[144] Second, correlating those lin-

---

139. Ibid., pp. 22-23. N.B. p. 23: 'No other redactor [but Mark] would have been in a position to have joined together separated parts of the gospel narrative'.

140. Ibid., pp. 24-26. Cf. p. 25: '[The] general procedure here in tracing the hand of the author of Mark has been to let the redactional *features* that function compositionally "take the lead" in drawing attention to *passages* in the gospel that are most likely to have come from the hand of the author rather than the more customary procedure of letting the passages that function compositionally draw attention to redactional features'. Here Peabody's divergence from Walker's approach is particularly noticeable.

141. Ibid., pp. 26-28.

142. Ibid., p. 27.

143. Ibid., pp. 115-58.

144. Thus ibid., pp. 163-65: (1) καί + εὐθύς; (2) παρὰ τὴν θάλασσαν; (3) ἐν τῇ θαλάσσῃ (4) καί + a verb of motion + εἰς Καφαρναούμ to introduce a pericope; (5) καί + a form of ἔρχομαι or its compounds + εἰς + accusative of συναγωγή (6) ὥστε + infinitive; (7) οἶκος/οἰκία used to set the stage for the subsequent pericope; (8) καί + a form of συνάγω + πρός;

guistic features with the verses in the Markan text in which they occur (with some verses containing more than one such feature), Peabody suggests as probable the issuance of 38 verses from the single hand of the author of the Gospel.[145] Peabody ends his study by suggesting that this kind of analysis could be extended further, that more redactional verses and stylistic features could be added to his lists by means of ever widening interlacings of evidence. At least on the basis of his work to this point, for him it is certain that 'the method proposed in . . . this study for isolating the redactional features of the author of Mark does produce significant results'.[146]

Peabody's study of putative redactional features in Mark has much to commend it. Thorough and meticulous,[147] his presentation evinces a logic

---

(9) ἀπέρχομαι + εἰς; (10) καί + aorist of ἔρχομαι or its compounds + εἰς + name of place + καί; (11) καί + historic present of verb of motion + πρὸς αὐτόν [= Ἰησοῦν]; (12) ἤρξατο/ἤρξαντο + infinitive; (13) ὥστε [μη]κέτι + infinitive to describe the curtailment of normal human activity which results from Jesus' presence or action; (14) ὁ λόγος used absolutely; (15) πάλιν used retrospectively uniting two or more separated pericopes; (16) a form of ἀκούω + ὅτι + [Ἰησοῦς] ἐστίν; (17) καί + a compound verb of motion with σύν + 'crowds' + ὥστε [μη]κέτι + infinitive + μηδέ (18) καὶ ἐδίδασκεν αὐτούς; (19) καὶ πᾶς ὁ ὄχλος; (20) καὶ ἔλεγεν αὐτοῖς as a linking and/ or introductory formula; (21) καί + τῆς Ἰουδαίας + καὶ πέραν τοῦ Ἰορδάνου + 'crowds' + 3rd person of verb of motion + πρὸς αὐτόν [= Ἰησοῦν]; (22) πρὸς τὴν θάλασσαν; (23) the motif of a boat being readied or used to protect Jesus from the crowd; (24) καὶ προσκαλεσάμενος τὸν ὄχλον/τοὺς μαθητάς/αὐτούς + 3rd singular of λέγω + αὐτοῖς; (25) καί + ἐν παραβολαῖς + verb of speaking + αὐτοῖς; (26) καὶ ἤρξατο διδάσκειν; (27) ὄχλος + πολύς; (28) εἰς τὸ πλοῖον; (29) ἐβαίνω + εἰς τὸ πλοῖον; (30) καὶ ὅτε + verb + phrase meaning 'privately' + [ἐπ]ηρώτων αὐτόν + phrase meaning 'disciples' + accusative of ἡ παραβολή + 3rd singular of λέγω + αὐτοῖς; (31) κατ' ἰδίαν/κατὰ μόνας; (32) εἰς τὸ πέραν; (33) retrospective passage looking back to the two feeding stories; (34) καί + a form of ἐμβαίνω + [εἰς τὸ πλοῖον] + a verb of motion + εἰς τὸ πέραν; (35) a conjunction + ἐκεῖθεν + ἀναστάς + 3rd singular of [ἀπ]έρχομαι + εἰς τὰ ὅρια + genitive of place + καί; (36) conjunction + a compound of ἔρχομαι + preposition + a form of τὰ ὅρια Τύρου as object; (37) καί + ἐμβάς + [εἰς τὸ πλοῖον] + [ἀπ]ῆλθεν εἰς + article; (38) the motif of crowds coming to Jesus; (39) the motif of the disciples questioning Jesus privately, usually in a house. In addition, Peabody believes that the following five features probably should be considered redactional in Mark: (1) καί + a verb of motion + εἰς + name of place + εἰς + name of place; (2) οἱ δώδεκα used absolutely to describe the inner core of the disciples; (3) ἐν τῇ ὁδῷ (4) καί + a verb of summoning + τοὺς δώδεκα + 3rd singular of λέγω + αὐτοῖς; (5) verb of motion + εἰς Ἱεροσόλυμα.

145. These verses are Mark 1.16, 21, 39, 45; 2.1-2, 13; 3.1, 7-10, 20, 23; 4.1-2, 10, 35; 5.1, 21; 6.34, 45, 55; 7.14, 17, 24, 31; 8.1, 10, 13, 19-21; 9.14, 28, 33; 10.1, 10 (Peabody, *Mark as Composer*, pp. 162-63).

146. Ibid., p. 165; cf. pp. 165-66.

147. For example, in Stage One of his procedure, Peabody starts at the beginning of Mark, combing the Gospel for recurrent literary features and reproducing them wherever

and discipline not to be found to the same degree in similar investigations (in Pryke's monograph, for example). Another strength of Peabody's work is its attempt to sharpen the investigator's criteria for identifying possible redactional elements: thus a given linguistic feature's frequency of occurrence no longer stands alone but is viewed in the context of both its distribution throughout the Gospel and its interweaving with other such linguistic features.[148] To the extent that recurrence, distribution, and interlacing actually measure what Peabody suggests that they measure, these criteria make a genuine contribution to the refinement of Markan *Redaktionsgeschichte*.[149] Finally, the credibility of Peabody's research is enhanced by its critical conversation with other investigators in the field, especially older researchers in Markan vocabulary and style. Peabody's conclusions about redactional material carry conviction when his linguistic and functional tests, applied to certain passages, appear to coincide with more conventional, form-critical judgments on those same passages: thus it is striking that so many verses deemed by Peabody as Markan — 1.16, 21, 39, 45; 2.1-2, 13; 3.1, 20; 4.1-2, 10, 35; 5.1, 21; 6.45; 7.14, 24, 31; 8.1, 10, 13; 9.14, 33; 10.1 — function as 'sutures' between pericopes, or seams (as form critics usually refer to them).[150]

---

they are found: thus his Table 1 considers καθὼς γέγραπται (the first 'literary feature' found in the Gospel), lists the verses in which that clause occurs (1.2; 9.13; 14.21), and reproduces in Greek the portion of each of those verses in which the feature appears. Ἰωάννης ὁ βαπτίζων, the second 'literary feature' in Mark, is the subject of Table 2, and its occurrence in Mark 1.4, 6.14, and 6.24 is displayed. After the application of additional criteria in Stage Two, these and 206 other linguistic elements (all of which have been carefully tabulated) are *discounted* from consideration as probably redactional features; by then, however, Peabody has left no stone unturned in moving toward that conclusion.

148. The criteria of recurrence, distribution, and interlacing appear to have originated, not with Peabody, but with his mentor, W. R. Farmer, who proposed them in an unpublished paper, 'A Proposed Methodology for Redaction Criticism of the Gospels' (1974; known to me through Walker, 'Method', pp. 87 n. 30, 89).

149. The same may be said of Peabody's supporting criterion that the greater the number of elements in a linguistic feature, the higher the probability that those elements may be traced to the same authorial hand. It is one thing to be told by Best and others that 'Jesus' private instruction of the disciples' is a Markan motif; it is quite another to be informed that, at Mark 4.10 and 7.17, one finds καὶ ὅτε + verb + phrase meaning 'privately' + [ἐπ]ηρώτων αὐτόν + phrase meaning 'disciples' + accusative of ἡ παραβολή + καί + 3rd singular of λέγω + αὐτοῖς!

150. Curiously (unless I failed to detect it), Peabody himself never indicates this corroboration of his results with those of scholars belonging to other methodological camps. In any event, he is conversant, not only with the research of Neirynck, Pryke, Walker, Turner, Zerwick, and Doudna, but with the all but forgotten works of Wilke, *Die neutestamentliche Rhetorik* (1843), and Zeller, 'Studien zur neutestamentlichen Theologie' (1843).

Yet, like those of his forerunners, Peabody's contribution to this field of inquiry is ultimately as rich in questions as it is in answers. To begin with, one might wish for greater clarity and precision in Peabody's procedure and reasoning at several points:

(a) Is there a sufficient distinction between Peabody's basic methodological Stages One and Two (the isolation of redactional features within the Markan text over against the discrimination of redactional features from Mark's tradition)? To be sure, Peabody appeals to different criteria in Stages One and Two; yet 'frequency of occurrence', or 'recurrence', figures significantly as a supporting criterion in *both* stages.

(b) Peabody seems inconsistent in the degree of credence he is willing to give to 'passages that function redactionally' in Mark: on the one hand, he wishes to make only 'minimal presuppositions' about such passages, regarding them as secondary to Markan linguistic features; on the other hand, two of the basic criteria in Stage Two of his method (the compositional function of redactional features and their distribution in different form-critical genres of material) rely heavily on the definition of just such functional passages.[151] To the extent that Peabody is more 'functionally' oriented than he might wish, his study tends to be subject to a nettlesome assumption: namely, that the final redactor of Mark was essentially faithful to, perhaps even constrained by, his traditions (else the redactor's functions cannot be discerned with confidence). Though not inconceivable, such an assumption would not sit well with those Markan interpreters who confer on the Evangelist the mantle of creative author.

(c) Peabody's various linguistic criteria are helpful, but for a number of reasons they are not conclusive in identifying the handiwork of the author of Mark. To argue, as does Peabody, that 'No other redactor [except for Mark] would have been in a position to have joined together separated parts of the gospel narrative', or to have forged links between pericopes that yield a narrative development, is virtually to transmute a form-critical hypothesis into an unimpeachable (and unverifiable) fact: we simply cannot be sure that pre-Markan tradition circulated only in pericopes and resisted all capacity, prior to the Evangelist, of being linked together into a more developed narrative.[152] Moreover, it is possible to envision situations

151. Peabody, *Mark as Composer*, pp. xv, 22-26. It should be recalled that virtually all of the verses identified by Peabody as redactional are known, in large measure, by their *function* of linking and summarizing.

152. Cf. ibid., p. 23. The passion narrative in the Gospels and the speeches in Acts — to

in which a linguistic phenomenon might well satisfy the criteria of recurrence and distribution without having come from the single hand of the Second Evangelist: theoretically, for instance, Mark could have appropriated one or more sources, each with its own redactional characteristics, which he then distributed widely throughout his Gospel. Similar imponderables blunt another of Peabody's criteria: in itself, the interlacing of various linguistic phenomena can neither demonstrate the presence of a single redactional hand nor identify any redactional hand as belonging to the final author of Mark, since such interlacing could indicate the copying of an earlier (pre-Markan) redactor by a later redactor — neither of whom, need we conclude, was the final author of the Second Gospel.[153]

(d) Although the thrust of Peabody's research is to be as discriminating as possible in distinguishing Mark's handiwork (identifying as redactional only 38 verses and not more than 44 linguistic elements), the concluding pages of his book broach the possibility of broadening that redactional base even further: 'it is unreasonable even to claim that I have identified the majority of the redactional features from the hand of the author of Mark within this study'.[154] In my opinion, this prospect tends to diminish the reliability of his procedure. Apparently, Peabody wants to be both discriminating and encompassing. Given the nature of his project, can he have it both ways?

Second, a critical eye should be cast on those arguments of Peabody that are based on recurrence or frequency of occurrence. (a) As we have seen, Peabody is careful to admit that the criterion of recurrence cannot be applied in isolation from other criteria in assessing possibly redactional material in Mark; still, this criterion seems to emerge preeminent in Peabody's method.[155] (b) This being so, does Peabody's definition of 'recur-

---

the extent that the latter reflect pre-Lukan, early Christian *kerygma* — both attest to pre-Gospel tradition that underwent early narrative linkage. Cf. H. Sawyerr, 'The Marcan Framework', *SJT* 14 (1961), pp. 279-94.

153. Cf. Walker, 'Method', p. 89. Clearly, Peabody is aware of the problems arising from our ignorance of the shape of pre-Markan tradition (*Mark as Composer*, pp. 22-23); nevertheless, he begs some fundamental questions by speaking of redactional features as 'favorite or habitual expressions' (ibid., p. 19): *Whose* redaction? *Whose* habitual or favorite features? Peabody tends to assume what he is trying to prove: namely, that these features are *Mark's*. Can we be so sure?

154. Peabody, *Mark as Composer*, p. 166.

155. Inasmuch as Peabody has framed his investigation as an inquiry into 'the favorite and habitual expressions of the author of Mark's gospel' (*Mark as Composer*, p. 15), this could hardly be otherwise.

rent phraseology' — 'all of the combinations of two or more literary elements that recur within the gospel of Mark two or more times' — afford us a reasonable degree of probability that such combinations occur with sufficient frequency so as to suggest factors other than chance? Peabody performs no statistical tests on his results by which this might be verified; yet preliminary analyses executed by James Little would cast doubt on the statistical significance of the recurrence of some of Peabody's 'redactional features'.[156]

Third, the cogency of Peabody's conclusions might be challenged. (a) Peabody's final listing of 39, and possibly 44, redactional features from the hand of Mark does not seem to incorporate elements of uniform quality: can item 24, καὶ προσκαλεσάμενος τὸν ὄχλον/τούς μαθητάς/αὐτούς + 3rd singular of λέγω + αὐτοῖς, be regarded as of the same critical stature as item 23, 'the motif of a boat being readied or used to protect Jesus from the crowd'?[157] (b) Furthermore, one wonders if the number of redactional elements, and therefore the significance of the occurrence of interlacing, has been somewhat inflated by the appearance, in Peabody's final list, of some items that seem to be essentially duplicative of other items.[158] (c) In light of Peabody's own caution that, not only frequency, but the number of words in a redactional feature should be seriously considered, should a one-word element like πάλιν be asked to serve as the linchpin for discerning 38 (or 43) other such elements? The apparent justification for this procedure — namely, that πάλιν bears a uniformly retrospective nuance in the semantics of the Second Evangelist — founders on the textual evidence: out of 28 occurrences of the word in Mark, 15 probably should be translated 'again' (2.13; 3.20; 4.1; 8.1, 25; 10.1, 24; 12.4; 14.61, 69, 70; 15.4, 12), while 10 could be sensibly rendered 'back' (2.1; 3.1; 5.21; 8.13; 10.10, 32; 11.3, 27; 14.39, 40) and 3 seem pleonastic if not ambiguous (7.14, 31; 15.13). (d) Finally, it is interesting that Peabody should emphasize, as one *raison d'être* for his work, the lack of consensus on Markan redaction among scholars cited by Frans Neirynck: as it turns out, Peabody's own decisions

---

156. Cf. Little, 'Redaction Criticism', pp. 173-80. Although writing prior to Peabody's study, Little's comment (ibid., p. 180) is germane in the present case: 'In other words, the various factors are sufficiently complex to forbid simplistic statements which amount to subjective judgments of significant frequency. Such judgments must be tested by proven statistical methods'.

157. Peabody, *Mark as Composer*, p. 164. The first of these two features occurs thrice (Mark 3.23; 7.14; 8.1); the second, twice (3.9; 4.1).

158. In note 144 above, cf. features (5) and (10), (28) and (34), (30) and (39).

about redactional verses agree with those of Gaston, Pesch, Gnilka, and Schmithals only twice (at Mark 8.13 and 8.17b-21).[159]

Like other critical works that have tackled the refinement of Markan redaction criticism, Peabody has tried to devise a method that, with a minimum of circularity, would isolate those verses and linguistic elements in the Second Gospel that are most probably redactional. Whether Peabody has significantly raised the level of probability for his designated verses and literary features remains an open question, the answer to which will be decided as Markan scholars grapple with the results and implications of his work. For myself, the theoretical and procedural problems that attend his study lead to doubts that the level of probability has been significantly elevated. Peabody has expanded our thinking about method and has contributed to our understanding of characteristic literary features in Mark; nevertheless, his proposal is ultimately no less circular than those of his precursors and has not demonstrated that those linguistic features are uniquely Markan.

B. The Refinement of Markan *Redaktionsgeschichte*: The Pursuit Assessed

What is the upshot of these half-dozen essays in reforming redaction criticism of the Second Gospel? To summarize and to conclude, I would suggest six outcomes, all negative, of the research that has been surveyed.

First, *the would-be refiners of Markan redaction criticism are in fundamental disagreement with each other over how that refinement should be conceived and executed.* Reedy and Pryke insist that any methodological retooling must begin with the supposed transitional sections of the Gospel, the seams and summaries; Little rejoins that such a perspective tends to restrict the Evangelist's creativity, and that one should start with the arrangements and interrelationships of stories and sayings within Mark. Walker proposes a method in which the function of certain Markan passages is regarded as being of primary importance, with linguistic features providing only confirmatory evidence; Peabody responds with a method emphasizing the ultimacy of Markan linguistic features, with putative redactional passages affording only secondary evidence. For Gaston and Reedy, the

---

159. Cf. Neirynck, 'Redactional Text', p. 145. Of course, with his results Peabody may intend to provide the basis for a new assessment. Whether his appraisal of redactional features in Mark becomes the center of a new scholarly consensus remains to be seen.

statistical significance of many words frequently occurring in Mark's Gospel can be verified, and the redactional significance of such words is clear; according to Little, only a handful of words in Mark recur with statistically significant frequency, and even those words' redactional significance is disputable. Though a reviewer's suspicion may be aroused by methodological proposals so much at odds with each other, such diversity in perspective would be admissible, even prized, if the different points of view converged to produce a consensus on the character of redaction in the Second Gospel. Unfortunately, to judge from the results of these studies, such a convergence does not occur.

Second, *the form-critical premises on which, in various ways, the proposed refinements of Mark and redaction criticism are based are currently being challenged or revised.* From its original conceptualization, *Redaktionsgeschichte* has been predicated on certain 'laws' that hypothetically governed the genesis and transmission of oral traditions about Jesus: among others, the supposed circulation of material in discrete pericopes (save, perhaps, for the passion narrative) and the assumption by these pericopes of recognizable forms or *Gattungen.* It was against this foil that Markan redaction was assumed to be perceptible; for the revisionist critics reviewed in this chapter, no less than for their antecedents, 'redaction criticism proper is dependent upon the ability to write a history of the tradition'.[160] Increasingly, however, Gospel investigators express less confidence in their own ability to produce such a *Traditionsgeschichte;* when the attempt has been made, the results have been considerably less tidy and predictable than the earlier reconstructions of Schmidt, Dibelius, and Bultmann.[161] Unfortunately, the proposed refinements of redaction criticism, considered here, all depend on this earlier model of the sources and traditions with which Mark had to work.[162] Insofar as this *formgeschicht-*

160. Perrin, *What Is Redaction Criticism?,* p. 13.

161. Güttgemanns, *Candid Questions Concerning Gospel Form Criticism,* pp. 291-92, 323-32, et passim; Kelber, *The Oral and the Written Gospel,* pp. 1-139.

162. A criticism made of Ernest Best by R. S. Barbour (reviewing Best's *Following Jesus* in *SJT* 36 [1983], p. 108) is equally *à propos* of the scholars considered in this chapter: 'Best writes of [the pre-Markan tradition] as if it were a single body of material, presumably handed on orally and not in written form, but nevertheless capable of being quoted very precisely in Greek. . . . [But] redaction criticism as practised on Mark's Gospel . . . seems to be leading us in the direction of a rather too easy assumption that there was a single coherent tradition on which he worked, each pericope of which came to him in one form and one form only. It may be even more difficult than a study like this suggests to isolate the tradition and contrast Mark's additions and alterations to it'.

lich model is regarded as untenable, the *redaktionsgeschichtlich* refinements presupposing that model are rendered comparably suspect.

Third, *current attempts to rehabilitate Markan redaction criticism differ from earlier practice of the method in their degree of awareness of the dangers of circular reasoning and fallacious argumentation; however, this awareness does not forestall their own engagement in such reasoning and argumentation.* Cautions against the circular, self-confirming interplay of 'redactional features' and 'redactional passages' in Mark, which characterizes Pryke's study, are voiced by Walker and Peabody, who proceed to advocate redaction-critical methods in which just such an interplay is ingredient. Gaston frankly admits the circular argumentation on which his computations and statistical tables are based; he is less direct in suggesting adequate controls for the flaw inherent in his method. Reedy chastises his scholarly precursors for building redaction criticism on a 'faulty methodological foundation'; he then offers a method of 'refinement' that is as confused in its conception as it is flawed in its execution. Except for Little, all of the investigators considered in this chapter ultimately regard a linguistic feature's frequency of occurrence as significant in forming redaction-critical judgments, and two among them (Gaston and Reedy) invest extraordinary industry in statistical analyses that purport to reveal the significance of those features' frequency. Only rarely is it granted (by Walker and Peabody) that the *redactional* significance of such frequency of occurrence remains open to question; even then, this admission does not realign the critical process in any substantive manner.

Fourth, *most of the attempts to renovate Markan redaction criticism are rooted, not in the primary text, but in various hypotheses concerning the character and extent of the Evangelist's editorial activity.* This is not to say that the works we have reviewed pay no attention to the Second Gospel; they do, and frequently in fine detail (vocabulary, stylistic features, percentages of occurrence, and so forth). Yet it is usually the case that the ground on which these often elegant studies stand is the shifting *opinio communis* of Markan scholarship. Gaston's statistical presentation begins with the examination of 'certain passages commonly agreed to be redactional'; Reedy and Pryke commence their projects with Markan passages that have been identified as redactional by a dozen or so scholars; the 'Maximal List' of Markan passages, from which Walker's method evolves and to which it continually returns, is compiled from material 'almost universally regarded as redactional by modern critical scholarship'. No one would reproach these investigators for their knowledge of, and interaction with, twentieth-century Markan research; on the contrary, that is one of the most laudable aspects of their procedure. The problem is the tendency of secondary scholarship to supersede the Second Gospel in importance, such that redaction-critical dialogue has begun and been conducted less with the text and more with scholars' assumptions about what is going on behind the text. Not only is this poor exegetical form; in the end it is unavailing, since there are precious few words, verses, or passages on which the majority of Markan scholars has reached a redaction-critical consensus.

Fifth, *it is doubtful that the various attempts to refine Markan redaction criticism have so sharpened the tool that it is nearer to achieving its avowed objective.* Perhaps the primary goal of all these researchers is the identification of the Second Evangelist's distinctive literary or theological contribution — 'distinctive' understood as 'unique' or 'distinct from other things' (*verschieden*, in German). Thus they are seeking '*where* Markan redaction is to be found in the Gospel and *how* it is to be identified' (Little), a differentiation 'between those cases where a redactor has simply taken over a word from a source and those in which he has written it of his own accord' (Gaston), 'a distinction between editorial contribution and the tradition of the primitive church' (Reedy), 'a very real distinction between traditional and redactional materials' (Walker), 'the isolation of those redactional features . . . which have the highest probability of coming from the hand of the author/composer of the gospel' (Peabody), or '[the] distinguishing [of] editorial and source material in the Gospel so as to lead on to a detection of the theology of the evangelist as redactor' (Pryke). Unfortunately, this mission, however articulated, has been convincingly accomplished by none of these scholars. Adopting different means of approach, they have presented us with phenomena that are undoubtedly 'distinctive', in the sense of being 'characteristic' *(bezeichnend),* of Mark: vocabulary, stylistic features, literary arrangements, functional passages, and whatnot. However, that which is 'characteristic' is by no means necessarily 'unique'. What the refiners of redaction criticism have sought is the latter; the most that their proposals — and perhaps all known forms of Markan *Redaktionsgeschichte* — are capable of yielding is the former.[163]

Sixth, *the more rigorously Markan scholars refine redaction criticism, the*

---

163. Cf. Hooker, 'On Using the Wrong Tool', p. 574. Note also Theissen's suggestion that, 'Once one stops looking at the relationship between tradition and redaction as a relationship between archaeological strata, and sees both as actualizations of a virtual genre structure, it becomes impossible to make a simple opposition between redaction and tradition' (*Miracle Stories*, p. 295).

more trivial or needless the method becomes. The potential for triviality is clearest in proposals like Walker's and Gaston's: the more narrowly they circumscribe the field that permissibly may be probed for Mark's redactional activity (for Walker, 'functional passages'; for Gaston, 'editorial sentences'), the lower their latitude for the interpreter's exploration of the Evangelist's compositional or theological artistry overall. The self-annihilating capacity of *Redaktionsgeschichte* is most evident in the work of Little and Pryke: the more elaborately the Evangelist is believed to have 'markanized' his sources, the less likely it becomes that those sources can be recognized or that any evidence of their existence has survived in the first place — which is, of course, the very *sine qua non* for redaction criticism.

Any one of these problems might be tolerable: for instance, from the method's inception it has been understood that the rationale and procedure of redaction criticism is fundamentally circular.[164] Compounded with the other difficulties suggested above, however, the circularity of the method becomes embarrassing. Add to that the tool's seeming incapability, when applied in a consistent manner, of producing coherent exegetical results, and that circularity arguably becomes vicious.

If redaction criticism of the Gospel of Mark be 'a matter of logical necessity',[165] 'an essential step toward perceiving the author's meaning',[166] 'an indispensable tool for assessing the total process by which the biblical text achieved its present form',[167] then the results of our study thus far are, to say the least, disconcerting. But *is* this method necessary, essential, or indispensable? Why have Markan investigators believed that it was? And are there methodological alternatives that might better address the issues with which *Redaktionsgeschichte,* in its original development and subsequent refinement, was intended to deal? It is the burden of the next and final chapter to ponder such questions as these.

---

164. Thus, for example, Marxsen, *Mark the Evangelist,* p. 25; Bultmann, *Synoptic Tradition,* p. 5; and C. L. Mitton, 'Some Further Studies in St. Mark's Gospel', *ExpTim* 87 (1976), p. 300.

165. Reedy, 'Redaction', p. 42.

166. R. T. Fortna, 'Redaction Criticism, NT', *IDBSup,* p. 733.

167. J. A. Wharton, 'Redaction Criticism, OT', *IDBSup,* p. 732. In context, Wharton is speaking of redaction criticism's value for biblical interpretation in general.

8. Method in Markan Study: Appraisal and Proposal

Any methodology is only as strong as its ability to answer questions which have been impervious to previous methodologies.

John R. Donahue[1]

Some years ago Norman Perrin averred, 'the way that redaction criticism is able to make sense of the phenomena demonstrably present in the texts is itself a validation of the methodology'.[2] *Pace* Perrin, I have argued that this, in itself, is not an adequate justification of the method, since redaction criticism seems capable of making sense of textual phenomena in ways that are widely discrepant and sometimes mutually exclusive.[3] Moreover, I have suggested that none of the recent attempts to curb the subjectivity with which *redaktionsgeschichtlich* judgments have been made is entirely or even sufficiently successful. In light of this perplexing state of affairs, and in view of the universally acknowledged difficulty of Markan *Redak-*

---

1. Donahue, *Are You the Christ?*, p. 31.

2. Perrin, *What Is Redaction Criticism?*, p. 40. Likewise, recall Best's caution: 'Without the control which [Markan style and vocabulary] supply it is possible to make Mark mean almost anything' (*Following Jesus*, p. 241). Surely the present study has demonstrated that even (or especially?) with the so-called control provided by redaction criticism, the meaning of discipleship in Mark is left almost entirely up in the air.

3. Nor is this phenomenon unique to the Second Gospel. Reviewing J. D. Kingsbury's *Matthew: Structure, Christology, Kingdom* (Philadelphia: Fortress, 1975), D. E. Garland observed, 'Perhaps it is an embarrassment that a method which purports to be especially suited for unearthing an author's purpose has produced so many purposes for Matthew. Kingsbury briefly passes over twelve proposals and then offers his own' (*RevExp* 74 [1977], pp. 567-68).

tionsgeschichte,[4] one wonders why this interpretive approach for so long has held so many Markan investigators in thrall.

A. *Redaktionsgeschichte*: Its Conceptualization Revisited

To understand the recent history of Markan exegesis, we might begin by recalling the fundamental concerns voiced by the first self-reflective redaction critics of the Second Gospel. Early on, and in contrast to the form-critical emphasis on the Gospel traditions as products of early Christian communities, redaction critics of Mark emphasized its production by *an individual author*. It is almost impossible to find a *redaktionsgeschichtlich* treatment of Mark and the other Gospels, of either older or more recent vintage, that does not stress this understanding of their literary origins. Thus Marxsen urges that Markan interpreters take into account 'an author personality [*sic*] who pursues a definite goal with his work, . . . an "individualistic" trait oriented to the particular interest and point of view of the evangelist concerned',[5] Repeatedly in the secondary literature the claim was made that, in *Redaktionsgeschichte*, 'We are dealing with individual authors not with the "community"',[6] 'evangelists [who] are genuine authors',[7] 'authors in their own right', whose existence 'must at all costs be stressed, even if the extent and delimitation of [each author's] sources, his share in shaping them, his name, his home, his fortunes could never be established with complete certainty'.[8]

Why were redaction critics so insistent in locating the Evangelist-author at the center of exegetical attention? In part, it reflected their commonsense judgment that only from the redactor's hands have we directly received the biblical literature; thus Franz Rosenzweig once suggested that

---

4. Thus Meye (*Jesus*, p. 38): 'attempts to differentiate between that which is Marcan and that which is traditional are at best precarious'; Best (*Following Jesus*, p. 241): 'the, admittedly, more difficult facts of Markan style and vocabulary'; Weeden (*Mark*, p. 3): 'it is not always easy to make judgments as to what is tradition and what is redaction'. Some such qualification of certitude is *de rigueur* among Markan redaction critics.

5. Marxsen, *Mark the Evangelist*, pp. 18, 24.

6. Stein, 'What Is *Redaktionsgeschichte?*', p. 49.

7. N. Perrin, 'The Evangelist as Author: Reflections on Method in the Study and Interpretation of the Synoptic Gospels and Acts', *BR* 17 (1972), p. 9. Notice also the very title of this article.

8. Rohde, *Rediscovering*, pp. 18, 33.

'R' (referring to the lowly esteemed redactor of the Hexateuch) should be interpreted as *rabbenu*, 'our master'.[9] In part, this accent on the author attempted to correct for the exaggerated importance conferred by form critics on *urchristliche Gemeinde* in the production of the Gospels, a perspective that virtually excluded any contribution by the individual Evangelists.[10] However, the principal reason for this emphasis on the Evangelist as author seems to have been its association with the idea of the Evangelist as *religious thinker* and his Gospel as the vehicle for *predominantly theological perspectives*. This connection between authorial and theological intention in the Evangelist's work is expressly wrought by Ernest Best in an early redaction-critical volume: 'All this means that we treat Mark seriously as an author. He has his place in the canon, not because he gives certain historical facts about the life of Jesus, but because, in the same sense as Paul, he preaches Christ'.[11]

Alongside regard for the Evangelists as genuine authors, this perception of Mark and the other Gospel writers as theologians might be considered the most significant redaction-critical concern. Certainly it has been one of the most frequently voiced: 'the evangelists were not merely *Sammler* but individual theologians',[12] 'their redactional work . . . undertaken to serve a theological conception and particular theological themes'[13] and reflecting 'a distinctive, definable theological outlook as it seeks to relate the story of Jesus in its own manner'.[14] The sort of religious coloration, applied to the narrative of Jesus, that had long been recognized in the Fourth Gospel now was acknowledged as pervading the Synoptics as well: 'Each Evangelist was a theologian in his own right and possessed a

---

9. Cited by G. von Rad, *Genesis: A Commentary* (rev. edn; OTL; Philadelphia: Westminster, 1972), pp. 42-43.

10. Thus Marxsen, pace Martin Dibelius (*Mark the Evangelist*, p. 20): 'Tradition is indeed the primary factor which we encounter, but it is the tradition of the evangelists, that is, the tradition laid down in the Gospels. When we reconstruct their world (and that means the world of the evangelists) we approach the individual tradition. Can it then be our first task to proceed to an investigation of the material of the synoptic tradition, ignoring the evangelists? Is not our primary task twofold — that of arriving at redaction *and* tradition?'

11. *Temptation*, p. xi. Cf. the subtitle of Haenchen's introductory section in *Der Weg Jesu*, pp. 32-37: 'Die Evangelisten als Schriftsteller und Theologen'.

12. Stein, 'What Is *Redaktionsgeschichte*?', p. 47.

13. Rohde, *Rediscovering*, p. 17; cf. Perrin, *What Is Redaction Criticism?*, p. 1; Schweizer, 'Die theologische Leistung'; idem, *Good News*, pp. 380-86.

14. J. H. Hayes and C. R. Holladay, *Biblical Exegesis: A Beginner's Handbook* (Atlanta: John Knox, 1982), p. 99; cf. Haenchen, *Der Weg Jesu*, p. 24.

theological purpose for writing his gospel'.[15] From this point of view, redaction-critical exegesis was often depicted as a process of textual threshing, separating the wheat of an Evangelist's theology from the chaff of his sources:

> . . . having ascertained the evangelist's redaction we seek to find: (1) What unique *theological views* does the evangelist present which are foreign to his sources? . . . (2) What unusual *theological emphasis or emphases* does the evangelist place upon the sources he received? . . . (3) What *theological purpose or purposes* does the evangelist have in writing his gospel?[16]

No less than the consideration of the Gospels as individual rather than communal products, this focus on the theology of the Evangelists was regarded as a departure from the form-critical approach: 'Form criticism did not investigate *primarily* the theological character and the theological conception of the existing written gospels, it did that only marginally'.[17] If, according to *Formgeschichte,* the Evangelist's role was understood as refinishing, dusting off, and rearranging the furniture of the Synoptic tradition, 'from the redaction critical viewpoint, . . . each evangelist functioned as the architect of his conceptual house of gospel, for which he chose, refurbished, and in part constructed the fitting furniture'.[18]

Beyond this slant on the Synoptists as authors and theologians, redaction criticism ostensibly emphasized two other aspects of the Gospels, one literary and the other sociological. The literary insight was expressed by different scholars in different ways: some spoke of the significance of the Gospel's narrative framework, overriding its constituent traditions; others expressed a critical concern for larger units of tradition up to and including the entire Gospel.[19] However they put the matter, redaction critics saw themselves as treating *the Gospels as unitary textual artefacts, to be interpreted holistically:*

---

15. Stein, 'Markan Redaction History', p. 181. See also Hooker, *Message,* p. 20.

16. Stein, 'What Is *Redaktionsgeschichte?*', p. 54; in the original, each of the numbered questions is italicized. Stein further indicates a fourth concern of the method, the *Sitz im Leben* out of which the Gospel was written; this we shall consider immediately below.

17. Rohde, *Rediscovering,* p. 16.

18. Kelber, 'Redaction Criticism', p. 12.

19. Cf. Marxsen, *Mark the Evangelist,* p. 23; Rohde, *Rediscovering,* pp. 14, 19; Perrin, *What Is Redaction Criticism?,* p. 34.

Redaction criticism served as a healthy corrective to certain trends within both tradition criticism and form criticism as they came to be preoccupied, if not obsessed, with the smaller literary units and sub-units within each Gospel. By contrast, redaction criticism emphasizes the wholeness of the Gospels, their literary integrity, and seeks to see not simply the individual parts, but what they were saying when arranged together as a single whole. Consequently, the redaction critic is never satisfied to analyze a single literary subunit or pericope in and of itself but rather, having done so, to relate it to the larger whole.[20]

Moreover, redaction critics claimed to contribute an important sociological insight: namely, an understanding of the Gospels in light of *the Evangelists' historical context and of the social setting of the community for which they were writing*. Most scholars concurred with Marxsen's characterization of this component of *Redaktionsgeschichte* as *der dritte Sitz im Leben*:

> If Joachim Jeremias differentiates the 'first situation-in-life' located in the unique situation of Jesus' activity, from the 'second situation-in-life' mediated by the situation of the primitive church (which form criticism seeks to ascertain), we are dealing here with the '*third* situation-in-life'.[21]

With allowance for minor modifications and varying shades of emphasis, these three ideas — the Evangelist as author and theologian, his Gospel as the immediate product of his and his community's 'setting in life', and that Gospel as a literary entity to be interpreted holistically — have been basic in the formulation of redaction criticism from its inception up to the present day. As such, redaction criticism was conceived to be, not merely another tool to be added to the arsenal of Gospel exegesis, but a comprehensive interpretive approach, equipped to address the theological, sociological, and literary issues raised by a text. Although comprehensive, the method did not intend, however, to award each of these concerns equal weight; for the center of gravity in redaction criticism, no less than in source and form criticism, remained with *the author-theologian*. Witness the research of Meye, Best, and Weeden: all are interested in questions of

---

20. Hayes and Holladay, *Biblical Exegesis*, p. 99. Cf. Haenchen, *Der Weg Jesu*, p. 23; S. S. Smalley, 'Redaction Criticism', in *New Testament Interpretation: Essays on Principles and Methods* (ed. I. H. Marshall; Exeter: Paternoster, 1977), pp. 191-92.

21. Marxsen, *Mark the Evangelist*, p. 23, referring to J. Jeremias, *The Parables of Jesus* (2nd rev. edn; New York: Charles Scribner's Sons, 1972), p. 22.

the Evangelist's literary achievement and social matrix, but the point of entry, as well as the confirmation, for both of these investigations reside with the identification of the redactor's theology.[22] Thus, if the focus and subsidiary concerns of redaction criticism were to be diagramed, the result would look something like this:

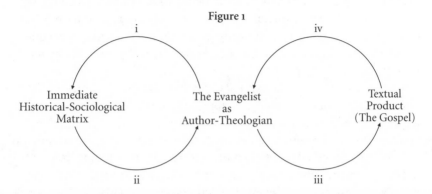

Figure 1

With this diagram I am suggesting several things. (a) Redaction criticism is a unified hermeneutical approach. (b) It is characterized by a reciprocal understanding: the identification of the redactor's theology enables one to intuit the particulars of the redactor's *Sitz im Leben* (i), which, in turn, corroborate specific elements of that theology (ii). (c) Another reciprocal understanding typifies redaction criticism: the identification of the redactor's theology enables one to interpret both the parts and the whole of the Gospel (iii), and that interpretation, in turn, confirms the primary aspects of the writer's theology (iv). (d) Standing at the point of intersection for these historical and literary investigations is the Evangelist, who is regarded as both author and theologian. For conventional redaction criticism, this last item is the most important. The redaction critic's conception of the Evangelist as author-theologian is both the starting-point for the total, critical inquiry as well as the terminus at which the method ultimately comes to rest.[23]

22. Thus D. M. Smith (*Interpreting the Gospels for Preaching* [Philadelphia: Fortress, 1980], p. 32): 'The basic insight of redaction criticism was that the evangelists were authors and theologians painting their own portraits of Jesus and addressing themselves to important theological issues, albeit in the church of the first century'.

23. On this point, John Barton's comments regarding Old Testament interpretation are no less accurate in describing the evolution of New Testament exegesis: 'It is important to

B. Redaction Criticism in the Context of Twentieth-Century Theology and Scholarship

Inasmuch as redaction critics of the Gospels have been absorbed in the delineation of the Evangelists' social and historical setting, it seems not inappropriate to inquire why redaction criticism itself has been pursued with such vigor, and what historical and cultural forces in this century have encouraged that pursuit. The following factors do not constitute a complete explanation; however, no explanation would be complete without mention of these.

1. Initially, at least, Markan redaction criticism was a somewhat late-blooming offshoot of the method's application to the other Synoptics. The impressive exegetical results of *Redaktionsgeschichte* when applied by Günther Bornkamm and his pupils to Matthew and by Hans Conzelmann to Luke were observed by Markan investigators,[24] and the conclusion was drawn by them, either openly or tacitly, that the method would yield equally impressive results when applied to the Second Gospel. Thus noted Norman Perrin:

> I may simply claim that the logical consequence of our most recent work is the conclusion that the evangelists Matthew and Luke have exercised the creative freedom of genuine authors with regard both to their model and their material. If this is true of Matthew and Luke, then it is certainly true of Mark. Whatever may have been the nature of the model Mark is following, whatever may have been the form or extent of the traditional material he is using, he is certainly exercising the creative freedom of an author.[25]

---

see that . . . form and redaction criticism . . . still belong firmly within the same family of critical approaches as source criticism. . . . [In] all three historical-critical methods, the original author in some sense is the place where the method comes to rest. Once we have found the meaning or intention of whoever first wrote the text, we have achieved our goal' (*Reading the Old Testament*, pp. 201-2).

24. Bornkamm, Barth, and Held, *Tradition and Interpretation;* Conzelmann, *The Theology of St. Luke.* Cf. Marxsen's expressions of indebtedness in *Mark the Evangelist*, pp. 16 n. 3, 28 n. 38.

25. Perrin, 'Evangelist as Author', p. 9. Notice that Perrin, like most Markan redaction critics, assumed the priority of the Second Gospel; thus it was natural for the origination and preliminary development of Synoptic *Redaktionsgeschichte* to occur with Gospels other than Mark.

In other words, what was sauce for the Matthean or Lukan goose was sauce for the Markan gander. The popularity of redaction criticism was accelerated further by the freedom and rapidity with which Anglo-Saxon and Continental scholarship could be exchanged and translated in the period following World War II.

2. To say that redaction criticism characterized the *Zeitgeist* of postwar Markan research as did no other interpretive tool is, while true, insufficient to explain why the method so thoroughly captured the imaginations of Synoptic scholars to start with. Surely one reason for the ascendance of *Redaktionsgeschichte* was its perceived continuity with previous exegetical methods. In the last section of his form-critical *magnum opus*, Bultmann himself had set the stage for this perception by suggesting that the composition of the Gospels 'involves nothing in principle new, but only completes what was begun in the oral tradition'.[26] Redaction critics ever since have debated among themselves the degree of continuity between their discipline and form criticism;[27] nevertheless, that there was *some* conceptual consonance between them, that *Redaktionsgeschichte* at least grew out of and presupposed the existence of the pre-literary, typical traditions analyzed by the form critics, has never been a serious subject of debate. Similarly, redaction-critical discussion of the Evangelists' distinctive literary traits and theological ideas was congenial with, and an extension of, the procedure adopted by such older source critics as Julius Wellhausen and B. H. Streeter.[28] However fruitful or abortive the attempt may be judged, however valuable or valueless the pursuit may be regarded, redaction criticism of Mark and the other Gospels promised to shed further light on the oral and literary history of those texts by means of a method based on accepted critical principles of analysis.

Continuity is esteemed no less by clerics than by scholars, and a *redaktionsgeschichtlich* point of view was perceived by some as congruous with ecclesial tradition. Years before the method was elaborated, its perspective was anticipated by Pius XII in *Divino Afflante Spiritu* (1943), a pa-

---

26. Bultmann, *Synoptic Tradition*, p. 321.

27. Contrast Best's postulation of the Second Evangelist's positive respect for, and conservative adaptation of, traditional material ('Mark's Preservation') with Kelber's argument for a radical disjunction between oral and literary transmission (*The Oral and the Written Gospel*, pp. 184-85 et passim).

28. Wellhausen, *Einleitung*; B. H. Streeter, *The Four Gospels: A Study of Origins* (New York: Macmillan, 1925).

pal encyclical that paved the way for the remarkable progress of Catholic biblical scholarship in this century:

> Let the interpreter then, with care and without neglecting any light derived from recent research, endeavor to determine the peculiar character and circumstances of the sacred writer, the age in which he lived, and the sources written or oral to which he had recourse and the forms of expression he employed. Thus he can better understand who was the inspired author, and what he wishes to express by his writings. There is no one indeed but knows that the supreme rule of interpretation is to discover and define what the writer intended to express. . . .[29]

3. Perhaps an even more significant reason for redaction criticism's hold upon Synoptic scholarship is this: the method ostensibly offered biblical theologians and preachers constructive theological insights at a time when two important theological movements were disintegrating, much to the chagrin of many adherents of historical criticism. These were the old quest of the historical Jesus and the 'biblical theology movement'.

a. The first of these movements was undergoing its death throes in the early decades of this century, and, in a real sense, a proleptic exercise in *Redaktionsgeschichte* was directly responsible for its demise. In the last half of the nineteenth century, the 'old quest' had been predicated largely on acceptance of 'the Markan hypothesis': the theory that Mark not only was the earliest Gospel and a source employed by Matthew and Luke, but also was the closest chronologically to the original eyewitnesses of Jesus and could therefore be regarded as historically trustworthy for information about the life and ministry of Jesus.[30] Although this position still claims some proponents,[31] its logic was sawn off at the root in the course of Wil-

---

29. Reproduced in *Rome and the Study of Scripture: A Collection of Papal Enactments on the Study of Holy Scripture Together with the Decisions of the Biblical Commission* (6th rev. and enlarged edn; Indiana: St. Meinrad, 1958), p. 97.

30. Though with varying modifications, this theory was most closely associated with C. G. Wilke *(Der Urevangelist)* and C. H. Weisse *(Die Evangelienfrage).*

31. Thus Taylor, *St. Mark,* pp. 148-49: 'Separated at the time of writing by little more than a generation from the death of Jesus, its contents carry us back farther into the oral period before Mark wrote to the tradition first of the Palestinian community and subsequently that of the Gentile Church at Rome. The historical value of Mark depends on the Evangelist's fidelity to that tradition, including his special advantages as a hearer of Peter's preaching. . . . Here is a writing of first-rate historical importance'. Recall also Meye, 'Messianic Didache', pp. 49-50.

liam Wrede's explosive and *redaktionsgeschichtlich*-clairvoyant presentation of the secrecy motif in the Gospels:

> It therefore remains true to say that as a whole the Gospel no longer offers a historical view of the real life of Jesus. Only pale residues of such a view have passed over into what is a supra-historical view for faith. In this sense the Gospel of Mark belongs to the history of dogma.[32]

When, some fifty years later, Ernst Käsemann reopened 'The Problem of the Historical Jesus' with the skeptical (and overstated) observation that 'the Gospels offer us primarily the primitive Christian kerygma, and . . . [historical] criticism can only help us to arrive at corrections and modifications in the kerygma but never at a word or action of the earthly Jesus himself',[33] he was adding in substance nothing new to Wrede's depiction of a historical-critical blind alley, which, if anything, looked by now even darker after form criticism.[34]

In the face of such increasing skepticism about history in the Gospels and the possibility of conventional *Leben-Jesu-Forschung*, Markan redaction critics could and did assume one of two postures. On the one hand, many joined Marxsen in simply bracketing out the bothersome historical questions and devoting themselves exclusively to the discernment of the Evangelist's theology: 'With this [redaction-critical] approach, the question as to what really happened is excluded from the outset. . . . [That question] is of interest only to the degree it relates to the situation of the primitive community in which the Gospels arose'.[35] Marxsen, in fact, was prepared to grant only minimal credence to the historicity of Mark's Gos-

32. Wrede, *Messianic Secret*, p. 131; see also pp. 115-45. Cf. the similar conclusions of Lightfoot, *History and Interpretation*, pp. 23-24, and consult the discussion in N. Perrin, 'The *Wredestrasse* Becomes the *Hauptstrasse*: Reflections on the Reprinting of the Dodd *Festschrift*', *JR* 46 (1966), pp. 296-300.

33. E. Käsemann, *Essays on New Testament Themes* (SBT 41; London: SCM, 1964), pp. 34-35; see also idem, 'Blind Alleys in the "Jesus of History" Controversy', *New Testament Questions of Today* (Philadelphia: Fortress, 1969), pp. 23-65.

34. Thus, for example, Dibelius: 'The first understanding afforded by the standpoint of *Formgeschichte* is that there never was a "purely" historical witness to Jesus' (*Tradition*, p. 295). Of course, other form critics maintained a guardedly positive estimation of the historicity of the Gospels' framework and contents: Dodd, 'Framework'; Jeremias, *Parables*.

35. Marxsen, *Mark the Evangelist*, pp. 23-24. Cf. the similar statement of purpose in Conzelmann, *Theology of St. Luke*, p. 9.

pel;[36] however, the secret of redaction criticism's success lay in the fact that one had not to agree with Marxsen's judgment in this matter in order to adopt the method and be repaid with positive exegetical results.

On the other hand, as *Redaktionsgeschichte* increasingly came to carry a certain scholarly cachet, it so fundamentally redefined what the Gospels were that no longer was the riddance of historical questions merely possible or permissible; it now was considered virtually mandatory. As a growing number of scholars came to accept the dictum that 'the gospels must be understood as *kerygma,* and not as biographies of Jesus of Nazareth',[37] the appropriation of the Gospels in a reprise of the old quest of the historical Jesus came to be regarded, not so much as problematic, but as illegitimate:

> The fact is that the very project of redaction criticism methodologically precludes the quest for the historical Jesus. . . . The historical Jesus forms the basis and presupposition of theology. Interestingly, what the gospels give us is not the presupposition, but the theologies.[38]

Although more conservative exegetes found slight consolation in the notion that neither Mark nor any of the Evangelists proclaimed the *historical* Jesus,[39] more liberal interpreters tended to regard this as a positive contribution of redaction criticism. It seemed to bridge the enormous temporal and hermeneutical gap between Mark as interpreter of the Jesus-traditions and the twentieth-century theologian as interpreter of the Second Gospel by functionally locating both in the same position: that of elucidator, not of Jesus of Nazareth, but of the early Christian *kerygma* about Jesus. As Eduard Schweizer expressed it:

> For Mark, . . . it is not the historical Jesus that he proclaims. It is not a Jesus who could be reconstructed and carried over from his to our time by

---

36. See Marxsen's *Introduction to the New Testament: An Approach to Its Problems* (Philadelphia: Fortress, 1968), pp. 120-45.

37. Rohde, *Rediscovering,* p. 11. Of course, this view had been anticipated by Wrede and, in 1915, by C. W. Votaw (*The Gospels and Contemporary Biographies in the Greco-Roman World* [FBBS; Philadelphia: Fortress, 1970], esp. pp. 1-5).

38. Kelber, 'Redaction Criticism', pp. 13-14. See also D. Blatherwick, 'The Markan Silhouette?', *NTS* 17 (1970/1971), pp. 184-92, esp. p. 192.

39. Naturally, some rejected such a formulation: thus T. W. Manson, *Studies in the Gospels and Epistles* (ed. M. Black; Philadelphia: Westminster, 1962), pp. 40-83.

historians. He can only be proclaimed and witnessed to by a believer like Mark. . . . [Although] the historical Jesus is, in the highest possible degree, essential for the faith of the church[,] . . . this does not mean that we could see anything which would really help us in the historical Jesus, without the miracle of God's Spirit who, in the word of the witness [i.e., Mark], opens our blind eyes to the 'dimension' in which all these events took place. The best historical reports, the best insights into the psychology of Jesus cannot replace or even support the evidence of the kerygma which calls us to faith and conveys faith to us.[40]

In short, redaction criticism responded to the problem of the historical Jesus either by completely ignoring it or by regarding it as of only tangential exegetical or theological consequence, since, on certain *redaktionsgeschichtlich* premises, the Evangelists themselves had responded to the matter in precisely the same way.

b. The waxing of redaction criticism during the middle of the twentieth century should be viewed also in the context of the waning of a second scholarly enterprise during the same period: the so-called 'biblical theology movement'.[41] In some respects the *redaktionsgeschichtlich* approach was antagonistic to some of the traits of that movement:[42] thus, given the nonchalance of the method toward matters historical, few proponents of 'revelation in history' found a home among Markan redaction critics, even though some of the earliest *redaktionsgeschichtlich* efforts considered the Second Evangelist's understanding of history.[43] And redaction criticism did nothing if not stimulate a heightened sensitivity to theological diversity among the Gospels, contrary to the emphasis of biblical theology on the unity of the Bible.[44]

On the other hand, so clearly in sympathy with other aspects of the

---

40. E. Schweizer, 'Mark's Contribution to the Quest of the Historical Jesus', *NTS* 10 (1963/1964), pp. 423, 431.

41. The growth and decline of this movement has been carefully chronicled by B. S. Childs, *Biblical Theology in Crisis* (Philadelphia: Westminster, 1967), pp. 13-87.

42. For a concise summary and assessment of the characteristics of postwar biblical theology, consult J. Barr, 'Biblical Theology', *IDBSup*, pp. 104-11.

43. Robinson, *Problem*; Burkill, *Mysterious Revelation*.

44. So Kelber, 'Redaction Criticism', p. 13: 'The concept of the evangelists as theologians sounds the death knell to any effort, conscious or unconscious, at gospel harmonization. To read one gospel through the eyes of another does violence to the integrity of both; to 'supplement' one gospel with features taken from the other three misapprehends all four of them. . . . Four evangelists equal four stories of Jesus'.

biblical theology movement was *Redaktionsgeschichte* that it proved to be the successor of the movement, in perspective if not in method. To those weary of the sort of biblical exegesis associated with 'liberal' theology (dry historical analysis, complacent or indifferent to theological concerns), redaction criticism promised, and often delivered, robust interpretations of the Evangelists' theologies,[45] based on the established exegetical principles of source and form criticism yet readily appropriable by both theologians and churchmen. Indeed, for the church and its ministry of preaching, a concern of vital importance for the biblical theology movement, redaction criticism was regarded as having immediate and positive implications: not only did it provide new exegetical content for preachers; it also offered them new paradigms for understanding the homiletical task. From Willi Marxsen's early, heuristic analogy between the Evangelist, his Gospel, and their *Sitz* with a modern preacher, sermon, and congregation,[46] it was but a short step to Leander Keck's characterization of biblical preaching as that which not only 'imparts [the Bible's] message-content, but . . . does so in a manner that repeats the Bible's own way of using normative tradition' — namely, 'in response to particular occasions (usually crisis situations) in the life of communities of faith'.[47]

To summarize: in the mid-twentieth century a number of forces conspired to promote the pursuit of Markan *Redaktionsgeschichte*. Especially significant were the apparent fruitfulness of the method when applied to the other Synoptics, its ostensible continuity with previous exegetical procedures, and its perceived theological fecundity during the decline of the biblical theology movement and the old quest of the historical Jesus.

---

45. Indeed, the very notion that the Synoptists displayed such developed and distinctive theological understandings was revolutionary: by contrast, Bultmann had used the Synoptics as the source only for 'The Message of Jesus' and 'The Kerygma of the Earliest Church' (*Theology of the New Testament* [vol. I; New York: Charles Scribner's Sons, 1951], pp. 3-62).

46. Marxsen, *Mark the Evangelist*, p. 24 n. 30.

47. L. E. Keck, *The Bible in the Pulpit: The Renewal of Biblical Preaching* (Nashville: Abingdon, 1978), p. 115. Notice that Keck considers this to be a distinctively *redaktionsgeschichtlich* insight: 'It is precisely at this point that especially redaction criticism becomes fruitful for preaching' (ibid.). Also cf. R. H. Fuller, *Preaching the New Lectionary: The Word of God for the Church Today* (Collegeville, MN: Liturgical Press, 1974), pp. xix-xxvi.

C. The Contributions and Liabilities of Redaction Criticism

Assets

So much of this book has been devoted to the drawbacks of Markan redaction criticism that the reader might wonder if anything complimentary can be said of it. As a matter of fact, the *redaktionsgeschichtlich* perspective on Mark and the other Gospels has offered, and continues to offer, some genuinely positive contributions. A return to Figure 1 on p. 259 should clarify this.

First, as we have witnessed, redaction criticism was intended to be a comprehensive method, melding concerns for the author, his historical and sociological background, and the literary features displayed by his text. Whether the method was in fact successful in holding together these various interests, particularly by regarding the author as the methodological fulcrum, is a moot point, and one to be considered presently. For the moment, let this much be underscored: by incorporating the historical, traditional, literary, and theological concerns of its methodological predecessors (especially source and form criticism), *Redaktionsgeschichte virtually 'set the agenda' for the full range of critical inquiry into the Gospels* during the second half of the twentieth century. Obviously, this amounts to no small contribution.

In the second place, *Redaktionsgeschichte* has drawn the attention of biblical scholars to the Evangelists as authors of literary products. At first blush, such an observation may seem self-evident if not trivial; in fact, it is of utmost significance in light of redaction criticism's methodological precursors and successors. Prior to *Redaktionsgeschichte* the primary critical tasks in the interpretation of the Gospels were the delineation of their literary sources (if any) and the discernment of their pre-literary traditions: that is, source and form criticism. While these approaches were not repudiated with the onset of redaction criticism, the critical perspective did become realigned toward the Evangelists as authors and their Gospels as literary wholes. Of course, a shift in perspective does not necessarily entail a substantive shift in exegetical method or results: many advocates of the so-called 'New Criticism' and other literary-critical strategies retort, with some justification, that redaction criticism remained every bit as 'disintegrating' of the Gospels, oblivious to their narrative wholeness, as were source and form criticism.[48] Nevertheless,

---

48. Among others, see Via, *Kerygma and Comedy,* pp. 72-78; R. M. Frye, 'Literary Criti-

without the countervailing stress of *Redaktionsgeschichte* on the synthesis of the Gospels by Evangelists who functioned as creative authors, the force of the literary critics' response might have been lost on us. Indeed, without the redaction-critical emphasis on authors and literary products, the current movement toward newer literary-critical approaches might not have been as expeditious.

Third, *Redaktionsgeschichte* has made a persuasive case for *the fundamentally theological character of Mark and of the other Gospels*. To say that various themes are interwoven by the author of Mark in his Gospel is, for the redaction critic, accurate but insufficient: these themes carry theological freight and communicate the Evangelist's distinctive *Tendenzen*.

To speak of the Evangelists' authorial intentions, and of the Gospels as vehicles of their creators' religious beliefs, has come to be regarded in some quarters as reflective of engagement in exegetical pursuits that are passé at best and spurious at worst. Against this *redaktionsgeschichtlich* understanding, at least three attacks have been mounted. (1) Some scholars, for instance, have adopted a position of critical agnosticism: in their view, the notion that the Evangelists molded their source materials in accordance with kerymatic convictions has been merely assumed, not demonstrated. As John Meagher has put it, '. . . we simply do not know how [the Gospels] were meant to be read'.[49] (2) Among interpreters influenced by New Criticism, the recovery of authorial intent, even if possible, is irrelevant, if not critically fallacious: for them, the meaning of a text resides in the sense or senses that the words bear or might come to bear, altogether apart from the intention of the author in penning those words or from other such extrinsic inquiries into the author's psychology or life-history.[50] To quote Monroe Beardsley: 'we must distinguish between the aesthetic object and

---

cism and Gospel Criticism', *TToday* 36 (1979), pp. 207-19; A. Stock, *Call to Discipleship: A Literary Study of Mark's Gospel* (GNS 1; Wilmington, DE: Michael Glazier, 1982), pp. 12-15. Despite its sobriquet, the movement known as 'New Criticism' flourished in the 1940s and 1950s; it is by now so old as to be considered dead in many quarters. Still, among biblical critics its influence persists.

49. Meagher, *Clumsy Construction*, p. 20.

50. The best-known exposition of this principle is that of W. K. Wimsatt, Jr, and M. C. Beardsley, 'The Intentional Fallacy', *SRev* 54 (1946), pp. 468-88 (repr. in W. K. Wimsatt, Jr, *The Verbal Icon: Studies in the Meaning of Poetry* [Lexington: University of Kentucky, 1954], pp. 3-18). Cf. Northrop Frye's dictum that all works of literary art 'are like a picnic to which the author brings the words and the reader the meaning' (cited in E. D. Hirsch, Jr, *Validity in Interpretation* [New Haven and London: Yale University Press, 1967], p. 1).

the intention in the mind of its creator'.[51] (3) Other scholars insist that Mark's Gospel, like any work of literary art, cannot and should not be mined for the historical data to which it purportedly refers or for such theological insights as are stressed by redaction critics; the meaning of Mark lies completely in its 'narrativity'. Representative of this perspective is Frank Kermode:

> We are so habituated to the myth of transparency that we continue, as Jean Starobinski neatly puts it, to ignore *what is written* in favor of *what it is written about.* . . . The claim that the gospels are truth-centered continues for many to entail the proposition that they are in some sense factual, even though the claim takes the form of saying that the fact they refer to is theology. It remains exceedingly difficult to treat them as stories, as texts totally lacking transparency on event.[52]

Collectively, these criticisms constitute a formidable attack on the redaction-critical understanding of the Gospels as conveyances of their author's theology. However, some things surely can be said in defense of the Evangelists' authorial and theological intentions.

(1) To respond first to what I have styled as 'critical agnosticism', we should concede, with Meagher, that it is possible to exaggerate the extent to which an Evangelist like Mark has 'orchestrated his received material to the tune of his special ideas and purposes'.[53] Moreover, we should be prepared to grant the existence of other motives behind the Second Gospel besides the proclamation of the *kerygma,* such as sheer curiosity about what Jesus had done and said. However, neither of these possibilities precludes or renders improbable the communication of a distinctive, theological point of view as a significant aspect of Mark's intentions (N.B. 1.1; 15.39),[54] And to discredit from the start the possibility of the Evangelists' theological interests on the basis of its potential for exaggeration is in itself a critical overstatement.

51. M. C. Beardsley, *Aesthetics: Problems in the Philosophy of Criticism* (New York: Harcourt, Brace, 1958), pp. 18-19.

52. F. Kermode, *The Genesis of Secrecy: On the Interpretation of Narrative* (Cambridge, MA, and London: Harvard University Press, 1979), pp. 118-19, 121.

53. Meagher, *Clumsy Construction,* p. 25.

54. If Meagher is correct (ibid., p. 22) that Mark's readers were just curious about Jesus, this very well might betoken a theological judgment among that readership that Jesus was an especially apt object of curiosity.

(2) Much ink has been spilled over 'the intentional fallacy', and this is no place to rehearse all of the pros and cons on the subject.[55] Let this much be said: in the interpretation of a text, some appeals to 'authorial intention' are invalid, and others may be quite valid indeed. The principal intention (!) of Wimsatt and Beardsley's essay on the subject was to refocus the attention of literary critics on *the literary work itself*: on the basis of the author's intention, the design or plan in the author's mind as it might be discerned from external evidence (letters or commentaries, for example), it is fallacious, argued Wimsatt and Beardsley, either to deduce textual meaning or to assess the author's artistic success in achieving whatever objective was sought in producing the text.[56] From this sensible observation, Wimsatt and Beardsley did not infer — nor need we infer — that the meaning intended by an author like Mark evaporated once the ink was dry, or that such meaning is unworthy of critical pursuit, or that a text is only some free-floating sequence of words whose meaning has nothing whatever to do with the author who wrote them.[57] To plead for the illegitimacy of redaction-critical inquiry into the Second Evangelist's intentions, and of the pursuit of that inquiry at the level of his Gospel's verbal meaning, is rather doctrinaire, and misunderstands the point of the anti-intentionalist critique.

(3) Like its assault on authorial intention, the New Critical stress on texts as artefacts, the product of a craft, arose in reaction to the Romanticist use of poems and other literary works as windows onto the psychological state or emotional experience of their authors.[58] In Continental biblical study of the eighteenth and nineteenth centuries, this assumption of 'textual transparency' was manifested in the pursuit of doctrinal or his-

55. For further discussion, see Hirsch, *Validity,* pp. 1-23 (see especially pp. 10-14), and Barton, *Reading the Old Testament,* pp. 147-51, 167-70.

56. 'We argued that the design or intention of the author is neither available nor desirable as a standard for judging the *success* of a work of literary art . . .' (Wimsatt and Beardsley, 'The Intentional Fallacy', p. 468).

57. Thus Hirsch (*Validity,* p. 13): 'If a text means what it says, then it means nothing in particular. Its saying has no determinate existence but must be the saying of the author or a reader'. No less a defender of semantic autonomy than Paul Ricoeur is in otherwise hearty agreement with Hirsch on this point: 'If the intentional fallacy overlooks the semantic authority of the text, the opposite fallacy forgets that a text remains a discourse told by somebody, said by someone to someone else about something' (*Interpretation Theory: Discourse and the Surplus of Meaning* [Fort Worth, TX: Texas Christian University Press, 1976], p. 30).

58. See W. K. Wimsatt, Jr, and C. Brooks, *Literary Criticism: A Short History* (New York: Knopf, 1957), pp. 657-80.

torical information conveyed by biblical narrative, with the result that interpretation of the narrative itself suffered eclipse.[59] In the New Critical view, all of this has amounted to a basic hermeneutical misplacement. Art is an end in itself; a poem is intended, not to transmit historical, philosophical, or any other kind of information, but simply to exist as a poem. By extrapolation, the meaning of a biblical narrative like Mark's Gospel cannot be reduced to the historical data or religious beliefs to which it purportedly refers; the meaning of Mark is utterly nonreferential and resides entirely in its own narrative shape. As Hans Frei puts it, 'the location of meaning in narrative of the realistic sort is the text, the narrative structure or sequence itself. . . . [In narrative,] the text, the verbal sense, and not a profound, buried stratum underneath constitutes or determines the subject matter itself'.[60]

Frei and the New Critics have put their finger on a significant aspect of much biblical literature: it tells stories. As such, the narrative form of Mark should be respected, not manipulated facilely as a convenient repository for historical or theological data. Still, this notion of the 'nonreferential' character of narrative harbors a dubious, if not mistaken, assumption: namely, that all literature, even all narrative, functions in the same manner — solely as works of art, rather than as discourse conveying something beyond itself. This may be true of poetry and imaginative fiction; it is less clear, and yet to be demonstrated, that narratives like the Gospels fall in the category of 'literature' in that sense *(Dichtungen)* and therefore should be evaluated *exclusively* according to the interpretive canons appropriate to poems and novels.[61] In other words, when Luke prefaces his narrative with the express intention that Theophilus 'may know the truth concerning the things of which [he has] been informed' (1.4), and when John concludes his narrative with the hope 'that you may believe that Jesus is the Christ, the Son of God, and that believing you may have life in his name' (20.31), is not the reader of these works[62] justified in moving beyond the acknowledged character of the Gospels as

---

59. H. W. Frei, *The Eclipse of Biblical Narrative: A Study in Eighteenth and Nineteenth Century Hermeneutics* (New Haven and London: Yale University Press, 1974).

60. Ibid., p. 280. Cf. M. Weiss, 'Die Methode der "Total-Interpretation"', *VTSup* 22 (1972), p. 91: 'Hier [in der Sprache der Dichtung] ist Gestalt selbst Gehalt. . . . Die "Form" des Kunstwerkes ist nicht nur ästhetische Hülle, sondern auch wesenhafter Ausdruck'.

61. Barton, *Reading the Old Testament,* pp. 159-67, develops this line of criticism in a lucid and penetrating manner.

62. The same would apply, *mutatis mutandis,* to Matthew and Mark.

works of narrative art, following their authors' lead in pursuing legitimately 'ostensive' theological issues?[63]

Notwithstanding these criticisms of their validity, three contributions of *Redaktionsgeschichte* as applied to Mark and to the other Gospels thus seem secure: its emphasis on the Evangelists as creative authors in their own right; its recognition of the fundamentally theological character of the Evangelists' intentions; and its multiple concerns for the history, tradition, theology, and literary character of the Gospels. To affirm these assets of *Redaktionsgeschichte* is not to deny the many procedural quandaries that have plagued Markan redaction criticism (or, for that matter, *Redaktionsgeschichte* when applied to the other Gospels). At this point, I am not speaking strictly of method or procedure as such. Redaction criticism has always been more than merely a step-by-step recipe for interpreting texts; often its practitioners have not even bothered to articulate such 'steps'. At heart, the term 'redaction criticism' has described a distinctive way of viewing biblical texts, the salient features of which were outlined at the beginning of this chapter. An interpretive approach to the Bible, or to any literature, can present a valid or at least defensible *point of view* on textual interpretation, apart from the success or validity of a particular *method* of interpretation that it may propose. For all of its problems, to which we now must turn, Markan redaction criticism has brought to bear on the text some distinctive perspectives: the importance of the author and his intention, the Gospel as expressive of theological interests, and the need for an exegetical approach incorporating concerns historical, theological, and literary. It is these hermeneutical *Tendenzen* that may prove to be the enduring contribution of redaction criticism of Mark and the other Gospels.

---

63. Historically, Christian readers have believed that they were so justified. Thus asserted Papias (c. 130): 'I did not rejoice in them who say much, but in them who teach the truth, nor in them who recount the commandments of others, but in them who repeated those given to the faith by the Lord and derived from truth itself' (Eusebius, *H.E.* 3.39.3: cf. Irenaeus's well-known comments on Mark's preservation of the preaching of Peter: Eusebius, *H.E.* 5.8.3). Note also Athanasius: 'Here, as indeed is expedient in all other passages of Sacred Scripture, it should be noted, on what occasion the Apostle spoke; we should carefully and faithfully observe to whom and why he wrote, lest, being ignorant of these points, or confounding one with the other, we miss the real meaning of the author' (*Contra Arianos* 1.54). Likewise, throughout the history of biblical exegesis, the assumption has been made that the Gospels are intended to call attention to what they are *about*.

Liabilities

On the other hand, the *redaktionsgeschichtlich* approach is not without its drawbacks. In most cases they are the obverse, or more accurately the overextension, of the very assets we have just observed.

1. To begin with, it is one thing to accent the Evangelists' authorial intention; it is something else to situate this concern at the center of one's interpretive procedure. As I have suggested, Markan redaction critics were justified in doing the former; the latter, however, has created nothing but problems for practitioners of the method:

a. By placing the author and his intention(s) at the methodological center, redaction criticism of Mark (on the assumption of Markan priority) has sought answers to exegetical questions that are, by definition, unverifiable.[64] This we have witnessed repeatedly in our investigations both of Markan discipleship and of the attempts devoted to methodological refinement: in order to discern the earliest Evangelists' redactional (= authorial) activity, every investigator has been compelled to engage in often highly speculative conjectures about the history of traditions *behind* the Evangelist, assumptions unamenable to empirical analysis yet invariably determinative of that researcher's exegetical or methodological results. Typically, those conclusions scatter in all directions and are impossible to validate, for they are primarily a function of their proponents' divergent perspectival starting-points, and only minimally the result of a controlled method of interpretation. In short, by locating the author at the center of critical attention, Markan redaction criticism has raised fundamental questions that it cannot answer, at least with any reasonable degree of confidence.[65]

b. Another problem flows directly from the preceding: by concentrating on the author, Markan redaction criticism (again presupposing Markan priority) has been forced to appeal to interpretive clues lying beyond the boundaries of the Gospel itself.[66] The paradox of Markan redac-

---

64. The same could be said of the redaction criticism of Matthew, predicated on the Griesbach hypothesis, and of John, on the assumption of its independence from the Synoptics.

65. Highlighting a different Markan motif (the destruction of the temple), and employing a procedure different from mine, Donald Juel has reached a similar conclusion: *Messiah and Temple: The Trial of Jesus in the Gospel of Mark* (SBLDS 31; Missoula, MT: Scholars, 1977), pp. 214-15.

66. More narrowly in connection with Markan Christology, this point has been made by J. D. Kingsbury, 'The "Divine Man" as the Key to Mark's Christology — The End of an Era?', *Int* 35 (1981), pp. 243-57.

tion criticism is that it must traffic in evidence that is not redactional: the key to the enterprise lies in the fragile reconstruction of the shape, development, and utilization of pre-Markan (non-textual) tradition. Since the method demands speculation about hypothetical sources, the *Geschichte* of whose *Redaktion* can be plotted, its practitioners are compelled to devise traditio-historical scenarios of greater or lesser plausibility, extrinsic to the actual content of the Gospel. Periodically, Markan scholars balk at such a dubious procedure and decide to treat the Gospel as a whole, taking it for what it says and refusing to quarry for pre-Markan strata; then, however, they are no longer practicing redaction criticism as it has been customarily defined — nor do they need to do so.

2. At least intuitively, many Markan redaction critics seem to be aware that their interpretations ultimately cannot be made to turn upon the author and his editorial activity. It is for this reason, I believe, that the focus of so many *redaktionsgeschichtlich* studies of the Second Gospel is not so much on precise redactional discriminations as on particular *themes* that are evident in the text: the mystery of the kingdom of God, the disciples' incomprehension, the suffering Son of man, and so forth. Of course, many exegetes have regarded the specification of such themes as an inherently redaction-critical operation;[67] however, this is a point of methodological confusion. Although the identification of the Gospel's themes could be incorporated into a larger redaction-critical paradigm, *such a determination is not an intrinsically redaction-critical criterion but a literary-critical assessment.*

It is equally misleading, I suspect, to follow the redaction-critical path of identifying Mark's thematic concerns as strictly theological in character. Doubtless many motifs in Mark *do* connote special theological interests of the author; yet such themes may also, or in some cases primarily, reflect the historical or social circumstances in Mark's environment or community, or may resonate at a deeper psychological level with the readers of that Gospel.[68] Furthermore, any one or a combination of these referents (the historical, social, theological, or psychological) may be addressed, not

---

67. To select one example among many: E. Schweizer has argued that the methodological starting-point for distinguishing tradition and redaction in Mark should be the delineation of such themes as *Wundercharakter*, teaching, and the suffering Son of man ('Anmerkungen', pp. 35-46).

68. For an insightful discussion of the subtle interconnections that can exist between an author and his readers in the realm of emotions, values, and beliefs, consult W. C. Booth, *The Rhetoric of Fiction* (2nd edn; Chicago and London: University of Chicago Press, 1983), pp. 89-147.

only by themes, but also by other literary devices, such as plot, settings, and characters. In any case, themes and other such literary characteristics rightly belong in the center of an interpretation of Mark in a way that 'theology' or 'theological themes' do not, if for no other reason than that the form of the Second Gospel is not that of a self-consciously theological treatise; Mark is first of all a narrative and, at least on initial approach, should be treated as such.

3. A third major liability of the redaction-critical approach has been its tendency toward 'methodological imperialism': by attempting to answer questions, not only of theology and *Traditionsgeschichte*, but of literary composition and socio-historical setting as well, redaction criticism has taken on more issues than its critical apparatus was designed to handle. Even more pointedly, it can be argued that the very procedure of *Redaktionsgeschichte* operates at cross-purposes with that method's intention to treat the Gospels as literary wholes:

> Literary criticism seeks to apprehend a text as a whole or as a totality. . . . From Marxsen up to the most recent times, however, redaction critics . . . have split Mark into tradition (sources) and redaction and have sought to establish chronological-genetic-causal relations between these two strata. . . . As provocative and interesting as these studies often are for historical purposes, the text as a whole, as a narrative, in the form in which it confronts the reader and needs explication, is lost sight of.[69]

Nor has redaction criticism adequately fulfilled its promise to illuminate the historical and sociological *Sitz im Leben* of Mark's Gospel. Thus, while reaping the fruits of *Redaktionsgeschichte* in his own study of the Second Gospel, Howard Clark Kee urges the adoption of more sophisticated tools of social analysis, since 'much of what passes for historical writing about the New Testament is docetic. It fails to take account of the full range of social and cultural factors that shaped the Christian communities and their ideas, their understanding of themselves, and their place in the universe'.[70]

---

69. Via, *Kerygma and Comedy*, pp. 72-73. Note also the similar criticisms of T. E. Boomershine, 'Mark the Storyteller: A Rhetorical-Critical Investigation of Mark's Passion and Resurrection Narrative' (Ph.D. diss., Union Theological Seminary [New York], 1974), pp. 23, 25, 31, 334-38; and N. Perrin, 'The Interpretation of the Gospel of Mark', *Int* 30 (1976), p. 120.

70. Kee, *Community*, p. ix. Likewise, L. E. Keck, 'On the Ethos of Early Christians', *JAAR* 42 (1974), pp. 435-42, upholds the corrective value of an ethological approach to the study of Christian origins.

Overall, redaction criticism has set forth most of the different kinds of critical questions that can reasonably be posed of the Gospels; it is doubt-ful, however, that *Redaktionsgeschichte,* or any methodological approach, is conceptually or practically equipped to answer all of those questions.

To sum up: Markan redaction criticism is neither a 'sacred cow' nor a 'white elephant'.[71] Born of the marriage of this century's scholarly occupa-tions and theological preoccupations, the *redaktionsgeschichtlich* point of view has schooled us in the appreciation of the Second Evangelist's literary creativity, the theological cast of his Gospel, and the need for critical breadth in the interpretation of Mark and the other Gospels. Corre-sponding to these contributions have been certain liabilities of the redaction-critical perspective: its misplacement of the author at the center of textual interpretation, occasioning tendentious and unverifiable exegeses; its overemphasis on the strictly theological quality of the Markan narrative; and its incompetence to answer all of the critical questions that it has raised. In pondering appropriate strategies in the study of Mark, we need not only to move beyond redaction criticism but also, and perhaps more important, to move forward in a manner respectful of the lessons it has taught us.

D. A Model for Synthetic Markan Interpretation

Toward the end of a penetrating review of recent redaction-critical com-mentaries on Mark's Gospel, Ulrich Luz draws five conclusions, three of which should chasten and guide our thinking about more adequate meth-ods in the interpretation of that Gospel:

1. Eine Bilanz [in der Markusforschung] scheint unmöglich.
2. *Hypothesenfreudigkeit sollte Grenzen haben,* zumal angesichts der wieder erstarkten Professorengläubigkeit in studentischen Kreisen.
3. Ein gemeinsames Kennzeichen der drei Kommentare . . . ist eine gewachsene Skepsis gegenüber der Tragfähigkeit traditionsgeschicht-licher Rekonstruktionen.[72]

71. The double metaphor is borrowed from V. P. Furnish, *The Moral Teaching of Paul: Selected Issues* (2nd edn, rev.; Nashville: Abingdon, 1985), pp. 11-28.

72. U. Luz, 'Markusforschung in der Sackgasse?', *TLZ* 105 (1980), pp. 653-54 (Luz's em-phasis). Of the other two conclusions, one concerns *traditionsgeschichtlich* hypotheses (that they should strive for simplicity [*Einfachheit*] and presuppose continuity with historical cir-

Previous chapters of the present study have contributed additional scraps of evidence in support of Luz's third conclusion: that skepticism concerning traditio-historical reconstructions of Mark is both growing and justified. Any formulation of fresh or revised approaches to the study of the Second Gospel must grapple with Luz's other two observations: that Markan research is in desperate need of a balance of perspectives, and that salutary limits should be imposed on the 'joy of hypothesizing', to which Markan scholars sometimes are disposed (and in which, as Luz candidly remarks, they often have been schooled). Actually, we have here two sides of the same coin: for a balance of hermeneutical perspectives would do much to demarcate appropriate boundaries for scholarly hypotheses, even as such limits would help Markan research to achieve the equilibrium that has been lacking.

Before that hermeneutical balance can be attained, first we must identify the various interpretive perspectives and remind ourselves of what each intends to help readers understand about Mark. Certainly there is a place for both the 'classical disciplines' as well as those of more recent vintage.

1. *Historical criticism,* the location of the text in time and space, may be subdivided into two distinct and complementary fields of investigation: 'the situation or situations described in the text itself and the situation or situations which gave rise to the document'.[73] The former, which is concerned with the internal historical aspects of the text, particularly the *Sitz im Leben* Jesu, we might refer to as historical analysis proper.[74] The latter, which addresses the external socio-historical forces that gave rise to the text, might be regarded as sociological analysis.[75]

---

cumstances wherever possible). This prescription is well-taken but need not concern us here. The other conclusion ('Für die Markusforschung scheint nach wie vor die *Vokabelstatistik* von . . . Wert zur Diagnose redaktioneller Bearbeitung zu sein' ['Sackgasse', p. 654]) I hesitate to accept, for the reasons detailed in Chapter 6.

73. Hayes and Holladay, *Biblical Exegesis*, p. 42.

74. In this category I would include, for example, the pioneering work of Johannes Weiss, *Jesus' Proclamation of the Kingdom of God* (ET and ed. R. H. Hiers and D. L. Holland; LJS; Philadelphia: Fortress, 1971), and the more recent studies of A. E. Harvey, *Jesus and the Constraints of History* (Philadelphia: Westminster, 1982), and E. P. Sanders, *Jesus and Judaism* (Philadelphia: Fortress, 1985). In the same vein are inquiries into the historical disciples: Cullmann, *Peter, Disciple — Apostle — Martyr,* and Klein, *Die Zwölf Apostel.*

75. Although this critical perspective has been acknowledged for years (cf. Marxsen's recognition of the 'second' and 'third' *Sitze im Leben*), only recently have the tools for its implementation begun to be refined. In the sociological study of Christian origins in general, the seminal works are J. G. Gager, *Kingdom and Community: The Social World of Early Chris-*

2. *Tradition criticism* is a rubric customarily applied to the study of biblical traditions, either oral or written, and how they have been employed, modified, and synthesized in the course of a community's history. Though often distinguished from source and form criticism,[76] and sometimes considered identical to redaction criticism,[77] tradition criticism is more than either of these definitions suggests. Perhaps this label could be adopted as a hermeneutical umbrella, encompassing the full range of development that culminates in a biblical text and embracing all of the oral and literary stages that purportedly underlie that text: source criticism, form criticism, redaction criticism, and perhaps even textual criticism. Like historical criticism (as that term has just been defined), *Traditionskritik* is essentially historical in orientation, but it is history of a different kind: if 'historical criticism' probes for the history *in* a text, then 'tradition criticism' incorporates the many disciplines that attempt to trace the history *of* a text.[78]

3. Though once associated with the excavation of sources within a composite document (a procedure usually known as source criticism), *literary criticism* currently denotes the disciplined analysis of the aspects of a narrative, with attention to such matters as the narrator and his point of view, narrative style, plot, time, settings, and characters.[79] Unlike historical

---

tianity (Englewood Cliffs, NJ: Prentice-Hall, 1975); A. J. Malherbe, *Social Aspects of Early Christianity* (Baton Rouge and London: Louisiana State University Press, 1977); G. Theissen, *Sociology of Early Palestinian Christianity* (Philadelphia: Fortress, 1978); and H. C. Kee, *Christian Origins in Sociological Perspective: Methods and Resources* (Philadelphia: Westminster, 1980). For sociological inquiries into the community behind the Second Gospel, see (among many others), Kee, *Community of the New Age;* J. A. Wilde, 'A Social Description of the Community Reflected in the Gospel of Mark' (Ph.D. diss., Drew, 1974); and Robbins, *Jesus the Teacher.*

76. Hayes and Holladay, *Biblical Exegesis,* pp. 85-93.

77. Thus J. C. Rylaarsdam (ed.), in W. Rast, *Tradition History and the Old Testament* (GBSOTS; Philadelphia: Fortress, 1972), p. vii.

78. Recent specimens include R. Riesner, *Jesus als Lehrer: Eine Untersuchung zum Ursprung der Evangelien-Überlieferung* (WUNT n.s. 7; Tübingen: Mohr [Siebeck], 1981); Kelber, *The Oral and the Written Gospel;* and J. D. M. Derrett, *The Making of Mark: The Scriptural Bases of the Earliest Gospel* (2 vols.; Shipston-on-Stour, Warwickshire: Drinkwater, 1985).

79. Scholarship in the realm of New Testament literary criticism is ever burgeoning, and not all of the contributions proceed from the same understanding of that discipline. Nevertheless, important among general contributions to the field are W. A. Beardslee, *Literary Criticism of the New Testament* (GBSNTS; Philadelphia: Fortress, 1970); N. R. Petersen, *Literary Criticism for New Testament Critics* (GBSNTS; Philadelphia: Fortress, 1978); and N. Frye, *The Great Code: The Bible and Literature* (New York and London: Harcourt Brace

and tradition criticism, this interpretive approach focuses on the structure and composition of a text when viewed in its own right, the 'world' or horizon of meaning generated by the text itself, apart from its historical or traditional context and determinants. Closely aligned with literary analysis is *rhetorical criticism.* The two are not identical: whereas the focus of literary criticism is on the internal dynamics of narrative, rhetorical criticism concentrates on discourse and its power to persuade (that is, either to induce action or to alter attitudes) through creative invention, arrangelent, and style.[80] Nevertheless, literary and rhetorical criticism are complementary and ultimately more like than unlike each other: both attend closely, if not exclusively, to the text itself as an aesthetic object; both are engaged in the analysis of structural conventions in a narrative or discourse; both are interested in the effect exerted by texts on their readers.

4. *Redaktionsgeschichte,* I have suggested, has rightly drawn our attention to the role of the Evangelists as genuine authors and creative theologians. Implicit in this insight is a legitimate, critical approach that is not necessarily antagonistic to the disciplines considered thus far, yet is identical with none of them. Here the accent would be, not on what the Evangelist is saying *in* a narrative (a literary-critical, or *kompositionskritisch,* concern), but on what the Evangelist as religious thinker is communicating *through* a narrative. Nor in this category would we assess the Evangelist's

---

Jovanovich, 1982). R. Alter, *The Art of Biblical Narrative* (New York: Basic Books, 1981), is a significant study of Old Testament narratives, full of insights for New Testament interpreters as well. Prominent among literary-critical analyses of the Second Gospel are Kermode, *Genesis of Secrecy;* Rhoads and Michie, *Mark as Story;* Kingsbury, *Christology;* Via, *Ethics;* and E. S. Malbon, *Narrative Space and Mythic Meaning in Mark* (San Francisco: Harper & Row, 1986). On Markan discipleship in narrative perspective, see Tannehill, 'Disciples in Mark'; W. Egger, *Nachfolge als Weg zum Leben: Chancen neuerer exegetischer Methoden dargelegt an Mk 10,17-31* (OBS 1; Klosterneuburg: Österreichisches Katholisches Bibelwerk, 1979); J. Dewey, 'Point of View and the Disciples in Mark', *SBL 1982 Seminar Papers* (Chico, CA: Scholars, 1982), pp. 97-106; and H.-J. Klauck, 'Die erzählerische Rolle der Jünger im Markusevangelium: Eine narrative Analyse', *NovT* 24 (1982), pp. 1-26.

80. The most serviceable treatments of rhetorical criticism based on classical standards are G. A. Kennedy, *Classical Rhetoric and Its Christian and Secular Tradition from Ancient to Modern Times* (Chapel Hill, NC: University of North Carolina Press, 1980), and idem, *New Testament Interpretation Through Rhetorical Criticism* (Chapel Hill, NC, and London: University of North Carolina Press, 1984). Among significant rhetorical investigations of the Second Gospel, see B. H. M. G. M. Standaert, *L'Evangile selon Marc: Composition et genre littéraire* (Brugge: Sint Andreisabdij, 1978): J. Dewey, *Markan Public Debate: Literary Technique, Concentric Structure, and Theology in Mark 2.1–3.6* (SBLDS 48; Chico, CA: Scholars, 1980); Robbins, *Jesus the Teacher.*

attitude *toward* tradition; here the emphasis would be on the writer's own theological point of view, potentially *irrespective* of the tradition and its development. Redaction criticism has tended to assume that, for discerning the Evangelist's theological perspective(s), the identification of his adjustments of received tradition was a practical necessity. This is not so. For instance, there is really no way to know for sure whether Mark's celebrated Christology of suffering was derived completely from his traditions, was present in those sources but augmented by the Evangelist, or was cut out of whole cloth by the author himself. Though this presents a pressing, if not insuperable, problem for *Traditionsgeschichte* (§2 above), it makes not the slightest bit of difference in the interpretive approach I am describing here: *regardless* of its origin, the motif is manifestly important for understanding Mark's overall point of view.

Though this theological interest has long been associated with redaction criticism,[81] to refer to this fourth critical discipline as *Redaktionsgeschichte* would muddy the methodological waters: the approach I envisage depends little, if at all, on the actual discrimination and analysis of a Gospel's tradition and redaction (which, in the case of Mark, is all but impossible to accomplish). Though I shudder at its syntactic clumsiness, this interpretive approach might be referred to as a *schriftstellerische Tendenzkritik*, an *authorial-theological criticism* of the Gospels (or other biblical literature).[82]

5. Finally, *reader-response criticism* could be used to describe forms of analysis that highlight neither the matrix of historical events nor the traditional conventions out of which texts evolved, neither a document's internal dynamics nor the theological meanings intended by its author, but rather the variety of meanings that it is possible and legitimate for readers to perceive in texts. In this category would fall those forms of literary criticism that emphasize the function of the reader in construing textual meaning: 'A literary text must . . . be concerned in such a way that it will engage the reader's imagination in the task of working out things for himself for reading is only a pleasure when it is active and creative'.[83] Though by no

---

81. Cf. Tagawa's comment that the purpose of redaction criticism is to rediscover 'l'orientation fondamentale' of each Evangelist's theology (*Miracles et Évangile*, p. 3).

82. Here 'author' is used in the sense of the 'incarnate author' (Via, *Kerygma and Comedy*, p. 78) or the 'implied author' (Booth, *Rhetoric of Fiction*, pp. 71-75, 151), rather than in reference to the historical Evangelist.

83. W. Iser, *The Implied Reader: Patterns of Communication in Prose Fiction from Bunyan to Beckett* (Baltimore: Johns Hopkins University Press, 1974), p. 275. Cf. also Kermode, *Genesis of Secrecy*, pp. 53-54.

means divorced from the surface features of a text (§3 above) or from the meanings intended by its author (§4), genre analysis in its various manifestations[84] qualifies as a type of reader-response criticism insofar as a genre is 'that sense of the whole by means of which an interpreter can correctly understand any part [of a text] in its determinacy'.[85] Similarly, structural exegesis[86] seems to represent a theory, not so much of writing, as of reading: thus Robert Polzin defines structural analysis as the intersection of 'the object investigated [that is, the text] and the operational laws of the subject [or reader] who constructs the model',[87] and Dan Via pursues an interpretation 'in which the narrative is realized [and] is completed only in the acts of the interpreter'.[88] Finally, under the heading of 'reader-response' strategies, one might locate canonical criticism: in accord with many forms of structuralist criticism (at least on this point), the canonical approach discovers or devises a particular genre, or social conventionality, by means of which Mark, or any biblical text, can be read with competence — the genre of 'canonical religious literature', or (more simply) 'scripture'.[89]

---

84. There have been almost as many proponents as *Gattungen* propounded for Mark: comedy (Via, *Kerygma and Comedy*); tragedy (E. W. Burch, 'Tragic Action in the Second Gospel: A Study in the Narrative of Mark', *JR* 11 [1931], pp. 346-58; G. G. Bilezikian, *The Liberated Gospel: A Comparison of the Gospel of Mark and Greek Tragedy* [BBM; Grand Rapids, MI: Baker Book House, 1977]; D. Gewalt, 'Die Verleugnung des Petrus', *LB* 43 [1978], pp. 113-44); catechesis (G. Schille, 'Bemerkungen zur Formgeschichte des Evangeliums: Rahmen und Aufbau des Markus-Evangeliums', *NTS* 4 [1957], pp. 1-24); aretalogy (M. Hadas and M. Smith, *Heroes and Gods: Spiritual Biographies in Antiquity* [Religious Perspectives 13; New York: Harper & Row, 1965]; J. M. Robinson, 'On the *Gattung* of Mark (and John)', *Jesus and Man's Hope* [I; ed. D. G. Miller and D. Y. Hadidian; A Perspective Book; Pittsburgh: Pittsburgh Theological Seminary, 1970], pp. 99-129); 'a parabolic miracle story' (Via, *Ethics*, p. 126 n. 12); biography (C. H. Talbert, *What Is a Gospel? The Genre of the Canonical Gospels* [Philadelphia: Fortress, 1977]).

85. Hirsch, *Validity*, p. 86 (entirely italicized in the original). Cf. Ricoeur, *Interpretation Theory*, p. 75: 'to understand is not merely to repeat the speech event in a similar event, it is to generate a new event beginning from the text in which the initial event has been objectified'.

86. D. Patte, *What Is Structural Exegesis?* (GBSNTS; Philadelphia: Fortress, 1976), is a general treatment of biblical structuralism. From a Marxist perspective, F. Belo, *A Materialist Reading of the Gospel of Mark* (Maryknoll, NY: Orbis Books, 1981), is a structuralist commentary on the Second Gospel. See also the analysis of Egger, *Nachfolge*.

87. R. M. Polzin, *Biblical Structuralism: Method and Subjectivity in the Study of Ancient Texts* (SemSup; Missoula, MT: Scholars, 1977), p. 33.

88. Via, *Ethics*, p. 17; cf. pp. 4-5, 179, and idem, *Kerygma and Comedy*, pp. 9-10.

89. Though B. S. Childs disavows involvement in so-called 'canonical criticism', as though it were only one more implement to be added to the arsenal of critical exegesis (thus idem, 'The Canonical Shape of the Prophetic Literature', *Int* 32 [1978], p. 54), he deftly cap-

How might one visualize this panoply of critical approaches to the interpretation of Mark? Years ago M. H. Abrams envisioned a triangular arrangement of four elemental coordinates of all theories of art criticism:

Figure 2

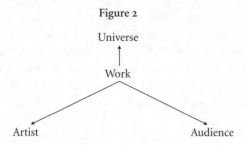

Abrams suggested that 'Although any reasonably adequate theory takes some account of all four elements, almost all theories . . . exhibit a discernible orientation toward one only': thus Romanticist critics probed the text for what it could tell us about its author; the critical school known as 'realism' emphasized the relation of the work to the universe of ideas or materialities that it was understood to reflect.[90]

Abrams's comparative framework of critical theories can assist us in conceptualizing the variety of interpretive strategies for Markan study, provided that we modify it in three ways: by differentiating and elaborating his coordinate of 'universe' into two separate but complementary coordinates; by extracting a chief 'idea' — 'theology' — from the 'universal' coordinate and pairing it with the 'artist' (= authorial intention); and by emphasizing even more than did Abrams the interrelation of the lateral vertices. With these modifications,[91] our synthetic model might be schematized in the following manner:

---

tures the spirit of the canonical approach: 'It belongs to the exegetical task that the modern reader takes his point of standing within the authoritative tradition by which to establish his identity with the Christian church' (*The New Testament as Canon: An Introduction* [Philadelphia: Fortress, 1985], p. 40). For a divergent approach to canonical exegesis, consult the books by J. A. Sanders: *Torah and Canon* (Philadelphia: Fortress, 1972); *Canon and Community: A Guide to Canonical Criticism* (GBSOTS; Philadelphia: Fortress, 1984); and *From Sacred Story to Sacred Text: Canon as Paradigm* (Philadelphia: Fortress, 1987).

90. M. H. Abrams, *The Mirror and the Lamp: Romantic Theory and the Critical Tradition* (New York: Oxford University Press, 1953), p. 6.

91. Another adaptation of this model is presented by Barton (*Reading the Old Testament*, pp. 201-4), whose discussion, while hewing more closely to Abrams's treatment, was suggestive in the creation of my own schema.

Figure 3

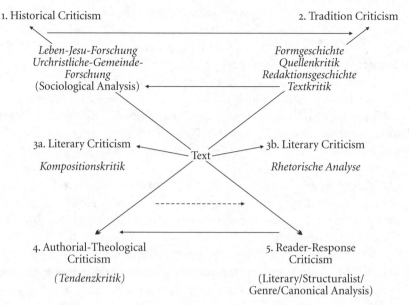

1. Historical Criticism 2. Tradition Criticism

Leben-Jesu-Forschung
Urchristliche-Gemeinde-
Forschung
(Sociological Analysis)

Formgeschichte
Quellenkritik
Redaktionsgeschichte
Textkritik

3a. Literary Criticism
Kompositionskritik

Text

3b. Literary Criticism
Rhetorische Analyse

4. Authorial-Theological
Criticism
(Tendenzkritik)

5. Reader-Response
Criticism
(Literary/Structuralist/
Genre/Canonical Analysis)

Some comments on the preceding diagram are in order:

1. Recalling the many difficulties encountered in redaction criticism's placement of the author at the center of interpretive concern, it seems more judicious to follow Abrams's lead and to locate the text and its 'surface' interpretation (via literary and rhetorical criticism) at the center (§3 of Figure 3). Regardless of the sort of exegesis to which a student of the Second Gospel may be attracted, the text and its interpretation must remain central in the hermeneutical enterprise.[92] However debatable our historical, traditional, theological, or generic hypotheses may be, indisputably the text lies before all of us: its reality is beyond debate, and repeatedly close readings of it afford the best corrective to the unbridled *Hypothesenfreudigkeit* against which Luz has cautioned us.[93] Stated differently, the

---

92. Sometimes it is said that literary-critical insights can extend the results of redaction criticism (thus F. J. Matera, reviewing Best's *Following Jesus* in *Int* 38 [1984], p. 94: 'the decade of the 80s will see narrative and literary approaches complement and advance the older disciplines'). Speaking chronologically, in terms of the history of scholarship, this is accurate; speaking procedurally, it gets the matter backwards: the older disciplines may extend those literary approaches on which they are based.

93. This is not to say that all literary or rhetorical critics will always agree; it is to say

Gospel narrative and its analysis is methodologically intrinsic to the interpretive task; the other four approaches, albeit valuable, are by definition hermeneutically extrinsic, since all are concerned with viewing the text in ways (historical, traditional, theological, generic) that are external to the surface concerns of the text itself.[94]

2. Although the text and its literary interpretation hold the center of this synthetic paradigm, such interpretation need not and ought not be regarded as the only, or even the 'best', hermeneutical approach to Mark or to the other Gospels.[95] Indeed, none of the five interpretive avenues in this model constitutes the 'best' or 'correct' way to read Mark. *All* of them have the potential for generating fresh ways of reviewing the Gospel, and they should be respected as such, regardless of those predilections of individual scholars that have been shaped by the internal logic of their chosen interpretive models. In other words, according to the terms laid down by the exegetical methods that they have opted to employ, the (old) New Critics and the structuralist exegetes are justified in repudiating the pursuit of the author and of his theological intentions; however, it is illegitmate for these interpreters to impose *their* hermeneutical ground rules on all other critics and to denounce, categorically, all pursuits undertaken on other exegetical bases (which are, in principle, equally valid

---

that the object of their investigation, the text, stands as the most ready and reliable control over all forms of interpretation.

94. It is ironic that structuralist interpreters sometimes reprove historical critics, and historical critics chide structuralist interpreters, for pursuing meaning beyond the confines of the text. The fact is, in their very different ways, critics in *both* camps are engaged in generating interpretations extrinsic to the text: historians pursue traditional developments behind the text; structuralists seek deep, socio-psychological structures underneath the text. Likewise, when literary critics such as Norman Petersen chastise historical critics for using biblical texts as 'windows' onto historical or traditional objects outside of the text (*Literary Criticism*, pp. 18-19, borrowing the famous metaphors coined by Murray Krieger in *A Window to Criticism: Shakespeare's Sonnets and Modern Poetics* [Princeton: Princeton University Press, 1964], pp. 3-4), they fail to recognize that their preferred use of texts as 'mirrors' is equally extrinsic, insofar as the interpreter's attention is thereby reflected — or deflected — onto those reading the text and their own world (§5 in Figure III).

95. At times this is suggested or implied by erstwhile tradition-critics who have been converted to literary-critical approaches. Cf. Perrin, 'Towards an Interpretation', pp. 1-2 (my emphasis): 'A *true* interpretation of the gospel must be built upon that which is peculiar to it as a discrete text [i.e., its structure, plot, characters, etc.]'. If by this Perrin means that such literary-critical considerations are foundational, I can agree; but if he means that such interpretation is 'true' in the sense of being 'uniquely valid', then he is presenting a value judgment or claim of faith that is beyond the province of biblical criticism to verify.

though different from their own). The same caveat, of course, applies in reverse.

3. Although the text and its surface interpretation intrinsically provide an indispensable control over hypotheses generated by the four extrinsic interpretive avenues, such proposals may be chastened as well by ongoing, critical dialogue between approaches historical and traditional (§1 and §2 in Figure 3), and between concerns for the author and his audience (§4 and §5).[96] That is to say, my suggested model would encourage the mutually corrective insights presently provided by historical and tradition criticism, as well as the potential for critical exchange between *Tendenzkritik* and reader-response criticism.[97]

4. The synthetic model that I am proposing claims the further advantage of acknowledging the past contributions of *Redaktionsgeschichte,* and other tradition-critical methods, while remedying their liabilities. Thus this paradigm balances the many virtues of the redaction-critical perspective — its emphasis on authors as theological thinkers, its desire to read texts holistically, and its recognition of the importance of interpreting

---

96. In many cases a 'longitudinal' corrective (e.g. of §1 over §4, or of §2 over §5) would be precluded, to the degree that many authorial or audience-response forms of criticism are intrinsically ahistorical. Still, a reciprocal corrective of the more literary approaches by their more historical counterparts could be indirectly, though partially, achieved through the critique by §3 of all the rest. This seems to be what Norman Perrin is driving at when he argues that literary criticism is necessary for a proper 'historical understanding' of a text in its literary form and language (*Jesus and the Language of the Kingdom: Symbol and Metaphor in New Testament Interpretation* [Philadelphia: Fortress, 1976], pp. 5-9).

97. In some cases the latter might be impossible (hence the hashed lateral line between §4 and §5 in Figure 3): for example, many forms of structuralist analysis rule out an interest in the author and the effect of his intentions on the reader. But this is not true in all cases: for instance, despite his stress on the exclusively linguistic object of New Testament theology, Erhardt Güttgemanns conceptualizes a text in terms of the correlation between its sender, receiver, subject matter, and verbal and non-verbal situational elements ('Theologie als sprachbezogene Wissenschaft', *Studia Linguistica Neotestamentica: Gesammelte Aufsätze zur linguistischen Grundlage einer Neutestamentlichen Theologie* [BET 60: Munich: Kaiser, 1971], pp. 213, 225-26). Moreover, Charles Talbert tacitly proposes a reciprocal corrective between what I have described as authorial and audience criticism (§§4 and 5) when he points out that 'redaction criticism can trace a theological theme throughout a gospel but what it cannot do is to arbitrate among the many competing themes in a gospel and assign positions of relative importance to them. Genre criticism holds out the possibility of such a task of arbitration' ('Introduction: Seminar on Gospel Genre', in *Colloquy on New Testament Studies: A Time for Reappraisal and Fresh Approaches* [ed. B. Corley; Macon, GA: Mercer University Press, 1983], p. 201).

texts in traditio-historical context — while relieving that single method of the burden of analyzing all such features, a task that redaction criticism has never been conceptually equipped to perform. For example, redaction critics often have gravitated in their interpretation of the Gospels to a type of *Kompositionskritik,* which they have been insufficiently prepared to execute; under such circumstances, the appropriate response would be, not for *Redaktionsgeschichte* to fade out of the exegetical framework altogether, but for it to yield to other methods (such as literary criticism) that are better fitted to address such *kompositionskritisch* questions.[98]

5. My suggested hermeneutical paradigm might be criticized as encouraging an exegetical eclecticism. Depending on how one defines that charge, it may or may not be valid. Thus, if one grants the existence of a variety of interpretive avenues that a critic might pursue in his or her reading of Mark, then one should feel no compunction in acknowledging the need for a variety of commensurate, critical disciplines and in deliberately selecting (ἐκλέγεσθαι) the vehicle that will best enable him or her to negotiate that particular approach to the Gospel. On the other hand, one is not thereby entitled to pick or choose one such approach and then to conduct one's scholarly passage as though the hermeneutical 'roads not taken' did not exist; in that sense, the synthetic model proposed here is quite definitely not eclectic. Contemporary exegesis of Mark, or of any of the Gospels, is a project of such vastness that a division of scholarly labor is both desirable and responsible; however, it is needful for the laborers in one area of the vineyard to stay in touch with, and to learn new skills from, those engaged in other aspects of the harvest.

Indeed, during the years to come, the quality of scholarly conversation about Mark may depend in large measure on the willingness of its exegetes to devote less energy to overworking any particular critical method (such as *Redaktionsgeschichte*) — less effort even to the arguably futile enterprise of forever generating novel interpretations of the Second Gospel that are

---

98. According to Petersen (*Literary Criticism,* p. 18), 'it [is] necessary to recognize that redaction criticism cannot answer the questions it has raised without becoming something else, namely, literary criticism. Redaction criticism is, in this respect, a victim both of its disciplinary ancestry and of its own designs'. With this estimate I both agree and disagree. Petersen has accurately perceived that *Redaktionsgeschichte* is poorly qualified to deal with many of the literary issues it raises: he assumes, inaccurately I think, that those are the only issues worth raising. If the Gospels' theological concerns are to be adequately addressed, the *tendenzkritisch* component of redaction criticism must not be forsaken in favor of literary criticism — for the latter is ill-equipped to grapple with *those* concerns.

not, at the same time, tenuous — and more energy to pondering the different kinds of questions, and their interrelationships, that might fruitfully be asked in reading that text.[99] In this regard, John Barton has issued some sane admonitions to Old Testament interpreters that are conspicuously pertinent to New Testament scholars as well, and to Markan redaction critics in particular:

> The task of criticism . . . is not to be always producing new interpretations, but to explain interpretations on which readers can agree. . . . Over and over again biblical critics seek *correct* methods, *prescriptive* answers to the question how we may read the Old Testament, successful procedures and techniques that we *ought* to be looking for. . . . Instead of asking which method is 'right', we might ask what is really going on in the reader when he is using each of them, what kind of reading they belong to.[100]

99. See C. Breytenbach, *Nachfolge und Zukunftserwartung nach Markus: Eine methodenkritische Studie* (ATANT 71; Zürich: Theologischer Verlag, 1984), for a superb example of the kind of interdisciplinary study that should be cultivated.

100. Barton, *Reading the Old Testament,* pp. 206-7.

Conclusion: Deductions and Directions

It remains for us to gather the threads of this investigation and to ponder their implications for the advancement of Markan research.

1. The task we set ourselves in this study was to evaluate the validity of the redaction-critical method in the interpretation of Mark's Gospel. As I suggested in the Introduction, a method receives its validation to the extent that it works, that is, to the degree that it produces interpretations that are reliable and confirmable. A restricted yet controlled analysis of different types of Markan *Redaktionsgeschichte* has demonstrated that, despite its widespread use and approbation by contemporary scholars, redaction criticism does not work when applied to the Second Gospel. When representative 'conservative', 'mediate', and 'liberal' exegetes have employed *Redaktionsgeschichte* in interpreting the role of the disciples in Mark, their conclusions have mirrored their preconceptions about what they more or less expected to find. Although virtually identical in procedure, their respective applications of redaction criticism appear to have bridled their assumptions, or to have verified their own and others' exegeses, little or none at all.

Even if this be granted, an incredulous reader might respond, So what? If three investigators use the same method in reading the same text and come up with three different interpretations, why should one have expected this to be otherwise? Is it not true that 'Exegetes working with the same texts, relying on the same methods, and adducing the same data reach differing conclusions only because they weigh the evidence differently and have varying sensibilities and insights'?[1]

---

1. L. E. Keck and G. M. Tucker, 'Exegesis', *IDBSup*, p. 297.

Well, yes and no. Certainly, differences in critical taste do account for many differences of interpretation. Yet to say that dissimilar conclusions are reached *only* because evidence is weighed in different ways, with varying levels of insight, is an overstatement. It is equally possible that 'the same methods' on which exegetes have relied are either so flawed or so unsuited to the texts being examined that they cannot channel their proponents' sensibilities or calibrate the interpretive scales on which the evidence is weighed.[2] This possibility, I suggest, has become a reality in the research of Meye, Best, and Weeden, in view of (a) the striking disparity of their exegetical outcomes, and (b) the remarkable correspondence of those results to their disparate presuppositions. At least in the work of these representative interpreters, 'the fundamental rule of biblical exegesis' (as enunciated here by Gene M. Tucker) appears to have been violated:

> The fundamental rule of biblical exegesis is that the interpreter must be obedient to the text itself, that is, he or she must allow the texts to determine their interpretation. Another way to put this is to say that understanding of a text must finally be "standing under", listening to, and hearing the text, and not one's own voice.[3]

To the degree that the method has not effectively inhibited the normal tendency of its practitioners to 'hear their own voice', Markan redaction criticism must be reckoned a failure.

2. Notwithstanding the care with which most of them have been undertaken, recent endeavors to refine Markan redaction criticism also fail to persuade. Among the half-dozen attempts that we have considered, the same problems recur: the scholarly premises on which they rest are subject to dispute; the modes of argumentation that they employ are at best circular and fallacious at worst, the rigor that they inject into Markan *Redaktionsgeschichte* tends, paradoxically, to undermine the worth of the method.

3. In a more positive vein, we have seen that redaction criticism pre-

---

2. In ruminating over critical method, most scholars assert or assume the necessity of exegesis in informing, correcting, or realigning the interpreter's assumptions: see E. Krentz, *The Historical-Critical Method* (GBSOTS; Philadelphia: Fortress, 1975), pp. 33-72; Keck and Tucker, 'Exegesis', p. 297; Hayes and Holladay, *Biblical Exegesis*, pp. 5-28. N.B. Peter Stuhlmacher's affirmation: 'The strength of the critical biblical sciences has always been their capacity for self-correction' (*Historical Criticism and Theological Interpretation of Scripture: Toward a Hermeneutics of Consent* [Philadelphia: Fortress, 1977], p. 76).

3. G. M. Tucker, 'Editor's Foreword' to Krentz, *The Historical-Critical Method*, p. v.

sents a distinctive and valuable point of view in the interpretation of Mark: a perspective that emphasizes the Evangelist's literary and theological creativity. While the particulars of the redaction-critical *method* seem to profit us little in Markan exegesis, this redaction-critical *perspective* has immeasurably enriched our appreciation of the kind of literature that Mark and the other Gospels typify.

4. The points at which Markan *Redaktionsgeschichte* has usually collapsed are those where the method has tried to treat certain issues without the conceptual equipment to resolve them. Irrespective of the method's competence to deal adequately with such concerns as the historical and social setting of the Gospel, its pre-literary background, or its literary and rhetorical power, Markan redaction criticism has rendered noteworthy service in drawing or recalling these issues to the attention of biblical exegetes. Though anchored in the historical-critical approach to the Bible, the *redaktionsgeschichtlich* perspective has reminded us of something that medieval interpreters simply took for granted: that biblical texts do not bear a single sense but harbor a rich plenitude of meaning.[4] They encourage not one but many different avenues of interpretation: investigations historical, sociological, and traditio-critical; inquiries into the author's intentions, the reader's responses, and the literary and rhetorical contours of the narrative itself. By posing critical questions that it cannot satisfactorily answer, redaction criticism has indirectly invited us to push beyond that method into interpretive realms that might enable us, in the felicitous expression of Bernhard W. Anderson, to listen more attentively to the various sonorities that resonate within a biblical text.[5]

5. In this study the interpretation of the disciples in Mark has functioned, not as an end in itself, but as the foil for examining these methodological concerns. Even so, the reader might wish to know where I come down, exegetically, on the subject. At the end of the day, I find most persuasive a Type II, or 'mediate', reading of Markan discipleship, such as that ex-

---

4. Cf. the *Quadriga*, the theory of the fourfold sense of Scripture — the literal, the allegorical, the tropological (moral), and the anagogical (eschatological) — to which the church subscribed from the time of John Cassian (d. ca. 435). To suggest that biblical (and other) texts are characterized by a multiplicity of meaning is *not* to sanction the reprehensible practice of construing a text to say whatever it pleases the interpreter to hear. Contrary to widespread belief, so-called precritical exegetes were as clear and unwavering on this principle as their twentieth-century counterparts: see B. Smalley, *The Study of the Bible in the Middle Ages* (3rd edn; Oxford: Basil Blackwell, 1983).

5. B. W. Anderson, 'The Problem and Promise of Commentary', *Int* 36 (1982), p. 350.

emplified by Ernest Best. As we have witnessed, Best's interpretation regards the disciples both positively and negatively: throughout the Markan narrative they fluctuate between success and failure, between approval and disapprobation. This, I think, is a more nuanced and cogent exegesis of Mark than that of either Robert Meye (representing our Type I, or 'conservative', position) or Theodore Weeden (in the Type III, or 'liberal', camp): the former tends to emphasize the disciples' merits (such as their special selection by Jesus [Mark 1.16-20; 3.13-19a] and their promotion of his ministry [6.7-13, 35]) at the expense of their blemishes; the latter accents their vices (such as their misapprehension of Jesus' messiahship [8.32b; 9.33-34; 10.35-41] and their desertion in Gethsemane [14.50-52]) without due regard for their virtues. Since the presentation of the disciples in the Second Gospel is characterized by a certain ambiguity and internal tension, Best's more complex treatment carries greater conviction. However — and here I would part company with Best — I do not believe that a 'mediate' interpretation depends on redaction-critical analysis: one may arrive at such an exegesis on the basis of a close reading of the text, mindful of its surface subtleties, without ever inviting *redaktionsgeschichtlich* conjectures into the discussion.

With these conclusions I hope to have established a basis, however slender, from which contemporary Markan interpretation may proceed. It is not my intention here to chart the course of that advance; however, some implications for future research might be suggested.

First, whatever else may have surfaced during the course of this inquiry, Markan redaction criticism has emerged as a rather hopeless, if not misbegotten, enterprise. I would not presume to declare a moratorium on the practice or refinement of the method; Markan scholars will, after all, pursue whatever studies they find interesting. *De gustibus non est disputandum.* Moreover, it would not be entirely without benefit for the kind of experiment I have conducted to be replicated, using different, representative interpreters, or perhaps even focusing on an altogether different Markan motif (for example, eschatology instead of discipleship). It would be interesting to observe the degree to which another such analysis corroborated, or failed to support, the results garnered in this study. On the whole, however, I am frankly skeptical of the benefits to be gained from the continued practice of *Redaktionsgeschichte* with Mark's Gospel, if undertaken on the same bases as those of most redaction-critical studies of the past thirty years. Learning which questions cannot be answered by the use of a particular method may not be as thrilling as discovering those which can, but the former is an aspect of scholarship no less important than the latter.

Second, the theological orientation of the Markan text, which the *redaktionsgeschichtlich* perspective has taught us to discern, summons interpreters in the twentieth century to recognize that exegesis inevitably entails a measure of theological reflection. This is not a rallying cry for a return to the interpretive practice of the Middle Ages, when exegesis and dogmatics were essentially undifferentiated. It is to suggest, however, that engagement with a biblical text must occur in the context of modernity no less than of antiquity. I would put an even finer point on it: when Mark the Evangelist presents us with certain claims about discipleship, viewed in the light of God's activity in the world through the ministry, death, and resurrection of Jesus, as exegetes we cannot forever shunt such *sachkritisch* considerations to systematic theologians without ultimately becoming irresponsible in our exegesis.[6]

Third, the tendency of *Redaktionsgeschichte* to point beyond its own province toward other investigative areas encourages contemporary Markan exegetes to continue their exploration of new and interdisciplinary forms of interpretation. For example, if one decides (with Best) that Mark's conception of discipleship is characterized by a dynamic interplay of faith and disbelief, this does not signal the end of the exegetical process. On the contrary, it has only begun: for it is then incumbent on the interpreter to contemplate a range of questions evoked by that interpretation. Speaking historically, what setting in the life of the Markan community most plausibly gave rise to so complex an understanding of discipleship? Does this perspective betoken a pastoral concern for a church under duress (Best), a polemical debate between 'orthodox' and 'heretical' factions in early Christianity (Weeden), or another situation entirely? From a tradition-critical perspective, is there any evidence to support the possibility that one strand of the Markan 'dialectic of discipleship' (the disciples' positive attributes, perhaps) distinguished the Evangelist's source materials, leaving him free to add or to elaborate the other, more severe presentation of the twelve?[7] In literary-critical terms, how do the structure of the

---

6. With Stuhlmacher (*Historical Criticism*, p. 85) I agree wholeheartedly: 'For hermeneutics and for dealing with our texts, this means that we may not use the traditional historical method merely to inquire in critically one-sided fashion how we relate to the texts and how the texts, gotten at through the principles of analogy and correlation, can be ranked in an ancient context of events. This line of inquiry obviously retains its full right. But in addition we must again learn to ask what claims of truth about man, his world, and transcendence we hear from these texts'. See also ibid., pp. 76-91.

7. To my knowledge, Best never attributes the Markan portrayal of the disciples to this

Gospel's plot and the development of its characters amplify the tension inherent in Markan discipleship? What are the effects of such narrative dis-
cord on the reader of the Gospel?[8] To what degree would the assessment of
the disciples by a first-century (or, for that matter, a twenty-first-century)
reader depend on the interpreter's assumptions about the literary genre to
which the Second Gospel belongs?[9] The answer to none of these questions
is self-evident; we are only beginning to learn how to respond to them.
This makes of the present a most exciting and fruitful time to be engaged
in the interpretation of Mark and the other Gospels. Truly, '[the] exegetical
process is complex and cannot be reduced to a single question or a single
method. Rather, the process must be guided by a number of factors, including the particularities of the text, and the exegete's own individuality,
as well as the context within which one reads and unfolds the text'.[10]

Fourth, after demarcating the different interpretive contexts within
which a text may be unfolded, much work remains to be done in clarifying
the nature, scope, and procedure of the critical disciplines appropriate to
those contexts. This should be implicit from the multiple meanings that
have been associated with the seemingly clear-cut term 'redaction criticism'.
As we have witnessed, this expression has been used by scholars to denote
both an exegetical *technique* and an interpretive *attitude;* moreover, the latter
embraces a cluster of perspectives on the nature of a Gospel (having to do
with such things as theology, authorial intention, and a religious *Sitz im
Leben*), while the former comprises a battery of no less than a dozen different
traditio-critical tests (for summaries, modifications, arrangements, and so
forth)! Obviously, 'redaction criticism' can mean, and has meant, a number
of different things, depending on the context in which the term is used.

---

particular kind of *traditionsgeschichtlich* development. He is well aware, however, of the potential theological dissonances that could have arisen from the Evangelist's preservation of a
tradition that was not totally malleable: see 'Mark's Preservation', pp. 21-34. Best opines,
moreover, that 'wherever we see the commentators in confusion this is a sign of the preservation of tradition' (ibid., p. 30) — a provocative suggestion in light of the tangled skein of
interpretation that Chapter 2 of this study has tried to unravel.

8. Tannehill, 'The Disciples in Mark', offers a thoughtful consideration of this question.

9. C. H. Talbert's proposed subtypes of Greco-Roman biography (among others, those
which provide a pattern to follow; those which dispel a false image of a teacher and substitute a true model in its place; those which validate or provide the key to a teacher's doctrine)
are suggestive, not only of the different images that they present of biographical subjects,
but also of the various responses that they might have induced in their readers. See his *What
Is a Gospel?*, especially pp. 92-98, 133-35.

10. Keck and Tucker, 'Exegesis', p. 299.

So it is with much of the nomenclature currently used in describing New Testament exegesis. For instance, take the phrase 'rhetorical criticism'. What does this mean? Presumably it refers to a disciplined process, by means of which judgments about rhetoric are rendered. Very well, then, what is 'rhetoric'? According to George A. Kennedy, 'Rhetoric is that quality in discourse by which a speaker or writer seeks to accomplish his purposes' through such techniques as invention, arrangement, and style; for Kennedy, the goal of rhetorical criticism is 'reading the Bible as it would be read by an early Christian, by an inhabitant of the Greek-speaking world in which rhetoric was the core subject of formal education and in which even those without formal education necessarily developed cultural preconceptions about appropriate discourse'.[11] Vernon K. Robbins's study, *Jesus the Teacher,* starts out with a definition of rhetoric similar to Kennedy's: 'Rhetoric refers to the art of persuasion. Rhetorical interpretation, therefore, is concerned with strategies that change attitudes and induce action'. However, as his book progresses, Robbins increasingly associates the 'rhetoric' of Mark with the interrelation of particular narrative forms, or culturally significant strategies of audience-identification, which have no direct counterparts in Kennedy's treatment: repetitive forms, which establish a basis of familiarity between Mark and his readers; conventional forms, which presuppose the familiar; and progressive forms, which build on repetitive and conventional forms.[12] In a work that anticipated current interest in rhetorical analysis by almost two decades, Amos N. Wilder explored 'the form and style of the New Testament writings', by which he meant such things as dialogue, stories, parables, poems, images, symbols, and myths. Wilder referred to the object of his analysis, generally, as 'early Christian rhetoric', since he intended to deal 'not only with the [New Testament] writings as such but with the oral speech that lies behind them'.[13] More recently, Northrop Frye has spoken of biblical rhetoric, particularly in its kerygmatic mode, as a linguistic idiom that is fundamentally oratorical; yet his conceptualization

---

11. Kennedy, *New Testament Interpretation,* pp. 3, 5; cf. pp. 12-33. See also idem, *Classical Rhetoric,* pp. 3-17.

12. Robbins, *Jesus the Teacher,* pp. 6 (quotation), 7-12, 20-73, 76-82, 197-209.

13. A. N. Wilder, *Early Christian Rhetoric: The Language of the Gospel* (Cambridge, MA: Harvard University Press, 1964), p. 2. Wilder equated 'rhetorical analysis' with a literary approach: 'One could call [this book] a study of the literary forms and genres of the Early Church'. In spite of its 'unfortunate connotations', the term 'rhetoric' had, for Wilder, 'the advantage of covering both written and oral discourse' (ibid.).

of rhetoric, adopting modern categories of language, myth, metaphor, and typology, is ultimately that of a twentieth-century literary critic.[14] While all of these are splendid studies that shed light on the language and structure of New Testament texts, manifestly they do not operate on the basis of the same understanding of 'rhetoric' or 'rhetorical interpretation'. No one would insist that Kennedy, Robbins, Wilder, and Frye must be interested in pursuing the same inquiries; I do believe, however, that it will be difficult for conventional New Testament exegesis to know what to make of 'rhetorical criticism' as long as that rubric is used by so many interpreters in so many different senses. Here and elsewhere, clarification is called for.[15]

Finally, a philosophical conundrum: do exegetical methods actually do what is attributed to them by their practitioners? This study has assumed that the validity of an interpretive method may be judged by its capacity to inform, to correct, and to restrain the interpreter's presuppositions, to the end that she or he may be made to 'stand under' — understand — the authority of the text. Yet *are* our methods capable of administering such presuppositional correction? If there can be no interpretation apart from some pre-understanding of what is to be interpreted, if there is no escaping the hermeneutical circle, then will not our exegetical methods necessarily function at the behest of our preconceptions, no matter how self-critical we intend for them to be? To push this disturbing line of inquiry a step further: is it not the case that interpretation is shaped by the very method that is applied, by the question with which the interpreter approaches his or her subject? At least one hermeneutical theorist thinks so:

14. Frye, *The Great Code*, pp. 27-29, 209, 214, 231. Cf. Dewey, who (in *Markan Public Debate*) virtually equates rhetorical with literary criticism: '[Rhetorical criticism] is the study of the literary techniques and rhetorical structure of a text to see what light such analysis sheds on the interrelationships of the parts of the text and the meaning of the text as a whole' (p. 1). The identification is complete in Stock's *Call to Discipleship*, p. 10: 'This new movement in Bible interpretation is Biblical Literary Criticism (also called Rhetorical or Composition Criticism)'.

15. The current debate over what is implied by 'canonical criticism', or 'a canonical approach to interpretation', is as needful as it is fascinating: among others, see J. Barr, *Holy Scripture: Canon, Authority, Criticism* (Philadelphia: Westminster, 1983); B. S. Childs, 'Childs versus Barr' (a review of the preceding book), *Int* 38 (1984), pp. 66-70; idem, *New Testament as Canon*, pp. 3-53; J. A. Sanders, review of Barr, *Holy Scripture*, in *JBL* 104 (1985), pp. 501-2; idem, *From Sacred Story to Sacred Text*. Surely, among the practitioners of New Testament 'literary criticism', a similar colloquy on method(s) and perspective(s) needs to be taking place.

Even when a literary interpreter turns toward the poem and, in effect, says, 'This is a poem; I shall understand it by doing thus and thus' — he has already interpreted his task and by extension shaped his seeing of the poem. And he has already, with his method, shaped the meaning of the object. Indeed, method and object cannot be separated: method has already delimited *what* we shall see. It has told us what the object is *as* object. For this reason, all method is already interpretation; it is, however, only one interpretation, and the object seen with a different method will be a different object.[16]

If Richard Palmer is right, then we should not be surprised by the tendency of Markan redaction critics to generate interpretations that conform to their presuppositions; according to Palmer, it could not be otherwise, whether we are dealing with *Redaktionsgeschichte* or with any other form of exegesis. Nor would it help to appeal to the text as the ultimate arbiter of our assumptions and methods: if this theory is correct, then the only text we can know is the text as interpreted — and that text shifts, chameleon-like, with the shifting of our interpretive methods.

Of course, Palmer may not be right: his assertions hang on a particular set of epistemological assumptions and on a theory of meaning that requires defense on philosophical grounds.[17] At the close of a book one cannot join a hermeneutical debate of such complexity; one can merely recognize the problem and the need for continuing discussion. Still, Palmer strikes the chord on which an investigation like this should end: a renewed appreciation for the difficulty of interpretation, of the fragility of our exegetical methods, and of the necessity for rigorous examination of the presuppositions on which are based, not only our methods, but our conception of understanding itself. In a modest way, these are the issues with which this study has attempted to grapple, and to which it points both its author and his readers for further reflection and research.

16. R. E. Palmer, *Hermeneutics: Interpretation Theory in Schleiermacher, Dilthey, Heidegger, and Gadamer* (NUSPEP; Evanston: Northwestern University Press, 1969), pp. 22-23.

17. Palmer lays the groundwork for that defense in *Hermeneutics*, pp. 223-41. For a tacit rebuttal, which accords greater weight to the determinacy of textual meaning, see Hirsch, *Validity*, pp. 1-23, 245-64; cf. pp. 24-67, 109-44.

Afterword: Mark's Disciples and
Markan Redaction After Twenty-Five Years

A person who publishes a book willfully appears before the populace
with his pants down.... If it is a good book nothing can hurt [him]. If
it is a bad book nothing can help [him].

Edna St. Vincent Millay[1]

The irrepressible Miss Millay was on the money. So, too, was the author of
2 Peter 2.22, whose motto I resist out of gratitude to the William B. Eerdmans Publishing Company for reissuing this volume. *The Disciples according to Mark* was a first scholarly monograph: originally published in 1989,
its *Vorleben* was a doctoral dissertation approved in 1986.[2] Though nothing
created at age thirty-one qualifies as juvenilia, neither is it a mature work.
It is a novice's offering on the guild's altar, whose aroma drifted south of
heaven.

My aim in this Afterword is fourfold. First, I wish to explain this
book's motivation and its academic lineage, to the degree I am conscious
of it. Second, anyone who has slogged this far has a right to know how

---

1. 'To Mrs. Cora B. Millay' (25 May 1927), in *The Letters of Edna St. Vincent Millay* (ed.
A. R. Macdougall; New York: Harper & Brothers, 1952), p. 220. Between these two sentences:
'Kathleen is about to publish a book'.

2. 'An Evaluation of the Investigative Method and Exegetical Results of Redaction Criticism of the Gospel of Mark: The Role of the Disciples as a Test-Case in Current Research'
(Ann Arbor: University Microfilms International [DA8624368], 1986). Immediately before
its publication I was startled to learn that the work had been dubbed *The Disciples according
to Mark:* a punchier name that I knew would mislead a reader of the book's contents. Even
so, I would never have insisted on the dissertation's title, which would choke a giraffe.

competent critics received the book upon its original publication. Third, the reader is also entitled to know how its twinned topics — the disciples in Mark and the place of redaction criticism in that Gospel's exegesis — fare in academic conversation in 2012, at least in my estimation. Finally, I shall offer some reflections on how my mind has changed, or remained the same, a quarter-century later.

A. Huntsman, What Query?

> You always need a springboard. *The Rules of the Game* . . . arose out of my desire to return to the classical spirit, to leave behind *La Bête humaine* and naturalism and even Flaubert — a desire to return to Marivaux, Beaumarchais, and Molière. It's very ambitious, but I'd like to point out, my dear friends, 'When choosing masters, it's best to choose a plump one.' It doesn't mean you're comparing yourself to them. It simply means you're trying to learn something from them.
>
> Jean Renoir[3]

My earliest seminar in Mark's Gospel was at Duke University three decades ago. Using that opportunity to devour Markan scholarship, its many off-hand references to 'Mark's redactional technique' confounded me. I had no quarrel with redaction criticism as such. I still do not.[4] Mine was the child's simple question: How do we know? If Mark's Gospel was the earliest written, how can one differentiate what the Evangelist wrote from what he borrowed, then edited? The casual confidence, the certainty of received opinion, was the itch that aggravated me. Writing my dissertation was a thirty-month scratch.

With that simple query clutched in my sweaty fist, my biggest problems were those every graduate student must confront. (a) How do you answer it? (b) On what material do you concentrate? Robert Stein's dis-

---

3. J. Renoir, introduction to *La Règle du jeu.* ©2004 The Criterion Collection.

4. Thus, my later reflections in 'Lightfoot, Robert Henry (1883-1953)', in *Dictionary of Biblical Interpretation* (ed. J. H. Hayes; 2nd edn; Nashville: Abingdon, 1999), pp. 77-78; 'Redaction Criticism', in *Encyclopedia of the Historical Jesus* (ed. C. A. Evans; New York and London: Routledge/Taylor & Francis, 2008), pp. 491-95; 'Redaction Criticism, New Testament', in *The Oxford Encyclopedia of Biblical Interpretation* (ed. S. McKenzie et al.; New York and Oxford: Oxford University Press, forthcoming 2013).

sertation, 'The Proper Method for Ascertaining a Marcan *Redaktions-geschichte*' (Princeton Theological Seminary, 1968), was my lifeline: its condensation into several articles, published in reputable venues,[5] provided a way into my question. The harder problem was limiting its scope. The project was conceived as an examination, not of Mark, but of Markan *scholarship*. By the 1960s virtually every theological commentary or monograph on the Second Gospel was redaction-critical; I did not relish the prospect of dissertating into middle age. Comparing different studies of a common topic seemed more manageable and more interesting than haphazard plowing through whole commentaries. By then Markan Christology had been flogged nearly to death; moreover, from that topic sprang so many tangled offshoots ('Messiah', 'Son of God', 'Son of man') that controlling all the variables promised migraines. Mark's presentation of the disciples, especially the twelve, seemed more feasible and almost as important. In the early 1980s Theodore Weeden's volume[6] was still churning the waters, and Ernest Best's studies had lately been synthesized.[7] Needing a third interlocutor, ideally one veering starboard of either Best or Weeden, I contemplated Rudolf Pesch's two-volume commentary on Mark.[8] I decided against Pesch for several reasons. To be frank, I feared that my German was not equal to the challenge. Even had it been adequate, my analysis had to test like with like. I knew that a dissertation microscoping method would lay itself open to keen scrutiny of its own procedure; placing a thousand-page commentary alongside trim monographs invited comparison of a cornucopia with kumquats. A practical compromise was Robert Meye's well-executed *Jesus and the Twelve: Discipleship and Revelation in Mark's Gospel*.[9] With that decided, off I went.

As a model for the kind of study I was attempting, Albert Schweitzer's

5. 'What Is *Redaktionsgeschichte?*' *JBL* 88 (1969), pp. 45-56; 'The "Redaktionsgeschichtlich" Investigation of a Markan Seam (Mc 1.21f.)', *ZNW* 61 (1970), pp. 70-94; 'The Proper Methodology for Ascertaining a Markan Redaction History', *NovT* 13 (1971), pp. 181-98. See above, Chapter 1.

6. *Mark — Traditions in Conflict* (Philadelphia: Fortress, 1971). See above, Chapter 5.

7. *Following Jesus: Discipleship in the Gospel of Mark* (JSNTSup 4; Sheffield Academic Press, 1981); *Disciples and Discipleship: Studies in the Gospel according to Mark* (Edinburgh: T. & T. Clark, 1986). See above, Chapter 4.

8. *Das Markusevangelium* (2 vols.; HTKNT; Freiburg, Basel, and Vienna: Herder, 1976, 1977). Pesch's earlier monograph, *Naherwartungen: Tradition und Redaktion in Mk 13* (KBANT; Düsseldorf: Patmos, 1968), was more preoccupied by the Gospel's eschatology than by discipleship.

9. Grand Rapids: Eerdmans, 1968. See above, Chapter 3.

The Quest of the Historical Jesus[10] likely lurked in my subconscious. Mind you, green hubris hadn't made away with common sense. Schweitzer's is immeasurably the more ambitious project, executed with brilliance and decisive results of durable impact. What fascinated me about that survey, which I first read as an undergraduate, was its probing of the questions beneath the quest: how a way of reading the Gospels became reflective of scholars' unexamined assumptions and thereby conventionalized. Tightly compressed, the first two chapters of *The Disciples according to Mark,* and much of Chapter 8, sketch outlines of 'the quest of Mark the redactor'[11]; my discussions of Meye, Best, and Weeden occupy somewhat the strategic positions that H. S. Reimarus, D. F. Strauss, and William Wrede did for Schweitzer's argument.[12] Beyond the prickly burden of a mantle fit only for genius, adopting Schweitzer as my 'plump master' entailed costly risks. I could not countenance his imperious tone: those Olympian aperçus,[13] which still make his book such a zesty read, had no business trailing from my pen. (Yes, I drafted my dissertation by hand.) More to the point: Schweitzer's *Quest* is carefully structured to demonstrate that all genuine progress toward a proper conception of its subject inexorably advanced toward his own conclusions. When I began formulating my modest offering, I was unsure where it was headed. By the time that direction was certain, I found myself locked into an argument of my own framing. I reached a point of no return and was virtually compelled by my reading of selected evidence to reckon Markan redaction criticism a failure. To admit otherwise, even had I believed otherwise, would have scuttled my thesis. The

---

10. First complete English edition, based on the first (1906), second (1913), and sixth (1950) German editions (ed. John Bowden; London and Minneapolis: SCM/Fortress, 2000). I am dumbfounded to discover no reference to Schweitzer in *The Disciples according to Mark. Sic transit intentus auctoriti.*

11. This was the title I gave to a revision of Chapter 8 as a freestanding 'teaser' in *JSNT* 33 (1988), pp. 19-39. Professor David Hill of the University of Sheffield was instrumental in Sheffield Academic's acceptance of both that article and my monograph. For his benevolence I remain grateful.

12. Schweitzer, *Quest,* pp. 14-26, 65-109, 296-314.

13. 'Hence the fiendish joy with which [Bruno] Bauer snatches away the crutches of this pseudo-science, hurls them to a distance, and makes merry over its helplessness' (ibid., p. 136). 'In the end [Wilhelm] Weiffenbach's critical principle proves to be merely a bludgeon with which he goes seal-hunting and clubs the defenceless Synoptic sayings right and left' (pp. 196-97). Had I accused Weeden of wresting crutches from the halt or envisioned Best's bludgeoning of baby seals, my *Doktorvater* would have slain such metaphors *tout de suite.*

burden of devising a foolproof argument vexed me. It still does. Accepting the foolproof will prove you a fool. Unlike Schweitzer, I had no breathtaking pronouncement on which to end my study. That bothered me less than the danger of being trapped inside my own argument. The ironic failure of Schweitzer's *magnum opus* is that he, no less than all his skewered precursors, ultimately discovered a Jesus to his own taste.[14] I now recognize that the deduction drawn at the end of my book's sixth chapter is similar to Schweitzer's, albeit applied to the Evangelist: 'In the end, the *redaktionsgeschichtlich* analysis of Markan discipleship appears to function less as a critical control . . . [and] more as a conduit, along which the investigator's assumptions can flow, without check or impediment'. Unlike Schweitzer, however, I did not finish my book by proposing a better way (in my case, of practicing a method found unsuited for Mark). I had little idea what to put in its place. With a magisterial flourish Schweitzer concluded, 'He comes to us as one unknown'.[15] Whimpering, my argument quit without quite knowing where it had come out. More on this presently.

Since the original publication of *The Disciples,* I've wondered if there may have been another, more attenuated influence on it: the dissertation written two decades previously by my director. Substantively, *The Composition and Order of the Fourth Gospel* has nothing to do with Mark or its redaction criticism. Formally, however, both concentrate on a Gospel's redaction-critical treatment, rather than on particulars of its exegesis. In his monograph[16] D. Moody Smith articulates the complicated literary theory on which Rudolf Bultmann's Johannine commentary was predicated: a project, never undertaken by Bultmann, which nevertheless guided his interpretation of that Gospel. Based on Bultmann's suggestions, Smith reconstructs in continuous Greek texts the conjectural 'revelation discourses' *(Offenbarungsreden),* a signs source, John's passion source, and other traditions. Smith also constructs what Bultmann conjectured had been the Evangelist's original text of the Fourth Gospel, which was damaged before its reconstitution by an 'ecclesiastical redactor'.[17] Smith himself does not evaluate Bultmann's method of identifying and separating sources, though he compiles the critiques of other schol-

---

14. 'Thus each successive epoch of theology found its own thoughts in Jesus; that was, indeed, the only way in which it could make him live' (ibid., p. 6).

15. Ibid., p. 487.

16. *The Composition and Order of the Fourth Gospel: Bultmann's Literary Theory* (Yale Publications in Religion 10; New Haven and London: Yale University Press, 1965).

17. Ibid., pp. 15-56, 179-212.

ars who had.[18] Without aiming to refute Bultmann's hypothesis, Smith identifies some of its weaknesses: its minimization of John's stylistic uniformity, the plausibility of recovering subterranean sources with such precision, and the possibility of restoring the original order of a Gospel as seriously disturbed as Bultmann believed it to have been.[19] While sympathetic to Bultmann's intention, Smith reasonably asks which text the exegete is responsible for interpreting: a scholarly reconstruction or the canonical product?[20] With hindsight it appears that many of the issues Smith raises of John in the hands of its most celebrated redaction critic — style as a slippery redactional indicator, deducing an Evangelist's theology by separating redaction from tradition, the practical impossibility of verifying elaborate hypotheses — resurfaced in my deliberation over Markan *Redaktionsgeschichte*. Not once, however, do I recall mention of Smith's *Composition and Order* in the same breath — or until now the same sentence — as *The Disciples according to Mark*.

B. The Best Was Yet to Come

> This is not a novel to be tossed aside lightly. It should be thrown with great force.
>
> Dorothy Parker[21]

It is a sadly ludicrous truism that doctoral dissertations in the humanities are written for an audience of one (the student's director), at most three to five (a committee). If the dissertation be approved, never again should an author with scholarly aspirations write for so few. Should Fortune smile and one's dissertation be accepted for publication, the potential readership is enlarged,

18. Namely, Joachim Jeremias, Martin Dibelius, Burton Scott Easton, Philippe-Henri Menoud, Ernst Käsemann, Eugen Ruckstuhl, Eduard Schweizer, Bent Noack, Heinz Becker, and Paul Niewalada (ibid., pp. 57-117).

19. Ibid., pp. 238-49.

20. Smith's most devastating assessment of Bultmann's procedure is quintessentially understated: '*Das Evangelium des Johannes* is actually a commentary, not upon the canonical Gospel of John, but upon a hypothetical original document which Bultmann constructed out of the materials provided by the traditional book' (p. 244). In fairness to Bultmann, Smith, and the scholars whose work the present book considers, I should note that the Second Gospel does not exhibit the Fourth's literary aporiae and seeming disarray, which prompted Bultmann's conjectures. See p. 10, above.

21. R. E. Drennan (ed.), *The Algonquin Wits* (Kensington: Citadel, 1985), p. 116.

though the royalties thereafter are dismal reminders that a closet of regular dimensions would accommodate that audience. *The Disciples according to Mark* was reviewed far beyond my expectation (that it would vanish without a trace). As far as I know, the book was critiqued in seventeen journals: mostly American or British, though some French and German. I marveled at reviews in Italian and Finnish; I would have fainted dead away had I been able to read them. Compensating for my linguistic deficiencies, I solicited the kind services of native speakers of those tongues.[22]

What did the book's first critics make of it? General patterns are traceable. Some found its analysis 'well-written and provocative' (Muddiman), 'trenchant . . . [and] sobering' (Collins), 'thoroughly researched and eminently readable . . . a model of careful scholarship' (Donahue), a 'sustained, penetrating critique . . . accomplished with a measured evenhandedness' (Green), 'judicious and systematic' as well as 'accurate' (Fowl), clear, orderly, and rigorous with good sense ('con chiarezza, ordine, rigore e buon senso': Fusco). One reviewer upheld the book's caution that all methods stand in service of the biblical text — 'et non le contraire' (Cuvillier). 'It is always fun to attack an established dogma', particularly when the assault jibes with a reviewer's own suspicions (Hooker).[23] One reviewer noted the book's 'measure of skepticism about history of traditions work on this gospel' (Morgan); others regarded its evaluation of *Redaktionsgeschichte* as too severe (Fusco; Taeger; Räisänen). '[A]t the end of the day, Black is probably too negative' (Hooker). The most lavish praise: *Disciples* was 'a brilliant and necessary critique . . . [so] fine and thought-provoking [that] it should be self-critically pondered by all New Testament scholars. . . . It shows the potential of studying the history of research in order to redraw the contours of biblical criticism' (Morgan). Dear me. That, surely, was the

---

22. E. Best, *JTS* 41 (1990), pp. 602-7; E. K. Broadhead, *PRelS* 17 (1990), pp. 83-84; A. Y. Collins, *Critical Review of Books in Religion* 4 (1991), pp. 169-71; E. Cuvillier, *Études théologiques et religieuses* 65 (1990), pp. 272-73; J. R. Donahue, *PSTJ* 42 (1989), pp. 11-12; S. F[owl], *JSNT* 40 (1990), p. 116; V. Fusco, *Biblica* 72 (1991), pp. 123-27; J. B. Green, *CBQ* 53 (1991), pp. 314-15; W. R. Herzog II, *TS* 51 (1990), pp. 513-15; M. D. Hooker, *Epworth Review* 18 (1991), pp. 86-87; J. E. Jones, *RevExp* 87 (1990), p. 129; E. S. Malbon, *Int* 45 (1991), pp. 82, 84; R. Morgan, *Theological Book Review* 1 (1989), p. 12; J. B. Muddiman, *ExpTim* (under the title, 'The End of Markan Redaction Criticism?') 101 (1990), pp. 307-9; H. Räisänen, *Teologisk tidskrift* 96 (1991), pp. 80-81; J.-M. Rousée, *RB* 96 (1989), pp. 474-75; J.-W. Taeger, *TLZ* 115 (1990), p. 590. Addressed in German and Italian to continental audiences, the reviews by Taeger and Fusco reported the book's contents in greatest detail, for which I remain appreciative.

23. This may have been Professor Hooker's idea of fun. For me the experience had all the amusement of a barefoot stroll on broken glass.

reviewer's estimate of another book, which by editorial snafu got attached to the title of mine. In any event, redrawing the contours of biblical criticism was the farthest thing from my mind. I was trying to complete a degree and, subsequently, hold on to a job.

Mission accomplished? Not a chance. In biblical studies no mission is ever accomplished for good and all, and reviewers of *The Disciples* were quick to blast its shortcomings. Though one scholar reckoned my coverage of German works and unpublished dissertations 'thorough indeed' (Malbon), others wanted more attention to European scholarship (Fusco, Taeger), which 'would significantly alter Black's findings at various points' (Broadhead). For Malbon, too many scholars were already clambering for attention: '[The book] is, in fact, a book about books. . . . [T]he sense of reading a series of book reviews, even though they are well arranged to present the author's argument, is disappointing'. Although some (Fowl; Morgan) were satisfied by its final recommendations for a coherent interpretation of Mark, coordinating historical and literary techniques, most judged those suggestions 'too brief' (Donahue), at best programmatic without 'deal[ing] adequately with the tensions between these methods of exegesis' (Green) and at worst disappointing (Hooker). 'While the detail of Black's study is impressive, the conclusion is not startling. . . . [He] points to . . . a way beyond redactional studies to a new type of gospel criticism . . . but offers no clear, original solutions' (Broadhead). Muddiman interpreted the book as suggesting that '[Markan] redaction criticism cannot evolve; it has to be toppled by revolution'. For Donahue, however, that revolution had already come and gone in the work of Pesch and of Donahue's own teacher, Norman Perrin[24]:

> Black . . . undervalues 'composition criticism' of Mark . . . which has often yielded more interesting and solidly grounded results, underscor[ing] Mark's creativity in arranging material for theological purposes (e.g. the recurrent threefold passion prediction and subsequent misunderstanding in 8:27–10:45) and in plotting overarching themes which span the whole gospel. . . . [T]he kind of redaction criticism pilloried by Black, while still frequent in German dissertations, never became the dominant approach in the English-speaking world, especially in the United States.[25]

24. 'The Interpretation of the Gospel of Mark,' *Int* 30 (1979), pp. 115-24, esp. p. 120.
25. *PSTJ* (October 1989), p. 12. Donahue developed this line of thought in 'Redaction

Writing in Münster, Taeger also complained of my one-sided conception of the method, observing that close readings of a text could be just as subjective and erroneously opinionated as its redaction criticism.[26] In effect, Taeger called Black's kettle potted.[27]

The jury was hung on the import of *Disciples* for reflecting on exegesis appropriate to Mark. For some, the book usefully reopened the hermeneutical question, 'un débat' that will never be closed (Cuvillier), confirming the need for a methodological rethinking of whose urgency many were unaware (Fusco). 'No longer can biblical interpreters presume they are engaged in research analogous to the experiments of ordinary science, carefully constructing assured results upon assured results. The task of biblical interpretation is much more akin to work in the social sciences and humanities, where results are relative to many and varied frames of reference, open to dispute and controversy' (Herzog). Another maintained that, though 'we [may] never reach consensus' on the extent of Markan priority, the nature of Mark's sources, and our conception of its oral *Vorlage*, 'as long as scholars continue to engage in reconstructing the history of the tradition, including the pre-gospel tradition, there will be a place for redaction criticism as defined by Stein' (Collins). Still others expressed dismay at the book's concern for reliable and confirmable interpretations. Malbon chastised its failure to appreciate readings that, in all their diversity, were interesting. Räisänen asked how redaction criticism of Mark could be judged unsuitable if the method was not in fact being used, in spite of its practitioners' claims.[28]

Later in this chapter I shall answer some of these criticisms, but the stage must now be cleared for the bow of a featured critic: the redoubtable

---

Criticism: Has the *Hauptstrasse* Become a *Sackgasse?*' in *The New Literary Criticism and the New Testament* (ed. Elizabeth Struthers Malbon and Edgar V. McKnight; JSNTSup 109; Sheffield: Sheffield Academic Press, 1994), pp. 27-57. Donahue's answer to his essay's titular question is that redaction criticism is neither main street nor dead end, but rather *Querstrasse*: a crossroad where historical, traditional, literary, and theological methods continue to intersect.

26. *TLZ* 115 (1990), p. 590.

27. Best notes the same, as we shall see.

28. A reviewer who shall remain nameless rendered the critique that most baffled me. Suggesting that mine was 'an honest attempt', he opined that my 'little faith in the redaction method lay perhaps . . . in the great difficulty of separating Mark's source material from [my] theological presuppositions'. Then and now I have held theological assumptions when approaching Mark, though in this book I remain unaware of how they directly bore on the labors of that Gospel's redaction critics. This critic concluded, 'The book offers a good exercise in redaction criticism'. I lament not having made my position transparent to all.

Ernest Best. Of all the principal interlocutors of *The Disciples*, only Best responded in print to my treatment of his scholarship. The longest published anywhere, his review sums up and extends the critiques of others. It also generated a private correspondence: I replied to his review by mail, and he answered my letter. The conversation was courteous, candid, substantive, and worth replicating here. For the sake of clarity and economy in presentation, I shall quote Professor Best's criticisms, then immediately quote my replies to him in a letter dated 4 April 1991.[29]

The defendant and the plaintiff[30] opened their remarks with the customary though sincere expressions of appreciation. Best thanked Black for a 'valuable', 'thought provoking piece of writing', whose flaws forbade the conclusion 'that the redaction critical method is not a useful tool in the hands of New Testament scholars'.[31] Graciously he expressed hope that I might forgive him if his review were overly critical, owing to his emotional investment. In return, Black thanked Best 'for the depth and care with which you have probed both my work as well as some of the issues that you judge to be implicated by it', and for helping all of us better to understand Mark's Gospel.

1. Best opened by rejecting my misinterpretation of his own work. 'Your reviewer would like to answer some of the criticisms made of him but if he did so this review would turn into a lengthy article. A few examples drawn from p. 130 will suffice. Black says that I regard γρηγορεῖν as Marcan on insufficient evidence. It occurs six times in Matthew, six in Mark, once in Luke, and not at all in John. What he does not notice is that at least five of the six occurrences in Matthew depend on Mark, and that if the word were also Matthean we should in fact (allowing for relative lengths of the two Gospels) expect nine independent occurrences.'[32]

My epistolary response to Professor Best: 'In the matter of γρηγορεῖν, an explanation such as you give . . . could account for a word's being considered "Markan," while appearing with the same frequency in Matthew and Mark. However, does that not still leave unresolved for us the puzzle of whether γρηγορεῖν is more than characteristically Markan but *distinguish-*

29. I have silently amended all page references to *The Disciples* in alignment with this edition's new pagination.

30. I leave for the reader to assign these *personae*. Years later most reviewers have become friends. I have no scores to settle, nor do I feel spurred to charge or to defend. Here my job is to report.

31. *JTS* 41 (1990), pp. 602, 607.

32. Ibid., p. 603.

ably Markan, that is, redactionally so? Given the word's recurrence in various eschatological texts of the New Testament (e.g., 1 Thess 5.6, 10; Matt 25.13; 1 Pet 5.8; Rev 3.2-3, all of which you helpfully cite in *Following Jesus,* p. 159 n. 47), could not one reasonably infer that γρηγορεῖν was inherited by the Second Evangelist from his traditions, not redactionally imported by him in material such as 13.35? (I should hastily enter the caveat that "inference" is by no means tantamount to "proof," with respect to the character and scope of either pre-Markan tradition or Markan redaction.)'

'When [Black] lists συνάγειν (24 times in Matthew, 5 in Mark) among the words I regard as Marcan favourites he has simply not read the context (*Following Jesus,* p. 49 n. 51) in which I gave the figures; I was not arguing the word was Marcan but seeking to eliminate it from an argument about Marcan favourite words.'[33]

My reply: 'I can understand your perplexity with my reading of your comments on συνάγειν in *Following Jesus.* On the other hand, I confess to similar perplexity in attempting to square those comments with your observation (ibid., p. 193) that συνάγειν, though not appearing frequently in Mark, occurs only in redactional seams and, for that reason, could be taken as supporting evidence of the redactional character of Mark 6:30 (p. 192). (At this point I begin to wonder if a third party could criticize both of us, in constructing very different arguments, of pressing equivocal evidence too hard!)'

'I cannot find where I claim that θαυμάζειν is a Marcan favourite; what I did claim was that the *theme* of amazement was Marcan. Inaccurate reading of those (I have not examined in detail his study of Meye and Weeden) he is criticizing does nothing to build up confidence in the ultimate result.'[34]

Answer: 'In reading p. 387 of your *NTS* article, "The Role of the Disciples in Mark," I was led to conclude that you regarded θαυμάζειν and ἐκπλήσσεσθαι as examples of Markan redactional vocabulary on the strength of (a) their parenthetical citation in support of your claim that "The amazement of the disciples . . . [was] entirely redactional," and (b) their immediate collocation with two other words (θαμβεῖσθαι and ἐκθαμβεῖσθαι) that elsewhere you judged to be "Markan word[s]" (*Following Jesus,* pp. 111, 116 n. 20). In short, however mistaken my belief, it seemed to me that you had introduced the disputed terms into the discussion of

33. Ibid.
34. Ibid., pp. 603-4.

"amazement" in Markan redactional theology, and that your acceptance of those words as redactional thus was warranted. Nevertheless, if that neither was nor is your intention, then I should simply retract the point and apologize to you for a critical question raised on its basis.'

'Some of the comparisons drawn are also inaccurate. On p. 91 [Black] lists the words which Meye considers redactional, and on p. 198 says that Meye and I have only six words in common. Had he looked at my work more closely he would have seen that with Meye I also regard διδαχή and κατ' ἰδιάν and some forms of πολύς as Marcan words.'[35]

'Returning to pp. 91-92 and 125-27 in my *Disciples*, I see that I recorded both διδαχή and κατ' ἰδιάν in Table 1 (Meye's identification of redactional vocabulary) but neither term in Table 3 (your own such identification). As a result, neither term recurs in my comparative assessment of the redactional vocabulary on which you and Meye agree (p. 198). Evidently, at least these two terms slipped through the net I cast across those of your publications that I examined for this test, and in the interest of accuracy I am happy to have the corrections brought to my attention. The same could be said of "some forms of 'πολύς,'" if by that you mean something other than the cognate, πολλά, used adverbially (which I accounted for in *Disciples*, p. 198 n. 41). Practically, I am not certain that these few additions would materially alter my conclusion, on p. 198, regarding the relatively minimal agreement on Markan redactional vocabulary among representative redaction critics. These additions do position you and Meye exegetically closer to each other than either of you to Weeden, a result that is scarcely surprising'.

2. Best also suggested that I had inadequately conveyed my own critical intentions. 'Black has little difficulty in showing that his three representatives come up with very different answers about the role of the disciples. He does not discuss their answers to the question of discipleship, how Mark expects his readers to behave, which to your reviewer at any rate is the more important question; the other is only incidental to it. I suspect that if he had considered this theme he might not have found his three representatives differed so greatly. At times indeed he does not preserve the necessary distinction between these two themes (e.g. p. 254 n. 2).'[36]

Response: 'I agree with you that Mark's portrayal of the disciples and Mark's understanding of discipleship can be usefully distinguished, and

35. Ibid., p. 604.
36. Ibid., p. 603.

your criticism of my lapse in conflating them on p. 254 n. 2 of *Disciples* is well-taken. (However, I am less sure that a consideration of representative redaction-critical treatments of "discipleship," not "the disciples," in Mark would yield, as you suspect, results that were far removed from the ones I document.)'

'Black compares and contrasts [the] results [of his three representatives] and concludes that if such different results appear when the method of redaction criticism is applied it probably indicates a flaw in the method itself. He draws this conclusion a little too hastily. Listing the criteria used in the direction of redaction, he indicates which each scholar has thought most important. There turns out to be only one which all three used extensively. It may then be the use of different criteria to detect redaction which has led to differing results rather than the use of the method as a whole, for some criteria may be more useful in detecting redaction than others. Until this possibility has been eliminated the method cannot be faulted.'[37]

Serve returned: 'In fact, on pp. 192-202 of my *Disciples,* I conjured with that possibility and found, on the contrary, that my three representative interpreters effectively *agreed* with one another in the employment of not one but four redaction-critical criteria: Markan modifications of traditional material as discerned through comparison with Matthew and Luke, Markan arrangement of traditional material, the Markan conclusion, Markan vocabulary and style.'

'[Black] claims these writers [in Chapter 7] realized the circularity of the [redaction-critical] method, as if his original three writers had not done so (e.g. see my *Mark: The Gospel as Story* [1983], p. 10), and consciously attempted to overcome this deficiency.'[38]

Answer: 'I do not recall claiming that you, Meye, or Weeden did not realize the inherent circularity of Markan redaction criticism. On the contrary, on p. 111 of *Disciples,* I quote your own acknowledgement of this circularity (in *Mark: The Gospel as Story,* p. 10); elsewhere [p. 253] I state, "from the method's inception it has been understood that the rationale and procedure of redaction criticism is fundamentally circular."'

'At one point (pp. 290-91) [Black] does confess that he agrees most closely with the conclusion I reached on the role of the disciples, but goes on to add that it is possible to reach this conclusion by a close reading of

37. Ibid., p. 604.
38. Ibid., p. 605.

the text without resort to redaction criticism. Now Black may be able to do this, but W. H. Kelber's *Mark's Story of Jesus* [1979] uses the kind of approach Black advocates and comes up with an entirely different result! It is not so easy just to read the text and understand it. It is necessary also to say that the realization of the importance of the role of the disciples in the Gospel is a result of redaction critical work.'[39]

'Notwithstanding your reservations, I continue to think it demonstrably the case, in recent scholarship, that "one may arrive at such exegesis [as you propose on redaction-critical grounds] on the basis of a close reading of the text, mindful of its surface subtleties, without ever raising *redaktionsgeschichtlich* conjectures into the discussion" (*Disciples*, p. 291). In support of this claim one might recall the recent work of Robert Tannehill and John Donahue, among others. The contrasting interpretation of Werner Kelber may be cited, as you have, as evidence that a literary critic will *not necessarily* arrive at an exegesis like Ernest Best's (especially if such an interpretation has been less than completely "mindful of Mark's surface subtleties"); that, however, is a very different matter.'

3. Other objections raised by Best seemed, as I wrote to him, 'not entirely germane to my own project; some from among these, however, are interesting and may be worthy of further pursuit by proponents of Markan redaction criticism.' 'Black has also not enquired whether the criteria [for ascertaining Markan redaction] are independent of one another (e.g. the selection of Marcanisms and seams); such independence is important in statistical work.'[40]

'The reason for this [I wrote] is that my research led me to the conclusion that Markan redaction critics themselves either were not conducting such an inquiry or (especially with regard to the method's attempted "rehabilitators": Chapter 7) had been unsuccessful, in my judgment, in making the case that such criteria *could* be adjudged as independent of one another.'

'Black fails to ask whether our theological and other presuppositions affected the way we operated the method. We may be predisposed to look for certain conclusions and manipulate the evidence so that the result [expected] appears. Because I started as a pastor rather than as an academic I may have tended to see Mark's Gospel as pastorally oriented; this would then affect my outlook on the disciples. Doubtless Meye and Weeden have

39. Ibid., p. 606.
40. Ibid., p. 604.

their own presuppositions and these may have affected the way they have looked at the evidence.'[41]

'I attempted to treat *in extenso* the methodological presuppositions that avowedly govern the redaction criticism of each of the scholars whose work I examined (especially pp. 69-75, 108-11, 142-49, 179-83). In fact, one of my conclusions (pp. 202-3) was rather similar to what you yourself conjecture: namely, that the exegetical results seem to be affected by the exegetes' varying presuppositions of what they generally expected to find. (For another of your hypotheses, however, I found no clear evidence: namely, that Markan redaction critics were "manipulating" either the Gospel of Mark or the practice of its redaction criticism [p. 199].) However, I did not think it appropriate to speculate on the personal, professional, or theological reasons for the various presuppositions made by different scholars, inasmuch as (a) such information is generally not in the public domain and for that reason is uncontrollable, and (b) even if such information were publicly accessible, its use could be misconstrued in all manner of *ad hominem* arguments. If this be a lacuna in my argument, then it is by design and not by accident.'

'I have indeed examined more sections of Mark than either Meye or Weeden so it is a priori probable that I will have identified a longer list of Marcanisms. This failure to check the base from which Meye, Weeden and I work seriously flaws Black's conclusions. He may still be correct, but a more rigorous proof is necessary. . . . It is in the light of [distinguishing Mark's theological presentation from the historical life of Jesus] that we can see the importance of Black's failure to list the criteria for determining [pre-Markan] tradition.'[42]

'With respect to [these] criticisms . . . I can only plead that it was the intention of *this* study to do neither; as stated in different ways on different occasions (e.g., *Disciples*, pp. 33, 64-67, 205), the task that I set for myself was not to propose ways by which Markan *Redaktionsgeschichte* might be rendered more trustworthy, but rather to observe carefully and critically the work of those who have attempted such a project (or who themselves have neglected to execute just such operations as you urge). If the majority of critics were to achieve principled agreement on the extent and material dimensions of Mark's traditional and redactional base, then this would be a considerable step forward in that Gospel's redaction criticism (on the as-

41. Ibid., pp. 604-5.
42. Ibid, pp. 604, 607.

sumption of its chronological priority). Although my own study does not suggest that such a critical consensus currently exists, its establishment, as well as the analytical bases on which it may be attained, could be a needful, next stage in the evolution of Markan redaction criticism.'

4. The positive yet insufficient proposals in Chapter 8 did not escape Professor Best's laser-like penetration. 'Regrettably [Black] gives us no indication how this method [he proposes] would work in practice so that we could see if it in fact would free those who use it from error: the proof of the pudding is in the eating, not in the recipe. . . . Black seems to imagine [circular reasoning] is a danger which appears only in the redaction criticism of Mark. It is a danger to almost all New Testament scholarship. . . . Even the use of five methods or tools will not eliminate the perils of circularity. I am sure that even if all Black's five methods were to be used scholars would still come up with different answers to the same problems. The whole history of the historical critical method shows how opinions have changed from generation to generation, very often because outside influences have played on the interpreters.'[43]

Again, with a heavy sigh, I flagellated myself. 'As suggested on p. 291 of *Disciples,* I admit, readily and with my own share of dissatisfaction, that my outline of methodological approaches and their possible correlations is slender and in need of development and practical confirmation; obviously, more work needs to be done, by myself and by others. (Perhaps you can understand and forgive that I did not prosecute this at the end of a work whose text and notes already had extended 296 pages!) However, in response to two comments you make . . . , I wish to emphasize that by no means do I believe it "so easy just to read the text and understand it,"[44] or that the hermeneutical circle can be escaped through the sheer accretion of methods. In my constructive methodological comments, I was attempting to suggest, rather, that *no single method,* operating independently of others, is ultimately sufficient for the task of interpreting complex texts. That for which I am groping, though it may prove chimerical, is something like the satisfaction of a "criterion of coherence," as observed in the recent quest for the historically reconstructed Jesus: an interpretation of a document like Mark may be accorded greater credibility to the degree that it coheres with the results of exegeses undertaken from different methodological perspectives. Put differently, it seems to me that different indicators,

43. Ibid., pp. 605, 606.
44. Ibid., p. 606.

pointing in a consistent direction, may prove to be more critically satisfying than an exegesis that operates only within one methodological framework (such as redaction criticism), no matter how elegantly wrought or defensible on its own terms such an exegesis may be. In any case, I am pleased that you did not charge me (as has another reviewer) with advocacy of a revolutionary toppling of Markan redaction criticism; on the contrary, that method indisputably has enhanced the modern study of that Gospel and retains, in my judgment, a significant (albeit chastened) position among the cluster of methods to be coordinated in the interpretation of that Gospel (*Disciples*, pp. 267-87).'

Near his review's end Best proffered two 'general reflections' I thought worth engaging.

1. 'Studying Mark is like dealing with a document in code which in wartime needs deciphering. More than one solution may be possible but there are some rough tests which may distinguish between them so that the correct one can be chosen. If one solution sets out a dinner menu and another the movement of troops the second may be accepted as correct because it belongs in the context of war.'[45]

'I wonder if this analogy oversimplifies the critical procedures involved. Can the Gospels, or any biblical literature, be "decoded" in the way you suggest? Given that Mark is a stylized portrayal of the ministry of Jesus, not an overt chronicle of its author's time, place, and circumstances, with what degree of confidence may its cultural context be construed *a priori* as war-torn, uneasily peaceful, or something else? Modifying your analogy in a fanciful way to make a serious point, I wonder at times if some Markan redaction critics — among whom I would not number Ernest Best — have handed us "a dinner menu" and have asked us to read it *as though it were* a communiqué concerning troop deployment. It was with some of the dimensions and implications of this problem that *Disciples* was intended to grapple.'

2. 'Black appears to operate with the assumption that [redaction criticism] is designed to discover the theology of the evangelists. I would agree that this is a part of its purpose but it is not the whole purpose. In the preface to my first attempt at redaction criticism I expressed the hope that what I wrote would "be useful in some small way in the quest of the historical Jesus" (*The Temptation and the Passion* [1965], p. xii). . . . The only way to Jesus is through the Gospels, but if we are to go that way then we need to

45. Ibid., p. 606.

know how the evangelists manipulated the tradition which they received; while this will not itself bring us to the historical Jesus it is a necessary first step. How do we shed what Mark has contributed to the material so that we can discover the form of an incident before Mark used it?'[46]

'As to your reflection on redaction criticism and the search for the Jesus of history, I am not without sympathy. You may recall that, in *Disciples* (pp. 277-86), I recognized both the validity and the needfulness of historical criticism (with respect both to the life of Jesus and to the social location of primitive Christian communities) and the constructive interaction of such historical research with various forms of tradition criticism. Again I should emphasize that my dissertation was intended to elicit, not indiscriminate derision of redaction criticism, but salutary skepticism of its overly ambitious claims and practices with regard to a Gospel whose sources are usually considered indeterminate (*Disciples,* p. 67). Conceivably, the recognition and appropriate correction of such claims and practices ultimately could eventuate, not in the abandonment of the critical quest for Jesus, but in more rigorous methods of its pursuit. Whether or not some forms of narrative and rhetorical criticism, now in their infancy, will make enduring contributions to historical investigation as such, only time will tell. It may be, as you suggest, that the work of some literary critics amounts to an evasion of historical research. Except for the more exotic streams of deconstruction, it is less clear to me that, in principle or in practice, such evasion is necessarily implicated in all forms of literary criticism, as Amos Wilder has argued with no little eloquence.[47] My suspicion is that, in the interpretation of texts and contexts, self-styled historical critics and literary critics have much to teach and to learn from one another.'

That was not the end of it. Professor Best replied to my missive in a letter, neatly typed with a faded ribbon (29 April 1991). I shall not weary the reader with all of its contents. Let it suffice that he opened with a gracious paragraph in which he expressed hope for no hard feelings in either direction. That hope was fulfilled. At varying length he responded precisely to several of my points: acknowledging those where, on reflection, he believed he had been inconsistent, pressing others where he thought my argument flabby. Chief among the latter was the 'statistical method' I had adopted. 'In statistical work it is important to ensure that categories and

---

46. Ibid., p. 607.

47. Here I was probably thinking of Wilder's collected essays, *The Bible and the Literary Critic* (Minneapolis: Fortress, 1991).

criteria are not interdependent. That you had not done so seemed to me to leave a gap in your work.' Fair enough, say I.[48] 'This is something that needs to be further examined if comparisons are to be made.' Agreed. To my knowledge that examination has yet to be undertaken. Neither Best nor I had the appetite for it; by that time both of us were knee-deep in other projects. Cheerfully he relinquished the metaphor of 'decoding' Mark: 'I heartily agree with you that this oversimplifies the matter. I was only hoping to provoke discussion; my suggestion was by way of flying a kite.' His penultimate paragraph is worth quoting in full: 'Finally may I say that I thoroughly enjoyed reading your book. It helped me to understand myself, or rather my work, better. I hope that my review does not stop others from reading what you wrote but will encourage them to examine more deeply the methods, all of them, that we use in our scholarly work.'

Affectionately known as 'Paddy,' Ernest Best was a pastor in Northern Ireland before accepting a lectureship in Biblical Literature and Theology at St Andrews. From 1974 until 1982 he held the chair in Divinity and Biblical Studies at the University of Glasgow, and was awarded an honorary D.D. in 1999. He died in 2004 at the age of eighty-seven. I never met him but wish very much that I had. He was a scholar and a gentleman.

Still with us, thankfully, are Robert Meye and Theodore Weeden. I have yet to meet the former, *emeritus* professor and dean at Fuller Theological Seminary. In a plot-twist that would raise Roger Ebert's guffaws, mere months after defending my dissertation I was teaching in Rochester, New York, and on Sundays attended a United Methodist church whose pastor was — wait for it — the Reverend Dr. Theodore J. Weeden, Sr. We enjoyed several friendly lunches together. Not once was my dissertation mentioned. Call me Coward if you like; I prefer Discretion. During one repast I remember asking Ted about his thesis, which in revised form was central to this book's fifth chapter. How had he come to write it? 'It was the Sixties,' he said. I cannot recollect the rest of his explanation well enough for quotation. Its gist was that his own graduate work had been done in an era, not only of miniskirts and flower power, but also of anti-establishmentarians. What happens if you read Mark's Gospel as a covert assault on Peter's authority? Whatever else, you have an interesting reading — the very thing one reviewer faulted *The Disciples* for failing to deliver. Best got it right:

48. Before turning to theology, Best had studied mathematics at Queen's University, Belfast. Unawares, I had crossed swords with a samurai. How my makeshift knowledge of statistics in Chapter 7 dodged his saber I shall never know.

'Doubtless Meye and Weeden have their own presuppositions and these may have affected the way they have looked at the evidence.'[49]

C. Marking Time

> The only thing anybody today knows about Chesterfield's [*Letters*] is that Johnson said of it that it taught the manners of a dancing-master and the morals of a whore, and it must be a century since anybody read it to find out whether Johnson was right.
>
> Bernard Levin[50]

Since few shall wait for a century's elapse, let's constrict our purview to the past twenty-five years. The following review cannot be comprehensive, and I tender apologies to all who have published in these areas and are disappointed to find their work undocumented here. I mean to shortchange none. The best I can do is trace some relevant scholarly tendencies since this book first appeared. Extending my storyline from 1989, I pose the questions thus: has Markan scholarship continued down a redaction-critical track? What other paths have been taken? Have the interpretive markers I associated with Meye, Best, and Weeden reappeared in more recent Markan investigation? Has one of their readings proved more popular among professional exegetes? What patterns have lately emerged?

The Continued Quest for Mark's Sources and Traditions

To speak of Mark as redactor implies some kind of assumption about what the Evangelist was editing. In this book it was not my original purpose to examine the oral traditions or written sources presupposed by this Gospel's redaction critics; nor shall I mount such an investigation here. Yet to ignore the matter entirely is irresponsible, and the reader may benefit from brief comments at this late juncture.[51]

---

49. Ibid., p. 605.

50. *Enthusiasms* (New York: Crown, 1983), pp. 41-42.

51. For more extensive surveys of this subject, consult W. R. Telford, 'The Pre-Markan Tradition in Recent Research (1980-1990)', in *The Four Gospels 1992: Festschrift Frans Neirynck* (ed. F. Van Segbroeck, C. M. Tuckett, G. Van Belle, and J. Verheyden; 2; BETL 100; Leuven: Leuven University Press/Peeters, 1992), pp. 693-723; A. Lindemann, 'Literatur zu den

In my view the most positive reconnaissance of this area in the past twenty-five years has entailed Mark's adaptation of a known, recognizable source: the Greek translation of the Hebrew Scriptures.[52] After Alfred Suhl's pioneering study in 1965,[53] Joel Marcus's *The Way of the Lord* (1992)[54] most vigorously reopened the question with special, though not exclusive, attention to the Second Gospel's appropriation of Isaiah. Rikki Watts has argued for an even more allusive, pervasive influence of Deutero-Isaiah on Mark's theology and narrative structure.[55] Thomas Hatina presses 'a model for reading scriptural quotations and allusions that is sensitive to both the narrative of Mark's Gospel and the historical setting in which it is written'.[56] Cilliers Breytenbach widens the scriptural lens by noting Mark's use of Deuteronomy in combination with other Pentateuchal books (e.g., Mark 7.10/Deut 5.16 + Exod 21.17; Mark 12.19/ Deut 25.5-6 + Gen 38.8).[57] Stephen Ahearne-Kroll puts the Psalms back into the picture, arguing (*pace* Watts) that the Davidic suffering king is more influential in Markan theology than the Deutero-Isaianic suffering servant.[58] Contrary to Mark 2.22, here new wine is profitably fermenting in old wineskins. Less influential have been the neo-Griesbachian offerings of Harold Riley[59] and the team formed by David Peabody, Lamar Cope,

---

Synoptischen Evangelien 1992-2000 (III): Das Markusevangelium', *Theologische Rundschau* 69 (2004), pp. 369-423; C. Breytenbach, 'Current Research on the Gospel according to Mark: A Report on Monographs Published from 2000-2009', in *Mark and Matthew I, Comparative Readings: Understanding the Earliest Gospels in Their First-Century Settings* (ed. E.-M. Becker and A. Runesson; WUNT 271; Tübingen: Mohr Siebeck, 2011), pp. 13-32.

52. For convenience I restrict myself to that general denotation, even though the precise or multiple forms of the Septuagint available to the Evangelist and other first-century writers is a matter of considerable debate.

53. *Die Funktion der alttestamentlichen Zitate und Anspielungen in Markusevangelium* (Gütersloh: Gütersloher).

54. Subtitled, *Christological Exegesis of the Old Testament in the Gospel of Mark* (Louisville: Westminster/John Knox). Though not restricted to Mark, D. H. Juel's *Messianic Exegesis: Christological Interpretation of the Old Testament in Early Christianity* (Philadelphia: Fortress, 1988) is another important contribution in this vein.

55. *Isaiah's New Exodus in Mark* (WUNT 88; Tübingen: Mohr Siebeck, 1997; republished, Grand Rapids: Baker Academic, 2001).

56. *In Search of a Context: The Function of Scripture in Mark's Narrative* (Library of New Testament Studies 232; London and New York: Sheffield Academic Press, 2002).

57. 'Die Vorschriften des Mose im Markusevangelium', *ZNW* 97 (2006), pp. 23-43.

58. *The Psalms of Lament in Mark's Passion: Jesus' Davidic Suffering* (SNTSMS 142; Cambridge: Cambridge University Press, 2007).

59. *The Making of Mark: An Exploration* (Macon: Mercer University Press, 1990).

and Allan J. McNicol.[60] While this research has sensibly concentrated on methodological clarity and justification, its ensuing interpretations of Mark as redactor of Matthew (and Luke) are so remote from the mainstream that most scholars have found them difficult to accept.[61]

'If we are frank', wrote Michael Goulder, 'we have no idea whether there was a pre-Marcan Gospel, in the sense of a continuous written account of Jesus'.[62] Goulder may not have known, but there are others who do. One is M.-É Boismard, who has reconstructed in Greek and in French an intermediate, or proto-, Mark, which was influenced by intermediary Matthean and Lukan sources.[63] Boismard's is a recondite theory, though it's simple as a stick compared with that of Delbert Burkett, whose *Rethinking the Gospel Sources: From Proto-Mark to Mark* (2004)[64] is, hands down, the most heroic measure to resuscitate *Urmarkus*. Burkett posits that none of the canonical Gospels used one another as a source. Instead, there was (1) a primitive Gospel, Proto-Mark, which was revised by (2) a Proto-Mark A and Proto-Mark B, which yielded (3) Markan C-material, which (4) each of the Synoptic Evangelists used independently of each

60. *One Gospel from Two: Mark's Use of Matthew and Luke: A Demonstration by the Research Team of the International Institute for Renewal of Gospel Studies* (Harrisburg: Trinity Press International, 2002). To date, C. S. Mann's *Mark: A New Translation with Introduction and Commentary* (AB 27; Garden City: Doubleday, 1986) remains the only technical commentary working within this redactional framework. It has now been replaced in the Anchor Bible by Joel Marcus's two-volume commentary, which is based on the two-source hypothesis (see below, n. 118). On Peabody's attempt to refine Markan redaction criticism, see above, Chapter 7.

61. See, for instance, the review of Riley by W. O. Walker, Jr, *JBL* 110 (1991), pp. 346-48, and of Peabody, Cope, and McNicol by H. T. Fleddermann in *CBQ* 66 (2004), pp. 498-500. I concur with C. A. Evans: '[I]t has been recognized over and again that Matthew and Luke make the greatest sense as *interpretations of Mark*. If the Griesbach-[William] Farmer Hypothesis were correct, one would expect major breakthroughs in Markan research. After all, we would know what Mark's sources were. But Farmer's following have not cast significant light on Mark' ('Source, Form and Redaction Criticism: The "Traditional" Methods of Synoptic Interpretation', in *Approaches to New Testament Study* [ed. S. E. Porter and D. Tombs; JSNTSup 120; Sheffield: Sheffield Academic Press, 1995], pp. 17-45 [quotation, p. 26]).

62. 'The Pre-Marcan Gospel', *SJT* 47 (1994), pp. 453-71 (quotation, 453).

63. *L'Évangile de Marc: Sa Préhistoire* (Études bibliques, n.s. 26; Paris: Gabalda, 1994). Boismard's reconstructed texts are presented, ibid., pp. 243-75. For an assessment, see F. Neirynck, 'Urmarcus Révisé: La Théorie Synoptique de M.-É. Boismard, Nouvelle Manière', *ETL* 71 (1995), pp. 166-75.

64. New York and London: T & T Clark. This is the first volume in a projected trilogy, whose second installment has appeared at this writing: *The Unity and Plurality of Q* (Early Christianity and Its Literature 1; Atlanta: Society of Biblical Literature, 2009).

other. In other words, canonical Mark is a fourth generation removed from the oldest Markan source: it is a redaction of a redaction (C) of collateral redactions (A and B). Burkett's argument is stunning in its creativity, diligence, caution, clarity, and (for the most part) logical coherence. Like Boismard, he is on to something true of Markan redaction and of the Synoptic problem: namely, our evidence implies traditional and literary developments whose complexity far outstrips the explanatory power of a simple two-source theory. My primary question, which will surprise no one who has read this book, is how on earth could one verify a hypothesis like this? It has no textual basis: that is to say, there's nothing one can recover and identify as an actual Proto-Mark or its recensions A, B, and C. They are all in Burkett's brain.[65] If you grant the probability of a development as complicated as he has proposed,[66] should you be prepared to grant the improbability of its ever being recovered, whether by Burkett or anyone else? A half-century later, Burkett's source-theory for Mark offers a hermeneutical reprise of Bultmann's for John. Even if either scholar were correct, which Gospel does one interpret: the canonical document or the theoretical reconstruction by its scholarly exegete?

The Disciples in Mark: A Survey More Up-To-Date

This study identified as Type I a generally positive assessment of the Second Evangelist's attitude toward history, pre-Gospel tradition, and the role

---

65. Burkett is aware of this problem (*From Proto-Mark to Mark*, pp. 263-66), but it must be faced squarely. Thus, D. W. Geyer (*Review of Biblical Literature* 5 [2005]; http://www.bookreviews.org/pdf/4520_4581.pdf): 'Yet it remains difficult to know what one has when one has a conclusion in this area of study. It appears not to be a historical conclusion, although its rhetoric is posturing as such. Source criticism seems to want to sound like it is setting straight the historical record. Outside of corresponding independent testimony, it can do no such thing'.

66. By concentrating on literary sources and neglecting vagaries of the Gospels' oral transmission, N. H. Taylor finds Burkett's argument *insufficiently* complicated (*JSNT* 28 [2006]: 57-58). H. Wansbrough (ed.), *Jesus and the Oral Gospel Tradition* (JSNTSup 64; Sheffield: Sheffield Academic Press, 1991; rpt. London: T & T Clark, 2004), is an important collection of essays on that subject from a diverse company of international scholars. In a review of Boismard's *L'Évangile de Marc* (*CBQ* 58 [1996], pp. 535-36), Craig Evans reminds us that about two centuries elapsed between codices of any of the Synoptics and their original compositions. During that time a perpetual process of editing and updating surely occurred, which could more simply account for the minor agreements of Matthew and Luke against Mark.

of the disciples in Mark. That point of view has not vanished. Its simplest expression may be reflected by Ekkehard Stegemann, who, in a fundamentally historical essay,[67] suggests that Mark remembered the triumvirate of Peter and the Zebedee brothers as martyrs who, like Jesus, gave their lives for the sake of the good news (Mark 8.35). A more complex account emerges from the comparative study of Mark and Matthew by John Riches, who draws upon Clifford Geertz's cultural anthropology.[68] For Riches, the Second Gospel evinces complementary cosmologies: one, cosmic-dualist, 'which [sees] the origin of evil as residing in the invasion of this world by hostile angelic forces, which enslaved or ensnared men and women'; the other, a forensic view that 'attributes evil to human disobedience'.[69] Congruent with these models are two different emphases in Mark's presentation of discipleship. Aligned with the dualist view of humanity's plight, the conversionist view 'stresses the giving of the mystery of the kingdom through private instruction to an in-group of followers, sharply distinguished from the parent group from which they come'.[70] As seen in Mark 3.20-35, 'Fictive ties [of discipleship] replace natural ties *as definitive of group membership*'.[71] The restorationist view, more exoteric and engaged with the public sphere, is concentrated on 'bringing the good news to the wider world and with directly engaging in conflict with the demonic powers'.[72] These two emphases are not neatly compartmentalized; instead, they are 'different moods and attitudes' that, intermingled, color discipleship in Mark 8:22–10:52. 'The darker mood of the [dualist-conversionist] images seems to have cast its spell over the [forensic and] restorationist account'.[73] For Riches, Mark's sectarian portrait of Jesus' followers is at bottom positive: disciples are responsible agents who, sadly, are blinded and possessed by demonic forces that can be overcome only by divine rescue.[74]

---

67. 'Zur Rolle von Petrus, Jakobus, und Johannes,' *Theologische Zeitschrift* 42 (1986), pp. 366-74.

68. *Conflicting Mythologies: Identity Formation in the Gospels of Mark and Matthew* (SNTW; Edinburgh: T & T Clark, 2000).

69. Ibid., p. 51. For these formulations Riches acknowledges his debt to Martinus de Boer's essays on Paul's Jewish apocalyptic eschatology.

70. Ibid., p. 77.

71. Ibid., p. 77 (Riches's italics). 'In this respect, one (but only one) of the key markers of Jewish identity is undermined.'

72. Ibid.

73. Ibid., pp. 87-89; quotations, pp. 88, 89.

74. Ibid., pp. 88-102.

Equally sensitive to Jewish apocalypticism, yet even more positive, is Suzanne Watts Henderson's interpretation, which proceeds from a blend of *Traditionsgeschichte* and narrative criticism.[75] In six passages from the Gospel's first half (1.16-20; 3.13-15; 4.1-34; 6.7-13; 6.32-44; 6.45-52), 'Mark predicates true discipleship not on full knowledge of Jesus' precise agenda but rather on his followers' full participation in his kingdom-of-God agenda'.[76] When failing to trust 'the prevailing promises of God's coming dominion', the disciples fall short; elsewhere, however, 'they emulate [Jesus'] paradigmatic exposition of God's rule' because he has empowered them to extend his Christological witness.[77] In a redaction-critical spin-off from the notion that biological families pale in significance before discipleship, Torsten Reiprich argues that Mark's Gospel presents a transformation of Jesus' own parent into an exemplary disciple among the *familia dei:* the previously unbelieving mother of 3.20-21, 31-35 reappears at the crucifixion as the vigilant 'Mary the mother of James the younger and Joses' (15.40).[78]

Epitomized by Weeden, Type III interpreters envision Mark as operating with a longer leash on antecedent traditions, unafraid to cast the disciples in unremitting gloom. As Robert Fowler comments, 'Weeden more than anyone else broke the grip of the strong readings of Mark that had enthralled readers for centuries. By arguing that the reader is led to distance himself from the Twelve instead of identifying closely with them, Weeden broke the ancient spell of the earliest and strongest of Mark's readers, namely, Matthew, Luke, and John. Weeden shattered these corrective lenses

75. *Christology and Discipleship in the Gospel of Mark* (SNTSMS 135; Cambridge: Cambridge University Press, 2006). Like Meye — and in striking contrast with Wrede — Henderson notes that 'the chasm between the historical and narrative worlds may not be so sprawling after all: ironically, Mark may preserve, even develop, authentic traditions of Jesus' reticence precisely in service of the evangelist's own Christological purpose' (p. 256 n. 20).

76. Ibid., p. 245.

77. Ibid.

78. *Das Mariageheimnis: Maria von Nazareth und die Bedeutung familiärer Beziehungen im Markusevangelium* (FRLANT 223; Göttingen: Vandenhoeck & Ruprecht, 2008). Sympathetic with this aspect of Riches's monograph, Reiprich makes no reference to it. With Reiprich's revelation of 'the Marian secret', one might compare the altogether positive portrayal of women in Mark proposed by Susan Miller (*Women in Mark's Gospel* [JSNTSup 259; London and New York: T & T Clark, 2004]). For her, female disciples in this Gospel act in a manner befitting God's new creation that the twelve never manage; '[Mark] records the accounts of women who live their lives in such a way that the kingdom of God is revealed in the earthly context' (p. 199).

for reading Mark, but we will take years to get accustomed to reading Mark with uncorrected vision'.[79]

Some have already tossed these glasses aside. Thus, Jeffrey Gibson's literary and theological assessment of the puzzling Mark 8.14-21: what Jesus rebukes here is not (à la Weeden) a heretical Christology but, rather, a parochial limitation of salvation to Israel. The disciples had conveniently 'forgotten' to take loaves because they denied Gentiles the salvation Jesus had demonstrated was theirs in the second feeding miracle (8.1-10).[80] Tradition-critically, William Telford refreshes a suggestion Joseph Tyson made in 1961[81]: through the *personae* of the disciples, Mark assails a primitive Jewish Christianity that accepted the risen Jesus as a Davidic sovereign without according any significance to his crucifixion. 'This theory', avers Telford, 'has much to commend it, although one has to add that an equally primitive view of Jesus as the exalted, apocalyptic Son of Man shortly to return in glory is in addition being modified by the evangelist in the light of his *theologia crucis*'.[82] In Telford's judgment Weeden correctly spotted conflicting Christologies in the early church as the tacit nub of controversy in Mark but misidentified the crux: not a high view of Jesus as Son of God (which, Telford believes, the miracle stories enhance), but, instead, a Jerusalem-based Christianity that sought to control nascent Gentile churches.[83]

The most relentlessly negative account of the disciples in recent Markan study may be that of Mary Ann Tolbert.[84] Her monograph adopts a modern narrative approach that acknowledges the techniques of Hellenistic rhetoric and novels.[85] For Tolbert the tension between the Markan Jesus and his disciples is not symptomatic of competing Christologies in early Christianity; rather, 'Mark's use of disciples to illustrate the rocky

---

79. *Let the Reader Understand: Reader Response Criticism and the Gospel of Mark* (Minneapolis: Fortress, 1991), pp. 256-57. For reasons I shall explain, Fowler's own reading of the disciples in Mark seems to me a Type II; still, his is the highest encomium of Weeden's contribution in recent scholarly literature.

80. Jeffrey B. Gibson, 'The Rebuke of the Disciples in Mark 8:14-21', *JSNT* 31 (1986), pp. 31-47.

81. 'The Blindness of the Disciples in the Gospel of Mark', *JBL* 80 (1961), pp. 261-68.

82. W. R. Telford, *The Theology of the Gospel of Mark* (New Testament Theology; Cambridge: Cambridge University Press, 1999), p. 136.

83. Ibid., pp. 88-103, 135-37.

84. *Sowing the Gospel: Mark's World in Literary-Historical Perspective* (Minneapolis: Fortress, 1989).

85. Ibid., pp. 35-126.

ground [4.5, 16-17] thwarts conventional expectations' in antiquity that a teacher's disciples will support him.[86]

> The disciples in Mark, as victims of constant and increasingly broad doses of situational irony, become at the same time increasingly removed from the audience's sympathy. If irony serves to bind more closely together the audience and the narrator (and, of course, Jesus, since he shares much of the narrator's status) by underscoring their joint knowledge and point of view, it also serves to distance the audience from the witless victims of irony, whether they be high priests or disciples. The rhetorical effect of irony, then, is twofold: it builds and strengthens community among those with superior knowledge, and it excludes those with inferior knowledge.[87]

Thus, by the Evangelist's narrative design, nothing good can be said of Peter and the rest of the twelve. They are arrogant, grasping, stubborn, fearful, treacherous, miserable, grieving failures.[88] Why? Such a negative depiction stirs Mark's audience to search for flaws among themselves: 'What type of earth am *I?* Will *I* go and tell?'[89] Even more: '[P]ortraying the *disciples* as failing foils to Jesus manipulates the reader to respond by becoming a *better disciple*. . . . Mark has created in the role of the authorial audience the perfect disciple'.[90]

Splitting the difference between I and III, Type II interpretations favor Mark's positive though chastened attitude toward history, tradition, and the role of Jesus' disciples. Over this 'mediate' realm Ambivalence rules. In a socio-theological exegesis of Mark 3.19b-35, John Painter observes that the twelve (3.19, 21) — like the crowd (3.20-21), Jerusalem's scribes (3.22-30), and the natural family (3.31-35) — are quite fallible followers.[91] Space is thus made for the reader to enter Jesus' family, open to all and based, not on this world's social networks, but on the eschatological reality created by God's

---

86. Ibid., pp. 154-56, 195-211, 218-27; quotation, p. 222.

87. Ibid., p. 103.

88. Ibid., pp. 201-2, 206, 211, 218, 226.

89. Ibid., pp. 224, 299 (quotation with Tolbert's italics).

90. Ibid., p. 224 (her emphasis), p. 297.

91. Elizabeth Struthers Malbon's alliterative coinage ('Fallible Followers: Women and Men in the Gospel of Mark', *Semeia* 28 [1983], pp. 29-48) has entered the scholarly literature as shorthand for a Type II presentation of the disciples in Mark. It aptly marries their durable qualities: though they fail, yet they follow; though they follow, still they fail.

kingdom.[92] The crossing of social boundaries by Jesus' disciples, especially their relinquishment of family (see Mark 10.29-31), also figures in Richard Strelan's comparison of the Second Gospel with a wide range of Jewish apocalyptic literature (including the Books of *Enoch, Jubilees, 2 Baruch,* Philo's *On Giants,* and Qumran's *Damascus Document*). These and other specimens of ancient Jewish literature cite the legend of the Fallen Watchers (Gen 6.1-4) to point up the sinfulness of the present generation, whose fidelity to God's law is tested. For Strelan, Mark 13.32-37 adapts the same myth for similar purpose: to encourage watchful hope among an unfaithful generation (8.11-13; 9.19; 14.32-42).[93] Analyzing Xenophon's *Memorabilia,* Iamblichus's *Pythagorean Life,* Philostratus's *Life of Apollonius of Tyana,* and the Wisdom of Ben Sira, Whitney Shiner compares their presentations of philosopher-student relationships with Mark's portrait of Jesus and the twelve. Viewing the Gospel in this light, Shiner concludes:

> [In contrast to the crowds and his opponents t]he disciples, on the other hand, provide a sympathetic human perspective seriously engaged with Jesus and his meaning. The difficulty that the disciples experience in understanding Jesus, in spite of their positive orientation and commitment, makes the hiddenness of his identity a reality for the listener. . . . The tragedy of Peter's recognizing his own cowardly denial of Jesus makes real the tragedy of humanity's denial of Jesus. The disciples represent the best human reaction to Jesus. It is that which brings their failures home so tellingly to Mark's listeners.[94]

The 'mediate' readings considered to this point are historical-critical in a classical sense: they regard the Second Gospel within the framework of its social world and religious traditions. A broad swath of other Type II specimens follows modern literary criticism. A good example of close reading of the text, sans thick theory, is Larry Hurtado's 'Following Jesus in the Gospel of Mark — and Beyond'.[95] Hurtado argues that Mark portrays the

92. J. Painter, 'When Is a House Not a Home? Disciples and Family in Mark 3:13-35', *NTS* 45 (1999), pp. 498-513.

93. R. E. Strelan, 'The Fallen Watchers and the Disciples in Mark', *Journal for the Study of the Pseudepigrapha* 20 (1999), pp. 73-92.

94. W. T. Shiner, *Follow Me! Disciples in Markan Rhetoric* (SBLDS 145; Atlanta: Scholars, 1995), p. 292.

95. In R. N. Longenecker (ed.), *Patterns of Discipleship in the New Testament* (Grand Rapids and Cambridge: Eerdmans, 1996), pp. 9-29.

twelve as having two roles, both positive and negative, and 'it is in this duality that the evangelist's purpose is served and disclosed'. That purpose is pedagogical: to warn readers away from the failures of discipleship and to reveal 'Jesus [as] the only adequate model of discipleship'.[96]

Other literary critics are Markedly fascinated by the duality on which Hurtado puts his finger. Thus, Elizabeth Struthers Malbon: 'I read the data [Werner] Kelber collects for "discipleship failure" as evidence of Markan pastoral concern for the difficulty of true discipleship, which affirms both the power and the suffering of Jesus'.[97] So stated, that is a neat paraphrase of Ernest Best's exegesis — though not for his reasons. Best and other redaction critics sought to identify the tensions between the Second Evangelist's style and substance and those of the inherited traditions and cultural situation. Without repudiating such interpretations but allowing them potential to correct her own, Malbon focuses on complicated interrelations of elements within the text. She advocates a reading of Mark that recognizes its techniques for eliciting readers' identification with the disciples and takes Jesus' predictions of their persecution, arraignment, and possible martyrdom (13.9-13) as seriously as their speechless fear at the empty tomb (16.8).[98] 'If there is a connotative coloring to Mark's Gospel, the disciples represent neither white nor black but gray. The shading of the Gospel of Mark — and especially of its portrait of the disciples — is thus more subtle than that to which a polemical reading is sensitive. And the challenge of being a follower of Jesus is thus more intricately drawn. The Markan Gospel discredits not the disciples, but the view of discipleship as either exclusive or easy'.[99]

Paul Danove registers 'a profoundly ambivalent estimation of the disciples for [Mark's] narrative audience'[100] that, unlike Malbon, tilts toward

---

96. Ibid., pp. 21-27; quotations, pp. 21, 25.

97. *Narrative Space and Mythic Meaning in Mark* (San Francisco: Harper & Row, 1986), p. 179 n. 26. The similarity between Kelber and Weeden's readings of Mark are noted in Chapters 2 and 5 of the present volume.

98. E. S. Malbon, 'Texts and Contexts: Interpreting the Disciples in Mark', *Semeia* 62.1 (1993), pp. 81-102; rpt., idem, *In the Company of Jesus: Characters in Mark's Gospel* (Louisville: Westminster John Knox, 2000), pp. 100-130.

99. Ibid., 'Texts and Contexts', p. 93. Variations on this theme may be found throughout Malbon's collection, *In the Company of Jesus*, esp. pp. 41-99, 166-225.

100. 'The Narrative Rhetoric of Mark's Ambiguous Characterization of the Disciples', *JSNT* 70 (1998), pp. 21-38 (quotation, p. 36); reprinted, with elaboration, as 'A Rhetorical Analysis of Mark's Construction of Discipleship', in *Rhetorical Criticism and the Bible* (ed. S. E. Porter and D. Stamps; JSNTSup 195; Sheffield: Sheffield Academic Press, 2002), pp. 280-96.

their abject failure and the narrative's deconstruction. '[T]he narrative audience is characterized by conflicting expectations; and cultivated positive and negative elements of the disciples' characterization simultaneously encourage the narrative audience to identify with and distance itself from the disciples'.[101] The means by which he arrives at this conclusion are theoretically dense. Danove bifurcates the now commonplace 'implied reader' into 'the authorial audience' (a narrator's construction of an actual readership with preexistent beliefs, knowledge, and familiarity with literary conventions)[102] and 'a narrative audience' (whose beliefs, knowledge, and literary competence are developed by the text).[103] The narrator cultivates the narrative audience's competence through 'semantic frames' and in that process modifies preexisting frames assumed by the authorial audience. Such frames provide '(1) points of information about the particular words accommodated by the frame, (2) relationships among these words and references to other frames containing them, and (3) perspectives for apprehending and evaluating the function of these words and expectations for their content'.[104] The words in these frames may carry a positive, negative, or ambiguous valence (respectively, in Mark 15.40-41; 16.8, ἀκολουθεῖν, φοβεῖσθαι, and θεωρεῖν).[105] Mark's narrative manipulates these semantic frames to achieve different rhetorical strategies, which Danove styles as 'neutral (the absence of repetition), sophisticating (repetition that builds on the authorial audience's pre-existing beliefs), and deconstructive (repetition that undercuts pre-existing beliefs)'.[106] The exegetical payoff: by marching its readers through these strategically arranged semantic fields, 'The Gospel as gospel seeks to persuade the original believing community to assume the ideology of the narrative audience and become the believing community proposed by the narration' — notwithstanding the fact 'that the formation of the believing community envisioned by the narration is

---

101. P. Danove, *The Rhetoric of the Characterization of God, Jesus, and Jesus' Disciples in the Gospel of Mark* (JSNTSup 290; New York and London: T & T Clark, 2005), p. 126.

102. Such as one finds in E. Best, 'Mark's Readers: A Profile', in Van Segbroeck et al. (eds.), *The Four Gospels 1992*, 2.839-55; cited by Danove in 'Narrative Rhetoric', p. 23 n. 5.

103. P. Danove, 'The Characterization and Narrative Function of the Women at the Tomb (Mark 15,40-41.47; 16,1-8)', *Biblica* 77 (1996), pp. 375-97, esp. p. 377.

104. Idem, 'Narrative Rhetoric', p. 22; also 'Characterization and Narrative Function', p. 376.

105. 'Characterization and Narrative Function', p. 394.

106. 'Narrative Rhetoric', p. 24. In 'The Rhetoric of the Characterization of Jesus as the Son of Man and Christ in Mark' (*Biblica* 84 [2003], pp. 16-34), Danove applies the same kind of analysis to study of Markan Christology.

frustrated'.[107] My reason for presenting Danove's method in such detail is to note a curious point: by differentiating 'positive' and 'negative' terms in these strategically distributed semantic frames, Danove has transposed old-fashioned redaction criticism into the newfangled semiotic analysis of C. J. Fillmore, Menakhem Perry, Umberto Eco, and P. J. Rabinowitz. Moreover, Danove is well aware of this: he correlates the semantic field attributed to the author's cultivation of his 'narrative audience' with the redactional vocabulary ascertained by E. J. Pryke.[108] Dress 'tradition' as 'authorial audience' and 'redaction' as 'narrative audience', keep the author firmly centered as 'rhetorical strategist' (instead of 'redactor'), and, with Danove, you have a reasonable facsimile of Best's technique and exegesis of Mark.

Cédric Fischer closely attends to the oscillating tension, generated by Markan segments (1.16–8.26; 8.27–10.52; 11.1–12.44; 13.3-37; 14.1–16.8), between a *pôle christologique* and a *pôle anthropologique*. Finally, however, his study is less diachronically literary, more synchronically theological.[109] For the disciples in Mark and their real-life counterparts in the Markan community, the incursion of God's unconsummated kingdom creates the paradox of the church's crucified-risen, now absent–still present Lord, mirrored by the disciples' believing infidelity. The Evangelist's anthropological determinism gives to his portrayal of the disciples a tragic aspect, correlative with Jesus' own tragic destiny; the disciples' incomprehension of Jesus reflects the fragility of the Christian's believing condition.[110] Fischer's exegesis intersects with that of Donald Juel,[111] who emphasizes the disciples' need to be released from the demonic, and with that of Juel's student Brent Driggers,[112] who stresses the sheer mystery of God and of God's hardening of the twelve.

The disciples' ambivalent conduct and the paradox of discipleship are

107. 'Rhetorical Analysis', p. 296. That frustration reaches its highest pitch at Mark 16.8: 'With the notice that the women never delivered the message and the implication that the disciples never became faithful proclaimers of that message, the parasite kills the host!' (p. 293).

108. Ibid., p. 281 n. 4; p. 282 nn. 5-6; p. 286 n. 17; p. 287 n. 20; p. 290 n. 31; p. 292 n. 37. On Pryke, see above, Chapter 7.

109. *Les Disciples dans l'Évangile de Marc: Une grammaire théologique* (Études bibliques n.s. 57; Paris: Gabalda, 2007), esp. pp. 19-24, 42-49, 142.

110. Ibid., pp. 107, 110, 171, 193-203.

111. *A Master of Surprise: Mark Interpreted* (Minneapolis: Fortress, 1994), pp. 70-75.

112. *Following God through Mark: Theological Tension in the Second Gospel* (Louisville and London: Westminster John Knox, 2007), pp. 99-106.

recurring motifs in recent theological studies of the Second Gospel. Interpreters differ, primarily, on whether there is for Mark a pedagogical takeaway — the need for candid reappraisal within the community of faith[113] — or whether (with Juel, Driggers, and Fischer) Mark intends to plunge its readers into what Christopher Burdon describes as 'the radiant obscurity' whose 'mystery is unveiled but not assimilated'.[114] Robert Fowler's exercise in reader-response criticism accepts the didactic option: 'Because Mark is willing to put the story and the discourse into tension with each other, he is able to offer a narrative that instructs the naratee in the challenges of discipleship without a full and explicit portrayal of successful discipleship in the story. In Mark the twelve are foils to Jesus at the story level so that at the discourse level the naratee can observe their mistakes and inadequacies and learn to behave differently'.[115] James Hanson disagrees that Mark's story and discourse are pedagogically at odds. For him, Mark presents God as heavily invested in disciples who are grasped by Satan; their fate 'rests not in their own capacity to overcome their failures, but in God's capacity to break through their unbelief and rescue them from their darkness'.[116]

What then shall we say to these things? Some patterns emerge. Here's what I see.

First: All three types of interpretation of the disciples in Mark, which I categorized some years ago, remain lively options in 2012. None of them has disappeared or supplanted the others. Each is represented by a recent, major monograph: Type I, by Suzanne Watts Henderson (2006); Type II, by Cédric Fischer (2007); Type III, by Mary Ann Tolbert (1989).

Second: Of these types, the second or mediate position is most heavily represented in the past quarter-century of scholarship. In the survey just

113. Thus, C. Latzoo, 'The Story of the Twelve in the Gospel of Mark,' *Hekima Review* [Nairobi] 13 (1995), pp. 25-33; P. M. Meagher, 'The Gospel of Mark: The Vulnerable Disciples,' *Vidjajyoti* 67 (2003), pp. 779-803.

114. *Stumbling on God: Faith and Vision through Mark's Gospel* (London and Grand Rapids: SPCK/Eerdmans, 1990), pp. 74, 106.

115. Fowler, *Let the Reader Understand*, pp. 259-60. See also M. C. Dippenaar, 'The Disciples in Mark: Narrative and Theology', *Toronto Journal of Theology* 17 (1995), pp. 139-209.

116. 'The Disciples in Mark's Gospel: Beyond the Pastoral/Polemical Debate', *Horizons in Biblical Theology* 20 (1998), pp. 128-55 (quotation, p. 137). 'Granted, the strong hint in 4:13 that the disciples may prove to be outsiders is borne out in the ensuing narrative; but if the reader's insider status is purchased at the expense of keeping the disciples out forever, the reader's inside status reveals itself as a Pyrrhic victory, for it suggests that human opposition and blindness can have the final word' (ibid., p. 154 n. 37).

presented, for every Type I or Type III reading, there are three or four among Type II. If one weighs the probabilities, this might be expected. By definition, 'mediate' positions are 'both/and', recognizing the measure of truth perceived in their 'conservative' or 'liberal' counterparts, which tend toward the 'either/or'.[117] In 1989 I thought — and still I think — that Type II readings of the disciples in Mark claim the strongest exegetical support. If one regards the disciples — whether reckoned as the twelve or more expansively — altogether positively, then satanic Peter at Caesarea Philippi (8.33) or the mute women at the tomb (16.8) will perplex. If one sees in them nothing but bad, then their abandonment of everything to follow Jesus (10.28) or their faithful ministry to him (15.40-41) will confound. If neither of these exclusive options satisfy, then your reading of Mark is probably somewhere in Type II.

Third: Whatever their type, few of the studies I have noted are redaction-critical in character. That is a big difference from mid-twentieth century scholarship. Some still so proceed (Telford, Reiprich); others' exegeses are vestigially *redaktionsgeschichtlich* while conducted on other bases (Stegemann, Henderson). Already we have noted the interesting case of Danove, who offers a semiotic redaction divested of tradition-history. Nevertheless, a majority of inquiries into the disciples in Mark do not proceed by separating, then weighing, tradition and redaction. No tumbling, please, into *post hoc, ergo propter hoc*: I find no evidence that my monograph made the slightest difference in others' methodological choices. Those still favoring Markan *Redaktionsgeschichte* continue with calm, without qualm. Those inclined toward different approaches haven't needed my encouragement. Continental scholars may display slightly greater propensity for Markan redaction criticism, though that is not universally demonstrable (see Telford and Fischer).[118] What's clear, a quarter

---

117. Though I tried to define them precisely, the labels 'conservative', 'mediate', and 'liberal' dissatisfied me in the 1980s (see above, Chapter 2, n. 38). They still do, not least because they invite mischievous confusion in the political and religious climate of the United States in the early twenty-first century. Aside from 'Types I, II, and III,' I still haven't landed on better shorthand. Neither did the book's reviewers. Hope springs eternal.

118. Though all cultural differences have not been effaced, the exegetical boundaries among European, British, North African, and North American Markan scholarship seem to me more porous today than they were three decades ago. For instance: Dieter Lührmann's *Das Markusevangelium* (Tübingen: Mohr-Siebeck, 1987), which replaced Erich Klostermann's commentary (1st edn, 1926; 4th edn, 1950) in the Handbuch zum Neuen Testament. While sensitive to Mark's traditions, sources, and redaction, Lührmann emphasizes the Gos-

century on, is that redaction criticism is no longer the automatic default setting in Markan scholarship.[119]

Is there a *different* default setting among Markan exegetes? That question leads to a fourth conclusion that may be drawn from my updated *Forschungsbericht:* methodologically, these studies of the disciples in Mark are all over the map. Irrespective of the ways in which I have typed them, one finds (1) historical and sociological investigations (see Stegemann, Painter, Riches), (2) *traditionsgeschichtlich* (Shiner, Strelan, Henderson) or redactional (Telford) analyses, (3) narrative or rhetorical examinations (Malbon, Tolbert, Dippenaar; Danove, to a degree), (4) *Tendenzkritik* (Burdon, Juel, Latzoo, Hanson, Meagher, Driggers, Fischer), (5) reader-response exercises (Fowler; Danove, to some extent), as well as studies that marry two or more of these approaches (most obviously, Gibson, Hurtado, Miller, and Reiprich). It is worth noting that representatives from each of these five converge on a Type II exegesis of Mark resembling Best's, which was undertaken on strenuously redaction-critical premises. From that one might conclude that the ambivalent portrait of the disciples in Mark is strengthened, or at least for now is most popular among scholars operating in five different methodological theaters.[120] Those are the same five that I mapped in Figure 3 of Chapter 8.[121] Many reviewers joined with me in faulting my model for composite exegesis. That model, however, has turned out to be reasonably predictive of the various ways my colleagues would proceed. No grove-decimating insight there, either. In 1989 I was of-

---

pel's narrative flow. The same may be said of Camille Focant's *L'évangile selon Marc* (Commentaire Biblique: Nouveau Testament 2; Paris: Cerf, 2004). On the Atlantic's western side, the history and redaction of traditions occupy an important place in the technical commentaries by A. Y. Collins (*Mark: A Commentary* [ed. H. W. Attridge; Hermeneia; Minneapolis: Fortress, 2007]) and J. Marcus (*Mark 1–8, 8–16: A New Translation with Introduction and Commentary* [AB 27, 27A; New York, New Haven, and London: Doubleday/Yale University Press, 2000, 2009]).

119. Telford notes: 'Redaction criticism is a discipline in tension with itself, seeking to remain an historical method but struggling in particular to come to terms with the literary aspects of its source material' ('The Pre-Markan Tradition in Recent Research (1980-1990)', p. 708).

120. Again, Telford (ibid., p. 712): 'Results are always strengthened when different methods produce similar conclusions'.

121. Best was 'sure that even if all Black's five methods were to be used scholars would still come up with different answers to the same problems' (*JTS* 41 [1990], p. 606). Of course they have, though at present the results are not as scattered as Best predicted. There is a working, exegetical consensus. Three decades from now things may look different.

fering, not a normative prescription of the multiple ways in which Markan scholarship ought to proceed, but rather a positive description of how in fact it did and could progress. The fact that it has done so demonstrates only that little, methodologically speaking, has radically changed in the past twenty-five years.[122] Would one expect otherwise?

Fifth: That said, a change is detectable. It is that which John Donahue charged me with underestimating:[123] redaction criticism's composition-critical dimension. Thirty years ago scholars theologically attentive to the Markan text naturally attempted to peel away the Evangelist's editorial embellishment from his inherited traditions. That exercise seemed natural, because such exegetes were the children of an antecedent generation of form criticism. In 2012 it seems just as natural for theologically sensitive interpreters to 'read Mark in its final form', as a narrative unity. So notes Telford, who is quite sympathetic to Markan *Redaktionsgeschichte*: 'Redaction criticism has been giving away, therefore, to a broader composition criticism in its search for Markan fingerprints. . . . There have been growing doubts about our ability to separate source from redaction in Mark, far less identify specific written sources or establish the earlier form of a proposed traditional unit. . . . There has been a growing recognition of the unity of the Gospel in its language, style, composition and theology, and a growing appreciation of its literary coherence at the global level, despite inconsistencies at the micro-level'.[124] For most interpreters this may be more a matter of recalibrated emphasis than of radical departure. Some

122. The exception to this assessment would be deconstructive analyses, which relocate the interpretive focus away from the text and onto its interpreter: several of the exercises, for example, in J. C. Anderson and S. D. Moore (eds.), *Mark and Method: New Approaches in Biblical Studies* (2nd edn; Minneapolis: Fortress, 2008). This, too, remains a lively option, though not one that has yet taken the field. Most historical and literary critics of Mark have reached rapprochement on the text's centrality, which is where most recent Markan commentaries operate: among others, J. R. Donahue and D. J. Harrington, *The Gospel of Mark* (Sacra Pagina 2; Collegeville: Liturgical, 2002); M. E. Boring, *Mark: A Commentary* (NTL; Louisville: Westminster John Knox, 2006); C. C. Black, *Mark* (Abingdon New Testament Commentaries; Nashville: Abingdon, 2011). Reviewing B. M. F. van Iersel's *Mark: A Reader-Response Commentary* (JSNTSup 164; Sheffield: Sheffield Academic Press, 1998), I reported surprise by how little exegetical difference it made that van Iersel wrote of 'reader response', not 'authorial intention' (*CBQ* 62 [2000], pp. 570-72).

123. *PSTJ* (October 1989), p. 12. There Donahue had me dead to rights. Best's spirited defense of the kind of Markan redaction criticism I challenged demonstrates, nevertheless, that the old method still had life in it and remained deeply attractive to some, even in English-speaking scholarship. It still does, as we have witnessed.

124. 'The Pre-Markan Tradition in Recent Research (1980-1990)', p. 707.

will always be interested in constructing levels of Markan exposition behind or beyond the text, be they traditional layers or semantic frames. Good on them. There is no inherently correct method of approach to any complex text; some methods are simply better suited than others to address particular questions that interest interpreters. If an approach throws light on a text as obscure as the Second Gospel, then let us embrace it and bless its practitioners' labors. And if in 2042 our reading of Mark as a narrative unity has become tendentious or blasé, we may rest assured that healthy scholarship will have kept pace to restore the balance or refresh the questions.

Sixth: The score of studies surveyed maintain a vibrant interest in the Second Evangelist as theologian,[125] a substantial bequest of redaction criticism. Recent scholarship tends to side more closely with Meye and Best, who construed Mark's aims as pedagogical or pastoral; in general it shows less sympathy for Weeden's view of Mark as polemicist. An interesting aspect of recent research on the disciples is how much stress Mark's interpreters lay on its apocalyptic eschatology (Tolbert, Burdon, Juel, Shiner, Hanson, Painter, Strelan, Telford, Riches, Miller, Henderson, Fischer, and Driggers). This, to be sure, is no new idea;[126] still, Markan apocalypticism was not highlit in the scholarship (roughly, 1950-1980) on which I originally concentrated.[127] I am not sure how to account for this; different kinds of cross-fertilization are possible. Juel and Marcus have probed Markan eschatology;[128] predictably, their students would follow their leads

---

125. Collins called me out on this characterization: 'The category "evangelist as religious thinker" seems to be straightforward and poses no major problems for those of us who think historically. The category "evangelist as theologian," however, has connotations related to the creeds of the church and the history of doctrine and dogma' (*Critical Review of Books in Religion* 4 [1991]: 171). I appreciate her fear of anachronism; like most theologians I know, however, I too think historically and suffer no fidgets by styling Mark as a theologian. Creedal and dogmatic connotations attend the term only if one chooses to import them, which in this case I do not. The claims (οἱ λόγοι) of this Gospel have fundamentally to do with the God (ὁ θεός) whose kingdom Jesus instantiates. Provided that the term is carefully defined, neither do I find 'historian' an impertinent description of Mark (C. C. Black, 'Mark as Historian of God's Kingdom', *CBQ* 71 [2009], pp. 64-83).

126. Timothy Colani, *Jésus Christ et les Croyances messianiques de son Temps* (2nd edn; Strasbourg: Treuttel et Wurtz, 1864).

127. Pesch's *Naherwartungen* (1968) and H. C. Kee, *Community of the New Age: Studies in Mark's Gospel* (Philadelphia: Westminster, 1977), were important exceptions.

128. Juel, *A Master of Surprise*; Marcus, *Mark 1–8, 9–16*. The same is true of Collins (*Mark: A Commentary*), though, to my knowledge, none of her students are here represented.

(the former, Driggers;[129] the latter, Miller and Henderson). *Wie der Doktorvater, so die Kinder.* Contemporaneous research in Jesus and in Paul has also been apocalyptically preoccupied.[130] The *Zeitgeist* at the century's turn could be influential, though that's impossible to prove. For whatever reason, the study of the disciples in Mark coheres with renewed appreciation of that Gospel's eschatology. That is an important scholarly development.[131] Coincident with this book's preoccupation, it is also fitting: among the earliest exercises in Markan *Redaktionsgeschichte* was James M. Robinson's *The Problem of History in Mark* (1957), which posited that Jesus' struggle with Satan shapes the Evangelist's perception of history.[132]

D. Mr. Popper's Falsifiable Penguins

> You must learn from the mistakes of others. You can't possibly live long enough to make all of them yourself.
>
> Attributed to Sam Levenson[133]

What are we doing, and why are we doing it? Trying to answer those questions sums up my reasons for writing *The Disciples according to Mark.* The

---

129. After Juel's death in 2003, Driggers's dissertation was completed the following year under Brian K. Blount's direction.

130. Representative are E. P. Sanders, *Paul and Palestinian Judaism: A Comparison of Patterns of Religion* (Philadelphia: Fortress, 1977); idem, *Jesus and Judaism* (Philadelphia: Fortress, 1985); J. L. Martyn, *Theological Issues in the Letters of Paul* (Nashville: Abingdon, 1997); D. C. Allison, *Jesus of Nazareth: Millenarian Prophet* (Minneapolis: Fortress, 1998).

131. *Pace* Breytenbach, for whom recent 'investigation [of discipleship in Mark] has resulted without significant progress in scholarship' ('Current Research on the Gospel according to Mark', p. 25). For Breytenbach, only that which is 'new' qualifies as progress. I disagree. Especially in the humanities, the testing, corroboration, and refinement of the old can be as valuable as the introduction of novelty. Sometimes the vaunted 'cutting edge' cannot dent warm butter.

132. SBT 21; London: SCM; rpt., *The Problem of History in Mark and Other Marcan Studies* (Philadelphia: Fortress, 1982). Robinson's dissertation was first published in German (*Das Geschichtsverständnis des Markusevangeliums* [Zürich: Zwingli]) in 1956, the same year in which Willi Marxsen's *Der Evangelist Markus* appeared (Göttingen: Vandenhoeck & Ruprecht).

133. Similar counsel is ascribed to Lao Tzu, Eleanor Roosevelt, and Hyman Rickover; in all cases the source has proven impossible to confirm. Levenson may be the least remembered today, and the author of *Everything but Money* (New York: Simon and Schuster, 1966) deserves rescue from obscurity.

same questions haunted the execution of my own labors. Even if many Markan exegetes no longer proceed redaction-critically, they operate by some critical light, and of that approach those questions are still worth raising. A critique of method, especially one's own methods, is like a colonoscopy. You need to know what's in there but wish that you might learn it more comfortably.

In the mid-1980s I may have heard of Sir Karl Raimund Popper (1902-1994); I knew little of his philosophy. I know only a smidgen now, though what I have learned chimes with my recollection of a dungeon carrel in Duke Divinity School's Library. Popper styled his philosophy of science as critical rationalism, 'the critical search for error'.[134] Theories 'are statements which are tested by being submitted to systematic attempts to falsify them'.[135] Contrary to the inductive method of classical empiricism,[136] 'scientific theories [are] not the digest of observations, but . . . inventions — conjectures boldly put forward for trial, to be eliminated if they [clash] with observations; with observations that [are] rarely accidental but as a rule undertaken with the definite intention of testing a theory by obtaining, if possible, a decisive refutation'.[137] Popper argued that corroboration and disproof are logically asymmetrical: one can never verify a theory's validity, no matter how many positive results issue from its testing, though a single negative outcome can demonstrate its falsity.[138] '[T]he criterion of the scientific status of a theory is its falsifiability, or refutability, or testability':[139] not a prejudgment that the theory is bogus or necessarily false but, rather, its *capability of being shown false* — if it is false — by severe testing. 'According to my proposal, what characterizes the empirical method is its manner of exposing to falsification, in every conceivable way, the system to be tested. Its aim is not to save the lives of untenable systems but, on the contrary, to select the one which by comparison is the fittest, by

---

134. K. R. Popper, *Conjectures and Refutations: The Growth of Scientific Knowledge* (3rd edn; London: Routledge and Kegan Paul, 1969), pp. 26-27. See also D. Miller, *Critical Rationalism: A Restatement and Defence* (Chicago and La Salle: Open Court, 1994).

135. K. R. Popper, *The Logic of Scientific Discovery* (New York: Basic Books, 1959), p. 313.

136. 'Induction, i.e. inference based on many observations, is a myth. It is neither a psychological fact, nor a fact of ordinary life, nor one of scientific procedure' (Popper, *Conjectures and Refutations*, p. 53).

137. Ibid., p. 46.

138. Popper, *The Logic of Scientific Discovery*, p. 33. '[I]t must be possible for an empirical system to be refuted by experience' (ibid., p. 41, italicized in the original).

139. Idem, *Conjectures and Refutations*, p. 37 (italicized in the original).

exposing them all to the fiercest struggle for survival.'[140] For Popper, the seeming 'explanatory power' of a theory proves nothing; 'It is easy to obtain confirmations, or verifications, for nearly every theory — if we look for confirmations.'[141]

> [T]he rationality of the sciences lies not in its habit of appealing to empirical evidence in support of its dogmas — astrologers do so too — but solely in the *critical approach:* in an attitude which, of course, involves the critical use, among other arguments, of empirical evidence (especially in refutations). For us, therefore, science has nothing to do with the quest for certainty or probability or reliability. We are not interested in establishing scientific theories as secure, or certain, or probable. Conscious of our fallibility we are only interested in criticizing them and testing them, hoping to find out where we are mistaken: of learning from our mistakes; and, if we are lucky, of proceeding to better theories.[142]

In the testing of theories, how does Popper propose we proceed? His basic rule is $PS_1 \rightarrow TT_1 \rightarrow EE_1 \rightarrow PS_2$. 'That is, we start from some problem PS_1, proceed to a tentative solution or tentative theory TT_1, which may be (partly or wholly) mistaken; in any case it will be subject to error-

---

140. Popper, *The Logic of Scientific Discovery,* p. 42. R. J. Ackermann disputes this Darwinian metaphor: 'The real evolutionary metaphor suggests that lots of theories (competing ones) ought to be present in any area of investigation — and that theories, like species, may survive the death of particular individuals that belong to them' (*The Philosophy of Karl Popper* [Amherst: University of Massachusetts Press, 1976], p. 58).

141. Popper, *Conjectures and Refutations,* p. 36. 'Our propensity to look out for regularities, and to impose laws upon nature, leads to the psychological phenomenon of *dogmatic thinking* or, more generally, dogmatic behaviour: we expect regularities everywhere and attempt to find them even where there are none; events which do not yield to these attempts we are inclined to treat as a kind of "background noise"; and we stick to our expectations even when they are inadequate and we ought to accept defeat' (ibid., p. 49).

142. Ibid., p. 229. W. W. Bartley's restatement clarifies: 'How then are hypotheses or theories to be confirmed? *They are not to be confirmed.* There is no way to confirm — that is, to prove, verify, make firmer, make more probable — any theory of interest. They are and remain forever conjectural. There is no certain knowledge. What *is* done — and what has been mistaken for confirmation — Popper calls 'corroboration.' For a theory to be corroborated is simply *to have been tested* severely and to have passed the test. Such a theory is not made more probable thereby: it may yet fail a more severe test tomorrow' ('A Popperian Harvest', in *In Pursuit of Truth: Essays on the Philosophy of Karl Popper on the Occasion of His 80th Birthday* [ed. P. Levinson; Atlantic Highlands, NJ, and Sussex: Humanities/Harvester, 1982], pp. 249-89; quotation, p. 264).

elimination, *EE1*, which may consist of critical discussion or experimental tests; at any rate, new problems *PS2*, arise from our creative activity; and these new problems are not in general intentionally created by us; they emerge autonomously from the field of new relationships which we cannot help bringing into existence with every action, however little we intend to do so'.[143] Therefore, '[t]he advance of knowledge consists, mainly, in the modification of earlier knowledge'.[144] Of decisive importance is the criticism of our conjectures: 'by bringing out our mistakes it makes us understand the difficulties of the problem we are trying to solve'.[145]

The scientist lives at the intersection of three interactive worlds. World 1 is the physical world of blastulas and wart hogs and galaxies, which science attempts to explain. World 2 is the subjective world of human affect and thought: our feelings, beliefs, and dispositions. World 3 is the world of objective human cognition — language and books, paintings and symphonies, myths and theorems and theories — by which the World 2 mind creates products out of World 1 materials. The knowledge grasped by the individual human mind (World 2) is as indebted to the accumulated fund of human culture (World 3) as to the aggregate sense of experience (World 1).[146]

The mind of the individual scientist is free to acknowledge 'that scientific discovery is impossible without faith in ideas which are of a purely speculative kind, and sometimes even quite hazy; a faith which is completely unwarranted from the point of view of science, and which, to that extent, is "metaphysical"'.[147] What the scientist dare not do is assume that her discoveries are secure foundations for further research: 'The empirical basis of objective science thus has nothing "absolute" about it. Science does not rest upon rock-bottom. The bold structure of its theories rises, as it were, above a swamp. It is like a building erected on piles. The piles are driven down from above into the swamp, but not down to any natural or

143. K. Popper, "Knowledge: Subjective versus Objective," in *A Pocket Popper* (ed. D. Miller; Oxford: Fontana, 1983), pp. 58-77; quotation, pp. 70-71.

144. Popper, *Conjectures and Refutations*, p. 28.

145. Ibid., p. vii.

146. K. Popper, *Objective Knowledge: An Evolutionary Approach* (rev. edn; Oxford and New York: Clarendon/Oxford University Press, 1979); idem, *Knowledge and the Mind-Body Problem: In Defence of Interaction* (ed. M. A. Notturno; London and New York: Routledge, 1994). Notes Ackermann (*The Philosophy of Karl Popper*, p. 55): 'The concept of intellectual evolution and of something like world 3 is not new with Popper. What is important here is Popper's use of these notions to ground an objective notion of the growth of scientific knowledge.'

147. Popper, *The Logic of Scientific Discovery*, p. 38.

"given" base; and when we cease our attempts to drive our piles into a deeper layer, it is not because we have reached firm ground. We simply stop when we are satisfied that they are firm enough to carry the structure, at least for the time being'.[148]

Well, then, Sir Karl: how *do* we know? On what basis can we assert any theory? '[M]y answer . . . would be: "I do *not* know: my assertion was merely a guess. Never mind the source, or the sources, from which it may spring — there are many possible sources, and I may not be aware of half of them; and the origins or pedigrees have in any case little bearing upon truth. But if you are interested in the problem which I have tried to solve by my tentative assertion, you may help me by criticizing it as severely as you can; and if you can design some experimental test by which you think you might refute my assertion, I shall gladly, and to the best of my powers, help you to refute it"'.[149]

At the age of seventeen Popper, a member of Austria's Social Democratic Worker's Party, watched while police shot eight, unarmed party comrades. His World 2 revulsion at World 1 atrocity led to his World 3 disavowal of Marxist historical materialism as pseudo-science. That may account, in part, for his plea at age sixty-one:

> What we should do, I suggest, is to give up the idea of ultimate sources of knowledge, and admit that all knowledge is human; that it is mixed with our errors, our prejudices, our dreams, and our hopes; that all we can do is to grope for truth even though it is beyond our reach. . . . If we thus admit that there is no authority beyond the reach of criticism to be found within the whole province of our knowledge, however far it may

148. Ibid., p. 111. '[T]he programme of tracing back all knowledge to its ultimate source in observation is logically impossible to carry through: it leads to an infinite regress. (The doctrine that truth is manifest cuts off the regress. This is interesting because it may help to explain the attractiveness of that doctrine.)' (*Conjectures and Refutations*, p. 23). Alternatively, Popper suggested, investigators cut short that regress by grounding their knowledge on the authority either of reason (the dogmatism of classical rationalism) or of experience (the psychologism of classical empiricism).

149. Idem, *Conjectures and Refutations*, p. 27. 'This answer applies, strictly speaking, only if the question is asked about some scientific assertion as distinct from a historical one. If my conjecture was an historical one, sources (in the non-ultimate sense) will of course come into the critical discussion of its validity. Yet fundamentally, my answer will be the same' (ibid.). '[A]ll theoretical or generalizing sciences make use of the same method, whether they are natural sciences or social sciences' (K. Popper, *The Poverty of Historicism* [2nd edn; London: Routledge & Kegan Paul, 1960], p. 130).

have penetrated into the unknown, then we can retain, without danger, the idea that truth is beyond human authority. And we must retain it. For without this idea there can be no objective standards of inquiry; no criticism of our conjectures; no groping for the unknown; no quest for knowledge.[150]

As best I can judge by Popper's criteria, 'strict editorial criticism'[151] of Mark's Gospel has failed and continues to fail.[152] That's the fundamental case made by this book. Restated in Popperian terms: given the problem of distinguishing the Second Evangelist's editorial hand from his traditions or sources (*PS1*: Chapters 1-2), I formulated a tentative theory (*TT1*) that redaction criticism, narrowly defined, was a deeply flawed method for Markan exegesis (Chapters 3-6). I subjected *TT1* to the highest level of error-elimination (*EE1*) of which I was capable (Chapter 7; later, the book's testing by a jury of peers). The result was a new set of problems (*PS2*) — how Markan exegesis might more fruitfully proceed (Chapter 8) — with which my reviewers and I have subsequently grappled. The fact that my outcomes were severely skeptical would be, for a Popperian, expected and even desirable: 'The conjectural character of scientific hypotheses lies not so much in the fact that they cannot be shown to be right as in the fact that they are ready to be shown to be wrong'.[153]

As best I can judge — and Best helped me reach this judgment — *The Disciples according to Mark* also failed, on Popper's terms. Indeed, *it failed in multiple ways*. For brevity's sake let's consider only three.[154] First: I had begun my study by asking, 'How do we know what the Evangelist wrote and what he borrowed from others and then edited?' Popper insists: "[T]here are all kinds of sources of our knowledge; but *none has author-*

---

150. Idem, *Conjectures and Refutations*, p. 30. Popper favored theories with 'verisimilitude' — approximation to truth — rather than claims of Truth with a capital T (ibid., pp. 233-35). See Miller, *Critical Rationalism*, pp. 194-209.

151. This term is Donahue's, which he suggests in differentiation from 'composition criticism' ('Redaction Criticism', pp. 29-34). As we have seen, classical redaction criticism comprised both elements.

152. Nevertheless, I confess that some Markan pericopae (e.g., 7.1-23) are almost impossible for me to understand without theoretical recourse to *Traditions-* and *Redaktionsgeschichte*. See Black, *Mark*, pp. 32-33, 169-77.

153. D. Miller, 'Conjectural Knowledge: Popper's Solution of the Problem of Induction', in Levinson (ed.), *In Pursuit of Truth*, pp. 17-49; quotation, p. 23.

154. I cannot recall having previously attempted, in print, a convincing refutation of my own argument. I've lost more than Edna Millay's trousers. I'm now almost buck naked.

ity. . . . Thus the empiricist's questions, "How do you know? What is the source of your assertion?" are wrongly put. They are not formulated in an inexact or slovenly manner, but *they are entirely misconceived:* they are questions that beg for an authoritarian answer".[155] As a blockheaded empiricist, I had sought to validate my conjecture, which for Popper is impossible; the best for which I could have hoped was its partial corroboration. Second: from Popper's vantage point, my critics denied me even that. Most of *The Disciples'* reviewers took its *PS2*, subjected their own *TT2* to strenuous *EE2*, and arrived at the *PS3* that one or another aspect of my tentative theory was erroneous. Even if a majority of reviewers agreed in the main with my new hypothesis, *all it took was one error* — for instance, my lack of clean statistical separation of categories and criteria — *to falsify it.* Q.E.D. Third: I certainly did not stick my neck out and advance a bold alternative for others to test. My representative redaction critics, as well as the method's rehabilitators, were far more courageous than I, though their conjectures could also be falsified. I called it Discretion. Popper might prefer, Cowardice.

Arguably, therefore, Meye, Best, Weeden, their successors — and Black — have *all* failed. There is yet another possibility: Popper's brand of critical rationalism is also flawed. I haven't the philosophical or scientific chops to demonstrate that, though I'd bet someone could. John Worrall argues that Popper seriously misidentified the nature of both the scientific process of identifying error and the process by which scientists generate 'tentative theories'.[156] Physicist and theologian John Polkinghorne agrees: '[S]cience does not in fact progress by continually drawing a bow at a refutable venture. . . . There is clearly much more to be said about science than Popper has been able to articulate.'[157]

There is more to be said about *Wissenschaft* than many biblical schol-

---

155. Popper, *Conjectures and Refutations*, pp. 24-25.

156. '"Revolution in Permanence": Popper on Theory-Change in Science', in *Karl Popper: Philosophy and Problems* (ed. A. O'Hear; Royal Institute of Philosophy Supplement 39; Cambridge: Cambridge University Press, 1995), pp. 75-102. For appreciative critiques of Popper's philosophy, the other essays in O'Hear's volume are well worth consulting, as are Ackermann, *The Philosophy of Karl Popper* (1976) and H. Keuth, *The Philosophy of Karl Popper* (Cambridge: Cambridge University Press, 2005).

157. *Beyond Science: The Wider Human Context* (Cambridge: Cambridge University Press, 1996), pp. 15-16. Both Polkinghorne and Worrall counterpropose a more gradual process, in which specific new theories are constructed from background theories regarded by scientists as well entrenched. Such a model is more in line with that suggested in Chapter 8, above.

ars often admit. Reviewing the last quarter-century of Markan scholarship, I am struck by how much of our work operates within World 3 while we genuflect before World 1. Save for archaeologists or textual critics who can sift physical materials, most of our socio-historical or literary-theological analysis remains grounded in theoretical construction. If that is unavoidable, perhaps other metaphors for our work would better serve us than the strictly scientific.[158] Are exegetes less akin to chemists with spectroscopes, more like judges applying statutes or pianists playing Chopin? If so, then jurists and musicologists may offer more help in disciplining our minds than we have credited them.[159] If not, Popper sobers and encourages us in a still salubrious humility: 'Science has no authority. It is not the magical product of the given, the evidence, the observations. It is not a gospel of truth. It is the result of our endeavours and mistakes. It is you and I who make science as well as we can. It is you and I who are responsible for it. . . . I may be wrong and you may be right, and by an effort we may get nearer to the truth'.[160]

158. Attempting to differentiate responsible historical criticism from flat-footed historicism, elsewhere I have made a case for scriptural interpretation as a relationship between the Lover and the beloved, not merely the investigator and her subject matter ('Trinity and Exegesis', *Pro Ecclesia* 19 [2010], pp. 151-80).

159. See R. A. Posner, *How Judges Think* (Cambridge, MA, and London: Harvard University Press, 2008); F. Dorian, *The History of Music in Performance: The Art of Musical Interpretation from the Renaissance to Our Day* (New York: Norton, 1966).

160. K. Popper, *Realism and the Aim of Science* (London: Routledge, 1983), pp. 259-60; idem, *The Open Society and Its Enemies*, volume 2: *The High Tide of Prophecy: Hegel, Marx, and the Aftermath* (London: Routledge & Sons, 1945), p. 238.

Selected Bibliography

I. Texts and Translations

Aland, Kurt, ed. *Synopsis Quattuor Evangeliorum: Locis parallelis evangeliorum apocryphorum et patrum adhibitis edidit.* 10th edn. Stuttgart Deutsche Bibelstiftung Stuttgart, 1971.

The Babylonian Talmud. Pt 2, Vol. VI: *Sukkah, Bezah.* Pt 4, Vols. III-IV: *Baba Bathra.* Edited and translated by I. Epstein. London: Soncino, 1938, 1935.

Eusebius. *The Ecclesiastical History.* 2 vols. Translated by Kirsopp Lake, J. E. L. Oulton, and H. J. Lawlor. Loeb Classical Library. Cambridge, MA and London: Harvard University Press/William Heinemann, 1926, 1932.

The Greek New Testament. 3rd edn. Edited by Kurt Aland, Matthew Black, Carlo M. Martini, Bruce M. Metzger, and Allen Wikgren. Stuttgart: United Bible Societies, 1975.

Josephus, Flavius. *The Jewish Wars.* 3 vols. Translated by H. St. J. Thackery. Loeb Classical Library. London and New York: William Heinemann/G. P. Putnam's Sons, 1927, 1928.

The Mishnah. Translated with introduction and brief explanatory notes by Herbert Danby. Oxford: Oxford University Press, 1933.

Novum Testamentum Graece. 26th edn. Edited by Eberhard Nestle, Kurt Aland, *et al.* Stuttgart: Deutsche Bibelgesellschaft, 1979.

Pesikta Rabbati: Discourses for Feasts, Fasts, and Special Sabbaths. 2 vols. Translated by William G. Braude. Yale Judaica Studies 18. New Haven and London: Yale University Press, 1968.

Philostratus, Flavius. *Life of Apollonius of Tyana.* 2 vols. Translated by F. C. Conybeare. Loeb Classical Library. London and New York: William Heinemann/G. P. Putnam's Sons, 1921, 1926.

II. Reference Works

Bauer, Walter. *A Greek-English Lexicon of the New Testament and Other Early Christian Literature.* 2nd edn, revised and augmented by W. F. Arndt, F. W. Gingrich, and F. W. Danker. Chicago and London: University of Chicago Press, 1979.

Crim, Keith, ed. *The Interpreter's Dictionary of the Bible.* Supplementary volume. Nashville: Abingdon, 1976.

Gaston, Lloyd. *Horae Synopticae Electronicae: Word Statistics of the Synoptic Gospels.* Society of Biblical Literature Sources for Biblical Study 3. Missoula, MT: Society of Biblical Literature, 1973.

Hawkins, John Caesar. *Horae Synopticae.* Oxford: Clarendon, 1909.

Kittel, Gerhard, and Gerhard Friedrich, eds. *Theological Dictionary of the New Testament.* 10 vols. Translated by Geoffrey W. Bromiley. Grand Rapids, MI: Eerdmans, 1964-76.

Morgenthaler, Robert. *Statistik des Neutestamentlichen Wortschatzes.* Zürich: Gotthelf, 1958.

III. Commentaries and General Works

Abrams, Meyer Howard. *The Mirror and the Lamp: Romantic Theory and the Critical Tradition.* New York: Oxford University Press, 1953.

Achtemeier, Paul John. '"And he followed him": Miracles and Discipleship in Mark 10.46-52'. *Semeia* 11 (1978), pp. 115-45.

———. '"He Taught Them Many Things": Reflections on Marcan Christology'. *Catholic Biblical Quarterly* 42 (1980), pp. 465-81.

———. *Invitation to Mark: A Commentary on the Gospel of Mark with Complete Text from the Jerusalem Bible.* Image Books. Garden City, NY: Doubleday, 1978.

———. *Mark.* 2nd edn, rev., and enlarged. Proclamation Commentaries. Philadelphia: Fortress, 1986.

———. 'Mark as Interpreter of the Jesus Traditions'. *Interpretation* 32 (1978), pp. 339-52. Reprinted in James Luther Mays, ed., *Interpreting the Gospels.* Philadelphia: Fortress, 1981, pp. 115-29.

———. 'The Origin and Function of the Pre-Marcan Miracle Catenae'. *Journal of Biblical Literature* 91 (1972), pp. 198-221.

———. 'Toward the Isolation of Pre-Markan Miracle Catenae'. *Journal of Biblical Literature* 89 (1970), pp. 265-91.

———. Review of *Redactional Style in the Marcan Gospel*, by E. J. Pryke. *Catholic Biblical Quarterly* 41 (1979), pp. 655-57.

Alter, Robert. *The Art of Biblical Narrative.* New York: Basic Books, 1981.

Ambrozic, Aloysius Matthew. *The Hidden Kingdom: A Redaction-Critical Study of the References to the Kingdom of God in Mark's Gospel.* Catholic Biblical Quarterly Monograph Series 2. Washington, D.C.: Catholic Biblical Association of America, 1972.

Anderson, Bernhard Ward. 'The Problem and Promise of Commentary'. *Interpretation* 36 (1982), pp. 341-55.

Anderson, Hugh. *The Gospel of Mark.* New Century Bible. Grand Rapids, MI, and London: Eerdmans/Marshall, Morgan & Scott, 1976.

Au, Wilkie. 'Discipleship in Mark'. *The Bible Today* 67 (1973), pp. 1249-51.

Baarlink, Heinrich. *Anfängliches Evangelium: Ein Beitrag zur näheren Bestimmung der theologischen Motive im Markusevangelium.* Kampen: Kok, 1977.

Bacon, Benjamin Wisner. *The Beginnings of the Gospel Story: A Historico-Critical Inquiry into the Sources and Structure of the Gospel According to Mark, with Expository Notes upon the Text, for English Readers.* New Haven: Yale University Press, 1920.

————. *The Gospel of Mark: Its Composition and Date.* New Haven: Yale University Press, 1925.

————. *Is Mark a Roman Gospel?* Harvard Theological Studies 7. Cambridge, MA and London: Harvard University Press, 1919.

Baltensweiler, Heinrich, and Reicke, Bo, eds. *Neues Testament und Geschichte: Historisches Geschehen und Deutung im Neuen Testament. Oscar Cullmann zum 70. Geburtstag.* Zürich and Tübingen: Theologischer Verlag/J. C. B. Mohr (Paul Siebeck), 1972.

Barbour, Robert Stewart. 'Recent Study of the Gospel According to Mark'. *Expository Times* 79 (1967/1968), pp. 324-29.

————. Review of *Following Jesus: Discipleship in the Gospel of Mark,* by Ernest Best. *Scottish Journal of Theology* 36 (1983), pp. 107-109.

Barr, James. 'Biblical Theology'. *The Interpreter's Dictionary of the Bible.* Supplementary volume. Edited by Keith Crim. Nashville: Abingdon, 1976, pp. 104-11.

————. *Holy Scripture: Canon, Authority, Criticism.* Philadelphia: Westminster, 1983.

————. *The Semantics of Biblical Language.* London: SCM, 1983.

Barton, John. *Reading the Old Testament: Method in Biblical Study.* Philadelphia: Westminster, 1984.

Bartz, Albert Edward. *Basic Statistical Concepts.* 2nd edn. Minneapolis: Burgess, 1981.

Beardslee, William Armitage. *Literary Criticism of the New Testament.* Guides to Biblical Scholarship, New Testament Series. Philadelphia: Fortress, 1970.

Beardsley, Monroe Curtis. *Aesthetics: Problems in the Philosophy of Criticism.* New York: Harcourt, Brace, 1958.

Belo, Fernando. *A Materialist Reading of the Gospel of Mark.* Maryknoll, NY: Orbis, 1981.

Best, Ernest. *Disciples and Discipleship: Studies in the Gospel According to Mark.* Edinburgh: T. & T. Clark, 1986.

————. 'Discipleship in Mark: Mark 8.22–10.52'. *Scottish Journal of Theology* 23 (1970), pp. 323-37.

————. *Following Jesus: Discipleship in the Gospel of Mark.* Journal for the Study of the New Testament, Supplement Series 4. Sheffield: JSOT, 1981.

————. *Mark: The Gospel as Story.* Studies of the New Testament and Its World. Edinburgh: T. & T. Clark, 1983.

————. 'Mark: Some Problems'. *Irish Biblical Studies* 1 (1979), pp. 77-98.

————. 'Mark III.20, 21, 31-35'. *New Testament Studies* 22 (1975/1976), pp. 309-19.

————. 'Mark's Preservation of the Tradition'. *L'Évangile selon Marc: Tradition et Rédaction.* Edited by M. Sabbe. Bibliotheca ephemeridum theologicarum lovaniensium 34. Gembloux and Louvain: Duculot/Leuven University Press, 1974, pp. 21-34. Reprinted in Rudolf Pesch, ed., *Das Markus-Evangelium.* Wege der Forschung 411. Darmstadt: Wissenschaftliche Buchgesellschaft, 1979, pp. 390-409. Reprinted in W. R. Telford, ed., *The Interpretation of Mark.* Issues in Religion and Theology 7. Philadelphia and London: Fortress/SPCK, 1985, pp. 119-33.

————. 'Mark's Use of the Twelve'. *Zeitschrift für die neutestamentliche Wissenschaft* 69 (1978), pp. 11-35.

————. 'Peter in the Gospel According to Mark'. *Catholic Biblical Quarterly* 40 (1978), pp. 547-58.

————. 'The Role of the Disciples in Mark'. *New Testament Studies* 23 (1977), pp. 377-401.

————. *The Temptation and the Passion: The Markan Soteriology.* Society for New Testament Studies Monograph Series 2. Cambridge: Cambridge University Press, 1965.

————. Review of *Redactional Style in the Marcan Gospel,* by E. J. Pryke. *Journal for the Study of the New Testament* 4 (1979), pp. 69-76.

Betz, Hans Dieter. *Nachfolge und Nachahmung Jesu Christi in Neuen Testament.* Beiträge zur historischen Theologie 37. Tübingen: J. C. B. Mohr (Paul Siebeck), 1967.

————. ed. *Christology and a Modern Pilgrimage: A Discussion with Norman Perrin.* Philadelphia: Fortress, 1971.

Bilezikian, Gilbert G. *The Liberated Gospel: A Comparison of the Gospel of Mark and Greek Tragedy.* Baker Biblical Monograph. Grand Rapids, MI: Baker Book House, 1977.

Birdsall, James Neville. Review of *The Last Twelve Verses of Mark,* by W. R. Farmer. *Journal of Theological Studies* n.s. 26 (1975), pp. 151-60.

Blatherwick, David. 'The Markan Silhouette?' *New Testament Studies* 17 (1970/1971), pp. 184-92.

Blevins, James Lowell. *The Messianic Secret in Markan Research,* 1901-1976. Washington, DC: University Press of America, 1981.

Boomershine, Thomas Eugene. 'Mark 16.8 and the Apostolic Commission'. *Journal of Biblical Literature* 100 (1981), pp. 225-39.

—————. 'Mark the Storyteller: A Rhetorical-Critical Investigation of Mark's Passion and Resurrection Narrative'. Ph.D. dissertation, Union Theological Seminary (New York), 1974.

Booth, Wayne Clayson. *The Rhetoric of Fiction.* 2nd edn. Chicago and London: University of Chicago Press, 1983.

Borg, Marcus J. 'The Currency of the Term "Zealot"'. *Journal of Theological Studies* n.s. 22 (1971), pp. 504-12.

Bornkamm, Günther, Gerhard Barth, and Hans-Joachim Held. *Tradition and Interpretation in Matthew.* Translated by Percy Scott. New Testament Library. Philadelphia: Westminster, 1963.

Bowman, John. *The Gospel of Mark: The New Christian Jewish Passover Haggadah.* Studia postbiblica 8. Leiden: E. J. Brill, 1965.

Bracht, Werner. 'Jüngerschaft und Nachfolge: Zur Gemeindesituation im Markusevangelium'. *Kirche im Werden: Studien zum Thema Amt und Gemeinde im Neuen Testament.* Edited by Josef Hainz. Munich: Ferdinand Schöningh, 1976, pp. 143-65.

Branscomb, Bennett Harvie. *The Gospel of Mark.* Moffatt New Testament Commentary. New York and London: Harper and Brothers, n.d.

Breytenbach, Cilliers. *Nachfolge und Zukunftserwartung nach Markus: Eine methodenkritische Studie.* Abhandlungen zur Theologie des Alten und Neuen Testaments 71. Zürich: Theologischer Verlag, 1984.

Brown, Raymond Edward. 'Jesus and Elisha'. *Perspective* 12 (1971), pp. 85-104.

Brown, Raymond Edward, Karl Paul Donfried, and John Reumann, eds. *Peter in the New Testament: A Collaborative Assessment by Protestant and Roman Catholic Scholars.* Minneapolis and New York: Augsburg/Paulist, 1973.

Brown, Schuyler. Review of *Mark — Traditions in Conflict,* by T. J. Weeden, Sr. *Theological Studies* 33 (1972), pp. 754-56.

Budesheim, T. L. 'Jesus and the Disciples in Conflict with Jerusalem'. *Zeitschrift für die neutestamentliche Wissenschaft* 62 (1971), pp. 190-209.

Bultmann, Rudolf. *Exegetica: Aufsätze zur Erforschung des Neuen Testaments.* Edited by E. Dinkler. Tübingen: J. C. B. Mohr (Paul Siebeck), 1967.

—————. 'Die Frage nach dem messianischen Bewusstsein Jesu und das Petrusbekenntnis'. *Zeitschrift für die neutestamentliche Wissenschaft* 19 (1919/1920), pp. 164-74. Reprinted in idem, *Exegetica: Aufsätze zur Erforschung des Neuen Testaments.* Edited by E. Dinkler. Tübingen: J. C. B. Mohr (Paul Siebeck), 1967, pp. 1-9.

—————. *The History of the Synoptic Tradition.* Rev. edn. Translated by John Marsh. New York: Harper & Row, 1963.

———. *Theology of the New Testament.* Vol. I. Translated by Kendrick Grobel. New York: Charles Scribner's Sons, 1951.

Bultmann, Rudolf, and Karl Kundsin. *Form Criticism: Two Essays on New Testament Research.* Translated by F. C. Grant. New York: Harper and Brothers, 1962.

Burch, Ernest Ward. 'Tragic Action in the Second Gospel: A Study in the Narrative of Mark'. *Journal of Religion* 11 (1931), pp. 346-58.

Burgers, Wim. 'De Instelling van de Twaalf in het Evangelie van Marcus'. *Ephemerides Theologicae Lovaniensis* 36 (1960), pp. 625-54.

Burkill, Thomas Alec. *Mysterious Revelation: An Examination of the Philosophy of St. Mark's Gospel.* Ithaca, NY: Cornell University Press, 1963.

———. *New Light on the Earliest Gospel: Seven Markan Studies.* Ithaca, NY and London: Cornell University Press, 1972.

Busemann, Rolf. *Die Jüngergemeinde nach Markus 10: Eine redaktionsgeschichtliche Untersuchung des 10. Kapitels im Markusevangelium.* Bonner biblische Beiträge 57. Bonn: Peter Hanstein, 1983.

Bussmann, Wilhelm. *Synoptische Studien.* 3 vols. Halle (Salle): Buchhandlung des Waisenhauses, 1925, 1929, 1931.

Cadoux, Arthur Temple. *The Sources of the Second Gospel.* New York: Macmillan, 1935.

Caird, George Bradford. Review of *Redactional Style in the Marcan Gospel,* by E. J. Pryke. *Expository Times* 90 (1978), p. 56.

Calvin, John. *A Harmony of the Gospels: Matthew, Mark, and Luke.* Calvin's Commentaries 1. Edited by D. W. Torrance and T. F. Torrance. Edinburgh: Saint Andrews, 1972.

van Cangh, Jean-Marie. 'La Galilée dans l'évangile de Marc: un lieu théologique?' *Revue biblique* 79 (1972), pp. 59-75.

Carrington, Philip. 'The Calendrical Hypothesis of the Origin of Mark'. *Expository Times* 67 (1956), pp. 100-103.

———. *The Primitive Christian Calendar: A Study in the Making of the Markan Gospel.* Cambridge: Cambridge University Press, 1952.

Catchpole, David R. 'The Fearful Silence of the Women at the Tomb: A Study in Markan Theology'. *Journal of Theology for Southern Africa* 18 (1977), pp. 3-10.

Childs, Brevard Springs. *Biblical Theology in Crisis.* Philadelphia: Westminster, 1976.

———. 'The Canonical Shape of the Prophetic Literature'. *Interpretation* 32 (1978), pp. 46-55.

———. 'Childs versus Barr'. Review of *Holy Scripture: Canon, Authority, Criticism,* by J. Barr. *Interpretation* 38 (1984), pp. 66-70.

———. *The New Testament as Canon: An Introduction.* Philadelphia: Fortress, 1985.

Christ, Felix, ed. *Oikonomia: Heilsgeschichte als Thema der Theologie*. O. Cullmann *Festschrift*. Hamburg-Bergstedt: Herbert Reich, 1967.

Conzelmann, Hans. *Die Mitte der Zeit*. Tübingen: J. C. B. Mohr (Paul Siebeck), 1953. ET idem, *The Theology of St. Luke*. Translated by Geoffrey Buswell. New York: Harper & Row, 1961.

Cook, Michael J. *Mark's Treatment of the Jewish Leaders*. Novum Testamentum Supplements 51. Leiden: E. J. Brill, 1978.

Corley, Bruce, ed. *Colloquy on New Testament Studies: A Time for Reappraisal and Fresh Approaches*. Macon, GA: Mercer University Press, 1983.

Coutts, John. 'The Authority of Jesus and of the Twelve in St. Mark's Gospel'. *Journal of Theological Studies* n.s. 8 (1957), pp. 111-18.

Cranfield, Charles Ernest Burland. *The Gospel According to St. Mark*. Cambridge Greek Testament Commentary. Cambridge: Cambridge University Press, 1959.

Crossan, John Dominic. 'Empty Tomb and Absent Lord (Mark 16.1-8)'. *The Passion in Mark: Studies on Mark 14–16*. Edited by Werner H. Kelber. Philadelphia: Fortress, 1976, pp. 135-52.

―――. 'Mark and the Relatives of Jesus'. *Novum Testamentum* 15 (1973), pp. 81-113.

Crum, John MacLeod Campbell. *St. Mark's Gospel: Two Stages of Its Making*. Cambridge: Cambridge University Press, 1936.

Cullmann, Oscar. *Peter, Disciple — Apostle — Martyr: A Historical and Theological Study*. Translated by Floyd V. Filson. Philadelphia: Westminster, 1953.

Culpepper, Richard Alan. *Anatomy of the Fourth Gospel: A Study in Literary Design*. New Testament Foundations and Facets. Philadelphia: Fortress, 1983.

Davies, William David. *The Gospel and the Land: Early Christian and Jewish Territorial Doctrine*. Berkeley: University of California Press, 1974.

―――. 'Reflections on Archbishop Carrington's "The Primitive Christian Calendar"'. *The Background of the New Testament and Its Eschatology: Studies in Honour of C. H. Dodd*. Edited by W. D. Davies and D. Daube. Cambridge: Cambridge University Press, 1956, pp. 124-52.

Davies, William David, and David Daube, eds. *The Background of the New Testament and Its Eschatology: Studies in Honour of C. H. Dodd*. Cambridge: Cambridge University Press, 1956.

Delorme, Jean. 'Aspects Doctrinaux du Second Évangile'. *Ephemerides Theologicae Lovanienses* 43 (1967), pp. 74-99.

―――. 'La mission des Douze en Galilée. Mk 6,7-13'. *Assemblées du Seigneur* 46 (1974), pp. 43-50.

Derrett, John Duncan Martin. *The Making of Mark: The Scriptural Bases of the Earliest Gospel*. 2 vols. Shipston-on-Stour: Drinkwater, 1985.

Dewey, Joanna. *Markan Public Debate: Literary Technique, Concentric Structure, and Theology in Mark 2.1–3.6*. Society of Biblical Literature Dissertation Series 48. Chico, CA: Scholars, 1980.

————. 'Point of View and the Disciples in Mark'. *Society of Biblical Literature Seminar Papers*. Chico, CA: Scholars, 1982, pp. 97-106.

Dewey, Kim E. 'Peter's Curse and Cursed Peter (Mark 14.53-54, 66-72)'. *The Passion in Mark: Studies on Mark 14–16*. Edited by Werner H. Kelber. Philadelphia: Fortress, 1976, pp. 96-114.

Dibelius, Martin. *From Tradition to Gospel*. Translated by Bertram Lee Woolf. New York: Charles Scribner's Sons, n.d.

Dinider, Erich, ed. *Zeit und Geschichte: Dankesgabe an Rudolf Bultmann zum 80. Geburtstag*. Tübingen: J. C. B. Mohr (Paul Siebeck), 1964.

Dodd, Charles Harold. *The Apostolic Preaching and Its Developments: With an Appendix on Eschatology and History*. Grand Rapids, MI: Baker Book House, 1980.

————. 'The Framework of the Gospel Narrative'. *Expository Times* 43 (1932), pp. 396-400.

Donahue, John Raymond. *Are You the Christ? The Trial Narrative in the Gospel of Mark*. Society of Biblical Literature Dissertation Series 10. Missoula, MT: Society of Biblical Literature, 1973.

————. 'Introduction: From Passion Traditions to Passion Narrative'. *The Passion in Mark: Studies on Mark 14–16*. Edited by Werner H. Kelber. Philadelphia: Fortress, 1976, pp. 1-20.

————. 'Jesus as the Parable of God in the Gospel of Mark'. *Interpretation* 32 (1979), pp. 369-88. Reprinted in James Luther Mays, ed., *Interpreting the Gospels*. Philadelphia: Fortress, 1981, pp. 148-67.

————. 'Temple, Trial, and Royal Christology (Mark 14.53-65)'. *The Passion in Mark: Studies on Mark 14–16*. Edited by Werner H. Kelber. Philadelphia: Fortress, 1976, pp. 61-79.

————. *The Theology and Setting of Discipleship in the Gospel of Mark*. The 1983 Père Marquette Theology Lecture. Milwaukee: Marquette University Press, 1983.

————. Review of *Following Jesus: Discipleship in the Gospel of Mark*, by Ernest Best. *Journal of Biblical Literature* 103 (1984), pp. 114-16.

Donaldson, J. '"Called to Follow": A Twofold Experience of Discipleship in Mark'. *Biblical Theology Bulletin* 5 (1975), pp. 67-77.

Dormeyer, Detlev. *Die Passion Jesu als Verhaltensmodell: Literarische und theologische Analyse der Traditions- und Redaktionsgeschichte der Markuspassion*. Münster: Aschendorff, 1974.

Doty, William Guy. *Contemporary New Testament Interpretation*. Englewood Cliffs, NJ: Prentice-Hall, 1972.

————. 'The Discipline and Literature of New Testament Form Criticism'. *Anglican Theological Review* 51 (1969), pp. 257-321.

————. 'Fundamental Questions about Literary-Critical Methodology: A Review Article'. *Journal of the American Academy of Religion* 40 (1972), pp. 521-27.

Doudna, John Charles. *The Greek of the Gospel of Mark*. Journal of Biblical Literature Monograph Series 12. Philadelphia: Society of Biblical Literature, 1961.

Ebeling, Hans Jürgen. *Das Messiasgeheimnis und die Botschaft des Marcus-Evangelisten*. Beihefte zur Zeitschrift für die neutestamentliche Wissenschaft 19. Berlin: Töpelmann, 1939.

Edwards, Richard Alan. 'A New Approach to the Gospel of Mark'. *Lutheran Quarterly* 22 (1970), pp. 330-35.

—————. Review of *Jesus and the Twelve: Discipleship and Revelation in Mark's Gospel*, by R. P. Meye. *Journal of Biblical Literature* 88 (1969), pp. 361-62.

Egger, Wilhelm. *Nachfolge als Weg zum Leben. Chancen neuerer exegetischer Methoden dargelegt an Mk 10, 17-31*. Österreiche Biblische Studien 1. Klosterneuburg: Österreichisches Katholisches Bibelwerk, 1979.

Ellis, Edward Earle. *The Gospel of Luke*. New Century Bible. Grand Rapids, MI, and London: Eerdmans/Marshall, Morgan & Scott, 1981.

Enslin, Morton Scott. 'The Artistry of Mark'. *Journal of Biblical Literature* 66 (1947), pp. 385-99.

Ernst, Josef. 'Noch einmal: Die Verleugnung Jesu durch Petrus (Mk 14,54.66-72)'. *Catholica* 39 (1976), pp. 207-26.

—————. 'Petrusbekenntnis — Leidensankündigung — Satanswort (Mk 8,27-33): Tradition und Redaktion'. *Catholica* 32 (1978), pp. 46-73.

—————. 'Die Petrustradition im Markusevangelium — ein altes Problem neu angegangen'. *Begegnung mit den Wort. Festschrift für Heinrich Zimmermann*. Edited by J. Zmÿewski and E. Nellessen. Bonner biblische Beiträge 53. Bonn: Peter Hanstein, 1980, pp. 35-65.

—————. 'Simon — Kephas — Petrus: Historische und typologische Perspektiven im Markusevangelium'. *Theologie und Glaube* 71 (1981), pp. 438-56.

Everitt, Brian Sidney. *The Analysis of Contingency Tables*. New York: Wiley, 1977.

Ezell, Doug. Review of *Mark — Traditions in Conflict*, by T. J. Weeden, Sr. *Southwestern Journal of Theology* 15 (1973), p. 98.

Farmer, William Reuben. *The Last Twelve Verses of Mark*. Society for New Testament Studies Monograph Series 25. Cambridge: Cambridge University Press, 1974.

—————. *The Synoptic Problem: A Critical Analysis*. New York: Macmillan, 1964.

—————. Review of *Redactional Style in the Marcan Gospel*, by E. J. Pryke. *Perkins School of Theology Journal* 32 (1978), pp. 46-48.

Farrer, Austin Marsden. *St. Matthew and St. Mark*. Westminster: Dacre, 1954.

—————. *A Study in St. Mark*. Westminster: Dacre, 1951.

Fitzmyer, Joseph Augustine. *The Gospel According to Luke (I–IX)*. Anchor Bible 28. Garden City, NY: Doubleday, 1981.

Fitzpatrick, M. 'Marcan Theology and the Messianic Secret'. *Australian Catholic Record* 59 (1982), pp. 404-16.

Fleddermann, Harry T. 'The Central Question of Mark's Gospel: A Study of Mark 8.29'. Ph.D. dissertation, Graduate Theological Union, 1978.

———. 'The Discipleship Discourse (Mark 9.33-50)'. *Catholic Biblical Quarterly* 43 (1981), pp. 57-75.

———. 'The Flight of a Naked Young Man (Mark 14.51-52)'. *Catholic Biblical Quarterly* 41 (1979), pp. 412-18.

Focant, Camille. 'L'incompréhension des disciples dans le deuxième évangile. Tradition et rédaction'. *Revue biblique* 82 (1975), pp. 161-85. Reprinted in translated condensation as idem, 'The Disciples' Blindness in Mark's Gospel', in *Theology Digest* 24 (1976), pp. 260-64.

Fortna, Robert Tomson. *The Gospel of Signs: A Reconstruction of the Narrative Source Underlying the Fourth Gospel.* Society for New Testament Studies Monograph Series 11. Cambridge: Cambridge University Press, 1980.

———. 'Redaction Criticism, NT'. *The Interpreter's Dictionary of the Bible.* Supplementary volume. Edited by Keith Crim. Nashville: Abingdon, 1976, pp. 733-35.

Fowler, Robert Marion. *Loaves and Fishes: The Function of the Feeding Stories in the Gospel of Mark.* Society of Biblical Literature Dissertation Series 54. Chico, CA: Scholars, 1981.

Freedman, David, Robert Pisani, and Roger Purves. *Statistics.* New York and London: W. W. Norton, 1974.

Frei, Hans. *The Eclipse of Biblical Narrative: A Study in Eighteenth and Nineteenth Century Hermeneutics.* New Haven and London: Yale University Press, 1974.

Freyne, Sean. 'At Cross Purposes: Jesus and the Disciples in Mark'. *Furrow* 33 (1982), pp. 331-39.

———. 'The Disciples in Mark and the *maskilim* in Daniel. A Comparison'. *Journal for the Study of the New Testament* 16 (1982), pp. 7-23.

———. *The Twelve: Disciples and Apostles. A Study in the Theology of the First Three Gospels.* Sheed and Ward Stag Book. London and Sydney: Sheed and Ward, 1968.

Frye, Northrop. *The Great Code: The Bible and Literature.* New York and London: Harcourt Brace Jovanovich, 1982.

Frye, Roland Mushat. 'Literary Criticism and Gospel Criticism'. *Theology Today* 36 (1979), pp. 207-19.

Fuller, Reginald Horace. *Preaching the New Lectionary: The Word of God for the Church Today.* Collegeville, MN: Liturgical, 1974.

Furnish, Victor Paul. *The Moral Teaching of Paul: Selected Issues.* 2nd edn, rev. Nashville: Abingdon, 1985.

Gager, John Goodrich. *Kingdom and Community: The Social World of Early Christianity.* Englewood Cliffs, NJ: Prentice-Hall, 1975.

Garland, David E. Review of *Matthew: Structure, Christology, Kingdom*, by J. D. Kingsbury. *Review and Expositor* 74 (1977), pp. 567-68.

Georgi, Dieter. *Die Gegner des Paulus im 2. Korintherbrief: Studien zur religiösen Propaganda in der Spätantike.* Wissenschaftliche Monographien zum Alten und Neuen Testament 11. Neukirchen-Vluyn: Neukirchener Verlag, 1964.

Gewalt, Dietfried. 'Die Verleugnung des Petrus'. *Linguistica Biblica* 43 (1978), pp. 113-44.

Gnilka, Joachim. *Das Evangelium nach Markus. 1. Teilband: Mk 1–8,26; 2. Teilband: Mk 8,27–16,20.* Evangelisch-katholischer Kommentar zum Neuen Testament 11/1-2. Zürich, Einsiedeln, and Cologne: Benzinger/Neukirchener Verlag, 1978-79.

Goulder, Michael Douglas. *Midrash and Lection in Matthew.* London: SPCK, 1974.

Grant, Frederick Clifton. *The Earliest Gospel: Studies of the Evangelic Tradition and its Point of Crystallization in Writing.* New York and Nashville: Abingdon, 1943.

Grobel, Kendrick. 'Idiosyncrasies of the Synoptists in Their Pericope-Introductions'. *Journal of Biblical Literature* 59 (1940), pp. 405-10.

Güttgemanns, Erhardt. *Candid Questions Concerning Gospel Form Criticism: A Methodological Sketch of the Fundamental Problematics of Form and Redaction Criticism.* Translated by W. G. Doty. Pittsburgh Theological Monograph Series 26. Pittsburgh: Pickwick, 1973.

————. 'Theologie als sprachbezogene Wissenschaft'. *Studia Linguistica Neotestamentica: Gesammelte Aufsätze zur linguistischen Grundlage einer neutestamentlichen Theologie.* Beiträge zur evangelischen Theologie 60. Munich: Kaiser, 1972, pp. 184-230.

Hadas, Moses, and Morton Smith. *Heroes and Gods: Spiritual Biographies in Antiquity.* Religious Perspectives 13. New York: Harper & Row, 1965.

Haenchen, Ernst. 'Die Komposition von Mk vii [read viii] 27-ix 1 und Par'. *Novum Testamentum* 6 (1963), pp. 81-109.

————. *Der Weg Jesu: Eine Erklärung des Markus-Evangeliums und der kanonischen Parallelen.* Berlin: Töpelmann, 1966.

Hainz, Josef, ed. *Kirche im Werden: Studien zum Thema Amt und Gemeinde im Neuen Testament.* Munich: Schöningh, 1976.

Hamilton, Neil Quinn. 'Resurrection Tradition and the Composition of Mark'. *Journal of Biblical Literature* 84 (1965), pp. 415-21.

Harrington, Daniel Joseph. 'A Map of Books on Mark (1975-1984)'. *Biblical Theology Bulletin* 15 (1985), pp. 12-16.

Harrisville, Roy Alvin. Review of *Mark — Traditions in Conflict,* by T. J. Weeden, Sr. *Dialog* 12 (1973), pp. 233-34.

Hartman, Lars. *Prophecy Interpreted: The Formation of Some Jewish Apocalyptic Texts and the Eschatological Discourse in Mark 13 Par.* Coniectanea biblica, New Testament 1. Lund: Gleerup, 1966.

Harvey, Anthony Ernest. *Jesus and the Constraints of History.* Philadelphia: Westminster, 1982.

Hawkin, David John. 'The Incomprehension of the Disciples in the Marcan Redaction'. *Journal of Biblical Literature* 91 (1972), pp. 491-500.

————. 'The Symbolism and Structure of the Marcan Redaction'. *Evangelical Quarterly* 49 (1977), pp. 98-110.

Hay, Lewis Scott. 'The Son-of-God Christology in Mark'. *Journal of Bible and Religion* 32 (1964), pp. 106-14.

Hayes, John Haralson, and Carl Roark Holladay. *Biblical Exegesis: A Beginner's Handbook*. Atlanta: John Knox, 1982.

Hedrick, Charles Webster. 'The Role of 'Summary Statements' in the Composition of the Gospel of Mark: A Dialog with Karl Schmidt and Norman Perrin'. *Novum Testamentum* 26 (1984), pp. 289-311.

Hickling, Colin J. A. 'A Problem of Method in Gospel Research'. *Religious Studies* 10 (1974), pp. 339-46.

Higgins, Angus John Brockhurst, ed. *New Testament Essays: Studies in Memory of T. W. Manson*. Manchester: University of Manchester Press, 1959.

Hirsch, Eric Donald, Jr. *Validity in Interpretation*. New Haven and London: Yale University Press, 1967.

Holladay, Carl Roark. Theios Anēr *in Hellenistic Judaism: A Critique of the Use of This Category in New Testament Christology*. Society of Biblical Literature Dissertation Series 40. Missoula, MT: Scholars, 1977.

Holtzmann, Hans Julius. *Die synoptischen Evangelien: Ihr Ursprung und geschichtlicher Charakter*. Leipzig: Engelmann, 1863.

Hooker, Morna Dorothy. 'In His Own Image?' *What About the New Testament? Essays in Honour of Christopher Evans*. Edited by Morna Hooker and Colin Hickling. London: SCM, 1975, pp. 28-14.

————. *The Message of Mark*. London: Epworth, 1983.

————. 'On Using the Wrong Tool'. *Theology* 65 (1972), pp. 570-81.

Hooker, Morna, and Colin Hickling, eds. *What About the New Testament? Essays in Honour of Christopher Evans*. London: SCM, 1975.

Iser, Wolfgang. *The Implied Reader: Patterns of Communication in Prose Fiction from Bunyan to Beckett*. Baltimore: Johns Hopkins University Press, 1974.

Jeremias, Joachim. *The Parables of Jesus*. 2nd rev. edn. Translated by S. H. Hooke. New York: Charles Scribner's Sons, 1972.

Jervell, Jacob, and Wayne Atherton Meeks, eds. *God's Christ and His People: Studies in Honour of Nils Alstrup Dahl*. Oslo: Universitetsforlaget, 1977.

Johnson, Sherman Elbridge. *A Commentary on the Gospel According to St. Mark*. Black's New Testament Commentaries. London: A. & C. Black, 1960.

Juel, Donald. *An Introduction to New Testament Literature*. Nashville: Abingdon, 1978.

————. *Messiah and Temple: The Trial of Jesus in the Gospel of Mark*. Society of Biblical Literature Dissertation Series 31. Missoula, MT: Scholars, 1977.

Kähler, Martin. *The So-Called Historical Jesus and the Historic Biblical Christ*.

Translated, edited, and with an introduction by Carl E. Braaten. Foreword by Paul Tillich. Philadelphia: Fortress, 1964.

Käsemann, Ernst. 'Blind Alleys in the "Jesus of History" Controversy'. *New Testament Questions of Today*. Translated by W. J. Montague. Philadelphia: Fortress, 1969, pp. 23-65.

————. 'The Problem of the Historical Jesus'. *Essays on New Testament Themes*. Translated by W. J. Montague. Studies in Biblical Theology 41. London: SCM, 1964, pp. 34-55.

Kazmierski, Carl R. *Jesus the Son of God: A Study of the Markan Tradition and Its Redaction by the Evangelist*. Forschung zur Bibel 33. Würzburg: Echter Verlag, 1979.

Kealy, Séan P. *Mark's Gospel: A History of Its Interpretation from the Beginning until 1979*. New York and Ramsey: Paulist, 1982.

Keck, Leander Earl. 'The Introduction to Mark's Gospel'. *New Testament Studies* 12 (1966), pp. 352-70.

————. 'Mark 3.7-12 and Mark's Christology'. *Journal of Biblical Literature* 84 (1965), pp. 341-58.

————. 'On the Ethos of Early Christians'. *Journal of the American Academy of Religion* 42 (1974), pp. 435-42.

Keck, Leander Earl, and James Louis Martyn, eds. *Studies in Luke-Acts*. Philadelphia: Fortress, 1980.

Keck, Leander Earl, and Gene Milton Tucker. 'Exegesis'. *Interpreter's Dictionary of the Bible*. Supplementary volume. Edited by Keith Crim. Nashville: Abingdon, 1976, pp. 296-303.

Kee, Howard Clark. *Christian Origins in Sociological Perspective: Methods and Resources*. Philadelphia: Westminster, 1980.

————. *Community of the New Age: Studies in Mark's Gospel*. Philadelphia: Westminster, 1977.

————. 'Mark as Redactor and Theologian: A Survey of Some Recent Markan Studies'. *Journal of Biblical Literature* 90 (1971), pp. 333-36.

————. 'Mark's Gospel in Recent Research'. *Interpretation* 32 (1978), pp. 353-68. Reprinted in James Luther Mays, ed. *Interpreting the Gospels*. Philadelphia: Fortress, 1981, pp. 130-47.

————. Review of *Jesus and the Twelve: Discipleship and Revelation in Mark's Gospel*, by R. P. Meye. *Interpretation* 24 (1970), pp. 116-17.

Kelber, Werner Heinz. 'Conclusion: From Passion Narrative to Gospel'. *The Passion in Mark: Studies on Mark 14–16*. Edited by Werner H. Kelber. Philadelphia: Fortress, 1976, pp. 153-80.

————. 'The Hour of the Son of Man and the Temptation of the Disciples (Mark 14.32-42)'. *The Passion of Mark: Studies on Mark 14–16*. Edited by Werner H. Kelber. Philadelphia: Fortress, 1976, pp. 41-60.

————. *The Kingdom in Mark: A New Place and a New Time.* Philadelphia: Fortress, 1974.

————. 'Mark 14.32-42: Gethsemane. Passion Christology and Discipleship Failure'. *Zeitschrift für die neutestamentliche Wissenschaft* 63 (1972), pp. 166-87.

————. 'Mark and Oral Tradition'. *Semeia* 16 (1979), pp. 7-55.

————. *Mark's Story of Jesus.* Philadelphia: Fortress, 1979.

————. *The Oral and the Written Gospel: The Hermeneutics of Speaking and Writing in the Synoptic Tradition, Mark, Paul, and Q.* Philadelphia: Fortress, 1983.

————. 'Redaction Criticism: On the Nature and Exposition of the Gospels'. *Perspectives in Religious Studies* 6 (1979), pp. 4-16.

————. ed. *The Passion in Mark: Studies on Mark 14–16.* Philadelphia: Fortress, 1976.

Kennedy, George Alexander. *Classical Rhetoric and Its Christian and Secular Tradition from Ancient to Modern Times.* Chapel Hill, NC: University of North Carolina Press, 1980.

————. *New Testament Interpretation through Rhetorical Criticism.* Chapel Hill, NC, and London: University of North Carolina Press, 1984.

Kermode, Frank. *The Genesis of Secrecy: On the Interpretation of Narrative.* Cambridge, MA, and London: Harvard University Press, 1979.

Kertelge, Karl. 'Die Epiphanie Jesu in Evangelium (Markus)'. *Gestalt und Anspruch des Neuen Testaments.* Edited by J. Schreiner. Würzburg: Echter Verlag, 1969, pp. 153-72. Reprinted in Rudolf Pesch, ed., *Das Markus-Evangelium.* Wege der Forschung 411. Darmstadt: Wissenschaftliche Buchgesellschaft, 1979, pp. 259-82. Reprinted in W. R. Telford, ed., *The Interpretation of Mark.* Issues in Religion and Theology 7. Philadelphia and London: Fortress/SPCK, 1985, pp. 78-94.

————. 'Die Funktion der 'Zwölf' in Markusevangelium: Eine redaktionsgeschichtliche Auslegung, zugleich ein Beitrag zur Frage nach dem neutestamentlichen Amtsverständnis'. *Trier Theologische Zeitschrift* 78 (1969), pp. 193-206.

Kingsbury, Jack Dean. *The Christology of Mark's Gospel.* Philadelphia: Fortress, 1983.

————. 'The "Divine Man" as the Key to Mark's Christology — The End of an Era?' *Interpretation* 35 (1981), pp. 243-57.

————. 'The Gospel of Mark in Current Research'. *Religious Studies Review* 5 (1979), pp. 101-107.

————. *Matthew: Structure, Christology, Kingdom.* Philadelphia: Fortress, 1975.

Kirby, M. F. 'Mark's Prerequisite for Being an Apostle'. *The Bible Today* 18 (1980), pp. 77-81.

Kittlaus, Lloyd R. 'John and Mark: A Methodological Evaluation of Norman Perrin's Suggestion'. *Society of Biblical Literature Seminar Papers.* Vol. II. Missoula, MT: Scholars, 1978, pp. 269-79.

Klauck, Hans-Josef. 'Die erzählerische Rolle der Jünger in Markusevangelium. Eine narrative Analyse'. *Novum Testamentum* 24 (1982), pp. 1-26.

Klein, Günther. 'Die Berufung des Petrus'. *Zeitschrift für die neutestamentliche Wissenschaft* 58 (1967), pp. 1-44.

————. 'Die Verleugnung des Petrus. Eine traditionsgeschichtliche Untersuchung'. *Zeitschrift für Theologie und Kirche* 58 (1961), pp. 285-328.

————. *Die Zwölf Apostel: Ursprung und Gehalt einer Idee*. Forschungen zur Religion und Literatur des Alten und Neuen Testaments, n.s. 59. Göttingen: Vandenhoeck & Ruprecht, 1961.

Klostermann, Erich. *Das Markusevangelium*. Handbuch zum Neuen Testament 3. 4th enlarged edn. Tübingen: J. C. B. Mohr (Paul Siebeck), 1950.

Knigge, Heinz-Dieter. 'The Meaning of Mark: The Exegesis of the Second Gospel'. *Interpretation* 22 (1968), pp. 53-70.

Knox, Wilfred Lawrence. *The Sources of the Synoptic Gospels*. Volume One: *St. Mark*. Cambridge: Cambridge University Press, 1953.

Koch, Klaus. *The Growth of the Biblical Tradition: The Form-Critical Method*. Translated by S. M. Cupitt. Scribner Studies in Biblical Interpretation. New York: Charles Scribner's Sons, 1969.

Krentz, Edgar. *The Historical-Critical Method*. 'Editor's Foreword', by Gene M. Tucker. Guides to Biblical Scholarship, Old Testament Series. Philadelphia: Fortress, 1975.

Krieger, Murray. *A Window to Criticism: Shakespeare's Sonnets and Modern Poetics*. Princeton: Princeton University Press, 1964.

Kuby, Alfred. 'Zur Konzeption des Markus-Evangeliums'. *Zeitschrift für die neutestamentliche Wissenschaft* 49 (1958), pp. 52-64.

Kühschelm, Roman. *Jüngerverfolgung und Geschick Jesu: Eine exegetisch-bibeltheologische Untersuchung der synoptischen Verfolgungsankündigungen Mk 13, 9-13 par und Mt 23, 29-36 par*. Österreichische Biblische Studien 5. Klosterneuburg Österreichisches Katholisches Bibelwerk, 1983.

Kümmel, Werner Georg. *Introduction to the New Testament*. 17th rev. edn. Translated by Howard Clark Kee. Nashville: Abingdon, 1973.

————. *The New Testament: The History of the Investigation of Its Problems*. Translated by S. McLean Gilmour and Howard C. Kee. London: SCM, 1972.

Kugelman, Richard. Review of *Jesus and the Twelve: Discipleship and Revelation in Mark's Gospel*, by R. P. Meye. *Catholic Biblical Quarterly* 31 (1969), pp. 589-90.

Kuhn, Heinz-Wolfgang. *Ältere Sammlungen im Markusevangelium*. Studien zur Umwelt des Neuen Testaments 8. Göttingen: Vandenhoeck & Ruprecht, 1971.

Kysar, Robert. *The Fourth Evangelist and His Gospel: An Examination of Contemporary Scholarship*. Minneapolis: Augsburg, 1975.

Lamarche, Paul. 'The Call to Conversion and Faith. The Vocation of Levi (Mk 2, 13-17)'. *Lumière et Vie* 25 (1970), pp. 301-12.

Lambrecht, Jan. *Die Redaktion der Markus-Apokalypse: Literarische Analyse und*

Strukturuntersuchung. Analecta biblica 28. Rome: Pontifical Biblical Institute, 1967.

———. 'The Relatives of Jesus in Mark'. *Novum Testamentum* 16 (1974), pp. 241-58.

Lampe, Geoffrey William Hugo. 'St. Peter's Denial'. *Bulletin of the John Rylands University Library of Manchester* 55 (1973), pp. 346-68.

Lane, William Lister. *The Gospel According to Mark: The English Text with Introduction, Exposition and Notes*. New International Commentary on the New Testament. Grand Rapids, MI: Eerdmans, 1974.

———. '*Theios Anēr* Christology and the Gospel of Mark'. *New Dimensions in New Testament Study*. Edited by R. N. Longenecker and M. C. Tenney. Grand Rapids, MI: Zondervan, 1974, pp. 144-61.

Lang, Friedrich Gustav. 'Kompositionsanalyse des Markusevangeliums'. *Zeitschrift für Theologie und Kirche* 74 (1977), pp. 1-24.

Lapide, Cornelius à. *The Great Commentary of Cornelius à Lapide: S. Matthew's Gospel — Chaps. XXII to XXVII; S. Mark's Gospel — Complete*. 3rd edn. Translated by Thomas W. Mossman. London: John Hodges, 1891.

Légasse, Simon. 'Approche de l'Épisode préévangélique des Fils de Zébédée (Marc x.35-40 par.)'. *New Testament Studies* 20 (1974), pp. 161-77.

———. 'Tout quitter pour suivre le Christ. Mc 10, 17-30'. *Assemblées du Seigneur* 59 (1974), pp. 43-54.

Lightfoot, Robert Henry. *The Gospel Message of St. Mark*. Oxford: Clarendon, 1950.

———. *History and Interpretation in the Gospels*. London: Hodder and Stoughton, 1935.

———. *Locality and Doctrine in the Gospels*. London: Hodder and Stoughton, 1938.

Linnemann, Eta. *Studien zur Passionsgeschichte*. Forschungen zur Religion und Literatur des Alten und Neuen Testaments 102. Göttingen: Vandenhoeck & Ruprecht, 1970.

———. 'Die Verleugnung des Petrus'. *Zeitschrift für Theologie und Kirche* 63 (1966), pp. 1-32.

Little, James Crichton. 'Redaction Criticism and the Gospel of Mark with Special Reference to Mark 4.1-34'. Ph.D. dissertation, Duke University, 1972.

Lohmeyer, Ernst. *Das Evangelium des Markus*. Kritisch-exegetischer Kommentar über das Neue Testament. Edited by H. A. W. Meyer. Göttingen: Vandenhoeck & Ruprecht, 1954.

———. *Galiläa und Jerusalem*. Göttingen: Vandenhoeck & Ruprecht, 1936.

Longenecker, Richard Norman, and Merrill Chapin Tenney, eds. *New Directions in New Testament Study*. Grand Rapids, MI: Zondervan, 1974.

Luz, Ulrich. 'Das Geheimnismotiv und die Markinische Christologie'. *Zeitschrift für die neutestamentliche Wissenschaft* 56 (1965), pp. 9-30. Reprinted in Christopher Tucker, ed., *The Messianic Secret*. Issues in Religion and Theology 1. Philadelphia and London: Fortress/SPCK, 1983, pp. 75-96.

————. 'Die Jünger im Matthäusevangelium'. *Zeitschrift für die neutestamentliche Wissenschaft* 62 (1971), pp. 141-71.

————. 'Markusforschung in der Sackgasse?' *Theologische Literaturzeitung* 105 (1980), pp. 642-55.

McKnight, Edgar Vernon. *Meaning in Texts: The Historical Shaping of a Narrative Hermeneutics.* Philadelphia: Fortress, 1978.

————. *What Is Form Criticism?* Guides to Biblical Scholarship, New Testament Series. Philadelphia: Fortress, 1969.

Malbon, Elizabeth Struthers. 'Fallible Followers: Women and Men in the Gospel of Mark'. *Semeia* 28 (1983), pp. 29-48.

————. 'Galilee and Jerusalem: History and Literature in Marcan Interpretation'. *Catholic Biblical Quarterly* 44 (1982), pp. 242-55.

————. *Narrative Space and Mythic Meaning in Mark.* New Voices in Biblical Studies. San Francisco: Harper & Row, 1986.

Malherbe, Abraham Johannes. *Social Aspects of Early Christianity.* Baton Rouge and London: Louisiana State University Press, 1977.

Maloney, Elliott Charles. *Semitic Interference in Marcan Syntax.* Society of Biblical Literature Dissertation Series 51. Missoula, MT: Scholars, 1981.

Manicardi, Ermenegildo. *Il cammino di Gesù nel Vangèlo di Marco: Schema narrativo e tema cristologico.* Analecta biblica 96. Rome: Pontifical Biblical Institute, 1981.

Mann, Christopher Stephen. *Mark: A New Translation with Introduction and Commentary.* Anchor Bible 27. Garden City, NY: Doubleday, 1986.

Manson, Thomas Walter. *Studies in the Gospels and Epistles.* Edited by Matthew Black. Philadelphia: Westminster, 1962.

Marshall, Ian Howard, ed. *New Testament Interpretation: Essays on Principles and Methods.* Exeter: Paternoster, 1977.

Martin, James Perry. Review of *Mark — Traditions in Conflict,* by T. J. Weeden, Sr. *Interpretation* 26 (1972), pp. 361-62.

Martin, Ralph Philip. *Mark: Evangelist and Theologian.* Contemporary Evangelical Perspectives. Grand Rapids, MI: Zondervan, 1972.

Martyn, James Louis. *History and Theology in the Fourth Gospel.* Revised and enlarged. Nashville: Abingdon, 1979.

Marxsen, Willi. *Der Evangelist Markus: Studien zur Redaktionsgeschichte des Evangeliums.* Forschungen zur Religion und Literatur des Alten und Neuen Testaments, NF 49. Göttingen: Vandenhoeck & Ruprecht, 1956. ET idem. *Mark the Evangelist: Studies on the Redaction History of the Gospel.* Translated by James Boyce, et al. Nashville and New York: Abingdon, 1969.

————. *Introduction to the New Testament: An Approach to Its Problems.* Translated by Geoffrey Buswell. Philadelphia: Fortress, 1968.

————. 'Redaktionsgeschichtliche Erklärung der sogenannten Parabeltheorie des Markus'. *Zeitschrift für Theologie und Kirche* 52 (1955), pp. 255-71.

————. Review of *Die Mitte der Zeit*, by Hans Conzelmann. *Monatsschrift für Pastoraltheologie* 6 (1954), p. 254.

Matera, Frank J. 'Interpreting Mark — Some Recent Theories of Redaction Criticism'. *Louvain Studies* 2 (1968), pp. 113-31.

————. *The Kingship of Jesus: Composition and Theology in Mark 15*. Society of Biblical Literature Dissertation Series 66. Missoula, MT: Scholars, 1981.

————. Review of *Following Jesus: Discipleship in the Gospel of Mark*, by Ernest Best. *Interpretation* 38 (1984), pp. 93-94.

Meagher, John Carney. *Clumsy Construction in Mark's Gospel: A Critique of Form and Redaktionsgeschichte*. Toronto Studies in Theology 3. New York and Toronto: Edwin Mellen, 1979.

————. '*Die Form- und Redaktionsungeschickliche Methoden*: The Principle of Clumsiness and the Gospel of Mark'. *Journal of the American Academy of Religion* 43 (1975), pp. 459-72.

Meier, John Paul. *The Vision of Matthew: Christ, Church, and Morality in the First Gospel*. New York: Paulist, 1979.

Metzger, Bruce Manning. *The Text of the New Testament: Its Transmission, Corruption, and Restoration*. 3rd edn. New York and Oxford: Oxford University Press, 1968.

————. *A Textual Commentary on the Greek New Testament*. N.p.: United Bible Societies, 1971.

Meye, Robert Paul. *Jesus and the Twelve: Discipleship and Revelation in Mark's Gospel*. Grand Rapids, MI: Eerdmans, 1968.

————. 'Mark 4,10: "Those About Him with the Twelve"'. *Studia Evangelica* 2 (1964), pp. 211-18.

————. 'Mark 16.8 — The Ending of Mark's Gospel'. *Biblical Research* 14 (1969), pp. 33-43.

————. 'Messianic Secret and Messianic Didache in Mark's Gospel'. *Oikonomia: Hellsgeschichte als Thema der Theologie*. O. Cullmann *Festschrift*. Edited by Felix Christ. Hamburg-Bergstedt: Herbert Reich, 1967, pp. 57-68.

Michaelis, Wilhelm. μιμέομαι, κ.τ.λ. *Theological Dictionary of the New Testament*. Vol. IV. Edited by Gerhard Kittel. Translated by Geoffrey W. Bromiley. Grand Rapids, MI: Eerdmans, 1967, pp. 359-74.

Miller, Donald George, and Dikran Y. Hadidian, eds. *Jesus and Man's Hope*. 2 vols. A Perspective Book. Pittsburgh: Pittsburgh Theological Seminary, 1970, 1971.

Minear, Paul Sevier. 'Audience Criticism and Markan Ecclesiology'. *Neues Testament und Geschichte: Historisches Geschehen und Deutung im Neuen Testament. Oscar Cullmann zum 70. Geburtstag*. Edited by Heinrich Baltensweiler and Bo Reicke. Zürich and Tübingen: Theologischer Verlag/J. C. B. Mohr (Paul Siebeck), 1972, pp. 79-89.

Minette de Tillesse, Georges. *Le Secret Messianique dans l'Évangile de Marc*. Lectio divina 47. Paris: Les Éditions du Cerf, 1968.

Mitton, Charles Leslie. 'Some Further Studies in St Mark's Gospel'. *Expository Times* 87 (1976), pp. 297-301.

Moloney, Francis J. 'The Vocation of the Disciples in the Gospel of Mark'. *Salesianum* 43 (1981), pp. 487-516.

Mosley, A. W. 'Jesus' Audiences in the Gospels of St. Mark and St. Luke'. *New Testament Studies* 10 (1963), pp. 139-49.

Moule, Charles Francis Digby. *The Birth of the New Testament.* 3rd edn, revised and rewritten. San Francisco: Harper & Row, 1982.

———. 'The Intention of the Evangelists'. *New Testament Essays: Studies in Memory of T. W. Manson.* Edited by A. J. B. Higgins. Manchester: Manchester University Press, 1959, pp. 165-79.

Mowery, Robert L. Review of *Redactional Style in the Marcan Gospel,* by E. J. Pryke. *Journal of Biblical Literature* 99 (1980), pp. 615-17.

Munro, Winsome. 'Women Disciples in Mark?' *Catholic Biblical Quarterly* 44 (1982), pp. 225-41.

Neirynck, Frans. *Duality in Mark: Contributions to the Study of Markan Redaction.* Bibliotheca ephemeridum theologicarum lovaniensium 31. Leuven: Leuven University Press, 1972.

———. 'L'Évangile de Marc: À propos d'un nouveau commentaire'. *Ephemerides Theologicae Lovanienses* 53 (1977), pp. 153-81; 55 (1979), pp. 1-42.

———. 'The Redactional Text of Mark'. *Ephemerides Theologicae Lovanienses* 57 (1981), pp. 144-62.

———. 'Synoptic Problem'. *The Interpreter's Dictionary of the Bible.* Supplementary volume. Edited by Keith Crim. Nashville: Abingdon, 1976, pp. 845-48.

Neotestamentica et Patristica: Eine Freundesgabe Herrn Professor Dr. Oscar Cullmann zu seinem 60. Geburtstag überreicht. Novum Testamentum Supplements 6. Leiden: E. J. Brill, 1962.

Neutestamentliche Studien für Rudolf Bultmann zu seinem siebzigsten Geburtstag am 20. August 1954. Edited by W. Eltester. Berlin: Töpelmann, 1954.

Nineham, Dennis Eric. *The Gospel of St. Mark.* The Pelican Gospel Commentaries. Baltimore: Penguin, 1963.

———. 'The Order of Events in St. Mark's Gospel — An Examination of Dr. Dodd's Hypothesis'. *Studies in the Gospels: Essays in Memory of R. H. Lightfoot.* Edited by D. E. Nineham. London: Blackwell, 1955, pp. 223-39.

———. ed. *Studies in the Gospels: Essays in Memory of R. H. Lightfoot.* London: Blackwell, 1955.

Nygren, Anders. *Agape and Eros. Part I: A Study of the Christian Idea of Love. Part II: The History of the Christian Idea of Love.* Vol. I. Philadelphia: Westminster, 1938.

———. *Meaning and Method: Prolegomena to a Scientific Philosophy of Religion and a Scientific Theology.* London: Epworth, 1972.

Osborne, B. A. E. 'Peter: Stumbing-Block and Satan'. *Novum Testamentum* 15 (1973), pp. 187-90.

Palmer, Richard E. *Hermeneutics: Interpretation Theory in Schleiermacher, Dilthey, Heidegger, and Gadamer.* Northwestern University Studies in Phenomenology and Existential Philosophy. Evanston: Northwestern University Press, 1969.

Parker, Pierson. *The Gospel Before Mark.* Chicago: University of Chicago Press, 1953.

Patte, Daniel. *What Is Structuralist Exegesis?* Guides to Biblical Scholarship, New Testament Series. Philadelphia: Fortress, 1976.

Peabody, David Barrett. *Mark as Composer.* New Gospel Studies 1. Macon, GA: Mercer University Press, 1987.

———. 'The Redactional Features of the Author of Mark: A Method Focusing on Recurrent Phraseology and Its Application'. Ph.D. dissertation, Southern Methodist University, 1983.

Peacock, Hebert F. 'Discipleship in the Gospel of Mark'. *Review and Expositor* 74 (1978), pp. 555-64.

Perrin, Norman. 'The Christology of Mark: A Study in Methodology'. *Journal of Religion* 51 (1971), pp. 173-87. Reprinted in M. Sabbe, ed., *L'Évangile selon Marc: Tradition et rédaction.* Bibliotheca ephemeridum theologicarum lovaniensium 34. Gembloux and Louvain: Duculot/Leuven University Press, 1974, pp. 471-85. Reprinted in W. R. Telford, ed., *The Interpretation of Mark.* Issues in Religion and Theology 7. Philadelphia and London: Fortress/SPCK, 1985, pp. 95-108.

———. 'The Creative Use of the Son of Man Traditions in Mark'. *Union Seminary Quarterly Review* 23 (1967/1968), pp. 357-65.

———. 'The Evangelist as Author: Reflections on Method in the Study and Interpretation of the Synoptic Gospels and Acts'. *Biblical Research* 17 (1972), pp. 5-18.

———. 'The Interpretation of the Gospel of Mark'. *Interpretation* 30 (1979), pp. 115-24.

———. *Jesus and the Language of the Kingdom: Symbol and Metaphor in New Testament Interpretation.* Philadelphia: Fortress, 1976.

———. *The Resurrection According to Matthew, Mark, and Luke.* Philadelphia: Fortress, 1977.

———. 'Towards an Interpretation of the Gospel of Mark'. *Christology and a Modern Pilgrimage: A Discussion with Norman Perrin.* Edited by Hans Dieter Betz. Philadelphia: Fortress, 1971, pp. 1-60.

———. *What Is Redaction Criticism?* Guides to Biblical Scholarship, New Testament Series. Philadelphia: Fortress, 1976.

———. 'The *Wredestrasse* Becomes the *Hauptstrasse:* Reflections on the Reprinting of the Dodd *Festschrift'. Journal of Religion* 46 (1966), pp. 296-300.

————, and Dennis C. Duling. *The New Testament: An Introduction.* 2nd edn. New York: Harcourt Brace Jovanovich, 1982.

Pesch, Rudolf. 'Berufung und Sendung, Nachfolge und Mission: Eine Studie zu Mk 1, 16-20'. *Zeitschrift für Katholische Theologie* 91 (1969), pp. 1-31.

————. *Das Markusevangelium.* 2 vols. Herders Theologischer Kommentar zum Neuen Testament. Freiburg, Basel, and Vienna: Herder, 1976, 1977.

————. 'Das Messiasbekenntnis des Petrus (Mk 8, 27-30). Neuverhandlung einer alten Frage'. *Biblische Zeitschrift* 17 (1973), pp. 178-95; 18 (1974), pp. 20-31.

————. *Naherwartungen: Tradition und Redaktion in Mk 13.* Kommentare und Beiträge zum Alten und Neuen Testament. Düsseldorf: Patmos, 1968.

————. 'Der Schluss der vormarkinischen Passionsgeschichte und des Markusevangeliums: Mk 15.42–16.8'. *L'Évangile selon Marc: Tradition et Rédaction.* Edited by M. Sabbe. Bibliotheca ephemeridum theologicarum lovaniensium 34. Gembloux and Louvain: Duculot/Leuven University Press, 1974, pp. 365-409.

————, ed. *Das Markus-Evangelium.* Wege der Forschung 411. Darmstadt: Wissenschaftliche Buchgesellschaft, 1979.

Petersen, Norman Richard. *Literary Criticism for New Testament Critics.* Guides to Biblical Scholarship, New Testament Series. Philadelphia: Fortress, 1978.

————. 'When Is the End Not the End? Literary Reflections on the Ending of Mark's Narrative'. *Interpretation* 34 (1980), pp. 151-66.

Polzin, Robert M. *Biblical Structuralism: Method and Subjectivity in the Study of Ancient Texts.* Semeia Supplements. Missoula, MT: Scholars, 1977.

Pryke, Edgar John. *Redactional Style in the Marcan Gospel: A Study of Syntax and Vocabulary as Guides to Redaction in Mark.* Society for New Testament Studies Monograph Series 33. Cambridge: Cambridge University Press, 1978.

Pudussery, Paul S. 'The Meaning of Discipleship in the Gospel of Mark'. *Jeevadhara* 10 (1980), pp. 93-110.

Quesnell, Quentin. *The Mind of Mark: Interpretation and Method through the Exegesis of Mark 6,52.* Analecta biblica 38. Rome: Pontifical Biblical Institute, 1969.

von Rad, Gerhard. *Genesis: A Commentary.* Rev. edn. Translated by John H. Marks. Old Testament Library. Philadelphia: Westminster, 1972.

Räisänen, Heikki. *Das 'Messiasgeheimnis' im Markusevangelium.* Helsinki and Leiden: Länsi-Suomi/E. J. Brill, 1976.

Rast, Walter. *Tradition History and the Old Testament.* 'Editor's Foreword' by J. Coert Rylaarsdam. Guides to Biblical Scholarship, Old Testament Series. Philadelphia: Fortress, 1972.

Rawlinson, Alfred Edward John. *The Gospel According to St. Mark.* Westminster Commentaries. London: Methuen, 1942.

Reedy, Charles Joseph. 'Redaction and the Messianic Secret in Mark: A Study of the Redaction Critical Method'. Ph.D. dissertation, University of St. Michael's College, 1976.

Reimarus, Hermann Samuel. *Reimarus: Fragments.* Edited by Charles H. Talbert. Lives of Jesus Series. Philadelphia: Fortress, 1970.

Rengstorf, Karl Heinrich. δώδεκα. *Theological Dictionary of the New Testament.* Vol. II. Edited by Gerhard Kittel. Translated by Geoffrey W. Bromiley. Grand Rapids, MI: Eerdmans, 1964, pp. 321-28.

―――. μανθάνω, κ.τ.λ. *Theological Dictionary of the New Testament.* Vol. IV. Edited by Gerhard Kittel. Translated by Geoffrey W. Bromiley. Grand Rapids, MI: Eerdmans, 1967, pp. 390-461.

Reploh, Karl-Georg. *Markus — Lehrer der Gemeinde: Eine redaktionsgeschichtliche Studie zu den Jüngerperikopen des Markus-Evangeliums.* Stuttgarter biblische Monographien 9. Stuttgart: Katholisches Bibelwerk, 1969.

Repo, Eero. *Der 'Weg' als Selbstbezeichnung des Urchristentums: Eine traditionsgeschichtliche und semasiologische Untersuchung.* Annales academiae scientarum fennicae B132/2. Helsinki: Soumalainen Tiedeakatemia, 1964.

Rhoads, David, and Donald Michie. *Mark as Story: An Introduction to the Narrative of a Gospel.* Philadelphia: Fortress, 1982.

Rhys, Howard. Review of *Mark — Traditions in Conflict,* by T. J. Weeden, Sr. *Anglican Theological Review* 54 (1972), pp. 368-69.

Ricoeur, Paul. *Interpretation Theory: Discourse and the Surplus of Meaning.* Fort Worth, TX: Texas Christian University Press, 1976.

Riesenfeld, Harald. 'Tradition und Redaktion im Markusevangelium'. *Neutestamentliche Studien für Rudolf Bultmann zu seinem siebzigsten Geburtstag.* Bern: Alfred Töpelmann, 1954, pp. 157-64. Reprinted in Rudolf Pesch, ed., *Das Markus-Evangelium.* Wege der Forschung 411. Darmstadt: Wissenschaftliche Buchgesellschaft, 1979, pp. 103-12.

Riesner, Rainer. *Jesus als Lehrer: Eine Untersuchung zum Ursprung der Evangelien-Überlieferung.* Wissenschafthche Untersuchungen zum Neuen Testament, 2nd series, 7. Tübingen: Mohr (Siebeck), 1981.

Robbins, Vernon Kay. *Jesus the Teacher: A Socio-Rhetorical Interpretation of Mark.* Philadelphia: Fortress, 1984.

―――. 'Last Meal: Preparation, Betrayal, and Absence (Mark 14.12-25)'. *The Passion in Mark: Studies on Mark 14–16.* Edited by Werner H. Kelber. Philadelphia: Fortress, 1976, pp. 21-40.

―――. Review of *Mark — Traditions in Conflict,* by T. J. Weeden, Sr. *Journal of Biblical Literature* 91 (1972), pp. 417-20.

Robinson, James McConkey. 'The Literary Composition of Mark'. *L'Évangile selon Marc: Tradition et rédaction.* Edited by M. Sabbe. Bibliotheca ephemeridum theologicarum lovaniensium 34. Gembloux and Louvain: Duculot/Leuven University Press, 1974, pp. 11-19.

―――. *A New Quest of the Historical Jesus.* Studies in Biblical Theology 25. London: SCM, 1971.

―――. 'On the *Gattung* of Mark (and John)'. *Jesus and Man's Hope.* Vol. I. Edited by D. C. Miller and D. Y. Hadidian. A Perspective Book. Pittsburgh: Pittsburgh Theological Seminary, 1970, pp. 99-129. Reprinted in idem, *The Problem of History in Mark and Other Marcan Studies*. Philadelphia: Fortress, 1982, pp. 11-39.

————. *The Problem of History in Mark.* Studies in Biblical Theology 21. London: SCM, 1957.

————. *The Problem of History in Mark and Other Marcan Studies*. Philadelphia: Fortress, 1982.

————. 'The Problem of History in Mark, Reconsidered'. *Union Seminary Quarterly Review* 20 (1965), pp. 131-47.

Robinson, William Childs, Jr. 'The Quest for Wrede's Secret Messiah'. *Interpretation* 27 (1973), pp. 10-30. Reprinted in Christopher Tuckett, ed., *The Messianic Secret.* Issues in Religion and Theology 1. Philadelphia and London: Fortress/ SPCK, 1983, pp. 97-115.

Rohde, Joachim. *Rediscovering the Teaching of the Evangelists*. Translated by Dorothea M. Barton. New Testament Library. Philadelphia: Westminster, 1968.

Roloff, Jürgen. *Apostolat — Verkündigung — Kirche: Ursprung, Inhalt, und Funktion des kirchlichen Apostelamtes nach Paulus, Lukas, und den Pastoralbriefen.* Göttingen: Vandenhoeck & Ruprecht, 1970.

————. 'Das Markusevangelium als Geschichtsdarstellung'. *Evangelische Theologie* 29 (1969), pp. 73-93.

Rome and the Study of Scripture: A Collection of Papal Enactments of the Study of Holy Scripture Together with the Decisions of the Biblical Commission. 6th edn, newly rev. and enlarged. Indianapolis: St. Meinrad, 1958.

Ropes, James Hardy. *The Synoptic Gospels.* Cambridge, MA: Harvard University Press, 1934.

Sabbe, M., ed. *L'Évangile selon Marc: Tradition et rédaction*. Bibliotheca ephemeridum theologicarum lovaniensium 34. Gembloux and Louvain: Duculot/ Leuven University Press, 1974.

Sanders, Ed Parrish. *Jesus and Judaism*. Philadelphia: Fortress, 1985.

————. *The Tendencies of the Synoptic Tradition.* Society for New Testament Studies Monograph Series 9. Cambridge: Cambridge University Press, 1969.

Sanders, James Alvin. *Canon and Community: A Guide to Canonical Criticism.* Guides to Biblical Scholarship, Old Testament Series. Philadelphia: Fortress, 1984.

————. *From Sacred Story to Sacred Text: Canon as Paradigm.* Philadelphia: Fortress, 1987.

————. *Torah and Canon*. Philadelphia: Fortress, 1972.

————. Review of *Holy Scripture: Canon, Authority, Criticism,* by J. Barr. *Journal of Biblical Literature* 104 (1985), pp. 501-502.

Sawyerr, Harry. 'The Marcan Framework'. *Scottish Journal of Theology* 14 (1961), pp. 279-94.

Schenk, Wolfgang. *Der Passionsbericht nach Markus: Untersuchungen zur Überlieferungsgeschichte der Passionstraditionen.* Gütersloh: Gerd Mohn, 1974.

Schenke, Ludger. *Auferstehungsverkundigung und leeres Grab.* Stuttgarter Bibelstudien 33. Stuttgart: Katholisches Bibelwerk, 1969.

————. *Der gekreuzigte Christus: Versuch einer literarkritischen und traditionsgeschichtlichen Bestimmung der vormarkinischen Passionsgeschichte.* Stuttgarter Bibelstudien 69. Stuttgart: Katholisches Bibelwerk, 1974.

————. *Studien zur Passionsgeschichte des Markus: Tradition und Redaktion in Markus 14, 1-42.* Forschung zur Bibel 4. Würzburg: Echter Verlag, 1971.

Schierling, Marla Jean. 'Women as Leaders in the Marcan Communities'. *Listening* 15 (1980), pp. 250-56.

Schille, Gottfried. 'Bemerkungen zur Formgeschichte des Evangeliums: Rahmen und Aufbau des Markus-Evangeliums'. *New Testament Studies* 4 (1957), pp. 1-24.

Schmahl, Günther. 'Die Berufung der Zwölf im Markusevangelium'. *Trier Theologische Zeitschrift* 81 (1972), pp. 203-13.

————. *Die Zwölf im Markusevangelium: Eine redaktionsgeschichtliche Untersuchung.* Trier Theologische Studien 30. Trier: Paulinus, 1974.

Schmidt, Hans, ed. *Eucharisterion: Hermann Gunkel zum 60. Geburtstag.* Göttingen: Vandenhoeck & Ruprecht, 1923.

Schmidt, Karl Ludwig. *Der Rahmen der Geschichte Jesu: Literarkritische Untersuchungen zur ältesten Jesusüberlieferung.* Berlin: Trowitzsch & Sohn, 1919.

————. 'Die Stellung der Evangelien in der allgemeinen Literaturgeschichte'. *Eucharisterion: Hermann Gunkel zum 60. Geburtstag.* Edited by H. Schmidt. Göttingen: Vandenhoeck & Ruprecht, 1923, pp. 50-134.

Schmithals, Walter. *Das Evangelium nach Markus.* Ökumenischer Taschenbuch Kommentar zum Neuen Testament 2/1, 2/2. Würzburg/Gütersloh: Gerd Mohn/Gütersloher & Echter Verlag, 1979.

————. 'Der Markusschluss, die Verklärungsgeschichte und die Aussendung der Zwölf'. *Zeitschrift für Theologie und Kirche* 69 (1972), pp. 379-411.

Schmitt, John J. 'Women in Mark's Gospel'. *The Bible Today* 19 (1981), pp. 228-33.

Scholes, Robert, and Robert Kellogg. *The Nature of Narrative.* London: Oxford University Press, 1966.

Schreiber, Johannes. 'Die Christologie des Markusevangeliums. Beobachtungen zur Theologie und Komposition des zweiten Evangeliums'. *Zeitschrift für Theologie und Kirche* 58 (1961), pp. 154-83.

Schreiner, Josef, ed. *Gestalt und Anspruch des Neuen Testaments.* Würzburg: Echter Verlag, 1969.

Schulz, Anselm. *Nachfolge und Nachahmen. Studien über das Verhältnis der neu-*

testamentlichen Jüngerschaft zur urchristlichen Vorbildethik. Studien zum Alten und Neuen Testament 6. Munich: Kösel, 1962.

Schweizer, Eduard. 'Anmerkungen zur Theologie des Markus'. *Neotestamentica et Patristica: Eine Freundesgabe Herrn Professor Dr. Oscar Cullmann zu seinem 60. Geburtstag überreicht.* Novum Testamentum Supplements 6. Leiden: E. J. Brill, 1962, pp. 35-46.

————. *The Good News According to Mark.* Translated by D. H. Madvig. Richmond, VA: John Knox, 1970.

————. 'Mark's Contribution to the Quest of the Historical Jesus'. *New Testament Studies* 10 (1963/64), pp. 421-32.

————. 'Neuere Markus-Forschung in USA'. *Evangelische Theologie* 33 (1973), pp. 533-37.

————. 'The Portrayal of the Life of Faith in the Gospel of Mark'. *Interpretation* 32 (1978), pp. 387-99. Reprinted in James Luther Mays, ed., *Interpreting the Gospels.* Philadelphia: Fortress, 1981, pp. 168-82.

————. 'Die theologische Leistung des Markus'. *Evangelische Theologie* 4 (1964), pp. 337-55. Reprinted in Rudolf Pesch, ed., *Das Markus-Evangelium.* Wege der Forschung 411. Darmstadt: Wissenschaftliche Buchgesellschaft, 1979, pp. 163-89. Reprinted in W. R. Telford, ed., *The Interpretation of Mark.* Issues in Religion and Theology 7. Philadelphia and London: Fortress/SPCK, 1985, pp. 42-63.

————. 'Towards a Christology of Mark?' *God's Christ and His People: Studies in Honour of Nils Alstrup Dahl.* Edited by Jacob Jervell and Wayne A. Meeks. Oslo: Universitetsforlaget, 1977, pp. 29-42.

————. 'Zur Frage des Messiasgeheimnis bei Markus'. *Zeitschrift für die neutestamentliche Wissenschaft* 56 (1965), pp. 1-8. Reprinted in Christopher Tuckett, ed., *The Messianic Secret.* Issues in Religion and Theology 1. Philadelphia and London: Fortress/SPCK, 1983, pp. 65-74.

Seal, Welton Ollie, Jr. 'Norman Perrin and His "School": Retracing a Pilgrimage'. *Journal for the Study of the New Testament* 20 (1984), pp. 87-107.

————. 'The Parousia in Mark: A Debate with Norman Perrin and His "School"'. Ph.D. dissertation, Union Theological Seminary (New York), 1982.

Selvidge, Marla Jean. '"And Those Who Followed Feared" (Mark 10.32)'. *Catholic Biblical Quarterly* 45 (1983), pp. 396-400.

Senior, Donald Paul. *The Passion of Jesus in the Gospel of Mark.* The Glazier Passion Series 2. Wilmington, DE: Michael Glazier, 1984.

————. 'The Struggle to Be Universal: Mission as Vantage Point for New Testament Interpretation'. *Catholic Biblical Quarterly* 46 (1984), pp. 63-81.

Sheridan, Mark. 'Disciples and Discipleship in Matthew and Luke'. *The Bible Today* 3 (1973), pp. 235-55.

Simonsen, Hejne. 'Mark 8,27–10,52: Markusevangeliets komposition'. *Dansk teologisk tidskrift* 27 (1964), pp. 83-99.

―――. 'Zur Frage der grundliegenden Problematik in form- und redaktions-geschichtlicher Evangelienforschung'. *Studia Theologica* 26 (1972), pp. 1-23.

Sjöberg, Erik Konstans Teodor. *Der verborgene Menschensohn in den Evangelien.* Lund: Gleerup, 1955.

Smalley, Beryl. *The Study of the Bible in the Middle Ages.* 3rd edn. Oxford: Blackwell, 1983.

Smalley, Stephen Stewart. 'Redaction Criticism'. *New Testament Interpretation: Essays on Principles and Methods.* Edited by I. Howard Marshall. Exeter: Paternoster, 1977, pp. 181-95.

Smith, Dwight Moody. *Interpreting the Gospels for Preaching.* Philadelphia: Fortress, 1980.

―――. *Johannine Christianity: Essays on Its Setting, Sources, and Theology.* Columbia, SC: University of South Carolina Press, 1984.

Smith, Morton. *Clement of Alexandria and a Secret Gospel of Mark.* Cambridge, MA: Harvard University Press, 1973.

―――. 'Comments on Taylor's Commentary on Mark'. *Harvard Theological Review* 48 (1955), pp. 21-64.

―――. 'Zealots and Sicarii: Their Origins and Relation'. *Harvard Theological Review* 64 (1971), pp. 1-19.

Smith, Robert Houston. 'New and Old in Mark 16.1-8'. *Concordia Theological Monthly* 43 (1972), pp. 518-27.

Sparks, Hedley Frederick Davis. Review of *Horae Synopticae Electronicae: Word Statistics of the Synoptic Gospels,* by Lloyd Gaston, *Journal of Theological Studies* n.s. 26 (1975), pp. 146-49.

Standaert, Benoît Herman Marguerite Ghislain Marie. *L'Evangile selon Marc: Composition et genre littéraire.* Brugge: Sint Andreisabdij, 1978.

Stanton, Graham. 'Introduction: Matthew's Gospel: A New Storm Centre'. *The Interpretation of Matthew.* Edited by Graham Stanton. Issues in Religion and Theology 3. Philadelphia and London: Fortress/SPCK, 1983, pp. 1-18.

―――. ed. *The Interpretation of Matthew.* Issues in Religion and Theology 3. Philadelphia and London: Fortress/SPCK, 1983.

Steichele, Hans-Jörg. *Der leidende Sohn Gottes: Eine Untersuchung einiger alttestamentlicher Motive in der Christologie des Markusevangeliums.* Biblische Untersuchung 14. Regensburg: Friedrich Pustet, 1980.

Stein, Robert Harry. 'The Proper Methodology for Ascertaining a Marcan *Redaktionsgeschichte*'. Th.D. dissertation, Princeton Theological Seminary, 1968.

―――. 'The Proper Methodology for Ascertaining a Markan Redaction History'. *Novum Testamentum* 13 (1971), pp. 181-98.

―――. 'The "Redaktionsgeschichtlich" Investigation of a Markan Seam (Mc 1.21f)'. *Zeitschrift für die neutestamentliche Wissenschaft* 61 (1970), pp. 70-94.

————. 'What Is *Redaktionsgeschichte?*' *Journal of Biblical Literature* 88 (1969), pp. 45-56.

Stemberger, Günter. 'Galilee — Land of Salvation?' Appendix to W. D. Davies, *The Gospel and the Land: Early Christian and Jewish Territorial Doctrine*. Berkeley: University of California Press, 1974, pp. 409-38.

Stock, Augustine. *Call to Discipleship: A Literary Study of Mark's Gospel*. Good News Studies 1. Wilmington, DE: Michael Glazier, 1982.

Stock, Klemens. *Boten aus dem Mit-Ihm-Sein: Das Verhältnis zwischen Jesus und den Zwölf nach Markus*. Analecta biblica 70. Rome: Pontifical Biblical Institute, 1975.

Stoldt, Hans-Herbert. *History and Criticism of the Markan Hypothesis*. Translated and edited by D. L. Niewyk. Macon, GA: Mercer University Press, 1980.

Strecker, Georg. 'Die Leidens- und Auferstehungsvoraussagen im Markusevangelium (Mk 8, 31; 9, 31; 10, 32-34)'. *Zeitschrift für Theologie und Kirche* 64 (1967), pp. 16-39. Reprinted, in English translation, as 'The Passion and Resurrection Predictions in Mark's Gospel'. *Interpretation* 22 (1968), pp. 421-42.

Streeter, Burnett Hillman. *The Four Gospels: A Study of Origins*. New York: Macmillan, 1925.

Stuhlmacher, Peter. *Historical Criticism and Theological Interpretation of Scripture: Toward a Hermeneutics of Consent*. Translated and with an introduction by Roy A. Harrisville. Philadelphia: Fortress, 1977.

————. 'Thesen zur Methodologie gegenwärtigen Exegese'. *Zeitschrift für die neutestamentliche Wissenschaft* 63 (1972), pp. 18-26.

Styler, G. M. 'The Priority of Mark'. Excursus in C. F. D. Moule, *The Birth of the New Testament*. 3rd edn, revised and rewritten. San Francisco: Harper & Row, 1982, pp. 285-316.

Suhl, Alfred. *Die Funktion der alttestamentlichen Zitate und Anspielungen in Markusevangelium*. Gütersloh: Gütersloher Verlagshaus, 1965.

Tagawa, Kenzo. *Miracles et Évangile: La pensée personnelle de l'Evangéliste Marc*. Etudes d'histoire et de philosophie religieuses 62. Paris: Presses Universitaires de France, 1966.

Talbert, Charles Harold. 'Introduction: Seminar on Gospel Genre'. *Colloquy on New Testament Studies: A Time for Reappraisal and Fresh Approaches*. Edited by Bruce Corley. Macon, GA: Mercer University Press, 1983, pp. 197-202.

————. *What Is a Gospel? The Genre of the Canonical Gospels*. Philadelphia: Fortress, 1977.

Tannehill, Robert Cooper. 'The Disciples in Mark: The Function of a Narrative Role'. *Journal of Religion* 57 (1977), pp. 386-405. Reprinted in W. R. Telford, ed., *The Interpretation of Mark*. Issues in Religion and Theology 7. Philadelphia and London: Fortress/SPCK, 1985, pp. 134-57.

————. 'The Gospel of Mark as Narrative Christology'. *Semeia* 16 (1979), pp. 57-95.

Taylor, Edward Lynn, Jr. 'The Disciples of Jesus in the Gospel of Mark'. Ph.D. dissertation, Southern Baptist Theological Seminary, 1979.

Taylor, Vincent. *The Gospel According to St. Mark: The Greek Text with Introduction, Notes, and Indexes*. 2nd edn. Thornapple Commentaries. Grand Rapids, MI: Baker Book House, 1966, 1981.

Telford, William R. 'Introduction: The Gospel of Mark'. *The Interpretation of Mark*. Edited by W. R. Telford. Philadelphia and London: Fortress/SPCK, 1985, pp. 1-41.

———. ed. *The Interpretation of Mark*. Issues in Religion and Theology 7. Philadelphia and London: Fortress/SPCK, 1985.

Theissen, Gerd. *The Miracle Stories of the Early Christian Tradition*. Translated by Francis McDonagh. Edited by John Riches. Philadelphia: Fortress, 1983.

———. *Sociology of Early Palestinian Christianity*. Translated by John Bowden. Philadelphia: Fortress, 1978.

———. '"Wir haben alles verlassen" (Mc. X.28). Nachfolge und soziale Entwurzelung in der jüdisch-palästinischen Gesellschaft des I. Jahrhunderts n.Ch.' *Novum Testamentum* 14 (1977), pp. 161-96.

Throckmorton, Burton Hamilton. 'Did Mark Know Q?' *Journal of Biblical Literature* 67 (1948), pp. 319-29.

Tiede, David Lenz. *The Charismatic Figure as Miracle Worker*. Society of Biblical Literature Dissertation Series 1. Missoula, MT: Society of Biblical Literature, 1972.

Trocmé, Etienne. *The Formation of the Gospel According to Mark*. Translated by Pamela Gaughan. Philadelphia: Westminster, 1975.

Tuckett, Christopher, ed. *The Messianic Secret*. Issues in Religion and Theology 1. Philadelphia and London: Fortress/SPCK, 1983.

Turner, Cuthbert Hamilton. 'Marcan Usage: Notes, Critical and Exegetical, on the Second Gospel'. *Journal of Theological Studies* o.s. 25 (1923), pp. 377-86; 26 (1924), pp. 12-20, 145-56, 225-40, 337-46; 27 (1925), pp. 58-62; 28 (1926), pp. 9-30, 349-62; 29 (1927), pp. 257-89, 346-61.

Tyson, Joseph B. 'The Blindness of the Disciples in Mark'. *Journal of Biblical Literature* 80 (1961), pp. 261-68. Reprinted in Christopher Tuckett, ed., *The Messianic Secret*. Issues in Religion and Theology 1. Philadelphia and London: Fortress/SPCK, 1983, pp. 35-43.

van Unnik, Willem Cornelis. 'Luke-Acts, A Storm Center in Contemporary Scholarship'. *Studies in Luke-Acts*. Edited by Leander E. Keck and J. Louis Martyn. Philadelphia: Fortress, 1980, pp. 15-32.

Vassiliadis, P. 'Behind Mark: Towards a Written Source'. *New Testament Studies* 20 (1974), pp. 155-60.

Via, Dan Otto, Jr. *The Ethics of Mark's Gospel — In the Middle of Time*. Philadelphia: Fortress, 1985.

————. *Kerygma and Comedy in the New Testament: A Structuralist Approach to Hermeneutic.* Philadelphia: Fortress, 1975.

Vielhauer, Philipp. 'Erwägungen zur Christologie des Markusevangeliums'. *Zeit und Geschichte: Dankesgabe an Rudolf Bultmann zum 80. Geburtstag.* Edited by E. Dinkler. Tübingen: J. C. B. Mohr (Paul Siebeck), 1964, pp. 155-69.

Votaw, Clyde Weber. *The Gospels and Contemporary Biographies in the Greco-Roman World.* Facet Books, Biblical Series. Philadelphia: Fortress, 1970.

Walker, William Oliver, Jr. 'A Method for Identifying Redactional Passages in Matthew on Functional and Linguistic Grounds'. *Catholic Biblical Quarterly* 39 (1977), pp. 76-93.

Weber, R. 'Christologie und "Messiasgeheimnis": ihr Zusammenhang und Stellenwert in der Darstellungsintention des Markus'. *Evangelische Theologie* 43 (1983), pp. 108-25.

Weeden, Theodore John, Sr. 'The Conflict Between Mark and His Opponents over Kingdom Theology'. *Society of Biblical Literature 1973 Seminar Papers.* Edited by George MacRae. Cambridge, MA: Society of Biblical Literature, 1973, pp. 203-41.

————. 'The Cross as Power in Weakness (Mark 15.20b-41)'. *The Passion in Mark: Studies on Mark 14–16.* Edited by Werner H. Kelber. Philadelphia: Fortress, 1976, pp. 115-34.

————. 'The Heresy That Necessitated Mark's Gospel'. *Zeitschrift für die neutestamentliche Wissenschaft* 59 (1968), pp. 145-58. Reprinted in Rudolf Pesch, ed., *Das Markus-Evangelium.* Wege der Forschung 411. Darmstadt: Wissenschaftliche Buchgesellschaft, 1979, pp. 238-58. Reprinted in W. R. Telford, ed., *The Interpretation of Mark.* Issues in Religion and Theology 7. Philadelphia and London: Fortress/SPCK, 1985, pp. 64-77.

————. *Mark — Traditions in Conflict.* Philadelphia: Fortress, 1971.

Weiss, Johannes. *Jesus' Proclamation of the Kingdom of God.* Translated and edited by Richard Hyde Hiers and David Larrimore Holland. Lives of Jesus Series. Philadelphia: Fortress, 1971.

Weiss, Meir. 'Die Methode der "Total-Interpretation"'. *Vetus Testamentum Supplements* 22. Leiden: E. J. Brill, 1972, pp. 88-112.

Weisse, Christian Hermann. *Die Evangelienfrage in ihrem gegenwärtigen Stadium.* Leipzig: Breitkopf & Härtel, 1856.

Wellhausen, Julius. *Einleitung in die drei ersten Evangelien.* Berlin: Reimer, 1905.

————. *Das Evangelium Marci.* 2nd edn. Berlin: Reimer, 1909.

Werner, Martin. *Der Einfluß paulinischer Theologie im Markusevangelium: Eine Studie zur neutestamentlichen Theologie.* Beihefte zur Zeitschrift für die neutestamentliche Wissenschaft und die Kunde der älteren Kirche 1. Gießen: Töpelmann, 1923.

Wharton, James A. 'Redaction Criticism, OT'. *The Interpreter's Dictionary of the Bi-*

ble. Supplementary volume. Edited by Keith Crim. Nashville: Abingdon, 1976, pp. 729-32.

Wilde, James Alan. 'A Social Description of the Community Reflected in the Gospel of Mark'. Ph.D. dissertation, Drew University, 1974.

Wilder, Amos Niven. *Early Christian Rhetoric: The Language of the Gospel.* Cambridge, MA: Harvard University Press, 1964.

Wilke, Christian Gottlob. *Die neutestamentliche Rhetorik.* Dresden and Leipzig: Arnoldische Buchhandlung, 1843.

————. *Der Urevangelist: oder, Exegetische kritisch-Untersuchung über das Verwandtschaftsverhältnis der drei ersten Evangelien.* Dresden and Leipzig: Fleischer, 1838.

Williamson, Lamar, Jr. *Mark.* Interpretation, A Bible Commentary for Teaching and Preaching. Atlanta: John Knox, 1983.

Wimsatt, William Kurtz, Jr, and Monroe Curtis Beardsley. 'The Intentional Fallacy'. *Sewanee Review* 54 (1946), pp. 468-88.

Wimsatt, William Kurtz, Jr, and Cleanth Brooks. *Literary Criticism: A Short History.* New York: Alfred Knopf, 1957.

Wrede, William. *The Messianic Secret.* Translated by J. C. G. Greig. Greenwood, SC: Attic, 1971.

Wuellner, Wilhelm. *The Meaning of 'Fishers of Men'.* New Testament Library. Philadelphia: Westminster, 1967.

Zeller, Eduard. 'Studien zur neutestamentlichen Theologie, 4. Vergleichende Übersicht über den Wörtervorrath der neutestamentlichen Schriftsteller'. *Theologische Jahrbücher* 2 (1843), pp. 443-543.

Zerwick, Maximilian. *Untersuchung zum Markus-Stil.* Scripta Pontificii Instituti Biblici. Rome: Pontifical Biblical Institute, 1937.

Zimmermann, Heinrich. *Neutestamentliche Methodenlehre: Darstellung der historisch-kritischen Methode.* 2nd rev. edn. Stuttgart: Katholisches Bibelwerk, 1968.

Zmÿewski, Josef, and Ernst Nellessen, eds. *Begegnung mit dem Wort: Festschrift für Heinrich Zimmermann.* Bonner biblische Beiträge 53. Bonn: Peter Hanstein, 1980.

Zumstein, Jean. *La Condition du croyant dans l'Évangile selon Matthieu.* Orbis biblicus et orientalis 16. Göttingen: Vandenhoeck & Ruprecht, 1977.

IV. Bibliography for the Afterword (2012)

Ackermann, Robert John. *The Philosophy of Karl Popper.* Amherst: University of Massachusetts Press, 1976.

Ahearne-Kroll, Stephen P. *The Psalms of Lament in Mark's Passion: Jesus' Davidic*

Suffering. Society for New Testament Studies Monograph Series 142. Cambridge: Cambridge University Press, 2007.

Allison, Dale C. *Jesus of Nazareth: Millenarian Prophet.* Minneapolis: Fortress, 1998.

Anderson, Janice Capel, and Stephen D. Moore, eds. *Mark and Method: New Approaches in Biblical Studies.* 2nd edn. Minneapolis: Fortress, 2008.

Bartley, W. W. 'A Popperian Harvest'. In *In Pursuit of Truth: Essays on the Philosophy of Karl Popper on the Occasion of His 80th Birthday,* edited by Paul Levinson, pp. 49-89. Atlantic Highlands, NJ, and Sussex: Humanities/Harvester, 1982.

Becker, Eve-Marie, and Anders Runesson, eds. *Mark and Matthew I, Comparative Readings: Understanding the Earliest Gospels in Their First-Century Settings.* Wissenschaftliche Untersuchungen zum Neuen Testament 271. Tübingen: Mohr Siebeck, 2011.

Best, Ernest. 'Mark's Readers: A Profile'. In *The Four Gospels 1992: Festschrift Frans Neirynck,* edited by F. Van Segbroeck, C. M. Tuckett, G. Van Belle, and Jack Verheyden, vol. 2, pp. 839-55. Bibliotheca ephemeridum theologicarum lovaniensium 100. Leuven: Leuven University Press/Peeters, 1992.

————. Review of C. C. Black, *The Disciples According to Mark* (1989). *Journal of Theological Studies* 41 (1990), pp. 602-7.

Black, C. Clifton. 'An Evaluation of the Investigative Method and Exegetical Results of Redaction Criticism of the Gospel of Mark: The Role of the Disciples as a Test-Case in Current Research'. Ann Arbor: University Microfilms International [DA8624368], 1986.

————. 'Lightfoot, Robert Henry (1883-1953)'. In *Dictionary of Biblical Interpretation,* edited by John H. Hayes, vol. 2, pp. 77-78. Nashville: Abingdon, 1999.

————. *Mark.* Abingdon New Testament Commentaries. Nashville: Abingdon, 2011.

————. 'Mark as Historian of God's Kingdom'. *Catholic Biblical Quarterly* 71 (2009), pp. 64-83.

————. 'The Quest of Mark the Redactor: Why Has It Been Pursued, and What Has It Taught Us?' *Journal for the Study of the New Testament* 33 (1988), pp. 19-39.

————. 'Redaction Criticism'. In *Encyclopedia of the Historical Jesus,* edited by Craig A. Evans, pp. 491-95. New York and London: Routledge/Taylor & Francis, 2008.

————. 'Redaction Criticism, New Testament'. In *The Oxford Encyclopedia of Biblical Interpretation,* edited by Steven McKenzie, et al. New York and Oxford: Oxford University Press, forthcoming 2013.

————. Review of B. M. F. van Iersel, *Mark: A Reader-Response Commentary* (1998). *Catholic Biblical Quarterly* 62 (2000), pp. 570-72.

————. 'Trinity and Exegesis'. *Pro Ecclesia* 19 (2010), pp. 151-80.

Boismard, M.-É. *L'Évangile de Marc: Sa Préhistoire.* Études bibliques n.s. 26. Paris: Gabalda, 1994.

Boring, M. Eugene. *Mark: A Commentary.* New Testament Library. Louisville: Westminster John Knox, 2006.

Breytenbach, Cilliers. 'Current Research on the Gospel according to Mark: A Report on Monographs Published from 2000-2009'. In *Mark and Matthew I, Comparative Readings: Understanding the Earliest Gospels in Their First-Century Settings,* edited by Eve-Marie Becker and Anders Runesson, pp. 13-32. Wissenschaftliche Untersuchungen zum Neuen Testament 271. Tübingen: Mohr Siebeck, 2011.

————. 'Die Vorschriften des Mose im Markusevangelium'. *Zeitschrift für die neutestamentliche Wissenschaft* 97 (2006), pp. 23-43.

Broadhead, Edwin K. Review of C. C. Black, *The Disciples According to Mark* (1989). *Perspectives in Religious Studies* 17 (1990), pp. 83-84.

Burdon, Christopher. *Stumbling on God: Faith and Vision through Mark's Gospel.* London and Grand Rapids, MI: SPCK/Eerdmans, 1990.

Burkett, Delbert. *Rethinking the Gospel Sources: From Proto-Mark to Mark.* New York and London: T & T Clark, 2004.

————. *Rethinking the Gospel Sources: The Unity and Plurality of Q.* Early Christianity and Its Literature 1. Atlanta: Society of Biblical Literature, 2009.

Colani, Timothy. *Jésus Christ et les Croyances messianiques de son Temps.* 2nd edn. Strasbourg: Treuttel et Wurtz, 1864.

Collins, Adela Yarbro. *Mark: A Commentary.* Edited by Harold W. Attridge. Hermeneia. Minneapolis: Fortress, 2007.

————. Review of C. C. Black, *The Disciples According to Mark* (1989). *Critical Review of Books in Religion* 4 (1991), pp. 169-71.

Cuvillier, Evian. Review of C. C. Black, *The Disciples According to Mark* (1989). *Études théologiques et religieuses* 65 (1990), pp. 272-73.

Danove, Paul. 'The Characterization and Narrative Function of the Women at the Tomb (Mark 15,40-41.47; 16,1-8)'. *Biblica* 77 (1996), pp. 375-97.

————. 'The Narrative Rhetoric of Mark's Ambiguous Characterization of the Disciples'. *Journal for the Study of the New Testament* 70 (1998), pp. 21-38.

————. *The Rhetoric of the Characterization of God, Jesus, and Jesus' Disciples in the Gospel of Mark.* Journal for the Study of the New Testament, Supplement Series 290. New York and London: T & T Clark, 2005.

————. 'A Rhetorical Analysis of Mark's Construction of Discipleship'. In *Rhetorical Criticism and the Bible,* edited by Stanley E. Porter and Dennis Stamps, pp. 280-96. Journal for the Study of the New Testament, Supplement Series 195. Sheffield: Sheffield Academic Press, 2002.

Dippenaar, Michaelis Christoffel. 'The Disciples in Mark: Narrative and Theology'. *Toronto Journal of Theology* 17 (1995), pp. 139-209.

Donahue, John R. 'Redaction Criticism: Has the *Hauptstrasse* Become a *Sackgasse?*'

In *The New Literary Criticism and the New Testament,* edited by Elizabeth Struthers Malbon and Edgar V. McKnight, pp. 27-57. Journal for the Study of the New Testament, Supplement Series 109. Sheffield: Sheffield Academic Press, 1994.

————. Review of C. C. Black, *The Disciples According to Mark* (1989). *Perkins School of Theology Journal* 42 (1989), pp. 11-12.

Donahue, John R., and Daniel J. Harrington. *The Gospel of Mark.* Sacra Pagina 2. Collegeville: Liturgical, 2002.

Dorian, Frederick. *The History of Music in Performance: The Art of Musical Interpretation from the Renaissance to Our Day.* New York: Norton, 1966.

Drennan, Robert E., ed. *The Algonquin Wits.* Kensington: Citadel, 1985.

Driggers, I. Brent. *Following God through Mark: Theological Tension in the Second Gospel.* Louisville and London: Westminster John Knox, 2007.

Evans, Craig A. Review of M.-É. Boismard, *L'Évangile de Marc* (1994). *Catholic Biblical Quarterly* 58 (1996), pp. 535-36.

————. 'Source, Form and Redaction Criticism: The "Traditional" Methods of Synoptic Interpretation'. In *Approaches to New Testament Study,* edited by Stanley E. Porter and David Tombs, pp. 17-45. Journal for the Study of the New Testament, Supplement Series 120. Sheffield: Sheffield Academic Press, 1995.

Evans, Craig A., ed. *Encyclopedia of the Historical Jesus.* New York and London: Routledge/Taylor & Francis, 2008.

Fischer, Cédric. *Les Disciples dans l'Évangile de Marc: Une grammaire théologique.* Etudes bibliques n.s. 57. Paris: Gabalda, 2007.

Fleddermann, Harry T. Review of D. B. Peabody, L. Cope, and A. J. McNicol, *One Gospel from Two* (2002). *Catholic Biblical Quarterly* 66 (2004), pp. 498-500.

Focant, Camille. *L'évangile selon Marc.* Commentaire Biblique: Nouveau Testament 2. Paris: Cerf, 2004.

F[owl], S[tephen]. Review of C. C. Black, *The Disciples According to Mark* (1989). *JSNT* 40 (1990), p. 116.

Fowler, Robert M. *Let the Reader Understand: Reader Response Criticism and the Gospel of Mark.* Minneapolis: Fortress, 1991.

Fusco, Vittorio. Review of C. C. Black, *The Disciples According to Mark* (1989). *Biblica* 72 (1991), pp. 123-27.

Geyer, Douglas W. Review of D. Burkett, *Rethinking the Gospel Sources: From Proto-Mark to Mark* (2004). *Review of Biblical Literature* 5 (2005). http://www.bookreviews.org/pdf/4520_4581.pdf.

Gibson, Jeffrey B. 'The Rebuke of the Disciples in Mark 8:14-21'. *Journal for the Study of the New Testament* 31 (1986), pp. 31-47.

Goulder, Michael. 'The Pre-Marcan Gospel'. *Scottish Journal of Theology* 47 (1994), pp. 453-71.

Green, Joel B. Review of C. C. Black, *The Disciples According to Mark* (1989). *CBQ* 53 (1991), pp. 314-15.

Hanson, James. 'The Disciples in Mark's Gospel: Beyond the Pastoral/Polemical Debate'. *Horizons in Biblical Theology* 20 (1998), pp. 128-55.

Hatina, Thomas R. *In Search of a Context: The Function of Scripture in Mark's Narrative*. Library of New Testament Studies 232. London and New York: Sheffield Academic Press, 2002.

Hayes, John H., ed. *Dictionary of Biblical Interpretation*. 2 vols. Nashville: Abingdon, 1999.

Henderson, Suzanne Watts. *Christology and Discipleship in the Gospel of Mark*. Society for New Testament Studies Monograph Series 135. Cambridge: Cambridge University Press, 2006.

Herzog, William R., II. Review of C. C. Black, *The Disciples According to Mark* (1989). *Theological Studies* 51 (1990), pp. 513-15.

Hooker, Morna D. Review of C. C. Black, *The Disciples According to Mark* (1989). *Epworth Review* 18 (1991), pp. 86-87.

Hurtado, Larry W. 'Following Jesus in the Gospel of Mark — and Beyond'. In *Patterns of Discipleship in the New Testament*, edited by Richard N. Longenecker, pp. 9-29. Grand Rapids, MI, and Cambridge: Eerdmans, 1996.

Jones, J. Estill. Review of C. C. Black, *The Disciples According to Mark* (1989). *Review and Expositor* 87 (1990), p. 129.

Juel, Donald H. *A Master of Surprise: Mark Interpreted*. Minneapolis: Fortress, 1994.

————. *Messianic Exegesis: Christological Interpretation of the Old Testament in Early Christianity*. Philadelphia: Fortress, 1988.

Keuth, Herbert. *The Philosophy of Karl Popper*. Cambridge: Cambridge University Press, 2005.

Latzoo, Cyril. 'The Story of the Twelve in the Gospel of Mark'. *Hekima Review* [Nairobi] 13 (1995), pp. 25-33.

Levenson, Sam. *Everything but Money*. New York: Simon and Schuster, 1966.

Levin, Bernard. *Enthusiasms*. New York: Crown, 1983.

Levinson, Paul, ed. *In Pursuit of Truth: Essays on the Philosophy of Karl Popper on the Occasion of His 80th Birthday*. Atlantic Highlands, NJ, and Sussex: Humanities/Harvester, 1982.

Lindemann, Andreas. 'Literatur zu den Synoptischen Evangelien 1992-2000 (III): Das Markusevangelium'. *Theologische Rundschau* 69 (2004), pp. 369-423.

Longenecker, Richard N., ed. *Patterns of Discipleship in the New Testament*. Grand Rapids, MI, and Cambridge: Eerdmans, 1996.

Lührmann, Dieter. *Das Markusevangelium*. Handbuch zum Neuen Testament 3. Tübingen: Mohr-Siebeck, 1987.

McKenzie, Steven, et al., eds. *The Oxford Encyclopedia of Biblical Interpretation*. New York and Oxford: Oxford University Press. Forthcoming, 2013.

Malbon, Elizabeth Struthers. *In the Company of Jesus: Characters in Mark's Gospel.* Louisville: Westminster John Knox, 2000.

———. Review of C. C. Black, *The Disciples According to Mark* (1989). *Interpretation* 45 (1991), pp. 82, 84.

———. 'Texts and Contexts: Interpreting the Disciples in Mark'. *Semeia* 62.1 (1993), pp. 81-102.

Malbon, Elizabeth Struthers, and Edgar V. McKnight, eds. *The New Literary Criticism and the New Testament.* Journal for the Study of the New Testament, Supplement Series 109. Sheffield: Sheffield Academic Press, 1994.

Marcus, Joel. *Mark 1–8, 8–16: A New Translation with Introduction and Commentary.* Anchor Bible 27, 27A. New York, New Haven, and London: Doubleday/ Yale University Press, 2000, 2009.

———. *The Way of the Lord: Christological Exegesis of the Old Testament in the Gospel of Mark.* Louisville: Westminster/John Knox, 1992.

Martyn, J. Louis. *Theological Issues in the Letters of Paul.* Nashville: Abingdon, 1997.

Meagher, P. M. 'The Gospel of Mark: The Vulnerable Disciples'. *Vidjajyoti* 67 (2003), pp. 779-803.

Millay, Edna St. Vincent. *The Letters of Edna St. Vincent Millay.* Edited by Allan Ross Macdougall. New York: Harper & Brothers, 1952.

Miller, David. 'Conjectural Knowledge: Popper's Solution of the Problem of Induction'. In *In Pursuit of Truth: Essays on the Philosophy of Karl Popper on the Occasion of His 80th Birthday,* edited by Paul Levinson, pp. 17-49. Atlantic Highlands, NJ, and Sussex: Humanities/Harvester, 1982.

———. *Critical Rationalism: A Restatement and Defence.* Chicago and La Salle: Open Court, 1994.

Miller, David, ed. *A Pocket Popper.* Oxford: Fontana, 1983.

Miller, Susan. *Women in Mark's Gospel.* Journal for the Study of the New Testament Supplement Series 259. London and New York: T & T Clark, 2004.

Morgan, Robert. Review of C. C. Black, *The Disciples According to Mark* (1989). *Theological Book Review* 1 (1989), p. 12.

Muddiman, John B. 'The End of Markan Redaction Criticism?' *Expository Times* 101 (1990), pp. 307-9.

Neirynck, Frans. 'Urmarcus Révisé: La Théorie Synoptique de M.-É. Boismard, Nouvelle Manière'. *Ephemerides theologicae lovanienses* 71 (1995), pp. 166-75.

O'Hear, Anthony, ed. *Karl Popper: Philosophy and Problems.* Royal Institute of Philosophy Supplement 39. Cambridge: Cambridge University Press, 1995.

Painter, John. 'When Is a House Not a Home? Disciples and Family in Mark 3:13-35'. *New Testament Studies* 45 (1999), pp. 498-513.

Peabody, David B., Lamar Cope, and Allan J. McNicol. *One Gospel from Two: Mark's Use of Matthew and Luke: A Demonstration by the Research Team of the International Institute for Renewal of Gospel Studies.* Harrisburg: Trinity Press International, 2002.

Polkinghorne, John. *Beyond Science: The Wider Human Context.* Cambridge: Cambridge University Press, 1996.

Popper, Karl R. *Conjectures and Refutations: The Growth of Scientific Knowledge.* 3rd edn. London: Routledge and Kegan Paul, 1969.

————. *Knowledge and the Mind-Body Problem: In Defence of Interaction.* Edited by Mark A. Notturno. London and New York: Routledge, 1994.

————. 'Knowledge: Subjective versus Objective'. In *A Pocket Popper,* edited by David Miller, pp. 58-77. Oxford: Fontana, 1983.

————. *The Logic of Scientific Discovery.* New York: Basic Books, 1959.

————. *Objective Knowledge: An Evolutionary Approach.* Rev. edn. Oxford and New York: Clarendon/Oxford University Press, 1979.

————. *The Open Society and Its Enemies.* Volume 2: *The High Tide of Prophecy: Hegel, Marx, and the Aftermath.* London: Routledge & Sons, 1945.

————. *The Poverty of Historicism.* 2nd edn. London: Routledge & Kegan Paul, 1960.

————. *Realism and the Aim of Science.* London: Routledge, 1983.

Porter, Stanley E., and Dennis Stamps, eds. *Rhetorical Criticism and the Bible.* Journal for the Study of the New Testament Supplement Series 195. Sheffield: Sheffield Academic Press, 2002.

Porter, Stanley E., and David Tombs, eds. *Approaches to New Testament Study.* Journal for the Study of the New Testament Supplement Series 120. Sheffield: Sheffield Academic Press, 1995.

Posner, Richard A. *How Judges Think.* Cambridge, MA, and London: Harvard University Press, 2008.

Räisänen, Heikki. Review of C. C. Black, *The Disciples According to Mark* (1989). *Teologisk tidskrift* 96 (1991), pp. 80-81.

Reiprich, Torsten. *Das Mariageheimnis: Maria von Nazareth und die Bedeutung familiärer Beziehungen im Markusevangelium.* Forschungen zur Religion und Literatur des Alten und Neuen Testaments 223. Göttingen: Vandenhoeck & Ruprecht, 2008.

Renoir, Jean. Introduction to *La Règle du jeu.* ©2004 The Criterion Collection.

Riches, John K. *Conflicting Mythologies: Identity Formation in the Gospels of Mark and Matthew.* Studies of the New Testament and Its World. Edinburgh: T & T Clark, 2000.

Riley, Harold. *The Making of Mark: An Exploration.* Macon, GA: Mercer University Press, 1990.

Robinson, James M. *Das Geschichtsverständnis des Markusevangeliums.* Zürich: Zwingli, 1956.

Rousée, Jourdain-Marie. Review of C. C. Black, *The Disciples According to Mark* (1989). *Revue biblique* 96 (1989), pp. 474-75.

Sanders, E. P. *Paul and Palestinian Judaism: A Comparison of Patterns of Religion.* Philadelphia: Fortress, 1977.

Schweitzer, Albert. *The Quest of the Historical Jesus*. First complete English edition, based on the first (1906), second (1913), and sixth (1950) German editions, edited by John Bowden. London and Minneapolis: SCM/Fortress, 2000.

Shiner, Whitney Taylor. *Follow Me! Disciples in Markan Rhetoric*. Society of Biblical Literature Dissertation Series 145. Atlanta: Scholars, 1995.

Smith, D. Moody, Jr. *The Composition and Order of the Fourth Gospel: Bultmann's Literary Theory*. Yale Publications in Religion 10. New Haven and London: Yale University Press, 1965.

Stegemann, Ekkehard W. 'Zur Rolle von Petrus, Jakobus, und Johannes'. *Theologische Zeitschrift* 42 (1986), pp. 366-74.

Strelan, Richard E. 'The Fallen Watchers and the Disciples in Mark'. *Journal for the Study of the Pseudepigrapha* 20 (1999), pp. 73-92.

Taeger, Jens-W. Review of C. C. Black, *The Disciples According to Mark* (1989). *Theologische Literaturzeitung* 115 (1990), p. 590.

Taylor, Nicholas H. Review of D. Burkett, *Rethinking the Gospel Sources: From Proto-Mark to Mark* (2004). *Journal for the Study of the New Testament* 28 (2006), pp. 57-58.

Telford, William R. 'The Pre-Markan Tradition in Recent Research (1980-1990)'. In *The Four Gospels 1992: Festschrift Frans Neirynck*, edited by F. Van Segbroeck, C. M. Tuckett, G. Van Belle, and Jack Verheyden, vol. 2, pp. 693-723. Bibliotheca ephemeridum theologicarum lovaniensium 100. Leuven: Leuven University Press/Peeters, 1992.

―――. *The Theology of the Gospel of Mark*. New Testament Theology. Cambridge: Cambridge University Press, 1999.

Tolbert, Mary Ann. *Sowing the Gospel: Mark's World in Literary-Historical Perspective*. Minneapolis: Fortress, 1989.

van Iersel, Bas M. F. *Mark: A Reader-Response Commentary*. Journal for the Study of the New Testament Supplement Series 164. Sheffield: Sheffield Academic Press, 1998.

Van Segbroeck, F., C. M. Tuckett, G. Van Belle, and Jack Verheyden, eds. *The Four Gospels 1992: Festschrift Frans Neirynck*. 3 vols. Bibliotheca ephemeridum theologicarum lovaniensium 100. Leuven: Leuven University Press/Peeters, 1992.

Walker, William O., Jr. Review of H. Riley, *The Making of Mark* (1990). *Journal of Biblical Literature* 110 (1991), pp. 346-48.

Wansbrough, Henry, ed. *Jesus and the Oral Gospel Tradition*. Journal for the Study of the New Testament Supplement Series 64. Sheffield: Sheffield Academic Press, 1991. Reprinted, London: T & T Clark, 2004.

Watts, Rikki. *Isaiah's New Exodus in Mark*. Wissenschaftliche Untersuchungen zum Neuen Testament 88; Tübingen: Mohr Siebeck, 1997. Republished, Grand Rapids, MI: Baker Academic, 2001.

Wilder, Amos N. *The Bible and the Literary Critic*. Minneapolis: Fortress, 1991.

Worrall, John. '"Revolution in Permanence": Popper on Theory-Change in Science'. In *Karl Popper: Philosophy and Problems,* edited by Anthony O'Hear, pp. 75-102. Royal Institute of Philosophy Supplement 39. Cambridge: Cambridge University Press, 1995.

Index of Modern Authors

Index of Subjects

Index of Biblical and Other References